AF323310

Computational Web Intelligence

Intelligent Technology for Web Applications

Series in Machine Perception and Artificial Intelligence – Vol. 58

Computational Web Intelligence

Intelligent Technology for Web Applications

Editors

Y.-Q. Zhang
Georgia State University, Atlanta, Georgia, USA

A. Kandel
Tel-Aviv University, Israel
University of South Florida, Tampa, Florida, USA

T. Y. Lin
San José State University, California, USA

Y. Y. Yao
University of Regina, Canada

World Scientific

NEW JERSEY · LONDON · SINGAPORE · BEIJING · SHANGHAI · HONG KONG · TAIPEI · CHENNAI

Published by

World Scientific Publishing Co. Pte. Ltd.

5 Toh Tuck Link, Singapore 596224

USA office: Suite 202, 1060 Main Street, River Edge, NJ 07661

UK office: 57 Shelton Street, Covent Garden, London WC2H 9HE

British Library Cataloguing-in-Publication Data
A catalogue record for this book is available from the British Library.

**COMPUTATIONAL WEB INTELLIGENCE: INTELLIGENT TECHNOLOGY
FOR WEB APPLICATIONS**
Series in Machine Perception and Artificial Intelligence (Vol. 58)

ISBN 981-238-827-3

Printed by FuIsland Offset Printing (S) Pte Ltd, Singapore

Preface

With explosive growth of data on wired and wireless networks, a significant need exists for a new generation of Web techniques with the ability to intelligently assist users in finding useful Web information and making smart Web decisions. Clearly, the future trend of the Web technology is from the bottom-level data oriented Web to the low-level information oriented Web, then to the middle-level knowledge oriented Web, and finally to the high-level intelligence oriented Web. Thus, it is urgent to develop new intelligent Web techniques for Web applications on wired and wireless networks.

Web Intelligence (WI), a new direction for scientific research and development, was introduced at the 24th IEEE Computer Society International Computer Software and Applications Conference in 2000. WI exploits Artificial Intelligence (AI) and advanced Information Technology (IT) on the Web and Internet. In general, AI-based Web techniques can improve Web QoI (Quality of Intelligence).

To promote the use of fuzzy Logic in the Internet, Zadeh highlights: "fuzzy logic may replace classical logic as what may be called the brainware of the Internet" at 2001 BISC International Workshop on Fuzzy Logic and the Internet (FLINT2001). So soft computing techniques can play an important role in building the intelligent Web brain. So soft-computing-based Web techniques can enhance Web QoI (Quality of Intelligence). In order to use CI (Computational Intelligence) techniques to make intelligent wired and wireless systems with high QoI, Computational Web Intelligence (CWI) was proposed at the special session on CWI at FUZZ-IEEE'02 of 2002 World Congress on Computational Intelligence. CWI is a hybrid technology of CI and Web Technology (WT) dedicating to increasing QoI of e-Business application systems on the wired and wireless networks. Main CWI techniques include (1) Fuzzy Web Intelligence (FWI), (2) Neural Web Intelligence (NWI), (3) Evolutionary Web Intelligence (EWI), (4) Granular Web Intelligence (GWI), (5) Rough Web Intelligence (RWI), and (6) Probabilistic Web Intelligence (PWI).

Since AI techniques and CI techniques have different strengths, so the broad question is how to combine the different strengths to make a powerful intelligent Web system. Hybrid Web Intelligence (HWI), a broad hybrid research area, uses AI, CI, BI (Biological Intelligence) and WT to build hybrid intelligent Web systems to serve wired and wireless users effectively and efficiently.

For clarity, the first two parts of the book introduce CWI techniques, and the third part presents HWI techniques.

Part I (Chapters 1-8) introduces basic methods dealing with Web uncertainty based on FWI, RWI and PWI. In Chapter 1, Yager describe a general recommender system framework for e-Business applications. Fuzzy techniques are used to analyze available users' profiles to make suitable recommendations for the users. In Chapter 2, Nikravesh and Takagi introduce a new intelligent Web search method using the Conceptual Fuzzy Set (CFS). The CFS-based search engine based on Google^{TM} is designed and implemented to generate more human-like search results. In Chapter 3, Berkan and Guner uses fuzzy logic and natural language processing to design a fuzzy question-answer Web system which can find out more satisfactory answers for users. In Chapter 4, Cai, Ye, Pan, Shen and Mark have designed the Content Distribution Networks (CDN) using fuzzy inference to transparently and dynamically redirect user requests to relevant cache servers. Simulation results have indicated that the fuzzy CDN can have higher network utilization and better quality of service. In Chapter 5, Wang presents a fuzzy Web recommendation system for Web users. The dynamic fuzzy method is used to generate fuzzy membership functions and rank candidates online. In Chapter 6, Chen, Chen, Gao, Zhang, Gider, Vuppala and Kraft use the fuzzy linear clustering approach to designing the intelligent search engine that can search for relevant fabrics based on users' queries. Simulations show that the fuzzy search engine is quite effective. In Chapter 7, Lingras, Yan and Jain propose a new complimentary fuzzy rough clustering method for Web usage mining. The conventional K-means algorithm, a modified K-means algorithm based on rough set theory, and a fuzzy clustering algorithm are compared. In Chapter 8, Butz and Sanscartier present the Web search methods using the probabilistic inference with context specific independence and contextual weak independence, respectively. Other traditional Bayesian networks are also discussed for comparison.

Part II (Chapters 9-13) introduces basic techniques of NWI, EWI and GWI. In Chapter 9, Fong and Hui develop a Web-based expert system using neural networks for convenient vehicle fault diagnosis. Simulation results have shown that the online neural expert system is effective in terms of speed and accuracy. In Chapter 10, Purvis, Harrington and Sembower present a genetic-algorithms-based optimization method to personalize Web documents on Web pages clearly. In Chapter 11, Loia, Senatore and Pedrycz propose a novel P-FCM (Proximity Fuzzy C-Means) to do Web page classification based on a user judgment in term of measure of similarity or dissimilarity among classified Web data. Such a hybrid human-computer Web search engine can simplify Web mining tasks. In Chapter 12, Abraham applies soft computing techniques to design i-Miner that is able to optimize the fuzzy clustering algorithm and analyze Web traffic data. The hybrid Web mining framework using neural networks, fuzzy logic and evolutionary computation is efficient according to simulation results. In Chapter 13, Liu, Wan and Wang propose a Web-based multimedia data retrieval system using the multimedia signal processing method and the content-based audio classification technique. Especially, the emerging audio ontology can be used in Web applications, digital libraries, and others.

Part III (Chapters 14-25) introduces HWI techniques and their applications. In Chapter 14, Zhou, Qin and Chen develop an effective Chinese Web portal for medical Web information retrieval using meta-search engines, cross-regional search technique, as well as post retrieval analysis technique. Importantly, mutli-language-based Web search techniques are beneficial to different people around the world. In Chapter 15, Chen designs tow new algorithms based on multiplicative query expansion strategies to adaptively improve the query vector. Performance analysis shows that the two new algorithms are much better than two traditional ones. In Chapter 16, Hu and Yoo apply data mining techniques and information technology to design a novel framework <u>B</u>iological <u>R</u>elationship *<u>EX</u>tract* (BRExtract) to find the protein–protein interaction from large collection of online biomedical biomedical literature. The simulations indicate that the new framework is very effective in mining biological patterns from online biomedical databases. In Chapter 17, Lee proposes a novel iJADE (intelligent Java Agent

Development Environment) based on intelligent multi-agent system to provide an intelligent agent-based platform for e-commerce applications. Useful functions are also described. In Chapter 18, Fong, Hui and Lee develop a Web content filtering system with low latency and high accuracy. Important potential applications include finding harmful Web materials, and fighting against Web-based terrorism. In Chapter 19, Serag-Eldin, Souafi-Bensafi, Lee, Chan and Nikravesh make a Web-based BICS decision support system using fuzzy searching technology to retrieve approximately relevant results and make relatively satisfactory decisions based on fuzzy decision criteria. Interesting simulation examples are given. In Chapter 20, Efe, Raghavan and Lakhotia introduce a novel link-analysis-based Web search method to improve Web search quality. This new search method is more effective than the keyword-based method in terms of Web search quality. In Chapter 21, Cao, Zhou, Chen, Chan and Lu discuss the mobile agent technology and its applications in electronic commerce, parallel computing, and information retrieval, Web Services and grid computing in widely distributed heterogeneous open networks. In Chapter 22, Panayiotopoulos and Avradinis combine computer graphics technology and Web technology to design intelligent virtual agents on the Web. Web-based intelligent virtual agents have many useful e-Applications. In Chapter 23, Wang introduces a network security technique using data mining techniques. In Chapter 24, Jin, Liu and Wang present a novel peer-to-peer grid model to mobilize distributed resources effectively and optimize global performance of the peer-to-peer grid network. In Chapter 25, Last, Shapira, Elovici, Zaafrany and Kandel propose a new intelligent Web mining based security technique to monitor Web contents.

Finally, we would like to express our sincere thanks to all authors for their important contributions. We world like to thank Ian Seldrup and others at World Scientific very much for great help for the final success of this book. This work was partially supported by the National Institute for Systems Test and Productivity at University of South Florida under the USA Space and Naval Warfare Systems Command Grant No. N00039-01-1-2248 and by the Fulbright Foundation that has granted Prof. Kandel the Fulbright Research Award at Tel-Aviv University, College of Engineering during the academic year 2003-2004.

Yan-Qing Zhang, Abraham Kandel, T.Y. Lin, Yiyu Yao

May, 2004

Contents

INTRODUCTION TO
COMPUTATIONAL WEB INTELLIGENCE
AND HYBRID WEB INTELLIGENCE

Yan-Qing Zhang

Department of Computer Science, Georgia State University
P.O. Box 4110, Atlanta, GA 30302, USA
E-mail: yzhang@cs.gsu.edu

Abraham Kandel

Department of Computer Science and Engineering, University of South Florida
4202 E. Fowler Ave., ENB 118, Tampa, FL 33620, USA
E-mail: kandel@csee.usf.edu
Faculty of Engineering, Tel-Aviv University, Tel-Aviv 69978, Israel

Tsau Young Lin

Department of Computer Science, San Jose State University
San Jose, CA 95192, USA
E-mail: tylin@cs.sjsu.edu

Yiyu Yao

Department of Computer Science, University of Regina
Regina, Saskatchewan, Canada S4S 0A2
E-mail: yyao@cs.uregina.ca

With explosive growth of data and information on wired and wireless networks, there are more and more challenging intelligent e-Application problems in terms of Web QoI (Quality of Intelligence). We mainly discuss Computational Web Intelligence (CWI) based on both Computational Intelligence (CI) and Web Technology (WT). In addition, we briefly introduce a broad research area called Hybrid Web Intelligence (HWI) based on AI (Artificial Intelligence), BI (Biological Intelligence), CI, WT and other relevant techniques. Generally, the intelligent e-brainware based on CWI and HWI can be widely used in smart e-Business applications on wired and wireless networks.

1. Introduction

AI techniques have been used in single-computer-based intelligent systems for almost 50 years, and in networked-computers-based intelligent systems in recent years. The challenging problem is how to use AI techniques in Web-based applications on the Internet. With explosive growth of the wired and wireless networks, Web users suffer from huge amounts of raw Web data because current Web tools still cannot find satisfactory information and knowledge effectively and make decisions correctly. So how to find new ways to design intelligent Web systems is very important for e-Business applications and Web users. Artificial Intelligence (AI) initially focuses on the research in single-computer intelligent systems, and then Distributed Artificial Intelligence (DAI) exploits the development on multi-computer intelligent systems. To use AI techniques to developing intelligent Web systems, WI (Web Intelligence), a new research direction, is introduced [Yao, Zhong, Liu and Ohsuga (2000)]. "WI exploits AI and advanced Information Technology (IT) on the Web and Internet [Yao, Zhong, Liu and Ohsuga (2000)]".

Now the Internet and wireless networks connect an enormous number of computing devices including computers, PDAs (Personal Digital Assistants), cell phones, home appliances, etc. CI is used in telecommunication network applications [Pedrycz and Vasilakos (2001a)]. Clearly, such a huge networked computing system on the world provides a complex, dynamic and global environment for developing the new distributed intelligent theory and technology based on AI, BI (Biological Intelligence) and CI.

2. Computational Intelligence and Computational Web Intelligence

Zadeh states that traditional (hard) computing is the computational paradigm that underlies artificial intelligence, whereas soft computing is the basis of CI. Based on the discussions on CI and AI [Bezdek (1994); Bezdek (1998); Fogel (1995); Marks (1993); Pedrycz (1999); Zurada, Marks and Robinson (1994)], the basic conclusion is that CI is different from AI, but CI and AI have a common overlap. In general, hard computing and soft computing can be used in intelligent hard Web applications and intelligent soft Web applications.

To promote the use of fuzzy Logic in the Internet, Zadeh stated "fuzzy logic may replace classical logic as what may be called the brainware of the Internet" at 2001 BISC International Workshop on Fuzzy Logic and the Internet (FLINT2001) [Nikravesh and Azvine (2001)]. The fuzzy intelligent agents are used in smart e-Commerce applications [Yager (2001)]. The conceptual fuzzy sets are applied to Web search engines to improve quality of Web service [Takagi and Tajima (2001)]. Clearly, the intelligent e-brainware based on soft computing plays an important role in smart e-Business applications.

To enhance QoI (Quality of Intelligence) of e-Business, Computational Web Intelligence (CWI) is proposed to use CI and Web Technology (WT) to make intelligent e-Business applications on the Internet and wireless networks [Zhang and Lin (2002)]. So the concise relation is given by

$$CWI = CI + WT.$$

Fuzzy logic, neural networks, evolutionary computation, granular computing, rough sets and probabilistic methods are major CI techniques for intelligent e-Applications on the Internet and wireless networks. Currently, seven major research areas of CWI are (1) Fuzzy WI (FWI), (2) Neural WI (NWI), (3) Evolutionary WI (EWI), (4) Probabilistic WI (PWI), (5) Granular WI (GWI), and (6) Rough WI (RWI). In the future, more CWI research areas will be added. The six current major CWI techniques are described below.

(1) FWI has two major techniques: fuzzy logic and WT. The main goal of FWI is to design intelligent fuzzy e-agents to deal with fuzziness of Web data, Web information and Web knowledge, and also make good decisions for e-Applications effectively.

(2) NWI has two major techniques: neural networks and WT. The main goal of NWI is to design intelligent neural e-agents that can learn Web knowledge from of Web data and Web information and make smart decisions for e-Applications intelligently.

(3) EWI has two major techniques: evolutionary computing and WT. The main goal of EWI is to design intelligent evolutionary e-agents to optimize e-Application tasks effectively.

(4) PWI has two major techniques: probabilistic computing and WT. The main goal of PWI is to design intelligent probabilistic e-agents to deal with probability of Web data, Web information and Web knowledge for e-Applications effectively.

(5) GWI has two major techniques: granular computing [Lin (1999); Lin, Yao, Zadeh (2001); Pedrycz (2001b); Zhang, Fraser, Gagliano and Kandel (2000)] and WT. The main goal of GWI is to design intelligent granular e-agents to deal with Web data granules, Web information granules and Web knowledge granules for e-Applications effectively.

(6) RWI has two major techniques: rough sets and WT. The main goal is to design intelligent rough e-agents to deal with roughness of Web data, Web information and Web knowledge for e-Applications effectively.

In summary, CWI technology is based on multiple CI techniques and WT. Relevant CI techniques and WT are selected to make a powerful CWI system for the special e-Business application.

3. Hybrid Intelligence and Hybrid Web Intelligence

In general, the hybrid intelligent architecture merging two or more techniques is more effective than the intelligent architecture using single technique [Kandel (1999)]. Hybrid Intelligence (HI) is a broad research area combining AI, BI and CI for complex intelligent applications. A clear relation is given below

$$HI = AI + BI + CI.$$

Hybrid Web Intelligence (HWI) is a broad research area merging HI and WT for intelligent wired and wireless mobile e-Applications. So we have a short relation:

$$HWI = HI + WT.$$

The main goal of HWI is to design hybrid intelligent wired and wireless e-Agents to process Web data, seek Web information and discover Web knowledge effectively. For example, (1) a hybrid neural symbolic Web agent can be designed using neural networks and traditional symbolic reasoning to do more complex Web search tasks than current Web search engines; (2) compensatory genetic fuzzy neural networks [Zhang and Kandel (1998)] can be used to design a hybrid intelligent Web systems for e-Applications.

HWI has a lot of intelligent Web applications on the Internet and wireless mobile networks. Main HWI applications include (1) intelligent Web agents for e-Applications such as e-Commerce, e-Government, e-Education and e-Health, (2) intelligent Web security systems such as intelligent homeland security systems, (3) intelligent Web bioinformatics systems, (4) intelligent grid computing systems, (5) intelligent wireless mobile agents, (6) intelligent Web expert systems, (7) intelligent Web entertainment systems, (8) intelligent Web services, (9) Web data mining and Web knowledge discovery [Schenker, Last and Kandel (2001a, 2001b)], (10) intelligent distributed and parallel Web computing systems based on a large number of networked computing resources, ..., and so on.

4. Conclusions

CWI can be used to increase the QoI of e-Business applications. CWI has a lot of wired and wireless applications in intelligent e-Business. Currently, FWI, NWI, EWI, PWI, GWI and RWI are major CWI techniques. CWI can be used to deal with uncertainty and complexity of Web applications. HWI, a more broad area than CWI, can be applied to more complex e-Business applications. In summary, HWI including CWI will play an important role in designing the smart e-Application systems for wired and wireless users.

Bibliography

Bezdek J.C. (1994). What is computational intelligence, *Computational Intelligence: Imitating Life*, J.M. Zurada, R.J. Marks II and C.J. Robinson (eds), IEEE Press, pp. 1-12.

Bezdek J.C., (1998). Computational Intelligence Defined – By Everyone!, *Computational Intelligence: Soft Computing and Fuzzy-Neuro Integration with Applications*, O. Kaynak, L.A. Zadeh, B. Turksen, I.J. Rudas (eds), pp. 10-37, Springer.

Fogel D. (1995). Review of "Computational Intelligence: Imitating Life," *IEEE Trans. on Neural Networks*, 6, pp.1562-1565.

Kandel A. (1992). *Hybrid Architectures For Intelligent Systems*, CRC Press.

Lin T.Y. (1999). Data Mining: Granular Computing Approach. *Proc. of PAKDD1999*, pp. *24-33*.

Lin T.Y., Yao Y.Y., Zadeh L. (eds). (2001). Data Mining, Rough Sets and Granular Computing, Physica-Verlag.

Marks R. (1993). Intelligence: Computational versus Artificial, *IEEE Trans. on Neural Networks*, 4, pp. 737-739.

Nikravesh M. and Azvine B. (2001). *New Directions in Enhancing the Power of the Internet (Proceedings of The 2001 BISC International Workshop on Fuzzy Logic and the Internet)*.

Schenker A., Last M., and Kandel A. (2001a). A Term-Based Algorithm for Hierarchical Clustering of Web Documents; Proceedings of IFSA / NAFIPS 2001, pp. 3076-3081, Vancouver, Canada, July 25-28.

Schenker A., Last M., and Kandel A. (2001b). Design and Implementation of a Web Mining System for Organizing Search Engine Results, Proceedings of the CAiSE'01 Workshop Data Integration over the Web (DIWeb01), pp. 62 -75, Interlaken, Switzerland, 4-5 June.

Takagi T. and Tajima M. (2001). Proposal of a Search Engine based on Conceptual Matching of Text Notes. Proceedings of The 2001 BISC International Workshop on Fuzzy Logic and the Internet, pp. 53-58.

Pedrycz W. (1999). Computational Intelligence: An Introduction, *Computational Intelligence and Applications*, P.S. Szczepaniak (Ed.), pp.3-17, Physica-Verlag.

Pedrycz W. and Vasilakos A. (eds). (2001). *Computational Intelligence in Telecommunications Networks*, CRC Press, 2001.

Pedrycz W. (eds). (2001). *Granular Computing - An Emerging Paradigm*, Physica-Verlag.

Yao Y.Y., Zhong, N., Liu, J. and Ohsuga, S. (2001). Web Intelligence (WI): Research challenges and trends in the new information age, *Proc. Of WI2001*, pp. 1-17.

Yager R.R. (2000). Targeted E-commerce Marketing Using Fuzzy Intelligent Agents. *IEEE Intelligent Systems*, Nov./Dec., pp. 42-45.

Zadeh L.A. (1997). Towards a theory of fuzzy information granulation and its centrality in human reasoning and fuzzy logic, *Fuzzy Sets and Systems*, 19, pp. 111-127.

Zhang Y.-Q. and Kandel A. (1998). *Compensatory Genetic Fuzzy Neural Networks and Their Applications*, Series in Machine Perception Artificial Intelligence, Volume 30, World Scientific.

Zhang Y.-Q. M. D. Fraser, R. A. Gagliano and A. Kandel. (2000). Granular Neural Networks for Numerical-Linguistic Data Fusion and Knowledge Discovery, *IEEE Transactions on Neural Networks*, 11, pp. 658-667.

Zhang Y.-Q. and Lin T.Y. (2002). Computational Web Intelligence (CWI): Synergy of Computational Intelligence and Web Technology, *Proc. of FUZZ-IEEE2002 of World Congress on Computational Intelligence 2002*, pp. 1104-1107.

Zurada J.M., Marks II R.J. and Robinson C.J. (1994). Introduction, *Computational Intelligence: Imitating Life*, J.M. Zurada, R.J. Marks II and C.J. Robinson (eds), IEEE Press, pp. v-xi.

Part I
**Fuzzy Web Intelligence, Rough Web Intelligence
and Probabilistic Web Intelligence**

CHAPTER 1

RECOMMENDER SYSTEMS BASED ON REPRESENTATIONS

Ronald R. Yager

Machine Intelligence Institute, Iona College
New Rochelle, NY 10801, USA
E-mail: yager@panix.com

We discuss some methods for constructing recommender systems. An important feature of the methods studied here is that we assume the availability of a description, representation, of the objects being considered for recommendation. The approaches studied here differ from collaborative filtering in that we only use preferences information from the individual for whom we are providing the recommendation and make no use the preferences of other collaborators. We provide a detailed discussion of the construction of the representation schema used. We consider two sources of information about the users preferences. The first are direct statements about the type of objects the user likes. The second source of information comes from ratings of objects which the user has experienced.

1.1 Introduction

Recommender systems [Resnick and Varian (1997)] are an important part of many websites and play a central role in the Ecommerce effort toward personalization and customization. The current generation of recommender systems predominantly use collaborative filtering techniques [Goldberg *et. al.* (1992); Shardanand and Maes (1995); Konstan *et. al.* (1997)]. These collaborative systems require preference information not only from the person being served but from other individuals. This community wide transmittal of preference information is used to determine similarity of interest between different individuals. This similarity of interest forms the basis of recommendations. An significant feature of these collaborative filtering approaches is that they do not require any representation of the objects being considered. He we focus on a class of recommender systems which are not collaborative. These types of recommender systems only use preference information about the person being served but they require some representation of the objects be considered. We refer to these as reclusive recommender systems. What is clear is that future recommender systems will incorporate both these perspectives. However, our focus here is on the development of tools necessary for this reclusive component.

1.2 Recommender Systems

The purpose of a recommender systems is to recommend to a user objects from a collection $D = \{d_1, ..., d_n\}$. An example we shall find convenient to refer to is one in which the objects are movies. The choice of technology for building a recommender system depends on the type of information available to it. In the following we discuss some types of information that may be available to a recommender system.

One source of information is knowledge about the objects in D. The quality of this information depends upon the representation used for the objects in D. The least information rich situation is one in which we just only have some unique identification of an object. For example, all we know about a movie is just its title. A richer information environment is one in which we describe an object with some attributes. For example, we indicate the year the movie was made, the type of movie, the stars. These attributes and their associated values provide a representation of an object. The richness of the representation will depend upon the features used to characterize the objects. Generally the more sophisticated the representation the better a system performs.

In addition to information describing the objects under consideration we must have some information about the user and more specifically their preferences with respect to the objects in D. Information about user preferences can be obtained in at least two different ways. We refer to these as **experientially** and **intentionally** expressed preference information. By experientially expressed preference information we mean information based upon the actions or past experiences of the user.

These are movies a user has previously seen and possibly some rating of these movies. In another domain we could mean the objects which the user has purchased. By intentionally expressed information we mean some specifications by the user of what they desire in objects of the type under consideration. To be of use these specifications must be expressed in a manner which can be related to the attributes used in the representation of the objects.

Another source of information is the preferences of other people. A system is collaborative if information about the preferences of other people is used in determining the recommendation to the current user.

Here we shall focus on non-collaborative recommender systems in which there exists a representation of the objects.

1.3 The Representation Schema

Our representation of an object will be based upon a set of primitive assertions about the object. We assume for each assertion and each object d in D we have available a value $\tau \in [0, 1]$ indicating the degree to which the assertion is compatible with what we know about the object d. In the movie domain a primitive assertion may be "this movie is a comedy." In this case for a given movie the value τ indicates the degree to which it is true that the movie is a comedy. Another assertion may be that "Robert DeNiro is a star in this movie." If the movie has Robert DeNiro as one of its stars then this assertion has validity one otherwise it is zero. Another assertion may be that "this movie was made in 1993," if the movie was made in 1995 this would have a validity of zero. If it was made in 1993, this assertion would have truth value one. We denote this set of primitive assertions as $A = \{A_1, ..., A_n\}$. For object d, $A_j(d)$ indicates the degree to which assertion A_j is satisfied by d. It is important to emphasize the value of $A_j(d)$ lies in the interval [0. 1].

Our representation of an object is the collection of valuations of these assertions for the object. For some purposes we can view the object d as a fuzzy subset d over the space A. Using this perspective the membership grade of A_j in d, $d(A_j) = A_j(d)$. As an alternative perspective an object can be viewed as an n dimensional vector whose jth component is $A_j(d)$. These different perspectives are useful in inspiring different information processing operations.

We call a subset V of a related assertions from A an attribute (or feature). For example V may consist of all the assertions of the form "this movie was made in the year *xyz*." We can denote this attribute as "the year the movie was made." Another notable subset of related assertions from *A* may consist of all the assertions of the form "*x* stars in this movie." This feature corresponds to the attribute of who are the stars of the movie.

In addition to the set *A* of primitive assertions we shall also assume the existence of a collection of attributes associated with the objects in *D*. We denote this collection of attributes as $F = \{V_1, V_2, ..., V_q\}$. Each attribute V_j corresponds to a subset of assertions which can be seen as constituting the possible values for the attribute. In some special cases a feature may consist of a single assertion. The quality of a recommender system is related to the sophistication of the primitive assertions and attributes used in the representation scheme.

We look at little more carefully at the relationship and differences between assertions and attributes. An assertion A_j is a declarative statement that can be assigned a value τ for a given object, indicating its degree of validity. This value always lies in the unit interval. An attribute, on the other hand, can be viewed as a variable that takes its value(s) from its associated universe. In our framework the universe associated with an attribute corresponds to the subset of primitive assertions that is used to define it. Furthermore for a given object the value of an attribute depends upon the truth values of the associated primitives. Let us look at this. If V_j is a attribute we denote the <u>variable</u> corresponding to this attribute for a particular object d as $V_j(d)$. We denote the <u>value</u> of this variable as G. Using the notation of approximate reasoning we express this as $V_j(d)$ *is* G. We obtain G in the following way. Let $A(V_j)$ indicate the subset of primitives associated with V_j. Let *d* represent the fuzzy of *A* corresponding to object d, then the value of the variable $V_j(d)$ is expressed as $V_j(d)$ *is* G where

$$G = A(V_j) \cap d.$$

G is the intersection of the attribute definition, the crisp subset $A(V_j)$, and the object representation, the fuzzy subset *d*. The collection of elements in the subset G determine the value of $V_j(d)$. What is important to emphasize is this value is generally **not** a truth value from the unit interval it is a fuzzy subset of V_j. One special case worth noting is when $G = \{A_k\}$. In this case $V_j(d)$ can be said to have the value A_k.

The primitive assertions can be classified with respect to the allowable truth values they can assume. For example binary type assertions are those in which τ must assume the value of either one or zero while other assertions can have truth values lying in the unit interval. Attributes can be classified by various characteristics [Zadeh (1997); Yager (2000a)]. They can be classified with respect to number of solutions they allow, is it restricted to having only one solution, does it allow multiple solutions, must it have a solution. For example the attribute corresponding to release year of a movie must have only one solution. On the other hand the attribute corresponding to the star of a movie can take on multiple values. In understanding the knowledge contained in G it is necessary to carefully distinguish between attributes that can only assume one unique value, such as date of release of a movie, and features that can assume multiple values, such as people starring in the movie. In the first case multiple assertions in G is an indication of uncertainty regarding our knowledge of the value of $V_j(d)$. In the second case multiple assertions in G is an indication of multiple solutions for $V_j(d)$. Here we shall not further pursue this important issue regarding different types of variables but only point to [Yager (2000a)] for those interested.

1.4 Intentionally Expressed Preferences

The basic functioning of a recommender system is to use **justifications** to generate recommendations to a user. By a justification we shall mean a reason for believing a user may be interested in an object. These justifications can be obtained either from preferences directly expressed by user or induced using data about the users experiences. In the following we shall look at techniques for obtaining recommendations which make use of preferences directly expressed by a user.

Here we consider the situation in which in addition to having a representation of the objects we assume the user has specified their preferences intentionally in a manner compatible with this representation. While availability of technologies in this environment is quite rich the quality of performance depends upon the capability of the system to allow the user to effectively express their preferences. This capability is dependent upon the representation schema as well as the language available to the user for expressing their preferences in terms of the basic assertions and attributes in the representational schema.

In the following we describe a language useful for expressing preferences. This language which, we introduce in [Yager (2000b)], is called Hi-Ret provides a very expressive language. Hi-Ret makes considerable use of the **O**rdered **W**eighted **A**veraging (OWA) operator [Yager (1988)].

We recall an OWA operator F of dimension n is mapping OWA: $R^n \rightarrow R$ characterized by an n–dimension vector W, called the weighting vector, such that its components w_j, j = 1 to n, lie in the unit interval and sum to one. The OWA aggregation is defined as

$$OWA(a_1,...,a_n) = \sum_{j=1}^{n} w_j b_j$$

where b_j is the jth largest of the a_i. The richness of the operator lies in the fact that by selecting W we can implement many different aggregation operators. In addition from an applications point of view an important feature of this operator is that the characterizing vector W can be readily related to nature language expressions of aggregation rules.

A number of different methods have been suggested for obtaining the weighting vector used in the aggregation. For our purpose we shall use an approach in the spirit of Zadeh's paradigm of computing with words [Zadeh (1996); Yager (To Appear)] which makes use of the concept of linguistic quantifiers. In anticipation of this we introduce the idea of a BUM function which is a mapping f: [0, 1]→[0, 1] such that f(0)=0, f(1)=1 and f(x)≥f(y) if x>y. Using such a function it can be shown [Yager (1996)] that we can generate the weights needed for an OWA operator by

$$w_j = f(\frac{j}{n}) - f(\frac{j-1}{n}).$$

The concept of linguistic quantifiers was originally introduced by Zadeh (1983). According to Zadeh a linguistic quantifier is a natural language expression corresponding to a proportional quantity. Examples of this are *at least one, all, at least α%, most, more than a few, some* and *all*. Zadeh (1983) suggested a method for formally representing linguistic quantifiers. Let Q be a linguistic expression corresponding to a quantifier such as *most*. Zadeh suggested representing this as a fuzzy subset Q over I = [0, 1] in which for any proportion r∈ I, Q(r) indicates the degree to which r satisfies the concept identified by the quantifier Q.

Yager (1996) showed how to use linguistic quantifiers to generalize the logical quantification operation. He considered the valuation of the statement $Q(a_1, ..., a_n)$ where Q is a linguistic quantifier and the a_j are truth values. It was suggested that the truth value of this type of statement could be obtained with the aid of the OWA operator. This process involved first representing the quantifier Q as a fuzzy subset Q and then using Q to obtain an OWA weighting vector W which was used to perform an OWA aggregation of the a_i. Formally we denote this as

$$Q(a_1, ..., a_n) = OWA_Q(a_1, ..., a_n)$$

Here we shall restrict ourselves to the class of linguistic quantifiers called RIM quantifiers. A RIM quantifier is represented by fuzzy subset Q: I→I which has the properties of a BUM function, These RIM quantifiers model the class in which an increase in proportion results in an increase in compatibility to the linguistic expression being modeled. Examples of these types of quantifiers are *at least one, all, at least α%, most, more than a few, some*. These are the type of quantifiers that are generally used by people in expressing their preferences.

We are now in a position to describe our language for allowing users to express their preferences in a manner that can be used for building recommender system. We assume available to the user for expressing their preferences are the assertions and attributes in the representational schema and a vocabulary of linguistic quantifiers $Q= \{Q_1, Q_2, ..., Q_q\}$. Transparent to the user is the representation of each quantifier as a fuzzy subset of the unit interval, $Q_k \equiv Q_k$.

We now introduce the idea of **primal preference module** (PPM). A PPM is of the form $<A_1, ..., A_q: Q>$. The components of a PPM, the A_i, are assertions associated with the objects in D and Q is a linguistic quantifier. With a PPM a user can express preference information by describing what properties they are interested in and then use Q to capture the desired relationship between these properties. For example do they desire *all* or *most* or *some* or *at least one* of these assertions be satisfied. If h is a PPM we can evaluate any object d in D with respect to this. In particular for object d we obtain the values $A_j(d)$ from our representation of d then use the OWA aggregation to evaluate it, h(d) = $OWA_Q(A_1(d), A_2(d), ..., A_q(d))]$.

While the PPM can be directly evaluated for any object the great significance of our system is that we can use these PPM to let users express their preferences in much more sophisticated ways. We now shall introduce the idea of a **basic preference module** (BPM). A BPM is a module of the form m = $<C_1, C_2, ..., C_p: Q>$ in which the C_i are called the components of the BPM. The only required property of these components are that they can be evaluated for each object in D. That is for any C_i we need to be able to obtain $C_i(d)$. Once having this we can obtain the valuation of the BPM as

$$m(d) = OWA_Q[C_1(d), ..., C_p(d)]$$

Let see what kinds of elements can constitute the C_i. Clearly the C_i can be any of the assertions in the set A. Furthermore the C_i can be any PPM as we know how to evaluate these. Even more generally the C_i can itself be a BPM. Additionally the C_i can be the negation of any of preceding types. For example if C is an object which we can evaluate then for $\overline{C}$ we have $\overline{C}(d) = 1 - C(d)$.

It is important to emphasize that all the components in a BPM are such that for any d, $C_j(d)$ takes it value in the unit interval. This allows us to evaluate objects within this logical framework and allows us to interpret m(d) as the degree to which m supports the recommendation of d. Attributes provide a natural conceptualization for users to describe preferences. In order to be able use descriptions of preferences using statements about attributes we must be able to convey their satisfaction by objects as values in the unit interval. As we pointed out earlier, however, attributes are such that their value for objects are not generally values from the unit interval but are drawn from the subset of assertions defining the attribute. However as we shall show BPM preferences specified using attribute values can be easily represented in this framework. Consider an attribute V_j and let $A(V_j) = \{A_{j1}, A_{j2},....A_{jn}\}$ be the subset of assertions related to the attribute V_j. With loss of generality we shall let A_{ji} indicate the assertion that V_{ji} *is* a_i. First let us consider the case where V_j is a variable which can take multiple solutions, such as the stars in a movie. The requirement that $V_j(d)$ has a_q as one of its values can be easily expressed by using the BPM with one component, the assertion A_{jq}. Consider now the situation where V_j is an attribute that assumes one and only one value. Consider the now the representation of the preference that V_j is a_1. We can represent this as the BPM m = <C_1, C_2: *all*> where C_1 is simply the assertion A_{j1}. The component C_2 is obtained as **not** C_3 where C_3 is the BPM defined by <A_{j2}, A_{j3}, ...A_{jn}: Q> where Q is the quantifier *any*. Using these basic modules we can model complex preference described in terms of attributes.

Using this framework based on BPM's we can express very sophisticated user preferences. Using a BPM we can express any type of user preference information as long as it can be evaluated by decomposing it into primitive assertions. Of particular value is the fact that a user can express their preferences even using concepts and language not within the given set of primitive assertions and associated attributes as long as they can eventually formulate their concepts using the primitive assertions. The general structure resulting from the use of BPM is a hierarchical type tree structure whose leafs are primitive assertions.

Let us see the process. A user expresses a predilection, C, for some types of objects. This predilection is formalized in terms of some BPM, a collection of components (criteria) and some quantifier relating these components. This components get further expressed (decomposed) by BPM's which are then further decomposed until we reach a component that is a primitive assertion which terminates a branch. This process can be considered as a type of grounding. We start at the top with the most highly abstract cognitive concepts we then express these these using less abstract terms and continue downward in the tree until we reach a grounded concept, a primitive assertion. Once having terminated each of the branches with a primitive assertion our tree provides an operational definition of the predilection expressed by the user. For any object d in D we can evaluate the degree to which it satisfies the predilection expressed. Starting at the bottom of the tree with the primitive assertions, whose validities can be obtained from our database, we then back up the tree using the OWA aggregation method. We stop when we reach the top of the tree, this is the degree to which the object d satisfies the expressed preference.

1.5 User Profiles

Using the basic preference modules introduced in the previous section we can now define a user profile to be included in a recommender system. One part of the user profile is the user *preference* profile $M = \{m_1, m_2, \ldots\ldots, m_K\}$ consisting of a collection of BPM's where each m_j describes a class of objects that the user likes. Satisfying any of the m_j provides a justification for recommending an object to the user. If $m_j(d)$ indicates the degree to which d satisfies the BPM m_j then $M(d) = \text{Max}_j [m_j(d)]$ is the degree of positive recommendation of d.

We can extend this to a situation where the user associates with each m_j a value $\alpha_j \in [0, 1]$ indicating the strength of this preference. Using this we calculate $M(d)) = \text{Max}_j[m_j(a) \wedge \alpha_j]$. We can also allow a user to supply negative or rejection information. We define a **Basic Rejection Module** (BRM) n_i to be a description of objects which the user prefers <u>not</u> to have recommended to him. A BRM is of the same form of BPM except it describes features which the user specifies as constituting objects he doesn't want. Thus a second component of the user profile is a collection $N=\{n_i\}$ of basic rejection modules. Using this we can calculate the degree of negative recommendation (rejection) of any object to a user, $N(d) = Max_i[n_i(d)]$. It is not necessary that a user have any negative modules. Additionally we can associate with each rejection module n_i a value $\beta_i \in [0, 1]$ indicating the weight associated with the rejection module n_i. Using this we get $N(d) = Max_i[n_i(d) \wedge \beta_j]$.

We must now combine these to two types of scores, recommendation and rejection. Let $\mathbf{R}(d)$ indicate the overall degree of recommendations of d. One possibility is a bounded subtraction $\mathbf{R}(d) = (M(d) - N(d)) \vee 0$. Another possibility is to assume that rejection has priority over preference $\mathbf{R}(d) = (1 - N(d)) \wedge M(d)$. Here we recommend things that are preferred and not rejected by the user. More expressive forms are possible.

1.6 Using Experience for Justification

We now consider the environment in which the user preference information is obtained using their previous experiences. We assume a user has a subset of E of D consisting of objects which it is known they have experienced. We also assume that for any object in E they provide a value $a \in [0, 1]$ indicating their scoring of that object. Our goal here is to suggest ways in which we can use this type of information to recommend new objects to our user. Again we also assume we have a representation schema over the objects in D.

One meta rational for recommending objects is to find objects which the user has experienced and liked and then recommend unexperienced objects similar to these. To implement this we need to have some measure of the similarity between objects. The availability of a representation for the objects allows for the construction of a measure of similarity between objects, hence we will assume the existence of a similarity relationship S over the set D. Thus for any two object di and dj in D we assume $S(d_i, d_j) \in [0,1]$ is available. Furthermore based on the users experiences we have for each d_i in E a rating, a_i, indicating the score the user has attributed to this object. We note these the totality of these ratings can be viewed as a fuzzy subset A over E in which $A(d_i) = a_i$. Semantically A corresponds to the subset of objects the user liked.

Our goal here is to use this information provide recommendations over the space $M = D - E$ of unexperienced objects. One approach is to provide a collection of justifications or circumstances which indicate that an object in M is suitable for recommendation. If R_j are a collection of justifications for recommending objects and $R_j(d_i)$ indicates the degree R_j supports the recommendation of d_i then the overall recommendation of d_i is

$$\mathbf{R}(d_i) = \text{Maxj}[R_j(d_i)].$$

Let us consider some guidelines that can be used to support recommendations based on the experiences of the user. Our goal here is not as much to provide a definitive listing of rules but to see how fuzzy logic can be used to enable the construction of some commonsense justifications which are expressed in a natural type language.

A simple yet basic rule of recommendation is the following
Rule 1: Recommend an object if there exists a *similar* object that the user *liked*. Under this rule the strength of recommendation of an unexperienced object d_i in $D - E$ can be obtained as

$$R_1(d_i) = \underset{j \in E}{MAX} \ [S(d_i, d_j) \wedge A(d_j)]$$

A second natural guideline for recommending objects is a softening of the first rule.
Rule 2: Recommend an object for which their are *at least several comparable* objects which the user *somewhat liked*.

Here we are softening the requirements of rule 1 by allowing a weaker indication of satisfaction, *somewhat liked* and allowing a weaker form of proximity between the objects as denoted by the use of the word **comparable** instead of similar. We are compensating for this softening by requiring *at least several* such objects instead of just a single object. Our goal now is to suggest a method to formalize this type of rule so that we can evaluate whether an object in M is recommendable under this guideline. In anticipation of modeling this rule we introduce some fuzzy subsets. First we note that the term *at least several* is an example of what Zadeh called a linguistic quantity, words denoting precise or imprecise quantities. Zadeh (1983) suggested that any linguistic quantity can be represented as a fuzzy subset Q over the set of integers. It is clear that *at least several* is monotonic in that $Q(k_1) \geq Q(k_2)$ if $k_1 > k_2$. We now must introduce a fuzzy subset to capture the idea of *somewhat liked*. This concept can be modeled in a number of different ways. With A being the fuzzy subset of E indicating the users satisfaction, $A(d_j) = a_j$ we let $\tilde{A}$ be a softening of this corresponding to the concept "somewhat liked." One way of defining $\tilde{A}$ is using a transformation function $T[0, 1] \rightarrow [0, 1]$ such that $T(a) \geq a$ and then defining $\tilde{A}(x_j) = T(A(x_j))$. One formulation for T is $T(a) = (T(a))^{\alpha}$ for $0 < \alpha < 1$. The smaller α the more the softening. The function T can also be expressed using a fuzzy systems modeling, for example

> if a is *low* then $T(a)$ is *medium*
> if a is *moderate* then $T(a)$ is *high*
> if a is *large* then $T(a)$ is *very large*

Finally we must define the concept **comparable**. As used, the term comparable is meant to indicate a softening of the concept of similar. Again if T is defined as in the preceding as a softening function we can use this to provide a definition for **comparable**. Thus if $S(x, y)$ indicates the degree of similarity between two objects then we can use $\text{Comp}(x, y) = T(S(x, y))$ to indicate the degree to which they are comparable. Here one possible definition for T in this case is

$$T(a) = 1 \text{ if } a \geq \beta \text{ and } T(a) = \beta \text{ if } a < \beta.$$

Once having satisfactorily obtained representations of these softening concepts we can use them to provide an operational formulation of this second rule. For any $d_i \in D - E$ we have

$$R_2(d_i) = \underset{F \subseteq E}{Max} [Q(|F|) \wedge \underset{d_j \subseteq F}{Min} (\tilde{A}(d_j)) \wedge \text{Comp}(d_j, d_i))]$$

In the preceding we can express

$$\tilde{A}(d_j) = T_1(A(d_j)) \text{ and } \text{Comp}(d_j, d_i) = T_2(S(d_j, d_i))$$

where T_1 and T_2 are two softening transformations. It is interesting to see that our first rule is a special case of this. If we let T_1 and T_2 be such that $T_1(a) = T_2(a) = a$ then

$$R_2(d_i) = \underset{F \subseteq E}{Max} [Q(|F|) \wedge \underset{d_j \subseteq F}{Min} (A(d_j)) \wedge S(d_j, d_i))]$$

Furthermore if Q is defined to be "at least one" then $Q(|F|) = 1$ if $F \neq \Phi$ and hence

$$R_2(d_i) = \underset{F \subseteq E}{Max} [\underset{d_j \subseteq F}{Min} (A(d_j)) \wedge S(d_j, d_i))].$$

This is equal to $\underset{d_j \subseteq E}{Max} [(A(d_j)) \wedge S(d_j, d_i))]$ which is $R_1(d_i)$.

It is interesting to consider the situation in which we have a collection of rules of this type, $R_k = <Q_k, \tilde{A}_k, Comp_k>$ where each is a softening of the preceding. Each one requiring more objects but softening either or both the requirements regarding satisfaction to the user and proximity to the object being evaluated. Here then, in this softening process, we are essentially increasing the radius about the object, decreasing the required strength but increasing the number of objects that need be found.

Another rational for justifying recommendation of objects is to look for unexperienced objects that have a lot of neighbors which the user has experienced regardless of the valuation which they have been given. This captures the idea that the user likes objects of this type regardless of their evaluation. For a example a person may see horror movies even if they think these movies are bad. As we shall see this type of rule can be expressed as an extreme case of the preceding recommendation rules. Again consider a rule $<Q, \tilde{A}, Comp>$ where we evaluate its relevance to an object d_i in M as

$$R_2(d_i) = \underset{F \subseteq E}{Max} \; [Q(|F|) \wedge \underset{d_j \subseteq F}{Min} \; (\tilde{A}(d_j)) \wedge Comp(d_j, d_i))].$$

To use this to model this new imperative we let

$\tilde{A}(d_j)) = 1$ if $d_j \in E$ and hence $R(d_i) = \underset{F \subseteq E}{Max} \; [Q(|F|) \wedge \underset{d_j \subseteq F}{Min} \; (Comp(d_j, d_i))].$

Letting $Comp(d_j, d_i) = S(d_j, d_i)$ we have

$$R(d_i) = \underset{F \subseteq E}{Max} \; [Q(|F|) \wedge \underset{d_j \subseteq F}{Min} \; (S(d_j, d_i))].$$

This can be seen as a type of fuzzy integral [Sugeno (1977)]. Let $S_{indexi(k)}$ be the kth most similar object in E to the object d_i. Furthermore let $q_k = Q(k)$ then

$$R(d_i) = Max_k[q_k \wedge S_{indexi(k)}].$$

The essential idea of the preceding methods for justifying recommendations was based on the process of discovering unexperienced items located in areas of the object space that are ***rich*** in objects that the user liked or experienced. We can capture this procedure in an alternative manner. For each unexperienced item, $d_i \in D - E$, we calculate $W(d_i) = \underset{d_j \in E}{\sum} a_j \, S(d_i, d_j)$. We can then map $W(d_i)$ into a value in the unit interval indicating the degree of recommendation for d_i Fuzzy systems modeling can be useful in constructing this mapping.

We should note that the preference profile introduced in the preceding section can be extended to include justifications of the type described here.

1.7 Conclusion

Here we have suggested some methodologies for constructing recommender systems. These approaches made use of the available description, representation, of the objects being considered for recommendation. We also only used preference information about the customer being served. We believe the future generation of recommender systems will recombine these techniques with the collaborative filtering approach.

Bibliography

Goldberg, D., Nichols, D., Oki, B. M. and Terry, D. (1992). Using collaborative filtering to weave an information tapestry, *Communications of the ACM* 35(12), pp. 61-70.

Konstan, J. A., Miller, B. N., Maltz, D., Herlocker, J. L., Gordon, L. R. and Riedl, J. (1997). Grouplens: Applying collaborative filtering to Usenet news, *Communications of the ACM* 40(3), pp. 77-87.

Resnick, P. and Varian, H. R. (1997). Recommender systems, *Communications of the ACM* 40(3), pp. 56-58.

Shardanand, U. and Maes, P. (1995). Social information filtering: algorithms for automating word of mouth, *Proceedings of the Computer Human Interaction-95 Conference*, Denver, pp. 210–217.

Sugeno, M. (1977). Fuzzy measures and fuzzy integrals: a survey, in *Fuzzy Automata and Decision Process,* Gupta, M.M., Saridis, G.N. & Gaines, B.R. (eds.), Amsterdam: North-Holland Pub, pp. 89-102.

Yager, R. R. (1988). On ordered weighted averaging aggregation operators in multi-criteria decision making, *IEEE Transactions on Systems, Man and Cybernetics* 18, pp. 183-190.

Yager, R. R. (1996). Quantifier guided aggregation using OWA operators," International Journal of Intelligent Systems 11, pp. 49-73.

Yager, R. R.(2000a). Veristic variables, *IEEE Trans on Systems, Man and Cybernetics* Part B: Cybernetics 30, pp. 71-84.

Yager, R. R. (2000b). A hierarchical document retrieval language, Information Retrieval 3, pp. 357-377.

Yager, R. R. (To Appear). On the retranslation process in Zadeh's paradigm of computing with words," *IEEE Transactions on Systems, Man and Cybernetics*.

Zadeh, L. A. (1983). A computational approach to fuzzy quantifiers in natural languages, *Computing and Math with Applications* 9, pp. 149-184.

CHAPTER 2

WEB INTELLIGENCE: CONCEPT-BASED WEB SEARCH

Masoud Nikravesh[1] and Tomohiro Takagi[2]

[1]BISC Program, EECS Department-CS Division
University of California, Berkeley, CA 94720, USA
[2] Dept. of Computer Science, Meiji University, Japan
Nikravesh@cs.berkeley.edu, Takagi@cs.meiji.ac.jp

Retrieving relevant information is a crucial component of cased-based reasoning systems for Internet applications such as search engines. The task is to use user-defined queries to retrieve useful information according to certain measures. Even though techniques exist for locating exact matches, finding relevant partial matches might be a problem. The objective of this paper is to develop an intelligent computer system with some deductive capabilities to conceptually cluster, match and rank pages based on predefined linguistic formulations and rules defined by experts or based on a set of known homepages. The Conceptual Fuzzy Set (CFS) model will be used for intelligent information and knowledge retrieval through conceptual matching of both text and links (here defined as "Concept"). The selected query doesn't need to match the decision criteria exactly, which gives the system a more human-like behavior. The model can be used for intelligent information and knowledge retrieval through Web-connectivity-based clustering. We will also present the integration of our technology into commercial search engines such as Google ™ as a framework that can be used to integrate our model into any other commercial search engines.

2.1 Introduction

The web environment is, for the most part, unstructured and imprecise.

To deal with information in the web environment what is needed is a logic that supports modes of reasoning which are approximate rather than exact. While searches may retrieve thousands of hits, finding decision-relevant and query-relevant information in an imprecise environment is a challenging problem, which has to be addressed. Another, and less obvious, is deduction in an unstructured and imprecise environment given the huge stream of complex information.

During the recent years, applications of fuzzy logic and the internet from web data mining to intelligent search engine and agents for internet applications have greatly increased [Nikravesh (2002); Nikravesh et al. (2002), (2003a), (2003b), (2003c), (2003d); Nikravesh, Choi (2003); Nikravesh, Azvine (2001), (2002); Takagi et al. (2002a), (2002b)]. The central tasks for the most of the search engines can be summarize as 1) query or user information request- do what I mean and not what I say!, 2) model for the Internet, Web representation-web page collection, documents, text, images, music, etc, and 3) ranking or matching function-degree of relevance, recall, precision, similarity, etc. There are two type of search engines that we are interested and are dominating the Internet. First, the most popular search engines that are mainly for unstructured data such as Google ™ and Teoma which are based on the concept of Authorities and Hubs (Figure 2.1). Second, search engines that are task specifics such as 1) Yahoo!: manually-preclassified, 2) NorthernLight: Classification, 3) Vivisimo: Clustering, 4) Self-organizing Map: Clustering + Visualization and 5) AskJeeves: Natural Languages-Based Search; Human Expert. Google uses the PageRank and Teoma uses HITS for the Ranking. Figure 2.1 shows the Authorities and Hubs concept and the possibility of comparing two homepages.

In this chapter, we will present an intelligent model that can mine the Internet to conceptually match, rank, and cluster the homepages based on predefined linguistic formulations and rules defined by experts or based on a set of known homepages. This model can be used to calculate conceptually the degree of match to the object or query. We will also present the integration of our technology into commercial search engines such as Google ™ as a framework that can be used to integrate our model into any other commercial search engines, or development of the next generation of search engines (Figure 2.2).

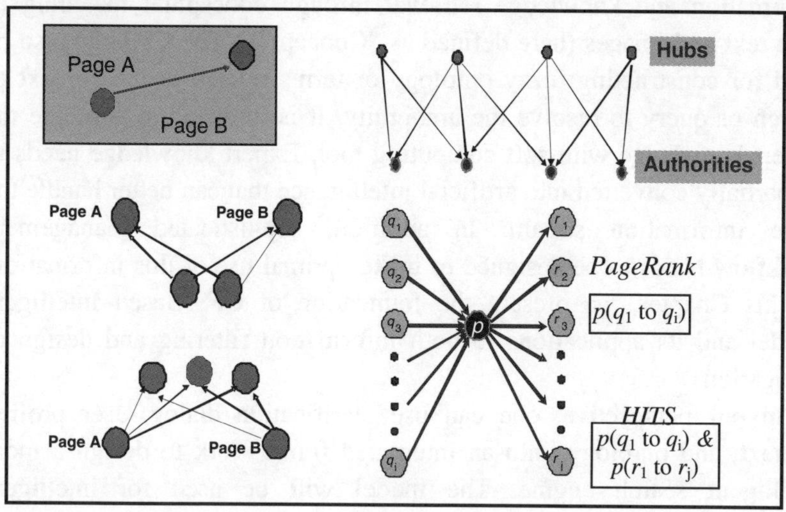

Fig. 2.1 Similarity of web pages.

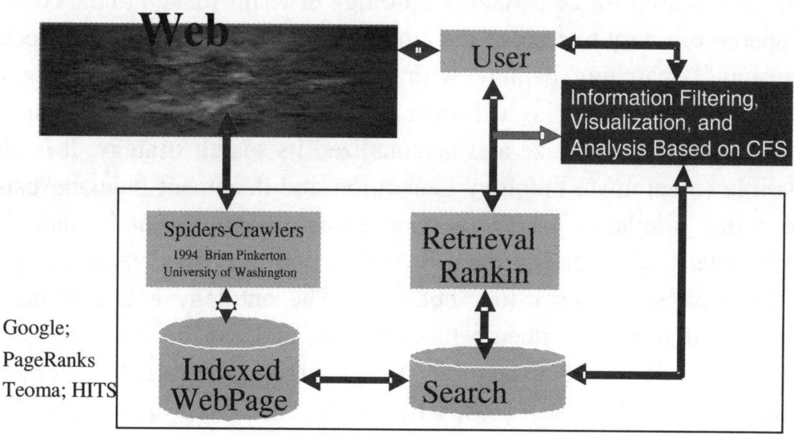

Fig. 2.2 Search Engines Architecture.

2.2 Fuzzy Conceptual Model and Search Engine

The Conceptual Fuzzy Set (CFS) model will be used for intelligent information and knowledge retrieval through conceptual matching of both text and images (here defined as "Concept"). The CFS can also be used for constructing fuzzy ontology or terms related to the context of search or query to resolve the ambiguity. It is intended to combine the expert knowledge with soft computing tool. Expert knowledge needs to be partially converted into artificial intelligence that can better handle the huge information stream. In addition, sophisticated management workflow needs to be designed to make optimal use of this information. In this Chapter, we present the foundation of CFS-Based Intelligent Model and its applications to both information filtering and design of navigation.

In our perspective, one can use clarification dialog, user profile, context, and ontology, into an integrated frame work to design a more intelligent search engine. The model will be used for intelligent information and knowledge retrieval through conceptual matching of text. The selected query doesn't need to match the decision criteria exactly, which gives the system a more human-like behavior. The model can also be used for constructing ontology or terms related to the context of search or query to resolve the ambiguity. The new model can execute conceptual matching dealing with context-dependent word ambiguity and produce results in a format that permits the user to interact dynamically to customize and personalized its search strategy. It is also possible to automate ontology generation and document indexing using the terms similarity based on Conceptual-Latent Semantic Indexing Technique (CLSI). Often time it is hard to find the "right" term and even in some cases the term does not exist. The ontology is automatically constructed from text document collection and can be used for query refinement. It is also possible to generate conceptual documents similarity map that can be used for intelligent search engine based on CLSI, personalization and user profiling. The user profile is automatically constructed from text document collection and can be used for query refinement and provide suggestions and for ranking the information based on pre-existence user profile. Given the ambiguity and imprecision of the "concept" in the Internet, which may be described by both textual and image information, the use of Fuzzy Conceptual Matching (FCM) is a necessity for search engines. In the FCM approach, the "concept" is defined by a series of keywords with different weights depending on the importance of each keyword. Ambiguity in concepts can be defined by a set of imprecise concepts. Each imprecise concept in fact can be defined by a set of fuzzy concepts. The fuzzy concepts can then be related to a set of imprecise words given the context. Imprecise words can then be translated into precise words given the ontology and ambiguity resolution through clarification dialog. By constructing the ontology and fine-tuning the strength of links (weights), we could construct a fuzzy set to integrate piecewise the imprecise concepts and precise words to define the ambiguous concept.

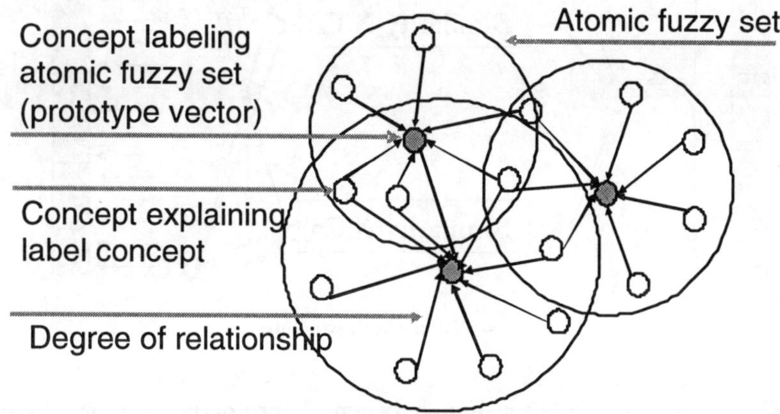

Fig. 2.3 CFSs based on RBF networks.

2.3 Construction of RBF network

In the CFSs, words may have synonymous, antonymous, hypernymous and hyponymous relation to other words. These relations are too complicated to be represented in a hierarchical structure. In this paper, we use RBF-like networks to generate CFSs. The image of CFSs is shown in Figure 2.3. The strength of the links between concepts reflects their degrees of relationship. The centered concept and its connected concepts constitute a fragment of concept description. A CFS is generated by overlapping the fragments of the activated concept description. A CFS expresses the meaning of a concept by the activation values of other concepts in these fragments.

2.4 Generation of CFSs

To generate CFSs, concepts are activated using the RBF networks as follows. In general, RBF networks have a structure shown in Figure 2.4.

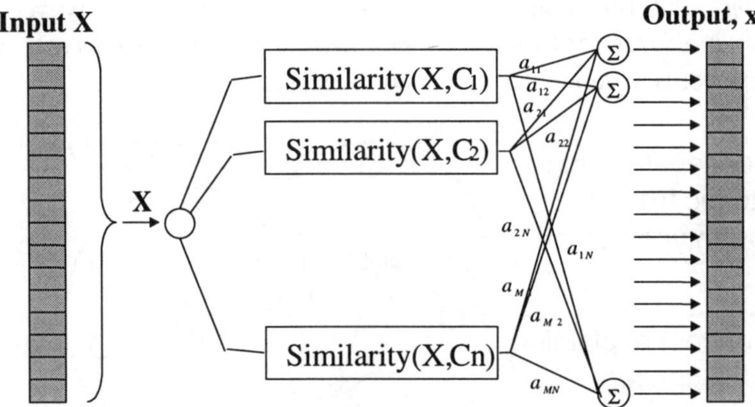

Fig. 2.4 RBF network structure.

The degree of relationship between a prototype vector c_i (i-th fragment of the concept description) and an input vector x is measured as,

$$\phi(dist(x, c_i))$$

and dist means the distance. Function φ translates the distance to the activation value of the prototype vector. Usually the distance is calculated by Euclidean distance.

$$dist(x, c_i) = \| x - c_i \|$$

The activation values of prototype vectors are weighted with degrees of relationship a_{ij}, and propagate to the relating nodes. So the activation value propagated to j-th node from i-th prototype vector c_i becomes,

$$a_{ij} \times \phi(dist(x, c_i))$$

Each node in output layer sums up values translated from all prototype vectors as,

$$\sum_{i=1}^{M} a_{ij} \times \phi(dist(x, c_i))$$

2.5 Illustrative Example of CFSs

Let's think about Java. If we are talking about computers, "java" will be understood as a programming language. If we are looking at a menu at a cafe, it will be understood as a kind of coffee. Its meaning is thus determined by context generated by the presence of related words, such as FORTRAN and C (Figure 2.5).

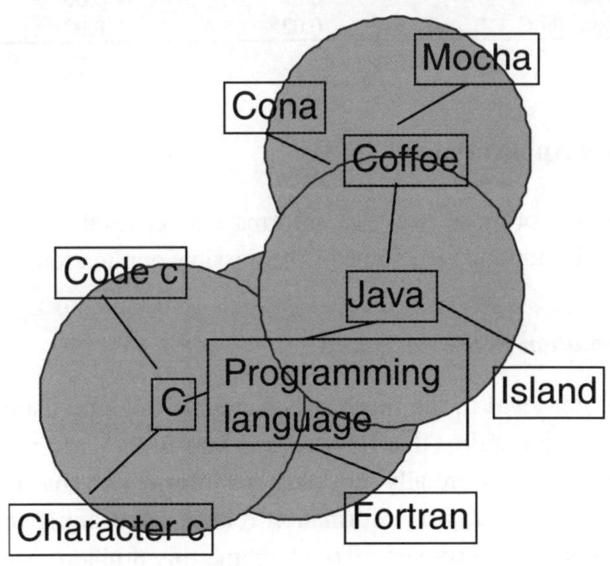

Fig. 2.5 Example of RBF, containing Java related fragments of concept.

Table 2.1 shows the propagated results in a network shown in Figure 2.5 starting from activation of "Java" and "C", and "Java" and "Mocha". After propagation of the activation of Java and C, coffee is 0.17 activated and programming language is 0.33 activated. In this case, Java is recognized as a programming language. In contrast, starting with the activation of Java and Mocha, Coffee is 0.47 activated, and programming language is 0.20 activated. Java is thus recognized as coffee.

Table 2.1 Propagated results starting from activation of "Java" and "C", and "Java" and "Mocha".

	Java&C	Java&Moca
Mocha	0.04	0.43
Cona	0.04	0.10
Coffee	0.17	0.47
Java	0.36	0.43
Island	0.22	0.27
Prog. lang.	0.33	0.20
Fortran	0.08	0.05
C	0.39	0.05
Code C	0.02	0.00
Character C	0.02	0.00

2.6 Previous Applications of CFSs

Previously, we proposed several information retrieval related systems using CFSs. Followings are some of the possible application areas.

2.6.1 *Information Retrieval System*

Information retrieval in the Internet is generally done by using keyword matching, which requires that for words to match; they must be the same or synonyms. But essentially, not only the information that matches the keywords exactly, but also information related in meaning to the input keywords should be retrieved. To overcome this problem, we proposed the architecture a search engine which conceptually matches input keywords and web pages. The conceptual matching is realized by context-dependent keyword expansion using conceptual fuzzy sets. We also we evaluated our proposed method through two simulations of retrieving actual web pages, and compared the proposed method with the ordinary TF-IDF method. We showed that our method could correlate seemingly unrelated input keywords and produce matching Web pages, whereas the simple TF-IDF method could not.

2.6.2 *Exposure of Illegal Web Sites Using : Conceptual Fuzzy Sets-Based Information Filtering System*

Usual information filtering system determines whether a document matches to a given topic or not comparing a word vector made from the original document with the topic. However, words relating to the topic do not exist in the document in general. We proposed an algorithm expanding keywords, emphasizing the expanded words relating to its subject and suppressing irrelevant ones. We developed a prototype system distinguishing illegal web sites from legal ones. It is achieved by describing what are considered to be illegal sites and by judging whether the objective web sites match the description of illegality. CFSs are used to describe the concept of illegal web sites. Currently, over 3,600 million or more web pages exist on the Internet. People can obtain necessary information from this huge network quickly and easily. On the other hand, various problems have arisen. For example, there are the adult sites, the criminal sites which illegally distribute software (Warez) and music (MP3) and the criminal promotion sites which promote illegal behavior such as making a bomb etc. Therefore, one of the technologies needed currently is the filtering of web sites.

Some software is put to practical use as an internet filter. However, typical software simply matches the web sites with illegal URL lists. This approach does not take their contents into consideration at all. These methods lack updating capabilities due to the drastic increase of illegal sites. Additionally, some software eliminates web sites that contain illegal words. They eliminate web sites by calculating confidence of the illegal words in documents by the TF-IDF method. The content-based approach using the TF-IDF method may eliminate any sites that contain harmful words. For example, news sites, which contain harmful words, may be eliminated. In this paper, we propose a filtering system that performs semantic analysis of a web document using conceptual fuzzy sets (CFSs). Our approach concerns not only the appearance of words in a document but also the meanings of words to recognize the harmful nature of a document.

2.6.2.1 *System Description*

We developed a system filtering web pages using conceptual fuzzy sets based on RBF networks and CFS (Figure 2.6).

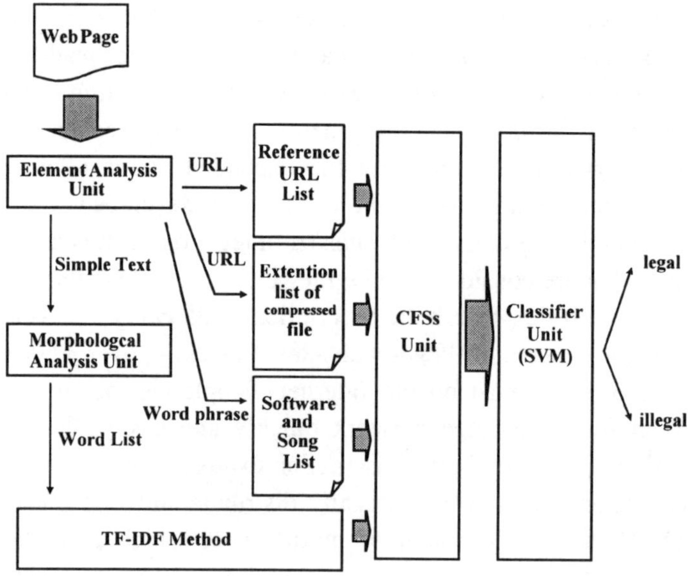

Fig. 2.6 Filtering system using CFSs.

2.6.2.2 *CFSs Unit*

A word vector, which consists of TF-IDF values, the link rates and the matching degree, is input into the CFSs unit. Propagation of activations occurs from input word vector throughout fragments of the concept descriptions and then abstract concepts "warez", "MP3" and "Emulator" are recognized. CFSs units consists of fragments of the concept descriptions, such as "warez", "MP3", etc as shown in Figure 2.7.

2.6.2.3 *Evaluations Procedure*

In this study, we randomly selected 300 actual web sites as samples for evaluation, and we compared the proposed method with the support

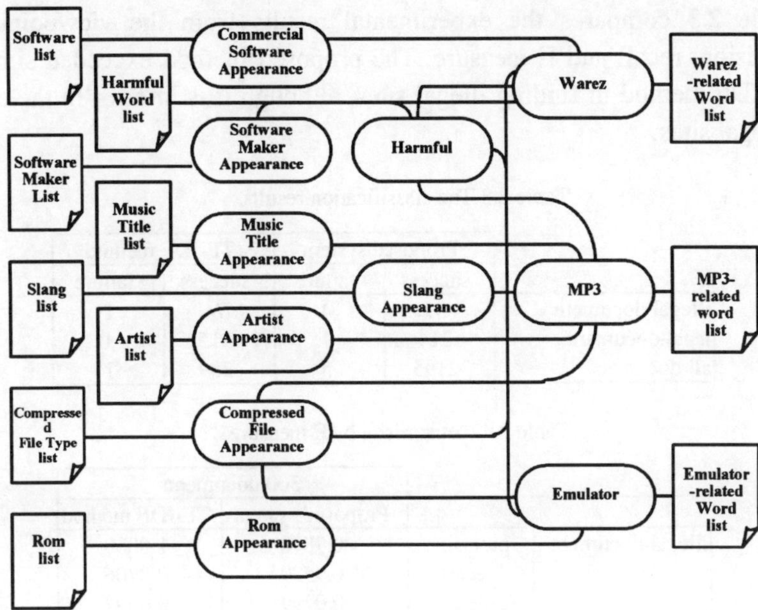

Fig. 2.7 Concept description in the CFS unit.

vector machine. The samples contained 85 illegal sites. We assumed seven types of the illegal sites shown in Table 2.2. This classification is not based on the law strictly but on common sense. We evaluated the system by filtering Warez, Emulator and MP3 sites in this study.

Table 2.2 Seven types of illegal sites.

Group	A classification criterion
Warez	Illegal distribution and sale of commercial software
Emulater	Illegal distribution of software, such as consumer games and video games
MP3	Distribution of music data which infringe on copyright
Adult	Dirty depictions and expressions
Hack & Crack	Distribution of illegal hacking and cracking software
	Instruction of technical know-how
Drug & Gun	Sale of drugs and guns
	Introduction of acquisition route
Killing	Expressions about murder, violate depiction, etc.

2.6.2.4 *Results*

The results of the experiments are shown in Table 2.3 and Table 2.4.

Table 2.3 compares the experimental results from the viewpoint of precision, recall and E measure. The proposed method exceeded simple TF-IDF method in finding illegal sites, although it is inferior in the case of legal sites.

Table 2.3 The classification results.

	Proposed system		TF-IDF method	
	success	failure	success	failure
illegal document	81	4	74	11
legal document	214	1	215	0
all document	2195	5	289	11

Table 2.4 Comparison by E measure.

		300 documents	
		Proposed system	TF-IDF method
illegal document	precision	0.9878	1.0000
	recall	0.9529	0.8706
	E measure	0.0299	0.0692
legal document	precision	0.9817	0.9556
	recall	0.9953	1.0000
	E measure	0.0115	0.0227

In this application, we applied the CFSs using RBF networks. Moreover, we proposed a system which is capable of filtering harmful web sites. We showed that the semantic interpretation of the concept by CFSs exceeded the TF-IDF method which is based on the superficial statistical information.

However, the proposed system has been evaluated using the limited number of target web documents. In our future work, we need to strengthen the conceptual descriptions and generalizations of CFSs that can be used in the entire Internet.

2.6.2.5 *Fuzzy-TF.IDF*

The use of Fuzzy-tf-idf is an alternative to the use of the conventional tf-idf. In this case, the original tf-idf weighting values will be replaced by a fuzzy set rather than original crisp value. To reconstruct such value both

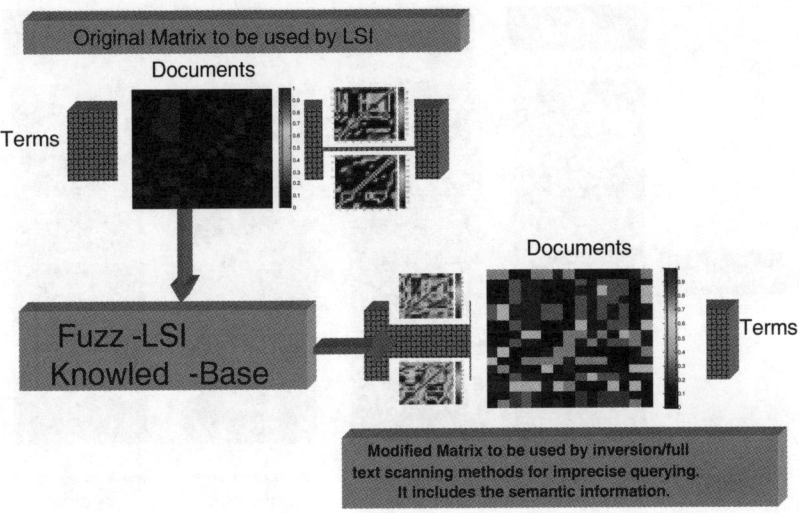

Fig. 2.8 Fuzzy-Latent Semantic Indexing-Based Conceptual Technique.

ontology and similarity measure can be used. To develop ontology and similarity one can used the conventional Latent Semantic Indexing (LSI). or Fuzzy-LSI [Nikravesh, Azvine (2002)]. The fuzzy-LSI (Figure 2.8), fuzzy-TF-IDF, and CFS can be used through an integrated system to develop fuzzy conceptual model for intelligent search engine. One can use clarification dialog, user profile, context, and ontology, into a integrated frame work to address some of the issues related to search engines were described earlier. In our perspective, we define this framework as *Fuzzy Conceptual Matching based on Human Mental Model* (Figure 2.9).

2.6.3 *Conceptual Fuzzy Sets-Based Navigation System for Yahoo!*

We proposed a menu navigation system which conceptually matches input keywords with all paths from a root category to leaf categories. Input keywords don't always match words on category menus directly.

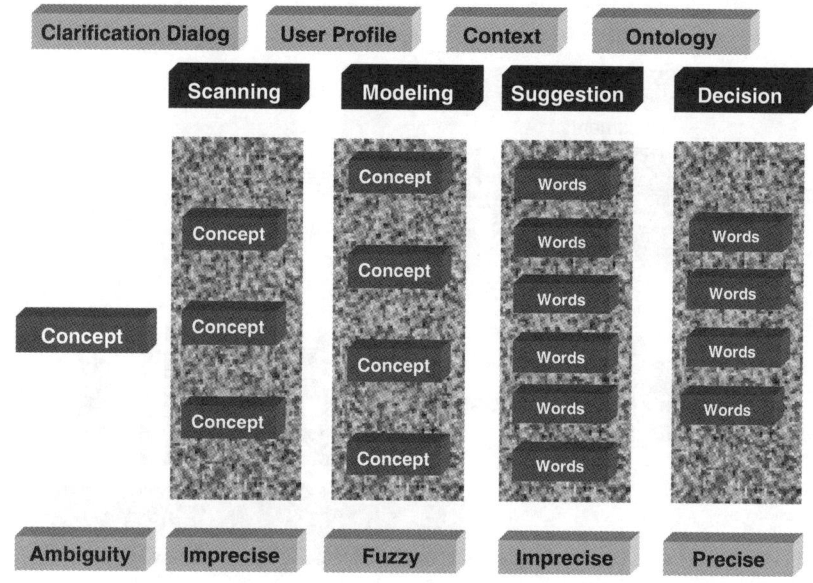

Fig. 2.9 Fuzzy Conceptual Matching and Human Mental Model.

Taking the meaning of a path into consideration and propagating activations of concepts recursively in CFS unit to associate relative words with input keywords enabled the system to search the path leading to an appropriate category.

2.6.3.1 *Navigation System for Yahoo!*

Many search engines such as Yahoo! classify a large number of web sites into their own large hierarchical categories (directories). Although category menus are provided for users, the users don't commonly know the hierarchical structure nor do they understand which item (categories) on the menus to select to find documents they want. In this section, we propose a navigation system which conceptually matches input keywords with all paths from a root category to leaf categories. Input keywords don't always match words on category menus directly. The proposed system conceptually matches keywords with paths by taking the meaning of a path into consideration and by expanding keywords. For conceptual matching, we use CFSs based on RBF networks.

2.6.3.2 *Navigation System*

In this section, we describe our navigation system which conceptually matches input keywords and all paths. The system consists of a CFS unit, a path base, a matching unit and a user interface. Figure 2.10 shows the architecture of the system.

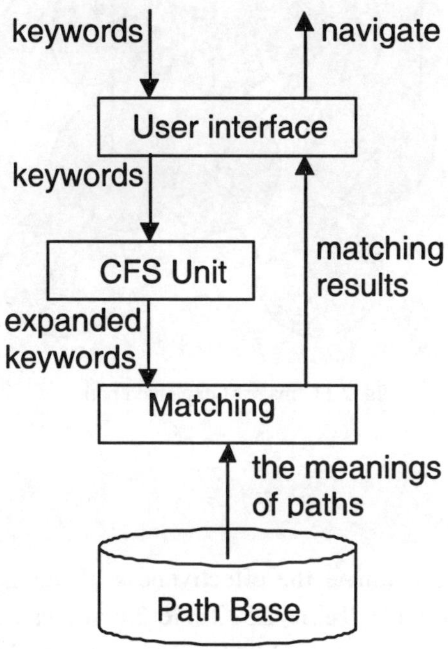

Fig. 2.10 Navigation System Architecture.

2.6.3.3 *Path base*

A path is a sequence of category labels from a root category to a leaf category. We take the meaning of a path into consideration to search paths to appropriate categories.

The meaning of a path is the result of expansion in the CFS unit from the category labels in the path. The path base stores all the paths and their corresponding meanings. Figure 2.11 shows the image of expanded paths.

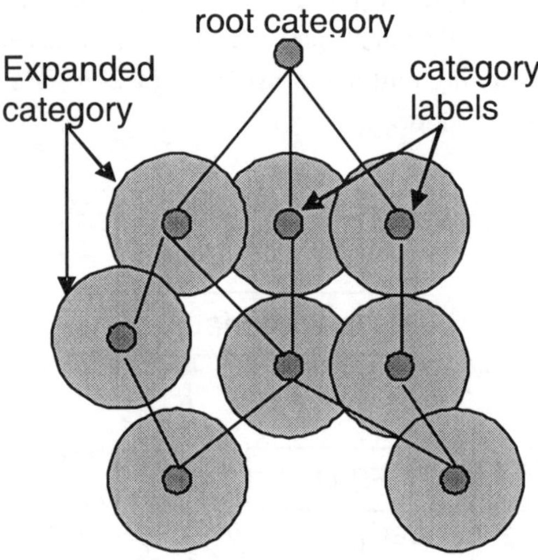

Fig. 2.11 Image of expanded paths.

2.6.3.4 *Experiments*

In this section, we evaluate the effectiveness of our navigation system using test data shown in Table 2.5. Table 2.6 shows some examples of paths. They referred *Yahoo! JAPAN*. First, we evaluated how many times the propagation of activation values should be carried out in the CFS unit. Second, we actually search the paths and evaluate the results.

Table 2.5 Test data.

the number of paths	213
the number of words	803
the number of headwords	214

Table 2.6 Example of paths.

Business and Economy > Cooperatives > Architecture > Software
Computer and Internet > Software > Internet
Government > Law > Tax
Science > Physics > Libraries

2.6.3.5 *Determine the repeat number of propagation*

Figure 2.12 shows the changes of activation values of some words with "personal computer" and "book" as input to the CFS unit. The activation value of the word "magazine" gets higher as the propagation is carried out and is at the peak in the third to fifth iteration. The word "magazine", which highly relates to "book", is associated by iterating propagation of activation values in CFS unit. The activation value of the word "information" is also at the peak in the third to fifth iteration. Although the word "information" is not connected directly to "personal computer" nor "book", the iteration of the propagation of activation values enables the association of the word.

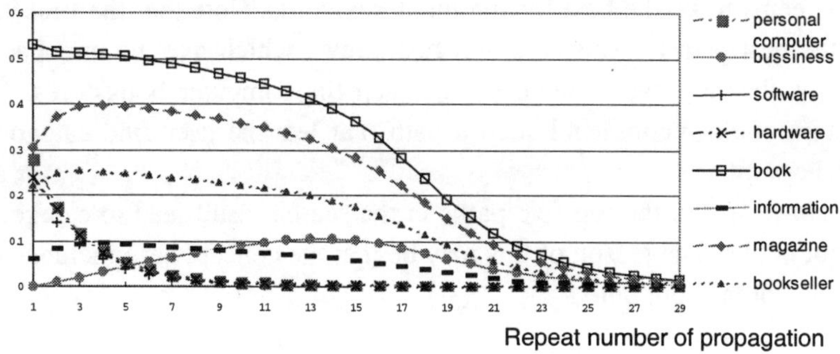

Fig. 2.12 Changes of activation values.

2.6.3.6 *Search the paths*

We assume that a user is interested in books about personal computers, and then he/she inputs "personal computer" and "book" as keywords. We fixed the repeat number of propagation in the CFS unit on three times and searched the paths with these keywords. The result is shown in Table 2.7.

Table 2.7 Matching results.

Business and Economy > Cooperatives > Books > Booksellers > Computers   Similarity = 0.951106
Business and Economy > Cooperatives > Books > Booksellers > Magazines   Similarity = 0.945896
Business and Economy > Cooperatives > Books > Booksellers > Movies   Similarity = 0.918033
Business and Economy > Cooperatives > Books > Booksellers > Architecture   Similarity = 0.9093
Business and Economy > Cooperatives > Books > Booksellers > Literature   Similarity = 0.904156

The top ranked path leads to the category which is assigned to web sites of online computer bookstores. The system could search the path that seems to be the best for the input keywords. Note that the first item in the best path is "Business and Economy", which may be unexpected for him/her to have to click on to reach the computer bookstores. Our system could recommend such a path that lets the user find categories he/she wants.

However, all the top five paths in the search result lead to categories about books. The reason of this may be that the concept base includes too many words about books.

2.6.3.7 *3D user interface*

We have developed a 3D user interface to navigate users effectively. The interface displays hierarchical structure in the same manner as Cone Tree (Robertson et al 90 and 91). Figure 2.13 is a screenshot of the user interface. Users can easily understand their position in large categorical hierarchy and the system can prevent them from getting lost. And for users who want to get more detail, functions such as rotation and zoom are also provided.

Paths with high similarities to input keywords are highlighted and the system can help users to reach appropriate categories.

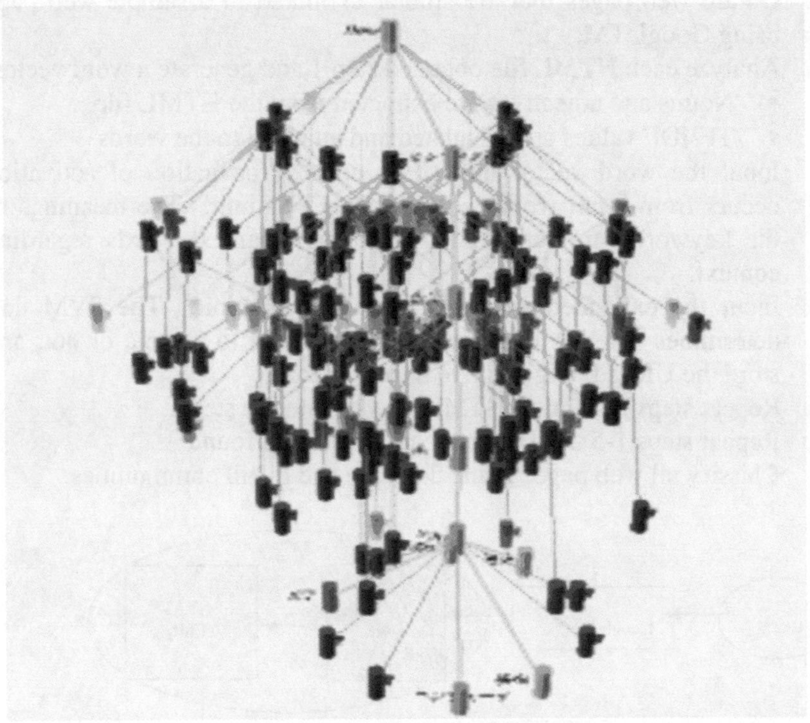

Fig. 2.13 3D user interface.

2.7 Concept-Based Web Communities for Google™ Search Engine

In this paper we apply CFSs to cluster web pages and distill their communities. In this section, we explain an outline of the proposed system and describe each module in our proposed model.

2.7.1 System Architecture

The proposed system processes web pages along with following steps and distills communities of pages. The system is roughly divided into two parts; filtering part (steps 1-6) and classifying part (step 7). Figure 2.14 shows the modules consisting of the proposed system.

1. Obtain web pages that are similar or linked to a sample web page using GoogleTM.
2. Analyze each HTML file obtained step 1 and generate a word vector.
   - Nouns and adjectives are extracted from the HTML file
   - TF-IDF values are calculated and attached to the words
3. Input the word vector into CFSs unit. Propagation of activation occurs from input word vector in the CFSs unit. The meanings of the keywords are represented in other expanded words regarding context.
4. Input the expanded word vector into SVM unit. The SVM unit determines whether the word vector matches to a topic or not, and store the URLs being positive into a database.
5. Repeat steps 2-4 for all HTML files resulted in step 1.
6. Repeat steps 1-5 until there are no new pages found.
7. Classify all web pages in the database and distill communities.

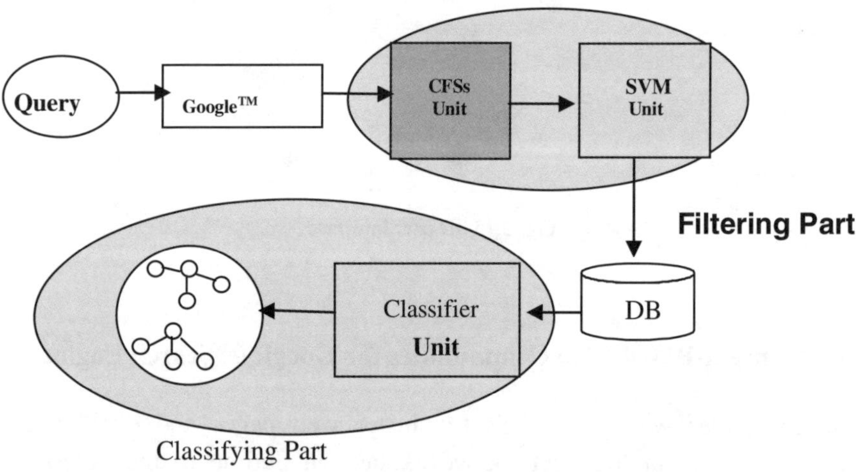

Fig. 2.14 Architecture of community distillation system.

2.7.2 CFSs Unit

This unit expands an input vector using CFSs based on RBF and transfers a resulted vector to the next SVM unit. The expansion brings the word vector to correct conceptual expression. In this experiment, we construct the CFSs with words that are frequently appeared in criminal web pages. Table 2.8 shows an example concept expression of "warez". For example, the pair "serial" and "0.8" means that the word "serial" relates to "wares" with a degree of relationship "0.8".

Table 2.8 An example concept expression "warez".

	WAREZ
warez	0.9
serial	0.8
serials	0.8
game	0.7
ames	0.7
app	0.7
apps	0.7
iso	0.5
zip	0.5
software	0.6
rom	0
emulator	0
...	
...	
...	

2.7.3 SVM Unit

This unit determines whether an input vector matches with a topic or not using a SVM (Support Vector Machine). Word vectors of actual criminal and non-criminal web pages previously train the SVM.

2.7.4 Classifier Unit

This unit generates word vectors of HTML files stored in the DB, expands these word vectors in a CFSs unit and classifies them in a SOM unit to distill web communities. Figure 2.15 shows modules and data flow in the classifier unit.

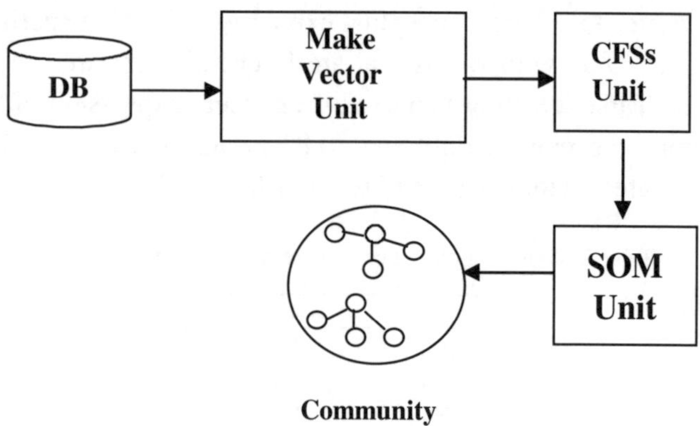

Fig. 2.15 Structure of classifier unit.

2.7.4.1 *Make Vector Unit*

This unit generates a word vector corresponding to each HTML file in the DB. Following three factors are taken into account to analyze the files and are aggregated to make a word vector.

1. The TF-IDF scores of the HTML file.
2. The TF-IDF scores of the pages that link to the original HTML file (scores of in-link files).
3. The TF-IDF scores of the pages that are linked by the original HTML file (scores of out-link files).

2.7.4.2 *CFSs Unit*

This unit is the same as the one explained in section 2.3.1. The CFSs add words relating to the words in the original word vector in its expansion process. The expansion enables conceptual matching of original HTML files, that is, conceptually close files close each other in SOM unit (see below).

2.7.4.3 *SOM Unit*

We used SOM (Self-Organization Map) to classify files. The SOM disposes large dimensional data in two or three dimension. Nodes that have short distance in the original dimension close in a result map. In this experiment, we made a two dimensional map with cosine-measure calculating a distance between two vectors.

2.7.5 *Experiment and Result*

To evaluate this system we executed filtering and classifying actual criminal web pages. A criminal URL was initially used to start gathering URLs of criminal web pages. Filtering process ended up with a DB including 19 files. Let's compare the results with and without CFSs unit. Page 1 and Page 2 in Table 2.9-1 and Table 2.9-2 are example "mp3" related web pages. Table 2.9-1 shows part of input vectors processed without CFSs unit and transferred to SOM unit, and Table 2.9-1 shows part of input vectors processed with CFSs unit. Each part contains 15 words with top 15 scores in a vector. Table 2.9-2 contains words that have stronger relations with mp3 and music than Table 2.9-1.

Table 2.9-1 Top 15 words in input vectors to SOM unit processed without CFSs unit.

Page 1		Page 2	
search	0.165674	search	0.262584
mp3	0.118774	mp3	0.095429
music	0.039699	download	0.055545
click	0.026133	music	0.038273
download	0.017919	free	0.021043
free	0.017091	click	0.018202
downloads	0.015728	audio	0.009763
ftp	0.01473	software	0.009372
vote	0.012558	album	0.009198
sound	0.011844	sound	0.009031
server	0.011095	song	0.008916
get	0.008173	artist	0.00849
game	0.007388	get	0.007687
advance	0.006955	vote	0.007396
software	0.00665	game	0.007114
...		...	
...		...	
...		...	

Table 2.9-2 Top 15 words in input vectors to SOM unit processed with CFSs unit.

Page 1		Page 2	
winmx	0.035209	winmx	0.027525
napster	0.035209	napster	0.027525
mp3z	0.032537	mp3z	0.02397
mp3s	0.031896	mp3s	0.023768
mp3	0.031511	mp3	0.023646
song	0.024038	song	0.017429
artist	0.024038	artist	0.017429
single	0.021033	dlz	0.016477
album	0.021033	dls	0.016275
music	0.021033	illegal	0.016153
titel	0.020638	dl	0.016153
cdz	0.020344	titel	0.015576
cds	0.019703	single	0.015251
cd	0.019318	album	0.015251
dlz	0.0189	music	0.015251
...		...	
...		...	
...		...	

That is, expansion with CFSs closed these two pages. As a result, these pages are put into the same cluster by classifier unit with CFSs unit, but are separated without CFSs. Table 2.10 shows the nodes in each cluster predicted by SOM unit. With CFSs unit the mp3 pages

Table 2.10 Nodes in each cluster.

CLUSTER	DATA No.
Adult	1
Driver	4
Ticket	11
Web search engines	9
Modified Web search engines	17
MP3	8,12,13,14,15
Modified	5,10
Image search	18
Image+MP3+softwere+web search	2,3,7,16
Crack+Serial+Wareze	6
Others	19

formed two clear clusters, one is for strictly mp3 and another is for mp3 related pages, on the other hand four different clusters were formed without CFSs. The result shows that conceptual expansion using CFSs has an effect to restrain needless words and to emphasize important words and brings better clustering results.

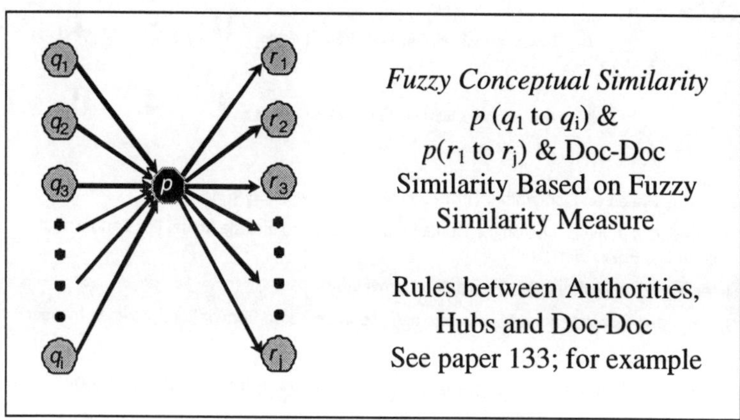

Fig. 2.16 Fuzzy Conceptual Similarity.

Figure 2.16 shows the possible model for similarity analysis is called "fuzzy Conceptual Similarity". Figure 2.17 shows the matrix representation of Fuzzy Conceptual Similarity model. Figure 2.18 shows the evolution of the Term-Document matrix. Figure 2.19 shows the structure of the Concept-based Google ™ search engine for Multi-Media Retrieval. To develop such models, state-of-the-art computational intelligence techniques are needed. These include and are not limited to:

- Latent-Semantic Indexing and SVD for preprocessing,
- Radial-Basis Function Network to develop concepts,
- Support Vector Machine (SVM) for supervised classification,
- fuzzy/neuro-fuzzy clustering for unsupervised classification based on both conventional learning techniques and Genetic and Reinforcement learning,
- non-linear aggregation operators for data/text fusion,

Webpages

$$RX' = \text{Webpages} \begin{pmatrix} 1_{\text{(Text\_Sim, In\_Link, Out\_Link, Rules, Concept)}} & 2_{(...)} & 0_{(...)} & 0_{(...)} \\ 0_{\text{(Text\_Sim, In\_Link, Out\_Link, Rules, Concept)}} & 1_{(...)} & 1_{(...)} & 6_{(...)} \\ 2_{\text{(Text\_Sim, In\_Link, Out\_Link, Rules, Concept)}} & 0_{(...)} & 5_{(...)} & 4_{(...)} \\ 0_{\text{(Text\_Sim, In\_Link, Out\_Link, Rules, Concept)}} & 1_{(...)} & 4_{(...)} & 0_{(...)} \end{pmatrix}$$

Text_sim: Based on Conceptual Term-Doc Matrix; It is a Fuzzy Set

In_Link & Out_Link: Based on the Conceptual Links which include actual links and virtual links; It is a Fuzzy Set

Rules: Fuzzy rules extracted from data or provided by user

Concept: Precisiated Natural Language definitions extracted from data or provided by user

Fig. 2.17 Matrix representation of Fuzzy Conceptual Similarity model.

- automatic recognition using fuzzy measures and a fuzzy integral approach
- self organization map and graph theory for building community and clusters,
- both genetic algorithm and reinforcement learning to learn the preferences,
- fuzzy-integration-based aggregation technique and hybrid fuzzy logic-genetic algorithm for decision analysis, resource allocation, multi-criteria decision-making and multi-attribute optimization.
- text analysis: next generation of the Text, Image Retrieval and concept recognition based on soft computing technique and in particular Conceptual Search Model (CSM). This includes
  - Understanding textual content by retrieval of relevant texts or paragraphs using CSM followed by clustering analysis.
  - Hierarchical model for CSM
  - Integration of Text and Images based on CSM
  - CSM Scalability, and
  - The use of CSM for development of
    - Ontology

- Query Refinement and Ambiguity Resolution
- Clarification Dialog
- Personalization-User Profiling

Term-Document Matrix

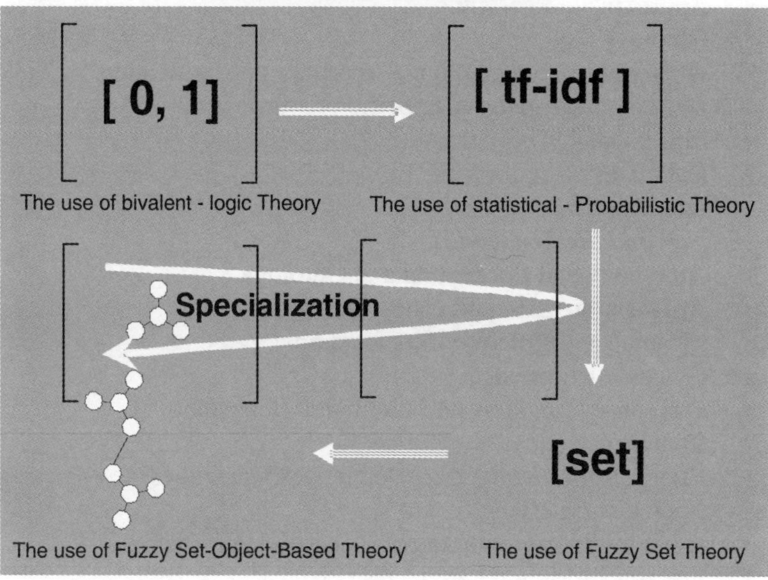

Fig. 2.18 Evolution of Term-Document Matrix representation.

Currently, our group has developed a model that is used for intelligent image retrieval (Google™-Concept-Based Image Retrieval) through conceptual matching of text, images, and links (Figures 2.20-1 and 20-2).

2.8 Challenges and Road Ahead

Following are the areas that were recognized as challenging problems and the new direction toward the next generation of the search engines and Internet. We summarize the challenges and the road ahead into four categories as follows:
- ***Search Engine and Queries:***
  - Deductive Capabilities

- Customization and Specialization
- Metadata and Profiling
- Semantic Web
- Imprecise-Querying
- Automatic Parallelism via Database Technology
- Approximate Reasoning
- Ontology
- Ambiguity Resolution through Clarification Dialog; Definition/Meaning & SpecificityUser Friendly
- Multimedia
- Databases
- Interaction
- ***Internet and the Academia:***
  - Ambiguity and Conceptual and Ontology
  - Aggregation and Imprecision Query
  - Meaning and structure Understanding
  - Dynamic Knowledge
  - Perception, Emotion, and Intelligent Behavior
  - Content-Based
  - Escape from Vector SpaceDeductive Capabilities
  - Imprecise-Querying
  - Ambiguity Resolution through Clarification Dialog
  - Precisiated Natural Languages (PNL)
- ***Internet and the Industry:***
  - XML=>Semantic Web
  - Workflow
  - Mobile E-Commerce
  - CRM
  - Resource Allocation
  - Intent
  - Ambiguity Resolution
  - Interaction
  - Reliability
  - Monitoring
  - Personalization and Navigation
  - Decision Support
  - Document Soul
  - Approximate Reasoning
  - Imprecise QueryContextual Categorization

- ***Fuzzy Logic and Internet; Fundamental Research:***
  - Computing with Words (CW) [Zadeh, (1996), (1999); Zadeh, Kacprzyk, (1999a) and (1999b)].
  - Computational Theory of Perception (CTP) [Zadeh, (2001); Zadeh, Nikravesh, (2002)].
  - Precisiated Natural Languages (PNL).

2.9 Conclusions

In this work, we proposed a search engine which conceptually matches input keywords and web pages. The conceptual matching is realized by context-dependent keyword expansion using conceptual fuzzy sets. First, we show the necessity and also the problems of applying fuzzy sets to information retrieval. Next, we introduce the usefulness of conceptual fuzzy sets in overcoming those problems, and propose the realization of conceptual fuzzy sets using Hopfield Networks. We also propose the architecture of the search engine which can execute conceptual matching dealing with context-dependent word ambiguity. Finally, we evaluate our proposed method through two simulations of retrieving actual web pages, and compare the proposed method with the ordinary TF-IDF method. We show that our method can correlate seemingly unrelated input keywords and produce matching Web pages, whereas the TF-IDF method cannot. In addition, the potentials of the FCS-based search engine to build communities have been investigated. Our new intelligent search engine can mine the Internet to conceptually match and rank homepages based on predefined linguistic formulations and rules defined by experts or based on a set of known homepages and then mine the information retrieved and to find cyber communities. Currently, the CFS models are build based on a semi-automated process, and needs a large datasets. In this study, however, we have used a small data set and explored the performance of the model. We expect large scale generalized CFSs resolve the difficulties and enable us to apply the proposed system to general kinds of web sites clustering.

Acknowledgement

Partial funding for this research was provided by the British Telecommunication (BT) and the BISC Program of UC Berkeley.

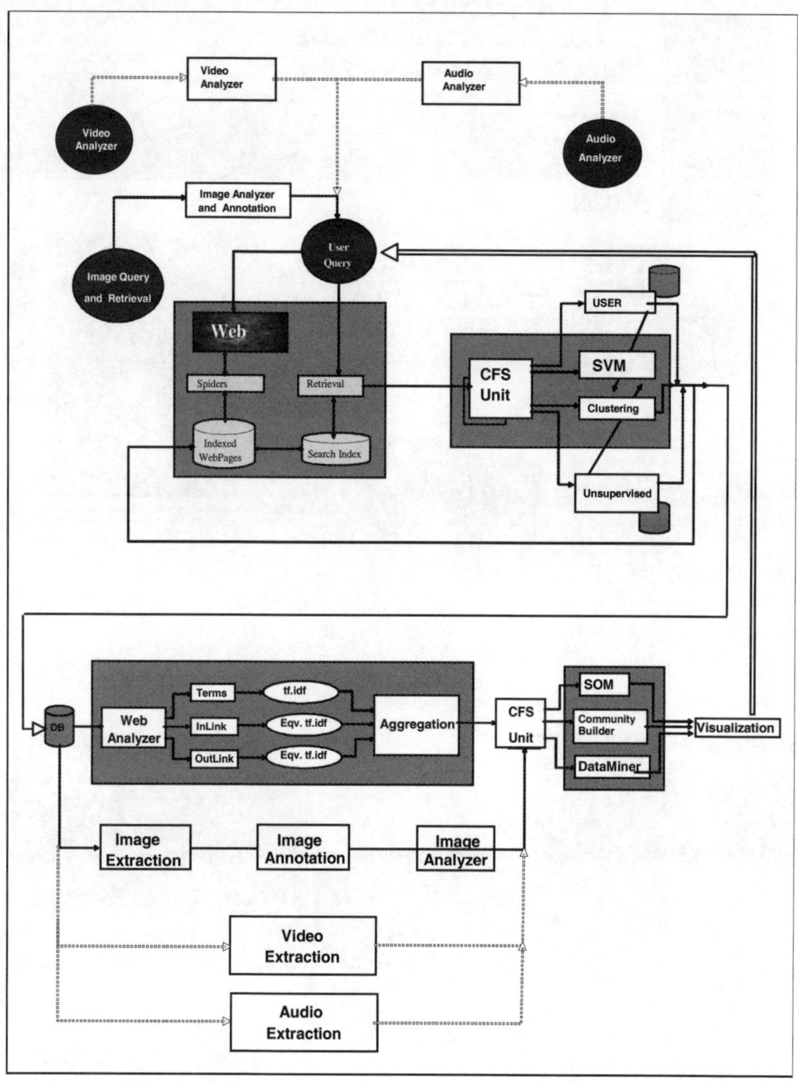

Fig. 2.19 Concept-Based Google™ Search Engine for Multi-Media Retrieval.

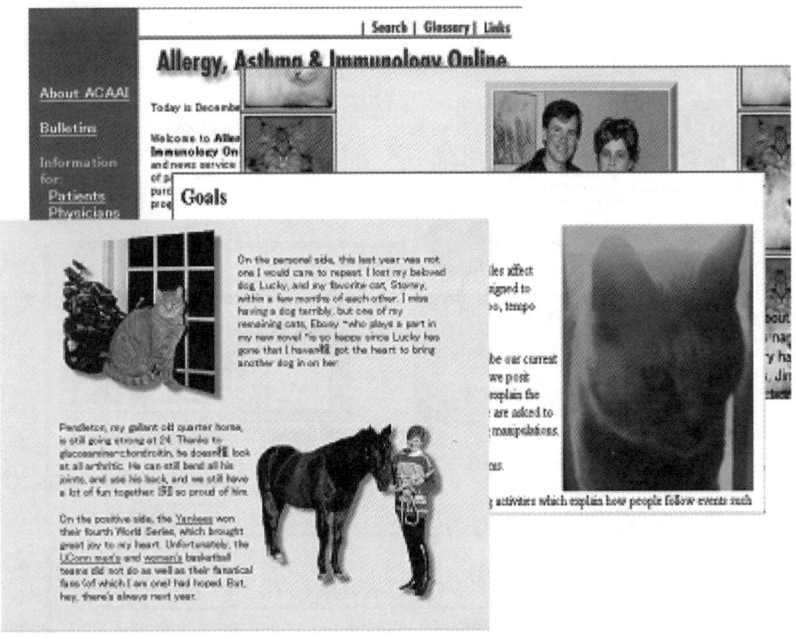

Fig. 2.20-1 CAT.

Fig. 2.20-2 Bill Gates.

Bibliography

Nikravesh M., (2002) Fuzzy Conceptual-Based Search Engine using Conceptual Semantic Indexing, *NAFIPS-FLINT*, June 27-29, New Orleans, LA, USA 2002.

Nikravesh, M. and Azvine, B., (2001) FLINT 2001, New Directions in Enhancing the Power of the Internet, UC Berkeley Electronics Research Laboratory, Memorandum No. UCB/ERL M01/28, August 2001.

Nikravesh, M. and Azvine, B., (2002) Fuzzy Queries, Search, and Decision Support System, *Journal of Soft Computing*, 6(5), August 2002.

Nikravesh, M., Azvine, B., Yager, R. and Zadeh, L. A. (2003a) "New Directions in Enhancing the power of the Internet", *in the Series Studies in Fuzziness and Soft Computing, Physica-Verlag, Springer,* August 2003.

Nikravesh, M. and Choi, D-Y., (2003) Perception-Based Information Processing, UC Berkeley Electronics Research Laboratory, Memorandum No. UCB/ERL M03/20, June 2003.

Nikravesh, M. et al., (2002) Fuzzy logic and the Internet (FLINT), Internet, World Wide Web, and Search Engines, *Journal of Soft Computing, Special Issue; fuzzy Logic and the Internet, Springer Verlag*, 6(5); August 2002.

Nikravesh, M. et al., (2003b) Perception-Based Decision processing and Analysis, UC Berkeley Electronics Research Laboratory, Memorandum No. UCB/ERL M03/21, June 2003.

Nikravesh, M. et al., (2003c) Web Intelligence: Conceptual-Based Model, UC Berkeley Electronics Research Laboratory, Memorandum No. UCB/ERL M03/19, June 2003.

Nikravesh, M. et al., (2003d) Web Intelligence, Conceptual-Based Model, Book Chapter in Enhancing the Power of the Internet, edited by Nikravesh et al., Studies in Fuzziness and Soft Computing, Springer-Verlag (To be Published, 2003).

Takagi, T. et al. (2002a) Exposure of Illegal Website using Conceptual Fuzzy Sets based Information Filtering System, the North American Fuzzy Information Processing Society - The Special Interest Group on Fuzzy Logic and the Internet NAFIPS-FLINT 2002, 327-332.

Takagi, T. et al. (2002b) Conceptual Fuzzy Sets-Based Menu Navigation System for Yahoo!, the North American Fuzzy Information Processing Society - The Special Interest Group on Fuzzy Logic and the Internet NAFIPS-FLINT 2002, 274-279.

Zadeh, L.A. (1996) Fuzzy Logic = Computing with Words," *IEEE Trans. on Fuzzy Systems* (4), 103-111, 1996.

Zadeh, L.A. (1999) From Computing with Numbers to Computing with Words-From Manipulation of Measurements to Manipulation of Perceptions, *IEEE Trans. On Circuit and Systems-I Fundamental Theory and Applications,* 45(1), Jan 1999, 105-119.

Zadeh, L.A. (2001) "A new direction in AI – Toward a computational theory of perceptions", *AI Magazine* 22(1): Spring 2001, 73-84

Zadeh, L. and Kacprzyk, J. (eds.) (1999a), Computing With Words in Information/Intelligent Systems 1: Foundations, Physica-Verlag, Germany, 1999.

Zadeh, L. and Kacprzyk, J. (eds.) (1999b), Computing With Words in Information/Intelligent Systems 2: Applications, Physica-Verlag, Germany, 1999.

Zadeh, L. A. and Nikravesh, M. (2002) Perception-Based Intelligent Decision Systems, AINS; ONR Summer 2002 Program Review, 30 July-1 August, UCLA.

## CHAPTER 3

A FUZZY LOGIC APPROACH TO ANSWER RETRIEVAL FROM THE WORLD-WIDE-WEB

Riza C. Berkan and N. Kartal Guner

AnswerChase, Inc.
141 Gibralter Ave., Annapolis, MD, 21401, USA
E-mail: berkan@answerchase.com

Most of the elaborate methods in natural language processing are not readily applicable to the automated acquisition of answers to questions asked by the Web user due to the particular problems of the Web domain, especially the stringent time constraint. A fuzzy sequence method is presented that takes advantage of the power of approximation in detecting sequence similarities in natural language. Linguistic and ontological elements are incorporated on top of the fuzzy sequence foundation for enhanced performance. This approach allows scaleable implementation such that the level of complexity can be adjusted to satisfy various constraints. The results show that fuzzy sequence solutions can accomplish a great deal of refinement of search engine results and yield a small set of evidence with which to form answers using sophisticated generation techniques.

3.1 Introduction

The ultimate form of acquiring useful information from the World Wide Web (Web) is the automated acquisition of answers to questions that are articulated in a free, natural form. We will refer to it as the question-answer paradigm (QAP) in this Chapter. When it works properly, QAP plays a revolutionary role in transforming the Web from its rather chaotic, commercial and black-box nature into something more useful with significant educational value. This is simply due to allowing freely-articulated questions, just as how a detective would conduct an investigation, or how a person would inquire during a social interaction, and the ability to acquire direct answers without being forced to make navigational choices and reading passages of text.

Retrieving answers to a question from a set of documents is a particular problem in Natural Language Processing (NLP). This is attributable to the QAP where the corresponding information domains (query, query explanation, text pool, candidate texts, etc.) are well defined. The task is also well defined: the expected outcome is a sentence (or a group of sentences) answering the question. The problem becomes even more particular considering the properties of the Web. Accordingly, the corresponding theories and methods must address the constraints of such particular problems, and they should utilize methods emerging from multiple disciplines, such as fuzzy logic, to take advantage of the various available approaches already developed and tested.

In this Chapter, we introduce a new fuzzy approach to answer retrieval from the Web that addresses the constraints involved, and employs a unique fuzzy sequence concept as the foundation of "approximate" language understanding. The method is an approximation at varying levels of complexity driven by the constraints.

3.2 Multi-Disciplinary Approach

QAP, as a particular problem specific to the Web, is comprised of problems that require solutions from multiple disciplines. These include, but not limited to, (1) knowledge mining, (2) fuzzy logic, (3) natural language processing, and (4) Web search. Although these disciplines cover the QAP related issues from their own perspectives, it is imperative that developing actual systems with success relies upon a more amalgamated approach shaped by the characteristics of the Web.

A handful of studies have recently emerged to establish such a particular discipline dedicated to the Web with suggested working concepts, terminology, and methods [Zhang and Lin (2002); Berkan and

Trubatch (2002); Yao (2002)]. The National Institute of Standards has dedicated a workshop on QAP under its TREC program [Vorhees (2000)]. By the time this manuscript was prepared, a few new companies have emerged in this branch of text retrieval such as AnswerBus.com, Language Computing Corporation, and AnswerChase, Inc.

In the context of knowledge mining, information extraction from text [Cowie and Lehnert (1996); Pazienza (1998)] has been the topic in a long list of research projects. Several extraction studies [Riloff (1996); Roark and Charniak (1998); Bagga, Chai and Biermann (2001)] have focused on automatically preparing linguistic resources for disambiguation for the generalized retrieval problem. These studies address the economic aspect of information retrieval and the importance of automation that are in concert with the typical limitations of the Web domain.

Fuzzy logic scholars, such as Profs Lotfi Zadeh and Paul P. Wang, have published on the recent concept of "computing with words" [Wang (2001)] that is directly related to QAP. Prof Zadeh went further to publish research results [Zadeh (2003)] focusing on a perception based computational approach to find answers to questions on the Web. The realm of "computing with words" and perception based search methods are all aimed at improving the accuracy of computerized language understanding, however, the corresponding implementations in the real world may require special optimizations to overcome various limitations of the Web.

In computational linguistics, or NLP, the retrieval problem [Strzalkowski (1995)] is one of the several known areas of research as outlined above. Significant progress has been made in tagging, lexical uses, disambiguation, ontological semantics, generation, and machine translation. Except for machine translation, all other areas of progress have direct applications to QAP. Especially, the generation studies including systematic grammar and unification frameworks [Mellish (1995)] allow generating answers from evidence that is the last step of QAP leading to a dialogue capability with the end user.

3.3 Practical Constraints

The QAP implementation over the Web is mandated by several constraints such as bandwidth, document format compatibility, indexing, *etc.* Nevertheless, all such constraints are, in fact, different manifestations of the trade-off between time versus quality, where time refers to the speed of obtaining results, and quality refers to the usefulness of the information presented. Interestingly, this trade-off is significantly tipped towards favoring "time" as evidenced by several market studies and the general knowledge about the successful search engines. Any search engine that would not produce results within the first 10 seconds is likely to be abandoned by its visitors before its usefulness is truly assessed.

There are two reasons for the "time" favoritism. First, a quick response to a query is a natural expectation in human dialogue. Thus, a rapidly responding system is perceived as more user-friendly. Second, there is no search technology today that rewards the end-user for his/her patience with a set of higher quality results. Thus, the social aspect of the Web is an unavoidable reality which determines one of its most important properties as set forth by time-constraint.

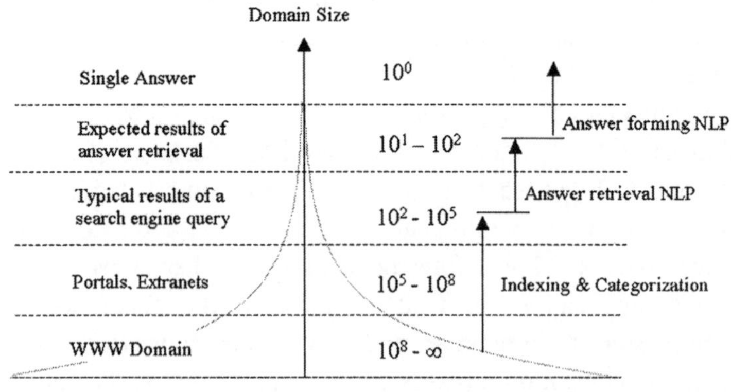

Fig. 3.1 Domain size characteristics of the retrieval systems operating on the Web.

Fig. 3.1 illustrates, to a gross approximation, the effect of time-constraint on the retrieval methods to implement. For example, it is not feasible to deploy a time consuming computation scheme for retrieval at the bottom of the graph, where the number of documents is in the billions. Using the same argument, it makes much more sense to deploy increasingly more complex analyses as we move to the top where the number of candidate documents, excerpts, paragraphs, or sentences are manageable in size to produce results in a reasonable time frame. Any method that can retrieve answers from the Web using methods more sophisticated than simple indexing must be based on a theory that addresses the structure shown in Fig. 3.1.

Time-constraint limits the applicability of complicated methods in the off-line mode as well. The time to prepare a solution using conventional theories of statistical linguistics, for example, which requires thorough corpus analysis, is likely to be longer than the dynamic changes of the documents on the Web. Accordingly, creating a Semantic Web by reforming the entire pool of Web documents with resource demanding methods may be unrealistic. This further validates the ladder approach shown in Fig. 3.1 where resource demanding methods are to be applied at the higher levels.

Given the considerations above, a solution to the answer retrieval problem must address the following issues:

- Time-constraint at all levels of Fig. 3.1.
- Deployment of methods at different complexity at different levels of Fig. 3.1 determined by domain size.
- Assumption that certain segments of the Web are no longer accessible in terms of implementing new methods.
- Assumption that factors affecting certain segments of the Web are biased and nothing can be done about it.

3.4 The Ladder Approach

It is imperative to take into account the history and the anticipated future of the Web in order to suggest feasible QAP solutions. In this respect, we assume that the future of QAP is only feasible via a ladder approach where the very bottom layer with respect to Fig. 1 has already been established by the existing and permanent Web infrastructure.

- Top Layer: Highly sophisticated NLP methods for answer formation (generation) and dialogue functions operating on a small set of evidence gathered from the middle layer.
- Middle Layer: A post-processing step where the search results of a bottom layer search engine are rapidly analyzed to extract sentences and/or paragraphs that contain evidence to support a possible answer.
- Bottom Layer: Search engines providing the first level of filtering by pre-indexing billions of Web documents.

Our main focus is the middle layer operations in which the search engine results are post-processed via client applications (it could also be a script pushed from the search engine's Web site or running on the Web server). However, the middle layer QAP solutions strongly depend on what is available from the bottom layer, and what is requested by the top layer. Accordingly, both domains are discussed in this Chapter as an integral part of the overall solution.

3.5 Handling the Bottom Layer: Indexing/Categorization

As alluded to earlier, the bottom-layer systems (*i.e.*, search engines) have already become irreplaceable bricks of the Web today. Any QAP solution starting from the bottom-layer would have to face the challenges of dealing with billions of documents in an organic-growth type environment. Thus, QAP that employs a variety of techniques to handle language understanding can only start from the middle-layer in reference to Fig. 3.1.

Search engines [Berry and Browne (1999)] operate based on simple Boolean-query algorithms and word indexing. Some of the well known search engines have wisely adopted single AND implementation as the query mechanism simply by banking on the fact that the number of documents pertaining each possible popular subject would, as a minimum, contain all the query words. To differentiate among the documents satisfying the same Boolean criteria, the most common modification is the voting system. Users who select a link to follow by viewing a small set of clues are actually voting for that result. The system encapsulates that action to increase the voting score of that particular document. Next time around, the same result is presented at a higher location when the same query is presented. Along the same caliber of enhancements, most search engines pre-process the user's query to eliminate insignificant words, and catch misspelled words. With such a pre-processing step, it is nowadays quite common to encounter search engines operating in the "ask" mode. These features mimic QAP without actually processing the results to extract answers. It is simply impossible to deploy a text analysis on-the-fly over billions of documents.

Among the troublesome features of search engines, the most significant drawback is the popularity phenomenon. Results adjusted by voting make search engines operate like newspapers in which the most popular topics have higher priorities. Another well known drawback is the lack of accuracy in pin-pointing the sentence (or paragraph) of interest due to the limitation of Boolean operation. A typical search engine user must follow the clues and read passages of texts to reach useful information. In this process, every page-click results in image downloading and other unnecessary actions that overload the bandwidth.

Although expecting a revolutionary change at the bottom layer operations may be unrealistic, new solutions emerge every day mostly related to the categorization aspect. XML and other database oriented formats show promise for more accurate indexing due to the selective indexing capability of the most important words per given category. It is fair to expect that the future indexing systems will be more semantically oriented due to better categorizations via XML type multi-level tags.

Another pitfall of the Web domain is that the search engine users are accustomed the freedom of forming incomplete or improper questions/queries. For example, it may be unrealistic to ask the search engine user to capitalize proper names as required by the English grammar. Similarly, it cannot be assumed that the user will enter proper punctuation. These are unavoidable realities of the Web domain that further challenges the developers of the QAP systems.

3.6 Middle Layer Solutions: Answer Retrieval

3.6.1 *Fuzzy Sequence Concept*

Fuzzy sequence is defined as a set of fuzzy elements that are lined up in a flexible order based on independent but related criteria. A good example of a fuzzy sequence is ill people lined up in an emergency room in the order of urgency. Each element (person) fits the "ill" set by a unique membership value representing the degree of illness. Yet, they are lined up for medical attention based on the urgency criteria, which is independent but related to illness. Note the importance of "lining up" that implies a sequential execution of an event (medical care in this case) as opposed to, for example, a fuzzy pattern in which elements are not executed one at a time, rather they are executed as groups as in image processing.

Natural language is an ideal fit to the fuzzy sequence concept. Language, either as an audio stimuli as in speech, or as a visual stimuli as in reading/writing a text, contains elements (i.e., words) that are fuzzy as to what they individually contribute to the overall meaning. To represent the world knowledge, language is comprised of flexible sequences of words, executed one after another, yielding a variety of meanings sometimes beyond the linear aggregation of their individual meanings.

The fuzzy sequence approach incorporates linguistic properties of natural language at its foundation level in a very limited manner. Instead, it uses the general notion of language as explained later in this section. On top of this foundation, morphology, semantic, and syntactic properties enter into the computations to augment the process in a controlled manner (at the design stage). Accordingly, the level of complexity and scalability can be set forth in concert with the constraints of the problem.

The fuzzy sequence concept deals with three basic forms of disambiguation: (1) linear conformity such as in "red car" where the first word simply modifies the second word, (2) exceptional conformity such as in "hot car" where both words map to a new concept of the second word, and (3) perception relationship such as "in your dreams" where the original meaning of the phrase is replaced by a context specific meaning (*i.e.,* "unlikely" in a conversational situation.) Whatever the nature of the sequence is, it is first treated as a mathematical sequence of literal meaning (linear conformity) then handled for disambiguation via resource libraries.

Fig. 3.2 illustrates the first part of the fuzzy sequence concept in application to language modeling. Every element of the symbol discourse (word domain) that belong to the sequence is the member of the fuzzy set *Meaning-A* with a membership value μ_i.

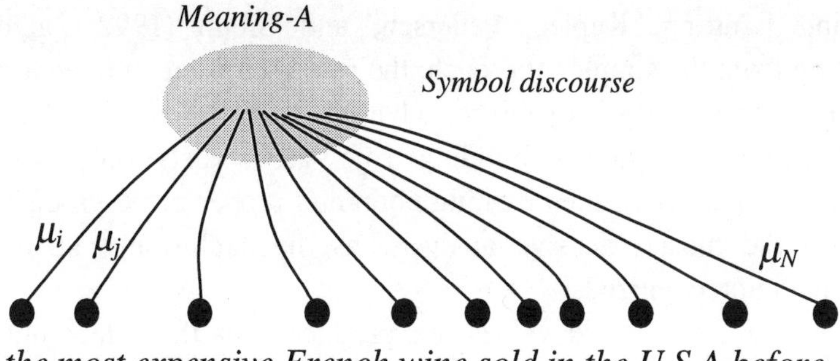

Fig. 3.2 The elements of a fuzzy sequence defining a meaning set
via simple membership.

According to conventional linguistics, the elements of each word in a sentence belong to its meaning set with full membership value. Removing one word will become grammatically and syntactically wrong, thus impairing the meaning of a sentence in an unpredictable way. In a fuzzy sequence approach, this gray area is explored such that every word is allowed to be a member of its meaning set at varying strength. Note that such an approach is taken here considering the particular problem of QAP and it may not be applicable to other NLP problems.

There are several ways to determine the membership values. In its simplest form, consider the example in Fig. 3.2.

the most expensive French wine sold in the USA before 1980

If we drop the word *wine* from the phrase, the meaning of the phrase becomes completely ambiguous (or meaningless). However, if we drop the word *French*, the meaning of the phrase is retained while losing its precision. The most expensive wine would also include French wine. Similarly, dropping other parts would produce different effects. Finally, dropping the article *the* would have a minimal impact.

The question of how to attain and preserve knowledge about the importance of each word in the absence of human supervision can be solved in a number of ways. One approach is to determine the roles of the words rather than their meaning by categorizing them into role groups. This can be a simple process with minimal resource requirements, or can be the outcome of a practical part-of-speech (POS) tagging [Cutting, Kupiec, Pedersen, and Sibun (1992)] algorithm. Starting from the simpler approach, the role groups are defined as nouns, proper names, verbs, adjectives, adverbs, stop words, *etc.* The fastest implementation requires building role group lists only for those involving small lists, then treating noun and proper name groups, which require the most extensive analysis, as the exclusion (*i.e.*, anything remained unrecognized.)

Next, a set of table values are produced for the role groups. For example, nouns and proper names are assigned the highest values whereas verbs, adjectives, adverbs, pronouns, etc., are assigned decreasingly smaller membership values all the way down to articles and stop words. The table values of the role groups merely differentiate importance without requiring precision. Such data can be gathered from a corpus analysis and/or constructed based on the general notion of natural language. More elaborate versions of role groups, such as sense tagging [Wilks and Stevenson (1997)], have been studied and are directly applicable for advanced disambiguation purposes.

The fuzzy sequence approach, then, incorporates the sequence relationships. This is illustrated in Fig. 3.3 using only one word for simplicity.

Fig. 3.3 shows the completion of the fuzzy sequence concept. In other words, the membership value of each element to belong to a meaning set is only valid in the presence of sequential relationships between each element.

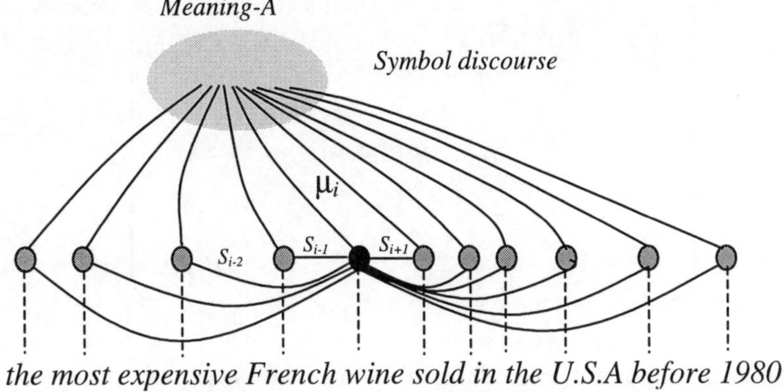

Fig. 3.3 Relationship of an element in a sequence with its neighbors.

This is easily justified considering the ongoing example. The phrase in Fig. 3.3 contains 11 words. If a computer had generated random sequences using these 11 words, the permutations would be 11!, more than 40 million. However, only one sequence, as shown above, retains the exact meaning. Therefore, the word *wine*, for example, would not have any valid membership to the meaning set A in a randomly constructed sequence using the same 11 words except for one permutation.

A word's membership to a meaning set is given by a vector

$$\{ S_{i,1}, \ldots , S_{i,i-2}, S_{i,i-1}, \mu_i, S_{i,i+1}, S_{i,i+2}, \ldots , S_{i,k} \} \qquad (3.1)$$

where S denotes sequence strength, expressed numerically between 0 and 1, and μ_i is the membership value of the *i*th word to belong to the meaning set A. The whole sequence is given by a matrix comprised of vectors such as in Eq. (3.1).

The sequence strength S is inversely proportional to distance, as one would expect from any sequentially coupled physical/information system based on a general scientific judgment. This can be verified in application to natural languages as well. In the ongoing example, *French wine* is obviously a stronger relationship than that of *most wine* because the word *most* modifies the adjective *expensive* in the original phrase.

$$\begin{pmatrix} \mu_{11} & S_{12} & S_{13} & \cdots & & & S_{1k} \\ S_{21} & \mu_{22} & S_{23} & \cdots & & & S_{2k} \\ & & \cdots & & & & \\ S_{i,1} & \cdots & S_{j,i-1} & \mu_{i,i} & S_{i,i+1} & \cdots & S_{i,k} \\ & & & \cdots & & & \\ & & & & \cdots & & \\ & & & & & & \mu_{k,k} \end{pmatrix} \tag{3.2}$$

Another important consideration about the sequence strength in application to QAP is the role of the words, just as in determining the membership value. In the ongoing example, consider the following partial sequences:

Good Sequences	Poor Sequences
most expensive	*expensive French*
French wine	*the most*
before 1980	*in the*
the U.S.A	*U.S.A before*

Taken from the same sentence, the partial sequences on the left are considered better than the sequences on the right per human inspection. This suggests that in every sentence of adequate length, there are natural divisions that the corresponding partial sequences are better sub-representations of the overall meaning than that of the partial sequences obtained randomly. Clearly, *French wine* is more descriptive than *expensive French,* thus the former must have a stronger neighborhood strength than the latter. Similar arguments can be extended to i-2, i+2 couplings (i.e., expensive wine, wine in) and beyond.

In the absence of human supervision, sequence strengths can be established, to an approximation, using the role groups again. However, in this case, table values are produced via rules (called tag-tag rules). For example, when a proper name is coupled with a noun, just as in *French wine*, the sequence strength must be higher than that of the coupling between an adjective and proper name, just as in *expensive French*. This approach is an approximation for fast implementation, but it has room for improvement by incorporating more elaborate techniques as long as the time-constraint is not violated.

As a result, sequence strength is a combination of factors that is modeled in the following ways:

$$S_{i,j} = (D_{i,j})^{-1} \cdot \mu_i(T_i) \cdot TT_{i,j} \tag{3.3}$$

$$S_{i,j} = (D_{i,j})^{-1} \wedge \mu_i(T_i) \wedge TT_{i,j} \tag{3.4}$$

where D is distance between the prime word and its neighbors, $\mu_i(T_i)$ is membership value based on role groups (Tags) and $TT_{i,j}$ is the effect produced by the tag-tag rules. Equation (3.3) is a more conservative representation than that of Eq. (3.4) due to the product operation that maintains significant numerical value only in the presence of a strong agreement among the three contributors.

A fuzzy sequence given by Eqs. (3.2), (3.3), and (3.4) is the simplest model that takes into account all possible relationships which can be extracted from a given sentence in the absence of human supervision. It further allows (1) to adjust knowledge embedding via Tags, and (2) to expand the model via more sophisticated techniques.

3.6.2 Sentence Scoring

The most important part of QAP is parsing of the sentences. Sentence enclosure represents completeness of both the meaning and structure. Given a candidate text (*i.e.*, retrieved via simple indexing methods from a large pool of Web documents) QAP requires scoring of each sentence by comparing it to the given question. In such an instance, the fuzzy sequence of the question is formed prior to the scoring operation.

Sentence scoring method investigates whether the given sentence has enough clues to support an answer in the following sentences, or if it includes the entire answer. This is assessed by word and sequence matching. Our earlier research [Berkan and Valenti (2000)] on this topic was based on a nonlinear sequence analysis technique that produced highly desirable results. The following is a more simplified and less resource demanding approach.

Single word matching produces what we call the "presence" score and is computed by

$$P_y = \frac{\sum_{i=1,f} \mu_i(T_i)^T}{\sum_{i=1,k} \mu_i(T_i)^Q} \tag{3.5}$$

where P is the presence score of the sentence y, $\mu_i(T_i)^T$ is the tag based membership value of the *ith* matching word of the text domain denoted by superscript label T, f is the number of matching words, k is the total number of words in the question, and superscript label Q denotes the question. The significance of Eq. (3.5) is that the fraction of match is not computed by the mere number of match, rather it is computed by the importance of the match which can be determined by a varying level of complexity embedded by T_i.

The presence of a word both in the question and in the parsed sentence is not an enough indication of whether the membership to the meaning set is valid. This is evaluated by sequence matching.

The QAP algorithm declares a sequence match when it finds a minimum of two adjacent words of the question in the parsed sentence. Note that these words may be separated in the parsed sentence. Then, the sequence score is evaluated using the fuzzy sequence matrix of the question. For example, sequence length of 3 (three adjacent words in any order) found in the parsed sentence means 3 by 3 section of the fuzzy sequence matrix of the question where that sequence was evaluated by the tag-tag rules.

$$\begin{bmatrix} \mu_{i,i-1} & S_{i,i} & S_{i,i+1} \\ S_{j,i-1} & \mu_{j,i} & S_{j,i+1} \\ S_{k,i-1} & S_{k,i} & \mu_{k,i+1} \end{bmatrix} \tag{3.6}$$

It should be immediately noted that the tag-tag rules make the fuzzy sequence matrix an asymmetric one; therefore, order mismatch (*i.e.*, *ijk* versus *kij*) will be detected inherently.

The sequence score of a parsed sentence is directly accessible from a segment such as in Eq. (3.6). If the sequence match is *ijk*, then the sequence score η is the summation of the first off-diagonal elements (i.e., $S_{i,i}$ + $S_{j,i+1}$) divided by the summation of all off-diagonal elements, called primer R which represents the exact entire sequence. In case of 3 by 3 section, the following possibilities exist:

$$\eta\,(\text{i j k}) = (S_{i,i} + S_{j,i+1})/R$$
$$\eta\,(\text{i k j}) = (S_{i,i+1} + S_{k,i})/R$$
$$\eta\,(\text{j i k}) = (S_{j,i-1} + S_{i,i+1})/R$$
$$\eta\,(\text{j k i}) = (S_{j,i+1} + S_{k,i-1})/R \qquad (3.7)$$
$$\eta\,(\text{k i j}) = (S_{k,1} + S_{i,i})/R$$
$$\eta\,(\text{k j i}) = (S_{k,i} + S_{j,i-1})/R$$
$$\eta\,(\text{i k}) = (S_{i,i+1})/R$$
$$\eta\,(\text{k i}) = (S_{k,1})/R$$

where the last two lines indicates the case in which the middle word denoted by j was not found in the parsed sentence. Note that η already includes P as shown in Eqs. (3.3) and (3.4). The presence score P and sequence score η, which are calculated for each sentence of the candidate document, are used to determine the final sentence score via a set of fuzzy rules. Some of these rules are outlined below along with their explanations to shed light onto why we use two parameters.

$$\textit{- If P is very low, THEN do not evaluate } \eta \qquad (3.8)$$

Obviously, if there are not enough important words matched between the question and the sentence, there is no need to look for sequences.

$$\textit{- If P is high AND } \eta \textit{ is very low,} \qquad (3.9)$$
$$\textit{THEN suspect a list}$$

For a given sentence, if most of the words are matched while none of the sequences are encountered, that means the sentence is ambiguous, or is comprised of a list of items (*i.e.*, grocery items listed in a random order).

$$- \textit{If P is high AND } \eta \textit{ is high,} \qquad\qquad (3.10)$$
THEN the sentence score is high and
reserve the sentence for generation
(see Section 3.8.3)

$$- \textit{If P is medium or high AND } \eta \textit{ is medium,} \qquad (3.11)$$
THEN the sentence score is medium

The last rule (3.11) represents bulk of the operation statistically speaking given a good candidate documents to analyze. These rules can be implemented using the standard fuzzy if-then rule structure [Berkan and Trubatch (1997)].

3.6.3 *Paragraph Scoring*

Paragraph scoring becomes important when none of the analyzed sentences show promise to have a direct answer to the question. In such a case, it means that the answer is spread over multiple sentences, or it simply does not exist.

Paragraph scoring assumes that if the answer is spilled over multiple sentences, the densities of medium quality sentences are likely to be high at around the answer. Thus, a cluster of sentences each containing some evidence is to be found. In such an analysis, it is important to track the captured sequences in each sentence and to make sure that all different sequences that would make up the answer are found. In other words, if the same sequence is repeating itself in different sentences while other sequences are not found, then there is not enough evidence to score that paragraph high. The paragraph score ϕ (a commonly used symbol to denote flux) is given by

$$\phi_n = (1/z) \sum_{i=1,z} \eta_i(\varepsilon_i) \qquad\qquad (3.12)$$

where z is the number of concomitant sentences in paragraph n that contain evidence $\eta_i(\varepsilon_i)$, and ε_i is the uniqueness factor eliminating repetition. Note that when the rule (3.11) dominates in a paragraph, which suggests the use of Eq. (3.12), all sentence scores are medium and low. Thus, Eq. (3.12) is expected to be a low number. One good criteria to detect an answer is to compare ϕ_n to the maximum $\eta_i(\varepsilon_i)$. When the two numbers are close to each other, it implies a well balanced spread of important sequences.

It must be obvious to the reader that sentence scoring and/or paragraph scoring as outlined here are not solid proofs of the existence of an answer. However, considering Fig 3.1, the refinement of results at the middle layer using this approach facilitates the final step of answer formation/generation.

3.6.4 Enhancements to Fuzzy Sequence Approach

Several factors play a major role in the implementation of the fuzzy sequence concept for the middle layer operations. Morphology-based matching of the words is the first factor (*i.e.,* matching the words swim, swimming, swam, *etc.)* which is solved via conventional methods or by simpler versions of stemming.

To improve disambiguation, different levels of ontological semantics [Kohout (1988)] can be used provided that time constraint (both for time-to-prepare a solution, and time to implement) is taken into consideration. A feasible approach is to develop a micro-ontology for each different vertical subject and to deploy a "topic-selected" retrieval. Such implementation will have a direct effect on $\mu_i(T_i)^T$, presence score P_y and sequence score η_y by increasing the number of matches. The level of matching capability is strictly related to the level of preparation as would be expected from any retrieval system.

3.7 Top Layer Solutions: Answer Formation

Also known as "generation", answer formation refers to creating a sentence from the evidence collected as the potential answer. This step can implement a sophisticated approach since the number of evidence propagated to the top will be manageable. Top layer operations involve the following analyses:

Forming an answer to a given question requires detecting the type of the question which helps determine which mapping rules must be fired in a generation strategy such as recursive descent. Computer algorithms such as PROTECTOR [Nicolov and Mellish (1997)] can accomplish answer generation given non-hierarchical input evidence that allows for flexible lexical choice. We have identified 26 question types as a preliminary set for detection. These types include confirmation-q "is XXX true?", causal-q "why is XXX true?", definitive-q "what is the XXX of XXX?", method-q "how does XXX XXX?" quantity-q "What is the (number) of XXX?", and their variations plus the unknown case. This type of detection is a straight forward task.

One practical and resource-optimized way of answer generation is to reverse mapping onto detected question types and appending the evidence collected from the middle-layer answer retrieval step. This requires an evidence validation method based on micro ontological semantics. Such evidence validation can be made fuzzy to produce "yes", "no", "may be yes", and "may be not" validations. For the confirm-q type questions, for example, this approach can produce fast and accurate results. Considering the confirm-q type question, a typical response can be in the form of

Is Shakespeare a legitimate author?

Shakespeare <u>may not be</u> a legitimate author because {Evidence-A}{Evidence-B}...{Evidence-N}

where the evidence set A thru N are retrieved by the middle-layer and validated to fall into "may not be" category. Many variations of this approach are possible, and the reader is encouraged to explore evidence based generation methods as candidate methods to enhance answer formation in AQP.

The dialogue function is essential to the overall QAP and it affects all layers. A sophisticated QAP application must implement a dialogue utility to talk back to the user and extract more useful information to answer the question. This is in concert with social interaction in which a question is often responded by an exploratory question to collect more clues. Dialogue process extends the original question into a set of question plus explanations that can be utilized in all layers of QAP. There are pure dialogue applications over the Web, also called chatterbots, and often attached to a limited database of responses [Wallace]. Making the dialogue utility an integral part of a retrieval system has yet to be explored.

3.8 Model Validation

Different versions of the QAP algorithm for the middle-layer operation have been tested through several parametric studies. The QAP performance relies on the following factors:

- Properly articulated questions with a significant level of specifity
- Assumption that the bottom-layer retrieval system, such as a search engine, will bring a good set of documents via simple but fast indexing methods
- Middle-layer retrieval process based on fuzzy sequence technique must employ basic morphological corrections
- Assumption that the text under analysis is written in proper writing style maintaining integrity and flow of ideas

Fig. 3.4 shows 1,248 cases of answer retrieval (in 24 blocks) to medical questions using the PubMed as the bottom layer search engine. The middle layer QAP has scored the retrieved paragraphs between 1 and 0 based on the fuzzy sequence algorithm and simple morphological corrections. The best sentence in each paragraph was highlighted which was used for evaluation purposes by human (*e.g.*, Answer and No Answer categories in Figs. 3.4 and 3.5) A lexical library of less than 200 entries was used. The minimum question length was set to 4 significant words whereas the maximum question length was set to 10. The embedded tag information and tag-tag rules only differentiated 4 role groups. As shown in Fig. 3.4., the score level between 0.39 and 0.32 is the interference region where the cases "Answer" and "No Answer" cannot be distinguished by the algorithm. This corresponds to a 7% error rate in answer detection.

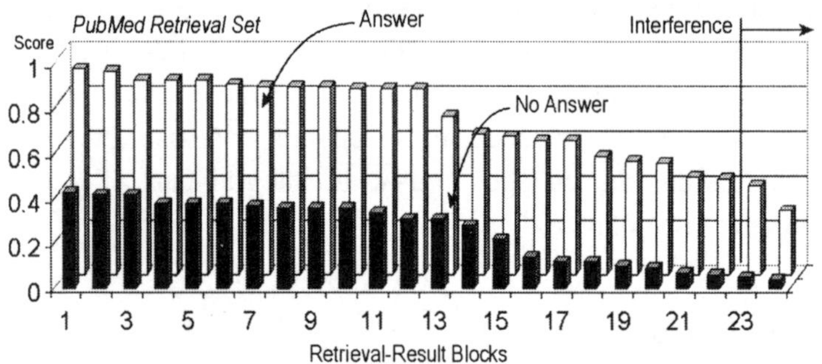

Fig. 3.4 PubMed answer retrieval results to medical questions

Fig. 3.5 shows 1,080 results using the major search engines on the Web (Google, Hotbot, Yahoo, AskJeeves) as the bottom layer search engines. The questions were compiled in business topics mainly about financial distress. The score level between 0.43 and 0.31 is the interference region where the cases "Answer" and "No Answer" cannot be distinguished. This corresponds to 12% error rate in answer detection. Business related lexicon libraries, again, included less than 200 terms.

These performances are favorable considering the fact that analyzing 500K text, after downloaded from the search engine results, takes less than 1 second and the foot print of the QAP algorithm is less than 100K (excluding the lexicon libraries). The paragraphs obtained with high scores are to be used by the answer formation process at the top layer.

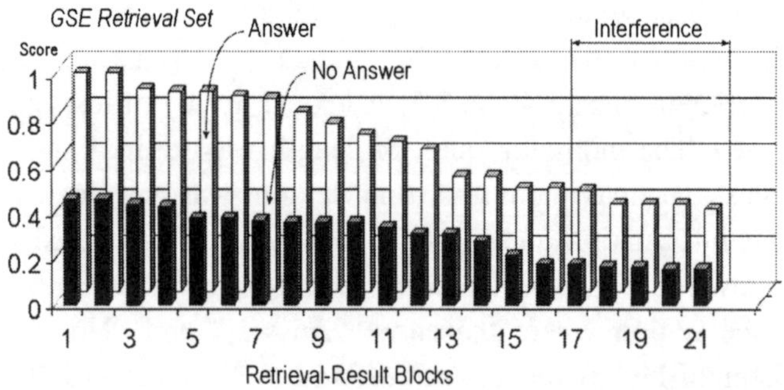

Fig. 3.5 GSE answer retrieval results to business questions

3.9 Conclusions

It is undisputable that useful information retrieval from the Web in an automated manner requires a post-processing step in which the search engine results are further analyzed. We have presented a three-layer architecture in this Chapter to retrieve answers to natural language questions, and to prepare an evidence set for answer formation to take place at the top layer using sophisticated methods.

The fuzzy sequence technique is as an approximated model for computerized language understanding. It is evident that utilizing sequence relationships embedded in the question, provided the question has an adequate number of significant words, and comparing them to those sequences found in the text, yield a highly effective extraction capability. Accordingly, paragraphs are detected and scored based on their potential to represent an answer to a given question. Enhancements are possible via micro-scale ontology that expands the sequences of the question into more valid sequences, thus providing a higher degree of detection capability. In concert with the stringent speed requirements of a typical Web application, this approach allows scaleable implementation. The processing speed of less than 1 second to analyze 500K text, and its less than 100K footprint, allows on-the-fly analysis capability that can be launched as a client application or as server scripts.

The approach presented in this Chapter assumes that the QAP implementation in the future will be a post-processing step, and it will pave the way for developing a dialogue interface through which the end-user experiences efficient and natural interaction to obtain answers to questions from the Web domain.

Bibliography

Bagga, A., J. Chai and A. Biermann (2001). "Extracting Information from text," Chp. 6., Computing with Words, Edited by Paul P. Wang, Wiley.

Berry, M. W., and M. Browne (1999). "Understanding Search Engines: Mathematical Modeling and Text Retrieval (Software, Environments, Tools)" Society for Industrial & Applied Mathematics, July.

Berkan, R.C., and M. Valenti (2000). " A nonlinear Answer Retrieval Technique" US Patent 09/741,749, December.

Berkan, R.C., and S. Trubatch (1997). "Fuzzy Systems Design Principles", IEEE Press.

Berkan, R. C., and S. L. Trubatch (2002). "Fuzzy Logic and Hybrid Approaches to Web Intelligence Gathering and Information Management", *Proc. of* FUZZ-IEEE'02 Special Session on Computational Web Intelligence, May.

Cowie, J., and W. Lehnert (1996). Information Extraction, Commun. ACM, Jan.

Cutting, D., J. Kupiec, J. Pedersen and P. Sibun (1992). "A practical part-of-speech tagger" In *Proc. of* ANLP-92, pp 133-140, Trento.

Kohout, L.J. (1998). Theories of possibility: meta-axiomatics and semantics, Fuzzy Sets Syst., 25:357-367.

Mellish, M. (1991). "Approaches to Realization in Natural Language Generation" Natural Language and Speech (ESPRIT Basic Research Series) ed. By Ewan Klein & Frank Veltman, 95-116. Berlin: Springler-Verlag.

Nicolov, N., C. Mellish (1997). "PROTECTOR: Efficient Generation with Lexicalized Grammars," Recent Advances in Natural Language Processing II, Edited by Nicholas Nicolov, Ruslan Mitkov, pp 221-243, John Benjamins Pub. Co., Vol 189.

Pazienza, M. (1998). "Information Extraction", Springer.

Riloff, E. (1996). "An empirical study of automated dictionary construction for information extraction in three domains", AI J., August.

Roark, B., and E. Charniak (1998). "Noun-phrase co occurrence statistics for semi-automatic semantic lexicon construction", in Proc. 36th Annual Meeting of the Association for Computational Linguistics.

Strzalkowski, T. (1995). "Natural Language Information Retrieval" *Information Processing and Management*, 31(3):1237-1248.

Voorhees, E. & Tice, D. (2000) "Building a Question Answering Test Collection", Proceedings of SIGIR-2000, pp. 200-207, July

Wallace, R.S. A.L.I.C.E AI Foundation, Web.alicebot.org.

Wang, P. (2001). "Computing with Words: Introduction, Implications, and Applications", Computing with Words, Wiley Series on Intelligent Systems.

Wilks, Y., and M. Stevenson (1997). "Combining Independent Knowledge Sources for Word Sense Disambiguation", Recent Advances in Natural Language Processing II, Edited by Nicholas Nicolov, Ruslan Mitkov, John Benjamins Pub. Co., Vol 189.

Yao, Y.Y. (2002). "Information Retrieval Support Systems", *Proc. of* FUZZ-IEEE'02 Special Session on Computational Web Intelligence, May.

Zadeh, L. (2003). "From Search Engines to Question-Answering System: The Need for New Tools" BISC Seminar, CS Division, EECS Dept. UC Berkeley, March.

Zhang, Y., and T.Y. Lin (2002). "Computational Web Intelligence (CWI): Synergy of Computational Intelligence and Web Technology" *Proc. of* FUZZ-IEEE'02 Special Session on Computational Web Intelligence, May.

CHAPTER 4

FUZZY INFERENCE BASED SERVER SELECTION IN CONTENT DISTRIBUTION NETWORKS

Lin Cai, Jun Ye, Jianping Pan, Xuemin Shen and Jon W. Mark

Centre for Wireless Communications
Department of Electrical and Computer Engineering
University of Waterloo, Waterloo, ON, N2L 3G1, Canada
E-mail: {cai, jye, jpan, xshen,jwmark}@bbcr.uwaterloo.ca

To accommodate the exponential growth of web traffic, Content Distribution Networks (CDN) have been designed and deployed to transparently and dynamically redirect user requests to different cache servers. Server selection is crucial to the functionality and performance of CDN. An appropriate server can be chosen according to the parameters such as user location, measured round trip time (rtt), and advertised server load. However, it is impractical to obtain accurate measurements of the above parameters. In addition, these parameters may have conflicting effects on decision making. In this chapter, a fuzzy inference system is designed to select servers based on partial measurements of rtts and historical information of servers' load. The performance of the fuzzy inference scheme is evaluated and compared with several existing schemes by simulations. The simulation results show that the fuzzy inference scheme can achieve higher network utilization, and provide better user perceived quality of service (QoS). In addition, the fuzzy inference scheme is fairly flexible to deal with network dynamics, due to its intrinsic capability of handling multiple, inaccurate and inconsistent decision inputs.

4.1 Introduction

Most Internet applications, *e.g.*, remote login, file transfer, and web browsing, are based on the so-called *client-server* application model, as shown in Fig. 4.1(a). After obtaining the server identifier which consists of the IP address, Well-Known-Service (WKS) protocol ID and port number in the Internet context, a client first initiates to establish a virtual two-way communication channel between itself and the designated server, and then exchanges the application layer messages in a *request-reply* manner with the server. In this paradigm, a single server presumably can support multiple clients distributed across the network. This application model works reasonably well until the Web becomes a ubiquitous platform to deliver almost all distributed Internet services to a very large user population. For instance, some popular web servers such as the news portal *cnn.com* and hot event site *saltlake2000.com* have to handle millions of simultaneous requests from users all over the world during a short time period. As shown in Fig. 4.1(b), this request surge can easily overload any single web server and its access network links. Excessive requests will either be queued in the network or at the server, or simply be dropped, and will be retried multiple times by transport protocols or applications, which can result in a very lengthy *click-to-display* latency.

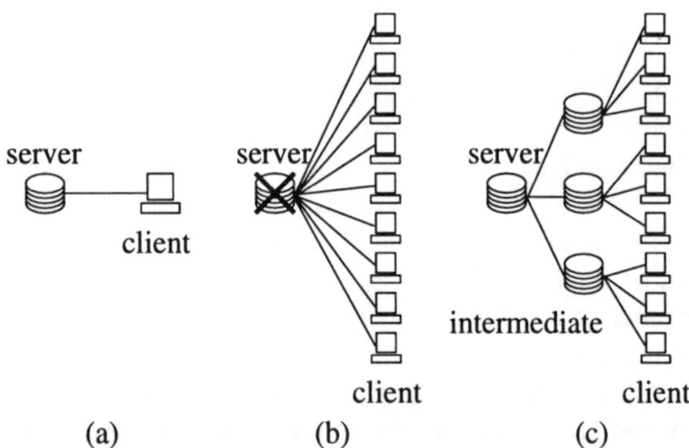

Fig. 4.1   Evolution of client-server models: (a) traditional model, (b) scalability burden with a large client population, and (c) client-intermediates-server model.

Because of this embedded scalability imperfection, World-wide Web (WWW) was unfortunately re-termed as *World-wide Wait* [Allison *et. al.* (1998)] during a certain period of the Internet popularization. Users have to endure an unexpected lengthy response time during their web browsing. Impatient users may be forced to resend their requests by pressing the reload button in their web browsers, which actually only worsens the already overloaded network or server, or simply leave those *hot-but-slow* web sites. There are other factors that are responsible for this poor user-perceived quality of online experience. They include software issues such as the vertical mismatch in HTTP/TCP transportation and application/OS adaptation, as well as hardware issues such as the physical limitation on network bandwidth and server capacity. Many studies have been done in recent years to introduce the persistent HTTP and non-blocking or thread-based implementations [Heidemann (1997)], besides the numerous investment on network bandwidth and server capacity. However, the underlying scalability issue due to the centralized client-server model still remains unchanged. This situation continues until web caching and content distribution were proposed and widely deployed in the last few years [Barish and Obraczka (2000)]. Both web caching and content distribution aim to shift the traditional client-server model into a distributed *client-intermediates-server* paradigm, as shown in Fig. 4.1(c). In web caching, requests from neighbor users are first aggregated at a nearby proxy server (or intermediate). If the requested object is cached at the proxy and is still valid, the cached object will be delivered to the users directly. Otherwise, the proxy will generate another request to the origin server of the requested object or another proxy server in a caching hierarchy. Essentially, web caching alleviates the scalability burden by reducing the amount and rate of user requests sent to the origin server. Due to the limited cache capacity and the fact that many cacheable objects are subject to change in content during their lifetime, cache maintenance (also known as cache replacement when a newly retrieved object has to be cached locally in a fully utilized cache) and consistency control (how to determine whether a cached object is still valid for user requests) have attracted many research interests in this area.

Different from the user-oriented approach in web caching, content distribution is a service provider based solution. Content Distribution Network (CDN) [Pan *et. al.* (2003)] providers distribute web content to their virtual overlay network of vast cache servers (or intermediate) in an *a priori* or *on-demand* manner. Although content distribution shares many common aspects in cache maintenance and consistency control with web caching, it is more concerned about how to direct a user request at a certain moment to a particular cache server, since there might be more than one server available to fulfill this request. This process is termed as *server selection*. CDN is expected to provide better flexibility, and hence better performance, than the ordinary web caching. For example, based on the current network traffic and server load, CDN can transparently redirect user requests, even from the same user, to different cache servers dynamically. However, it is almost impossible, or at most only available in a much coarser granularity that users can change their proxy servers on a per-request basis. Therefore, server selection is crucial in terms of both functionality and performance in CDN. The benefit of CDN is three-fold.

First, with proper server selection, users are more likely to have a quicker response, or shorter *click-to-display*, from a *better* cache server, instead of the faraway origin server or a overloaded proxy server. Second, for network providers, a proper server selection can globally balance traffic flows in their network with better link utilization and avoid a single point of failure or congestion around the origin server. Third, with a proper server selection, service providers can offer more reliable services to their customers over the virtual server overlay network: even if one or some cache servers or a part of the network become unavailable, CDN can still choose a reachable server for users with *best* possible effort.

In this chapter, we propose a fuzzy inference based server selection scheme for CDNs. There are several advantages of adopting the fuzzy inference based scheme. First, fuzzy logic is inherently capable to infer the relation among *multiple* information sources, no matter they are explicitly or implicitly related. Second, a fuzzy inference based engine is intrinsically tolerable to noises and even errors in these information sources. It also performs reasonably well when some information sources are temporarily unavailable. Third, a fuzzy inference based implementation of decision processes can be generic and be trained individually with respect to its actual location to adjust control parameters properly. Simulation results show that the fuzzy inference scheme can achieve higher network utilization, and provide better user perceived quality of service (QoS). In addition, the fuzzy inference scheme is flexible to deal with network dynamics, due to its intrinsic capability of handling multiple, inaccurate and inconsistent decision inputs. The remainder of this chapter is organized as follows. In Sec. 4.2, the server selection techniques in CDN and the incapabilities of the deterministic-logic based decision process are discussed. In Sec. 4.3, a fuzzy inference based system for server selection in CDN is proposed. The performance of the proposed fuzzy inference scheme is evaluated and compared with other four existing schemes by simulations in Sec. 4.4, followed by concluding remarks and future research issues in Sec. 4.5.

4.2   Server Selection in Content Distribution Networks

4.2.1   *A Server Selection Model*

A CDN server selection model and two practical implementations of the model with the regular user request process are shown in Fig. 4.2. The relationship among those involved in user request and server selection is shown in Fig. 4.2(a). Here, we identify four abstract entities: user (U), reference (R), server (S) and decision maker (D). Since origin server and

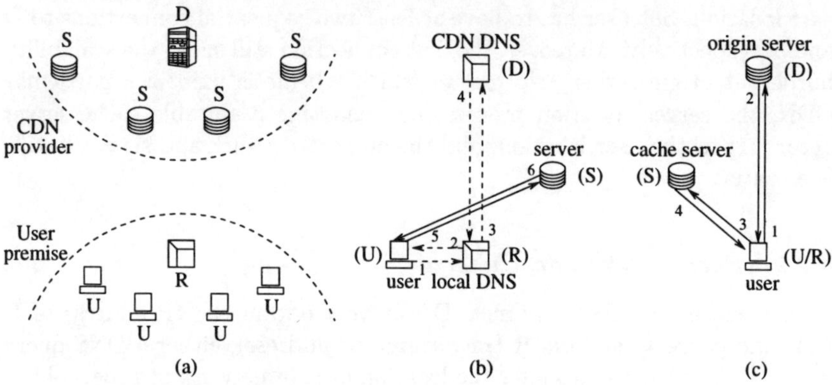

Fig. 4.2   CDN server selection: (a) model, (b) out-of-band DNS resolution, and (c) in-band HTTP redirection.

cache servers are externally identical in functionality from the viewpoint of end users, they are all denoted as S. Reference (R) is the location used by (or visible to) the decision maker (D) to identify individual users (U). R can be in the finest granularity, *e.g.*, a R for each U, or in a coarser granularity, *i.e.*, a group of users share a common R. D is responsible for getting server and network status, locating user requests, and determining which server will be used to serve a particular user request. In a practical CDN, D and S are owned and maintained by the CDN provider, and U and R are in the user premise, *i.e.*, they are not under the control of the CDN provider.

In the Web context, the server selection process can occur during the out-of-band DNS (Domain Name System) name resolution, or by using the in-band HTTP redirection scheme. For the DNS resolution [Pan *et. al.* (2003)], as shown in Fig. 4.2(b), user (U) first contacts its local DNS server (R) for the mapping of a generic CDN host name. R then contacts the CDN DNS servers (D) to map this host name into an IP address dynamically. Based on the location of R, and the status about network links and cache servers, D returns R the IP address of a chosen server; this mapping will then be relayed back to U. After this out-of-band DNS resolution process, U then contacts the chosen server (S) directly. In this approach, all users using the same local DNS server R will be treated equally by D.

For the HTTP redirection, as shown in Fig. 4.2(c), user (U) first contacts the origin server. Here, U is also R from the viewpoint of the origin server that acts as D. Based on the user location (U/R), network and server status, D returns an HTTP redirect primitive with the IP address of a chosen cache server (S). Then U contacts the chosen S that finally fulfills its request. For this in-band HTTP redirection process, D can have a better resolution on user location, but user has to have at least two sequential connections to D and S, respectively. Moreover, the first connection still suffer the scalability burden at origin server. No matter which scheme is used in a particular CDN, the server selection process, *i.e.*, choosing a suitable cache server according to the user location, and the current network and server status, is essential.

4.2.2   *Server Selection Criteria*

In the packet switched Internet, D can only obtain the IP address of R from the packet sent from R (*i.e.*, source IP address), either a DNS query or an HTTP request. To infer the location of R in network or geographical space, D has to rely on other assistances, *e.g.*, reverse name resolution, address block lookup, Autonomous System (AS) number, or longest Border Gateway Protocol (BGP, a *de facto* inter-domain routing protocol) prefix [Krishnamurthy and Wang (2000)]. The country-code top-level domain (ccTLD) names usually can give a good hint on geographical location, but this approach is less effective for generic top-level domain (gTLD) names. IP address allocation authorities keep a record of the owner information for allocated address. However, for many large ISP networks and organizations, a single block of addresses can spread throughout the Internet worldwide. AS number and BGP prefix usually can give a better proximity in terms of network route reachability. Therefore, user location information inferred by D may contain considerable noises and even errors. However, once the location of an IP address is determined, it rarely changes when comparing to the network or server dynamics.

The network and server status has to be measured periodically by D (or by someone else and then the status is fed to D). Based on the measurement history, the status of network links and cache servers can be predicted with a certain confidence for the near future by using a statistical estimator. Here, the tradeoff between how frequent the measurement is and how accurate the prediction is should be carefully balanced. Normally, the more frequent the measurement is, the better prediction D can probably have. However, a more frequent prediction implies higher measurement overhead, especially in CDN where there are thousands of cache servers need to be measured. More importantly, there is always an upper bound on how frequent the measurement can be done. On the other hand, usually all estimators give higher prediction errors if there are less measurements. Obviously, less measurement overhead and better prediction accuracy are contradicting in many aspects. Better performance can be achieved only if an appropriate tradeoff can be made.

Another troubling issue in server selection is how to synthesize network status and server status collected at D but from the viewpoint of the users. For example, a user may not have a proper network connectivity to a lightly loaded server, and a nearby server (in terms of network connectivity) might be already highly overloaded. Traditionally, network links and cache server are measured in different metrics with different disciplines, such as available bandwidth of a link and available processing capability of a server. In the Web context, user-perceived quality of experience can be highly characterized by the *click-to-display* latency. Since D usually is faraway from U or R, it is important to ensure that a *good* decision made by D is still valid at U or R, especially when the decision may lag behind the network/server dynamics.

4.2.3 *Related Work*

Existing server selection schemes are based on the *deterministic* (or *crisp*) control logic, *i.e.*, the factors considered in the decision process are quantized deterministically. For example, a user's request can be directed to a nearby server, based on the proximity of IP address, host name, AS number, or BGP prefix, or other metrics such as hop count or round-trip time (*rtt*) [Guyton and Schwartz (1995); Carter and Crovella (1997)] between them. Alternatively, a user's request can be directed to a lightly loaded server, based on the available resources of server processor, memory capacity, and I/O bandwidth. Besides the possible embarrassing scenarios such as a nearby but highly loaded server or a lightly loaded but unreachable server, traditional deterministic logic is facing other challenges during the decision process. For instance, the Internet measurement shows that *rtt* and router or AS hop counts are highly clustered and cannot offer a fine granularity to distinguish *near* or *far* servers. This fact implies that *rtt* or hop count approach alone cannot lead to a good server selection. Moreover, heterogeneous servers may have different capabilities to serve further requests even with the same amount of available resources. This fact indicates that it is quite difficult to compare two heterogeneous servers directly to determine which one is indeed a *better* server.

There are many other related work in server selection. [Stemm *et. al.* (2001)] evaluates a measurement architecture named SPAND which is collocated with users. The user-perceived performance is monitored passively and will be used for server selection in the future. However, this approach is inadequate for CDN where the provider does not have control in the user premise. An application-layer anycast approach to direct a request to one of all cache servers that share the same anycast domain name (ADN) is proposed in [Zegura *et. al.* (2000)]. It follows in a similar way as DNS lookup, and the local ADN server has to further determine the performance metrics associated with the returned server list. However, this approach requires a major infrastructure upgrade, as well additional resolve servers near users. IDMap [Jin *et. al.* (2000)] and Webmapper [Andrews *et. al.* (2002)] are other two approaches to offer new location-based services such as Internet distance and client cluster, but they also face the same problem: how to place these new instruments in a network with arbitrary topology properly. On the contrary, the server selection in a commercial CDN should be able to transparently and dynamically direct user requests to a *good* cache server according to user location, network traffic, and server load. Also this selection should be easily deployed and efficiently maintained by CDN provider, instead of individual users.

Table 4.1   Information sources involved in decision process

source	metrics	possible noises/errors
user location	reverse DNS, AS number, BGP prefix	coarse granularity, inaccurate database
network traffic	round-trip time, router/domain hops	poor resolution in the Internet
server load	processor load, memory capacity, I/O speed	difficult to compare heterogeneous servers

The inability of a deterministic logic to produce reliable and consistent results in the context of server selection is due to several factors. First, there are multiple information sources for the decision process, including IP address, host name, AS number, BGP prefix, round-trip time, hop count, and available server resources. Many of these sources are correlated, but it is very unlikely to obtain a universal correlation among them to reduce the number of independent information sources. Second, these information sources can contain considerable noise and errors, either due to the measurement limitation or the metric definition itself, and sometimes are even contradicting each other. For instance, a small hop count usually implies a small *rtt*, but for slow access links, a path with a small hop count can even have a higher round-trip time than another path that consists of a few more high-speed links. Third, the decision process can be location-dependent, *i.e.*, the location of D becomes an information source in the decision process. This fact results in additional complexity and performance deficiency in a deterministic logic based decision process when there are multiple D's involved.

Ideally, a *good* decision process should be effective when there are multiple information sources, robust when the information sources contain considerable noises and errors, and consistent even when the relationship among these information sources is location-dependent. In addition, a *good* decision process should be easy to develop, quick to evaluate, and scalable to deploy.

4.3   Fuzzy Inference Based Server Selection Scheme

Traditionally, deterministic server selection schemes explore a set of specific measured parameters to make decisions for server selection. This type of schemes has little or no allowance for measurement uncertainties [Klir and Yuan (1995); Wang (1994)]. For instance, when a measured rtt is used to represent the state of distance between a client and a server, two thresholds are defined, one indicates nearby state and the other indicates faraway state. The distance corresponds to the nearby state if the rtt is below the lower threshold, and to the faraway state if the rtt exceeds the higher threshold. When the measured rtt falls between the two thresholds, the decision that the distance corresponds to only one state will inevitably have some uncertainty.

The logic that determines belong to or not belong to a particular state is called crisp logic. Conversely, the uncertainty of measurement can be represented by using fuzzy logic in defined fuzzy variables. In addition, fuzzy logic has the capability to take into account random errors in measurements in making decisions, which mimics the intuition of a trained human expert. This intuition is not easily captured with tradition crisp logic. Fuzzy logic, unlike the crisp (deterministic) logic in which a proposition is either true or false, utilizes the ideas of fuzzy set which aims to describe and process vague concepts that are difficult to formulate mathematically though commonly used. The definition of fuzzy set and fuzzy logic allows the gradual transition between states. Unlike in crisp set, a variable falls into one state determined by virtue of the mathematical definition of each crisp set, hence processing a natural capacity to express and deal with observation and measurement uncertainties [Shen *et. al.* (2000)]. Its ability to approximate reasoning process makes it possible to derive fuzzy inference rules of a system which are expressed in natural language based on knowledge of its functioning which is often imprecise or incomplete [Munakata and Jani (1994)]. Fuzzy systems are multi-input-single-output mappings from a real-valued vector to a real-valued scalar (a multiple output mapping can be decomposed into a collection of single-output mappings) and the precise mathematical formulas of these mappings can be obtained. Fuzzy systems are knowledge-based systems constructed from human knowledge in the form of fuzzy IF-THEN rules, and provide a systematic procedure for transforming a knowledge base into a nonlinear mapping.

For the server selection, *rtt* and server load are two most important information to be used. However, due to the dynamics of the network, it is impractical if not impossible to get the real time values of *rtt* and server load. To reduce the information collection overhead, a small portion of the servers are chosen as probers, and the probers periodically collect the load information from all servers for D. Therefore, the load information known to D is a historical one which cannot capture the changes occurring since the most recently probing. For the *rtt* measurements, only the *rtts* between the client and the probers are measured to reduce the *rtt* measurement traffic. In the highly dynamic networks, the *rtt* between two nodes is time-varying due to changes in network resources, network topology, competing traffic, *etc.*. Thus, given the *rtt* values between the client and the probers, one can only get some rough information on how far is the client from the probers as well as the servers.

The imprecision and uncertainty of the input values of *rtt* and server load measurements affect the decision of the server selection algorithm based on the input values. To tackle this difficulty, fuzzy inference system, which is an expert system, can be used to solve the problems with uncertainty and imprecision by allowing it to represent qualitatively expressed control rules quite naturally with the linguistic description. Another aspect of fuzzy inference system is that when it is applied to appropriate problems, the fuzzy system often shows a faster and smoother response than conventional systems due to the fact that fuzzy control rules are usually relatively simpler and do not require heavy computational complexity.

Fig. 4.3 shows the block diagram of the fuzzy inference system. The fuzzy inference system estimates the likelihood that a request served by a server according to the *rtt* measurements from the probers and the server load measurements. The server with the maximum likelihood value is selected to serve the request. The design of the fuzzy inference system is given as follows.

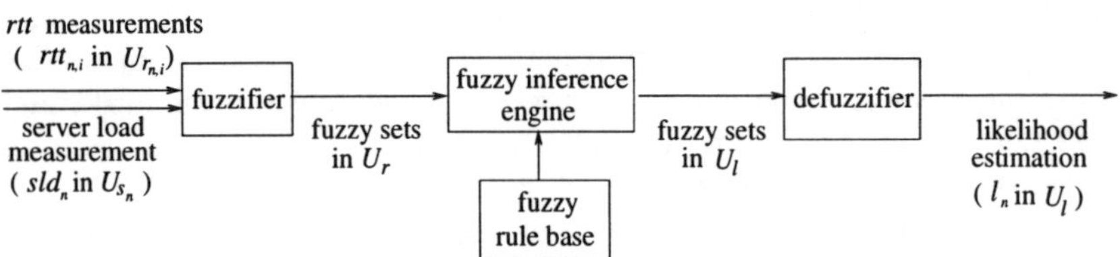

Fig. 4.3   Fuzzy inference system

The fuzzy inference system employs a knowledge base, expressed in terms of fuzzy inference rules and an appropriate inference engine, to estimate the likelihood that a request served by a specific server. The estimation is based on the partial measurements of *rtts* and the historical information of the server's load. The system is capable of utilizing knowledge elicited from human operators. The knowledge is expressed using natural language, a cardinal element of which is linguistic variables. Let the linguistic variable $rtt_{n,i}$, $i = 1, \cdots, M$, be the *rtt* measurement from prober i at time t_n, then the corresponding universe of discourse is the set of all possible *rtt* levels. We choose the term set of $rtt_{n,i}$, denoted by $U_{rtt_{n,i}}$, to contain the following elements: very close (VC), close (C), not faraway (NF), faraway (F), and very faraway (VF). Let the linguistic variable sld_n be the server load measurement of a specific server, then the corresponding universe of discourse is the set of all possible *sld* levels. We choose the term set of sld_n, denoted by U_{sld_n}, to be the set containing the following elements: slightly loaded (SL), lightly loaded (LL), loaded (L), heavily loaded (HL), and extremely loaded (EL). Let the linguistic variable l_n be the likelihood of a request served by a specific server with the universe of discourse being the interval $[0, 1]$. We choose the term set of l_n, denoted by U_{l_n}, to be the set containing the following element: very unlikely (VU), unlikely (UL), uncertain (UC), likely (L), and very likely (VL). The number of terms in $U_{rtt_{n,i}}$, U_{sld_n} and U_{l_n}, respectively, is chosen to achieve a compromise between complexity and fuzzy inference system performance. The membership functions of the input (the *rtt* measurements from M probers and server load measurement) and the output (the likelihood) depend on network structure, network coverage area, server rate, and server capacity *etc.*.

In the fuzzifier, each specific value of the measured $rtt_{n,i}$ is mapped to the fuzzy set $U^1_{r_{n,i}}$ with degree $\mu^1_{x_i}(rtt_{n,i})$ and to the fuzzy set $U^2_{r_{n,i}}$ with degree $\mu^2_{x_i}(rtt_{n,i})$, and so on, where $U^J_{r_{n,i}}$ is the name of the Jth term or fuzzy set value in $U_{r_{n,i}}$; and each specific value of the measured server load sld_n is mapped to the fuzzy set $U^1_{s_n}$ with degree $\mu^1_y(sld_n)$ and to the fuzzy set $U^2_{s_n}$ with degree $\mu^2_y(sld_n)$, and so on, where $U^L_{s_n}$ is the name of the Lth term or fuzzy set value in U_{s_n}.

The fuzzy rules describe the fuzzy logic relationship between the measured data and the likelihood information, *i.e.*, the kth rule has the following form.

$R_k :$

If $rtt_{n,0}$ is R_{0k} and ... and $rtt_{n,M}$ is R_{Mk} and sld_n is S_k

then l_n is L_k

where $k = 1, 2, \ldots, K$, K is the total number of the fuzzy rules, $(rtt_{n,0}, \ldots, rtt_{n,M}, sld_n) \in U_{r_{n,0}} \times \ldots \times U_{r_{n,M}} \times U_{s_n} = U_r$ and $l_n \in U_{l_n} = U_l$ are linguistic variables, R_{ik}, S_k and L_k are fuzzy sets in $U_{r_{n,i}}$, U_{s_n} and U_{l_n}, respectively.

In the fuzzy inference engine, the product inference engine is employed to combine the fuzzy rules in the fuzzy rule base into a mapping from fuzzy sets in U_r to fuzzy set in U_l, that is:

> Given Fact:
>
> $rtt_{n,0}$ is $\tilde{R}_0$ and $\ldots$ and $rtt_{n,M}$ is $\tilde{R}_M$ and sld_n is $\tilde{S}_n$
>
> Consequence:
>
> l_n is $\tilde{L}_n$

where $\tilde{R}_i$, $\tilde{S}_n$ and $\tilde{L}_n$ are linguistic terms for $rtt_{n,i}$, sld_n and l_n, respectively.

The fuzzy rule base is created by training data sequence (measured input-output pairs). To avoid tedious field trials, the training data can be generated in computer simulation, based on network structure and traffic model. The look-up table approach is deployed to generate the fuzzy IF-THEN rules. The degree assigned to rule k is calculated by using product operations

$$Q_k = \mu_k \prod_{i=0}^{M} \mu_{I_{ik}}(rtt_{n,i}) \mu_{I_k}(sld_n) \mu_{O_k}(l_n) \tag{4.1}$$

where I_{ik} denotes the input region of rule k for $rtt_{n,i}$, I_k denotes the input region for sld_n, O_k denotes the output region for l_n, $\mu_{I_{ik}}(rtt_{n,i})$ is the degree of $rtt_{n,i}$ in I_{ik} obtained from the membership functions, $\mu_{I_k}(sld_n)$ is the degree of sld_n in I_k, $\mu_{O_k}(l_n)$ is the degree of l_n in O_k, and μ_k, which is between 0 and 1, is the degree assigned by human operators.

The defuzzifier performs a mapping from fuzzy set $l_n \in U_l$ to a crisp point $l_n \in U_l$. Among the commonly used defuzzification strategies, the center average defuzzification method yields a superior result [Braae and Rutherford (1978)]. Let $\tilde{l}_n$ denote the estimation (generated by the fuzzy inference system at time t_n) of the likelihood l_n. The formula for the estimation at the defuzzifier output is

$$\tilde{l}_n = \frac{\sum_{k=1}^{K} \bar{Q}_k \prod_{j=1}^{M} \mu_{I_{jk}}(rtt_j) \mu_{I_k}(sld_k) \bar{l}_k}{\sum_{k=1}^{K} \bar{Q}_k \prod_{j=1}^{M} \mu_{I_{jk}}(rtt_j) \mu_{I_k}(sld_k)} \tag{4.2}$$

where $\bar{l}_k$ is the center value of the output region of rule k, and $\bar{Q}_k$ is the degree (normalized to 1) of rule k.

4.4 Performance Evaluation

4.4.1 *Simulation Topology and Parameters*

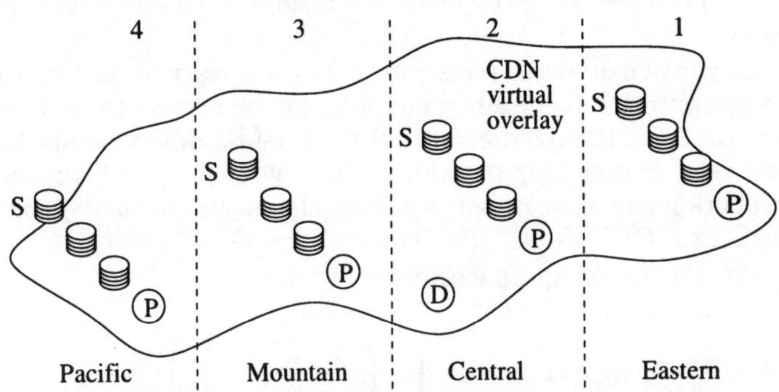

Fig. 4.4   Network topology

To evaluate the performance of the proposed fuzzy inference-based server selection scheme, extensive simulations have been performed. The network topology used in our simulation is shown in Fig. 4.4. 12 CDN cache servers (S) are equally located in 4 timezones, and there is 1 prober (P) in each zone. The probers collect the number of requests buffered from all servers every P_I seconds. When a user initiates a request, the *rtts* between all probers and this user are measured.

Since a client may be located anywhere, the *rtt* between a client and all servers are randomly distributed. In the simulation, if a user and a server are in the same zone, their *rtt* is normally distributed between 5 ms to 50 ms, with mean 10 ms and variance 10 ms; if a user and a server are k ($k = 1, 2, 3$) zones away, their *rtt* will be normally distributed from $10k$ ms to $100k$ ms, with mean $50k$ ms and variance $20k$ ms. All servers have the same processing power and the size of requested objects is exponentially distributed, so the service time is exponentially distributed with a mean of 100 ms. Each server can buffer at most 40 requests.

At different times, the request pattern among different zones in a CDN can be different and uneven. For instance, at 9AM EST, the request arrival in the Eastern timezone is much more intensive than that in the Pacific timezone. To examine the system performance in a wide spectrum of network scenarios, simulations are performed with traffic intensity increasing from 10% to 90% for both the even and uneven request patterns.

4.4.2   *Simulated Fuzzy System*

Before presenting the simulation results, we first show how the designed fuzzy system is trained and tuned. After 4 probers are chosen, the fuzzy inference system takes 4 *rtt* measurements from 4 probers and the load history at a specific server to estimate the likelihood that a request is served by this server.

For the type of membership functions, it is necessary to take into account both the computational efficiency and adaption easiness of the fuzzy inference system. Gaussian, triangular and trapezoidal functions are the most commonly used membership functions. Here, we choose the Gaussian membership function since it can better reflect the nature of the *rtt* and server load status in a CDN. With the Gaussian function, the degree $\mu_{I_{jk}}(rtt_j)$ and $\mu_{I_k}(sld_n)$ in (4.1) can be expressed as

$$\mu_{I_{jk}}(rtt_j) = \exp\left(-\left(\frac{rtt_j - \overline{rtt}_{jk}}{\sigma_{jk}^r}\right)^2\right) \tag{4.3}$$

$$\mu_{I_k}(sld_k) = \exp\left(-\left(\frac{sld_k - \overline{sld}_k}{\sigma_k^s}\right)^2\right) \tag{4.4}$$

where $\overline{rtt}_{jk}$, σ_{jk}^r, $\overline{sld}_k$, and σ_k^s are adjustable parameters for each Gaussian function.

Substituting (4.3) and (4.4) into (4.1), the estimate at the defuzzifier output is

$$\bar{l}_n = \frac{\sum_K \bar{Q}_k \Pi_j \exp\left(-\left(\frac{rtt_j - \overline{rtt}_{jk}}{\sigma_{jk}^r}\right)^2\right) \exp\left(-\left(\frac{sld_k - \overline{sld}_k}{\sigma_k^s}\right)^2\right) \bar{l}_k}{\sum_K \bar{Q}_k \Pi_j \exp\left(-\left(\frac{rtt_j - \overline{rtt}_{jk}}{\sigma_{jk}^r}\right)^2\right) \exp\left(-\left(\frac{sld_k - \overline{sld}_k}{\sigma_k^s}\right)^2\right)}. \tag{4.5}$$

The initial center values for elements in $U_{l_n}(\bar{l}_k)$ are 0, 0.25, 0.50, 0.75, and 1.0, respectively. In order to determine $\overline{rtt}_{jk}$ and σ_{jk}^r, the possible *rtt*s are divided into 5 ranges, and the initial values of $\overline{rtt}_{jk}$ and σ_{jk}^r are determined based on the mean and variance of the *rtt* in each range, denoted respectively as $\overline{rtt}_{jk}(0)$ and $\sigma_{jk}^r(0)$. The initial values of $\overline{sld}_k$, and σ_k^s, denoted respectively as $\overline{sld}_k(0)$, and $\sigma_k^s(0)$, are set in a similar way. To obtain the initial fuzzy inference rules, $10,000$ requests are generated by computer. During training process, it is assumed that the object size and *rtt*s from user to all servers are readily available, so that the decision can be made based on the accurate *click-to-display* latency t_d. When there is a request, the decision of which server is selected is based on the value of t_ds for a user w.r.t. all servers. All t_ds are sorted and the likelihood values are assigned as follows: the server with the minimum t_d is assigned as VL;

the servers with the second and third minimum t_ds are assigned as L; the servers with fourth to sixth minimum t_ds are assigned as UC; the servers with seventh to ninth minimum t_ds are assigned as UL, and the servers with the three maximum t_ds are assigned as VU. After the initial fuzzy inference rules have been generated, the total number of fuzzy rules K is known. In order to determine the optimal fuzzy inference rules, the back propagation training method, which is an iterative gradient algorithm, is employed to train the fuzzy system, *i.e.*, given a set of training input-output sequences (rtt_j, sld_k, l_k), $j = 1, 2, 3, 4$, the parameters in (4.5) are adjusted so that the decision error

$$\mathrm{err}(n) = \frac{1}{2}(\tilde{l}_n - l_n)^2 \tag{4.6}$$

is minimized. Since $\tilde{l}_n$ is a function of $\overline{rtt}_{jk}$, σ^r_{jk}, $\overline{sld}_k$, σ^s_k and $\bar{l}_k$, the optimization problem becomes the one by training the parameters $\overline{rtt}_{jk}$, σ^r_{jk}, $\overline{sld}_k$, σ^s_k and $\bar{l}_k$ to minimize $\mathrm{err}(n)$. At each step, the gradient of $\mathrm{err}(n)$ with respect to the adjusted parameter is calculated by differentiating $\mathrm{err}(n)$ with respect to the concerned parameter, then the parameter is adjusted based on the gradient value.

Let $z_k = \Pi^4_{j=1} \exp\left(-\left(\frac{rtt_j - \overline{rtt}_{jk}}{\sigma^r_{jk}}\right)^2\right) \exp\left(-\left(\frac{sld_k - \overline{sld}_k}{\sigma^s_k}\right)^2\right)$, $b = \sum^K_{k=1} z_k$, $c = \sum^K_{k=1}(\bar{l}_k z_k)$, then $\tilde{l}_n = c/b$. To adjust $\bar{l}_k$, we use,

$$\bar{l}_k(n) = \bar{l}_k(n-1) - \alpha \frac{\partial \mathrm{err}(n)}{\partial \bar{l}_k} \tag{4.7}$$

where α is a positive real-valued constant step-size.

Using the chain rule, we have

$$\frac{\partial \mathrm{err}(n)}{\partial \bar{l}_k} = (\tilde{l}_n - l_n)\frac{\partial \tilde{l}_n}{\partial c}\frac{\partial c}{\partial \bar{l}_k} = (\tilde{l}_n - l_n)\frac{1}{b}z_k. \tag{4.8}$$

Hence, the algorithm to adjust $\bar{l}_k$ is

$$\bar{l}_k(n) = \bar{l}_k(n-1) - \alpha(\tilde{l}_n - l_n)\frac{1}{b}z_k, \tag{4.9}$$

where $n = 1, 2, \cdots, N$. Similarly, we can obtain the algorithms to adjust $\overline{rtt}_{jk}$, σ^r_{jk}, $\overline{sld}_k$, and σ^s_k, where $n = 1, 2, \cdots$, $j = 1, 2, 3, 4$, and $k = 1, 2, \cdots, K$.

After the parameters of $\overline{rtt}_{jk}$, σ^r_{jk}, $\overline{sld}_k$, σ^s_k and $\bar{l}_k$ have been adjusted with these algorithms, the fuzzy inference rules can be tuned further according to the adjusted values of parameters and the same data set which is used to generate the initial fuzzy inference rules.

Figs. 4.5(a) and (b) show the final membership functions of $rtt_{n,i}$ and sld_n, respectively. The center values of the elements in U_{l_n}, $\bar{l}_k$, are set to be 0, 0.233, 0.489, 0.762, and 1.0, respectively, after the training process.

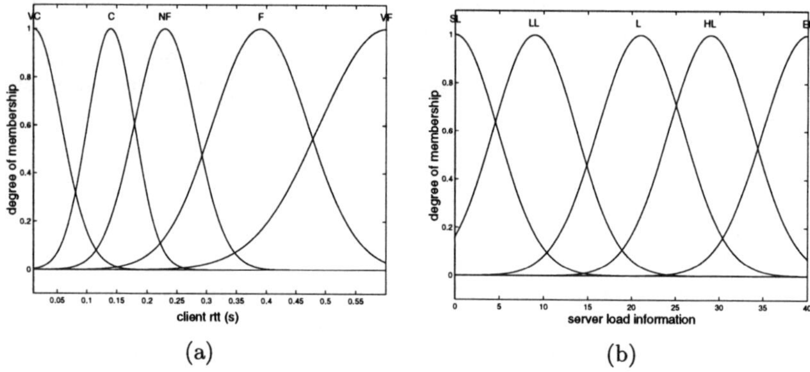

Fig. 4.5   Membership functions of (a) *rtt* and (b) *sld*.

4.4.3   *Performance Comparison*

The performance of the designed fuzzy inference scheme is compared with four other schemes: 1) *random*, randomly selecting from all servers with equal likelihood; 2) *min-load*, selecting the one (or a random one of those) with minimum load according to the load history known to D; 3) *inzone*, randomly selecting from all servers in the same zone as the requesting user; 4) *min-rtt*, randomly selecting from all servers in the zone where the prober has the least *rtt* to the user.

The system performance comparison includes request blocking rate P_B and average network load. A request is blocked when the server's buffer overflows. Since network load is proportional to the *rtt* for a given request, the average serving *rtt* is chosen to represent network load. User-perceived QoS is measured by the average *click-to-display* latency. Simulation results are presented in Sec. 4.4.3.1 when requests are evenly distributed across the network, and in Sec. 4.4.3.2 when requests are unevenly distributed in different zones. The measurement overhead for different schemes are compared in Sec. 4.4.3.3.

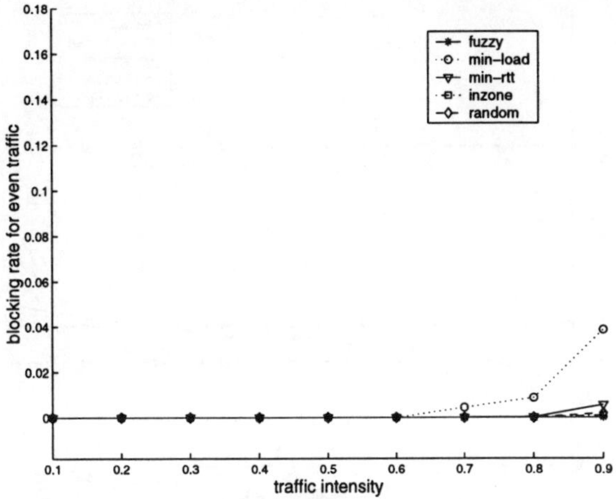

Fig. 4.6　Blocking rate with even request pattern ($P_I = 0.5s$).

4.4.3.1　*Even Request Pattern*

When requests are evenly generated in the network, for the random and in-zone schemes, the request arrival rate for each server is the same. Therefore, their blocking rates, P_Bs, should be the same, and they are also the optimal schemes when D has no status information about each server. Fig. 4.6 shows P_B (y-axis) for all schemes when the traffic intensity ρ (x-axis) is from 0.1 to 0.9. In this simulation, the probers update server status every $P_I = 0.5$ second. It can be seen that the random, inzone, min-rtt, and fuzzy schemes have no request blocking until $\rho = 0.8$. When $\rho = 0.9$, the blocking rates for the random, inzone, and fuzzy schemes are below 0.2%, while the min-rtt scheme has a blocking rate of 0.5%. The min-load scheme, however, starts to block requests when ρ is as low as 0.7, and P_B increases to 4% when $\rho = 0.9$. The reason is that D only knows the historical load information about all servers, and some recently assigned requests may easily overload a server which had the minimum load previously. On the other hand, based on the same historical load information, with the fuzzy inference system, D can intelligently distribute requests to different servers according to their previous load and the *rtts* between the user and probers. The simulation results show that the blocking rate for the fuzzy scheme is the lowest, which indicates the importance of appropriate interpretation of inaccurate inputs.

Fig. 4.7 shows the average network load, which is normalized to the load of the random scheme, w.r.t. traffic intensity. The simulation results

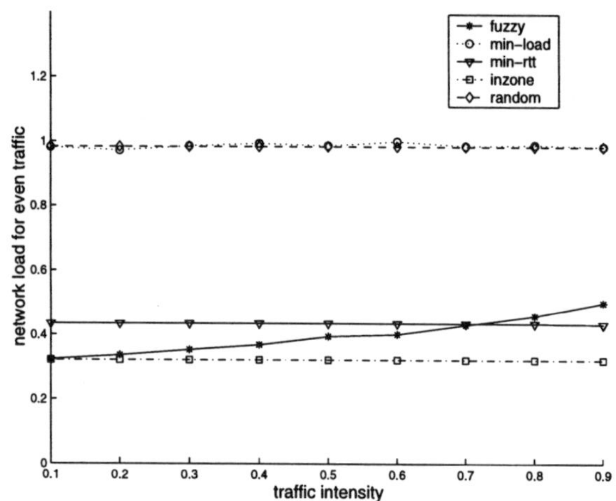

Fig. 4.7   Average network load with even request pattern ($P_I = 0.5s$).

in Fig. 4.7 show that the average network loads (in terms of *rtt*) of the random and inzone schemes remain constant, which give the upper and lower bounds, respectively. The min-load scheme does not consider *rtt* when selecting a server; thus, its average network load fluctuates around that of the random scheme. When the zone information is unavailable, D has to estimate the user location based on the measured *rtt* between the user and all probers. The estimation may not be accurate since, in network space, a user might be quite close to one prober, but not that close to any server in the same zone. Given the estimation error, the average network load of the min-rtt scheme is consistently higher than that of the inzone scheme, but much smaller than that of the random scheme. The fuzzy scheme can approach the lower bound when the traffic intensity is low, and its average network load slowly increases when there are more requests, which is an expected behavior. When requests become intensive, the fuzzy scheme makes a trade-off between blocking rate and network load, by intentionally choosing some faraway servers when nearby servers are very busy.

Fig. 4.8 shows the average of user experienced latency, which has two components: the *rtt* between the user and the server, and the delay in the server. When the traffic intensity is light, the latency is dominated by *rtt*; when requests become intensive, the latency is dominated by queueing delay. Therefore, the average latency for the inzone scheme is the optimal one when the request intensity is small, but it increases faster than the

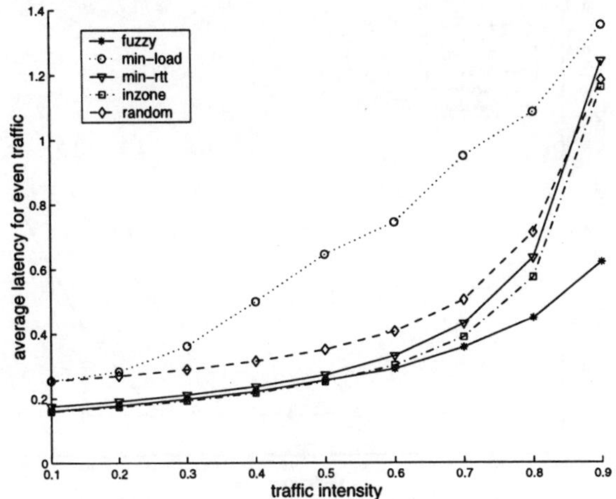

Fig. 4.8   Average latency with even request pattern ($P_I = 0.5s$).

random scheme when there are more requests, and they meet when $\rho = 0.9$. The latency for the min-rtt scheme is slightly higher than the inzone scheme due to the estimation error of user location. The min-load scheme has the highest delay for two reasons: it does not consider the user location, so it performs as bad as the random scheme when traffic is light; the non-realtime load status is not well interpreted, so the allocated traffic to a server is very bursty, and the average queueing delay becomes very large when traffic is heavy. The performance of the fuzzy scheme is very respectful, which approaches the lower bound when the traffic intensity is light, and the latency increases much slower than all the other schemes and remains the lowest all the time, which shows the significant advantages of the fuzzy scheme.

4.4.3.2 *Uneven Request Pattern*

In this set of simulations, the request arrival ratio from Eastern (zone 1) to Pacific timezone (zone 4) is $0.4 : 0.3 : 0.2 : 0.1$. Under this scenario, the performance for the random and min-load schemes is unaffected. However, as shown in Fig. 4.9, blocking occurs for the inzone and min-rtt scheme when $\rho \geq 0.6$, and their blocking rates are as high as 14% and 9.5% when $\rho = 0.9$, respectively. Since the traffic intensity in Eastern timezone equals $0.4\rho/0.25$, it exceeds 1 when $\rho \geq 0.625$, and equals 1.6 when $\rho = 0.9$. Similarly, the traffic intensity in zone 2 reaches 1 when $\rho = 5/6$. Therefore, it is not surprising to see the severe blocking rate with uneven requests for

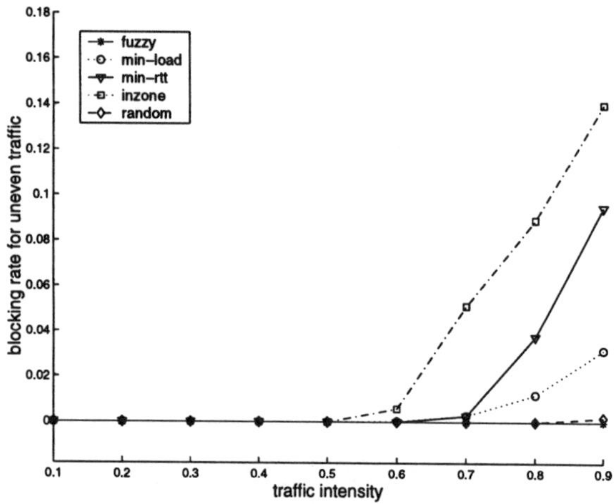

Fig. 4.9   Blocking rate with uneven request pattern ($P_I = 0.5s$).

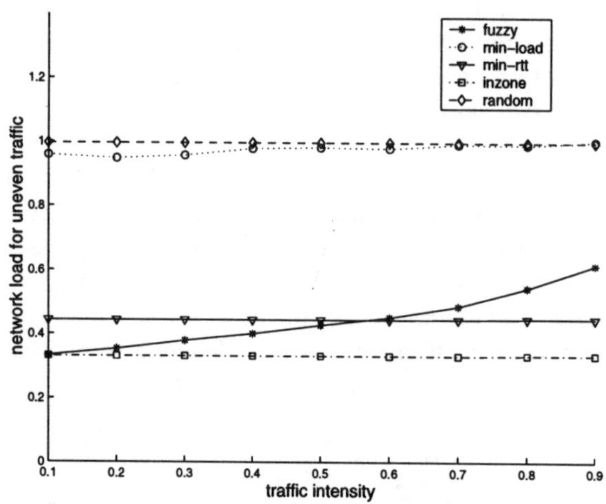

Fig. 4.10   Average network load with uneven request pattern ($P_I = 0.5s$).

the inzone and min-rtt schemes. Also, the average latency of these two schemes increases quickly and exceeds that of the min-load scheme when $\rho \geq 0.7$, as shown in Fig. 4.11. The network load for these two schemes remains unchanged, since they choose the server based on *rtt* only, as shown in Fig. 4.10. On the other hand, the fuzzy scheme has the least blocking rate

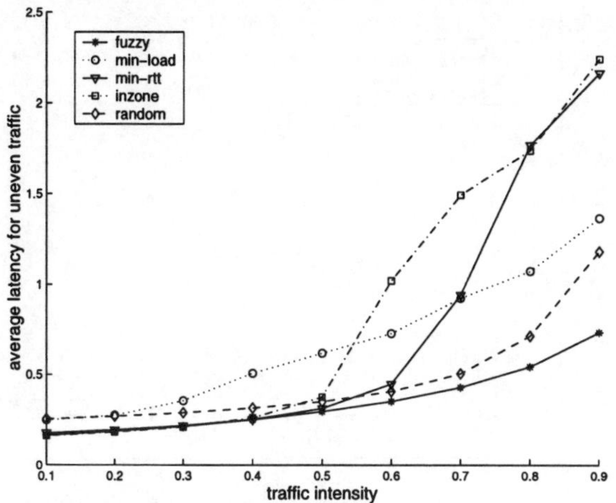

Fig. 4.11   Average latency with uneven request pattern ($P_I = 0.5s$).

and average latency among all schemes. Its average network load slightly increases since it directs some requests from Eastern zones to the servers in other zones to alleviate the congestion. Therefore, the fuzzy scheme is very robust with different traffic patterns.

4.4.3.3   *Measurement Overhead Comparison*

Both the fuzzy and min-load schemes require the server load information which is collected by the probers periodically. The frequent probing itself may produce a considerable amount of extra traffic which is the overhead for these schemes. On the other hand, the larger the probing interval P_I is, the less accurate the load information is. Therefore, it is more difficult to select a server appropriately. Fig. 4.12 shows the blocking rate of these two schemes when the probing intervals are 0.5 s and 1 s, respectively. With the probing frequency halved to 1 per second, the blocking becomes very severe for the min-load scheme which blocks 16% of the requests when $\rho = 0.9$. For the fuzzy scheme with the same probing frequency, there is no blocking until $\rho = 0.9$, where the blocking rate is only 0.6%. Fig. 4.13 shows the average latency of the fuzzy scheme is also much smaller than that of the min-load scheme. The network load with these two schemes are almost unchanged, although it is not presented here due to the limited space. In summary, the fuzzy scheme works well with inaccurate load information and can tolerate a larger P_I.

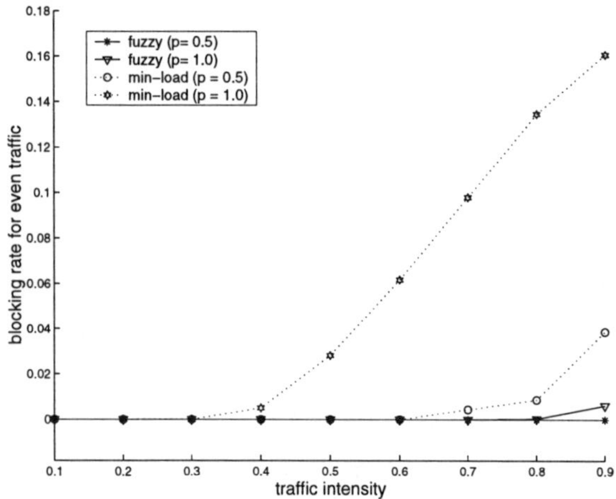

Fig. 4.12   Blocking rate for $P_I = 0.5s$ vs. $P_I = 1s$ (even request).

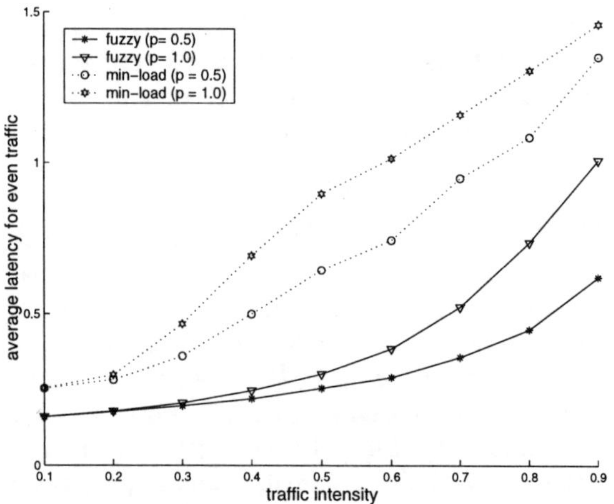

Fig. 4.13   Average latency for $P_I = 0.5s$ vs. $P_I = 1s$ (even request).

4.5   Conclusions and Future Work

A fuzzy inference system has been designed to select the appropriate DNS
cache server with limited knowledge of network status. With the fuzzy
inference system, decisions can be made based on multiple inaccurate and

imprecise measurements, and the server can be chosen quickly and intelligently. It has been shown that the more uncertainty of the measurements is, the more performance gains the fuzzy inference scheme can achieve over the deterministic schemes. In conclusion, the fuzzy inference scheme is a very promising solution for DNS cache server selection in highly dynamic networks.

Future research work includes a) how to deal with link/server dynamics, since some links and servers may up/down without any notice; b) how to optimally place CDN servers and probers, and how to obtain the optimal probing intervals, according to the traffic intensity statistics, user QoS requirements, and desired system utilization.

Acknowledgement

This work has been supported by a grant from Bell Canada under the Bell-University Laboratories Program.

Bibliography

Allison, C., Bramley, C. and Serrano, J. (1998). The world wide wait: where does the time go? *Proc. Euromicro'98*, pp. 932-940.

Andrews, M., Shepherd, B., Srinivasan, A., Winkler, P. and Zane, F. (2002). Clustering and server selection using passive monitoring, *Proc. IEEE INFOCOM' 02*.

Barish, G. and Obraczka, K. (2000). World wide web caching: trends and techniques, *IEEE Communications Magazine*, **38**, 5, pp 178–184.

Braae, M. and Rutherford, D. A. (1978). Fuzzy relations in a control setting, *Kybernetes: An International Journal of Cybernetics and General Systems*, **7**, pp. 185–188.

Carter, R. and Crovella, M. (1997). Dynamic server selection using bandwidth in wide area networks, *Proc. IEEE INFOCOM'97*.

Guyton, J. and Schwartz, M. (1995). Locating nearby copies of replicated Internet servers, *ACM SIGCOMM'95*, pp. 288–298.

Heidemann, J. (1997). Performance interactions between P-HTTP and TCP implementations, *ACM Computer Communication Review*, **27**, 2, pp 65–73.

Jin, Y., Shavitt, D., Jamin, S., Jin, C. and Zhang, L. (2000). On the placement of Internet instrumentation, *Proc. IEEE INFOCOM'00*.

Klir, G. J. and Yuan, B. (1995). *Fuzzy Sets and Fuzzy Logic: Theory and Applications*, Prentice-Hall.

Krishnamurthy, B. and Wang, J. (2000). On network-aware clustering of web clients, *ACM SIGCOMM'00*, pp. 97–110.

Munakata, T. and Jani, Y. (1994). Fuzzy systems: an overview, *Communications of the ACM*, **37**, pp. 69–76.

Pan, J., Hou, Y. T. and Li, B. (2003). An overview of DNS-based server selections in content distribution networks, *Computer Networks*, to appear.

Shen, X., Mark, J. W., and Ye, J. (2000). User Mobility Profile Prediction: An Adaptive Fuzzy Inference Approach, *Wireless Networks*, **6**, pp. 363–374.

Stemm, M., Seshan, S. and Katz, R. (2001). A network measurement architecture for adaptive applications, *Proc. IEEE INFOCOM'01*, pp. 285–294.

Wang, L. X. (1994). *Adaptive Fuzzy Systems and Control: Design and Stability Analysis*, Prentice Hall.

Zegura, E., Ammar, M., Fei, Z., and Bhattacharjee, S. (2000). Application-layer anycasting: a server selection architecture and use in a replicated Web service, *IEEE/ACM Trans. on Networking*, **8**, 4, pp. 455-466.

CHAPTER 5

RECOMMENDATION BASED ON PERSONAL PREFERENCE

Pei Wang

Department of Computer and Information Sciences
Temple University, Philadelphia, PA 19122, USA
E-mail: pei.wang@temple.edu

This chapter first defines a recommendation process, which helps the user to select products from a large number of candidates according to personal preference. Though both conventional database and fuzzy database have been used for this task, none of the two provide a proper solution. A new approach is introduced, which is easy to design and maintain, and provides well justified results. The central idea of this approach is to interpret user preference as consisting of multiple criteria, each of which is relative to available data. The procedure introduced here forms a membership function at run-time according to user request and available data, then use it to rank the candidates.

5.1 Introduction

In web-based e-commerce and on-line shopping, people often meet the "selection problem", that is, the user is looking for a product of a certain type, with flexibility or uncertainty in the details of the request. Typically, the user has certain "constraints" that must be satisfied, as well as certain ``preference" that are desired, but not specified in absolute terms.

For example, if the user is looking for a home computer, then most requests are in the form of preference: almost everyone prefers a fast CPU, a large hard drive, a cheap price, and so on, but few of the requests really has a fixed range. If the user is search for a flight, then the

101

departure and arrival airports may be determined, while the other parts of the request (such as departure date and time, arrival time, number of transfers, and so on) may be flexible to different degrees.

In this situation, if there are M products satisfying the constraints, and all of them are displayed to the user, then often it is too much information, and the user gets little help in using the preferences to get a final decision. For this situation, a "recommendation system" (also called "recommender system") is desired [Jameson et. al. (2002); Kautz (1998)]. Briefly speaking, the function of a recommendation system is to reduce the size of the displayed list from M to N (which is a much smaller number), under the condition that the user's preference is respected in the process.

Obviously, we do not want N to be too large, otherwise the recommendation system does not help much. On the other side, we do not want N to be too small — if N is one, then the "recommendation system" is actually making decision for the user. This is not desired, under the assumption that not all the relevant factors about the final decision can be included in the constraints and preferences, therefore the user still want to compare the top candidates, and to make the final decision, by taking all relevant factors into consideration. This is exactly what we usually expect when asking friends or experts for "recommendations" — we hope them to reduce the number of candidates to a manageable level, without making the final decisions for us.

Of course, the desired N may be different from situation to situation, and from user to user, but in general, we can take a default value in the range between five and ten. Such a choice is consistent with the psychological research on human memory (the well known "7 ± 2" phenomenon), as well as the common practice of picking the "top ten" in various categories.

If we can assume that the user only need one product from the M candidates (which is usually true), and that given sufficient time for analysis, comparison, and actual evaluation, the user would select product P_i, then a "good" recommendation system should almost always provides a top-N list containing P_i in it. With the help of such a system, the user's decision-making process is simplified, but still get (usually) the same result.

According to the above definition of the problem, there are still several ways of making recommendations, which have been explored to various degrees [Jameson et. al. (2002); Kautz (1998)]. For example, recommendation can be made according to a top-N list determined by the voting of domain experts or users for each category. Such votes can be collected explicitly or implicitly, such as through a "collaborative filtering". Or, recommendations can be made according to the similarity among users and similarity among products. For example, according to the selections the users have made before, they are classified into several groups, and the preference of each group is determined by statistics. When a new user is classified into a certain group, recommendations are made according to the preference of the members of the same group.

What we study in this chapter is a special situation, where we assume that there is no historical information available (such as votes, comments, reviews, past selections, and so on), and the recommendation is only based on the constraints and preferences provided by the current user. Since these requirements are highly personal and change from case to case, there is no way to anticipate them, and to determine a top-N list for every case in advance. Instead, the recommendation has to be formed at run-time according to user's requests.

Formally, the problem is defined as the following. DB is a database (or an information system of another type) that contains descriptions about products of certain category. Each product d_i is specified as a vector $d_i = <d_{i1}, d_{i2}, \cdots, d_{it} >$, in which each d_{ij} is the value of the product on an attribute A_j.

In the simplest form, the user's request consists of a constraint vector $c = <c_1, c_2, \cdots, c_t >$ and a preference vector $p = <p_1, p_2, \cdots, p_t >$. Each element of these two vectors is a condition for the corresponding attribute value.

A condition in constraint, c_j, is a binary expression of the form "X *relation* v", where X is a variable representing an attribute value, v is a constant value of the corresponding attribute, and *relation* is one of the following relations: $=, \neq, <, \leq, >, \geq$, where the last four are only defined on attributes whose values form a total order (therefore $X \neq Y$ can always be further specified as $X < Y$ or $X > Y$). The value of such an expression is either 1 (for "true") or 0 (for "false").

A condition in preference has the same form as a constraint, except that the relation is "$\approx$", for "similar to", and the expression is not binary, but has a value in a certain range. That is, to what extent a preference is satisfied is a matter of degree. Without losing generality, we take the range to be the interval $[0, 1]$. As a special case, "$X \approx v$" has value 1 if and only if "$X = v$" is true. Therefore, the similarity relation can be seen as a generalization of the equality relation, from binary to multi-valued. For attributes whose values form a total order, we define two new relations: "$X \ll$" is defined as "$X \approx v_{min}$", and "$X \gg$" is defined as "$X \approx v_{max}$", where "v_{min}" and "v_{max}" are the minimum and maximum value of the corresponding attribute, respectively (they do not need to be a finite value). Intuitively, these preferences mean "has a small value" and "has a large value", respectively.

Therefore, constraints and preferences correspond to different ways to assign a "score" to a value of a product on an attribute. After applying on a value d_{ij}, a constraint c_j provides a score in $\{0, 1\}$, a preference p_j provides a score in $[0, 1]$.

Since the variable X in above requirements is just a place holder, it can be omitted without causing confusion. In the following, therefore, we will use "*relation v*" for a constraint, and use "$\approx v$", "$\ll$", or "$\gg$" for a preference. There is a special condition "*null*" for "no constraint/preference", which should be ignored in the recommendation procedure.

For example, if each flight (from a city to another in a given date) is specified only by departure time, arrival time, and prices, then the preference "leave around 9 AM, arrive early, with a low price" is represented as "≈ 9, $\ll$, $\ll$". Similarly, if each computer is specified only by its CPU speed, hard-drive size, and price, then the preference "fast and cheap" is represented as "$\gg$, *null*, $\ll$".

Given these definitions, we can represent a recommendation procedure for top-N products as the following:

(1) Apply the user constraint $c = <c_1, c_2, \cdots, c_t>$ on the database DB. For each product $d_i = <d_{i1}, d_{i2}, \cdots, d_{it}>$, if its value d_{ij} satisfies condition c_j for all $j = 1 \cdots t$, then it becomes a candidate for recommendation.

(2) The above step produces a set of candidates of size M. If $M \leq N$, then recommendation is unnecessary, and the procedure ends. Otherwise the procedure continues.

(3) Apply the user preference $p = <p_1, p_2, \cdots, p_t>$ to each product d_i in the candidate set, and get a vector of scores $<s_{i1}, s_{i2}, \cdots, s_{it}>$, where s_{ij} is the return value of applying preference p_j to value d_{ij}.

(4) Apply a summarizing function $f(x)$ to the score vector of each product d_i in the candidate set to get a total score $s_i = f(<s_{i1}, s_{i2}, \cdots, s_{it}>)$, which is a numerical value.

(5) Select the top N products according to their total scores, and return them as the recommendation to the user.

5.2   The Existing Techniques

Described in this way, recommendation can be seen as *selective information retrieval*. Can we just use existing techniques, such as relational database, to carry out this process?

Obviously, the constraints we defined above are very close to conditions in database queries. Now the question is: can the preferences defined above be properly handled as conventional database queries? Obviously, a direct mapping does not exist, because database queries are based on binary logic, that is, whether a data item satisfies a condition is a matter of true or false, not a matter of degree. But how about approximative mapping? Maybe we can translate a preference into a query condition without losing too much information.

Such an approximation is possible — actually people are forced to do so on a daily basis. If a user prefers a flight departing around 9 AM, she often has to specify her preference as a query condition for a time interval $[9\text{-}\Delta, 9\text{+}\Delta]$, where Δ is a constant, like 30 minutes or so. If a user prefers a fast and cheap computer, he has to specify the CPU speed as above a certain threshold (such as 2 GHz) and the price as below a certain threshold (such as $1000).

Since the query language of conventional database only uses binary conditions, what happened above is that preferences are converted into constraints, then represented as query conditions. Of course this is an approximation, but is it good enough?

We say that the very idea of "recommendation" is lost in such an approximation, so it is unacceptable as a way to build a recommendation system. Here the problem is: if preference is treated as constraints, whether a product satisfies the user's request is a matter of true or false, and there is no way to rank the candidates that satisfying all the conditions. Consequently, the user simply gets all products that returned by the query, or a random subset of it as the "top-N" list, which is not really based on user preference.

When the user is forced to specify an interval for each attribute value, two extreme cases often happen: the query either returns no product or returns too many. For example, when the user is looking for a "fast and cheap notebook computer", if the request is "translated" into query for "faster than 3 GHz and cheaper than $500", there may be nothing available, but if it is treated as a query for "faster than 1 GHz and cheaper than $3000", then there may be five hundred of them. If we really want a certain number (say 5 to 10) of products returned by the query, the conditions in it should be tuned properly. For example, a query for "faster than 2 GHz and cheaper than $1250" returns five products, which looks like a good recommendation — until we think about the following issues.

To translate the preferences into a query which returns data items around a certain number, the user must be either very familiar with the distributions of the attribute values, or willing to try many different intervals/thresholds. In the former case, the user is an expert in the domain, so rarely needs any recommendation at all. In the latter case, the process is very time-consuming and often frustrating — many readers of this book may have such personal experience. Recommendation system cannot assume either of the two cases, because it is designed exactly to help the users who neither are experts in the field, nor have the time and patience to evaluate many possibilities.

Furthermore, even when "faster than 2 GHz and cheaper than \$1250" returns 5 products, the list may exclude some good candidates. For example, there may be a product which is a little bit slower than 2 GHz, but much cheaper than all the five products in the list, or a product which is a little bit more expensive than \$1250, but much faster than the five products in the list. No matter how the query condition is determined, such possibilities always exist.

This is the case, because binary query cannot handle trade-off among multiple preferences. When a user preference contains multiple components, it is normal, rather than exceptional, for them to conflict with each other. For example, in almost all shopping situations, users prefer products which are cheap and with high quality, even when we all know that these two preferences usually cannot be optimized together. Without a quantitative measurement on "degree of satisfying" or something like that, trade-off becomes arbitrary.

What it means is that even though database query is still the most often used technique for the users to request for data items, it does not provide much help for selective retrieval, because of the binary expressions used in the query language.

If we want to directly process the preference defined before, we need conditions that different values satisfy to different degrees. Under this consideration, the most obvious solution is to apply fuzzy logic [Zadeh (1975)] into database query, which leads to the idea of "fuzzy database" [Yang and Lee-Kwang (2000); Yang et. al. (2001)].

A recommendation system based on fuzzy logic can be designed according to the "recommendation procedure" defined previously, where the processing of the constraints are just like in conventional database. The preferences are specified using "linguistic variables", such as "$\approx fast$" for speed, and "$\approx cheap$" for price. Each linguistic value corresponds to a fuzzy set, with a membership function to calculate the score for each attribute value. Finally, the total score of a product is the minimum of all the individual scores, because in fuzzy logic the (default) function for "AND" (i.e., conjunction of conditions) is "min".

In this way, we can indeed get a recommendation system satisfying our previous description, and it no longer suffers from the problem in conventional database discussed above. Since the idea of fuzzy logic has been well known for many years, and this application is not that difficult, why have not we seen many such systems?

Among all reasons, a major issue is the design and maintenance of the membership functions. According to the common interpretation of membership function, it measures a subjective opinion on the "compatibility" between the linguistic value and numerical values [Zadeh (1975)]. For example, it can be said that "The membership of $1000 to *cheap* is 0.9", "The membership of $1250 to *cheap* is 0.85", and so on. Therefore, the designer of the recommendation system is responsible for specifying membership functions for every linguistic value.

Furthermore, it is well known that the same linguistic value, such as "cheap", corresponds to very different membership functions when used on different categories. Clearly, what can be labeled as "cheap" can have radically different prices for categories like notebook computer, super computer, house, notebook, pencil, and so on. Consequently, a separate membership function is needed for each linguistic value on each category. Even if that can be provided, there is still trouble — these functions may need to be adjusted from time to time. For example, what is considered as "a cheap notebook computer" two years ago is no longer "cheap" according to the current situation in the market.

In summery, though it is possible to build a recommendation system using fuzzy logic, the design and maintenance process is complicated (because of the *relative* nature of the membership functions), and the recommendations are hard to justify (because of the *subjective* nature of the membership functions).

All these problem comes from a common root, that is, though fuzzy logic *represents* and *processes* fuzziness in various ways, it does not properly *interpret* fuzziness. Since this problem has been analyzed in detail in a previous publication [Wang (1996)], we will not repeat the discussion here. We just want to say that because of this problem, fuzzy logic does not work well in recommendation systems, except in special situations where only a few membership functions are needed, and they do not change over time.

5.3   A New Approach

The main content of this chapter is to introduce a new approach for recommendation system design. This approach is similar to the fuzzy-logic approach discussed above, except that the membership functions are automatically generated from the available data by an algorithm, therefore the results are well justified, and the design and maintenance of the system is relatively easy.

This approach of recommendation is a by-product, a practical application, of the author's research on general-purpose intelligent system [Wang (1995)]. In the following, we only introduce the aspects of the research that is directly related to the recommendation procedure. For how this procedure is related to the big picture of artificial intelligence, please visit the author's website at `http://www.cis.temple.edu/~pwang/` for related materials.

Again, here we treat the constraints in the same way as in conventional database. After the M candidates are returned by the query, the recommendation task is treated as a task of selecting "good" instances of a given concept among given candidates.

Concretely, a preference vector $p = <p_1, p_2, \cdots, p_t>$ defines a concept C_p, the instance of which is what the user is looking for. For example, "fast and cheap notebook computers" is such a concept, and "flights (from one given city to another) leaving around 9 AM (on a certain day) and arrive as early as possible" is another. Such a concept is defined by the preference vector, as a set of properties. That is, "fast and cheap notebook computers" is a subset of notebook computers that have properties as being "fast" and being "cheap".

According to the model of categorization used in this approach, in the recommendation process the concept C_p is defined collectively by all the given properties, each of which contributes to the meaning of the concept, and none of which is sufficient or necessary for the membership by itself. Furthermore, whether an attribute value satisfy a corresponding property is a matter of degree.

Unlike in fuzzy logic, where degree of membership is a subjective judgment that cannot be further analyzed, in our approach the "score" of each value for a given preference is the *proportion of positive evidence among all evidence*, that is, $s = w^+/(w^+ + w^-)$, where w^+ and w^- are the amount of *positive* and *negative* evidence, respectively, for the preference to be satisfied by the value.

How is evidence defined and measured? Let us start from a concrete example. If the price of a notebook computer is \$1250, then to what extent it belongs to the concept of "cheap notebook computers"? According to our theory [Wang (1996)], such a question cannot be answered without a "reference class", that is, it depends on the answer of another question: "Compare to what?". Adjectives like "cheap" get their meaning from relations like "cheaper than", though the object of the comparison is often omitted in the expression. In the recommendation process, we assume that the default objects of comparison are the other candidates. Therefore, we interpret "cheap" as "cheaper than the other candidates". Since usually there are multiple candidates, and some of them may be cheaper, and others more expensive, than the product under consideration, whether it is "cheaper than the other candidates" is usually a matter of degree.

If there are M candidates that satisfy the constraints, then they are used to score one another for the preferences. To decide the score for a

$1250 computer to be labeled as "cheap", the other $M - 1$ candidates are compared to it one by one in price, where more expensive ones are counted as positive evidence, and cheaper ones as negative evidence, for the labeling (candidates with the same price provide no evidence). The total amount of evidence is the sum of the amount of positive evidence and the amount of negative evidence. Therefore, among the M candidates, if there are m_1 of them are more expensive than $1250, and m_2 of them are cheaper than $1250, then the score for a $1250 computer to be labeled as "cheap" can be simply taken as $m_1/(m_1 + m_2)$ [Wang (1996)]. Especially, the cheapest candidate gets a score 1.0, and the most expensive one get 0.0, for the given preference.

The above approach can be applied to a preference as far as the values of the corresponding attribute form a total order, even if the values are not numerical. The following is a general definition of evidence in the recommendation process:

- When a value d_{ij} is evaluated according to a preference p_j of the form "$\approx v$" ("similar to v"), if another value d_{kj} (of another candidate) is farther away from v than d_{ij} is, it is positive evidence; if d_{kj} is closer to v than d_{ij} is, it is negative evidence.
- When a value d_{ij} is evaluated according to a preference p_j of the form "$\ll$" ("has a small value"), if another value d_{kj} (of another candidate) is larger than d_{ij}, it is positive evidence; if d_{kj} is smaller than d_{ij}, it is negative evidence.
- When a value d_{ij} is evaluated according to a preference p_j of the form "$\gg$" ("has a large value"), if another value d_{kj} (of another candidate) is smaller than d_{ij}, it is positive evidence; if d_{kj} is larger than d_{ij}, it is negative evidence.

After separating positive and negative evidence from non-evidence among the other candidates, their number can be used as the above m_1 and m_2, respectively, then from them the score of the given value can be calculated according to the previous formula.

For a given attribute, if its values are not only comparable, but also numerical, sometimes the distance between values should be taken into account when scores are calculated. For example, to evaluate the score for $1250 to be labeled as "cheap", the existence of a $750 and a $1200, as the prices of other candidates, are very different. Though both are negative evidence, the former is clearly a much "stronger" one than the latter. For this situation, a more meaningful way to calculate the amount of evidence is to give each piece of evidence a "weight", which is the difference of that value and the given value. For the above case, the weights of the two pieces of evidence are 1250 - 750 = 500 and 1250 - 1200 = 50, respectively. Now the amount of (positive and negative) evidence m_1 and m_2 are weighted sum of pieces of evidence.

For a product d_i, after its attribute values get their scores as a vector $<s_{i1}, s_{i2}, \cdots, s_{it}>$ according to a given preference $p = <p_1, p_2, \cdots, p_t>$, the next step is to combine them into a total score s_i, which represents the membership for the product to be an instance of the concept C_p. Here we treat each preference p_i as an independent channel to collect (positive and negative) evidence for the membership relation. Therefore, evidence collected in each channel should be pooled together. As a default rule (assume all the preferences are equally weighted and each score is obtained from the same number of comparisons), the total score is simply the average of the individual scores, that is, $s_i = (\sum_{j=1}^{t} s_{ij})/t$.

Now let us give a complete and general algorithm for the recommendation procedure described above.

The database DB is a collection of data items, each of which is a vector $d_i = <d_{i1}, d_{i2}, \cdots, d_{it}>$, in which each d_{ij} is the value of d_i on an attribute A_j. In other words, DB is a matrix, where each row is a data item, and each column corresponds to an attribute.

A recommendation request r consists of two components, a constraint vector $c = <c_1, c_2, \cdots, c_t>$ and a preference vector $p = <p_1, p_2, \cdots, p_t>$. Each c_j has the form "*relation$_j$ v_j*", where v_j is a constant value, and *relation$_j$* is one of the following relations: $=$, $\neq$, $<$, $\leq$, $>$, $\geq$. The evaluation of c_j against a value d_{ij} should return 1 (*true*) or 0 (*false*). Each p_j has the form '$\approx v_j$", "$\ll$", or "$\gg$". The evaluation of p_j against a value d_{ij} should return a real number in $[0, 1]$.

For a given DB and a given r, the recommendation procedure, for a top-N list of data items satisfying r in DB, is the following:

(1) Translate c into a (conventional) database query on DB, and get the candidate set, which includes all data items in DB satisfying c.

(2) Assume the size of the candidates set M. If $M \leq N$, then recommendation is unnecessary, and the procedure may ends here. Otherwise the procedure continues.

(3) Apply the user preference $p = <p_1, p_2, \cdots, p_t>$ to each data item d_i, and get a vector of scores $<s_{i1}, s_{i2}, \cdots, s_{it}>$, where s_{ij} is the return value of applying preference p_j to value d_{ij}.

(4) Let the total score of a candidate d_i to be $(\sum_{j=1}^{t} s_{ij})/t$.

(5) Select the top N data items according to their total scores, and return them as the recommendation to the user. As options, the total score of each may be displayed, and they may be sorted according to their total scores.

In the above step (3), for each value d_{ij} and preference p_j, the score s_{ij}

is the ratio of positive evidence among all evidence, that is, $s_{ij} = w^+/(w^+ + w^-)$. The (positive and negative) evidence is collected by comparing d_{ij} to each d_{kj} in the candidate set, as the following:

- p_j has the form "$\approx v_j$": d_{kj} is positive evidence if $|d_{kj} - v_j| > |d_{ij} - v_j|$. d_{kj} is negative evidence if $|d_{kj} - v_j| < |d_{ij} - v_j|$. The weight of the evidence is $||d_{kj} - v_j| - |d_{ij} - v_j||$.
- p_j has the form "$\ll$": d_{kj} is positive evidence if $d_{kj} > d_{ij}$. d_{kj} is negative evidence if $d_{kj} < d_{ij}$. The weight of the evidence is $|d_{kj} - d_{ij}|$.
- p_j has the form "$\gg$": d_{kj} is positive evidence if $d_{kj} < d_{ij}$. d_{kj} is negative evidence if $d_{kj} > d_{ij}$. The weight of the evidence is $|d_{kj} - d_{ij}|$.

The last two cases are the special cases of the first with v_j to be v_{min} and v_{max}, respectively.

If the values of each attribute form a total order (so that "$>$" and "$<$" are defined between any pair of them), but the distance between them are not defined, then the definition of evidence for the first case is modified as the following: d_{kj} is positive evidence if $d_{kj} > d_{ij} \geq v_j$, or $d_{kj} < d_{ij} \leq v_j$. d_{kj} is negative evidence if $d_{ij} > d_{kj} \geq v_j$, or $d_{ij} < d_{kj} \leq v_j$. Furthermore, in all the three cases, each piece of evidence is equally wighted.

5.4 Discussion

The above recommendation procedure is based on the opinion that selection among candidates are usually carried out according to multiple relatively defined criteria, and the goal is to achieve an overall optimum, which does not always coincide with optimum on each criteria. Recommendation helps selection by reducing the number of candidates that need to be presented to the user according to given selection criteria.

Most shopping websites still use conventional database query to carry out the selection process. As a result, non-expert users have to spend lots of time in fine tuning their query to get a desired number of candidates for the final comparison and selection. Compared to that process, the recommendation procedure introduced in this chapter has the following advantages:

- Both (binary) constraints and (fuzzy) preferences are allowed, where the former is expressed in absolute term, while the latter in relative term. This is a more natural way to set selection criteria for most users, especially for users who are not expert in the field. For them, what really matters is often the relative value, not the absolute value, of a data item on an attribute.

- Trade-off and compromise among multiple preference are allowed and supported. Actually, all difficult selection problems happen in the cases where different criteria have to be balanced against each other. Using the concept of evidence (for membership relation), the above algorithm maps values of different attributes (with different units) into a common (unit-free) dimension.
- By presenting a top-N list to the user, the selection process is simplified without losing promising candidates. Still, the user can bring new factors (that are not in the recommendation request) into account in the final stage of the selection.

Compared to the similar solution based on fuzzy logic, this recommendation procedure has the following advantages:

- The degree of membership for an instance to belong to a concept is no longer a subjective opinion, but a measurement justified according to a theory on cognition and intelligence [Wang (1995); Wang (1996)].
- The scores are determined by the available data according to a domain-independent algorithm. Consequently, there is no need to manually design and maintain the membership functions. Instead, such functions are automatically learned from the data, and so are adaptive to the changes in data.

Because of the adaptive nature of the membership function, the system treats "cheap computer" and "cheap notebook" with different standards, simply because the available instances in these two categories have different price distributions. When a new product with the lowest price is added into the system, all other products in the same category automatically become "more expensive", as the result of comparing to it. This is closer to how the human mind works in these situations. Also, this "maintenance-free" solution is easier to be used in practical situations.

What we have introduced so far is the core procedure of a recommendation system, which is simple and domain-independent, and can be extended and customized for various purposes. When this approach is applied in a concrete system, there are still many additional issues, which we will only briefly mention here:

- For certain applications, the preferences on different attributes should not be treated equally. In such a situation, the final score for a data item can be changed from the average of the individual scores to the weighted sum of the individual scores. The weights of the attributes can either be specified by the user as part of recommendation request, or take default values determined by the designer according to the nature of each attribute.

- Some changes should be made in the algorithm to handle incomplete or uncertain data. For example, such data should make the corresponding score "weaker" in the recommendation decision. No matter what data is involved, its net effect should be reflected in the amount of evidence for the membership function.

- The constraint processing part can be simply replaced by the standard relational database query mechanism. In this way, the processing of preference can be designed as a frond-end of database, or even as an extension of SQL.

- In the previous procedure, we assume that there is a total order among the values of an attribute. If that is not the case, the recommendation system still can work after some domain-specific modification. For example, in a flight reservation system, if the (departure or arrival) airport is not part of the constraint, but part of preference, then nearby airports should be taken into consideration. In this case, the "degree of similarity" between two airports can be determined by distance, easiness of access, and so in.

- The (preference-based) recommendation technique introduced above can be combined with other recommendation techniques mentioned at the beginning of the chapter. For example, expert opinions, peer reviews, and so on, can all be taken as evidence collected from different channels for the same membership relation.

- The recommendation system can be connected to an intelligent reasoning system, such as the one from which this approach comes [Wang (1995)]. Since both systems are based on the same theoretical foundation, the reasoning system can use background knowledge to evaluate similarity relations between non-numerical values of attributes, then let the recommendation system use them in the evaluation of scores.

- The recommendation system can be further personalized by remembering and generalizing user preferences from past requests, and using these learned parameters in future recommendations.

- For advanced users, the system can allow them to override the default functions used in each stage of the recommendation process (for the calculation of degree of similarity, amount of evidence, individual scores, total scores, final recommendations, and so on) with their specially designed functions.

- Since the final result of recommendation is the top-N list, not the absolute values of concrete scores, various approximation algorithms can be used in each stage of the process, especially for the collection of evidence. These algorithms can improve the efficiency of the system, without losing the quality of the result too much.

In general, we believe that the preference-based recommendation technique defined in this chapter can greatly improve the efficiency of on-line shopping and other information selection processes, and make the huge amount of available data more accessible and manageable for common users, especially the users without expert knowledge.

Bibliography

Jameson, A., Konstan, J., and Riedl, J. (2002). *AI Techniques for PersonalizedRecommendation:* Tutorial presented at AAAI. URL: http://www.dfki.de/~jameson/aaai02-tutorial/

Kautz, H. (editor) (1998). *Recommender Systems*, AAAI Technical Report. URL: http://www.aaai.org/Press/Reports/Workshops/ws-98-08.html

Wang, P. (1995). *Non-Axiomatic Reasoning System: Exploring the Essence of Intelligence.* PhD thesis, Indiana University. URL: http://www.cogsci.indiana.edu/farg/peiwang/papers.html

Wang, P. (1996). The interpretation of fuzziness. *IEEE Transactions on Systems, Man, and Cybernetics*, 26:321-326.

Yang, J. and Lee-Kwang, H. (2000). Treating Uncertain Knowledge-Based Databases. *Academic Press International Theme Volumes on Knowledge-Based Systems Techniques and Applications*, 1:327-351.

Yang, Q. *et. al.* (2001). E.cient Processing of Nested Fuzzy SQL Queries in a Fuzzy Database. *IEEE Transactions on Knowledge and Data Engineering*, 13:884-901.

Zadeh, L. (1975). The concept of a linguistic variable and its application to approximate reasoning. *Information Sciences*, 8:199-249, 8:301-357, 9:43-80.

CHAPTER 6

FUZZY CLUSTERING AND INTELLIGENT SEARCH FOR A WEB-BASED FABRIC DATABASE

Jianhua Chen [1], Yan Chen [2], Wei Dong Gao [3], Bin Zhang [4], Ayse Gider [2], Sreeram Vuppala [1] and Donald H. Kraft [1]

[1] *Department of Computer Science, Louisiana State University*
Baton Rouge, LA 70803-4020, USA
[2] *School of Human Ecology, Louisiana State University*
Baton Rouge, LA 70803-4020, USA
[3] *College of Textiles and Clothing, Jiang Nan University*
Wu Xi, P.R. China
[4] *Department of Information Systems and Decision Science*
Louisiana State University
Baton Rouge, LA 70803-4020, USA
E-mail: Ychen@lsu.edu, bnzhang1@lsu.edu, agider@lsu.edu,
svuppal@bit.csc.lsu.edu, kraft@bit.csc.lsu.edu

In this chapter, we present our on-going work on a web-based online database for fabric sourcing. The objective of the database and its intelligent search engine is to address the urgent needs of cloth manufacturers, clothing designers and retailers to quickly find suitable fabric materials and fabric manufacturers. The intelligent search engine allows users to enter flexible queries in search for fabrics according to fabric mechanical property, the intended garment appearance, as well as tailorability of the fabrics. We also apply fuzzy linear clustering method of Hathaway and Bezdek to the task of fabric drape property prediction which is useful for selecting suitable fabrics. We show that the fuzzy linear clustering method is quite effective for this task. A hybrid method combining K-nearest neighbor method and fuzzy linear clustering improves the prediction accuracy further.

6.1   Introduction

The explosive development of Information Technology (IT), in particular the Internet and the Web, has revolutionized the way business is conducted today. IT has offered the business world tremendous on-line business opportunities. The traditional textile industry has already benefited from these opportunities significantly. Increasingly more and more cloth manufacturers, clothing designers and retailers are going on-line to track fashion, search for suitable fabric materials, locate fabric manufacturers, and sell products. For example, websites such as Worth Global Style Network (WGSN) (www.wgsn.com) established in London provide fashion and style industries with news and services including resources of yarn, fabrics, garment accessories, and graphics of new design styles and fashion trend. The cloth retailer Neiman Marcus launched a 24 million dollars Web site investment with new multimedia capabilities in the hope to make customer's on-line shopping experience more realistic.

There is a tremendous need for on-line fabric databases storing detailed information about fabric properties and fabric manufacturers. Moreover, an intelligent search engine should be built with such a database so that garment designers and manufacturers can search for fabrics which are suitable for the designed garment appearance and tailoring. To address this need, we have established an on-line database and an intelligent search engine accessible through the World Wide Web. The first batch of fabrics, consisting of about 300 samples from several fabric manufacturers in China, are stored in the database. Cloth manufacturers can use the search engine to find desired fabrics that match fashion trends in color, drape, and style, and to locate fabrics with good physical properties that assure high garment quality. The search engine and the fabric sourcing database have the following characteristics: First, it supports flexible queries more powerful than ordinary exact query as in conventional database search. Range queries and queries with relevance feedback are supported. This significantly benefits the users in case exact match to the user's query is not available in the database. Second, the search engine incorporates data mining techniques such as fuzzy clustering (and potentially decision trees) to support the capability of fabric property prediction and thus fabric selection based on the fuzzy clusters. Third, the online database and the search engine represent a first-step toward a real-world online application which provides an important link between cloth designers/manufactures and fabric suppliers.

Obviously, the search criteria for fashion trend and suitable fabric materials are often fuzzy. For example, the answer to whether or not a particular garment design is "fashionable" depends on many factors and can not be easily quantified. Similarly, the judgement of whether or not (or how much) a fabric material is "suitable" for a specific garment is a fuzzy one. Moreover, various fabric properties are related to each other in a fuzzy way. Thus it is natural to use fuzzy logic techniques for building such a search engine for our online database. In this work, the fuzzy linear clustering method[Hathaway and Bezdek (1993)] is used to predict fabric appearance (drape) from fabric mechanical properties.

The fabrics stored in the online database are characterized by more than a dozen mechanical properties (such as shear, tensile, ect.) and fabric contents, structure and end-use information. In addition, a fabric also has other properties such as appearance and tailorability. Intuitively, these "more intangible" properties are related to mechanical properties of a fabric in a subtle way. In selecting suitable fabrics from the online database, we often need the capability of predicting fabric appearance and tailorability from its mechanical properties. A systematic prediction method is desired so that "fuzzy" queries for fabrics with desired appearance and tailorability can be answered. In spite of some works on fabric evaluation and classification[Chen *et. al* (2000); Chen *et. al* (1999)], little is known in textile study literature for predicting fabric appearance and tailorability from its mechanical properties. In the current work, Fuzzy linear clustering method by Bezdek and Hathaway[Hathaway and Bezdek (1993)] is used to discover correlations between fabric drape coefficient (which can be viewed as a fabric appearance property) and fabric mechanical/structural properties. Our experiments indicate that fuzzy linear clustering is quite effective for this purpose. Our study also sheds some insight on the issue of selecting the number of fuzy clusters and that of overfitting. Moreover, we develop a hybrid method combining fuzzy linear clustering with K-nearest neighbor for fabric drape coefficient prediction. We show that the hybrid method improves the prediction accuracy.

This chapter is organized as follows. In Section 2, we briefly describe the on-line fabric database and the intelligent search engine for the database. In Section 3, the fuzzy linear clustering method used in this work is presented. The experimental studies on the prediction accuracy of the fuzzy linear clustering method and the hybrid method are presented in Section 4. We conclude and discuss future works in Section 5.

6.2   The On-line Database and Search Engine

An on-line database with a search engine has been established using DB2 database and Microsoft Active Page Server. The database is accessible from the World Wide Web. The search engine supports several types of queries to the database, from simple queries for fabrics with specific mechanical/structural property value requirements, to "fuzzy" queries for fabrics with vague fabric appearance (drape, etc.) and tailorability requirements. The users can also see drape images of fabrics, and check out details about fabric manufacturers. Currently the database contains about 300 fabrics from several fabric manufacturers. Each fabric is characterized by a number of physical (mechanical/structural) properties such as tensile, shear, and structure, and its contents (cotton, polyester, etc.) and end-use (such as suit, blouse, coat, etc.). Drape coefficients and drape images of the fabrics are also stored in the database. Tailorability information about the fabrics will be researched and added later on to the database. The following figures show the architecture and some of the interface screens of the on-line database. More details about the on-line database and its search engine can be found at the website http://tam4.huec.lsu.edu/.

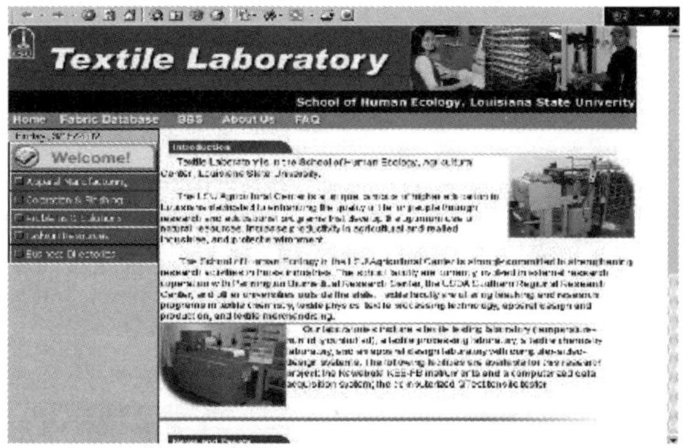

Fig. 6.1   The On-line Database Web Page

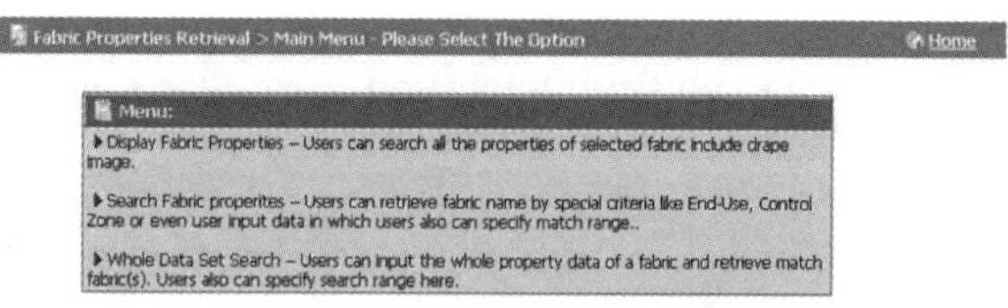

Fig. 6.2   The Search Menu

Users can ask several types of queries to the search engine. The simplest query is to select fabrics according to individual fabric property (mechanical, structural, end-use, drape) requirement or a combination of such properties. However, such queries alone are not sufficient to meet the user's

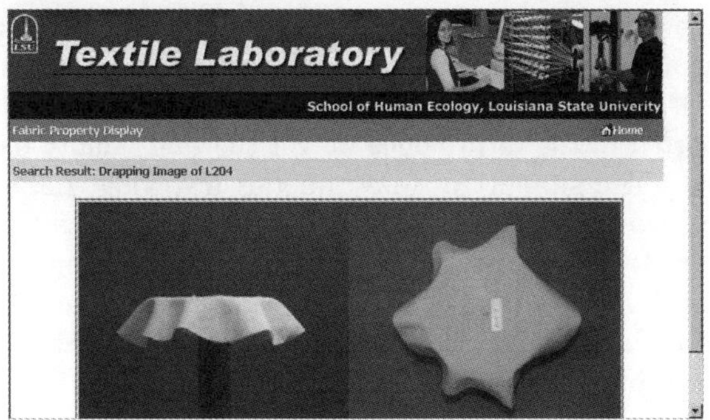

Fig. 6.3   Fabric Drape Image

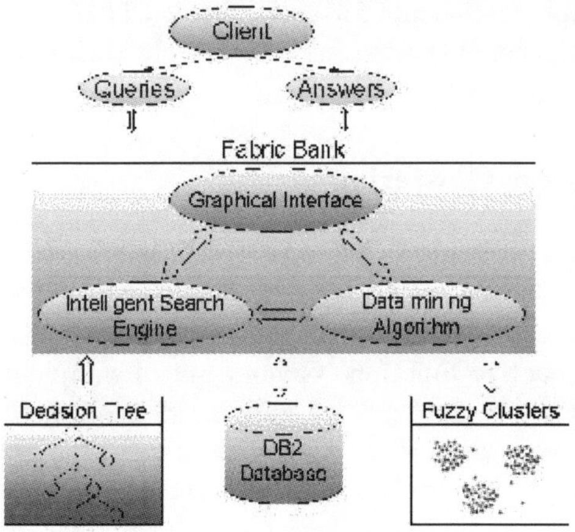

Fig. 6.4   System Architecture

need. The system also allows users to specify range queries so that fabrics
which approximately match the user's requirement can be returned to the
user. In range queries, the user specifies each desired property (numerical) value and a tolerance range (say X percent). Then the fabrics whose
specific property values are within the given range of the desired property
value (plus/minus X percent) are selected. Query processing by relevance-
feedback method is planned and will be implemented in the near future.

Moreover, the search engine also provides support to fuzzy queries that specify fabric appearance (such as drape) using vague terms (such as "high drape value"). Fuzzy queries involving vague specification of tailorability will be supported in the future once we get the tailorability data from relevant sources. The support of fuzzy queries involving drape property is conducted in two ways: One is to define simple fuzzy sets ("high drape", "medium drape", "low drape") over the drape property domain, and simply return the fabrics according to the fuzzy membership value of the fabric's drape in the required fuzzy set. The other approach, which is applicable when we do not have the fabric's drape data in the database, is to first predict the fabric's drape value, and then decide whether to select the fabric according to its predicted drape value.

Although drape coefficient data can be obtained for each fabrics by using the Cusick Drape Tester, it is a tedious process. Thus it would be desirable to have the ability to predict the drape property of a fabrics from its other physical properties so that we probably do not have to physically measure the drape coefficients for every fabric. That is why we conducted the prediction experiments with fuzzy linear clustering in this research.

6.3   Fuzzy Linear Clustering

The fuzzy linear clustering method of Hathaway and Bezdek is a generalization of fuzzy C-means of Bezdek[Bezdek (1980)]. The fuzzy C-means algorithm is a family of algorithms which form fuzzy clusters by iteratively optimizing an objective function. Given a set of sample data points $\{p_i = < x_{i1}, x_{i2}, ..., x_{is} > : 1 \leq i \leq n\}$ and the desired number of clusters C (≥ 2), the algorithm produces C fuzzy clusters A_k, $1 \leq k \leq C$, by finding cluster center v_k for each cluster A_k, and the membership values $\mu_{ki} = \mu_k(p_i)$ for each point p_i and cluster A_k. It chooses the μ_{ki} so that the following objective function (where $m > 1$ is a fixed constant)

$$J_m = \sum_{k=1}^{C} \sum_{i=1}^{n} (\mu_{ki})^m \|p_i - v_k\|^2 \tag{6.1}$$

is minimized under the constraints that $\sum \mu_{ki} = 1$ (summed over all k) for each i, and each $\mu_{ki} \geq 0$. Here, $\|p_i - v_k\|$ denotes the Euclidean distance between the points p_i and v_k and v_k is visualized as the center of the cluster A_k. The equations for determining μ_{ki} to minimize J_m are given by

$$\mu_{ki} \; = \; \frac{\left[||p_i - v_k||^2\right]^{-1/(m-1)}}{\sum_{j=1}^{C}\left[||p_i - v_j||^2\right]^{-1/(m-1)}} \tag{6.2}$$

$$1 \leq k \leq C \; and \; 1 \leq i \leq n,$$

together with the following equations for v_k (which are to be considered coordinate-wise for p_i and v_k):

$$v_k \; = \; \frac{\sum_{i=1}^{n}\left(\mu_{ki}\right)^m p_i}{\sum_{i=1}^{n}\left(\mu_{ki}\right)^m} \tag{6.3}$$

In fuzzy linear clustering[Hathaway and Bezdek (1993)] the input to the algorithm would still be a set of data points $X = \{p_i,\ 1 \leq i \leq n\}$ and $C \geq 2$, the number of clusters. Each given data point p_i is of the form $p_i = <x_i,\ y_i>$, where x_i is a real-valued vector of dimension $s \geq 1$, and y_i is a real number. The fuzzy linear clustering algorithm will search for fuzzy clusters A_k $(1 \leq k \leq C)$ which are characterized by linear functions $g_k(x) = a_{k0} + a_{k1}x_1 + ... + a_{ks}x_s$. The algorithm finds the membership values μ_{ki} and the coefficients in the linear functions $g_k(x)$ such that the objective function (6.4) is minimized:

$$J_m \; = \; \sum_{k=1}^{C}\sum_{i=1}^{n}(\mu_{ki})^m [y_i - g_k(x_i)]^2 \tag{6.4}$$

The constraints $\sum \mu_{ki} = 1$ (summed over all k) and $\mu_{ki} \geq 0$ apply here as well. The essential difference here is the replacement of the center v_k for the cluster A_k by the hyperplane $y = g_k(x)$. The distance $||p_i - v_k||$ is now replaced by the distance of p_i from the hyperplane $y = g_k(x)$, which is $|y_i - g_k(x_i)|$. We call the resulting clusters fuzzy linear clusters .

The computation of the fuzzy linear clusters proceeds from an initial randomly generated membership values. The algorithm iteratively computes the linear coefficients by linear regression from the current membership values and then computes the membership values from the current linear coefficients according to the following equation:

$$\mu_{ki} \; = \; \frac{\left[(y_i - g_k(x_i))^2\right]^{-1/(m-1)}}{\sum_{j=1}^{C}\left[(y_i - g_j(x_i))^2\right]^{-1/(m-1)}} \tag{6.5}$$

$$1 \leq k \leq C \; and \; 1 \leq i \leq n,$$

The algorithm terminates when the maximum change of the membership values between consecutive iterations falls below a given threshold.

Hathaway and Bezdek developed the fuzzy linear clustering method. Kundu and Chen independently discovered it[Kundu and Chen (1994)] and showed that the fuzzy linear clusters defined possess the nice property of being invariant under linear transformations. The applications of fuzzy linear clustering in fuzzy control rule learning have also been investigated[Chen and Kundu (1996); Mikulcic and Chen (1996); Sabharwal and Chen (1996)] These results indicate that fuzzy linear clustering method is very useful for capturing linear patterns in data, and that the method has a strong generalization capability for function approximation.

6.4   Experiments On Fuzzy Clustering

In [Chen *et. al* (2002)], we presented a preliminary result of our work on using fuzzy linear clusters for drape prediction from fabric mechanical properties. But at that time the amount of experiment data was too small. Now that we have obtained more data (300+ data points), a series experiments have been performed on application of fuzzy linear clustering to discover patterns from the larger dataset. Here each data point is of the form <x, y>, where x = <x_1, ..., x_{16}>, a vector of dimension 16 corresponding to 16 mechanical properties of a fabric, and y is the fabric's drape coefficient. The objective here is to predict a fabric's drape coefficient value from its mechanical property values.

Application of fuzzy linear clustering for data prediction typically involves two steps: The training step and the prediction step. In the training step, we apply fuzzy linear clustering algorithm (with the number of clusters C specified) to a training data set with n data points. This will produce the cluster centers g_k (in the form of linear equations) for $1 \leq k \leq C$ and the fuzzy membership values μ_{ki} for $1 \leq k \leq C$ and $1 \leq i \leq n$. The training step will also generate a predicted y value for each training data point $< x_i, y_i >$. In the prediction step, given only the x-part of a data point (x = <x_1, ..., x_{16}>), the prediction algorithm will produce an estimated y-part. The y value is computed by first computing $g_k(x)$ for each linear equation g_k, and then combining the results of all clusters by the following equation:

$$y = \sum_{k=1}^{C} g_k(x)\mu_{ki} \tag{6.6}$$

Here the membership value μ_{ki} comes from the training data point $< x_i,$ $y_i >$, which is the nearest neighbor of x.

In the training step, we have experimented with various number of clusters in observation of the resulting prediction accuracy on the training data. As we expected, the prediction accuracy (on training data) is already quite high (nearly 95 percent) when we use 3 clusters. The prediction accuracy on training data increases when the number of clusters is increased. When we use 6 clusters (with a training data size = 150), the accuracy (on training data) exceeds 98 percent.

In the prediction step, to test the generalization capability of the discovered fuzzy cluster patterns, we apply the trained fuzzy models to predict drape values for unseen test data. Overall, the results are quite encouraging. Without any further fine tuning, we achieved a prediction accuracy of about 88 percent on test data. Subsequently, a new prediction method using multiple nearest neighbors is used, which leads to a prediction accuracy about 92 percent.

In the initial prediction study, two experiments have been conducted. In one experiment, we observe the prediction accuracies on testing data (disjoint from training data) in connection with various number of clusters used in training. We observed that using too many clusters in training is not helpful to reduce prediction error on unseen test data. As can be seen by the following Figure 6.5, prediction accuracy on testing data initially increases with the increase of number of clusters, but then it starts getting worse. This suggests that using too many clusters for the training is likely to "overfit" the training data, and the clusters obtained actually lose generalization power and thus causing the drop in prediction accuracy. In the other experiment, we tried different sizes for the training and testing data split, and observed the resulting prediction accuracy on testing data. The following Figure 6.6 shows the prediction accuracy in connection with training data size (we totally have 300 data points). It is obvious that the prediction accuracy initially improves with the growth of training data size, but after the training data size reaches 150 (half of the total data), the prediction accuracy deteriorates. Again, here we observe the effect of "overfitting". The lesson is that training with too many data points is not necessarily a blessing - the models discovered may not generalize well.

After the initial experiments that confirmed the viability of applying fuzzy linear clustering for fabric drape coefficient prediction, we develop a hybrid method combining K-nearest neighbor approach with fuzzy linear clustering for the drape prediction task. The hybrid method differs from the initial method described earlier only in one place: The prediction step. Instead of using only one nearest neighbor to obtain the membership values of a new data point x to the fuzzy clusters, multiple nearest neighbors

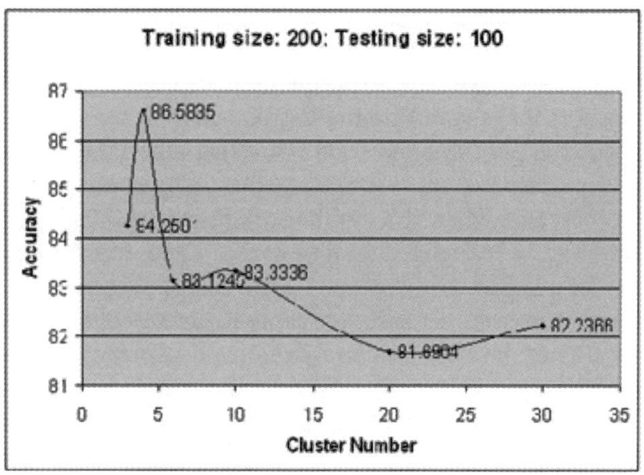

Fig. 6.5   Number of clusters vs. prediction accuracy

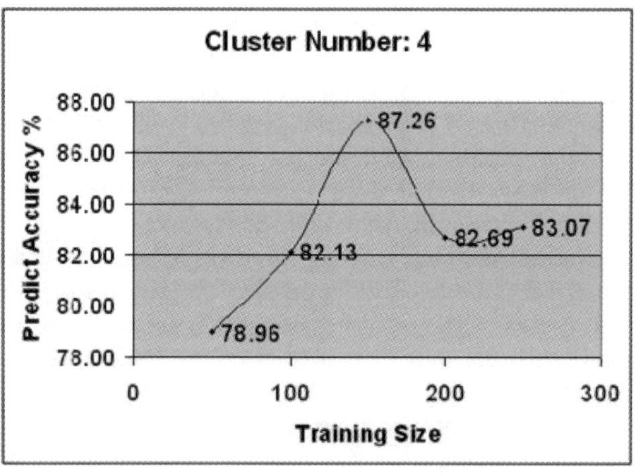

Fig. 6.6   Training data size vs. prediction accuracy

are used for this purpose. Thus the hybrid method combines ideas from K-Nearest neighbor and fuzzy linear clustering in performing the data prediction task.

K-nearest neighbor method, studied widely in machine learning and data analysis, is a simple yet powerful approach for pattern recognition and classification tasks. In its simplest form, the K-nearest neighbor method solves the classification problem by classifying a new input data x to class

c, if class c is the most numerous class among all nearest neighbors of x. To be more precise, assume we have a set T of (training) data points each of the form $< x, y >$, where x is a vector of values for the independent variables, and y is the classification of x (y takes discrete values from the set $\{c_1, c_2, ..., c_z\}$ indicating the class of x). The classification task is: Given a new input data x, classify the new data to be one of the possible classes. Let $N(x) = \{< x_1, y_1 >, ..., < x_k, y_k >\}$ be the the set of k nearest neighbors of x from the training data T. Let count(c_j) denote the number of points $< x_i, y_i >$ in $N(x)$ such that $y_i = c_j$ for each class lable c_j. The classification of x by K-nearest Neighbor method will be equal to c_j such that count$(c_j) = $ Max$\{$count$(c_1), ..., $count$(c_z)\}$.

In our application, we are not interested in using K-Nearest Neighbor method for classification of data points. Instead, we would like to use K-Nearest Neighbor method to obtain the membership values of a new data point in each of the fuzzy linear clusters, so that we can predict the fabric drape using the clusters linear equations weighted by the membership values. Thus we use a generalization of the simplest K-Nearest Neighbor method here. Recall that in fuzzy linear clustering, the training data set is of the form $\{< x_1, y_1 >, ..., < x_n, y_n >\}$. After the training step by fuzzy linear clustering, membership values of the training data points in fuzzy clusters are established. Let v_i be the (row) vector representing the membership values of training data point $< x_i, y_i >$ in the fuzzy clusters, namely, $v_i = (\mu_{1i}, \mu_{2i}, ..., \mu_{Ci})$ where μ_{li} is the membership value of $< x_i, y_i >$ in cluster l. Now, in the prediction step, given an input data x_0, we first need to compute μ_{j0} $(1 \leq j \leq C)$, the membership values of x_0 in the C fuzzy clusters. Let $N(x_0) = \{< x_{i1}, y_{i1} >, ..., < x_{ik}, y_{ik} >\}$ be the set of K-nearest neighbors of x_0. The membership values are computed from $v_{i1}, ..., v_{ik}$ by the formula

$$\mu_{j0} = \frac{\sum_{t=1}^{k} \mu_{j,it}}{k} \quad , 1 \leq j \leq C \tag{6.7}$$

The final predicted y_0 value is obtained by

$$y_0 = \sum_{j=1}^{C} g_j(x_0)\mu_{j0} \tag{6.8}$$

We have implemented the hybrid method combining K-nearest neighbor method with fuzzy linear clustering for fabric drape prediction. We find that the hybrid approach improves prediction accuracy further to about 92 percent. The Figure 6.7 and Figure 6.8 show the prediction accuracy versus training data size. In these two experiments, the total data set size is 183 (rather than 300). Again one can in some sense observe that a bigger training data size may not be always produce better performance, and overfitting must be avoided.

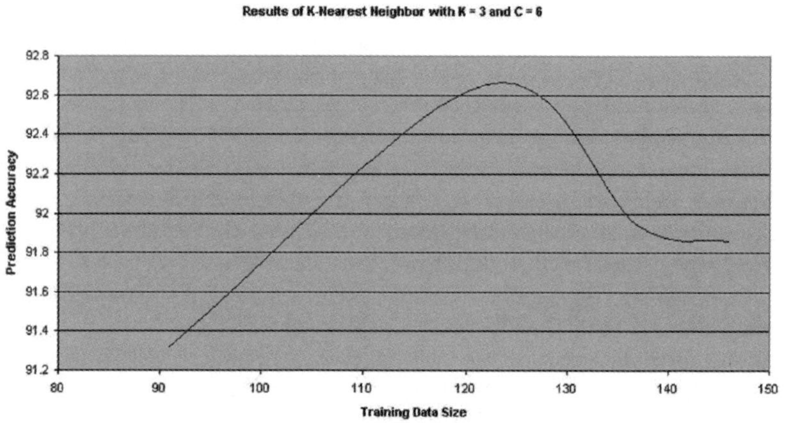

Fig. 6.7   Results using Hybrid Method with K Nearest Neighbors

6.5   Conclusions and Future Work

Information Technology is bringing tremendous opportunities to the textile and garment industry. Our online database and its intelligent search engine provides cloth designer, manufactures and retailers a useful and convenient tool to quickly find suitable fabric materials that best fit their need. The flexible queries supported by our system enhance the system's usability. Data mining methods such as fuzzy clustering are applied effectively to discover patterns relating fabric properties. The system can be seen as a first step toward a comprehensive online business exchange system for cloth designers, manufacturers, retailers and fabric manufacturers.

Fuzzy linear clustering appears to be quite effective for predicting fabric appearance from fabric physical properties. The experiments indicate a

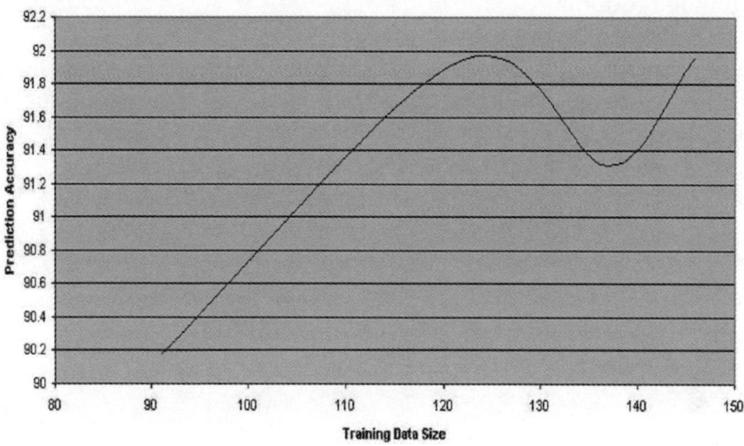

Fig. 6.8   Results using Hybrid Method with K Nearest Neighbors

promising application of fuzzy approach to discovery of patterns relating fabric properties. Moreover, the experiments show that we need to guard against overfitting in applying fuzzy linear clustering: trying to fit the training data with too many clusters or training with too many data points may cause a loss of generalization power. Our study also indicate that the hybrid method combining K-nearest neighbor method with fuzzy linear clustering produces superior prediction accuracy.

Besides further experiments and validations of the fuzzy linear clustering method, we see several ways to extend our works of applying fuzzy approach to the search engine on the fabric database. These include application of fuzzy linear clustering to discover new patterns among fabric properties, the use of fuzzy C-means algorithm for fabric classification and query answering, and development of hybrid approaches combining fuzzy methods with decision tree learning to predict fabric appearance and tailorability.

We are investigating hybrid methods that combine fuzzy clustering with decision tree learning for predicting fabric appearance and tailorability. The idea is to first apply fuzzy C-means algorithm for discretizing numerical valued fabric properties, and then construct a decision tree from the fabric property data. The decision tree can be used for prediction of fabric appearance or tailorability, which will be incorporated into the search engine.

Acknowledgement

We are grateful to Professor Sukhamay Kundu for helpful discussions on topics related to this work and for letting us to use his program for fuzzy linear clustering. This work is supported in part by the Louisiana Board of Regents grant LEQSF(2001-04)-RD-A-03.

Bibliography

Bezdek J.C. (1980) A convergence theorem for the fuzzy ISODATA clustering algorithms, *IEEE Transactions on Pattern Analysis and Machine Intelligence* (2), pp. 1-8.

Chen J., Chen Y., Zhang B., Gider A. (2002). Fuzzy linear clustering for fabric selection from online database, *Proceedings of NAFIPS-FLINT 2002*, New Orleans, LA, pp. 518–523.

Chen J., Kundu S. (1999). Fuzzy control system design by fuzzy clustering and self-organization, *Proceedings of NAFIPS'96 Conference*, Berkeley, CA.

Chen Y., Collier B.J., Collier J.R. (1999). Application of cluster analysis to fabric classification, *International Journal of Clothing Science and Technology*, **11** (4), pp. 206–215.

Chen Y., Hu P., Quebedeaux D., Collier B.J. (2000). Objective evaluation of fabric softness, *Textile Research Journal*, **70** (5), pp. 443–448.

Hathaway R.J., Bezdek J. (1993). Switching regression models and fuzzy clustering, *IEEE Transactions on Fuzzy Systems*, **1**, 3, pp. 195–204.

Kraft D., Chen J., Mikulcic A. (2000). Combining fuzzy clustering and fuzzy inferencing in information retrieval, *Proceedings of FUZZ'IEEE 2000*, San Antonio, TX.

Kundu S., Chen J. (1994). Fuzzy linear invariant clustering with applications in fuzzy control, *Proc. of NASA/NAFIPS*.

Mikulcic A., Chen J. (1996). Experiments on application of fuzzy clustering in fuzzy system design, *Proceedings of FUZZ'IEEE 1996*, New Orleans, LA.

Sabharwal J., Chen J. (1996). Intelligent pH control using fuzzy linear invariant clustering, *Proceedings of Southeastern IEEE Symposium on Systems Theory*, Baton Rouge, pp. 514–518.

Zadeh L.A. (1965). Fuzzy sets, *Information and Control* (8), pp. 338–353.

CHAPTER 7

WEB USAGE MINING: COMPARISON OFCONVENTIONAL, FUZZY, AND ROUGH SET CLUSTERING

Pawan Lingras, Rui Yan, and Adish Jain

Department of Mathematics and Computing Science,
Saint Mary's University,
Halifax, Nova Scotia, Canada, B3H 3C3
E-mail: Pawan.Lingras@stmarys.ca

Noise and incompleteness are two of the major issues with web related data. Fuzzy set and rough set theories provide complimentary methods for accommodating, noisy, incomplete, and approximate information. Non-conventional clustering techniques based on fuzzy set and rough set theories may be more suitable for web mining applications. This chapter compares the results of clustering obtained using the conventional K-means algorithm, a modified K-means algorithm based on rough set theory, and a fuzzy clustering algorithm. The modifications to the K-means algorithm are based on the properties of rough sets. The resulting clusters are represented as interval sets. The paper describes results of experiments used to create conventional, fuzzy, and interval set representations of clusters of web users on three educational websites. The experiments used secondary data consisting of access logs from the World Wide Web. This type of analysis is called web usage mining, which involves applications of data mining techniques to discover usage patterns from the web data. Analysis shows the advantages of fuzzy and interval set representation of clusters over crisp clusters.

133

7.1 Introduction

The World Wide Web (WWW) can provide an unprecedented insight into the behaviour of users. It is possible to track the movement of each customer in a web-based store, which is not possible in a conventional store. The resulting explosion of information has created new challenges for the computing science. Data from the World Wide Web can be broadly categorized as content, structure, and usage. Content data consist of the physical resources on the web, such as documents and programs. Structural data are related to the organization of a website, and links and relationships between various web resources. Content and structural data represent primary data on the web. Web usage data correspond to the secondary data generated by users' interaction with the web. Web usage data include data from web server access logs, proxy server logs, browser logs, user profiles, registration files, user sessions or transactions, user queries, bookmark folders, mouse clicks and scrolls, and any other data generated by the interaction between users and the web.

Based on the data sources, web mining can be divided into three classes: content mining, structure mining, and usage mining [Srivastava *et. al.* (2000)]. Web usage mining applies data mining techniques to discover usage patterns from web data, in order to understand and better serve the needs of web-based applications. Web usage mining includes creation of user profiles, user access patterns, and navigation paths. The results of web usage mining are used by e-commerce companies for tracking customer behavior on their sites. Web usage mining consists of three phases, namely preprocessing, pattern discovery, and pattern analysis.

Clustering analysis is an important function in web usage mining, which groups together users or data items with similar characteristics. The clustering process is an important step in establishing user profiles. User profiling on the web consists of studying important characteristics of web visitors. Due to the ease of movement from one portal to another, web users can be very mobile. If a particular website does not satisfy the needs of a user in a relatively short period of time, the user will quickly move on to another website. Therefore, it is very important to understand the needs and characteristics of web users. Clustering in web mining faces several additional challenges, compared to traditional applications [Joshi and Krishnapuram (1998)]. Clusters tend to have fuzzy or rough boundaries. The membership of an object in a cluster may not be precisely defined. There is likelihood that an object may be a candidate for more than one cluster. In addition, due to noise in the recording of data and incomplete logs, the possibility of the presence of outliers in the data set is high. Joshi and Krishnapuram [Joshi and Krishnapuram (1998)] argued that the clustering operation in web mining involves modelling an unknown number of overlapping sets. They proposed the use of fuzzy clustering [Hathaway and Bezdek (1993); Krishnapuram (1995); Krishnapuram and Keller (1993)] for grouping the web documents.

Lingras [Lingras (2001)] described how a rough set theoretic clustering scheme could be represented using a rough set genome. The resulting genetic algorithms (GAs) were used to evolve groupings of highway sections represented as interval or rough sets. Lingras [Lingras (2002)] applied the unsupervised rough set clustering based on GAs for grouping web users of a first year university course. He hypothesized that there are three types of visitors: studious, crammers, and workers. Studious visitors download notes from the site regularly. Crammers download most of the notes before an exam. Workers come to the site to finish assigned work such as lab and class assignments. Generally, the boundaries of these clusters will not be precise. The preliminary experimentation by Lingras [Lingras (2002)] illustrated the feasibility of rough set clustering for developing user profiles on the web. However, the clustering process based on GAs seemed computationally expensive for scaling to a larger data set. Lingras and West [Lingras and West (2002)] provided a theoretical and experimental analysis of a modified K-means clustering based on the properties of rough sets. It was used to classify the visitors of an academic website into upper and lower bounds of the three classes mentioned above. The modified K-means approach is suitable for large data sets. The Kohonen neural network or self-organizing map [Kohonen (1988)] is another popular clustering technique. The Kohonen network is desirable in some applications due to its adaptive capabilities. Lingras *et. al.* [Lingras *et. al.* (2002)] introduced the interval set clustering, using a modification of the Kohonen self-organizing maps, based on rough set theory. The proposed algorithm was used to find cluster intervals of web users. Three websites that were used for the experimentation catered to two first year and one second year courses. The students used the website for downloading class-notes and lab assignments; downloading, submitting and viewing class assignments; checking their current marks; as well as for accessing a discussion board. These websites were accessed from a variety of locations. Only some of the web accesses were identifiable by student ID. Therefore, instead of analyzing individual students, it was decided to analyze each visit. This also made it possible to guarantee the required protection of privacy. Lingras *et. al.* [Lingras *et. al.* (2002)] also provided a comparison of user behavior among first and second year students. The experiments showed that the modified Kohonen network provides reasonable interval sets of clusters by adjusting to the changing user behaviour. Lingras *et. al.* [Lingras *et. al.* (2003)] applied the concept of fuzzy C-means [Cannon *et. al.* (1986);

Cheng *et. al.* (1995)] to the three educational websites analyzed earlier by Lingras *et. al.* [Lingras *et. al.* (2002)]. The resulting fuzzy clusters also provide a reasonable representation of user behaviours for the three websites. This chapter compares the clusters obtained from the conventional clustering, the modified K-means and fuzzy clustering algorithms.

7.2   Literature Review

7.2.1   *Review of K-Means*

Let us assume that the objects are represented by m-dimensional vectors. The objective is to assign these n objects to k clusters. Each of the clusters is also represented by an m-dimensional vector, which is the centroid vector for that cluster. The process begins by randomly choosing k objects as the centroids of the k clusters. The objects are assigned to one of the k clusters based on the minimum value of distance $d(\mathbf{x}, \mathbf{v})$ between the object vector $\mathbf{v}$ and cluster vector $\mathbf{x}$. The distance $d(\mathbf{x}, \mathbf{v})$ can be the standard Euclidean distance. After the assignment of all the objects to various clusters, the new centroid vectors of the clusters are calculated as:

$$x_j = \frac{\sum_{object\ \mathbf{v}\ was\ assigned\ to\ cluster\ \mathbf{x}} v_j}{|\mathbf{x}|}, \tag{7.1}$$

where $1 \le j \le m$ Here $|\mathbf{x}|$ is the cardinality of cluster $\mathbf{x}$. The process stops when the centroids of clusters stabilize, i.e. the centroid vectors from previous iteration are identical to those generated in the current iteration.

7.2.2   *Modified K-Means based on Rough Set Theory*

Rough sets were proposed using equivalence relations. However, it is possible to define a pair of upper and lower bounds $(\underline{A}(X), \overline{A}(X))$ or a rough set for every set $X \subseteq U$ as long as the properties specified by Pawlak [Pawlak (1982)] are satisfied. The basic rough set properties are:

- (P1) An object $\mathbf{v}$ can be part of at most one lower bound
- (P2) $\mathbf{v} \in \underline{A}(\mathbf{x_i}) \Rightarrow \mathbf{v} \in \overline{A}(\mathbf{x_i})$
- (P3) An object $\mathbf{v}$ is not part of any lower bound $\Longleftrightarrow \mathbf{v}$ belongs to two or more upper bounds

It is important to note that, (P1)-(P3) are not necessarily independent or complete. Yao *et. al.* [Yao *et. al.* (1994)] described various generalizations of rough sets by relaxing the assumptions of an underlying equivalence relation. Skowron and Stepaniuk [Skowron and Stepaniuk (1999)] discussed a similar generalization of rough set theory. If one adopts a more restrictive view of rough set theory, the rough sets developed in this paper may have to be looked upon as interval sets.

Incorporating rough sets into K-means clustering requires the addition of the concept of lower and upper bounds. Calculations of the centroids of clusters need to be modified to include the effects of lower as well as upper bounds. The modified centroid calculations for rough sets are given by:

$$
x_j = \begin{cases} w_{lower} \times \frac{\sum_{v \in \underline{A}(\mathbf{x})} v_j}{|\underline{A}(\mathbf{x})|} + w_{upper} \times \frac{\sum_{v \in (\overline{A}(\mathbf{x}) - \underline{A}(\mathbf{x})} v_j}{|\overline{A}(\mathbf{x}) - \underline{A}(\mathbf{x})|} & \text{if } \overline{A}(\mathbf{x}) - \underline{A}(\mathbf{x}) \neq \phi; \\ w_{lower} \times \frac{\sum_{v \in \underline{A}(\mathbf{x})} v_j}{|\underline{A}(\mathbf{x})|} & \text{otherwise.} \end{cases}
$$

$$(7.2)$$

where $1 \leq j \leq m$. The parameters w_{lower} and w_{upper} correspond to the relative importance of lower and upper bounds. It can be shown that eq. 7.2 is a generalization of eq. 7.1. If the upper bound of each cluster were equal to its lower bound, the clusters will be conventional clusters. Therefore, the boundary region $\overline{A}(\mathbf{x}) - \underline{A}(\mathbf{x})$ will be empty, and the second term in the equation will be ignored. Thus, eq. 7.2 will reduce to the conventional K-means calculations given by eq. 7.1. Following rough mereology [Skowron and Stepaniuk (1999)], rough sets are used as patterns for classification. Relevant patterns are discovered by tuning the parameters in such a way that the lower approximation, boundary region, and complement of the upper approximation are relevant, i.e. they are sufficiently included in (or close to) target concepts.

The next step in the modification of the K-means algorithms for rough sets is to design criteria to determine whether an object belongs to the upper or lower bound of a cluster. For each object vector, $\mathbf{v}$, let $d(\mathbf{v}, \mathbf{x}_i)$ be the distance between itself and the centroid of cluster X_i. The differences $d(\mathbf{v}, \mathbf{x}_i) - d(\mathbf{v}, \mathbf{x}_j)$, $1 \leq i, j \leq k$, were used to determine the membership of $\mathbf{v}$ as follows. Let $d(\mathbf{v}, \mathbf{x}_i) = \min_{1 \leq j \leq k} d(\mathbf{v}, \mathbf{x}_j)$ and $T = \{j : d(\mathbf{v}, \mathbf{x}_i) - d(\mathbf{v}, \mathbf{x}_j) \leq threshold$ and $i \neq j\}$.

(1) If $T \neq \emptyset$, $\mathbf{v} \in \overline{A}(\mathbf{x}_i)$ and $\mathbf{v} \in \overline{A}(\mathbf{x}_j), \forall j \in T$. Furthermore, $\mathbf{v}$ is not part of any lower bound. The above criterion gurantees that property (P3) is satisfied.
(2) Otherwise, if $T = \emptyset$, $\mathbf{v} \in \underline{A}(\mathbf{x}_i)$. In addition, by property (P2), $\mathbf{v} \in \overline{A}(\mathbf{x}_i)$.

It should be emphasized that the approximation space A is not defined based on any predefined relation on the set of objects. The upper and lower bounds are constructed based on the criteria described above.

The rough K-means algorithm, described above, depends on three parameters, w_{lower}, w_{upper}, and *threshold*. Experimentation with various values of the parameters is necessary to develop a reasonable rough set clustering. Section 7.3 describes the design and results of such experiments.

7.2.3 *Fuzzy C-means Clustering*

Conventional clustering assigns various objects to precisely one cluster. A fuzzy generalization of the clustering uses a fuzzy membership function to describe the degree of membership (ranging from 0 to 1) of an object to a given cluster. There is a stipulation that the sum of fuzzy memberships of an object to all the clusters must be equal to 1.

Cannon *et. al.* [Cannon *et. al.* (1986)] described an efficient implementation of an unsupervised clustering mechanism that generates the fuzzy membership of the objects to various clusters.

The objective of the algorithm is to cluster n objects into c clusters. Given a set of unlabeled patterns : $X = \{x_1, x_2, ..., x_n\}$, $x_i \in R^s$, where n is the number of patterns, and s is the dimension of pattern vectors (attributes). Each cluster is represented by the cluster center vector $\mathbf{V}$. The FCM algorithm minimizes the weighted within group sum of the squared error objective function $J(\mathbf{U}, \mathbf{V})$:

$$J(\mathbf{U}, \mathbf{V}) = \sum_{k=1}^{n} \sum_{i=1}^{c} u_{ik}^m d_{ik}^2. \tag{7.3}$$

where:

- $\mathbf{U}$:the membership function matrix.
- u_{ik}: the elements of U. $u_{ik} \in [0, 1]$, $i = 1, ...n$, $k = 1, ...c$. $\sum_{k=1}^{c} u_{ik} = 1$, $0 < \sum_{i=1}^{n} u_{ik} < n$.
- $\mathbf{V}$:the cluster center vector, $\mathbf{V} = \{v_1, v_2, ..., v_c\}$
- n :the number of patterns.
- c :the number of clusters.
- d_{ik} :the distance between x_i and v_k.
- m :the exponent of u_{ik} that controls fuzziness or amount of cluster overlap. Gao *et. al.* [Gao *et. al.* (2000)] suggested the use of $m = 2$ in the experiments.

The Fuzzy C-means algorithm is as follows:

- Step 1: Given the cluster number c, randomly choose the initial cluster center $\mathbf{V}^0$. Set $m = 2$, s, the index of the calculations, as 0, and the threshold ϵ , as a small positive constant.

- Step 2: Based on **V**, the membership of each object U^s is calculated as:

$$u_{ik} = \frac{1}{\sum_{j=1}^{c} \left(\frac{d_{ik}}{d_{jk}}\right)^{\frac{2}{(m-1)}}}, i = 1, ...n, k = 1, ...c. \qquad (7.4)$$

$$d_{ik} = \mid x_k - v_i \mid > 0, \forall i, k. \qquad (7.5)$$

for $d_{ik} = 0$, $u_{ik} = 1$ and $u_{jk} = 0$ for $j \neq i$.

- Step 3: Increment s by one. Calculate the new cluster center vector $\mathbf{V}^s$ as:

$$v_i = \frac{\sum_{k=1}^{n} (u_{ik})^m x_k}{\sum_{k=1}^{n} (u_{ik})^m}, \forall i, i = 1, ..n. \qquad (7.6)$$

- Step 4: Compute the new membership U^s using the equation (4) and (5) in step 2.
- Step 5: If $\mid U^s - U^{(s-1)} \mid < \epsilon$, then stop, otherwise repeat step 3, 4, and 5.

7.3   Study Data and Design of the Experiment

7.3.1   *Data Description*

The study data was obtained from web access logs of three courses. These courses represent a sequence of required courses for the computing science programme at Saint Mary's University. The first and second courses were for first year students. The third course was for second year students. The first course is "Introduction to Computing Science and Programming" offered in the first term of the first year. The initial number of students in the course was 180. The number reduced over the course of the semester to 130 to 140 students. The students in the course come from a wide variety of backgrounds, such as computing science major hopefuls, students taking the course as a required science course, and students taking the course as a science or general elective. As is common in a first year course, students' attitudes towards the course also vary a great deal. The second course is "Intermediate Programming and Problem Solving" offered in the second term of the first year. The initial number of students in the course was around 100. The number reduced over the course of the semester to about 90 students during the semester. The students have similar backgrounds and motivations as in the first course. However, the student U^s population is less susceptible to attrition. It was hoped that these subtle changes between the two courses would be reflected in the fuzzy C-means and rough K-means clustering methods. These results were also compared with the third course, "Data Structures", offered in the second year. This course consisted of core computing science students. The number of students in this course was around 23 students. It was hoped that the profile of visits would reflect some of the distinctions between the students. Lingras [Lingras (2002)] and Lingras and West [Lingras and West (2002)] showed that visits from students attending the first course could fall into one of the following three categories:

- Studious: These visitors download the current set of notes. Since they download a limited/current set of notes, they probably study class-notes on a regular basis.
- Crammers: These visitors download a large set of notes. This indicates that they have stayed away from the class-notes for a long period of time. They are planning for pretest cramming.
- Workers: These visitors are mostly working on class or lab assignments or accessing the discussion board.

The fuzzy C-means algorithm was expected to provide the membership of each visitor to the three clusters mentioned above. The modified K-means provided the lower bound, upper bound and boundary of each visitor to the three clusters.

7.3.2 *Data Preparation*

Data quality is one of the fundamental issues in data mining. Poor data quality always leads to poor quality of results. Data preparation is an important step before applying data mining algorithms. The data preparation in this paper consisted of two phases: data cleaning and data transformation.

Data cleaning involved removing hits from various search engines and other robots. Some of the outliers with large number of hits and document downloads were also eliminated. This reduced the first data set by 5%. The second and third data sets were reduced by 3.5% and 10%, respectively. The details about the data can be found in table 7.1.

The data transformation required the identification of web visits [Lingras (2002)]. Certain areas of the website were protected, and the users could only access them using their IDs and passwords. The activities in the restricted parts of the website consisted of submitting a user profile, changing a password, submission of assignments, viewing the submissions, accessing the discussion board, and viewing current class marks. The rest of the website was public. The public portion consisted of viewing course information, a lab manual, class-notes, class assignments, and lab assignments. If users only accessed the public website, their IDs would be unknown. Therefore, web users were identified based on their IP address. This also made sure that the user privacy was protected. A visit from an IP address started when the first request was made from the IP address. The visit continued as long as the consecutive requests from the IP address had sufficiently small delay.

The web logs were preprocessed to create an appropriate representation of each user, corresponding to a visit. The abstract representation of a web user is a critical step that requires a good knowledge of the application domain. Previous personal experience with the students in the course suggested that some of the students print preliminary notes before a class and an updated copy after the class. Some students view the notes on-line on a regular basis. Some students print all the notes around important days such as midterm and final examinations. In addition, there are many accesses on Tuesdays and Thursdays, when in-laboratory assignments are due. On and off-campus points of access can also provide some indication of a user's objectives for the visit. Based on some of these observations, it was decided to use the following attributes for representing each visitor [Lingras (2002)]:

- On campus/Off campus access.
- Day time/Night time access: 8 a.m. to 8 p.m. were considered to be the daytime.
- Access during lab/class days or non-lab/class days: All the labs and classes were held on Tuesdays and Thursdays. The visitors on these days are more likely to be workers.
- Number of hits.
- Number of class-notes downloads.

The first three attributes had binary values of 0 or 1. The last two values were normalized. The distribution of the number of hits and the number of class-notes was analyzed for determining appropriate weight factors. Different weighting schemes were studied. The numbers of hits were set to be in the range of [0,10]. Since the class-notes were the focus of the clustering, the last variable was assigned higher importance, where the values fell in the range [0, 20].

Total visits were 23,754 for the first data set, 16,255 for the second data set, and 4,248 for the third data set. The visits where no class-notes were downloaded were eliminated, since these visits correspond to either casual visitors or workers. Elimination of outliers and visits from the search engines further reduced the sizes of the data sets. The fuzzy C-means clustering was applied to the remaining visits: 7,619 for the first data set, 6,030 for the second data set, and 1,274 for the third data set, as shown

Table 7.1   Descriptions of data sets

Data Set	Hits	Hits after cleaning	Visits	Visits after cleaning
First	361609	343000	23754	7619
Second	265365	256012	16255	6030
Third	40152	36005	4248	1274

in table 7.1. The threshold for stopping the clustering process was set at 10^{-11} and m was equal to 2. For rough K-means, $w_{lower} = 0.75$ and $w_{upper} = 0.25$.

7.4   Results and Discussion

Table 7.2 shows the cardinalities of conventional clusters, the modified K-means based on rough set theory, and the sets with fuzzy memberships greater than 0.6. The actual numbers in each cluster vary based on the characteristics of each course. For example, in the fuzzy C-means clustering results, the first term course had significantly more workers than studious visitors, while the second term course had more studious visitors than workers. The increase in the percentage of studious visitors in the second term seems to be a natural progression. It should be noted that the progression from workers to studious visitors was more obvious with fuzzy clusters than the conventional clusters and the rough K-means clusters. Interestingly, the second year course had significantly large number of workers than studious visitors. This seems to be counter-intuitive. However, it can be explained based on the structure of the websites. Unlike the two first year courses, the second year course did not post the class-notes on the web. The notes downloaded by these students were usually sample programs that were essential during their laboratory work.

Table 7.3 shows cluster center vectors from the conventional K-means. It was possible to classify the three clusters as studious, workers, and crammers, from the results obtained using the conventional K-means algorithm. The crammers had the highest number of hits and class-notes in every data set. The average number of notes downloaded by crammers varied from one set to another. The studious visitors downloaded the second highest number of notes. The distinction between workers and studious visitors for the second course was also based on other attributes. For example, in the second data set, the workers were more prone to come on lab days, access websites from on-campus locations during the daytime.

It is also interesting to note that the crammers had higher ratios of document requests to hits. The workers, on the other hand, had the lowest

Table 7.2 Cardinalities of the clusters for three techniques

Course	Cluster Name	FCM memberships >0.6	RKM Lower bound	Conventional Clusters
First	Studious	1382	1412	1814
	Crammers	414	288	406
	Workers	4354	5350	5399
Second	Studious	1750	1197	1699
	Crammers	397	443	634
	Workers	1322	1677	3697
Third	Studious	265	223	318
	Crammers	84	69	89
	Workers	717	906	867

Note: FCM: *Fuzzy C-Means*; RKM: *The modified K-Means based on rough set theory.*

Table 7.3 The conventional K-means cluster center vectors

Course	Cluster Name	Campus Access	Day/Night Time	Lab Day	Hits	Document Requests
First	Studious	0.67	0.76	0.44	2.97	2.78
	Crammers	0.62	0.72	0.32	4.06	8.57
	Workers	0.67	0.74	0.49	0.98	0.85
Second	Studious	0.00	0.68	0.28	0.67	0.55
	Crammers	0.66	0.72	0.36	2.43	2.92
	Workers	1.00	0.82	0.46	0.66	0.51
Third	Studious	0.69	0.75	0.50	3.87	3.15
	Crammers	0.60	0.71	0.44	5.30	10.20
	Workers	0.62	0.74	0.50	1.41	1.10

ratios of document requests to hits. Table 7.4 shows the modified K-means center vectors. The fuzzy center vectors are shown in table 7.5. These center vectors are comparable to the conventional centroid vectors. In order to compare fuzzy and conventional clustering, visits with fuzzy membership greater than 0.6 were grouped together. Similar characteristics can be found in these tables. For the second data set, the modified K-means is more sensitive to the differences between studious and crammers in the first three attributes than the other two techniques.

Table 7.6 shows average vectors for the fuzzy C-means with memberships > 0.6. As expected, tables 7.5 and 7.6 are similar. Table 7.7 and 7.8 shows the average cluster vectors for lower bound and upper bound from the modified K-means. The lower bounds seemed to provide more distinctive vectors than any other representations of clusters. Comparison of tables 7.4, 7.7, and 7.8 shows that the centroid vectors for the conventional vectors seemed to lie between the upper and the lower bounds of the

Table 7.4   The modified K-means cluster center vectors

Course	Cluster Name	Campus Access	Day/Night Time	Lab Day	Hits	Document Requests
First	Studious	0.67	0.75	0.43	3.16	3.17
	Crammers	0.61	0.72	0.33	4.28	9.45
	Workers	0.67	0.75	0.49	1.00	0.86
Second	Studious	0.14	0.69	0.03	0.64	0.55
	Crammers	0.64	0.72	0.34	2.58	3.29
	Workers	0.97	0.88	0.88	0.66	0.49
Third	Studious	0.70	0.74	0.48	4.09	3.91
	Crammers	0.55	0.72	0.43	5.48	10.99
	Workers	0.62	0.75	0.51	1.53	1.13

clusters.

Table 7.5   Fuzzy C-Means cluster center vectors

Course	Cluster Name	Campus Access	Day/Night Time	Lab Day	Hits	Document Requests
First	Studious	0.68	0.76	0.44	2.30	2.21
	Crammers	0.64	0.72	0.34	3.76	7.24
	Workers	0.69	0.77	0.51	0.91	0.75
Second	Studious	0.60	0.75	0.13	0.63	0.52
	Crammers	0.64	0.73	0.33	2.09	2.54
	Workers	0.83	0.87	0.75	0.62	0.47
Third	Studious	0.69	0.75	0.50	3.36	2.42
	Crammers	0.59	0.72	0.43	5.14	9.36
	Workers	0.62	0.77	0.52	1.28	1.06

Intersections between conventional clusters and the sets with fuzzy memberships greater than 0.6 provides another indication of the similarity between fuzzy C-means clustering and the modified clusters. Table 7.9 shows the ratios of cardinalities of intersections: $\frac{|G_c \cap G_k|}{|G_c \cup G_k|}$, where G_c is the set of objects with memberships greater than 0.6 for the corresponding fuzzy segment, and G_k is the modified K-means cluster. If both the groupings were identical, we will get identity matrices. The higher values along the diagonal confirm similarity between the two methods. Somewhat lower values for the first two data sets indicate that the clustering of the first year courses is fuzzier than the third data set (second year course). This observation seems reasonable. It is easier to characterize the behavior of senior students. The fuzzy representation seems more appropriate for first year students. Similar observations can also be made from table 7.10, which compares fuzzy C-means clusters with the conventional K-means clusters.

Table 7.6 Average vectors for fuzzy C-means with membership>0.6

Course	Cluster Name	Campus Access	Day/Night Time	Lab Day	Hits	Document Requests
First	Studious	0.70	0.78	0.45	2.37	2.41
	Crammers	0.65	0.72	0.33	3.74	7.92
	Workers	0.67	0.75	0.50	0.82	0.67
Second	Studious	0.52	0.89	0.00	0.49	0.40
	Crammers	0.65	0.75	0.34	2.18	0.96
	Workers	1.00	1.00	1.00	0.52	0.36
Third	Studious	0.69	0.75	0.51	3.69	2.28
	Crammers	0.58	0.70	0.43	5.38	10.39
	Workers	0.60	0.75	0.52	1.19	1.00

Table 7.7 Average vectors for the lower bounds of the modified K-means

Course	Cluster Name	Campus Access	Day/Night Time	Lab Day	Hits	Document Requests
First	Studious	0.67	0.75	0.43	3.23	3.23
	Crammers	0.60	0.72	0.33	4.29	9.60
	Workers	0.67	0.75	0.49	0.98	0.83
Second	Studious	0.00	0.69	0.00	0.61	0.54
	Crammers	0.63	0.72	0.33	2.64	3.44
	Workers	1.00	0.91	1.00	0.63	0.47
Third	Studious	0.70	0.74	0.48	4.13	4.00
	Crammers	0.55	0.73	0.44	5.49	11.09
	Workers	0.62	0.75	0.51	1.50	1.11

7.5 Summary and Conclusions

This research compares experimental results from the conventional K-means algorithm with a fuzzy C-means algorithm and a modified K-means algorithm. Web visitors for three academic courses were used in the experiments. Since some of the visitors may not precisely belong to one of the groups, the visitors were represented using fuzzy membership functions and rough sets. There were many similarities and a few differences between the characteristics of conventional, fuzzy clusters, and rough set clusters for the three websites. The fuzzy set representation of clusters and rough sets made it easier to identify these subtle differences between the three courses than the conventional K-means approach. The groups considered in this study are imprecise. Therefore, the use of fuzzy sets and rough sets seemed to provide good results.

Table 7.8   Average vectors for the upper bounds of the modified K-means

Course	Cluster Name	Campus Access	Day/Night Time	Lab Day	Hits	Document Requests
First	Studious	0.67	0.75	0.43	2.96	2.97
	Crammers	0.61	0.73	0.32	4.23	9.10
	Workers	0.67	0.75	0.48	1.08	0.93
Second	Studious	0.55	0.71	0.14	0.73	0.59
	Crammers	0.65	0.72	0.35	2.39	2.83
	Workers	0.88	0.80	0.52	0.73	0.56
Third	Studious	0.69	0.74	0.48	3.97	3.65
	Crammers	0.56	0.71	0.43	5.46	10.70
	Workers	0.62	0.75	0.51	1.63	1.18

Table 7.9   Ratios of cardinalities of intersections between FCMs and RKMs

Courses	Cluster Name	Studious (RKMs)	Crammers (RKMs)	Workers (RKMs)
First	Studious (FCM)	0.37	0.00	0.03
	Crammers (FCM)	0.06	0.60	0.00
	Workers (FCM)	0.00	0.00	0.81
Second	Studious (FCM)	0.40	0.00	0.00
	Crammers(FCM)	0.00	0.71	0.00
	Workers (FCM)	0.00	0.00	0.79
Third	Studious (FCM)	0.37	0.00	0.07
	Crammers (FCM)	0.00	0.82	0.03
	Workers (FCM)	0.00	0.00	0.79

Table 7.10   Ratios of cardinalities of intersections between FCMs and KMs

Courses	Cluster Name	Studious (RKMs)	Crammers (RKMs)	Workers (RKMs)
First	Studious (FCM)	0.56	0.00	0.04
	Crammers (FCM)	0.02	0.82	0.00
	Workers (FCM)	0.00	0.00	0.81
Second	Studious (FCM)	0.32	0.00	0.20
	Crammers(FCM)	0.00	0.63	0.00
	Workers (FCM)	0.00	0.00	0.36
Third	Studious (FCM)	0.83	0.00	0.00
	Crammers (FCM)	0.00	0.94	0.00
	Workers (FCM)	0.03	0.00	0.67

Bibliography

Cannon, R., Dave, J. and Bezdek, J. (1986). E.cient Implementation of the Fuzzy C-means Clustering Algorithms. *IEEE Trans.* PAMI, Vol. 8, pp: 248-255.

Cheng, T., Goldgof, B. D. and Hall, L.O. (1995). Fast Clustering with Application to Fuzzy Rule Generation. *In the proceedings of 1995 IEEE International Conference on Fuzzy Systems*, Vol. 4, pp: 2289-2295.

Gao, X., Li, J. and Xie, W. (2000). Parameter Optimization in FCM Clustering Algorithms. *In the Proceedings of 2000 IEEE 5th International Conference on Signal Processing,* Vol. 3, pp: 1457-1461.

Hathaway, R. and Bezdek, J. (1993) . Switching Regression Models and Fuzzy Clustering. *IEEE Transactions of Fuzzy Systems*, Vol. 1, No. 3, pp: 195-204.

Joshi, A. and Krishnapuram, R. (1998). Robust Fuzzy Clustering Methods to Support Web Mining. *In the Proceedings of the workshop on Data Mining and Knowledge Discovery*, SIGMOD '98, pp: 15/1-15/8.

Kohonen, T. (1988). Self-Organization and Associative Memory. *Springer Verlag,* Berlin.

Krishnapuram, R., Frigui, H. and Nasraoui, O. (1995). Fuzzy and Possibilistic Shell Clustering Algorithms and their Application to Boundary Detection and Surface Approximation, Parts I and II. *IEEE Transactions on Fuzzy Systems*, Vol. 3, No. 1, pp: 29-60.

Krishnapuram, R. and Keller, J. (1993). A Possibilistic Approach to Clustering. *IEEE Transactions*, Vol. 1, No. 2, pp: 98-110.

Lingras, P. (2001). Unsupervised Rough Set Classi.cation using GAs. *Journal of Intelligent Information Systems.* Vol. 16, No. 3, pp: 215-228.

Lingras, P. (2002). Rough Set Clustering for Web Mining. *Proceedings of 2002 IEEE International Conference on Fuzzy Systems.*

Lingras, P. and West, C. (2002). Interval Set Clustering of Web Users with Rough K-means. *To appear in the Journal of Intelligent Information Systems.*

Lingras, P., Hogo, M. and Snorek, M. (2002). Interval Set Clustering of Web Users using Modi.ed Kohonen Self-Organization Maps based on the Properties of Rough Sets. *Submitted to Web Intelligence and Agent Systems: an International Journal.*

Lingras, P., Yan, R. and West, C. (2003). Fuzzy C-means Clustering of Web Users for Educational Sites. *Proceedings of* 16th *Canadian Conference on Aritificial Intelligence*, AI' 2003, Halifax, Nova Scotia, Canada, pp: 557-562.

Pawlak, Z. (1982). Rough Sets. *International Journal of Information and Computer Sciences,* Vol. 11, pp: 145-172.

Skowron, A. and Stepaniuk, J. (1999). Information Granules in Distributed Environment. *in New Directions in Rough Sets, Data Mining, and Granular-Soft Computing,* Setsuo Ohsuga, Ning Zhong, Andrzej Skowron, Ed., Springer-Verlag, Lecture notes in Arti.cial Intelligence 1711, Tokyo, pp: 357-365.

Srivastava, J., Cooley. R., Deshpande. M. and Tan. P. (2000). Web Usage Mining. *Discovery and Applications of Usage Patterns from Web Data, in SIGKDD Explorations*, Vol. 1, Issue 2, pp: 1-12.

Yao, Y. Y., Li, X., Lin, T. Y. and Liu, Q. (1994). Representation and Classification of Rough Set Models. *in the proceedings of third International Workshop on Rough Sets and Soft Computing*, pp: 630-637.

CHAPTER 8

TOWARDS WEB SEARCH USING CONTEXTUAL PROBABILISTIC INDEPENDENCIES

Cory J. Butz and Manon J. Sanscartier

Department of Computer Science
University of Regina, Regina, SK, S4S 0A2, Canada
E-mail: {butz, sanscarm}@bbcr.uwaterloo.ca

Several researchers have suggested that Bayesian networks be used in web search (information retrieval). One advantage of this approach is that Bayesian networks are more general than the probabilistic models previously used in information retrieval. In practice, experimental results demonstrate the effectiveness of the modern Bayesian network approach. On the other hand, since Bayesian networks are defined solely upon the notion of probabilistic conditional independence, these encouraging results do not take advantage of the more general probabilistic independencies recently proposed in the Bayesian network community. In this chapter, we begin by demonstrating that probabilistic inference with *context specific independence* (CSI) can be more efficient than a traditional Bayesian network approach. The use of CSI involves the *union-product* operator for combining partial distributions. We then show that the union-product operator is not sufficient for factorizations based on *contextual weak independence* (CWI), which is a generalization of CSI. We subsequently introduce a new operator, called *weak-join*, for CWI factorizations and show that it is both associative and commutative. Finally, we explicitly demonstrate that probabilistic inference using CWIs can be more efficient than when CSIs are used.

8.1   Introduction

In practice, probabilistic inference would not be feasible without making independency assumptions. Directly specifying a joint probability distribution is not always possible as one would have to specify 2^n entries for a distribution over n binary variables. However, *Bayesian networks* [Pearl (1988); Wong and Butz (2001); Wong *et. al.* (2000)] have become a basis for designing probabilistic expert systems as the *conditional independence* (CI) assumptions encoded in a Bayesian network allow for a joint distribution to be indirectly specified as a product of *conditional probability distributions* (CPDs). More importantly, perhaps, this factorization can lead to computationally feasible inference in some applications. Thereby, Bayesian networks provide an elegant framework for the formal treatment of uncertainty.

One problem domain that involves reasoning under uncertainty is *information retrieval* [Baeza-Yates and Ribeiro-Neto (1999); Dominich (2001); Salton and McGill (1983); van Rijsbergen (1979)]. Several researchers have naturally suggested that Bayesian networks be applied in traditional information retrieval [Fung and Del Favero (1995); Ribeiro-Neto *et. al.* (2000); Turtle and Croft (1990); Wong and Yao (1995)], web search [Silva *et. al.* (2000)] and user profiling [Wong and Butz (2000)]. Although encouraging results have been reported, these works are based on the strict notion of probabilistic conditional independence. In the Bayesian network community, *context-specific independence* (CSI) [Boutilier *et. al.* (1996)] and *contextual weak independence* (CWI) [Wong and Butz (1999)] have been recently suggested as generalizations of probabilistic conditional independence. In [Butz (2002)], it was suggested that contextual independencies be exploited in web search.

In this chapter, we begin by demonstrating that probabilistic inference with CSI can be more efficient than a traditional Bayesian network approach [Zhang and Poole (1999)]. The use of CSI involves the *union-product* operator for combining partial distributions. We then examine the notion of CWI, which is a more general independency than CSI. It is explicitly demonstrated that the union-product operator is not sufficient for factorizations based on CWI. We subsequently introduce a new operator, called *weak-join*, for CWI factorizations. Our main result is that the weak-join operator is both associative and commutative. This is important as it allows the terms in a CWI factorization of a distribution to be written in any order. Finally, we explicitly demonstrate that probabilistic inference using CWIs can be more efficient than when CSIs are used [Butz and Sanscartier (2002)].

This chapter is organized as follows. Section 2 reviews Bayesian networks. In Section 3, the notion of CSI is presented. Important properties related to web search using CWI are given in Section 4. The conclusion is given in Section 5.

8.2 Bayesian Networks

It has already been shown how a single Bayesian network can be used to model information retrieval concepts [Ribeiro-Neto *et. al.* (2000)] and web search concepts [Silva *et. al.* (2000)]. Thus, we begin our discussion with a review of Bayesian networks.

Consider a finite set $U = \{A_1, A_2, \ldots, A_n\}$ of discrete random variables, where each variable $A \in U$ takes on values from a finite domain V_A. We may use capital letters, such as A, B, C, for variable names and lowercase letters a, b, c to denote specific values taken by those variables. Sets of variables will be denoted by capital letters such as X, Y, Z, and assignments of values to the variables in these sets (called configurations or tuples) will be denoted by lowercase letters x, y, z. We use V_X in the obvious way. We shall also use the short notation $p(a)$ for the probabilities $p(A = a)$, $a \in V_A$, and $p(z)$ for the set of variables $Z = \{A, B\} = AB$ meaning $p(Z = z) = p(A = a, B = b) = p(a, b)$, where $a \in V_A, b \in V_B$.

Let p be a *joint probability distribution* (jpd) [Pearl (1988)] over the variables in U and X, Y, Z be subsets of U. We say Y and Z are *conditionally independent* given X, if given any $x \in V_X$, $y \in V_Y$, then for all $z \in V_Z$,

$$p(y \mid x, z) = p(y \mid x), \quad \text{whenever } p(x, z) > 0. \tag{8.1}$$

We write Eq. (8.1) as $p(Y \mid X, Z) = p(Y \mid X)$ for convenience.

Based on the *conditional independence* (CI) assumptions encoded in the Bayesian network in Fig. 8.1, the jpd $p(A, B, C, D, E)$ can be factorized as

$$p(A, B, C, D, E) = p(A) \cdot p(B) \cdot p(C|A) \cdot p(D|A, B) \cdot p(E|A, C, D). \tag{8.2}$$

Using the CPDs $p(D|A, B)$ and $p(E|A, C, D)$ shown in Fig. 8.2, we conclude this section with an example of probabilistic inference.

The distribution $p(A, B, C, E)$ can be computed from Eq. (8.2) as

$$
\begin{aligned}
p(A, B, C, E) &= \sum_D p(A, B, C, D, E) \\
&= \sum_D p(A) \cdot p(B) \cdot p(C|A) \cdot p(D|A, B) \cdot p(E|A, C, D) \\
&= p(A) \cdot p(B) \cdot p(C|A) \cdot \sum_D p(D|A, B) \cdot p(E|A, C, D).
\end{aligned}
$$

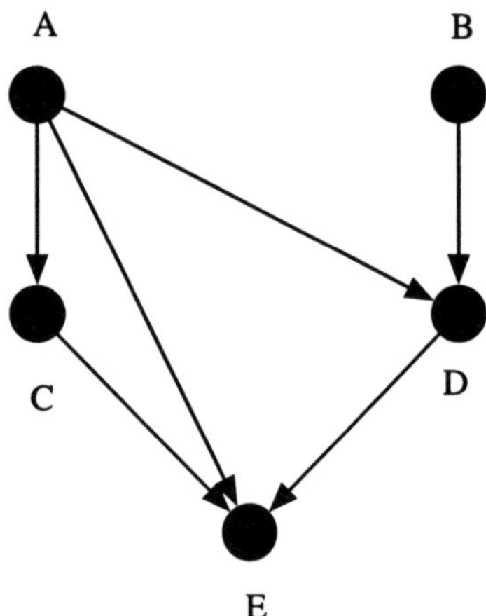

Fig. 8.1   A Bayesian network.

Computing the product $p(D|A, B) \cdot p(E|A, C, D)$ of the two distributions in Fig. 8.2 requires 32 multiplications. Marginalizing out variable D from this product requires 16 additions. The resulting distribution can be multiplied with $p(A) \cdot p(B) \cdot p(C|A)$ to obtain our desired distribution $p(A, B, C, E)$.

8.3   Context Specific Independence

The Bayesian network factorization of $p(A, B, C, D, E)$ in Eq. (8.2) only reflects conditional independencies $p(y|x, z) = p(y|x)$ which hold for *all* $x \in V_X$. In some situations, however, the conditional independence may only hold for certain *specific* values in V_X.

Consider again the CPD $p(D|A, B)$ in Fig. 8.2. Although variables D and B are *not* conditionally independent given A, it can be seen that D and B are independent in context $A = 0$, that is,

$$p(D = d|A = 0, B = b) \;=\; p(D = d|A = 0),$$

as shown in Fig. 8.3. Similarly, for the CPD $p(E|A, C, D)$ in Fig. 8.2, it can be seen that variables E and D are independent given C in context $A = 0$, while E and C are independent given D in context $A = 1$, i.e.,

$$p(E = e|A = 0, C = c, D = d) \;=\; p(E = e|A = 0, C = c)$$

A	B	D	$p(D|A,B)$
0	0	0	0.3
0	0	1	0.7
0	1	0	0.3
0	1	1	0.7
1	0	0	0.6
1	0	1	0.4
1	1	0	0.8
1	1	1	0.2

A	C	D	E	$p(E|A,C,D)$
0	0	0	0	0.1
0	0	0	1	0.9
0	0	1	0	0.1
0	0	1	1	0.9
0	1	0	0	0.8
0	1	0	1	0.2
0	1	1	0	0.8
0	1	1	1	0.2
1	0	0	0	0.6
1	0	0	1	0.4
1	0	1	0	0.3
1	0	1	1	0.7
1	1	0	0	0.6
1	1	0	1	0.4
1	1	1	0	0.3
1	1	1	1	0.7

Fig. 8.2   The conditional probability distributions $p(D|A,B)$ and $p(E|A,C,D)$ in Eq. (8.2).

and

$$p(E = e|A = 1, C = c, D = d) \ = \ p(E = e|A = 1, D = d),$$

as depicted in Fig. 8.4.

A	B	D	$p(D|A,B)$
0	0	0	0.3
0	0	1	0.7
0	1	0	0.3
0	1	1	0.7
1	0	0	0.6
1	0	1	0.4
1	1	0	0.8
1	1	1	0.2

$\rightarrow$

A	D	$p(D|A = 0)$
0	0	0.3
0	1	0.7

Fig. 8.3   Variables D and B are conditionally independent in context $A = 0$.

This kind of contextual independency was formalized as *context-specific*

A	C	E	$p(E\|A=0,C)$
0	0	0	0.1
0	0	1	0.9
0	1	0	0.8
0	1	1	0.2

$p(E|A,C,D)$

A	D	E	$p(E\|A=1,D)$
1	0	0	0.6
1	0	1	0.4
1	1	0	0.3
1	1	1	0.7

Fig. 8.4   Variables E and D are conditionally independent given C in context $A = 0$, while E and C are conditionally independent given D in context $A = 1$.

independence (CSI) by Boutilier et al. [Boutilier *et. al.* (1996)] as follows. Let X, Y, Z, C be pairwise disjoint subsets of U and $c \in V_C$. We say Y and Z are *conditionally independent* given X in *context* $C = c$, if

$$p(y \mid x, z, c) = p(y \mid x, c), \quad \text{whenever } p(x, z, c) > 0.$$

Recall the conditional probability distribution $p(E|A,C,D)$ in Fig. 8.2. The parents of node E in the Bayesian network in Fig. 8.1 are A, C, and D. As previously mentioned, variables E and D are independent given C in $p(E|A = 0, C, D)$, while E and C are independent given D in $p(E|A = 1, C, D)$. These contextual independencies can be represented by *two* Bayesian networks. One Bayesian network is constructed for $A = 0$ in which the parents of E are $\{A, C\}$. A second Bayesian network is constructed for $A = 1$ in which the parents of E are $\{A, D\}$. (See [Wong and Butz (1999)] for a more detailed discussion on modeling contextual independencies.) The other given CPDs can be examined for contextual independencies in a similar fashion using the detection algorithm in [Boutilier *et. al.* (1996)]. Before turning our attention from modeling to inference, we note that Zhang and Poole [Zhang and Poole (1999)] also pointed out that the notion of CSI can also be applied in the problem of constructing a Bayesian network [Wong and Butz (2001)].

In order to utilize the above three context-specific independencies for more efficient probabilistic inference, Zhang and Poole [Zhang and Poole (1999)] generalized the standard product operator $\cdot$ as the *union-product* operator $\odot$. The *union-product* $p(Y, X) \odot q(X, Z)$ of functions $p(Y, X)$ and $q(X, Z)$ is the function $p(y, x) \odot q(x, z)$ on YXZ defined as

$$
\begin{cases}
p(y, x) \cdot q(x, z) & \text{if both } p(y, x) \text{ and } q(x, z) \text{ are defined} \\
p(y, x) & \text{if } p(y, x) \text{ is defined and } q(x, z) \text{ is undefined} \\
q(x, z) & \text{if } p(y, x) \text{ is undefined and } q(x, z) \text{ is defined} \\
\text{undefined} & \text{if both } p(y, x) \text{ and } q(x, z) \text{ are undefined}
\end{cases}
$$

Note that $\odot$ is commutative and associative [Zhang and Poole (1999)].

The union-product operator allows for a single CPD to be horizontally partitioned into more than one CPD, which, in turn, exposes the contextual independencies. Returning to the factorization in Eq. (8.2), the CPD $p(D|A, B)$ can be rewritten as

$$
\begin{aligned}
p(D|A, B) &= p(D|A = 0, B) \odot p(D|A = 1, B) \\
&= p(D|A = 0) \odot p(D|A = 1, B),
\end{aligned} \tag{8.3}
$$

while $p(E|A, C, D)$ is equivalently stated as

$$
\begin{aligned}
p(E|A, C, D) &= p(E|A = 0, C, D) \odot p(E|A = 1, C, D) \\
&= p(E|A = 0, C) \odot p(E|A = 1, D).
\end{aligned} \tag{8.4}
$$

By substituting Eq.s (8.3) and (8.4) into Eq. (8.2), the factorization of the jpd $p(A, B, C, D, E)$ using CSI is

$$
\begin{aligned}
p(A, B, C, D, E) = {} & p(A) \cdot p(B) \cdot p(C|A) \odot p(D|A = 0) \odot p(D|A = 1, B) \\
& \odot\ p(E|A = 0, C) \odot p(E|A = 1, D).
\end{aligned} \tag{8.5}
$$

The use of CSI leads to more efficient probabilistic inference. Computing $p(A, B, C, E)$ from Eq. (8.5) involves

$$
\begin{aligned}
p(A, B, C, E) = {} & \sum_D p(A) \cdot p(B) \cdot p(C|A) \odot p(D|A = 0) \odot p(D|A = 1, B) \\
& \odot p(E|A = 0, C) \odot p(E|A = 1, D) \\
= {} & p(A) \cdot p(B) \cdot p(C|A) \odot p(E|A = 0, C) \\
& \odot \sum_D p(D|A = 0) \odot p(D|A = 1, B) \odot p(E|A = 1, D).
\end{aligned}
$$

Computing the union-product $p(D|A = 0) \odot p(D|A = 1, B) \odot p(E|A = 1, D)$ requires 8 multiplications. Next, 8 additions are required to marginalize out variable D. Eight more multiplications are required to compute the union-product of the resulting distribution with $p(E|A = 0, C)$. The resulting distribution can be multiplied with $p(A) \cdot p(B) \cdot p(C|A)$ to give $p(A, B, C, E)$.

The important point in this section is that computing $p(A, B, C, E)$ from the CSI factorization in Eq. (8.6) required 16 fewer multiplications and 8 fewer additions compared to the respective number of computations needed to compute $p(A, B, C, E)$ from the CI factorization in Eq. (8.3).

8.4   Contextual Weak Independence

CSI is a special case of a more general independence called *contextual weak independence* (CWI) [Wong and Butz (1999)]. Contextual weak independence is the most general contextual independence currently known in the Bayesian network community.

Let R be a finite set of variables, X, Y, Z, C, be pairwise disjoint subsets of R, and let $c \in V_C$. We say Y and Z are *weakly independent* [Wong and Butz (1999)] given X in context $C = c$, if both of the following two conditions are satisfied: (i) there exists a maximal disjoint compatibility class $\pi = \{t_i, \dots, t_j\}$ in the relation $\theta(X, Y, C = c) \circ \theta(X, Z, C = c)$, and (ii) given any $x \in V_X^\pi$, $y \in V_Y^\pi$, then for all $z \in V_Z^\pi$,

$$p(y \mid x, z, c) = p(y \mid x, c), \text{ whenever } p(x, z, c) > 0,$$

where $\theta(W)$ denotes the equivalence relation induced by the set W of variables, $\circ$ denotes the composition operator, and V_W^π denotes the set of values for W appearing in π.

Consider another JPD $p'(A, B, C, D, E)$, which also satisfies the conditional independencies in the Bayesian network in Fig. 8.1:

$$p'(A, B, C, D, E) \;=\; p'(A) \cdot p'(B) \cdot p'(C|A) \cdot p'(D|A, B) \cdot p'(E|A, C, D) \quad (8.6)$$

The CPD $p'(D|A, B)$ is shown in Fig. 8.5 (i).

In the CPD $p'(D|A, B)$, there are *no* context-specific independencies holding in the context $A = 0$ or $A = 1$. In other words, $p'(D|A = 0, B)$ and $p'(D|A = 1, B)$ cannot be further decomposed. Let us partition the CPD $p'(D|A, B)$ in Fig. 8.5 (i) into the four blocks shown in Fig. 8.5 (ii). In the two blocks where $A = 0$, variables D and B are conditionally independent given A. Hence, using a CWI approach, variable B can be dropped as shown in Fig. 8.5 (iii). For simplicity, $p'_{B \in \{0,1\}}(D|A = 0)$, and $p'_{B \in \{2,3\}}(D|A = 0)$, are written as $p'_1(D|A = 0)$, and $p'_2(D|A = 0)$, respectively. Also, for clarity and consistency in the table, $p'(D|A = 1, B)$ has been divided into the two blocks $p'_1(D|A = 1, B)$, and $p'_2(D|A = 1, B)$. In practice, the three partial functions $p'_1(D|A = 0)$, $p'_2(D|A = 0)$, $p'(D|A = 1, B)$, will be stored in place of the single CPD $p'(D|A, B)$.

Unfortunately, the union-product operator $\odot$ for combining partial functions is not sufficient for CWI.

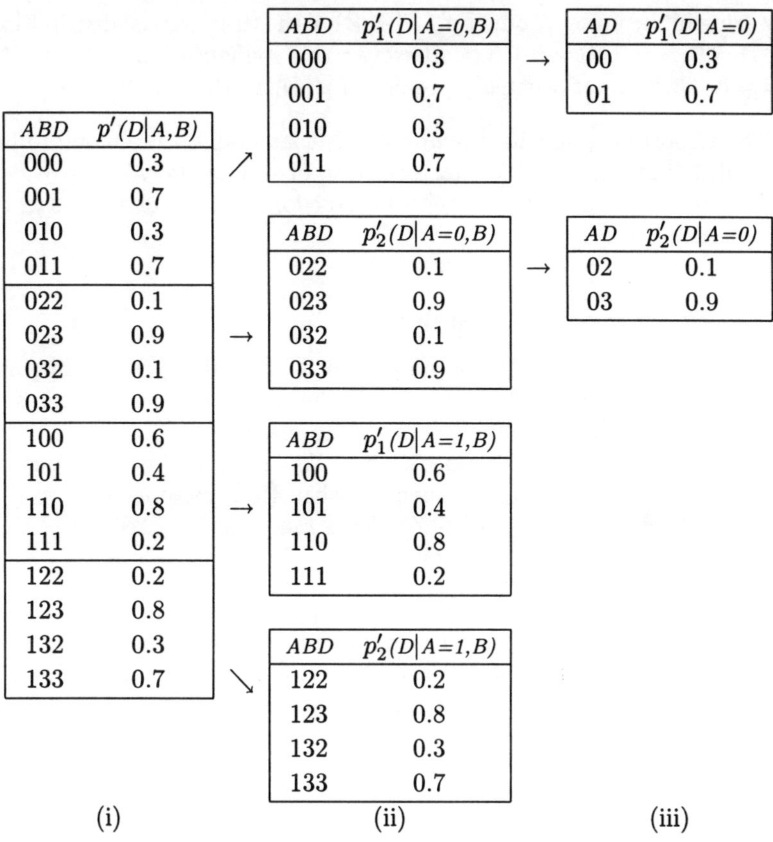

Fig. 8.5   Variables D and B are *weakly* independent in context $A = 0$.

Example 8.1   Recall $p'(D|A, B)$ will be stored as the three partial distributions $p'_1(D|A = 0)$, $p'_2(D|A = 0)$, and $p'(D|A = 1, B)$. Consider the union-product of these three distributions

$$p''(D|A, B) \;=\; p'_1(D|A = 0) \odot p'_2(D|A = 0) \odot p'(D|A = 1, B).$$

One partial row in $p''(D|A, B)$ is $< A = 0, B = 2, D = 0 >$. For this row, $p'_1(D|A = 0)$ is *defined* with probability value 0.3. However, $p'_2(D|A = 0)$ is *undefined* (as $D = 0$ in the partial row while it is either 2 or 3 in $p'_2(D|A = 0)$). By case (ii) in the $\odot$ definition, the partial row is completed as $< A = 0, B = 2, D = 0, 0.3 >$. In the next union-product with $p'(D|A = 1, B)$, $p'(D|A = 1, B)$ is *undefined* (as $A = 0$ in $< A = 0, B = 2, D = 0, 0.3 >$ while $A = 1$ in $p'(D|A = 1, B)$). Again, by case (ii), the final configuration appearing in the union-product $p''(D|A, B)$ of the three partial distributions is $< A = 0, B = 2, D = 0, 0.3 >$. However, this configuration $< A = 0, B = 2, D = 0, 0.3 >$ is *not* originally present in $p'(D|A, B)$.

The important point in Example 8.1 is that taking the union-product of the distributions in a CWI factorization of $p(X|Y)$ may not give back $p(X|Y)$. Thus, we introduce a new operator for CWI factorizations in the next section.

8.4.1 *The Weak-Join Operator*

In order to manipulate CWI decompositions, the union-product operator $\odot$ needs to be generalized. We propose the *weak-join* operator $\oplus$ as an extension to $\odot$. Some terminology is first required.

Let variable $A \in X$ be dropped in $p(Y, X)$. The function $p(y, x)$ is said to be *inconsistent*, if $p(y, x)$ is undefined when V_A is considered.

The *weak-join* $p(Y, X) \oplus q(X, Z)$ of the functions $p(Y, X)$ and $q(X, Z)$ is the function on YXZ defined as

$$\begin{cases} p(y, x) \cdot q(x, z) & \text{if both } p(y, x) \text{ and } q(x, z) \text{ are defined} \\ p(y, x) & \text{if } p(y, x) \text{ is defined and } q(x, z) \text{ is undefined} \\ q(x, z) & \text{if } p(y, x) \text{ is undefined and } q(x, z) \text{ is defined} \\ \text{undefined} & \text{if both } p(y, x) \text{ and } q(x, z) \text{ are undefined} \\ 0.0 & \text{if } p(y, x) \text{ or } q(x, z) \text{ is inconsistent.} \end{cases}$$

The next example illustrates the weak-join operator.

Example 8.2   Recall the situation where $p'(D|A, B)$ is stored as the three partial distributions $p'_1(D|A = 0)$, $p'_2(D|A = 0)$, and $p'(D|A = 1, B)$. Consider the weak-join of these three distributions

$$p''(D|A, B) \;=\; p'_1(D|A = 0) \oplus p'_2(D|A = 0) \oplus p'(D|A = 1, B).$$

One partial row in $p''(D|A, B)$ is $< A = 0, B = 2, D = 0 >$. Since the dropped variable B has values 0 or 1 in $p'_1(D|A = 0)$, by definition, $p'_1(D|A = 0)$ is *inconsistent*. Thus, by case (v) in the $\oplus$ definition, the partial row is completed as $< A = 0, B = 2, D = 0, \ 0.0 >$. For the weak-join with $p'(D|A = 1, B)$, the latter is *undefined*. By case (ii) of $\oplus$, the final configuration in the weak-join is $< A = 0, B = 2, D = 0, \ 0.0 >$. This agrees with the original distribution $p'(D|A, B)$.

Example 8.2 demonstrates that the weak-join operator $\oplus$ assigns the correct probability value to the configuration $< A = 0, B = 2, D = 0 >$, unlike the union-product operator in Example 8.1. The reader can verify that the weak-join

$$p'_1(D|A = 0) \oplus p'_2(D|A = 0) \oplus p'(D|A = 1, B), \qquad (8.7)$$

produces the distribution in Fig. 8.5 (i).

The important point to remember is that the union-product $\odot$ was generalized as the weak-join operator $\oplus$ in order to correctly reason with CWI decompositions.

Unlike the definition of CSI [Boutilier *et. al.* (1996)], the definitions of CWI [Wong and Butz (1999)] and the weak-join operator $\oplus$ do *not* require a CPD to be horizontally partitioned as a dichotomy (see Fig. 8.3). On the contrary, by the definition of $\oplus$, the CPD $p'(D|A, B)$ in Eq. (8.6) can be written as

$$p'(D|A, B)$$
$$= p'_1(D|A = 0, B) \oplus p'_2(D|A = 0, B) \oplus p'_1(D|A = 1, B) \oplus p'_2(D|A = 1, B),$$

as illustrated in Fig. 8.5 (i,ii). Variables D and B are conditionally independent in context $A = 0$ in both $p'_1(D|A = 0, B)$ and $p'_2(D|A = 0, B)$, as depicted in Fig. 8.5 (iii). Thus, the previous equation can be refined as

$$p'(D|A, B)$$
$$= p'_1(D|A = 0) \oplus p'_2(D|A = 0) \oplus p'_1(D|A = 1, B) \oplus p'_2(D|A = 1, B) \qquad (8.8)$$

Before discussing efficient inference using CWI factorizations in the next section, we conclude this section by showing the weak-join operator is associative and commutative.

Lemma 8.1   The weak-join operator $\oplus$ is associative and commutative.
Proof: Consider the weak-join $p(y, x) \oplus q(x, z)$. In case (i) of the definition of $\oplus$, we have

$$p(y, x) \cdot q(x, z).$$

Since the multiplication operator $\cdot$ is commutative [Pearl (1988)], we obtain

$$p(y, x) \cdot q(x, z) = q(x, z) \cdot p(y, x).$$

Hence,

$$p(y, x) \oplus q(x, z) = q(x, z) \oplus p(y, x). \qquad (8.9)$$

Now, consider the weak-join

$$(p(y, x) \oplus q(x, z)) \oplus r(z, w).$$

In case (i) of the $\oplus$ definition, we have

$$(p(y, x) \cdot q(x, z)) \cdot r(z, w).$$

Again, since the multiplication operator $\cdot$ is associative [Pearl (1988)],

$$p(y, x) \cdot (q(x, z) \cdot r(z, w)).$$

Thus,

$$(p(y, x) \oplus q(x, z)) \oplus r(z, w) = p(y, x) \oplus (q(x, z) \oplus r(z, w)). \qquad (8.10)$$

By Eqs. (8.9) and (8.10), the weak-join operator $\oplus$ is commutative and associative in case (i).

In case (ii) of the $\oplus$ definition, we have $p(y, x)$. Since the function $q(x, z)$ is undefined, it may be viewed as the constant 1. By case (i), we obtained our desired result. Case (iii) can be obtained in a similar fashion to (ii).

In case (iv), since both $p(y, x)$ and $q(x, z)$ are undefined, they can both be viewed as the constant 1. The claim holds by case (i).

The last case to consider is (v). Here $p(y, x) \oplus q(x, z)$ is assigned the value 0.0. Hence, case (v) is trivially commutative and associative.

Lemma 8.1 is important as it allows the terms in a CWI factorization of a distribution to be written in any order.

8.4.2 *The CWI Inference Process*

Recall the joint distribution $p'(A, B, C, D, E)$ in Section 4. As previously mentioned, the conditional probability distribution $p'(D|A, B)$ is shown in Fig. 8.5. The CPD $p'(E|A, C, D)$ is depicted in Fig. 8.6.

In the CPD $p'(E|A, C, D)$, there are *no* context-specific independencies holding in context $A = 0$ or $A = 1$. The partial functions $p'(E|A = 0, C, D)$ and $p'(E|A = 1, C, D)$ cannot be further decomposed. Let us now partition the CPD $p'(E|A, C, D)$ in Fig. 8.6 (i) into the four blocks shown in Fig. 8.6 (ii). For this CPD, independencies are found in all four blocks. In the two blocks where $A = 0$, variables E and D are weakly independent given C. Hence, using a CWI approach, variable D can be dropped in those two blocks as shown in Fig. 8.6 (iii). Similarly, in the two blocks where $A = 1$, variables E and C are independent given D, so variable C can be dropped in those two blocks as shown in Fig. 8.6 (iii). For simplicity, $p'_{D \in \{0,1\}}(E|A = 0, C)$, $p'_{D \in \{2,3\}}(E|A = 0, C)$, $p'_{C \in \{0,1\}}(E|A = 1, D)$, and $p'_{C \in \{2,3\}}(E|A = 1, D)$, are written as $p'_1(E|A = 0, C)$, $p'_2(E|A = 0, C)$, $p'_1(E|A = 1, D)$, $p'_2(E|A = 1, D)$, respectively. In practice, the four partial functions $p'_1(E|A = 0, C)$, $p'_2(E|A = 0, C)$, $p'_1(E|A = 1, D)$,

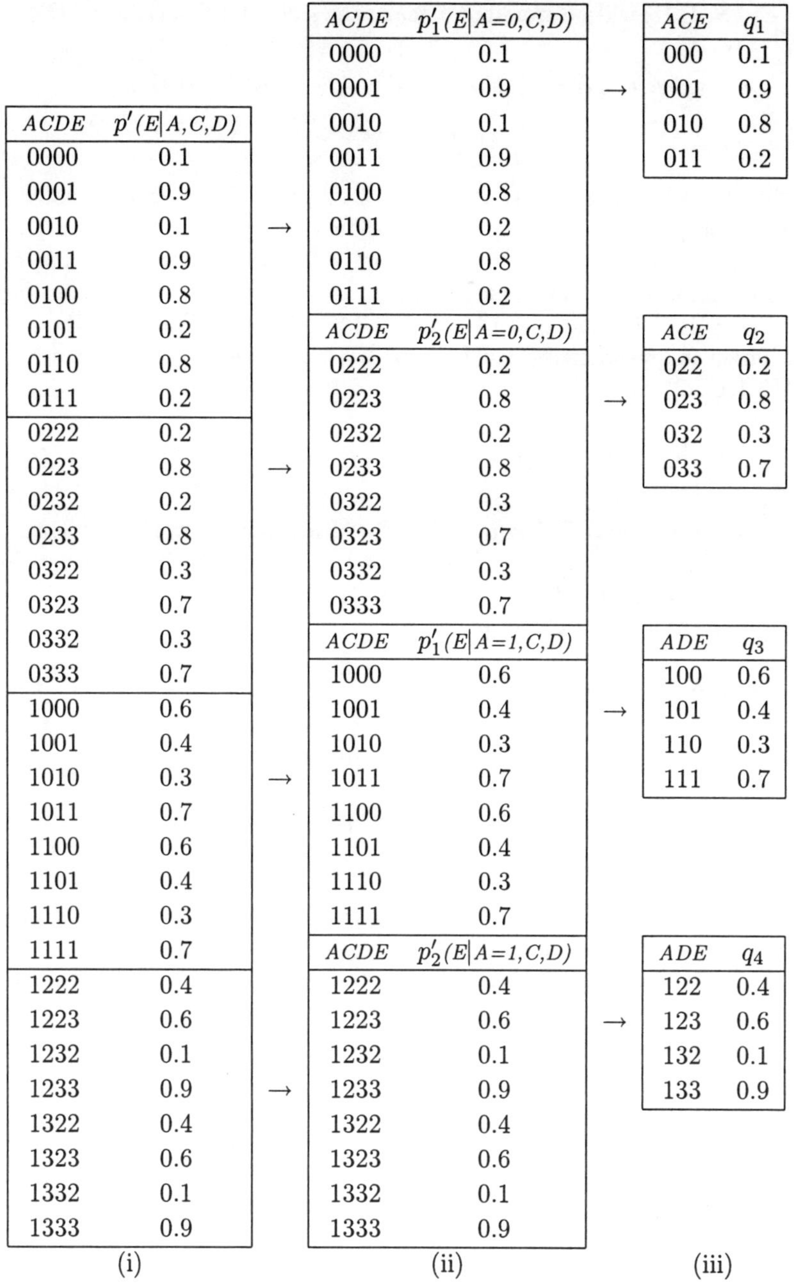

(i)

ACDE	$p'(E|A,C,D)$
0000	0.1
0001	0.9
0010	0.1
0011	0.9
0100	0.8
0101	0.2
0110	0.8
0111	0.2
0222	0.2
0223	0.8
0232	0.2
0233	0.8
0322	0.3
0323	0.7
0332	0.3
0333	0.7
1000	0.6
1001	0.4
1010	0.3
1011	0.7
1100	0.6
1101	0.4
1110	0.3
1111	0.7
1222	0.4
1223	0.6
1232	0.1
1233	0.9
1322	0.4
1323	0.6
1332	0.1
1333	0.9

(ii)

ACDE	$p'_1(E|A{=}0,C,D)$
0000	0.1
0001	0.9
0010	0.1
0011	0.9
0100	0.8
0101	0.2
0110	0.8
0111	0.2

ACDE	$p'_2(E|A{=}0,C,D)$
0222	0.2
0223	0.8
0232	0.2
0233	0.8
0322	0.3
0323	0.7
0332	0.3
0333	0.7

ACDE	$p'_1(E|A{=}1,C,D)$
1000	0.6
1001	0.4
1010	0.3
1011	0.7
1100	0.6
1101	0.4
1110	0.3
1111	0.7

ACDE	$p'_2(E|A{=}1,C,D)$
1222	0.4
1223	0.6
1232	0.1
1233	0.9
1322	0.4
1323	0.6
1332	0.1
1333	0.9

(iii)

ACE	q_1
000	0.1
001	0.9
010	0.8
011	0.2

ACE	q_2
022	0.2
023	0.8
032	0.3
033	0.7

ADE	q_3
100	0.6
101	0.4
110	0.3
111	0.7

ADE	q_4
122	0.4
123	0.6
132	0.1
133	0.9

Fig. 8.6   Variables E and D are *weakly* independent given C in context $A = 0$, while E and C are *weakly* independent given D in context $A = 1$. Here q_1, q_2, q_3 and q_4 are labels for $p'_1(E|A = 0, C)$, $p'_2(E|A = 0, C)$, $p'_1(E|A = 1, D)$, and $p'_2(E|A = 1, D)$.

$p'_2(E|A = 1, D)$ will be stored in place of the single CPD $p'(E|A, C, D)$, i.e.,

$$p'(E|A, C, D) = p'_1(E|A = 0, C, D) \oplus p'_2(E|A = 0, C, D)$$
$$\oplus\, p'_1(E|A = 1, C, D) \oplus p'_2(E|A = 1, C, D), \quad (8.11)$$

as illustrated in Fig. 8.6 (i,ii). Variables E and D are conditionally independent given C in context $A = 0$ in both $p'_1(E|A = 0, C, D)$ and $p'_2(E|A = 0, C, D)$, as depicted in Fig. 8.6 (iii). Furthermore, E and C are conditionally independent given D in context $A = 1$ in both $p'_1(E|A = 1, C, D)$ and $p'_2(E|A = 1, C, D)$, as shown in Fig. 8.6 (iii).

These independencies can be used to refine the CWI factorization of $p'(E|A, C, D)$ as

$$p'_1(E|A = 0, C) \oplus p'_2(E|A = 0, C) \oplus p'_1(E|A = 1, D) \oplus p'_2(E|A = 1, D).$$

The notion of CWI can *refine* the Bayesian network factorization of $p'(A, B, C, D, E)$ in Eq. (8.6). By substituting the factorizations of $p'(D|A, B)$ and $p'(E|A, C, D)$ into Eq. (8.6), the factorization of $p'(A, B, C, D, E)$ in a CWI approach is

$$p'(A, B, C, D, E)$$
$$= p'(A) \cdot p'(B) \cdot p'(C|A) \oplus$$
$$p'_1(D|A = 0) \oplus p'_2(D|A = 0) \oplus p'_1(D|A = 1, B) \oplus\ p'_2(D|A = 1, B) \oplus$$
$$p'_1(E|A = 0, C) \oplus p'_2(E|A = 0, C) \oplus p'_1(E|A = 1, D) \oplus p'_2(E|A = 1, D).$$

Since we are interested in comparing the results obtained from CSI inference and CWI inference, we consider computing $p'(A, B, C, E)$ in a CSI approach followed by a CWI approach.

In a CSI approach, no refinement of the BN factorization in Eq. (8.6) is possible. Thereby, computing $p'(A, B, C, E)$ from Eq. (8.6) in a CSI approach involves

$$p'(ABCE) = \sum_D p'(A) \cdot p'(B) \cdot p'(C|A) \cdot p'(D|A, B) \cdot p'(E|A, C, D)$$
$$= p'(A) \cdot p'(B) \cdot p'(C|A) \cdot \sum_D p'(D|A, B) \cdot p'(E|A, C, D). \quad (8.12)$$

Computing $\sum_D p'(D|A, B) \cdot p'(E|A, C, D)$ requires 64 multiplications and 32 additions.

On the contrary, computing $p'(A, B, C, E)$ in a CWI approach involves

$$
\begin{aligned}
p'(A, B, C, E) \\
= \quad & \sum_D p'(A) \cdot p'(B) \cdot p'(C|A) \oplus p'_1(D|A = 0) \oplus p'_2(D|A = 0) \\
& \oplus p'_1(D|A = 1, B) \oplus p'_2(D|A = 1, B) \oplus p'_1(E|A = 0, C) \\
& \oplus p'_2(E|A = 0, C) \oplus p'_1(E|A = 1, D) \oplus p'_2(E|A = 1, D) \\
= \quad & p'(A) \cdot p'(B) \cdot p'(C|A) \oplus p'_1(E|A = 0, C) \oplus p'_2(E|A = 0, C) \\
& \oplus \sum_D p'_1(D|A = 0) \oplus p'_2(D|A = 0) \oplus p'_1(D|A = 1, B) \\
& \oplus p'_2(D|A = 1, B) \oplus p'_1(E|A = 1, D) \oplus p'_2(E|A = 1, D).
\end{aligned}
\tag{8.13}
$$

32 multiplications and 16 additions are required to compute the distribution to be multiplied with $p'(A) \cdot p'(B) \cdot p'(C|A)$, as opposed to the needed 64 multiplications and 32 additions in the CSI factorization in Eq. (8.12).

Observe that computing $p'(A, B, C, E)$ from the CWI factorization in Eq. (8.13) required 32 fewer multiplications and 16 fewer additions compared to the respective number of computations needed to compute $p'(A, B, C, E)$ in the CSI factorization in Eq. (8.12). Methods for acquiring CWIs from an expert or data are given in [Butz and Sanscartier (2002)].

8.5   Conclusions

Although several researchers have reported encouraging results on applying Bayesian networks to web search (information retrieval), these results do not utilize the more general forms of conditional independence recently proposed. *Context specific independence* (CSI) [Boutilier *et. al.* (1996)] was first introduced in the Bayesian network community and shown to be useful in probabilistic inference [Zhang and Poole (1999)]. The use of CSI involves the *union-product* operator for combining partial distributions.

In this chapter, we explicitly demonstrated that the union-product operator is not sufficient for factorizations based on *contextual weak independence* (CWI) [Wong and Butz (1999)], which is a generalization of CSI. We subsequently introduced a new operator, called *weak-join*, for CWI factorizations. Our main result (Lemma 8.1) is that our weak-join operator is both associative and commutative. This is important as it allows the terms in a CWI factorization of a distribution to be written in any order. Finally, we demonstrated that probabilistic inference using CWIs can be more efficient than when CSIs are used [Butz and Sanscartier (2002)].

Bibliography

Baeza-Yates, R. and Ribeiro-Neto, B. (1999). *Modern Information Retrieval*, Addison Wesley, New York.

Boutilier, C., Friedman, N., Goldszmidt, M. and Koller, D. (1996). "Contextspecific independence in Bayesian networks," Twelfth Conference on Uncertainty in Artificial Intelligence, 115-123.

Butz, C.J. (2002). "Exploiting Contextual Independencies in Web Search and User Profiling", World Congress on Computational Intelligence, 1051-1056.

Butz, C.J. and Sanscartier, M.J. (2002). "On the Role of Contextual Weak Independence in Probabilistic Inference", Fifteenth Canadian Conference on Artificial Intelligence, 185-194.

Butz, C.J. and Sanscartier, M.J. (2002). "Acquisition Methods for Contextual Weak Independence", 3rd International Conference on Rough Sets and Current Trends in Computing, 339-343.

Chickering, D.M., Heckerman, D. and Meek, C. (1997). "A Bayesian approach to learning Bayesian networks with local structure," Thirteenth Conference on Uncertainty in Artificial Intelligence, 80-89.

Dominich, S. (2001). *Mathematical Foundations of Information Retrieval*, Kluwer Academic Publishers, Dordrecht.

Friedman, N. and Goldszmidt, M. (1996). "Learning Bayesian networks with local structure," Twelfth Conference on Uncertainty in Artificial Intelligence, 252-262.

Fung, R. and Del Favero, B. (1995). Applying Bayesian networks to information retrieval. *Communication of ACM*, **38**, 3:42-48, **38**, 3:57.

Pearl, J. (1988). *Probabilistic Reasoning in Intelligent Systems: Networks of Plausible Inference*, Morgan Kaufmann Publishers, San Francisco.

Ribeiro-Neto, B., Silva, I. and Muntz, R. (2000). "Bayesian network models for information retrieval", Soft Computing in Information Retrieval: Techniques and Applications. F. Crestani and G. Pasi (Eds.), Springer Verlag, 259-291.

Salton, G. and McGill, M. (1983). *Introduction to Modern Information Retrieval*, McGraw Hill, New York.

Silva, I., Ribeiro-Neto, B., Calado, P., Moura, E. and Ziviani, N. (2000). Linkbased content-based evidential information in a belief network model. *Twenty-third International Conference on Research and Development in Information Retrieval,* 96-103.

Turtle, H.R. and Croft, W.B. (1990). Inference networks for document retrieval. *Thirteenth International Conference on Research and Development in Information Retrieval,* 1-24.

van Rijsbergen, C.J. (1979). *Information Retrieval,* Butterworths, London.

Wong, S.K.M. and Butz, C.J. (1999) "Contextual weak independence in Bayesian networks," Fifteenth Conference on Uncertainty in Artificial Intelligence, 670-679.

Wong, S.K.M. and Butz, C.J. (2000). A Bayesian Approach to User Profiling in Information Retrieval. *Technology Letters,* **4**, 1:50-56.

Wong, S.K.M. and Butz, C.J. (2001). Constructing the dependency structure of a multi-agent probabilistic network. *IEEE Transactions on Knowledge and Data Engineering,* **13**, 3:395-415.

Wong, S.K.M., Butz, C.J. and Wu, D. (2000). On the implication problem for probabilistic conditional independency, *IEEE Transactions on Systems, Man and Cybernetics,* SMC-A, **30**, 6:785-805.

Wong, S.K.M. and Yao, Y.Y. (1995). On modeling information retrieval with probabilistic inference, *ACM Transactions on Information Systems,* 13:38-68.

Zhang, N. and Poole, D. (1999). "On the role of context-specific independence in probabilistic inference," Sixteenth International Joint Conference on Artificial Intelligence, 1288-1293.

Part II
Neural Web Intelligence, Evolutionary Web Intelligence and Granular Web Intelligence

CHAPTER 9

NEURAL EXPERT SYSTEM FOR VEHICLE FAULT DIAGNOSIS VIA THE WWW

A.C.M. Fong and S.C. Hui

School of Computer Engineering, Nanyang Technological University,
Blk N4, Nanyang Ave., Singapore 639798
Email: {ascmfong;asschui}@ntu.edu.sg

The present trend in vehicle fault diagnosis is toward automation. Modern motor vehicles can often be modeled as a complex system made up of many components, making fault diagnosis difficult. Traditionally, effective vehicle fault diagnosis relies heavily on the experience and knowledge of human experts. This chapter presents the development of an expert system whose aim is to provide useful aid to human users in their attempts at vehicle fault diagnosis, even at remote locations via the WWW. The system employs a hybrid data mining process to effectively mine data stored in a vehicle service database, which contains past service records. Through the learning capability of a neural network, the system is able to generalize knowledge stored in the database. Performance evaluation of the system confirms its effectiveness both in terms of speed and accuracy.

9.1 Introduction

The increasing demand for vehicle fault diagnostic information has led to the development of effective techniques for fault diagnosis. For example, in [Lu *et. al.*, (2000)], the authors describe a fuzzy model that learns automotive diagnostic knowledge using machine learning techniques. In [Guo *et. al.*, 2000)], the authors propose a three-step approach to vehicle engine diagnosis, which combines wavelet multi-resolution analysis with inter-signal analysis and machine learning. Lai has applied time-domain

169

modal analysis to engine fault diagnosis based on vibration data of the crank system [Lai (1993)].

While the above techniques apply to specific vehicle components, the research presented in this chapter is concentrated on developing techniques for mining general fault descriptions. These fault descriptions are stored in the vehicle service database of a company that services and repairs different makes of vehicle models. The database contains a wealth of information on faults and solutions accumulated over a period of several years. The mining technique, which exhibits human-like intelligence, comprises three main components: neural network (NN) and rule-based reasoning (RBR) and case-based reasoning (CBR). In particular, NN and RBR are incorporated into the framework of a CBR cycle for knowledge extraction and vehicle fault diagnosis.

NNs have been investigated for data mining [Bigus (1996)], as well as for fault diagnosis [Kuhlmann *et. al.*, (1999)]. Although CBR has demonstrated its suitability to fault diagnosis in different domains [Patterson and Hughes (1997)], traditional CBR systems are inefficient for large case-bases because they use flat memory structure for indexing and k-nearest neighbor algorithm for retrieval. The NN approach provides an efficient learning capability from detailed examples. It generalizes the knowledge through training, thereby reducing the search space. Hence, NN is used for case indexing and retrieval. In addition, the hybrid technique has been implemented for online vehicle fault diagnosis over the WWW. Tests have been conducted by both service technicians and casual users to gauge the effectiveness of the system based on the hybrid data mining technique.

9.2 Intelligent Data Mining for Vehicle Fault Diagnosis

Data mining is a rapidly emerging field motivated by the need to analyze large amounts of stored in large databases that are becoming commonplace in businesses [Chen *et. al.* (1996)]. This section provides a brief background of the various techniques that are related to the development of the data mining techniques for intelligent vehicle fault diagnosis, namely Case-Based Reasoning, Rule-Based Reasoning and Neural Networks. This is followed by an outline of the proposed intelligent data mining process. It will become apparent that the new method offers superior performance compared to other methods reported.

9.2.1 *Case-based reasoning*

The CBR methodology is characterized by the CBR cycle [Aamodt and Plaza (1994)] that consists of four phases RETRIEVE, REUSE, REVISE and RETAIN as shown in Fig. 9.1.

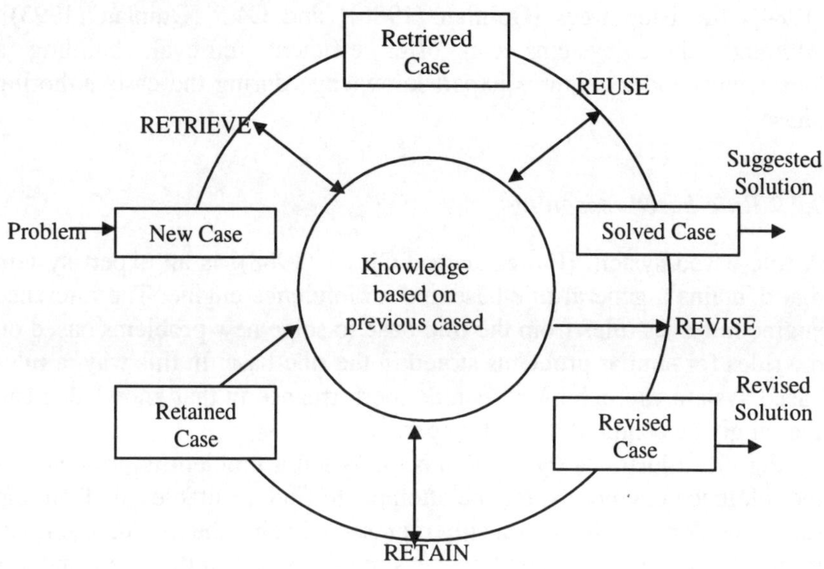

Fig. 9.1 The CBR cycle

First, a problem is presented as a new case to the CBR cycle. RETRIEVE is then applied to retrieve the most similar case from the stored knowledge. REUSE is then used to reuse the solution of the retrieved case for the current problem. Next, REVISE is applied to revise the proposed solution based on the current problem. Finally, RETAIN is to retain the current experience for future problem solving.

CBR systems rely on building a large repository of diagnostic cases (i.e. past service reports) in order to circumvent the difficult task of extracting and encoding expert domain knowledge [Riesbeck and Schank (1989)]. It is one of the most appropriate techniques for fault diagnosis as it learns with experience in solving problems and hence emulates human-like intelligence.

However, the performance of CBR systems critically depends on the adequacy and organization of cases, and the algorithms used for retrieval from a large case database [Althoff *et. al.* (1995)]. Most CBR systems use the nearest neighbor algorithm for retrieval from a flat-indexed case database, which is inefficient especially for large case databases. Other CBR systems use hierarchical indexing such as CART [Breiman *et. al.* (1984)], decision trees [Quinlan (1986)] and C4.5 [Quinlan (1993)]. Although these systems can offer efficient retrieval, building a hierarchical index requires expert knowledge during the case-authoring phase.

9.2.2 *Rule-based reasoning*

A rule-based system [Bowerman and Glover (1988)] is an expert system that contains a general rule-base and an inference engine. The inference engine retrieves rules from the rule-base to solve new problems based on the rules for similar problems stored in the rule-base. In this way, a rule-based system can exhibit humanlike performance in that knowledge can seemingly be acquired through experience.

Fig. 9.2 illustrates the RBR model. When a problem is presented at the inference engine, the engine attempts to find a suitable rule from the rule base. A rule is most typically represented using the *if ... then* format. If no existing rule is found to be suitable, a new rule is created for solving the current problem. This new rule is then stored into the rule base for future use.

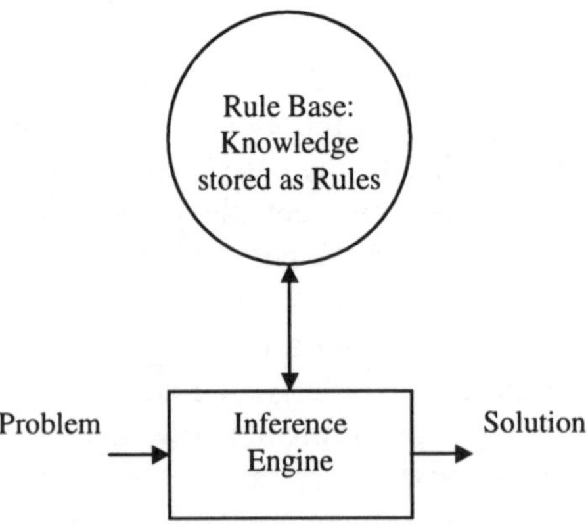

Fig. 9.2 A rule-based expert system model

9.4.1 *Neural network model generation*

Preprocessing is implemented using word-list, stop-list and algorithms from Wordnet [Fellbaum (1998)]. The purpose of preprocessing is to obtain a set of keywords by parsing the fault-descriptions stored in the vehicle service database. The keywords generated in this way are used to initialize and train the NN. A NN indexing database is generated consisting of the list of keywords, NN weight matrix and the fault-descriptions to keywords links.

The weights of the SOM NN are initialized with random real numbers in the closed interval [0,1]. The performance of SOM retrieval depends on the number of clusters generated and the average number of fault- descriptions within a cluster. Subsequently, an input vector is formed for each unique fault- description. These input vectors are then presented to the SOM for training and formation of clusters.

After the training process, the weight matrix generated represents the clusters. Linear topology is used to determine the neighborhood in the SOM. The initial neighborhood size is set to half the number of clusters, whereas the number of iterations and the initial learning rate are set to 100 and 0.5, respectively. The SOM training algorithm is summarized below.

SOM Training Algorithm:

For each input vector $x(t)$ selected in a random order, repeat steps 1-4 for 100 times:

1. Match the input vector with weight vectors of the output nodes and compute the winner output node as the one with minimum normalized Euclidean distance.

2. Update weight vectors, $w_i(t)$, as

$$w_i(t+1) = w_i(t) + \alpha(t)\,[x(t) - w_i(t)] \qquad \text{for each } i \in N_c(t),$$
$$w_i(t+1) = w_i(t) \qquad\qquad\qquad \text{otherwise,}$$

3. Update the cluster membership by adding the input vector to the winner cluster.

4. Reduce the neighborhood size and the learning rate. The rate of reduction is linear, so that the neighborhood radius will be 1 and the learning rate will be 0.05 in the last iteration.

In the above SOM training algorithm, t is the discrete-time index of the variables, the factor $\alpha(t) \in [0,1]$ is the learning rate, and $N_c(t)$ specifies the neighborhood around the winner in the map.

9.4.2 *Rule base generation*

As each service record in the vehicle service database contains a fault-description and corresponding solutions to be exercised for diagnosing the fault-description, suggested solution rules can be generated automatically to provide specific diagnostic instructions towards solving a particular fault.

The rule-base consists of control rules and solution rules. Control rules are coded manually to specify the diagnostic procedure for the firing of solution rules so that the suggested solutions can be exercised one by one according to their priorities. Using these two types of rules, the rule-based inference engine under the C Language Integrated Production System (CLIPS) environment can provide a step-by-step guidance to the user in diagnosing a fault- description.

9.5 Online Vehicle Fault Diagnosis

Online fault diagnosis follows the CBR cycle with four phases: RETRIEVE, REUSE, REVISE and RETAIN. The RETRIEVE process looks for the past service records having similar fault- descriptions to the input fault description from the knowledge base. The user's fault description is first preprocessed before retrieval can be performed. The NN performs retrieval by computing the winner through a competitive learning process. The winning cluster is the one that corresponds to the weight vector with minimum distance from the input vector. Retrieval of a specific fault- description is based on the nearest Euclidean distance of all the fault- descriptions in the retrieved cluster.

The REUSE process reuses the solutions of the retrieved service records that contain fault-descriptions closest to the user's fault description. The rule-based engine will guide the user to exercise the suggested solutions of the retrieved service records in an effective manner to arrive at a solution that solves the problem. In the REVISE process, the current problem description and its solution are revised with user feedback. Finally, in the RETAIN process, the revised information is retained by updating the relevant databases.

9.5.1 *The user's experience*

From the user's perspective, the first step needed to initialize an online query is to enter an input into the system via a web-based interface. If the user knows the error code, then no other information is required from the user for further processing. The corresponding fault- description can be identified and its suggested solutions can be retrieved. Otherwise, the fault description can be entered in natural language or as a set of keywords. In addition, the user can also provide the names of components and their states as input.

Next, the neural network retrieval process recalls similar fault-descriptions experienced in the past and ranks them based on the score that signifies the similarity of the retrieved fault- description to the user input. The retrieval algorithm is based on the matching process discussed in the training algorithm. In particular, competitive learning is used to compute the winning cluster as in the training process. The Euclidean distance of fault- descriptions within the cluster is used to rank them in terms of closeness to the input fault-description. The user can browse the fault- descriptions of each of the clusters. The fault- descriptions from these clusters are ranked.

The reuse of service records entails reusing the solutions of the fault-descriptions retrieved during the retrieval process. In the NN retrieval process, the displayed fault- descriptions that match most closely to the input fault description provided by the user are ranked according to their matching scores. The solutions are presented in the order according to the solution rules fired. The rules operate in a competitive manner to display the solutions in the order of their priority in solving the fault-description.

After the reuse phase, it is necessary to update the NN indexing database, the solution rules and the service records in the vehicle service database. The update is based on user feedback on the effectiveness of the fault diagnosis process. The input problem description and its past solutions are revised through user's feedback and updated into the relevant databases. The user provides feedback on whether the problem is resolved or not. If the problem is resolved, then the NN indexing database and the suggested solution rule-base are updated. If the problem is not resolved after trying all the solutions of the retrieved fault-descriptions, then the user will make a failure report and the problem will be further investigated by service personnel.

9.6 Experiments

Experiments have been conducted on the NN to retrieve cases and rule-based reasoning to reuse cases in the CBR cycle. The measures of performance are retrieval efficiency and retrieval accuracy. This approach is also compared with the k Nearest Neighbor (kNN) technique used in the traditional CBR systems for retrieval.

The following data were used in the experiments. The number of unique sets of fault-descriptions in the vehicle service database = 1,966 and the total number of fault-descriptions = 31,750, of which 23,600 were used for training (the unique set) and the rest of testing (the testing set). The number of keywords in the keyword list = 1,325. The number of words to be searched in the Wordnet's dictionary = 121,962 and the maximum allowable number of keywords in a fault-description or in the user input = 15.

The retrieval efficiency of the NN can be measured based on the time taken in preprocessing the fault-descriptions, the total training time and the average online retrieval speed by the NN. Preprocessing of all fault-descriptions took a total of 261s, offline training of the SOM NN took 4775s and the average online retrieval speed was 0.6s.

The retrieval precision depends on the accuracy of preprocessing, the frequency of new keywords being added, the number of incorrect winners computed by the NN, and the degree of precision of the user input. In terms of SOM, the retrieval accuracy can be based on the closest matched fault- description of the retrieved cluster. If the user input consists of many new keywords, which are not part of the keyword list, the accuracy will be affected. However, the NN learns to improve its accuracy in time.

The learning rate is another important factor in determining the number of iterations required for convergence. In particular, convergence was found to be optimal with a learning rate of 0.5. Any increase in the learning rate led to instability (i.e. no convergence achieved), whereas reducing it made the number of iterations needed to converge unacceptably high. The retrieval accuracy was found to be about 90% using the testing set mentioned above.

9.6.1 *Comparison with tradition kNN*

Comparison between the NN retrieval technique and the k-nearest neighbor (kNN) retrieval technique in traditional CBR systems has also been conducted in terms of both efficiency and accuracy. Two popular variations of kNN techniques were chosen for comparison. The first variation, denoted kNN1, stores cases in a flat memory structure, extracts keywords from the textual descriptions and uses normalized Euclidean distance for matching. The second variation, denoted kNN2, uses the fuzzy-trigram technique for matching. Two experiments were carried out. The first experiment was based on the testing set mentioned above, while the second experiment was based on user fault descriptions. The results are summarized in Table 9.1.

Table 9.1 Performance comparison

Technique	Average Retrieval Time	Retrieval Accuracy	
		Based on Service Records for Testing	Based on User Input
kNN1	14.3 s	81.3%	72.1%
kNN2	15.6 s	76.8%	76.2%
SOM NN	0.6 s	91.2%	89.4%

From Table 9.1, it is clear that SOM performed better than either variation of kNN for retrieval in terms of both speed and accuracy. Another major drawback of these kNN techniques is that new cases retained are indexed separately into the flat memory structure and thus the search space keeps on increasing, further decreasing the efficiency.

In the second experiment, a total of 50 fault descriptions were taken from non-expert users. The purpose of this experiment was to test the performance when the input was less precise in describing the fault-description. Expectedly, all retrieval techniques were found to have lower retrieval accuracy compared to the first experiement due to the impreciseness and grammatical variation in the user input.

9.7 Conclusion

A hybrid data mining process has been presented for knowledge extraction from the unstructured data in a vehicle service database for intelligent fault diagnosis. It is accomplished by incorporating neural network and rule-based reasoning within the framework of case-based reasoning. The data mining process consists of an offline knowledge extraction process to extract knowledge from the unstructured textual data of the service database and an online fault diagnosis process to support vehicle fault diagnosis over the World Wide Web. Performance evaluation has been conducted which has shown that the hybrid approach using NN technique outperforms traditional kNN techniques of CBR systems in both accuracy and efficiency of retrieval.

Bibliography

Aamodt, A. and Plaza, E. (1994). Case-Based Reasoning: Foundational Issues, Methodological Variations, and System Approaches. *Proceedings of AICom - Artificial Intelligence Communications*, 7, pp. 39-59.

Althoff, K.-D., Auriol, E., Barletta, R. and Manago, M. (1995). A review of Industrial Case-Based reasoning Tools. AI Perspectives Report, Artificial Intelligence, Oxford, U.K.

Bigus, J.P. (1996). Data Mining with Neural Networks: Solving Business Problems from Application Development to Decision Support. McGraw Hill, New York.

Bowerman, R.G. and Glover, D.E. (1988). Putting Expert Systems into Practice. Van Nostrand Reinhold Company, New York.

Breiman, L. Friedman, J., Olshen, R. and Stone, C. (1984). Classification of Regression Trees. Wadsworth.

Chen, M.S., Han, J. and Yu. P.S. (1996). Data Mining: An overview from a database perspective, *IEEE Transactions on Knowledge and Data Engineering*, 8, pp. 866-883.

Fellbaum, C. (Editor). Wordnet: An Electronic Lexical Database. The MIT Press, (1998)

Guo, H., Crossman, J.A., Murphey, Y.L. and Coleman, M. (2000) Automotive signal diagnostics using wavelets and machine learning, *IEEE Trans. Vehicular Tech.*, 49, pp. 1650-1662.

Kohonen, T. (1997). Self-Organizing Maps. Second Extended Edition, Springer Series in Information Sciences, 30, Springer, Berlin, Heidelberg, New York.

Kuhlmann, D, Handschin, E and Hoffmann, W. (1999). ANN based fault diagnosis system ready for practical application, Engineering Intelligent systems for electrical engineering and communications, 7, pp. 29-39.

Lai, S.H.-Y. (1993). Engine system diagnosis using vibration data. *Computers & Industrial Engineering*, 25, pp. 135-138.

Lu, Y, Chen, T.Q. and Hamilton, B. (2000). A fuzzy system for automotive diagnosis: fast rule generation and self-tuning, *IEEE Trans. Vehicular Tech.*, 49, pp. 651-660.

Patterson, D.W.R. and Hughes, J.G. (1997) Case-based reasoning for fault diagnosis, *The New Review of Applied Expert Systems*, 3, pp. 15-26.

Quinlan, J.R. (1986). Induction of Decision Trees. *Machine Learning*, 1, pp. 81-106.

Quinlan, J.R. (1993). C4.5: Programs for Machine Learning. Morgan Kaufmann.

Riesbeck, C.K. and Schank, R.C. (1989). Inside Case-Based Reasoning. Lawrence Erlbaum Associates, Inc.

CHAPTER 10

DYNAMIC DOCUMENTS IN THE WIRED WORLD

Lisa Purvis, Steven Harrington, Neil Sembower

Xerox Corporation
800 Phillips Road, 128-27E, Webster, NY 14580, USA
E-mail: {lpurvis, sharrington, sembower}@crt.xerox.com

The digital networked world is enabling and requiring a new emphasis on personalized document creation. Traditional methods of producing documents have become insufficient, since most are aimed at producing static results, and require time-consuming and knowledge-intensive processes. As new untrained users start producing documents for a wide audience, the old publishing tools prove too demanding. The new, more dynamic digital environment demands tools that can find, filter, and layout the content automatically, tailored to personal needs and transformed for the presentation device, and can enable novices or entirely automated workflows to easily create such documents. In order to enable such automated document assembly, we have formalized custom document creation as a constrained optimization problem, and use a genetic algorithm to assemble and transform compound personalized documents. This enables new personalized document workflows that are necessary to be productive in the wired world.

10.1 Introduction

The digital networked world is a sea of information. Individuals need this information in different forms, at different times, on different devices. While there is a lot of information, only a portion of it is relevant to each individual at a particular time, and the information needs of an individual change over time. Businesses are also finding that personalized information is more effective in keeping customers, both in e-commerce and traditional settings. The new, more dynamic digital environment demands tools that can automatically create documents, tailored to personal needs and transformed for the presentation device.

We have formalized the custom document creation problem as a multiobjective constrained-optimization problem, and use a genetic algorithm to assemble personalized documents. We begin in Section 10.2 by providing a background on other approaches to custom document creation. In Section 10.3, we describe our formulation of the problem as a constrained optimization problem solved with a genetic algorithm, along with examples of new workflows in the wired world which we can enable by using this approach. Section 10.4 describes the areas of focus for our future work, and we then conclude in Section 10.5 with a summary.

10.2   Background and Related Work on Dynamic Document Creation

10.2.1 *Variable Information Documents*

Current approaches to dynamic document creation are either non-automated, or limited in scope. One current approach to the non-automated means of dynamic document creation is in the realm of printed custom documents, called "variable information" documents. Simple examples of such documents are bills and statements, which contain different information for each individual (e.g. account number, address, name), while still adhering to the same basic layout. Variable documents are also beginning to become more complex documents such as brochures and catalogs, which include images and color, customized for each individual.

In traditional variable information (VI) document creation applications, the creation is accomplished by an expert in graphic arts, databases, layout, document design, etc. This expert document creator develops an overall layout for the document that includes slots for the customized data. The creator also finds or creates appropriate content pieces, and specifies rules for how to fill in the custom slots with this content, or places the content in a database and then links the slots to particular fields in the database. The VI application then creates a document for each customer by inserting the data for the customer into its linked slot. These types of templates are typically called "lick and stick", because the template has "art holes" which are defined by the document creator, and then the variable data is placed into those art holes to form different instances of the document.

The resulting set of documents is typically quite similar: each custom slot has one piece of content of about the same size, and the general layout is the same for all instances, regardless of the available content pieces. Thus, the traditional process not only requires extensive time and expertise from the document creator, but it also does not respond dynamically to varying amounts or types of content pieces, or to different output devices. Furthermore, the template creator is responsible for ensuring that the final document will adhere to good design principles, and is therefore aesthetically pleasing.

It is with these limitations in mind that we began our research to automate the creation of personalized documents. With an automated approach, novices can easily create personalized documents, and the documents themselves can transform themselves for different sets of content, different individuals, and different devices.

For example, consider a document such as the catalog page shown in Figure 10.1A. We have created a design for the set of content shown, but then at a later time, certain content in the document may become out of date, at which point we would like to remove it from the document to keep the contents up to date. When we remove some document elements as shown in Figure 10.1B, the original design of the document no longer works well. Our system can fix the bad design to create the new layout shown in Figure 10.1C.

10.2.2 *Scripts, Dynamic HTML, and Active Server Pages*

Dynamic documents are also now prevalent on the World Wide Web. The definition of dynamic, however, relates mostly to the data and not to the layout. A classic solution for creating dynamic web content is to write a specialized program (i.e. a "script") following the Common

Gateway interface (CGI) standard for communication between a client browser and a server application.

Fig. 10.1 Original catalog page, changed to remove outdated content, and then redesigned to be aesthetically pleasing again.

As the HTML page goes through the web server, the server dynamically interprets the "script" (or program) that is embedded in the HTML file. Since the server executes the CGI script in real time, it can output dynamic information such as a weather reading or the latest results from a database query.

Other approaches to scripting involve JavaScript or VBScript, which are scripts that are executed on the client side rather than on the server. Another more recent approach to scripting is called Active Server Pages (or ASP). ASPs are executed on the server, and are used for selecting content to insert into an existing HTML page. In this sense, ASPs are similar to CGI scripts. The difference is that ASPs are multithreaded, leading to faster speeds than CGI scripts can achieve, and the ability to handle large numbers of users.

Dynamic HTML (or DHTML) is a term that describes the combination of HTML, scripts, and style sheets, thereby allowing documents to be animated and self-modified. Since the Dynamic HTML approach includes style sheets, it enables a script to modify any aspect of the loaded page (style or content). The scripts can communicate with the user making the document interactive, further blurring the distinction between document and program.

The assumption in such approaches is that while the content is dynamic, the layout is limited to what the program has been designed for. In order to achieve different results, the programs must be changed. Thus, maintaining an attractive and dynamic web site in this way can be both costly and inefficient.

10.2.3 *Style Sheets and Transformational Languages*

Recent standards efforts are creating new types of styling and layout methods for use on the web. Style sheet technology provides a separation between document content and document style/layout information. By replacing or changing the style sheet, all web pages using that style sheet will change their rendering accordingly. The most well known style sheet language is probably the Cascading Style Sheets (CSS), developed by the World Wide Web Consortium (W3C), and supported in a wide range of web browsers. The next generation of style sheet languages, based on CSS is XSL (Extensible Style Sheet Language), currently being standardized by the W3C.

The drawback of using style sheets to specify and handle dynamic documents is that the styling cannot easily be dynamic, changing with the document contents. Thus if you require different styles for different sets of content, you would require a style sheet for each different output style. This is problematic in terms of anticipating all potential content scenarios, as well as a difficult maintenance problem. Furthermore, a single style sheet cannot easily handle both output device and creator's intent, since intent is known during creation while output device is known at presentation.

A more advanced approach to styling that is beginning to emerge is to combine style and transformation languages. There are several transformation languages, including the Extensible Style Sheet Language (XSLT) [Clark (1999)] that is currently being standardized by the W3C, and the Document Style Semantics and Specification Language (DSSSL). These transformation languages offer, in addition to the styling possibilities of style sheets, the possibility of transforming data from one thing to another. These transformations, however, are straight mappings from data to presentable document, and need to be changed if some aspect of the data changes. Style sheets address the presentation of the content, but not the selection or generation of the content (other than perhaps filtering out some of it). Thus, they aren't ideal for creating truly dynamic documents that respond to user preferences and changing document content.

10.2.4 *Personalized Information Services*

Another related application domain is in the area of personalized information services. Such services have the capability to compose content in various forms (e.g. for web, for print, for wireless).

Work in this area has been done on personalization of web sites for mobile devices [Anderson (2001)]. The PROTEUS system allows an addition or removal of links to web documents, as well as eliding of certain content. This is done in such a way as to maximize the expected utility for a given visitor, based on a visitor model obtained from mining web access logs and site content.

Another related domain is in adaptive web sites, which improve their organization and presentation by learning from visitor access patterns. One example of work in this area is the synthesis of index pages using clustering techniques [Perkowitz (2000)]. In their work, web logs are analyzed in order to find groups of pages that often occur together in user visits, and then these groups of pages are turned into index pages.

Our work focuses on taking sets of content elements (text paragraphs, images), and arranging them into an aesthetically pleasing document without using fixed templates. As such, we are focused on automating document intensive processes and enabling more dynamic documents.

10.2.5 *Constraint-Based Research*

Constraints have long been used to describe properties of user interfaces that should be enforced, such as ensuring that the left side of a window should always be to the left of the right side. A pioneering work in the area of interfaces and interactive systems is Ivan Sutherland's Sketchpad system [Sutherland (1963)]. There are numerous systems that use constraints for widget layout [Myers (1990,1997)], while Badros [Badros

(1999)] uses constraints for window layout. A Java-based GUI toolkit that incorporates constraints is subArctic, which provides building blocks for developing constraint-based user interfaces [Hudson (1996)]. Various approaches to personalizing user interfaces such as using version spaces, first-order logic-based goal specification, programming by demonstration, and machine learning are described by Weld et al in [Weld (2003)]. Other work related to constraint-based user interfaces is in the area of intelligent computer aided design (CAD) [Young (1991), Gross (1988), Nourani (1993)].

There has been work in the creation of documents using constraint-based approaches. Dengler et al use a constraint-based approach to generate diagrams [Dengler (1993)]. Another related work is in the adaptation of synchronized multimedia presentations [Rousseau (1999)], where they explore extensions to HTML that enable adapting web documents to different conditions and user needs. Graf has developed a constraint-based layout framework called LayLab [Graf (1995)], and applied it to various applications such as flowchart layout and pagination of yellow pages. Kroener has explored the combination of several AI techniques (constraint processing included) to achieve dynamic document layout [Kroener (1999)]. The constraints research group at the University of Washington has explored constraint-based document layout for the web [Borning (2000)].

Our work is focused on document design using a multiobjective optimization approach where design qualities are encoded as soft constraints. This in turn allows us to find document designs that not only satisfy certain spatial and physical style constraints, but also optimize the softer design constraints.

10.3 Dynamic Document Assembly as a Multiobjective Constrained Optimization Problem

10.3.1 *Initial Constraint Satisfaction Based Approach*

Our initial approach to solving the automated document assembly problem was to model the problem as a simple constraint satisfaction problem, which stopped when it found a solution that satisfied the constraints.   Our constraints were primitive layout constraints such as left-of, right-of, left-align, top-align, width < 350, etc. We found that in document creation, this approach did not create output documents that looked acceptable.   Furthermore, it required the document creator to specify a large number of low-level constraints, which defeated our goal of making the process simple. As an example, consider the document shown in Figure 10.2.   We had specified simple content and layout constraints: we wanted a title, a number of images about flowers, and an advertisement. Furthermore, we wanted the title to be above the images, and the images above the advertisement, we wanted the three content areas to be the same width, and none of the content items could overlap one another. The result adheres to the constraints, but there are problems in that the images are all sandwiched together, the document isn't balanced, etc.

What we needed was a means to find a solution that not only satisfied the basic content and layout constraints, but that was the "best" solution according to some aesthetic design criteria. We also desired to make the entire process easy for the document creator, and thus didn't want to require the creator to enter more specific constraints to achieve better-looking results.   Therefore we decided to model the problem as a constrained multiobjective optimization problem, using a genetic algorithm approach that combines both traditional hard constraints with soft constraints that measure the aesthetic properties of the document.

Fig. 10.2 Solution Satisfying Basic Layout Constraints

This enables better-looking output documents, as well as eases the burden on the document creator.

10.3.2 *Genetic Algorithm Based Constrained Multiobjective Optimization Approach*

Over the last few years, much research has been devoted to applying genetic algorithms in constrained optimization problems [Coello (1999)]. We chose the genetic algorithm approach because it provides us with a means to easily combine hard and soft constraints, as well as to easily combine several types of problem variables (real, integer, boolean). In addition, our initial work on using a systematic constraint satisfaction approach indicated that our problem would be too complex to be practically solved using a systematic approach. As is typical in real life constraint satisfaction problems, the large numbers of variables and large domains coupled with a limited time to solve the problem preclude a complete algorithm from being practical. Thus we opted for an approach that would be both easy to implement and had promise in terms of flexibility and efficiency.

10.3.2.1 *Document Parameters as Genes*

Our methodology specifies the document, its content components, its layout requirements, and its desired aesthetic criteria as elements of a multiobjective optimization problem. Solving this problem results in an automated document layout for the set of content components that satisfies not only certain primitive content and layout constraints, but also advantageously fulfills desired design properties that provide a way to ensure that the generated document is well designed.

As such, we model each of the document parameters that can be modified as genes in the genome. As an example, consider the document template shown in Figure 10.3. This document template specifies that the positions and sizes of both areaA and areaB can be changed.

Thus, the genes in this example are: areaA-topLeftX, areaA-topLeftY, areaB-topLeftX, areaB-topLeftY, areaA-width, areaA-height, areaB-width, areaB-height. The resulting genome contains these eight genes.

We also model each of the desired design qualities as objectives to maximize. If more than one design quality is desired (as is typically the case), the problem becomes a multiobjective optimization problem. In this case, we sum the individual objective function scores to produce the overall optimization score for a particular solution. We can furthermore weight each of the desired qualities with a priority, so that the overall optimization score becomes a weighted sum of the individual objective function scores.

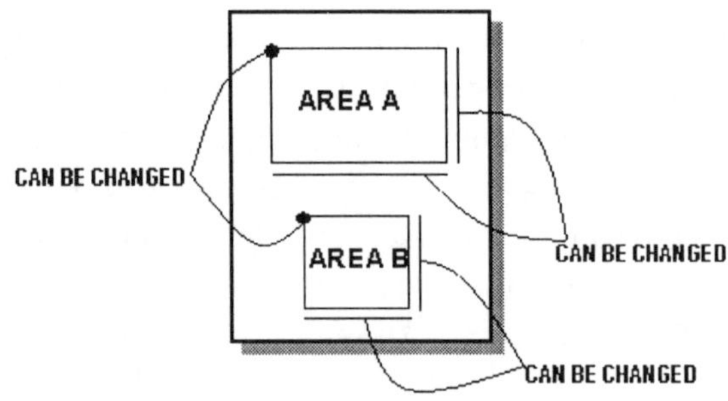

Fig. 10.3 Example Document Template

The genetic algorithm allows us to explore the search space of possible documents, evolving towards the one that best meets the desired design objectives.

10.3.2.2 *Design Qualities as Objectives*

What we needed was a means to find a solution that not only satisfied the basic content and layout constraints, but that was the "best" solution according to some aesthetic design criteria.

We began by encoding some of the basic design criteria that one might find in any book on basic design principles [Williams (1994)]. We encoded such principles as alignment, balance, legibility, compactness, text and image balance, etc. Each design criterion measures one aspect of the document. For instance, the alignment criterion provides scores that indicate how well the edges of the elements within a document align to one another. Each criterion ranges from 0 to 1, with 1 being a perfect, maximized score for that particular design quality. For instance, the documents shown in Figure 10.4 range in alignment value from close to 0 for the most unaligned, to close to 1 for the most aligned.

Fig. 10.4   Examples of Alignment Scores

10.3.2.3 *Optimizing Design Qualities*

We then combine the individual scores for each design quality into an overall measure of how "optimal" the document is for all of the design measures combined. We currently use a simple weighted sum to compute the overall score. For example, if we are optimizing the document layout based on the qualities of balance and alignment, and each are weighted the same, we obtain the scores as shown in Figure 10.5, with the document on the right side considered best because it has the higher total score.

If, however, we weight Balance 5 times higher than Alignment, the document on the left is considered best (score of 4.6733 versus 4.4209).

We also have "required" constraints in our document layout problem, which describe properties that must be satisfied in the resulting solution. Such required constraints specify, for example, that document elements cannot overlap, and must stay within the page margins.

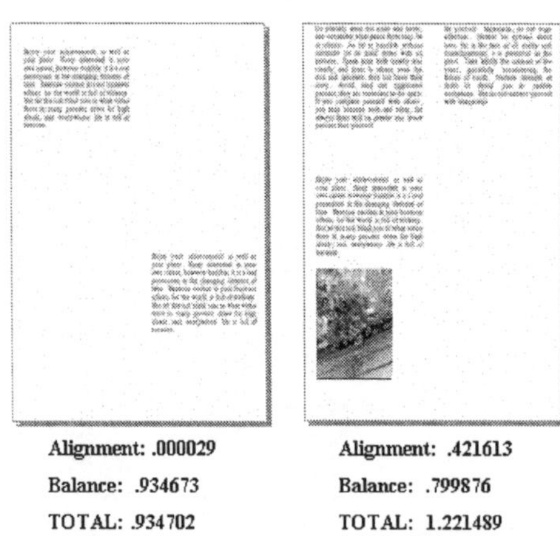

Alignment: .000029	Alignment: .421613
Balance: .934673	Balance: .799876
TOTAL: .934702	TOTAL: 1.221489

Fig. 10.5   Example of Two Equally Weighted Objectives

The interaction between these required and desired properties results in a complex search space. Furthermore, as the number of competing objectives increases and less well-behaved objectives are considered, the problem rapidly becomes increasingly complex [Fonseca (1994)]. In our empirical testing, we have verified that our application domain indeed exhibits many of the difficult behaviors of a typical multiobjective optimization problem. This has enabled us to take advantage of several existing techniques to improve the behavior of our approach [Purvis (2003)].

10.3.3 *Benefits of the Multiobjective Optimization Approach*

Overall, the multiobjective optimization approach gives us the flexibility to provide several features in personalized document creation that aren't available today, even beyond the automated personalization factor.

10.3.3.1 *Easier Document Specification*

In the wired world there is a lot of information and a lot of different situations in which users need to access this information. One inhibitor to achieving truly dynamic document presentation is that it is difficult for the user to specify what he would like the document to look like under all possible circumstances. For instance, perhaps he would like a very compact version of the document to take along on a long trip, so it doesn't take many pages. Alternatively, maybe he would like a very colorful and eye-catching document in order to show it to a customer. But how would one specify such document criteria? The genetic algorithm approach helps us to make the document specification process easy for the user.

Whereas the simple constraint satisfaction approach required many low-level layout constraints to be specified in order to achieve a reasonable result, the genetic algorithm approach allows a specification of a few high-level desired constraints and qualities – a much more intuitive and less user-demanding process. As an example, consider the document shown in Figure 10.6.

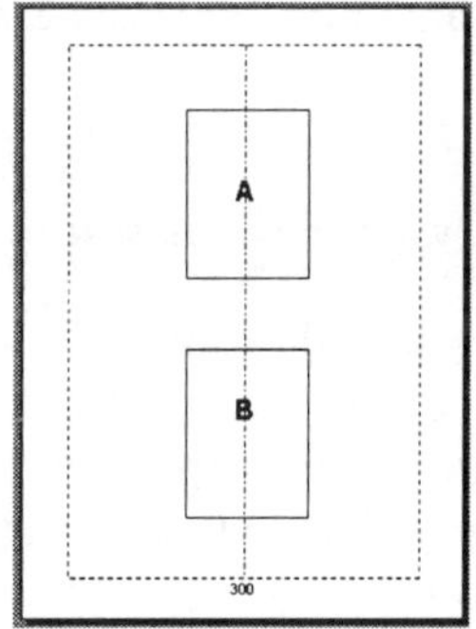

Fig. 10.6   Example Document

The low-level constraints necessary with the constraint satisfaction approach to enable the simple two-item document to look reasonably good are:

A above B
A left-align B

> **A right-align B**
> **50 < AWidth < 300**
> **50 < BWidth < 300**
> **AMiddleX = 300** (for centering)
> **BMiddleX = 300** (for centering)
> **BTopRightY – AbottomRightY < 50** (for spacing)

Alternatively, the few high-level design qualities and constraints that can be specified to achieve good results with the new genetic algorithm approach are:

> **NoOverlap**
> **Stay In Margins**
> **Balance**
> **Consistency Of Order** (to keep A above B)
> **Spatial Compactness** (to limit space between A and B)

Furthermore, the genetic algorithm approach allows the same high-level specification to apply easily to different content. For instance, if we add another content item, the same set of high-level constraints and design qualities can be used, whereas in the constraint satisfaction approach, another set of low-level constraints would need to be added to solve the problem in a reasonable way. Furthermore, a default set of design qualities and constraints can be pre-selected, such that the user doesn't need to specify anything, unless he would like to have more control over the process.

10.3.3.2 *Enabling More Dynamic Document Instances*

Similarly in the wired world the content is changing very fast, and different content may be desired under different circumstances. Another advantage of the automated layout approach is that we can find pleasing solutions for any combination of content, thereby enabling more dynamic custom document instances. As an example, consider the two different documents shown in Figure 10.7. Both were created from the same document template. The automated system queried the customer and content databases to find the appropriate content, and was able to arrange the varying types and amounts of content into documents that still adhere to all of the hard layout constraints as well as the aesthetic criteria of balance and alignment.

Another advantage of the constrained-optimization approach over existing approaches is that we can weight the various aesthetic criteria, and result in a different output document based on the weightings. A simple example of that is shown in Figures 10.8 and 10.9, where we have a document containing two images and two paragraphs.

Fig. 10.7 Different Documents from the Same Template

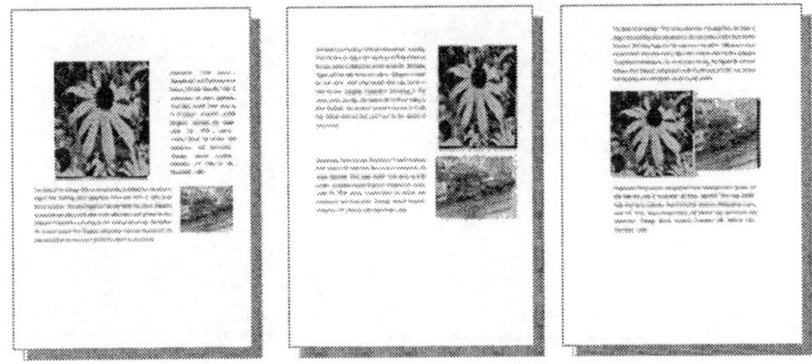

Fig. 10.8 Compactness Aesthetic Criteria Weighted with High Importance

If we weight compactness with high importance, we get solutions such as those shown in Figure 10.8. If on the other hand, we weight page utilization high and compactness low, we get solutions such as those shown in Figure 10.9.

We can furthermore take advantage of the dynamic nature of such an automated document system in order to automatically produce different layouts for different devices. As an example, consider the document shown in Figure 10.10A. If we have originally created such a document for display on a traditional computer display screen, but then want to display it on a smaller screen such as a cell phone or a PDA (personal digital assistant), we can change the layout to make the document easily readable on the small screen, as shown in Figure 10.10B, where the outlined area represents the screen of a small device such as a cell phone or PDA.

Fig. 10.9   Page Utilization Aesthetic Criteria Weighted with High Importance

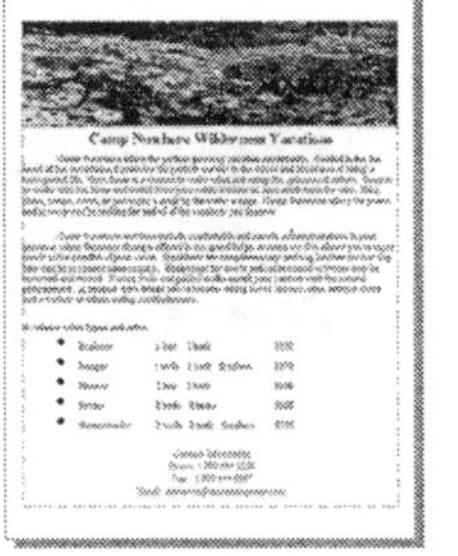
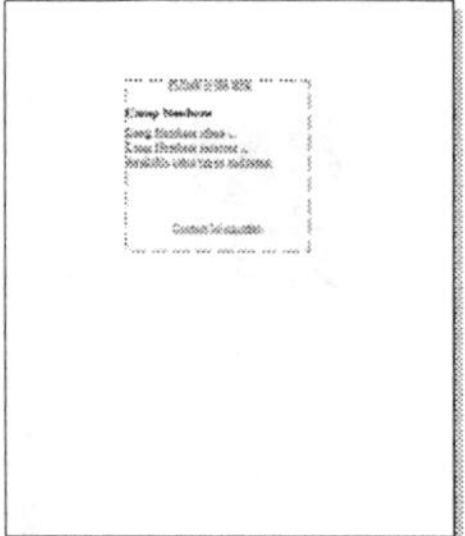

Fig. 10.10   Document Originally Intended for Typical Screen Display, and Layed Out
Differently for a Small Screen Device

10.3.4 *New Workflows Enabled by the Approach*

10.3.4.1 *Prepress Workflow Issues*

The multiobjective optimization approach for automated document layout allows the expensive task of composing a page to be decoupled from the rest of the document creation process thus enabling workflows for personalized documents that today aren't possible.

Documents have particular audiences and specific requirements, and each audience measures the value of a document in terms of how well the document meets those requirements. Publishers differentiate themselves by providing products that are valued higher by their audience. Through careful prioritization of user requirements and understanding of how document value is measured we can change document production workflows to emphasize those areas of the production that are essential to the success of the document.

Today's typical document production workflows generate documents for vertical markets such as magazines and newspapers, where the content and presentment is chosen to satisfy as large of an audience as possible. These workflows do not make it practical to produce personalized documents for smaller audiences (e.g. audiences of one, or individual customers). In the networked and digital world documents generated for more selective markets can meet exacting requirements such as size, shape, media, content and fulfillment. By relaxing layout requirements and allowing automation of the layout prepress step publishers can supply targeted content to each reader.

Multiple objectives may be structured to emphasize different aspects of page layout. Document look and feel guidelines allow organizations to present a common face that facilitate usage of the documents and help to establish branding. Some of these look and feel guidelines may be expressed in terms of multiple objectives allowing organizations to maintain the common look and feel. By offering a layout service that applies look and feel it frees the authors to focus on the content and reduces the amount of time spent dealing with layout issues.

By focusing on users specific requirements of content and presentment we can create documents that have a higher customer value and more utility. As the per document variability of the content increases, workflows need to automate prepress steps to sustain throughput, and page layout is a production bottleneck that demands attention to detail. As short production cycles and appropriateness of content increase in importance the difference between a page layout that is 'good enough' and 'perfect' will not affect how users measure the value of the document, and this product quality tolerance can be leveraged into new products and workflows.

10.3.4.2 *New Workflow Example*

One example of such an automated personalized document workflow is the automated creation of documents that have high customer value because they contain information of interest to the user, obtained from a wide variety of content sources, and then pushed out to the user as necessary. Today's typical information gathering services either use a fixed template in which to pour in the results of a query, or they simply provide a list of relevant information. Our approach enables a richer, more valuable document to be automatically synthesized for a user.

Let's take as an example the creation of a personalized newspaper. Each individual may wish to subscribe to a daily or weekly edition of the news, but is only interested in those articles of relevance to the individual's work or leisure interests. Thus, each instance of the newspaper will be different.

Furthermore, if the content for this customized newspaper comes from the world-wide-web, then we must anticipate that the content returned from a search will be of widely varying forms (e.g. large images, small images, full articles, paragraphs, sentences, etc.). We cannot pre-select or pre-instantiate a database with content that will fit appropriately into a predesigned template.

With our multiobjective optimization approach, we can take the wide variety of content elements returned from a personalized search and arrange them into a pleasing document for the end customer, automatically. This in turn will drive more frequent information requests due to the results being of high value to the customer, thereby creating a new document workflow.

As an example, consider the custom newspaper samples created by our system, as shown in Figure 10.11. Here we can see that as we allow true customization of the content, the layout must also change in order to accommodate that content. Figure 10.11A, for instance, shows an instance of the newspaper where the individual has three custom news categories of interest (as evidenced by the three columns). Figure

10.11B shows an instance where the user has only one custom news category of interest, on a different topic, such that the image also is different, having a different aspect ratio, and thus requiring a different layout.

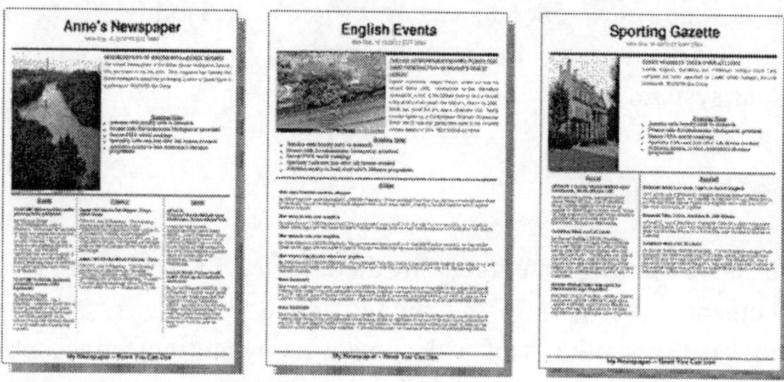

Fig. 10.11   Samples of a Custom Newspaper, with varying content and layout from instance to instance

Figure 10.11C shows yet another combination of content, which has been automatically arranged into a pleasing layout with the given content.

Automated search, filtering, and layout technologies together can provide an end-to-end customized information push service, thus expanding the realm of today's personalized document workflows.

10.4 Future Work

The multiobjective optimization approach to document personalization has provided us with many benefits beyond what is available today in such workflows.   The multiobjective optimization problem itself, however, is a complex problem.   Although the Genetic Algorithm (GA) has been shown to outperform other search procedures on large, complex search spaces, certain problem features are known to still cause difficulty for the GA.   Such features as multi-modality, deception, isolated optimum, collateral noise, and a mixture of hard and soft constraints are all known to impact the performance of the genetic algorithm [Deb (1999)].   These features often prohibit the GA from accomplishing its two most important tasks: guiding the search towards the global Pareto-optimal region, and maintaining population diversity.   On a complex, real-world problem such as ours, all of these difficulties emerge. Our current and future work entails exploring the many current techniques and devising new ones to ensure efficient scalability of the algorithm such that documents of arbitrary complexity can be efficiently designed by our system.

10.5 Summary

We are exploring intelligent methodologies by which to enable new document workflows in the digital, wired world. As such, we have modeled the synthesis of a document as a multiobjective optimization problem, and use a genetic algorithm to compose the content of a document into an aesthetically pleasing document layout.

This approach provides several advantages over traditional custom document creation approaches: we can ensure that the automatically assembled output document adheres to certain specified aesthetic qualities, we can make the specification process simple for the user, we enable a more dynamic output document, and we can modify the appearance of the output document according to weightings on our design criteria.

This approach has therefore enabled a flexible and automated means to create customized documents which reduces costs in existing personalized document workflows, and produces higher value documents that increase knowledge worker productivity. This in turn enables new document workflows, thereby expanding the market space for personalized document creation.

Bibliography

Anderson, A., Domingos, P., and Weld, D. (2001) Personalizing Web Sites for Mobile Users, in *Proceedings of the World Wide Web Conference*, WWW'01.

Badros, G. and Stachowiak, M. (1999) Scwm – The Scheme Constraints Window Manager, web page, http://scwm.sourceforge.net/

Borning, A., Lin R., and Marriott, K. (2000) Constraint-Based Document Layout for the Web, in *Multimedia Systems*, Vol. 8 No. 3, pp. 177-189.

Clark, James (1999). XSL Transformations (XSLT) 1.0, Work In Progress, World Wide Web Consortium.

Coello C. (1999) A Comprehensive Survey of Evolutionary-Based Multiobjective Optimization Techniques. *Knowledge and Information Systems Journal*, Volume 1(3), 129-156.

Deb, K. (1999) Multi-objective Genetic Algorithms: Problem Difficulties and Construction of Test Problems. *Evolutionary Computation*, Volume 7(3), 205-230.

Dengler, E. Friedell, M., Marks, J. (1993) Constraint-Driven Diagram Layout, in *Proceedings of the 1993 IEEE Symposium on Visual Languages*, pages 330-335, Bergen, Norway.

Fonseca, C.M., Fleming, P.J. (1994). An Overview of Evolutionary Algorithms in Multiobjective Optimization. *Evolutionary Computation* 3(1):116.

Graf, W.H. (1995) *The* Constraint-Based Layout Framework LayLab and its Applications, in *Electronic Proceedings of the ACM Workshop on Effective Abstractions in Multimedia*. (http://www.cs.tufts.edu/~isabel/graf/mm95.html)

Gross, M., Ervin, S., Anderson, J., and Fleisher, A. (1988) Constraints: Knowledge Representation in Design, *Design Studies*, 9(3):133-143. Butterworth & Co (Publishers) Ltd.

Hudson, S. and Smith, I. (1996) SubArctic UI Toolkit User's Manual, Technical Report, College of Computing, Georgia Institute of Technology.

Kroener, A. (1999) The DesignComposer: Context-Based Automated Layout for the Internet, in *Proceedings of the AAAI Fall Symposium Series: Using Layout for the Generation, Understanding, or Retrieval of Documents*.

Myers, B., Giuse, D., Dannenberg, R., VanderZanden, B., Kosbie, D., Pervin, E., Mickish, A., and Marchal, P. *(1990)* Garnet Comprehensive support for graphical highly interactive user interfaces, *IEEE Computer*.

Myers, B., McDaniel, R., Miller, R., Ferrency, A., Faulring, A., Kyle, B., Mickish, A., Klimovitski, A., and Doane, P. (1997) The Amulet Environment: New Models for

Effective User Interface Software Development, *IEEE Transactions on Software Engineering*, 23(6):347-365.

Nourani, F. and Magalhaes, L. (1993) Management of Consistency Constraints in a CAD Database System, in Zesheng Tang, editor, *New Advances in Computer Aided Design & Computer Graphics*, volume 2, pages 770-776, Beijing, China.

Purvis, L., Harrington, S., O'Sullivan, B., Freuder, E. (2003) "Creating Personalized Documents: An Optimization Approach", *Proceedings of the ACM Symposium on Document Engineering*, Grenoble, France.

Rousseau,F., Garcia-Macias, A. Valdeni de Lima, J. and Duda, A. (1999) User Adaptable Multimedia Presentations for the WWW, in *Electronic Proceedings from the 8th International World Wide Web Conference.*

Sutherland, I. (1963). Sketchpad: A man-machine graphical communication system, In *Proceedings of the Spring Joint Computer Conference*, pages 329-346.

Weld, D., Anderson, C., Domingos, P., Etzioni, O., Gajos, K., Lau, T., Wolfman, S. (2003). Automatically Personalizing User Interfaces, in *Proceedings of the 18th Joint Conference on Artificial Intelligence*, Acapulco, Mexico.

Williams, R. (1994). The Non-Designers Design Book. Peachpit Press. Berkeley, CA.

Young, R.E., Greef, A., O'Grady, P. (1991) SPARK: An Artificial Intelligence Constraint Network System for Concurrent Engineering, In J.S.Gero, editor, *Artificial Intelligence in Design '91*, pages 79-94. Butterworth Heinemann, Oxford, UK.

CHAPTER 11

PROXIMITY-BASED SUPERVISION FOR FLEXIBLE WEB PAGES CATEGORIZATION

Vincenzo Loia[1], Sabrina Senatore[1], and Witold Pedrycz[2]

[1]Department of Mathematics & Informatics
University of Salerno
Via S. Allende - 84081 Baronissi (SA), Italy

[2]Department of Electrical & Computer Engineering
University of Alberta
Edmonton T6R 2G7 Canada
and
Systems Research Institute, Polish Academy of Sciences
Warsaw, Poland
E-mail: loia@unisa.it, ssenatore@unisa.it, pedrycz@ee.ualberta.ca

Nowadays Internet has become a universal repository of human knowledge and information, it turns the Web into a new publishing medium accessible to everybody. As an immediate consequence, any Web user can look for information, pushes his personal data with little effort and almost without costs. This universe without frontiers has attracted millions of people causing a revolution in the way people use computers and perform their daily tasks. For instance, e-commerce and home banking are becoming very popular and have generated meaningful revenues. Anyway, despite so much success, the web suffers of some problems of its own, making the reliability of Internet-based retrieval systems more complex; finding proper information on the Web becomes a troublesome activity. Sometimes, to satisfy user's information need, a meticulous surfing in the WWW hyperspace becomes a fundament activity, in order to search for information of interest. However, since the hyperspace is vast and almost unknown, such a navigation task is usually inefficient, because information definition and structure is frequently of low quality. There are different

205

problems concerning Web searching activity, one among these falls in the query phase. Often, the searching process returns a huge list of answers that are irrelevant, unavailable, or outdated. The tedium of querying, due to the fact the queries are too weak to cope with the user's expressiveness, has stimulated the designers to enrich the human-system interaction with new searching metaphors, new criteria of matching: as instance, defining a kind of comparition among "similar" pages, as offered by Google, Yahoo and others. The idea is very good, since the similarity gives an easy and intuitive mechanism to express a complex relation. We believe that this approach could become more effective if the user can rely on major flexibility in expressing the similarity dependencies with respect the current and available possibilities. In this chapter, we introduce a novel method for considering and processing the userdriven proximity/similarity during Web navigation. We define an extension Fuzzy C-Means algorithm, namely P-FCM (Proximity Fuzzy C-Means) incorporating a user judgment in term of measure of similarity or dissimilarity among clusterized data. We present the theoretical framework of this extension and then we observe, through a suite of Web-based experiments, how significant is the impact of user's feedback during P-FCM functioning. These observations suggest that the P-FCM approach can offer a relatively simple way of improving the Web page classification according with the user interaction with the search engine.

11.1 Introduction

Most The demand of effective systems and tools for information retrieval, filtering and analysis is becoming more evident with the incessant and rapid development of information sources and information users. It is aware of the user's ability to access, assimilate, and act upon available information, so it becomes predominant the exigency to realize, develop, refine and expand models, technologies and methods in order to retrieve and deliver relevant information. Information Retrieval (IR) techniques are used in this domain, in order to satisfy operator's information need by a retrieval of potentially relevant information; the IR concerns with the study of systems for indexing, searching, and recalling data, particularly text or other unstructured forms. Users report difficulties in finding the information they need, in assessing the general structure of the network they are browsing and it is common the feeling of getting lost and not knowing where to go [Edwards and Hardman (1989)]. The activity concerned with improving human information retrieval from hypertext systems, however, has since then mainly been involved with other issues such as search engines using lexical matching rules, user modeling for adaptive information access and presentation [Brusilovsky (1996)], visualization techniques, automated browsing agents, browsing assistance, indexing, classification, etc. Today the main problem with the development of automated tools is related to finding, extracting, parsing, and filtering the user requirements from web knowledge. The IR approach to retrieval from hypertext networks and the WWW has conduct to the implementation of keyword-based search engines for automated retrieval, based on the word match approach in which documents are retrieved by lexically matching a set of provided keywords. This approach has a number of fundamental problems with polysemy and synonymy in which a same word can have different meanings and the same meaning can be expressed by different keywords [Johan *et. al.* (1999)]. Indexing of web pages to facilitate retrieval is an interesting task, but becomes a challenging problem, considering the dimension and the changing of the Web, it becomes evident that any kind of manual classification and categorization of Web sources (sites, pages, etc.) will be prohibitively time consuming. Innovative resource discovery systems make use of automatic text categorization technology to classify web document into categories.

Even though it is still unfeasible to fully extract the meaning of a HTML document, clustering provides a powerful tool to categorize the document without a deep, *a priori* knowledge of categories (unsupervised clustering). There are many clustering algorithms where the similarity measure is a distance (or objective) function that is iteratively minimized to obtain the final partition. The objective function is chosen depending on the geometric structure of the cluster [Jain and Dubes (1988)]. Fuzzy C-means (FCM) clustering algorithm, proposed by Bezdek [Bezdek (1981)], and other researchers can provide an unsupervised approach to the cluster analysis of data. There have been a number of interesting developments along the main line see [Hathaway *et. al.* (2000)], [Runkler and Bezdek (1999)], [Hoppner *et. al.* (1999)], [Hoppner (1997)].

In response to the inadequacies of the IR systems, researches are directed towards an interactive approach to retrieving. IR interaction is a promising research paradigm that stresses the iterative nature of information searching: it tries to better understand phenomena such as search strategies, search term generation and use, and successive searches by users for the same research problem. Methods employed to study these phenomena include observation of users in naturalistic environments, discourse analysis, and other speech-based analyses such as think aloud protocols. The focus is to gain an understanding of end-user and mediated searching that will guide the development of "intelligent" IR systems that will act as guides to information searching to end users. The traditional model of IR holds that IR systems are comprised of texts that are represented and organized to facilitate retrieval; on the other side, users approach IR systems claiming information requirements in form of research questions that must be further reduced to a query in order to meet IR protocol features. Interactive IR (IIR) provides a rich research agenda. It includes human behavior elements, but it also requires a basic understanding of how IR systems work so that realistic IIR researchers can collaborate with IR system designers. The future of IIR is in interdisciplinary collaboration and research. Researchers from disciplines, such as psychology, sociology, business, computer science, library and information science, and communications, to name a few, are needed to give full description to IIR [Robins (2000)].

11.2   P-FCM algorithm

The FCM algorithm accepts a collection of data (patterns). This process is completely guided by some underlying objective function. The result depends exclusively upon the data to be analyzed. There is no further user/designer intervention (with an exception of setting up the parameters of the algorithm and deciding upon the number of clusters to be formed). There is another important, yet quite often overlooked source of information coming directly from the potential user of the results of the clustering process. Our intent in to augment the basic FCM model so that it can accept such hints about proximity of the object (Web pages). In a nutshell, the proposed algorithm consists of two main phases that are realized in interleaved manner. The first phase is data driven and is primarily the standard FCM applied to the patterns. The second concerns an accommodation of the proximity-based hints and involves some gradient-oriented learning.

11.2.1   *Problem formulation and underlying notation*

The high level-computing scheme comprises of two phases that are nested, as shown in Fig. 11.1. The upper level deals with the standard FCM computing (iterations) while the one nested there is aimed at the accommodation of the proximity requirements and optimizes the partition matrix on this basis. The upper part (phase) of the P-FCM is straightforward and

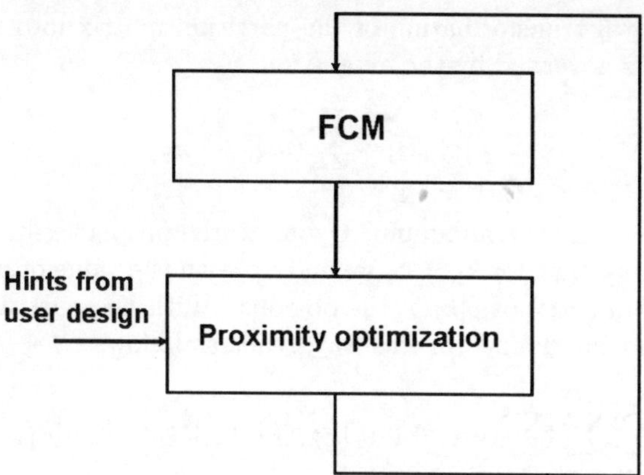

Fig. 11.1   An overall scheme of P-FCM algorithm

follows the well known scheme encountered in the literature. The inner part deserves detailed discussion. The accommodation of the proximity requirements is realized in the form of a certain performance index whose minimization leads us to the optimal partition matrix. As stated in the problem formulation, we are provided with pairs of patterns and their associated level of proximity. The partition matrix U (more specifically the induced values of the proximity) should adhere to the given levels of proximity. Bearing this in mind, the performance is formulated as the following sum.

$$V = \sum_{k_1=1}^{N} \sum_{k_2=1}^{N} (\hat{p}[k_1, k_2] - p[k_1, k_2])^2 b[k_1, k_2] d[k_1, k_2] \qquad (11.1)$$

The notation $\hat{p}[k_1, k_2]$ is used to describe the proximity level induced by the partition matrix. It becomes apparent that using directly the values of the membership (corresponding entries of the partition matrix) is not suitable. Simply, if two patterns k_1 and k_2 have the same distribution of membership grades across the clusters, these membership grades are usually not equal to 1 as the proximity value could be close or equal to 1. The value $d[k_1, k_2]$ denotes the distance between the two corresponding patterns while $p[k1, k2]$ is the proximity level provided by the user or data analyst. Subsequently, the entries of the binary matrix B are defined as follows:

- $b[k_1, k_2]$ assumes binary value: it returns 1 if there is a proximity hint for this specific pair of the patterns, that is k_1 and k_2;
- otherwise the value of $b[k_1, k_2]$ is set up to zero (meaning that there is no proximity hint for the specific pair of data).

The well-known transformation of the partition matrix into its proximity counterpart is governed by the expression

$$\hat{p}[k_1, k_2] = \sum_{i=1}^{c} (u_{ik_1} \wedge u_{ik_2}) \tag{11.2}$$

where $\wedge$ represents the minimum. Owing to the properties of the partition matrix, we note that for $k_1 = k_2$ we end up with the value of $\hat{p}[k_1, k_2]$ equal to 1. The symmetry of $\hat{p}[k_1, k_2]$ is obvious. With the partition-proximity dependency being defined in this way, reads as follows

$$V = \sum_{k_1=1}^{N} \sum_{k_2=1}^{N} (\sum_{i=1}^{c} (u_{ik_1} \wedge u_{ik_2}) - p[k_1, k_2])^2 b[k_1, k_2] d[k_1, k_2] \tag{11.3}$$

The optimization of V with respect to the partition matrix does not lend itself to a closed-form expression and requires some iterative optimization. The gradient-based scheme comes in a well-known format

$$u_{st}(iter + 1) = [u_{st}(iter) - \alpha \frac{\partial V}{\partial u_{st}(iter)}]_{0,1} \tag{11.4}$$

$s = 1, 2, \ldots, c, t = 1, 2, \ldots, N$ where $[\ ]_{0,1}$ indicates that the results are clipped to the unit interval; α stands for a positive learning rate. Successive iterations are denoted by "iter".

The detailed computations of the above derivative are straightforward. Taking the derivative with u_{st}, s=1, 2, $\ldots$, c, t =1, 2, , N, one has

$$\frac{\partial V}{\partial u_{st}(iter)} = \sum_{k_1=1}^{N} \sum_{k_2=1}^{N} \frac{\partial}{\partial u_{st}} (\sum_{i=1}^{c} (u_{ik_1} \wedge u_{ik_2}) - p[k_1, k_2])^2 b[k_1, k_2] d[k_1, k_2] =$$

$$2b[k_1, k_2] d[k_1, k_2] \sum_{k_1=1}^{N} \sum_{k_2=1}^{N} (\sum_{i=1}^{c} (u_{ik_1} \wedge u_{ik_2}) - p[k_1, k_2]) \frac{\partial}{\partial u_{st}} \sum_{i=1}^{c} (u_{ik_1} \wedge u_{ik_2})$$

$$\tag{11.5}$$

The inner derivative assumes binary values depending on the satisfaction of the conditions:

$$\frac{\partial}{\partial u_{st}} \sum_{i=1}^{c} (u_{ik_1} \wedge u_{ik_2}) = \begin{cases} 1 \text{ if t=}k_1 \text{ and } u_{sk_1} \leq u_{sk_2} \\ 1 \text{ if t=}k_2 \text{ and } u_{sk_2} \leq u_{sk_1} \\ 0 \text{ otherwise} \end{cases} \tag{11.6}$$

Making this notation more concise, we can regard the above derivative to be a binary (Boolean) predicate $\varphi[s, t, k_1, k_2]$ and plug it into (11.5) that leads to the overall expression

$$\frac{\partial V}{\partial u_{st}(iter)} = 2 \sum_{k_1=1}^{N} \sum_{k_2=1}^{N} (\sum_{i=1}^{c}(u_{ik_1} \wedge u_{ik_2}) - p[k_1, k_2])\varphi[s, t, k_1, k_2] \quad (11.7)$$

11.3   Some illustrative examples

As a simple, yet highly illustrative example we consider a two-dimensional dataset, Fig. 11.2 and Table 1.

1	1.1
2.3	1.8
2.1	2.2
2.6	1.9
5.7	6.1
4.8	5.5
5.1	4.9
9.1	9.7
9.4	10
10	9.5
9.5	9.8
9.9	10

Table 1. Two-dimensional data set

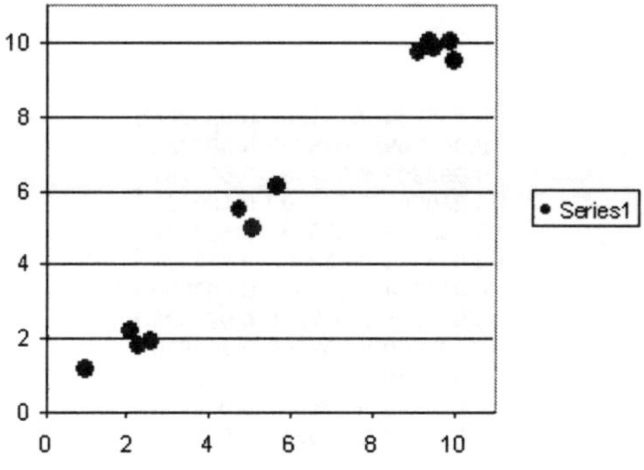

Fig. 11.2   Related graphical representation

(a) The structure is self-evident: we can easily identify three clusters; by looking at Fig. 11.2 we note that patterns {1, 2, 3, 4} form the first cluster, while the second cluster is formed by 5, 6, 7. The rest of the patterns, 8, 9,

10,11, 12 build the third cluster. The results of the standard FCM quantifies our observation. For c = 3 we obtain three clearly distinguishable clusters described by the following partition matrix

$$
\begin{bmatrix}
0.952520 & 0.038084 & 0.009395 \\
0.995613 & 0.003693 & 0.000694 \\
0.988632 & 0.009640 & 0.001728 \\
0.978916 & 0.017923 & 0.003161 \\
0.018723 & 0.960182 & 0.021095 \\
0.006886 & 0.989496 & 0.003618 \\
0.018021 & 0.974067 & 0.007912 \\
0.002099 & 0.007198 & 0.990703 \\
0.000587 & 0.001888 & 0.997525 \\
0.002142 & 0.006752 & 0.991106 \\
0.000052 & 0.000169 & 0.999779 \\
0.001093 & 0.003341 & 0.995566
\end{bmatrix}
$$

and the prototypes located at the centers of these clusters, that is $\mathbf{v}_1 = [2.02\ 1.76]$, $\mathbf{v}_2 = [5.19\ 5.49]$ and $\mathbf{v}_3 = [9.57\ 9.80]$. These results are not surprising at all.

(b) Now let us consider that three patterns are linked and the proximities are given for two pairs of patterns, namely (6 9 0.6) and (5 4 0.7). These two proximities indicate that patterns 6 and 9 are related quite strongly (at the level of 0.6). A similar effect happens to the pair (5, 4). The learning is completed for α=0.05 for 30 iterations. The resulting partition matrix has the entries

$$
\begin{bmatrix}
0.815730 & 0.151003 & 0.033266 \\
0.943769 & 0.048793 & 0.007437 \\
0.962309 & 0.032901 & 0.004791 \\
0.250000 & 0.250000 & 0.500000 \\
0.333333 & 0.333333 & 0.333333 \\
0.333333 & 0.333333 & 0.333333 \\
0.017614 & 0.975387 & 0.007000 \\
0.008718 & 0.017956 & 0.973325 \\
0.500000 & 0.250000 & 0.250000 \\
0.019438 & 0.038529 & 0.942033 \\
0.014405 & 0.028845 & 0.956749 \\
0.023423 & 0.045394 & 0.931182
\end{bmatrix}
$$

The prototypes are equal to $\mathbf{v}_1 = [2.76\ 2.74]$, $\mathbf{v}_2 = [5.15\ 5.09]$, and $\mathbf{v}_3 = [8.95\ 9.06]$. What becomes quite visible from the partition matrix is a change in the revealed structure; because of the proximity constraints the second cluster (the one involving patterns 4, 5 and 6) is "destroyed" and the patterns are no longer identified with high membership grades.

prototypes –

2.766809   2.747653

5.148547   5.093493

8.952405   9.065768

(c) Let us consider the set of proximity constraints: (1 10 0.7), (2 12 0.9), (5 3 1), (2 3 0.1), (5 6 0.0). It is noticeable that patterns 1 and 10 are very similar; the same happens for 2 and 12. Likewise patterns 5 and 3 are put in the same group. The two patterns, 2 and 3, whose geometric similarity is quite high are considered to be disjoint with regard to the proximity. The resulting partition matrix is equal to

$$\begin{bmatrix} 0.250000 & 0.500000 & 0.250000 \\ 0.216394 & 0.563724 & 0.219882 \\ 0.487244 & 0.259879 & 0.252878 \\ 0.555156 & 0.066086 & 0.378758 \\ 0.487545 & 0.259394 & 0.253061 \\ 0.000000 & 0.000000 & 1.000000 \\ 0.247161 & 0.007887 & 0.744952 \\ 0.034209 & 0.924941 & 0.040849 \\ 0.049668 & 0.891651 & 0.058681 \\ 0.333333 & 0.333333 & 0.333333 \\ 0.045453 & 0.900899 & 0.053648 \\ 0.390388 & 0.219224 & 0.390388 \end{bmatrix}$$

The prototypes are $\mathbf{v}_1 = [4.75\ 4.61]$, $\mathbf{v}_2 = [7.83\ 8.15]$, and $\mathbf{v}_3 = [5.15\ 5.36]$. It is noticeable that the first cluster does not have any profound representative; the highest membership value in the first column is 0.55.

(d) Now consider the following proximity constraints: (1 2 0.1), (9 10 0.4), (5 3 1), (6 8 0.8), (5 6 0.0). The gradient-based learning leads to oscillations; to dampen them we reduce the learning rate to 0.01. This leads to the results

$$\begin{bmatrix} 0.135113 & 0.817769 & 0.047118 \\ 1.000000 & 0.000000 & 0.000000 \\ 0.467040 & 0.446195 & 0.086765 \\ 0.632342 & 0.362025 & 0.005632 \\ 0.478827 & 0.453825 & 0.067348 \\ 0.253063 & 0.253063 & 0.493873 \\ 0.417849 & 0.488535 & 0.093616 \\ 0.173759 & 0.208402 & 0.617839 \\ 0.000000 & 0.000000 & 1.000000 \\ 0.007163 & 0.007502 & 0.985335 \\ 0.001086 & 0.001142 & 0.997771 \\ 0.005370 & 0.005630 & 0.989000 \end{bmatrix}$$

prototypes: $\mathbf{v}_1 = [3.09\ 2.79]$, $\mathbf{v}_2 = [2.92\ 2.98]$, $\mathbf{v}_3 = [9.35\ 9.55]$. As a result of optimization, we learn that some bonding between the patterns is stronger than the direction of weak proximity constraint imposed on them. This effect is profoundly visible in case of the pair 9-10 (refer to the partition matrix). It is instructive to note an effect of the proximity constraints on the boundaries between the clusters (they are built in a usual manner by identifying regions in the input space where a membership grade to the given cluster is the highest). We learn, Fig. 11.3, that these boundaries

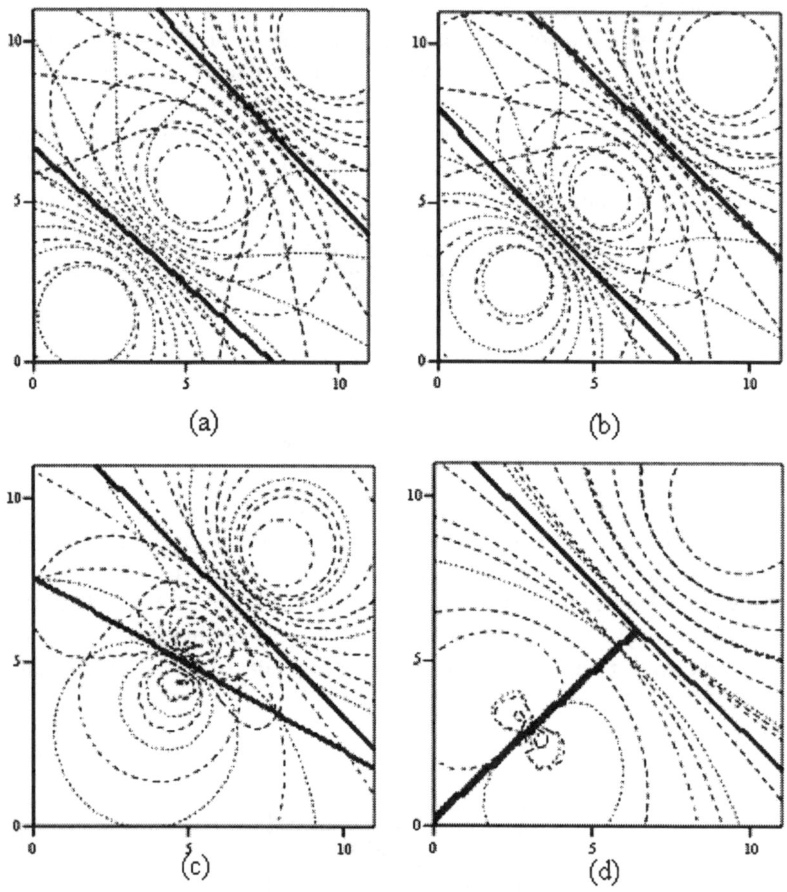

Fig. 11.3   Boundaries between clusters for the discussed collections of the proximity constraints - (a) visualizes the case without any proximity information, cases (b) - (d) involve the proximity constraints discussed above.

vary significantly depending upon the collections of the proximities. This underlines that they exhibit a direct impact on the geometry of the clusters and their potential classification characteristics.

11.4   Benchmark

Our test activity is applied to web pages classified by ODP (Open Directory Project, http://www.dmoz.org informally known as Dmoz, e.g. Mozilla Di-

Table 11.1   Selected keywords chosen as features of data set

Category	*Selected Keywords*
Top:Computers:Education	learn*, teach*, computer, knowledge, tutor*, howto, software.
Top:Computer:Software:Retailers	retail*, business, sell, product, software
Top:Reference:Education:Distance_Learning	learn*, distance, software, online, guide

rectory); it is a open web database, widely distributed, classified by volunteer force of more 8000 editors.

Our testbed are based on web pages extracted from three ODP categories:

(1) Top:Computers:Education
     http://www.dmoz.com/Computers/Education
(2) Top:Computer:Software:Retailers
     http://www.dmoz.com/Computers/Software/Retailers
(3) Top:Reference:Education:Distance_Learning
     http://www.dmoz.com/Reference/Education/Distance_Learning

For each category, Dmoz gives a descriptive web page, explaining the arguments related to the category. Through the analysis of these pages, we extracted some keywords that seem to represent good candidate to became terms of the feature space. Table 11.1 shows keywords used in this case study, associated with each category.

The real set of terms (the feature space) is compound of 15 words. Some keywords appear in more of one category: we stress the classification algorithm to prove its performance to distinguish different typologies of pages. For some keywords we apply the stemming technique, to consider all the words with common prefix, too.

Each web page is represented as a 15-dimensional vector, where each component is a normalized value given by the frequency of occurrence of the term in the page. Although in our approach the features can be keywords, hyperlinks, images, animations, etc., in this experiment we consider just keyword-based features, in order to be compliant with Dmoz static classification, based on term-frequency analysis. Our test has been performed on 30 web pages per category, for an amount of 90 pages. As first step we applied a standard FCM algorithm on the 90 pages considering three clusters (Fig. 11.4).

The Fig. 11.4 shows the distribution of membership grades of the Web pages in each cluster: the figure is divided in four parts: initially shows the overall FCM distribution, then separated clusters representations are

Table 11.2   User's evaluation of proximity between some Web pages

Pages (couple)		Proximity
4	23	0.9
4	25	0.8
4	43	0.1
4	79	0.1
25	36	0.1
36	19	0.2
14	15	0.9
65	26	0.2
12	8	0.8
28	4	0.9
82	30	0.1
30	14	0.9
13	65	0.1
6	42	0.1
25	42	0.1
8	15	0.1

evidenced (by a line joins all cluster's points); we can observe that the page 31-60 are wholly in right cluster (cluster 1 in the figure); instead some problem arise in the valuation of first 30 pages (representing by the cluster 3), where the membership grades not higher than the others (especially if compared with membership distribution of cluster 3). Last 30 pages (61-90) belong to cluster 2, as shown their distribution. The worst classification is verified for the cluster 3; in particular there are some pages that are completely out of this cluster: for example pages 6 has highest membership in the cluster 1; in the same way, pages 13, 25 are better represented as pages respectively of clusters 2 and 1 (in the figure they are highest value in the first 30 pages). In order to improve the classification of web pages, we insert some proximity values (see Table 11.2) and valuate obtained results. Anyway we can not insert some values of proximity for the atypical pages as 6, 13, while we give some proximity values for the page 25 (it is similar to page 4 and dissimilar to page 42) in the cluster 3; in fact, from a more scrupulous analysis, we observe that some pages are different if compared with to other pages of the same category:

page 6: http://www.learnlots.com/ is a site that provides customer service and knowledge management software;

page 13: http://cadtechseminars.com/ presents some seminaries for Auto-CAD application;

page 25: http://207.21.245.66/RHSGroup/DesktopDefault.aspx is a site on software developer's Resource for Training.

As shown in Fig. 11.5, it is evident that some pages improve their membership in the right cluster: the average membership of cluster 3 is increased, the pages belonged to cluster 1 (black line) are strongly enclosed in the right cluster and a rather similar situation is presented for the cluster 2. We can note the web page 25 decreases the membership in the wrong cluster: now it appears in cluster 1 with membership 0.474383, against 0.56004, the value in the same cluster of FCM distribution (see Fig. 11.4) while web pages as 6, 13 do not improve very considerable their membership in this cluster.

In many real life cases the user may disagree with a textual Web search classification: in our test, this situation may occur since the categorization has been realized considering only textual information and no other media have been taken into consideration. Automatic user model can be used in this kind of approach: customized classification can be realized to reflect the user preferences and interests.

For example, let us suppose the user's intention is to assert that some pages classified in the category Top:Computer:Education are, according personal judgment, different. In fact, Fig. 11.6 represents this situation: the user asserts that pages 16 and 17 are different, because the first one deals with information about computer schools while the second page represents a course about the art management. So his feedback contribute to classification is a proximity measure 0.1 between pages 16 and 17. At the same way the user appraises the pages 27 and 68, shown in Fig. 11.6, belonged to different categories, are close: he assesses that they are inherent the same topic, in fact both of them are pages of sites propose educational and tutoring approach. In the following the Table 11.3 shows the proximity value given in input to P-FCM algorithm and the Fig. 11.7 represents the correspondent classification results

The Fig. 11.7 shows the clusterization after the P-FCM, with the proximity values, given in the table 11.3: it can observe the pages 16 and 17 are in different clusters; in fact the page 17 changes its cluster: now it strongly belongs to cluster 2; on the other side, the pages 27 and 68 (whose proximity value is high in the table 11.3), although by the DMOZ classification they are in two different categories, now they are in the same cluster (cluster2), as shown in the figure. Fig. 11.8 represents the same classification results, where an analogous situation is better evidenced for pages 18 and 19, 77 and 78, 4 and 8. Some proximity values given by user do not strongly impact on the classification distribution, expecially for web pages in the category Top:Computer:Software:Retailers; here the pages have a distribution forcefully enclosed in their cluster, so the influence of user's evaluation is not relevant.

Table 11.3 Proximity values
between some Web pages

Pages (couple)		Proximity
77	78	0.0
77	53	0.9
55	61	0.9
16	17	0.1
84	20	0.9
89	75	0.1
68	70	0.1
18	19	0.1
34	35	0.1
53	54	0.1
8	4	0.0
27	68	0.9
27	23	0.0
27	34	0.0

11.5 Related Works

Today web search engine are able to return ranked list of relevant documents, in response to keyword-based queries, but most of results may not
be valuable to a user: which documents are useful depends on the context
of the query, but sometimes the results for a given request are identical,
independent of the user or the context in which the user made the request
[Lawrence (2000)]. A remarkable progress could be to realize a complete
personalization of searching activity that is aware of previous user's request
and interests, and uses that information in order to obtain a better model of
the users interests [Budzik and Hammond (2000)], [Budzik *et. al.* (2000)].
At the same time, advanced search engine technology can be a fundamental
key to appreciate how semantic information can be mined from the content and link based metrics. In this direction semantic mapping [Menczer
(2003)] are employed to define topological space on the Web. The semantic
maps envisage data collected from billions of pairs of Web pages and then
provide an estimation of relevance/similarity among web pages, comparing
the relative content and the context. A crucial issue is the selection of the
terms to include in the patter representing the Web page. Given P as a
generic Web page, many approaches follows these basic trends:

- content-based approach: in this case we treat the words appearing in
  P;
- link-based approach: the useful information of the document are the
  identifiers (for instance URLs) for each document linking to P;

- anchor-based approach: words appearing inside or near an anchor in a web page P', when the anchor links to P;

The first approach has been widely adopted since it can be easily implemented by applying a traditional text categorization method directly, based on term frequency. The typical text categorization process consists of the steps: lexical preprocessing of web pages, indexing of them to facilitate the data retrieval, dimensionality reduction of features space and finally classification. Anyway, clustering of web search results by taking account of some features of web page:

(1) Most web pages in search results usually are pages of introduction, top pages of web sites, which mean that they probably include some links and pictures instead of concrete contents, with consequence that the term-based clustering algorithms poorly works.
(2) Often Web pages are written in multiple languages, or in languages other than English, so term-based clustering algorithms are difficult to be applied to this kind of web pages.
(3) Ignoring the hyperlink feature leads to various drawbacks, in particular a pure content-based technique reveals very sensible to spam.

Considering hyperlinks in Web pages is an interesting technique that has been explored in different works [Dean and Herzinger (1999); Chakrabarti *et. al.* (1998); Oh *et. al.* (2000)]. The base idea is simple: pages that share common links each other are very likely to be tightly related. In general the links in Web pages are divided into two types: links of inter-site and links of intra-site. The difference we treat these information specifies the contextuality of the page, an important notion that recently is assuming a relevant role in Web page categorization [Attardi *et. al.* (1998) ; Loia and Luongo (2001); Kwon and Lee (2003)].

About the third approach, known also as "anchor-window" technique [Chakrabarti *et. al.* (1998)], it appears very useful for similarity-search task since anchor-based information represents a hand-built summary of the target Web page. By analysis of the text surrounding the link, a short phrase or sentence they provide hints as to what might be found on the target page. Extracting the anchors to a web document from the documents pointing at it could be indicative of the content of the target web documents, to give succinct descriptions of the page [Amitay (1998); Haveliwala *et. al.* (2000)].

The role played by semantic map combined with term selection, as approximated by textual similarity, is estimably present in the Web, and provides a background environment on which various web systems, including search engines [Lawrence and Giles (1999)], focused crawlers [Chakrabarti *et. al.* (1999)] and intelligent web agents [Menczer and Belew (1999)] are based.

11.6   Conclusion

Clustering, or grouping sets of related pages, is one of the crucial web-related information-retrieval problems. In order to guarantee appropriate clustering of web search results, some features can be required [Zamir and Etzioni (1998)]:

- Relevance: Clustering should separate related web pages from irrelevant ones.
- Overlap: One web page could belong to more than one cluster since it could have more than one topic.
- Incrementally: In order for speed, clustering procedure should start to process one page as soon as it arrives instead of waiting all information available.

Sometime these requirements are not simple to reach, or in worst case, there is no guarantee to obtain accurate web classification; unfortunately, most of clustering activities consider a fixed threshold for resemblance, forcing to decide in advance if some documents are included in the clusters. Recently, the approaches to web clustering can be nearly divided into two topologies: 1) offline clustering, in which the entire web crawl information is used to precomputed sets of pages that are related according to some metric and 2) online clustering, in which clustering is built on the results of search queries, according to given topic. Anyway the web situation is continuously changing, so it is not possible to characterize a universally better searching paradigm. The need to further enrich the user interaction during Web navigation is characterizing the design of recent web-based systems. Our approach aims to reach this goal, focusing on effect and the impact of users feedback on Web page categories: the system can modeled information according users preference and knowledge so to provide a better tailor classification of web pages. The P-FCM approach intends to give the users a fundamental role contributing to add useful, personal information to categorization of Web pages. Ultimately, the challenge is that it possible to have so many options to take into account around web searching activities that both the user and the search engines can get really overwhelmed of a cognitive and operative overhead.

11.7   Acknowledgments

Support from the Natural Sciences and Engineering Research Council of Canada (NSERC) is gratefully acknowledged.

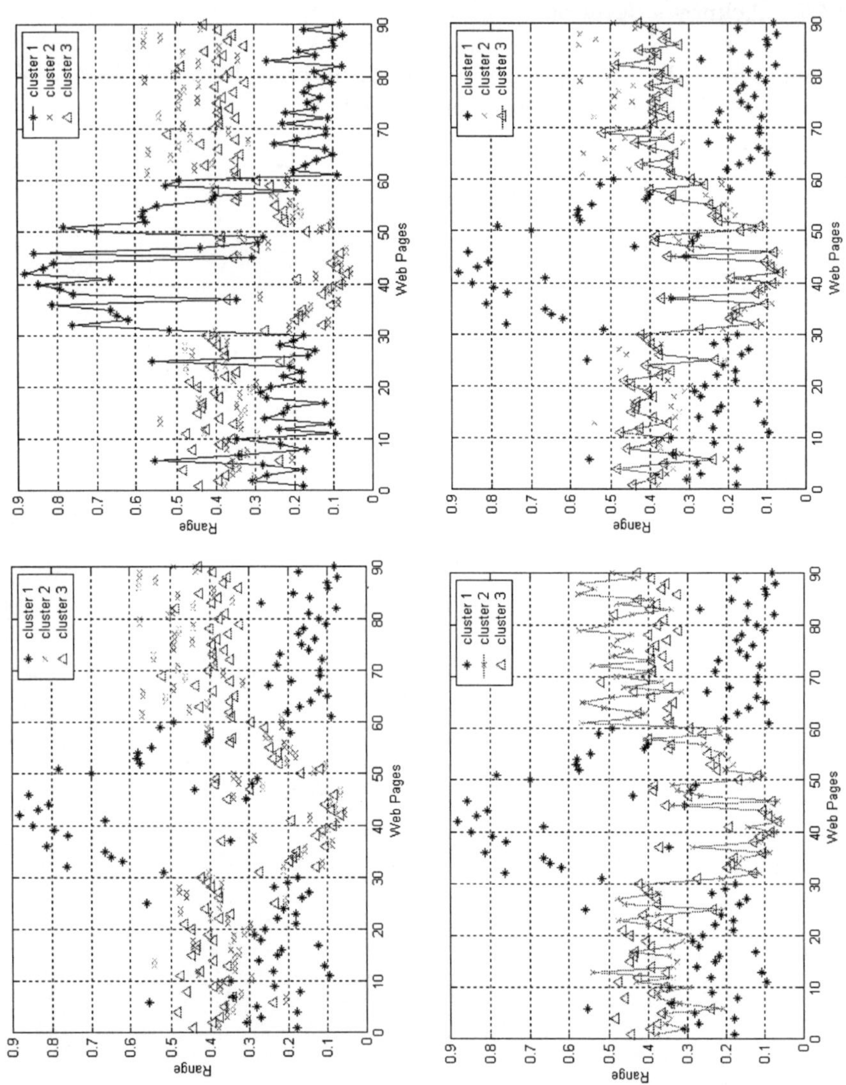

Fig. 11.4   FCM classification of web pages with evidenced single cluster representation

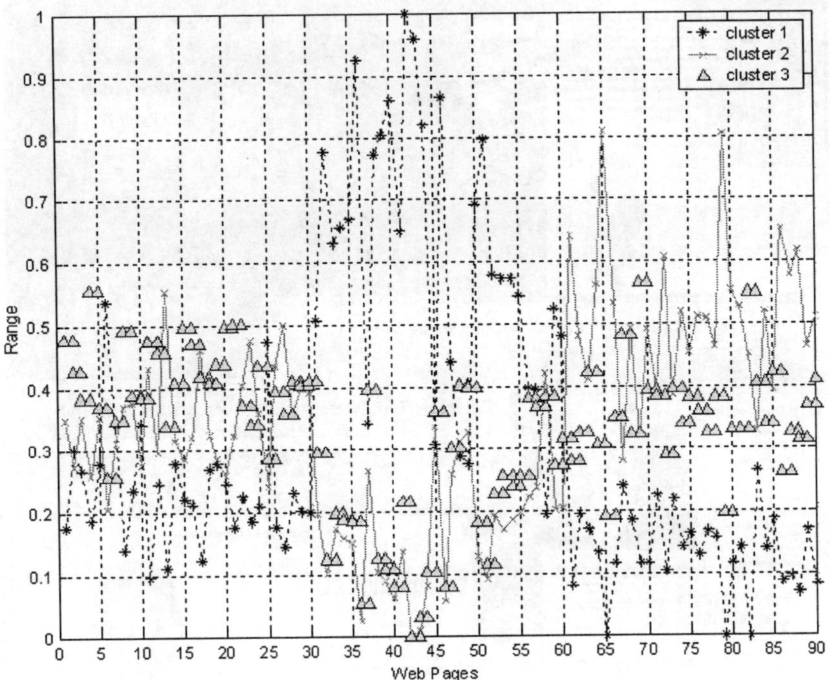

Fig. 11.5   The results of the P-FCM clustering

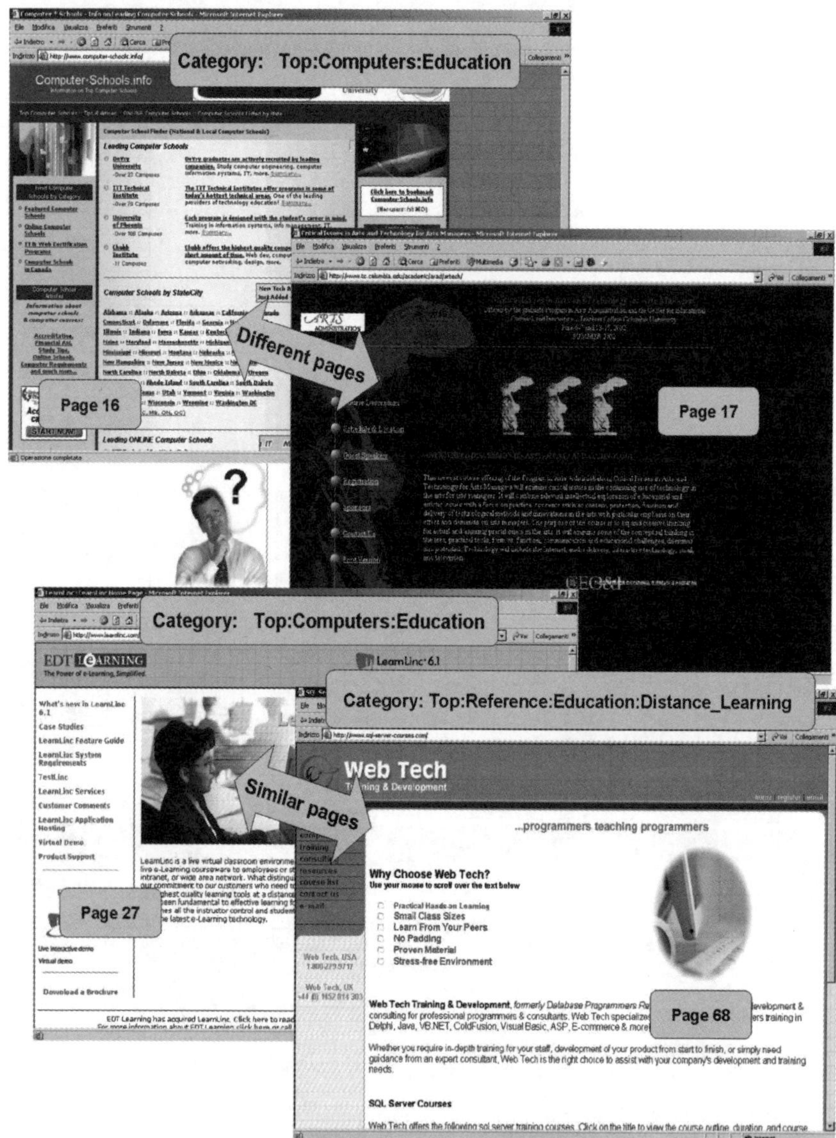

Fig. 11.6   User's assessment about two pages of the same/different category

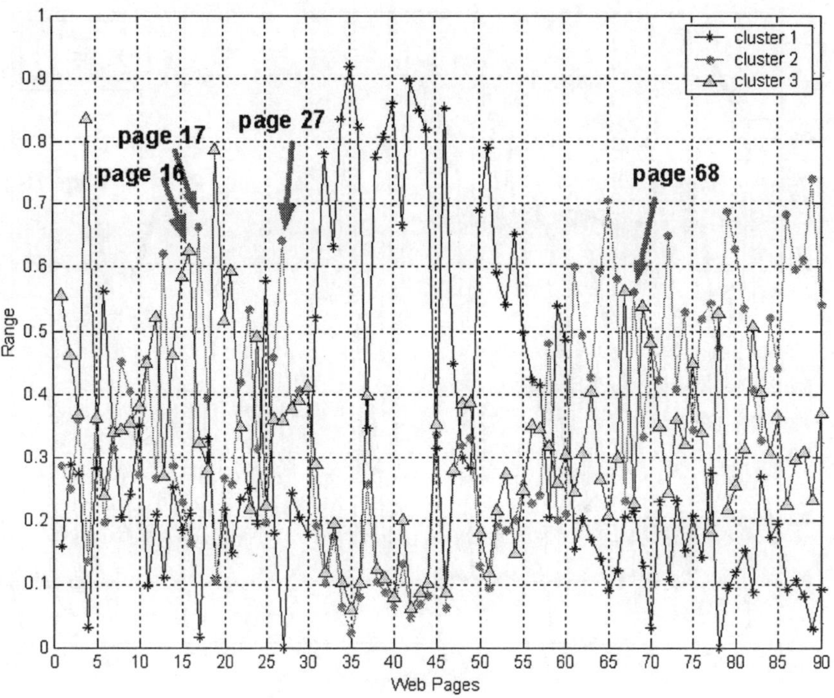

Fig. 11.7   The results of P-FCM clustering:

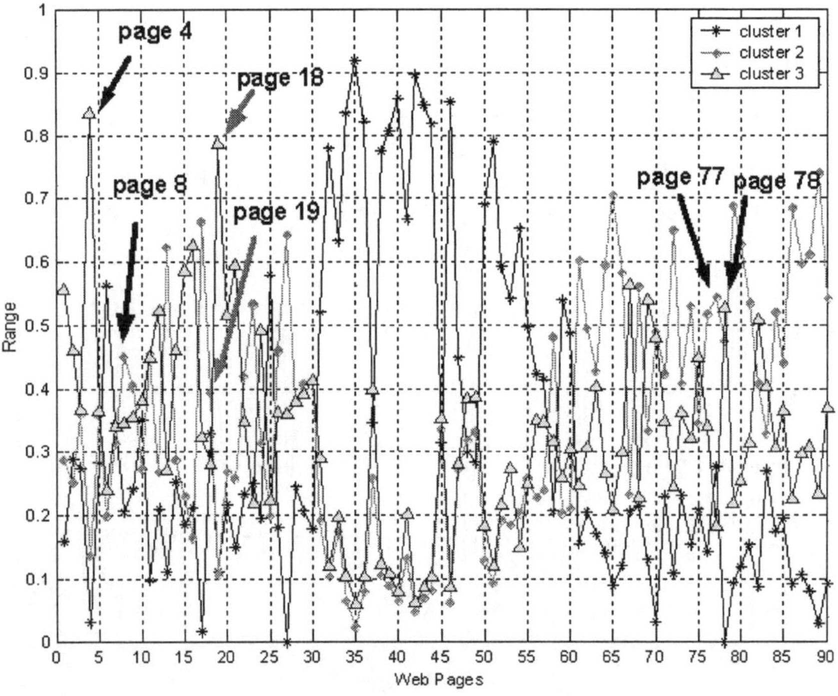

Fig. 11.8   The effect of P-FCM clustering: similar pages change classification

Bibliography

Amitay E. Using common hypertext links to identify the best phrasal description of target web documents. In *SIGIR'98 Post-Conference Workshop on Hypertext Information Retrieval for the Web*, Melbourne, Australia, 1998.

Attardi, G., Di Marco S., and Salvi, D. Categorisation by context. *Journal of Universal Compouter Science*, 4:719–736, 1998.

Bezdek, J.C. *Pattern Recognition and Fuzzy Objective Function Algorithms*. Plenum Press, N. York, 1981.

Brusilovsky P. Methods and techniques of adaptive hypermedia. *User Modeling and User*, 6(2-3):87–129, 1996.

Budzik J.,Hammond K.J. . User interactions with everyday applications as context for just-in-time information access. In ACM Press, editor, *Proceedings of the 2000 International Conference on Intelligent User Interfaces*, New Orleans, Louisiana, 2000.

Budzik J.,Hammond K.J., Birnbaum L., Krema M. Beyond similarity. In AAAI Press, editor, *Proceedings of the 2000 Workshop on Artificial Intelligence and Web Search*, 2000.

Chakrabarti S., Dom B. E., Indyk P. Enhanced by hypertext categorization using hyperlyinks. In *Proccedings of ACM Knowledge discovery and data mining (KDD'98)*, pages 169–173, New York, USA, 1998.

Chakrabarti S., Dom B. E., Ravaghan P., Rajagopalan S., Gibson D. and Kleinberg, J. Automatic resource compilation by analyzing hyperlink structure and associated text. In *Proceedings of WWW7*, 1998.

Chakrabarti S., van den Berg M., Dom B. E. Focused crawling: a new approach to topic-specific web resouce descovery. In *Proccedings of Seventh International Word Wide web Conference*, Toronto, Canada, May 1999.

Dean J. and Herzinger M. Finding Related Pages in the World Wide Web. In *Proceedings of WWW8*, 1999.

Edwards D.M., Hardman L. Lost in cyberspace: Cognitive mapping and navigation in a hypertext environment. In *R. McAleese Hypertext: Theory into practice*, chapter 7. Ablex Publishing Corporation, New Jersey, 1989.

Hoppner F. Fuzzy shell clustering in image processing - fuzzy c-rectangular and two rectangular shells. *IEEE Trans. on Fuzzy Systems*, vol.5, no.5:599–613, 1997.

Hathaway R.J., Bezdek J.C., Hu Y. Generalized fuzzy c-means clustering strategies using lp norm distances. *IEEE Trans. on Fuzzy Systems*, 8 no. 5:576–582, 2000.

Haveliwala T. H., Gionis A., Indyk P. Scalable Techniques for Clustering the Web. In *WebDB (Informal Proceedings)*, pages 129–134, 2000.

Hoppner F., Klawonn F., Kruse R., Runkler T. *Fuzzy Cluster Analysis – Methods for Image Recognition*. J. Wiley, N. York, 1999.

Jain A. K., Dubes R. C. *Algorithm for Clustering Data*. Prentice-Hall, 1988.

Johan B., Sompel H. and Rocha L. Mining associative relations from website logs and their application to context-dependent retrieval using spreading activation, 1999.

Kwon O., Lee J. Text categorization based on k-nearest neighbor approach for Web site classification. In *Information Processing and Management*, volume 39, pages 25–44, 2003.

Lawrence S. Context in Web Search. *IEEE Data Engineering Bulletin*, 23(3):25 32, 2000.

Lawrence S., Giles L. Accessibility and Distribution of Information on theWeb. In *Proceedings of The International Symposium on Language for Intensional Programming*, volume 400, pages 107–109. Nature, 1999.

Loia V., Luongo P. An Evolutionary Approach to Automatic Web Page Categorization and Updating. In *Proceedings of 2001 International Conference on Web Intelligence*, volume 2198 of *Lecture Notes in Artificial Intelligence*, pages 292–302, Maebashi City, Japan, October 23-26 2001. Springer.

Menczer F. Semi-Supervised Evaluation of Search Engines via Semantic Mapping. In *Proceedings of WWW2003*, Budapest, Hungary, 2003.

Menczer F., Belew R. K. Adaptive Retrieval Agents: Internalizing Local Context and Scaling up the Web. *Machine Learning*, pages 1–45, 1999.

Oh H. J., Myaeng S. H., Lee M. H. A practical hypertext categorization method using links and incrementally available class information. In *Proceedings of the 23rd annual international conference on Research and Development in Information Retrieval (SIGIR2000)*, pages 264–271, Athens, Greece, 2000.

Robins D. Interactive Information Retrieval: Context and Basic Notions. *Informing Science*, 3(2):57–62, 2000.

Runkler T. A., Bezdek J.C. Alternating cluster estimation: a new tool for clustering and function approximation. *IEEE Trans. on Fuzzy Systems*, 7 no. 4:377–393, 1999.

Zamir O., Etzioni O. Web document clustering: A feasibility demonstration. In *SIGIR 98*, Melbourne, Australia, 1998.

CHAPTER 12

WEB USAGE MINING: BUSINESS INTELLIGENCE FROM WEB LOGS

Ajith Abraham

Department of Computer Science, Oklahoma State University, USA
E-mail: ajith.abraham@ieee.org

Web usage mining attempts to discover useful knowledge from the secondary data obtained from the interactions of the users with the Web. Web usage mining has become very critical for effective Web site management, creating adaptive Web sites, business and support services, personalization, network traffic flow analysis and so on. This chapter presents a divide and conquer approach (*i-Miner*) to optimize the concurrent architecture of a fuzzy clustering algorithm (to discover web data clusters) and a fuzzy inference system to analyze the Web server traffic trends. A hybrid evolutionary fuzzy clustering algorithm is used to optimally segregate similar visitors. The clustered data is then used to analyze the trend patterns using a Takagi-Sugeno fuzzy inference system learned using a combination of evolutionary algorithm and neural network learning. Proposed approach is compared with other clustering and function approximation techniques. The results are graphically illustrated and the practical significance is discussed in detail. Empirical results clearly show that the proposed Web usage-mining framework is efficient.

12.1 Introduction

The WWW continues to grow at an amazing rate as an information gateway and as a medium for conducting business. Web mining is the extraction of interesting and useful knowledge and implicit information

229

from artifacts or activity related to the WWW [Cooley (2000); Kosala and Blockeel (2000)]. Based on several research studies we can broadly classify Web mining into three domains: content, structure and usage mining [Chakrabarti (2003); Chang *et. al.* (2001)].

Web servers record and accumulate data about user interactions whenever requests for resources are received. The rapid e-commerce growth has made both business community and customers face a new situation. Due to intense competition on one hand and the customer's option to choose from several alternatives business community has realized the necessity of intelligent marketing strategies and relationship management. Analyzing the Web access logs can help understand the user behavior and the web structure. From the business and applications point of view, knowledge obtained from the Web usage patterns could be directly applied to efficiently manage activities related to e-business, e-services, e-education and so on [Chen and Kuo (2000); Cheung *et. al.* (1997)].

Accurate Web usage information could help to attract new customers, retain current customers, improve cross marketing/sales, effectiveness of promotional campaigns, tracking leaving customers and find the most effective logical structure for their Web space [Heer and Chi (2001); Jespersen *et. al.* (2002)]. User profiles could be built by combining users' navigation paths with other data features, such as page viewing time, hyperlink structure, and page content [Cho et. al. (2003)]. What makes the discovered knowledge interesting had been addressed by several works [Hay *et. al.* (2003); Heinrichs and Lim (2003); Runkler and Bezdek (2003)]. Results previously known are very often considered as not interesting. So the key concept to make the discovered knowledge interesting will be its novelty or unexpectedness appearance [Aggarwal *et. al.* (1999); Agrawal and Srikant (1994); Coenen *et. al.* (2000); Nanopoulos *et. al.* (2002)].

A typical Web log format is depicted in Figure 12.1. When ever a visitor access the server it leaves the IP, authenticated user ID, time/date, request mode, status, bytes, referrer, agent and so on. The available data fields are specified by the HTTP protocol. There are several commercial software that could provide Web usage statistics [Analog, (2003)] [ClickTracks, (2003)] [Hitbox (2003); LogRover, (2003); Website Tracker, (2003); WebStat, (2003)]. These stats could be useful for Web administrators to get a sense of the actual load on the server. For small web servers, the usage statistics provided by conventional Web site trackers may be adequate to analyze the usage pattern and trends. However as the size and complexity of the data increases, the statistics provided by existing Web log file analysis tools may prove inadequate and more intelligent mining techniques will be necessary [Piramuthu (2003); Roussinov and Zhao (2003); Yang and Zhang (2003); Abraham (2003); Zhang and Dong (2003)].

```
64.68.82.66 - - [17/May/2003:03:41:23 -0500] "GET /marcin HTTP/1.0" 404 318
192.114.47.54 - - [17/May/2003:03:41:33 -0500] "GET /~aa/isda2002/isda2002.html HTTP/1.1" 404 350
216.239.37.5 - - [17/May/2003:03:41:43 -0500] "GET /~ijcr/Vols/vol10no1.html HTTP/1.0" 200 4568
218.244.111.106 - - [17/May/2003:03:41:51 -0500] "GET /~aa/his/ HTTP/1.1" 404 332
64.68.82.18 - - [17/May/2003:03:42:15 -0500] "GET /~pdcp/cfp/cfpBookReviews.html HTTP/1.0" 304 -
212.98.136.62 - - [17/May/2003:03:43:21 -0500] "GET /cs3373/programs/pgm03.dat HTTP/1.1" 200 498
212.98.136.62 - - [17/May/2003:03:43:26 -0500] "GET /cs3373/programs/pgm04.html HTTP/1.1" 200 55722
212.98.136.62 - - [17/May/2003:03:43:38 -0500] "GET /cs3373/images/WaTor.gif HTTP/1.1" 200 39021
212.29.232.2 - - [17/May/2003:03:43:40 -0500] "GET /welcome.html HTTP/1.0" 200 5253
```

Fig. 12.1. Sample entries from a Web server access log

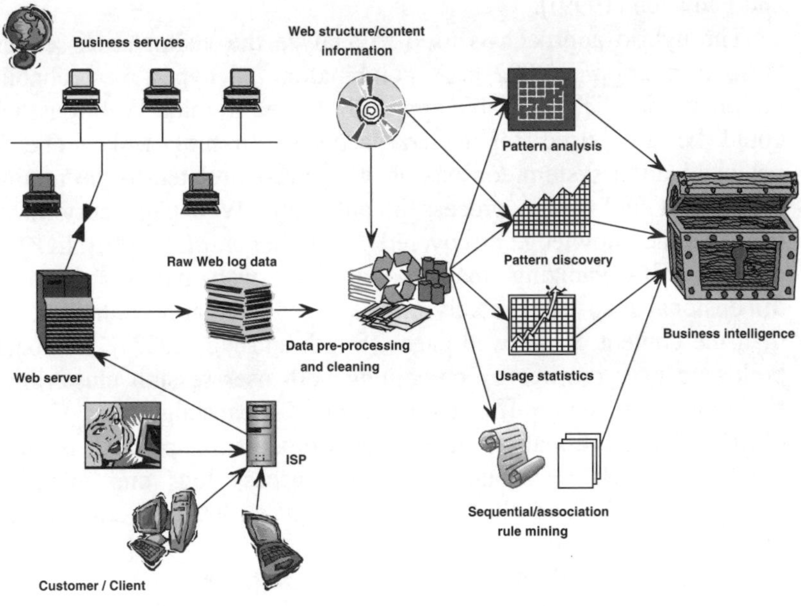

Fig. 12.2. Web usage mining framework

A generic Web usage-mining framework is depicted in Figure 12.2. In the case of Web mining, data could be collected at the server level, client level, proxy level or some consolidated data. These data could differ in terms of content and the way it is collected etc. The usage data collected at different sources represent the navigation patterns of different segments of the overall Web traffic, ranging from single user, single site browsing behavior to multi-user, multi-site access patterns. As evident from Figure 12.2, Web server log does not accurately contain sufficient information for inferring the behavior at the client side as they relate to the pages served by the Web server. Pre-processed and cleaned data could be used for pattern discovery, pattern analysis, Web usage statistics and generating association/ sequential rules [Kitsuregawa *et. al.* (2002)]; Masseglia *et. al.* (1999); Pal *et. al.* (2002)]. Much work has been performed on extracting various pattern information from Web logs and the application of the discovered knowledge range from improving the design and structure of a Web site to enabling business organizations to function more efficiently [Paliouras *et. al.* (2000); Pazzani and Billsus (1997); Perkowitz and Etzioni (1998); Pirolli *et. al.* (1996); Spiliopoulou and Faulstich (1999)].

The hybrid approach is used to analyze the visitor click sequences [Jespersen *et. al.* (2002)]. A combination of hypertext probabilistic grammar and click fact table approach is used to mine Web logs, which could be also used for general sequence mining tasks. The Web personalization system consists of offline tasks related to the mining of usage data and online process of automatic Web page customization based on the knowledge discovered [Mobasher *et. al.* (1999)]. LOGSOM utilizes self-organizing map to organize web pages into a two-dimensional map based solely on the users' navigation behavior, rather than the content of the web pages [Smith and Ng (2003)]. LumberJack builds up user profiles by combining both user session clustering and traditional statistical traffic analysis using K-means algorithm [Chi *et. al.* (2002)]. The relational online analytical processing approach is used for creating a Web log warehouse using access logs and mined logs (association rules and clusters) [Joshi *et. al.* (1999)]. A comprehensive overview of Web usage mining research is found in [Cooley (2000; Kosala and Blockeel (2000); Srivastava *et. al.* (2000)].

To demonstrate the efficiency of the proposed frameworks, Web access log data at the Monash University's Web site [Monash (2003)] were used for experimentations. The University's central web server receives over 7 million hits in a week and therefore it is a real challenge to find and extract hidden usage pattern information. Average daily and hourly access patterns for 5 weeks (11 August'02 – 14 September'02) are shown in Figures 12.3 and 12.4 respectively. The average daily and hourly patterns even though tend to follow a similar trend (as evident from the figures) the periodic differences tend to increase during high traffic days (Monday – Friday) and during the peak hours (11:00-17:00 Hrs). Due to the enormous traffic volume and chaotic access behavior, the prediction of the user access patterns becomes more difficult and complex. Web data is first clustered using an evolutionary fuzzy clustering algorithm. The clustered data is then used to analyze the trends using a Takagi-Sugeno fuzzy inference system learned using a combination of evolutionary algorithm and neural network learning. Proposed approach is compared with self-organizing maps (to discover patterns) and several function approximation techniques like neural networks, linear genetic programming and Takagi-Sugeno fuzzy inference system (to analyze the clusters).

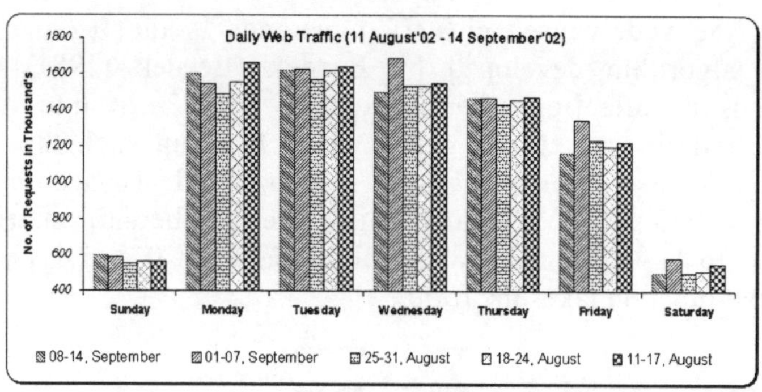

Fig. 12.3. University's daily Web traffic pattern for 5 weeks

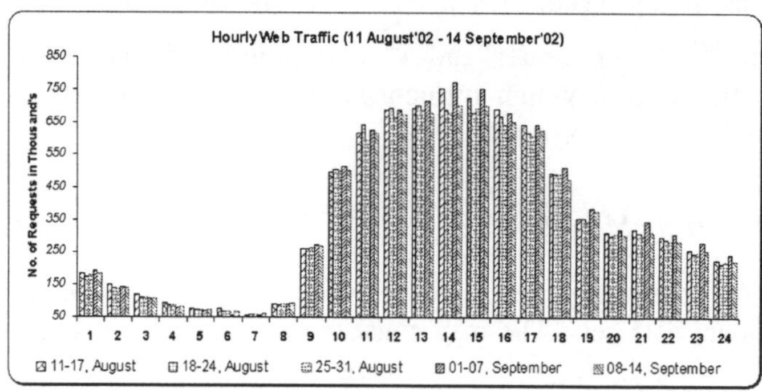

Fig. 12.4. Average hourly Web traffic patterns for 5 weeks

Experimental results have clearly shown the importance of the clustering algorithm to analyze the user access trends [Wang et. al. (2002)]. In the subsequent section, we present some theoretical concepts of clustering algorithms and various computational intelligence paradigms. Experimental results are provided in Section 12.3 and some conclusions are provided towards the end.

12.2. Mining Framework Using Hybrid Computational Intelligence Paradigms (CI)

12.2.1 *Clustering Algorithms for Segregating Similar Visitors*

Fuzzy Clustering Algorithm

One of the widely used clustering methods is the fuzzy c-means (FCM) algorithm developed by Bezdek [Bezdek (1981)]. FCM partitions a collection of n vectors x_i, $i= 1,2...,n$ into c fuzzy groups and finds a cluster center in each group such that a cost function of dissimilarity measure is minimized. To accommodate the introduction of fuzzy partitioning, the membership matrix U is allowed to have elements with values between 0 and 1.The FCM objective function takes the form

$$J\ (U,c_1,...c_c) = \sum_{i=1}^{c} J_i = \sum_{i=1}^{c}\sum_{j=1}^{n} u_{ij}^m d_{ij}^2 \tag{1}$$

Where u_{ij}, is a numerical value between [0,1]; c_i is the cluster center of fuzzy group i; $d_{ij} = \|c_i - x_j\|$ is the Euclidian distance between i^{th} cluster center and j^{th} data point; and m *is* called the exponential weight which influences the degree of fuzziness of the membership (partition) matrix.

Self Organizing Map (SOM)

The SOM is an algorithm used to visualize and interpret large high-dimensional data sets. The map consists of a regular grid of processing units, "neurons". A model of some multidimensional observation, eventually a vector consisting of features, is associated with each unit. The map attempts to represent all the available observations with optimal accuracy using a restricted set of models. At the same time the models become ordered on the grid so that similar models are close to each other and dissimilar models far from each other.

Fitting of the model vectors is usually carried out by a sequential regression process, where $t = 1,2,...$ is the step index: For each sample $x(t)$, first the winner index c (best match) is identified by the condition

$$\forall_i, \|x(t) - m_c(t)\| \le \|x(t) - m_i(t)\| \tag{2}$$

After that, all model vectors or a subset of them that belong to nodes centered around node $c = c(x)$ are updated as

$$m_i(t+1) = m_i(t) + h_{c(x),i}(x(t) - m_i(t)) \tag{3}$$

Here $h_{c(x),i}$ is the neighborhood function, a decreasing function of the distance between the ith and c^{th} nodes on the map grid. This regression is usually reiterated over the available samples.

12.2.2 *Computational Intelligence (CI) for Analysis of Visitor Trends*

CI substitutes intensive computation for insight into how complicated systems work. Artificial neural networks, fuzzy inference systems, probabilistic computing, evolutionary computation etc were all shunned by classical system and control theorists. CI provides an excellent framework unifying them and even by incorporating other revolutionary methods.

Artificial Neural Network (ANN)

ANNs were designed to mimic the characteristics of the biological neurons in the human brain and nervous system. Learning typically occurs by example through training, where the training algorithm iteratively adjusts the connection weights (synapses). Backpropagation (BP) is one of the most famous training algorithms for multilayer perceptrons. BP is a gradient descent technique to minimize the error E for a particular training pattern. For adjusting the weight (w_{ij}) from the ith input unit to the jth output, in the batched mode variant the descent is based on the gradient ∇E ($\dfrac{\delta E}{\delta w_{ij}}$) for the total training set

$$\Delta w_{ij}(n) = -\varepsilon^* \frac{\delta E}{\delta w_{ij}} + \alpha^* \Delta w_{ij}(n-1)$$

(4)

The gradient gives the direction of error E. The parameters ε and α are the learning rate and momentum respectively.

Linear Genetic Programming (LGP)

Linear genetic programming is a variant of the GP technique that acts on linear genomes [Banzhaf et. al. (1998)]. Its main characteristic when compared to tree-based GP lies in that the evolvable units are not the expressions of a functional programming language (like LISP), but the programs of an imperative language (like c/c ++). An alternate approach is to evolve a computer program at the machine code level, using lower level representations for the individuals. This can tremendously hasten up the evolution process as, no matter how an individual is initially represented, finally it always has to be represented as a piece of machine code, as fitness evaluation requires physical execution of the individuals. The basic unit of evolution here is a native machine code instruction that runs on the floating-point processor unit (FPU). Since different instructions may have different sizes, here instructions are clubbed up together to form instruction blocks of 32 bits each. The instruction blocks hold one or more native machine code instructions, depending on the sizes of the instructions. A crossover point can occur only between instructions and is prohibited from occurring within an instruction. However the mutation operation does not have any such restriction.

Fuzzy Inference Systems (FIS)

Fuzzy logic provides a framework to model uncertainty, human way of thinking, reasoning and the perception process. Fuzzy *if-then* rules and fuzzy reasoning are the backbone of fuzzy inference systems, which are the most important modelling tools based on fuzzy set theory. We made use of the Takagi Sugeno fuzzy inference scheme in which the conclusion of a fuzzy rule is constituted by a weighted linear combination of the crisp inputs rather than a fuzzy set [Takagi and Sugeno, (1985)]. In our experiments we optimized the fuzzy inference system using the Adaptive Network Based Fuzzy Inference System

(ANFIS) [Jang (1992)] and EvoNF framework [Abraham (2002)], which implements a Takagi Sugeno fuzzy inference system.

Optimization of Fuzzy Clustering Algorithm

Usually a number of cluster centers are randomly initialized and the FCM algorithm provides an iterative approach to approximate the minimum of the objective function starting from a given position and leads to any of its local minima. No guarantee ensures that FCM converges to an optimum solution (can be trapped by local extrema in the process of optimizing the clustering criterion). The performance is very sensitive to initialization of the cluster centers. An evolutionary algorithm is used to decide the optimal number of clusters and their cluster centers. The algorithm is initialized by constraining the initial values to be within the space defined by the vectors to be clustered. A very similar approach is given in [Hall et. al. (2001)].

Optimization of Fuzzy Inference System

We used the EvoNF framework [Abraham (2002)], which is an integrated computational framework to optimize fuzzy inference system using neural network learning and evolutionary computation. Solving multi-objective scientific and engineering problems is, generally, a very difficult goal. In these particular optimization problems, the objectives often conflict across a high-dimension problem space and may also require extensive computational resources. The hierarchical evolutionary search framework could adapt the membership functions (shape and quantity), rule base (architecture), fuzzy inference mechanism (T-norm and T-conorm operators) and the learning parameters of neural network learning algorithm [Abraham (2001)]. In addition to the evolutionary learning (global search) neural network learning could be considered as a local search technique to optimize the parameters of the rule antecedent/consequent parameters and the parameterized fuzzy operators. The hierarchical search could be formulated as follows:

For every fuzzy inference system, there exist a global search of neural network learning algorithm parameters, parameters of the fuzzy operators, *if-then* rules and membership functions in an environment decided by the problem. The evolution of the fuzzy inference system will evolve at the slowest time scale while the evolution of the quantity and type of membership functions will evolve at the fastest rate. The function of the other layers could be derived similarly. Hierarchy of the different adaptation layers (procedures) will rely on the prior knowledge (this will also help to reduce the search space). For example, if we know certain fuzzy operators will work well for a problem then it is better to implement the search of fuzzy operators at a higher level. For fine-tuning the fuzzy inference system all the node functions are to be parameterized. For example, the Schweizer and Sklar's T-norm operator can be expressed as:

$$T(a,b,p) = \left[\max \left\{ 0, (a^{-p} + b^{-p} - 1) \right\} \right]^{-\frac{1}{p}} \tag{5}$$

It is observed that

$$\lim_{p \to 0} T(a,b,p) = ab$$
$$\lim_{p \to \infty} T(a.b,p) = \min\{a,b\} \tag{6}$$

which correspond to two of the most frequently used T-norms in combining the membership values on the premise part of a fuzzy *if-then* rule.

12.2.3 *Mining Framework Using Intelligent Miner (i-Miner)*

The hybrid framework optimizes a fuzzy clustering algorithm using an evolutionary algorithm and a Takagi-Sugeno fuzzy inference system using a combination of evolutionary algorithm and neural network learning. The raw data from the log files are cleaned and pre-processed and a fuzzy C means algorithm is used to identify the number of clusters. The developed clusters of data are fed to a Takagi-Sugeno fuzzy inference system to analyze the trend patterns. The *if-then* rule structures are learned using an iterative learning procedure [Cordón et. al. (2001)] by an evolutionary algorithm and the rule parameters are fine-tuned using a backpropagation algorithm.

Architecture of *i-Miner* is depicted in Figure 12.5. The hierarchical computational framework of *i-Miner* is further illustrated in Figure 12.6. The arrow direction depicts the speed of the evolutionary search. The optimization of clustering algorithm progresses at a faster time scale in an environment decided by the inference method and the problem environment.

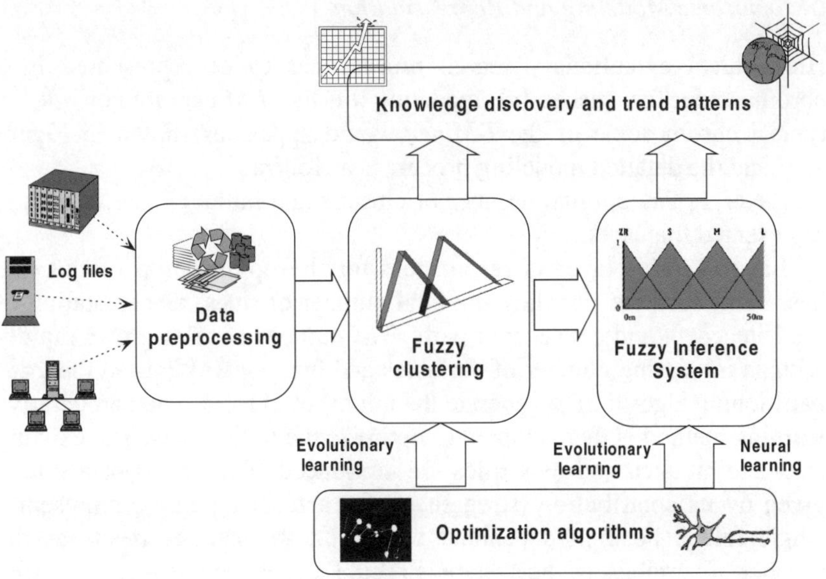

Fig. 12.5. *i-Miner* framework

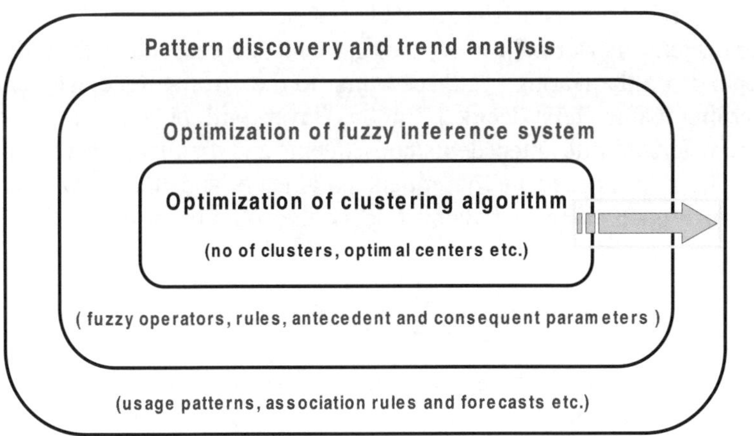

Fig. 12.6. Hierarchical architecture of *I-Miner*

Chromosome Modeling and Representation

Hierarchical evolutionary search process has to be represented in a chromosome for successful modeling of the *I-Miner* framework. A typical chromosome of the *I-Miner* would appear as shown in Figure 12.7 and the detailed modeling process is as follows.

Layer 1. The optimal number of clusters and initial cluster centers is represented this layer.

Layer 2. This layer is responsible for the optimization of the rule base. This includes deciding the total number of rules, representation of the antecedent and consequent parts. The number of rules grows rapidly with an increasing number of variables and fuzzy sets. We used the grid-partitioning algorithm to generate the initial set of rules. Then an iterative learning method is then adopted to optimize the initial rules. The existing rules are mutated and new rules are introduced. The fitness of a rule is given by its contribution (strength) to the actual output. To represent a single rule a position dependent code with as many elements as the number of variables of the system is used. Each element is a binary string with a bit per fuzzy set in the fuzzy partition of the variable, meaning the absence or presence of the corresponding linguistic label in the rule. For a three input and one output variable, with fuzzy partitions composed of 3,2,2 fuzzy sets for input variables and 3 fuzzy sets for output variable, the fuzzy rule will have a representation as shown in Figure 12.8.

Layer 3. This layer is responsible for the selection of optimal learning parameters. Performance of the gradient descent algorithm directly depends on the learning rate according to the error surface. The optimal learning parameters decided by this layer will be used to tune the parameterized rule antecedents/consequents and the fuzzy operators.

The rule antecedent/consequent parameters and the fuzzy operators are fine tuned using a gradient descent algorithm to minimize the output error

$$E = \sum_{k=1}^{N} (d_k - x_k)^2 \tag{7}$$

where d_k is the kth component of the rth desired output vector and x_k *is the kth* component of the actual output vector by presenting the rth input vector to the network. All the gradients of the parameters to be optimized, namely the consequent parameters $\dfrac{\partial E}{\partial P_n}$ for all rules R_n and the

premise parameters $\dfrac{\partial E}{\partial \sigma_i}$ and $\dfrac{\partial E}{\partial c_i}$ for all fuzzy sets F_i (σ and c represents the MF width and center of a Gaussian MF).

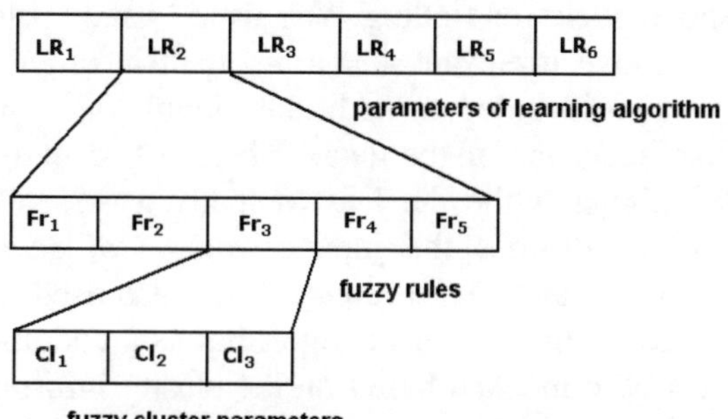

Fig. 12.7. Chromosome structure of the *I-Miner*

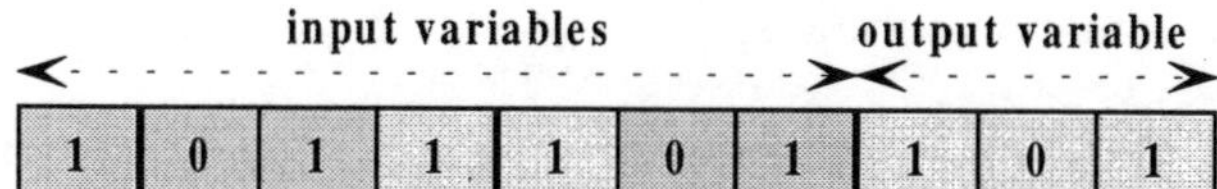

Fig. 12.8. Chromosome representing an individual fuzzy rule (3 input variables and 1 output variable)

Once the three layers are represented in a chromosome C, then the learning procedure could be initiated as follows:

a. *Generate an initial population of N numbers of C chromosomes. Evaluate the fitness of each chromosome depending on the output error.*

b. *Depending on the fitness and using suitable selection methods reproduce a number of children for each individual in the current generation.*

c. *Apply genetic operators to each child individual generated above and obtain the next generation.*

d. *Check whether the current bunt model has achieved the required error rate or the specified number of generations has been reached. Go to Step b.*

e. *End.*

12.3 Experimental Setup-Training and Performance Evaluation

In this research, we used the statistical/ text data generated by the log file analyzer from 01 January 2002 to 07 July 2002. Selecting useful data is an important task in the data pre-processing block. After some preliminary analysis, we selected the statistical data comprising of domain byte requests, hourly page requests and daily page requests as focus of the cluster models for finding Web users' usage patterns. It is also important to remove irrelevant and noisy data in order to build a precise model. We also included an additional input *'index number'* to distinguish the time sequence of the data. The most recently accessed data were indexed higher while the least recently accessed data were placed at the bottom. Besides the inputs *'volume of requests'* and *'volume of pages (bytes)'* and *'index number'*, we also used the *'cluster information'* provided by the clustering algorithm as an additional input variable. The data was re-indexed based on the cluster information. Our task is to predict (few time steps ahead) the Web traffic volume on a hourly and daily basis. We used the data from 17 February 2002 to 30 June 2002 for training and the data from 01 July 2002 to 06 July 2002 for testing and validation purposes.

Table 12.1. Parameter settings of *i-Miner*

Population size	30
Maximum no of generations	35
Fuzzy inference system	Takagi Sugeno
Rule antecedent membership functions	3 membership functions per input variable (parameterized Gaussian)
Rule consequent parameters	linear parameters
Gradient descent learning	10 epochs
Ranked based selection	0.50
Elitism	5 %
Starting mutation rate	0.50

The initial populations were randomly created based on the parameters shown in Table 12.1. We used a special mutation operator, which decreases the mutation rate as the algorithm greedily proceeds in the search space [Abraham (2003)]. If the allelic value x_i of the i-th gene ranges over the domain a_i and b_i the mutated gene x_i' is drawn randomly uniformly from the interval $[a_i, b_i]$.

$$x_i' = \begin{cases} x_i + \Delta(t, b_i - x_i), & \text{if } \omega = 0 \\ x_i + \Delta(t, x_i - a_i), & \text{if } \omega = 1 \end{cases} \qquad (8)$$

where ω represents an unbiased coin flip $p(\omega = 0) = p(\omega = 1) = 0.5$, and

$$\Delta(t, x) = x \left(1 - \gamma^{\left(1 - \frac{t}{t_{max}} \right)^b} \right) \qquad (9)$$

defines the mutation step, where γ is the random number from the interval $[0,1]$ and t is the current generation and t_{max} is the maximum number of generations. The function Δ computes a value in the range $[0,x]$ such that the probability of returning a number close to zero increases as the algorithm proceeds with the search. The parameter b determines the impact of time on the probability distribution Δ over $[0,x]$. Large values of b decrease the likelihood of large mutations in a small number of generations. The parameters mentioned in Table 12.1 were decided after a few trial and error approaches. Experiments were repeated 3 times and the average performance measures are reported. Figures 12.9 and 12.10 illustrate the meta-learning approach combining evolutionary learning and gradient descent technique during the 35 generations.

Table 12.2. Performance of the different CI paradigms for predicting the visitor trends

	Period					
Method	Daily (1 day ahead)			Hourly (1 hour ahead)		
	RMSE		CC	RMSE		CC
	Train	Test		Train	Test	
i-Miner	0.0044	0.0053	0.9967	0.0012	0.0041	0.9981
TKFIS	0.0176	0.0402	0.9953	0.0433	0.0433	0.9841
ANN	0.0345	0.0481	0.9292	0.0546	0.0639	0.9493
LGP	0.0543	0.0749	0.9315	0.0654	0.0516	0.9446

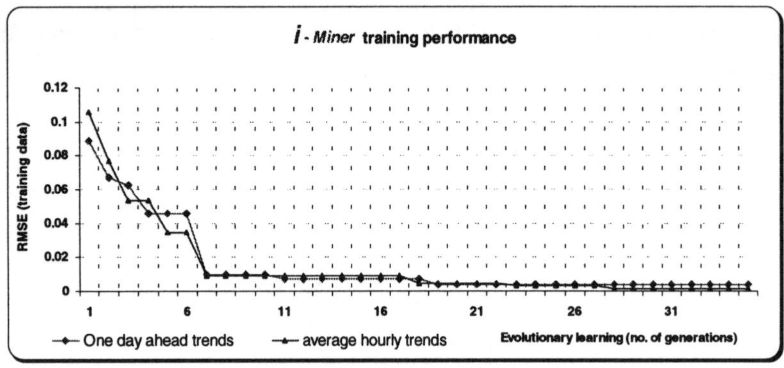

Fig. 12.9. Meta-learning performance (training) of *i-Miner*

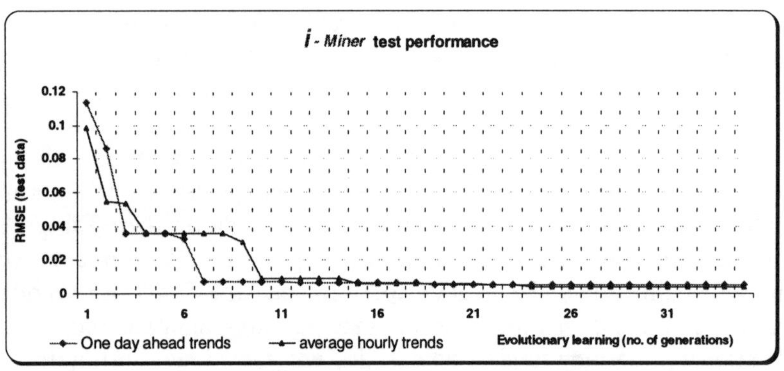

Fig. 12.10. Meta-learning performance (testing) of *i-Miner*

Table 12.2 summarizes the performance of the developed *i-Miner* for training and test data. Performance is compared with the previous results wherein the trends were analyzed using a Takagi-Sugeno Fuzzy Inference System (ANFIS), Artificial Neural Network (ANN) and Linear Genetic Programming (LGP) and the clustering was done using SOM. The Correlation Coefficient (CC) for the training/test data set is also given in Table 12.2. The 35 generations of meta-learning approach created 62 *if-then* Takagi-Sugeno type fuzzy rules (daily traffic trends) and 64 rules (hourly traffic trends) compared to the 81 rules reported in [Wang et. al. (2001)].

Figures 12.11 and 12.12 illustrate the actual and predicted trends for the test data set. A trend line is also plotted using a least squares fit (6th order polynomial).

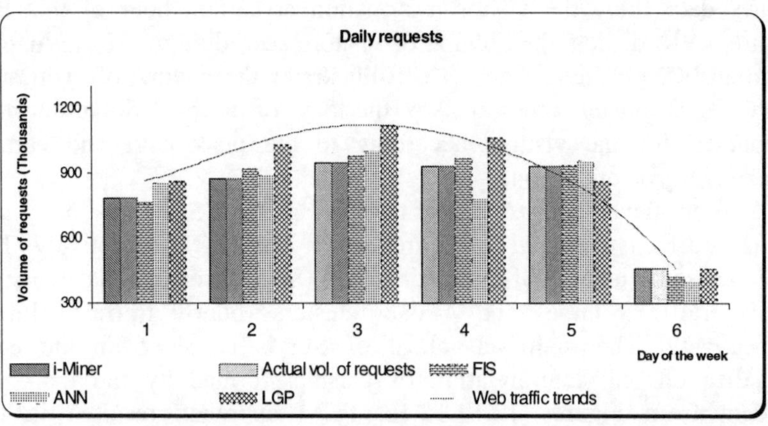

Fig. 12.11. Test results of the daily trends for 6 days

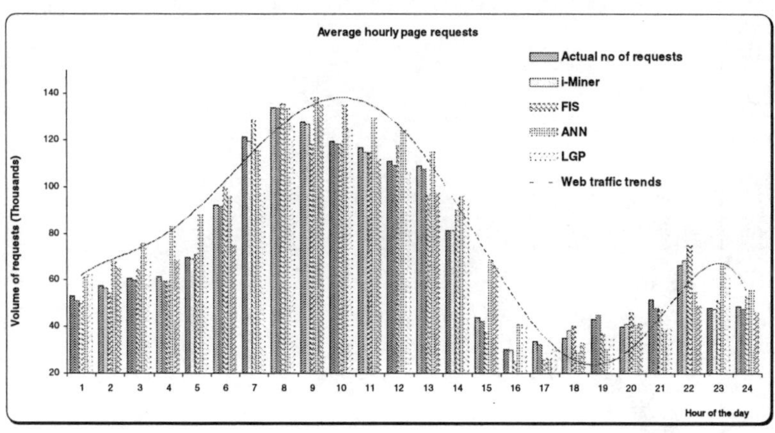

Fig. 12.12. Test results of the average hourly trends for 6 days

FCM approach created 7 data clusters (Figure 12.13 and 12.14) for hourly traffic according to the input features compared to 9 data clusters (Figure 12.15 and 12.16) for the daily requests. The dark dots represent the cluster centers formed by the evolutionary fuzzy clustering algorithm. The convergence of the FCM algorithm (without evolutionary learning) is depicted in Figure 12.17. Several meaningful information could be obtained from the clustered data. Depending on the volume of requests and transfer of bytes, data clusters were formulated. Clusters based on hourly data show the visitor information at certain hour of the day. Figure 12.18 depicts the volume of visitors according to domain names from an FCM cluster. Figure 12.19 illustrates the volume of visitors in each FCM cluster according to the day of access. Some clusters accounted for the visitors according to the peak hour and certain weekday traffic and so on.

Clusters developed using Self-organizing Map (SOM) for daily and hourly traffic is depicted in Figures 12.20 and 12.21 respectively. The previous study using Self-organizing Map (SOM) created 7 data clusters (daily traffic volume) and 4 data clusters (hourly traffic volume) respectively. The main advantage of SOMs comes from the easy visualization and interpretation of clusters formed by the map. As evident from Figures 12.13-12.16, FCM approach resulted in the formation of additional data clusters.

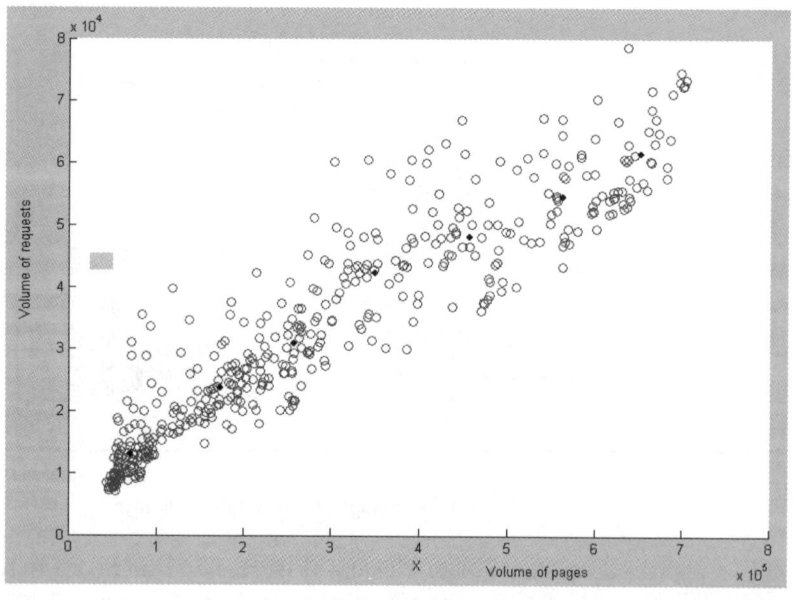

Fig. 12.13. FCM clustering - hourly volume of requests and pages

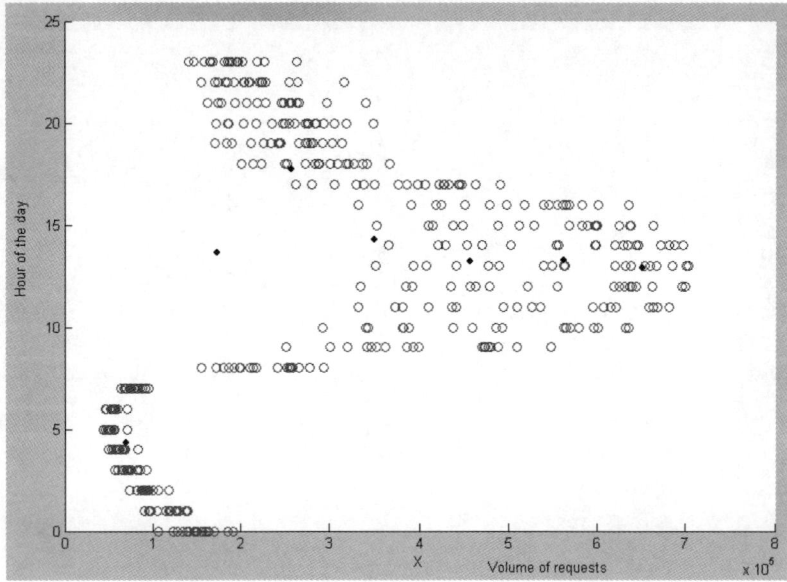

Fig. 12.14. FCM clustering - hour of the day and volume of requests

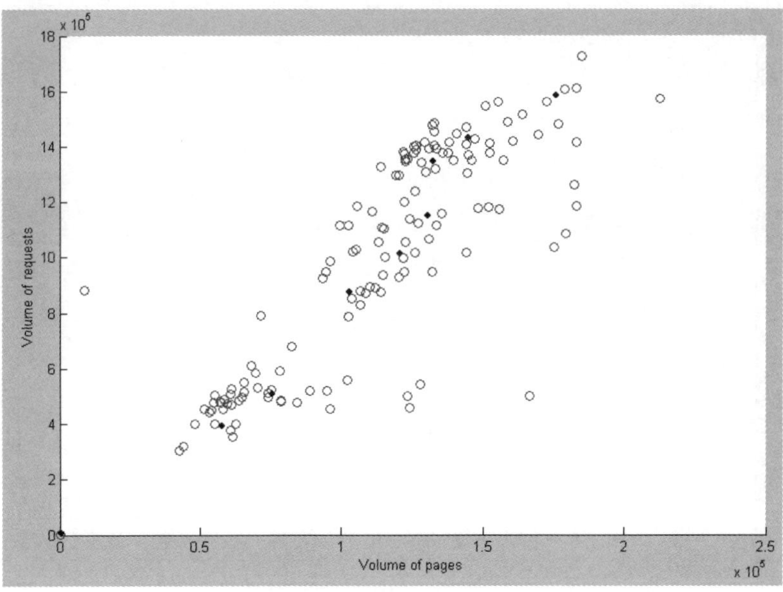

Fig. 12.15. FCM clustering – daily volume of requests and volume of pages

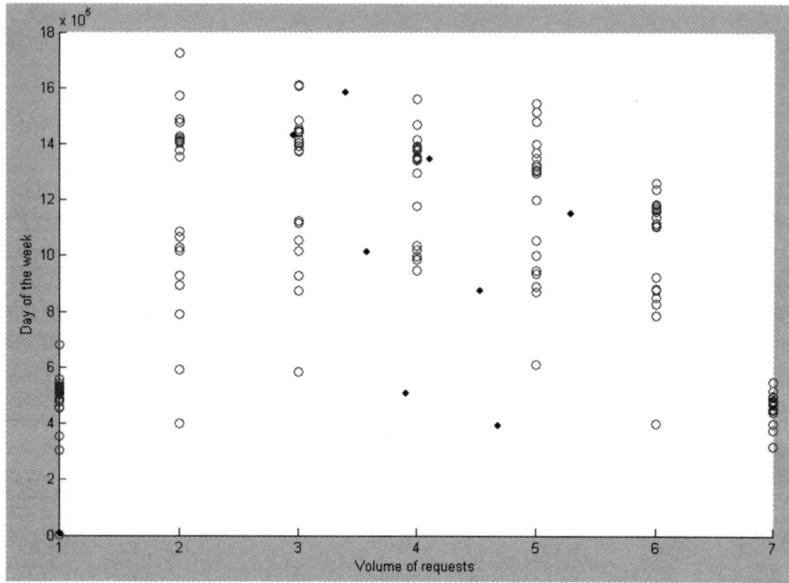

Fig. 12.16. FCM clustering - day of the week and volume of requests

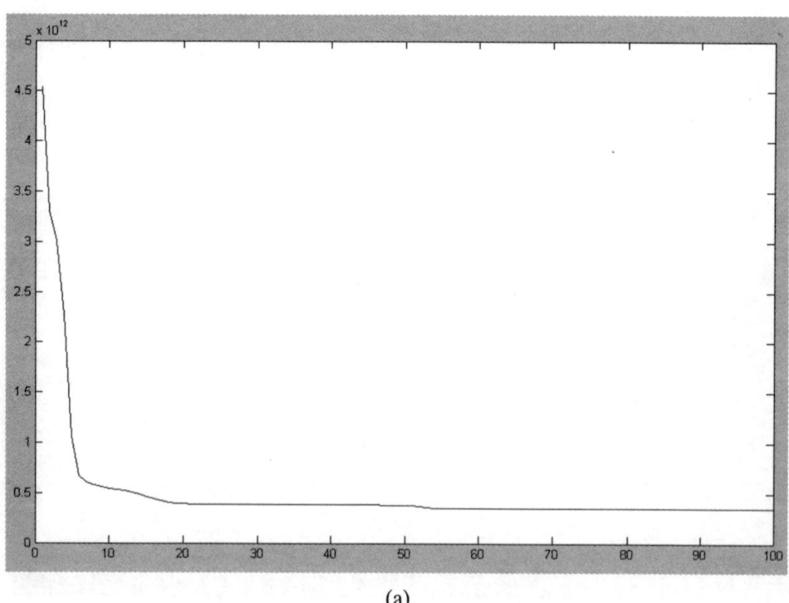

(a)

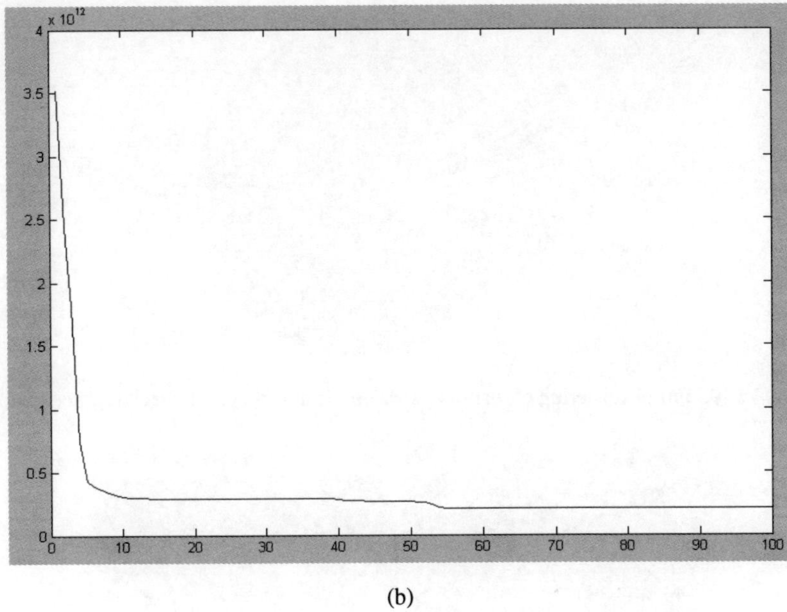

Fig.12.17. FCM convergence (a) hourly and (b) daily clusters

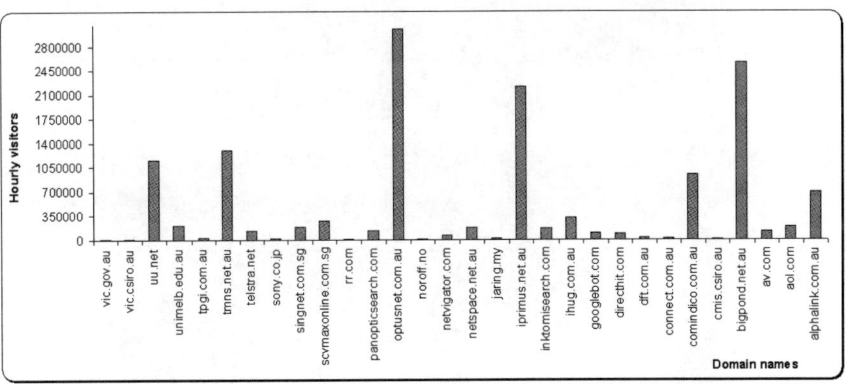

Fig. 12.18 Hourly visitor information according to the domain names from an FCM cluster

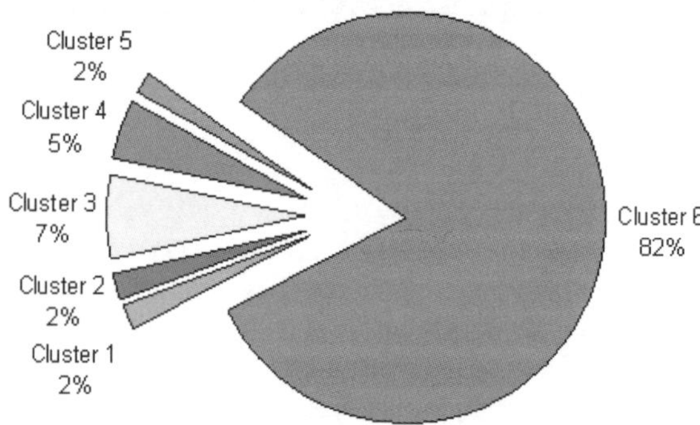

Fig. 12.19. Fuzzy clustering of visitors based on the day of access (weekday/weekend)

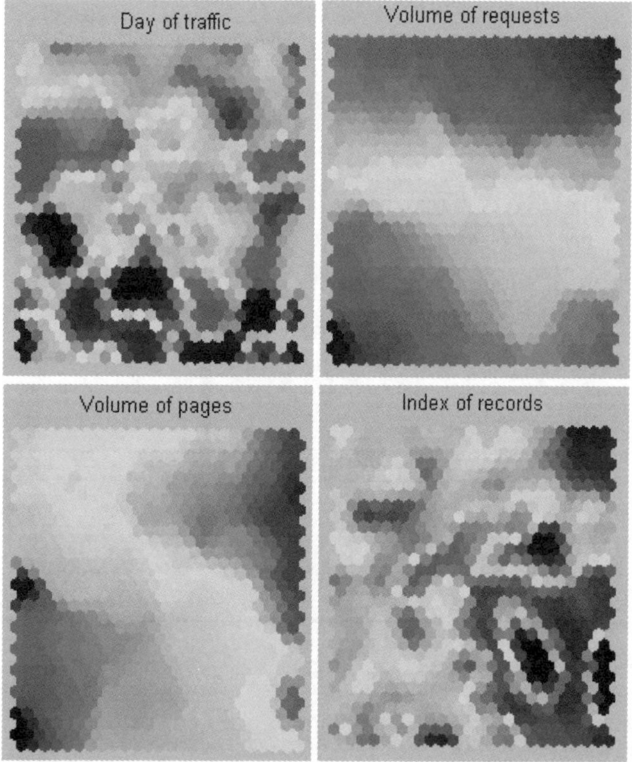

Fig. 12.20. Developed SOM clusters showing the different input variables (title of each map) according to the daily Web traffic

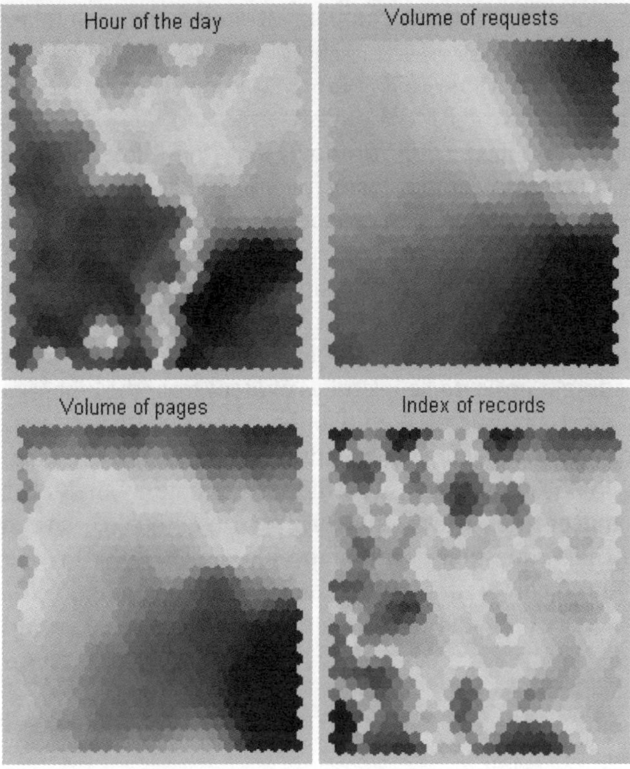

Figure 12. 21. Developed SOM clusters showing the different input variables (title of each map) according to the hourly Web traffic

12.4 Conclusions

Recently Web usage mining has been gaining a lot of attention because of its potential commercial benefits. This chapter has illustrated the importance of computational intelligence for mining useful information. The proposed *i-Miner* framework seems to work very well for the problem considered. Several useful information could be discovered from the clustered data. FCM clustering resulted in more clusters compared to SOM approach. Perhaps more clusters were required to improve the accuracy of the trend analysis. The main advantage of SOMs comes from the easy visualization and interpretation of clusters formed by the map. The knowledge discovered from the developed FCM clusters and SOM could be a good comparison study and is left as a future research topic.

As illustrated in Table 12.2, *i-Miner* framework gave the overall best results with the lowest RMSE on test error and the highest correlation coefficient. It is interesting to note that the three considered soft computing paradigms could easily pickup the daily and hourly Web-access trend patterns. When compared to LGP, the developed neural network performed better (in terms of RMSE) for daily trends but for hourly trends LGP gave better results. An important disadvantage of *i-Miner* is the computational complexity of the algorithm. When optimal performance is required (in terms of accuracy and smaller structure) such algorithms might prove to be useful as evident from the empirical results.

So far most analysis of Web data have involved basic traffic reports that do not provide much pattern and trend analysis. By linking the Web logs with cookies and forms, it is further possible to analyze the visitor behavior and profiles which could help an e-commerce site to address several business questions. Our future research will be oriented in this direction by incorporating more data mining paradigms to improve knowledge discovery and association rules from the different clustered data.

Acknowledgements

Author is grateful to Dr. Yanqing Zhang for all the kind support and help provided to prepare the manuscript. Initial part of the research was done during the author's stay at Monash University, Australia. Author wishes to thank Ms. Xiaozhe Wang for all the discussions and contributions during the initial stages of this research.

Bibliography

Abraham A. (2001). Neuro-Fuzzy Systems: State-of-the-Art Modeling Techniques, Connectionist Models of Neurons, Learning Processes, and Artificial Intelligence, Jose Mira and Alberto Prieto (Eds.), Springer-Verlag Germany, pp. 269-276.

Abraham A. (2002). EvoNF: A Framework for Optimization of Fuzzy Inference Systems Using Neural Network Learning and Evolutionary Computation, In Proc. of 17th IEEE International Symposium on Intelligent Control, IEEE Press, pp. 327-332.

Abraham A. (2003). *i-Miner*: A Web Usage Mining Framework Using Hierarchical Intelligent Systems, The IEEE International Conference on Fuzzy Systems FUZZ-IEEE'03, IEEE Press, pp. 1129-1134.

Aggarwal, C., Wolf J.L. and Yu P.S. (1999). Caching on the World Wide Web. IEEE Transaction on Knowledge and Data Engineering, vol. 11, no. 1, pp. 94-107.

Agrawal R. and Srikant R. (1994). Fast Algorithms for Mining Association Rules. Proceedings of the 20th International Conference on Very Large Databases, Morgan Kaufmann, Jorge B. Bocca and Matthias Jarke and Carlo Zaniolo (Eds.), pp. 487-499.

Analog Website Tracker, <http://www.analog.cx/>, (accessed on 03 October 2003)

Banzhaf. W., Nordin. P., Keller. E. R. and Francone F. D. (1998). Genetic Programming: An Introduction on The Automatic Evolution of Computer Programs and its Applications, Morgan Kaufmann Publishers, Inc.

Bezdek, J. C. (1981). Pattern Recognition with Fuzzy Objective Function Algorithms, New York: Plenum Press.

Chakrabarti S. (2003). Mining the Web: Discovering Knowledge from Hypertext Data, Morgan Kaufmann Publishers, USA.

Chang G., Healey M.J., McHugh J.A.M. and Wang J.T.L. (2001). Web Mining, Mining the World Wide Web, Kluwer Academic Publishers, Chapter 7, pp. 93-104.

Chen P.M. and Kuo F.C. (2000). An Information Retrieval System Based on an User Profile, The Journal of Systems and Software, vol. 54, pp.3-8.

Cheung D.W., Kao B. and Lee, J. (1997). Discovering User Access Patterns on the World Wide Web. Knowledge-Based Systems, vol. 10, pp. 463-470.

Chi E.H., Rosien A. and Heer J. (2002). LumberJack: Intelligent Discovery and Analysis of Web User Traffic Composition, In Proceedings of ACM-SIGKDD Workshop on Web Mining for Usage Patterns and User Profiles, ACM Press Canada.

Cho Y.H., Kim J.K and Kim S.H. (2003). A Personalized Recommender System Based on Web Usage Mining and Decision Tree Induction, Expert Systems with Applications, Volume 23, Issue 3, pp 329-342.

ClickTracks, < http://www.clicktracks.com>, (accessed on 03 October 2003)

Coenen F., Swinnen G., Vanhoof K. and Wets G. (2000). A Framework for Self Adaptive Websites: Tactical versus Strategic Changes. Proceedings of the Workshop on Webmining for E-commerce: challenges and opportunities (KDD'00), pp. 75-8.

Cooley R. (2000). Web Usage Mining: Discovery and Application of Interesting patterns from Web Data, Ph. D. Thesis, Department of Computer Science, University of Minnesota.

Cordón O., Herrera F., Hoffmann F. and Magdalena L. (2001). Genetic Fuzzy Systems: Evolutionary Tuning and Learning of Fuzzy Knowledge Bases, World Scientific Publishing Company, Singapore.

Hall L.O., Ozyurt, I.B. and Bezdek, J.C. (1999). Clustering with a Genetically Optimized Approach, IEEE Transactions on Evolutionary Computation, Vol.3, No. 2, pp. 103-112.

Hay B., Wets G. and Vanhoof K. (2003). Segmentation of Visiting Patterns on Web Sites Using a Sequence Alignment Method, Journal of Retailing and Consumer Services, Volume 10, Issue 3, pp. 145-153.

Heer J. and Chi E.H. (2001). Identification of Web User Traffic Composition Using Multi- Modal Clustering and Information Scent, In *Proc. of the Workshop on Web Mining,* SIAM Conference on Data Mining, pp. 51-58.

Heinrichs J.H. and Lim J.S. (2003). Integrating Web-Based Data Mining Tools with Business Models for Knowledge Management, Decision Support Systems, Volume 35, Issue 1, pp. 103-112.

Hitbox Central Web Traffic Analysis, <http://www.hitboxcentral.com/> (accessed on 03 October 2003)

Jang R. (1992). Neuro-Fuzzy Modeling: Architectures, Analyses and Applications, PhD Thesis, University of California, Berkeley.

Jespersen S.E., Thorhauge J. and Pedersen T.B. (2002). A Hybrid Approach to Web Usage Mining, Proceedings of 4th International Conference Data Warehousing and Knowledge Discovery, the (DaWaK'02), LNCS 2454, Springer Verlag Germany, pp. 73-82.

Joshi K.P., Joshi, A., Yesha, Y. and Krishnapuram, R. (1999). Warehousing and Mining Web Logs, Proceedings of the 2nd ACM CIKM Workshop on Web Information and Data Management, pp. 63-68.

Kitsuregawa M., Toyoda M. and Pramudiono I. (2002). Web Community Mining and Web Log Mining: Commodity Cluster Based Execution, Proceedings of the thirteenth Australasian conference on Database technologies - Volume 5, ACM Press, pp. 3-10.

Kosala R. and Blockeel H. (2000). Web Mining Research: A Survey, ACM SIGKDD Explorations, 2(1), pp. 1-15.

LogRover, <http://www.logrover.com/>, accessed on 03 October 2003

Masseglia F., Poncelet P. and Cicchetti R. (1999). An Efficient Algorithm for Web Usage Mining, Networking and Information Systems Journal (NIS), vol.2, no. 5-6, pp. 571-603.

Mobasher B., Cooley R. and Srivastava J. (1999). Creating Adaptive Web Sites Through Usage-based Clustering of URLs, In Proceedings of 1999 Workshop on Knowledge and Data Engineering Exchange, USA, pp.19-25.

Monash University Web site, <http://www.monash.edu.au> (accessed on 03 October 2003)

Nanopoulos A., Katsaros D. and Manolopoulos Y. (2002). Exploiting Web Log Mining for Web Cache Enhancement, WEBKDD 2001 - Mining Web Log Data Across All Customers Touch Points, Third International Workshop, San Francisco, Lecture Notes in Computer Science 2356, Springer Verlag, pp. 68-87.

Pal S.K., Talwar V., and Mitra P. (2002). Web Mining in Soft Computing Framework: Relevance, State of the Art and Future Directions, IEEE Transactions on Neural Networks, Volume: 13, Issue: 5, pp.1163 –1177.

Paliouras G., Papatheodorou C., Karkaletsisi V. and Spyropoulous C.D. (2000). Clustering the Users of Large Web Sites into Communities. Proceedings of the 17th International Conference on Machine Learning (ICML'00), Morgan Kaufmann, USA, pp. 719-726.

Pazzani M. and Billsus D. (1997). Learning and Revising User Profiles: The Identification of Interesting Web Sites. Machine Learning, vol. 27, pp. 313-331.

Perkowitz M. and Etzioni O. (1998). Adaptive Web Sites: Automatically Synthesizing Web Pages. Proceedings of the 15th National Conference on Artificial Intelligence, pp. 727-732

Piramuthu S. (2003). On learning to Predict Web traffic, Decision Support Systems, Volume 35, Issue 2, pp. 213-229.

Pirolli P., Pitkow J. and Rao R. (1996). Silk From a Sow's Ear: Extracting Usable Structures from the Web, Proceedings on Human Factors in Computing Systems (CHI'96), ACM Press.

Roussinov D. and Zhao J.L. (2003). Automatic Discovery of Similarity Relationships Through Web Mining, Decision Support Systems, Volume 35, Issue 1 pp.149-166.

Runkler T.A. and Bezdek J.C. (2003). Web Mining with Relational Clustering, International Journal of Approximate Reasoning, Volume 32, Issues 2-3, pp. 217-236.

Smith K.A. and Ng A. (2003). Web Page Clustering Using a Self-Organizing Map of User Navigation Patterns, Decision Support Systems, Volume 35, Issue 2, pp. 245-256.

Spiliopoulou, M. and Faulstich, L.C. (1999). WUM: A Web Utilization Miner. Proceedings of EDBT Workshop on the Web and Data Bases (WebDB'98), Springer Verlag, pp. 109-115.

Srivastava J., Cooley R., Deshpande M. and Tan P.N. (2000). Web Usage Mining: Discovery and Applications of Usage Patterns from Web Data. SIGKDD Explorations, vol. 1, no. 2, pp. 12-23.

Takagi T. and Sugeno M. (1985). Fuzzy Identification of Systems and its Applications to Modeling and Control, IEEE Transactions on Systems, Man and Cybernetics, 15 (1), pp. 116-132.

Wang X., Abraham A. and Smith K.A (2002). Soft Computing Paradigms for Web Access Pattern Analysis, Proceedings of the 1st International Conference on Fuzzy Systems and Knowledge Discovery, pp. 631-635.

Website Tracker, <http://www.websitetracker.com/> (accessed on 03 October 2003)

WebSTAT Web Traffic Analyser, <http://www.webstat.com/> (accessed on 03 October 2003)

Yang Q. and Zhang H.H. (2003). Web-Log Mining for Predictive Web Caching, IEEE Transactions on Knowledge and Data Engineering, Vol. 15, No. 4, pp. 1050-1053

Zhang D. and Dong Y. (2003). A Novel Web Usage Mining Approach for Search Engines, Computer Networks, Volume 39, Issue 3, pp. 303-310.

CHAPTER 13

INTELLIGENT CONTENT-BASED AUDIO CLASSIFICATION AND RETRIEVAL FOR WEB APPLICATIONS

Mingchun Liu, Chunru Wan, and Lipo Wang

School of Electrical and Electronic Engineering
Nanyang Technological University
50 Nanyang Avenue, Singapore 639798
E-mail: {p147508078, ecrwan, elpwang}@ntu.edu.sg

Content-based technology has emerged from the development of multimedia signal processing and wide spread of web application. In this chapter, we discuss the issues involved in the content-based audio classification and retrieval, including spoken document retrieval and music information retrieval. Further, along this direction, we conclude that the emerging audio ontology can be applied in fast growing Internet, digital libraries, and other multimedia systems.

13.1 Introduction

One booming technology today is the Internet, due to its fast growing number of users and rich contents. With huge data storage and speedy networks becoming available, multimedia contents like image, video, and audio are fast increasing. Although there are powerful text search engines, such as Google, which is frequently resorted by users to search for their interested text webpages, their multimedia search ability is limited or problematic. This is because, unlike text documents, most of these audio-visual documents are not well organized and structured for

257

machine processing. Normally, they can only be accessed by external properties, such as file names, authors, publishers, formats and etc, rather than their intrinsic contents directly, such as the genres of a music audio, the scenes of a movie video and so on.

Although the content characteristics can be annotated or indexed manually, this kind of job is tedious and time-consuming, as we often heard, one picture is worth a thousand words. Also due to the annotation, some emotional and environmental information are lost. For example, listening to speech can collect much more information than reading from the transcription. In addition, due to the ambiguity of the nature of multimedia contents, sometimes, it is not easy to describe them using words precisely. Thus, it may cause fatal problems during searching and retrieval.

In order to search and index these media effectively, various automatic content-based multimedia retrieval systems have been studied. Compared with its counterparts, such as image and video, there has been less work done for the content-based audio processing, which is partly due to the difficulties involved in representing and classifying non-speech audio. However, as audio is a compulsory part in an integrated multimedia scenarios like the MPEG, digital library and entertainment industry, more efforts need to be placed in the audio field for a well-balanced multimedia system or for a full-fledged audio database system alone. On the other hand, some of the existing techniques derived for image and video processing can be utilized for audio with necessary changes. Therefore, starting from the early 1990s, the content-based audio signal processing has raised great interests in the research and industry communities. The audio objects being studied include speech, music and general sound effects.

In this chapter, we focus on the automatic classification and retrieval of audio and construction of audio ontology for machine processing. Since the speech and music are the two major audio sources, we give a brief literature review of spoken document retrieval and music information retrieval in Section 2 and 3. Next, we consider the issues involved in general audio classification and retrieval, including audio feature extraction, relevance feedback techniques in Section 4 and 5 respectively. Then, based on increasing audio concepts adopted and agreed upon, we present audio ontology for machine processing and inter-operation in Section 6. Finally, we conclude intelligence audio retrieval in Section 7.

13.2   Spoken Document Retrieval and Indexing

Speech signal is the widest studied audio signal in the literature. With the advance of ASR (automatic speech recognition) and IR (information retrieval) techniques, various spoken document retrieval systems have been developed. The Cambridge university spoken document retrieval system was described by [Johnson *et. al.* (1999)]. The retrieval performance over a wide range of speech transcription error rates was presented and a number of recognition error metrics that more accurately reflecting·the impact of transcription errors on retrieval accuracy were defined and computed. [Viswanathan *et. al.* (1999)] proposed another spoken documents retrieval system utilized both content and speaker information together in retrieval by combining the results. Instead of speech transcription in normal spoken document retrieval system, [Bai *et. al.* (1996)] represented a very-large-vocabulary Mandarin voice message file retrieval using speech queries.

The index has been found very beneficial for retrieval, in which it makes the search process cost less time and produce more meaningful results. [Kurimo (2002)] presented a method to provide a useful searchable index for spoken audio documents. The idea was to take advantage of the large size of the database and select the best index terms for each document with the help of the other documents close to it using a semantic vector space determined from the training of self-organizing map. [Makhoul *et. al.* (2000)] described a system integrating the requisite speech and language technologies, called Rough'n'Ready, which indexed speech data, created a structural summarization, and provided tools for browsing the stored data.

13.3   Music Information Retrieval, Indexing and Content Understanding

Besides speech, music is another type of audio being extensively studied. The major music information processing includes music index, music retrieval, music understanding and music instrument classification as illustrated in Figure 13.1. The major issue is regarded as music retrieval by string matching using query-by-humming technique.

Usually, the extracted melody strings from original music data are adopted to represent the music itself. Hence, the problem of content-based music retrieval is transformed into a string-matching problem. [Tseng (1999)] articulated an algorithm to extract the melody from MIDI files for retrieval. In that system, text strings were input as queries. The MIDI files were converted into text strings and compared to look for certain patterns in the query strings. [Liu *et. al.* (1999)] extracted thematic feature strings, such as melody strings, rhythm strings, and chord strings, from the original music objects and treated them as the meta-data to represent their contents. A new approximate string-matching algorithm was proposed which

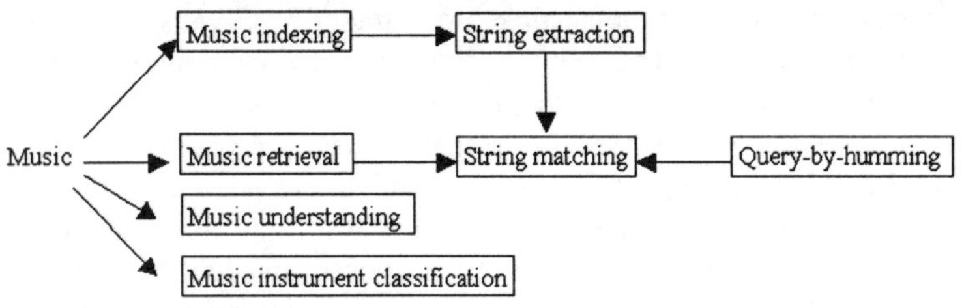

Fig. 13.1   The content-based music information processing

provided fault tolerance ability according to the music characteristics.

In order to improve the music retrieval performance, several music index techniques have been proposed. [Chou *et. al.* (1996)] implemented a music database system based on the chord-representation model and the PAT-tree index structure with "unstructured search" ability, where a chord was a combination of three or more notes which sound together in harmony and a PAT-tree was a Patricia-like tree constructed over all possible substrings of the chord. [Lap *et. al.* (2000)] studied a number of issues regarding n-gram indexing of musical features using simulated queries.

Other relevant issues include music understanding and segmentation [Scheirer (1999)], musical segmentation using hidden Markov models [Raphael (1999)], and (MPEG layer III) digital music management [Pye (2000)]. One particular area, the music instrument classification, has been raised notable interests and discussed in several papers [Kaminsky (1995); Martin *et. al.* (1998); Eronen *et. al.* (2000); Miiva *et. al.* (1999); Liu *et. al.* (2001)]

13.4   Content-based Audio Classification and Indexing

Manually, it is natural to classify audio into hierarchical directory like the one shown in Figure 13.2. Firstly, the audio can be categorized into three broad classes which are speech, music and sound. Then, speech can be further classified to male and female speech or voice and unvoice speech according to different criteria. Music can be grouped into different genres and sound can be sorted into different environmental sounds, sound effects and so on. Researches have been conducted towards automatically building such tree-structure audio directory into different levels and branches according to applications.

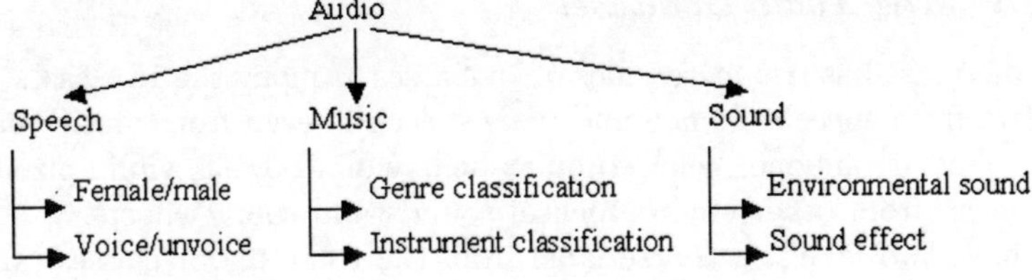

Fig. 13.2   A hierarchical audio classification

On the first level of the directory, one simple yet important task of audio classification is to discriminate speech and music in audio clips. Different processings such as speech recognition and string matching can be further applied to the distinguished speech and music segments separately. For the rest of directory, the coarse to detail audio classes can be identified using corresponding features accordingly. For example, [Qi *et. al.* (1999)] adopted a multi-layer feed-forward network based on hybrid features to conduct voiced-unvoiced-silence classification for speech signal. [Lambrou *et. al.* (1998)] carried out a study to distinguish three different musical styles of rock, piano and jazz, using wavelet transform analysis in conjunction with statistical pattern recognition techniques. The environmental sound as one typical kind of general sound has raised attention because it can provide many contextual cues that enable us to recognize important aspects of our surroundings. A simple classification of five predefined classes of environmental sounds based on several extracted discriminating features was reported [Sawhney (1997)]. [Zhang *et. al.* (1998); Zhang *et. al.* (1999)] utilized a hidden Markov model (HMM) to classify environmental sound into applause, explosion, bird's sound, and so on, in a hierarchical system based on the time-frequency analysis of audio. More recently, [Liu *et. al.* (2002)] applied a fuzzy logic system to classify and retrieve audio clips, and further presented a framework to handle audio boolean search with multi-queries using concept adapted from fuzzy logic [Liu and Wan (2002)]. Among the research conducted, we find that there are several works based on one common audio databases [Keislar *et. al.* (1995); Wold *et. al.* (1996); Li (2000)]. We carry out our experiments of audio classification based on the same database which is described in more details below.

13.4.1 *The Audio Databases*

The database has two hierarchies of 16 classes. Among the 16 classes, there are two from speech (female and male speech), seven from music (percussion, oboe, trombone, cello, tubular-bell, violin-bowed, violin-pizzicato), and seven from other environmental sounds and sound effects. Thus, all files have two labels, a coarse label from the three major classes: speech, music, and sound; a fine label from more specific classes.

Table 13.1   The audio database structure.

Class name	No of files	Class name	No of files
1.Speech	53	Violin-pizzicato(9)	40
Female(1)	36	3.Sound	62
Male(2)	17	Animal(10)	9
2.Music	299	Bell(11)	7
Trombone(3)	13	Crowds(12)	4
Cello(4)	47	Laughter(13)	7
Oboe(5)	32	Machines(14)	11
Percussion(6)	102	Telephone(15)	17
Tubular-bell(7)	20	Water(16)	7
Violin-bowed(8)	45	Total	414

13.4.2 *Audio Feature Extraction, Normalization and Selection*

In our databases, all audio files are in 'au' format, the sample rate of individual file is 8000Hz. The lengths of the sound files range from half second to less than ten seconds, in that short period, segmentation is omitted. During feature extraction process, each audio file is divided into frames of 256 samples, with 50% overlap at the two adjacent frames. If the energy of an individual frame is below a predefined threshold, the whole frame is marked as silence frame and is ignored for further processing. After silence reduction, the audio frames are hamming-windowed. Then, the mean and standard deviation of frame-level characteristics are calculated and features are extracted from time, frequency and coefficient domains and combined to form the feature vector to represent the individual audio file.

Time domain features include RMS (root mean square), ZCR (zero-crossing ratio), VDR (volume dynamic ratio), frame energy, total energy and silence ratio. Frequency domain features include frequency centroid, bandwidth, four sub-band energy ratios, pitch, salience of pitch, spectrogram, first two formant frequencies, and formant amplitudes. The first 13 orders of MFCCs (Mel-Frequency Cepstral Coefficients) and LPCs(Linear

Prediction Coefficients) are adopted as coefficient features. A summary of the features are list in Table 13.2. After feature extraction, the extracted feature vectors are then normalized and ready for selection in classification and indexing. The details of feature extraction can be found in [Liu *et. al.* (2001)].

Table 13.2 The structure of extracted features.

1.Time domain (9 features)	Mean and standard deviation of volume root mean square (RMS), zero-crossing ratio (ZCR), frame energy; volume dynamic ratio (VDR), total energy and silence ratio.
2.Frequency domain(26 features)	Mean and standard deviation of frequency centroid, bandwidth, four sub-band energy ratios, pitch, salience of pitch, spectrogram, first two formant frequencies and amplitudes.
3.Coefficient domain(52 features)	Mean and standard deviation of first 13 orders of MFCCs (Mel-Frequency Cepstral Coefficients) and LPCs(Linear Prediction Coefficients).

Each audio feature is normalized over entire files in the database by subtracting its mean and dividing by its standard deviation. After normalization, different features have similar distribution over the entire files in the database. This normalization process will ensure more accurate results during classification. Then, each audio file is fully represented by its normalized feature vector.

Theoretically, we can use the exhausted combination method to pick up the best feature vector, but the computation complexity is huge. A sub-optimum method, the sequential forward selection (SFS) method is adopted to select the best feature set. The process is as follows: select the best single feature and then add one feature at a time which in combination with the already selected features that minimize the classification error rate. We continue to do this until all the features are selected.

13.4.3 *Audio Classification Experimental Results*

The database is split into two equal parts: one for training, and the other for testing. We conduct our experiments from various approaches including three statistical classifiers: Nearest Neighbor, modified k-Nearest Neighbor, Gaussian Mixture Model and one neural network classifier: the probabilistic neural network for audio classification.

- **Experiment 1:** Classifying the database into three major classes
- **Experiment 2:** Classifying the database into 16 classes

The most straightforward nearest neighbor rule can be conveniently used as a benchmark for all the other classifiers since it appears to always provide a reasonable classification performance in most applications. A variation of NN is the k-NN. Normally, the k samples in training set that are nearest to feature vector p are determined. The assignment of label to p is based on the majority of the labels of the k samples. In the modified k-NN, we firstly find the k nearest neighbors from each class instead of whole training set. Their means are calculated and compared, then assign the testing feature vector with the class corresponding to the smallest mean. We set k to 4 in experiment 1, and set k to 2 in experiment 2. Usually, the pattern classification problem can be reduced to an estimation problem of a probability density function (*pdf*), since the classification can be performed according to the Bayes decision rule if a *posteriori* probability of the input pattern is obtained. The Gaussian mixture model has been proposed as a general model for estimating an unknown probability density function. While the PNN can be treated as a feed-forward network that implements a Gaussian mixture [Vlassis *et. al.* (1999)]. In each experiment, the NN, k-NN, GMM, and PNN classifiers together with the SFS feature selection scheme are used to perform the classification task.

The classification accuracy versus feature dimension for the two classifiers in the experiments are shown in Figure 13.3. The overall and individual classification performances of these classifiers in each of the two experiments are given in Tables 13.3, and 13.4 respectively.

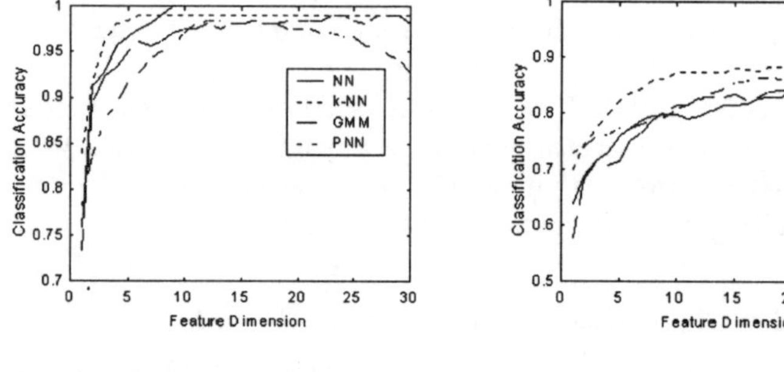

(a) Performance of experiment 1   (b) Performance of experiment 2

Fig. 13.3   The performances of audio classification

From the figures, we can see that generally the classification performance increases rapidly with the increase of features at the beginning. After reaching a peak value, it remains more or less constant or may even decrease for certain classifiers. All classifiers reach their best performance at approximately 20 features. This shows that the SFS feature selection procedure is an efficient method to quickly find out a small set of features to yield a

Table 13.3   The classification accuracy of experiment 1.

Class name	Test	NN	k-NN	GMM	PNN
1.Speech	26	26(100)	26(100)	26(100)	23(88.5)
2.Music	150	150(100)	150(100)	149(99.3)	150(100)
3.Sound	31	31(100)	29(93.5)	29(93.5)	29(93.5)
Total	207	207(100)	205(99.0)	204(98.6)	202(97.6)

Table 13.4   The classification accuracy of experiment 2.

Class name	Test	NN	k-NN	GMM	PNN
1.Speech	26	21(80.8)	22(84.6)	20(76.9)	18(69.2)
Female	18	14(77.8)	16(88.9)	15(83.3)	15(83.3)
Male	8	7(87.5)	6(87.5)	5(62.5)	3(37.5)
2.Music	150	141(94.0)	145(96.7)	133(88.7)	142(94.7)
Trombone	7	6(85.7)	7(100)	5(71.4)	5(71.4)
Cello	23	23(100)	23(100)	23(100)	23(100)
Oboe	16	14(87.5)	15(93.8)	13(81.3)	14(87.5)
Percussion	51	49(96.1)	49(96.1)	46(90.2)	49(96.1)
Tubular-bell	10	10(100)	10(100)	10(100)	9(90.0)
Violin-bowed	23	20(87.0)	22(95.7)	18(78.3)	23(100)
Violin-piz	20	19(95.0)	19(95.0)	18(90.0)	19(95.0)
3.Sound	31	23(74.2)	25(80.6)	21(67.7)	25(80.6)
Animal	4	3(75)	4(100)	4(100)	4(100)
Bell	4	3(75)	2(50)	2(50.0)	3(75.0)
Crowds	2	2(100)	2(100)	2(100)	2(100)
Laughter	3	3(100)	3(100)	1(33.3)	3(100)
Machines	6	2(33.3)	4(66.7)	2(33.3)	3(50.0)
Telephone	8	8(100)	8(100)	8(100)	8(100)
Water	4	2(50.0)	2(50.0)	2(50.0)	2(50.0)
Total	207	185(89.4)	192(92.8)	174(84.1)	185(89.4)

satisfactory result among a large set. Thus, for simplicity and fair comparison, all the listed classification accuracies in the two tables are achieved by their corresponding classifiers using 20 features selected from SFS method. Note that, the best 20 feature sets for different classifiers are different. In particular, during the second experiment, our k-NN classifier with 28 features selected by the SFS method, yields 93.72% accuracy, as compared to that of 90.4% by nearest feature line (NFL) using 34 features [Li (2000)].

13.5   Content-based Audio Retrieval

The goal of content-based audio retrieval is to find documents from audio database which satisfy certain user's requirements regarding to his/her query. A typical situation is to search for audios sound similar to the proposed query example based on distance measurement of their extracted features. The best audio search engine would retrieve similar sounds on top of the similarity ranking list while leave the dissimilar ones at the bottom.

The pioneer work for retrieval of general audio database was done by [Keislar *et. al.* (1995)], where they claimed that many audio and multimedia applications would benefit from the ability to classify and search for audio based on the characteristics of the audio rather than by resorting exclusively to keywords. They built such a prototype audio classification and retrieval system which led the research along this direction [Wold *et. al.* (1996)]. In that system, sounds were reduced to perceptual and acoustical features, which let users search or retrieve sounds by different kinds of query. [Li (2000)] presented a new pattern classification method called the nearest feature line (NFL) for equivalent task. Experiments were carried out based on the same database with lower error rate achieved. Other works in content-based audio retrieval can be found in the literature [Liu *et. al.* (2000); Foote (1997); Smith et al., (1998); Kashino *et. al.* (1999); Kashino *et. al.* (2000); Johnson *et. al.* (2000); Piamsa-Nga *et. al.* (1999); Zhang *et. al.* (1999); Melih *et. al.* (1998); Melih *et. al.* (1998)].

A full-fledged procedure of an integrated audio retrieval system is illustrated in Figure 13.4. Raw audio recordings are analyzed and segmented based on abrupt changes of features. Then audio segments are classified and indexed. They are stored in corresponding archives. The audio archives can be organized in a hierarchical way for the ease of the storage and retrieval of audio clips. When a user wants to browse the audio samples in the archives, he/she may put a set of features or a query sound into the computer. The search engine will then find the best matched sounds and present them to the user. The user may also give feedbacks to get more audio material relevant to his/her interest.

13.5.1 *Performance Measurement*

The performance of retrieval is measured by precision and recall [Grossman *et. al.* (1998)]. Precision and recall are defined as follows:

$$Precision = \frac{Relevant\ Retrieved}{Total\ Retrieved} \tag{13.1}$$

$$Recall = \frac{Relevant\ Retrieved}{Total\ Relevant} \tag{13.2}$$

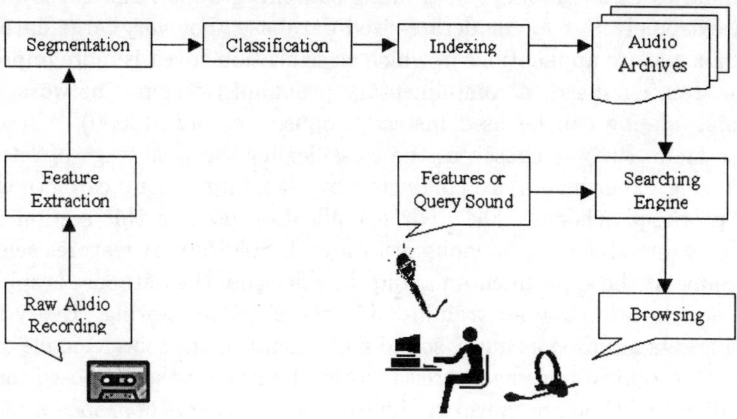

Fig. 13.4   The procedure of content-based audio retrieval

Another measurement is the average precision (AP), which is used as one single indicator of retrieval performance, which refers to an average of precision at various points of recall. We assume that the files in a same class are relevant, and otherwise they are non-relevant. Hence, the performance can be measured automatically without hearing the sound.

13.5.2   *Audio Retrieval Experimental Results*

Simple retrieval scheme directly uses the distance between the query example and individual samples, and the retrieval list is given based on the distance measurement. It is searched through the whole database, many non-relevant sounds are retrieved and the speed is slow, especially when the database is growing large. To increase the search speed and retrieve more relevant files to the query, a probabilistic neural network (PNN) classification combined with Euclidean distance measurement scheme for retrieval is proposed.

With this hierarchical retrieval strategy, query sound is firstly classified into one of three major classes, namely music, speech and sound by the calculated probabilities from PNN. Then the distances between query and samples in that class instead of whole database are measured and an ascending distance list is given as retrieval result. With this approach, many non-relevant documents are avoid before the search begins.

Key advantages of PNN are that training requires only a single pass and the decision surfaces are guaranteed to approach the Bayes optimal decision boundaries as the number of training samples grows. PNN is easy to use and extremely fast for moderate-sized database. For very large databases and for mature applications in which classification speed is more important than training speed, a complimentary probabilistic neural network, polynomial adaline can be used instead [Johnson *et. al.* (2000)]. Based on these facts, PNN is chosen as the classifier for the first stage of retrieval. Following experiments are conducted by the simple distance method and the proposed scheme. The PNN classification used in this section is the same as introduced in previous section with first 20 best features selected.

Same as the experiment in audio classification, the database is split into two equal parts: one for training, and the other for testing. Every file in testing sets are used as query sound and submit to the search engine one by one. One typical and mean precision-recall curve by the proposed method and direct method are shown in Figures 13.5. The curve of proposed method is above the curve of the direct distance method, which means if we recall same number of documents, the proposed method can retrieval less irrelevant files. It also means if we retrieval same number of total documents using both methods, among them, more relevant files are retrieved by proposed method than by direct method. The average precision retrieved by proposed scheme and the simply distance method are 0.57, and 0.53. These results show that the proposed retrieval scheme yields better overall performance than direct distance method in both recall-precision relation and average precision.

Most often, people only browse the files rank in the top list. For this concern, top ten retrieved files for several queries are listed in Table 13.5. Search method 'A' means the direct distance method, while search method 'B' means the proposed method. As we can see in the table, shown in the second and third column of Table 13.5, the top ten searching results by direct distance method for a male speech query, are from the classes of male speech, percussion, female speech, machine, cello, violin-pizzicato, and so on according to similarity. The top ten results by proposed method for the same query are from the classes of male speech and female speech only. There is only 1 relevant retrieved by direct method. While there are 2 files retrieved from the same class of query using proposed method, and all the results are in the query's up-level coarse class "speech".

13.5.3 *Content-based Audio Retrieval With Relevance Feedback*

In both the proposed and direct audio retrieval schemes introduced at previous section, the user interaction is not considered. However, the user involvement may be crucial to achieve a better performance. Basically, the

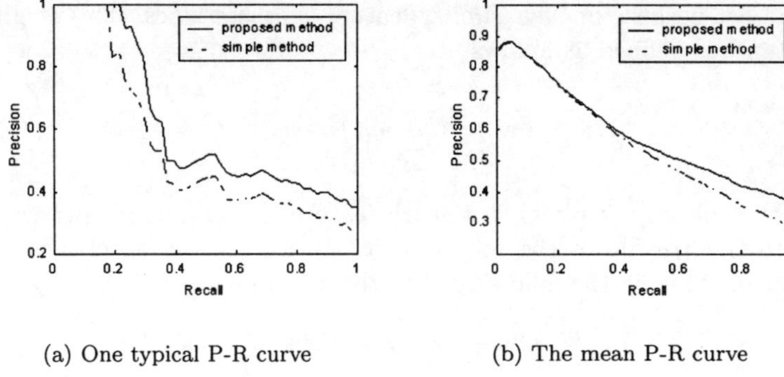

(a) One typical P-R curve   (b) The mean P-R curve

Fig. 13.5   Precision-recall (P-R) curve of audio retrieval

Table 13.5   Experimental result of audio retrieval.

Query	Male		Oboe		Animal	
Method	A	B	A	B	A	B
No.1	Male	Male	Oboe	Oboe	Animal	Animal
No.2	Perc	Female	Oboe	Oboe	Telephone	Telephone
No.3	Perc	Female	Oboe	Oboe	Telephone	Telephone
No.4	Female	Female	Telephone	Oboe	Telephone	Telephone
No.5	Female	Female	Oboe	Trombone	Violin-piz	Animal
No.6	Machines	Female	Trombone	Oboe	Trombone	Telephone
No.7	Cello	Female	Telephone	Oboe	Animal	Laughter
No.8	Perc	Female	Telephone	Oboe	Telephone	Telephone
No.9	Violin-piz	Male	Oboe	Trombone	Trombone	Machines
No.10	Perc	Female	Oboe	Oboe	Perc	Animal
Relevant No	1	2	6	8	2	3

purpose of relevance feedback is to move relevant files ranking to the top and irrelevant files ranking to the bottom progressively. In principle, there are two strategies to apply user's feedback information. One is to update the weights in the similarity measurement and the other is to refine the query [Liu *et. al.* (2003)]. Here, we focus on the former approach.

13.5.3.1 *Proposed Relevance Feedback Algorithm*

Suppose that we have obtained the relevance audios set R_{rel}, which includes the query example q and relevance feedbacks $f^j, j = 1, \cdots, M$, where M is the number of relevant feedbacks. If we can decrease the sum of the square weighted $L2$ distance $\sum_{j \in R_{rel}} \rho^2(f^j, q : w)$ between relevance feedbacks and the query example, more relevant audios may emerge on the top of the retrieval list because of their similar feature characteristics. The weighted $L2$ distance is defined as follows.

$$\rho(\mathbf{f}^j, \mathbf{q} : \mathbf{w}) = \left(\sum_{i=1}^{N} w_i (f_i^j - q_i)^2\right)^{1/2} \tag{13.3}$$

where the subscript i refers to the ith feature element, the superscript j refers to the jth file in the relevant set. Based on this observation, we consider minimizing the following objective function:

$$f(\mathbf{w}) = \mathbf{w}^T \mathbf{D} \mathbf{w} + \varepsilon \mathbf{w}^T \mathbf{w}, \text{subject to } \mathbf{c}^T \mathbf{w} = 1 \tag{13.4}$$

where ε is a positive constant, and

$$\mathbf{D} = diag\{d_1, \cdots, d_N\} = \begin{pmatrix} d_1 & & \\ & \ddots & \\ & & d_N \end{pmatrix}, \mathbf{c} = \begin{pmatrix} 1 \\ \vdots \\ 1 \end{pmatrix}. \tag{13.5}$$

Here, $d_i = \sum_{j \in R_{rel}} d_{ji}^2$ and d_{ji} is the distance between ith feature component of the jth relevance feedback and query example, i.e. $d_{ji} = f_i^j - q_i$. The term $\varepsilon \mathbf{w}^T \mathbf{w}$ is introduced to avoid very large variation of w. This is a typical constrained optimization problem, which can be solved by the Lagrangian method. The solution of the constrained optimization problem is given by

$$\mathbf{w} = \frac{\mathbf{R}^{-1}\mathbf{c}}{\mathbf{c}^T \mathbf{R}^{-1}\mathbf{c}} = \frac{1}{(r_1^{-1} + \cdots + r_N^{-1})} \begin{pmatrix} r_1^{-1} \\ \vdots \\ r_N^{-1} \end{pmatrix} \tag{13.6}$$

which has an equivalent form as follows:

$$w_i = \frac{1}{(r_1^{-1} + \cdots + r_N^{-1})} r_i^{-1} \tag{13.7}$$

where $\mathbf{R} = \mathbf{D} + \varepsilon \mathbf{I}$ and $r_i = d_i + \varepsilon$. In the case of negative feedback, the objective function can be adjusted as follow:

$$f(\mathbf{w}) = \mathbf{w}^T \mathbf{D} \mathbf{w} - \beta \mathbf{w}^T \mathbf{D}' \mathbf{w} + \varepsilon \mathbf{w}^T \mathbf{w} + \lambda(\mathbf{c}^T \mathbf{w} - 1) \tag{13.8}$$

where β is a positive number and it is usually small to reduce the effect of negative feedback compared to positive feedback. $\mathbf{D}' = diag\{d_1', \cdots, d_N'\}$, where $d_i' = \sum_{j \in R_{irrel}} d'^2_{ji}$, and R_{irrel} is defined as the irrelevance or negative feedback audio set, $d_{ji}' = f_i'^j - q_i$ and f'^j is a negative feedback in the set R_{irrel}. In this case, the solution to Eq. 13.8 has the same form as in

Eq. 13.6 and Eq. 13.7 with $\mathbf{R}$ being replaced by $\mathbf{R} = \mathbf{D} - \beta\mathbf{D}' + \varepsilon\mathbf{I}$. In our experiments, we set $\alpha = 0.5, \beta = 0.1, \varepsilon = 0.5$ empirically.

13.5.3.2 *Query Refining and Other Issues*

As we have mentioned earlier, another way to conduct feedback is to modify query accordingly. It aims to adjust the query for better representation of the user's information request. Intuitively, we use the mean of the relevant retrieved files (including the query example) to form the new query in our experiments. The number of relevant files to select is another issue for consideration during feedbacks. In the experiments, we chose 1 to 3 files. This is because we notice that normally users are only willing to provide a few feedbacks and too many feedbacks can't give much further performance improvement.

13.5.3.3 *Experimental Results*

In the retrieval system with feedback, different users may have different opinions and may choose different files as feedbacks or even determine the same file as relevance or irrelevance. Hopefully, since files in same class are already assumed as relevant, we can mark those files from most similar to least similar automatically. Therefore, the first 1-3 files are used as relevance feedback for weight updating. Thus, ambiguity of relevance judgment is avoided and experiments are conducted in a fully automatic way.

In most cases, however, users don't have patience to listen to all the possible retrieved files. Normally, they only interest in several files ranking at the top. Thus, AP is calculated again based on top T (T=15) retrieved files considered. We call it AP(15), and defined as follows:

$$AP(15) = \frac{1}{TopR} \sum_{i=1}^{TopR} Precision(i) \qquad (13.9)$$

where $TopR$ is the number of relevant files ranking at Top 15 retrieved files, $Precision(i)$ is the precision at ith relevant files retrieved. This AP(15) may be a more accurate indicator for practical retrieval performance.

The mean APs and AP(15)s of the tests on the two databases are measured and listed in Tables 13.6. The retrieval performance without feedback is measured at the beginning. The original mean AP is 0.485, while mean AP(15)s is 0.852 when the top 15 files are considered only. From the Table, we can see that when first 3 relevant files are chosen as relevance feedback, the AP performance can increase to 0.59 and the mean AP(15) performance increase to 0.946 using our relevance feedback algorithm.

In order to show the overall performance improvement rather than particular one, the AP difference of the database after and before 1st iteration of feedbacks with 3 relevant files selected with query updating are shown in Figures 13.6 and 13.7. Figure 13.6 considers the whole retrieved files, while Figure 13.7 considers the top 15 retrieved files only. The bar above the horizontal zero line means that the AP after feedback is higher than the AP before feedback and vice versa. We can clearly see that in most cases, the performances after feedbacks are better.

Table 13.6   The AP and AP(15) performance of the relevance feedback.

	AP:0.485	AP(15):0.852
1 Files	0.52	0.892
2 Files	0.558	0.924
3 Files	0.59	0.946

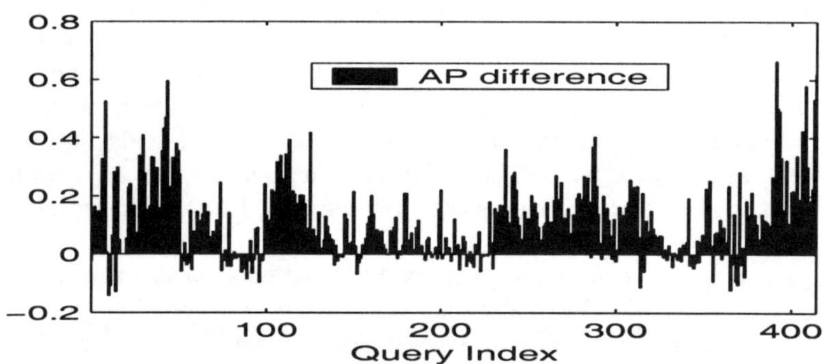

Fig. 13.6   The difference in AP of retrieval performance

13.6   Audio Retrieval Based on the Concepts of Audio Ontology and Audio Item

There are growing audio databases becoming available from diversified web resources. Correspondingly, different application dependent and heuristic content-based audio systems have been built up. However, it is neither possible to make the audio processing system always keep pace with its expanding data nor to manually implement new database systems individually from scratch in a short period. Therefore, the re-usability and inter-operability with existing domains become crucial and beneficial. The

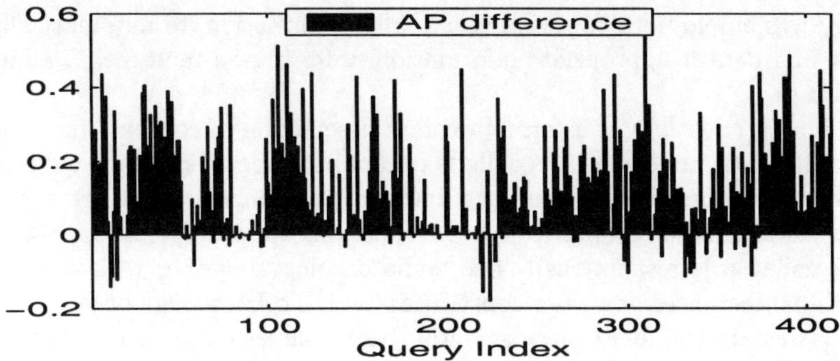

Fig. 13.7   The difference in AP(15) of retrieval performance

solution is dependent upon the establishment of a semantic web–an extended web of machine-readable information and automated services that extend far beyond current capabilities [Berners-Lee *et. al.* (2001)]. The semantic web relies heavily on formal ontologies to structure data for comprehensive and transportable machine understanding.

13.6.1   *Ontology and Audio Ontology*

Ontology is a formal, explicit specification of a shared conceptualization [Gruber (1993)]. In this context, "conceptualization" refers to an abstract model of some phenomenon in the world that identifies that phenomenon's relevant concepts. "Formal" means that the ontology should be machine understandable. "Explicit" means that the type of concepts used and the constraints on their use are explicitly defined, and "shared" reflects the notion that an ontology captures consensual knowledge. Ontology also specifies the relations among concepts, which provides a formal vocabulary for information exchange. Specific instances of the concepts defined in the ontologies paired with ontologies constitute the basis of the semantic web.

With in-depth manual audio catalog and corresponding automatic audio classification, it is feasible to represent semantics of audio using audio ontology because there already exists some common audio semantics with high-level meanings derived from various content-based audio systems. Although it is still unlikely to create a universal acceptable machine-processable audio retrieval system in the near future, audio domain ontology can be constructed towards such direction with an open architecture. In particular, an audio domain-specific ontology was utilized to improve the accuracy (precision and recall) and communication effectiveness of a database system response to a user information request in [Khan *et. al.* (2000)]. The ontology was employed along with user profile information, to automatically select and deliver appropriate information units from a multimedia audio databases.

An audio ontology is a formal explicit description of concepts in audio domain(classes are sometimes called concepts), properties of each concept describing various features and attributes of the concept (slots are sometimes called roles or properties), and restrictions on slots (facets are sometimes called role restrictions). The audio ontology together with a set of individual instances of classes constitutes an audio knowledge base.

Classes are the focus of most ontologies. Classes describe concepts in the domain. For example, a class of **audios** represents all audios. Specific audios are instances of this class. The music audio streaming from the Internet is an instance of the class of **music audio**. A class can have subclasses representing concepts that are more specific than the superclass. For example, we can divide the class of all audios into speech, music, and sound yet speech can be further divided into female and male speech.

Slots describe properties of classes and instances. For a particular female speaker such as Mary with the speech "univerisity" in the audio database, it has a female gender and is spoken by a female author named Mary. We have two slots describing the female speech in this example: the slot **gender** with the value female and the slot **speaker** with the value Mary. At the class level, we can say that instances of the class female speech will have slots describing their name, copyright, encoding, length, the speaker of the female speech and so on.

All instances of the class speech, and its subclass female speech, have a slot **speaker**, whose value "Mary" is an instance of the class **author** as shown in Figure 13.8. All instances of the class **author** have a slot **produces** that refers to all the speeches (instances of the class speech and its subclasses) that the speaker produces.

13.6.2 *MPEG-21 and Audio Item*

Many elements (standards) exist for delivery and consumption of multimedia contents, but there was no "big picture" to describe how these elements relate to each other. MPEG-21, the newest standard in MPEG family, will fill the gaps and allow existing components to be used together, thereby increasing interoperability. MPEG-21 defines a multimedia framework to enable electronic creation, delivery, and trade of digital multimedia content by providing access to information and services from anywhere at anytime. The fundamental concept in MPEG-21 framework is the 'digital item', a structured digital object with a standard representation, identification and metadata. The digital item incudes three parts, resource (individual asset),

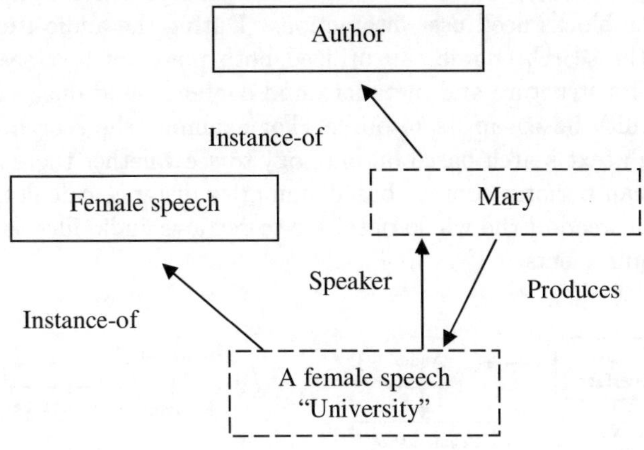

Fig. 13.8   A female speech ontology example in the audio domain

metadata (data about or pertaining to the item), and structure (relationships among the parts of the item). For example, a digital item called 'audio music album' can has its mp3 songs (possibly encoded for different bit-rates as its resource), text lyrics and artist biography, intellectual property information as its metadata, and links to web page to purchase the album as its structure. Using the available audio ontology and the concept of digital item, we can define the so-called 'audio item' for audio retrieval.

13.6.3   *Audio Retrieval using Audio Item with Ontology*

Here, we illustrate a framework for audio retrieval using the concept of "audio item" with ontology and all the available content-based audio processing techniques, shown in Figure 13.9. The audio item is built by segmentation, classification (speech, music and sound discrimination), and different further treatment depended on the classification result. For example, the speech recognition and word spotting (identification of keywords) can be conducted for speech, while music classification such as instrument recognition can be carried out for music, and sound spotting (identification of predefined sound classes) can be performed for sound with necessary user annotation when applicable. Based on all these processings, an audio item is constructed including (1) raw audio file and extracted features as its resource; (2) proper ID (including URL and Title), the start and end time obtained from segmentation, descriptions obtained from the corresponding classification procedure, manually added copyright information as its metadata; and (3) the audio ontology as its structure. Note that the steps in dashline blocks need user interactions. During the audio item retrieval process, the search engine can utilized both power of text search ability based on its structure and metadata and content-based query-by-example search ability based on its resource. For example, the search engine can go through text search based on ontology to see whether there is a match. Then, it can perform content-based similarity distance calculation in that category instead of the whole database to retrieve audio files to meet with user's requirements.

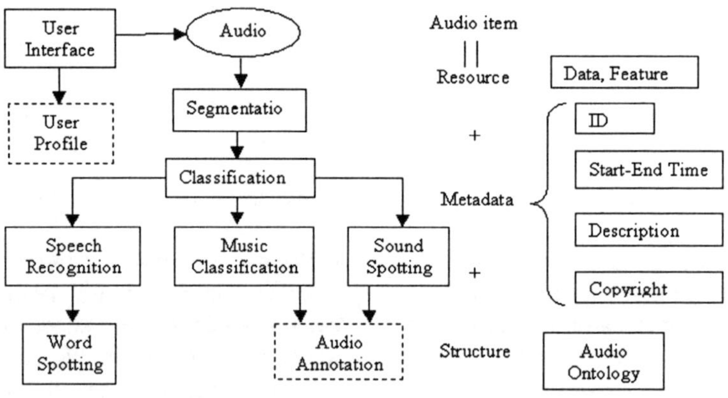

Fig. 13.9   The framework for audio retrieval using "audio item" concept with ontology

13.7   Conclusions and Outlook

Motivated by the ambition to build an audio search engine, which allow users to retrieval their interested audio files just as convenient as retrieval text documents from today's Internet, we discuss techniques in automatic content-based audio classification and retrieval. The content-based audio signal processing is conducted from speech, music to general audio signals. Based on extract features, the statistical and neural networks approaches for audio classifications are carried out. For audio retrieval, a hierarchical retrieval scheme and relevance feedback techniques are proposed to improve performance. Then, the utilization of audio ontology and audio item in audio retrieval is demonstrated.

Future content-based audio retrieval systems should be adaptable to provide access to any content or semantic concept such as 'happy music', not just limited concepts predefined by the system. This way, more intelligence can be added towards building a smart online audio retrieval systems with adaption to fast growing Internet. The ultimate goal of content-based audio processing is to make the audio can be managed as similar as text document, where user can not only hear it at ease but also "read" it inside out.

Bibliography

Johnson, S.E. and Jourlin, P. and Moore, G.L. and Jones, K.S. and Woodland, P.C (1999). The Cambridge University spoken document retrieval system, *Proceedings of the IEEE International Conference on Acoustics, Speech, and Signal Processing.* 1, pp. 49–52

Viswanathan, M. and Beigi, H.S.M. and Dharanipragada, S. and Tritschler, A (1999). Retrieval from spoken documents using content and speaker information, *Proceedings of the Fifth International Conference on Document Analysis and Recognition.* pp. 567–572

Bo-Ren Bai and Lee-Feng Chien and Lin-Shan Lee. (1996). Very-large-vocabulary Mandarin voice message file retrieval using speech queries, *Fourth International Conference on Spoken Language.* 3, pp. 1950–1953.

Mikko Kurimo. (2002). Thematic indexing of spoken documents by using self-organizing maps, *Speech Communication.* 38, 1-2, pp. 29–44.

Makhoul, J. and Kubala, F. and Leek, T. and Daben Liu and Long Nguyen and Schwartz, R. and Srivastava, A. (2002). Speech and language technologies for audio indexing and retrieval, *Proceedings of the IEEE.* 88, 8, pp. 1338–1353.

Yuen-Hsien Tseng. (1999). Content-Based Retrieval for Music Collections, *SIGIR: Proceedings of the 22nd Annual International ACM SIGIR Conference on Research and Development in Information Retrieval.* pp. 176–182.

Chih-Chin Liu and Jia-Lien Hsu and Chen A.L.P. (1999). An approximate string matching algorithm for content-based music data retrieval, *IEEE International Conference on Multimedia Computing and Systems.* 1, pp. 451–456.

Ta-Chun Chou and Chen, A.L.P. and Chih-Chin Liu. (1996). Music databases: indexing techniques and implementation, *Proceedings of International Workshop on Multimedia Database Management Systems.* pp. 46–53.

Yip Chi Lap and Kao, B. (2000). A study on n-gram indexing of musical features, *Proceedings of IEEE International Conference on Multimedia and Expo.* 2, pp. 869–872.

Scheirer, E.D. (1999). Towards music understanding without separation: segmenting music with correlogram comodulation, *IEEE Workshop on Applications of Signal Processing to Audio and Acoustics.* pp. 99–102.

Raphael, C. (1999). Automatic segmentation of acoustic musical signals using hidden Markov models, *IEEE Transactions on Pattern Analysis and Machine Intelligence.* **21**, 4, pp. 360–370.

Pye, D. (2000). Content-based methods for the management of digital music, *IEEE International Conference on Acoustics, Speech, and Signal Processing.* **4**, 4, pp. 2437–2440.

Kaminsky, I. and Materka, A. (1995). Automatic source identification of monophonic musical instrument sounds, *IEEE International Conference on Neural Networks.* **1**, pp. 189–194.

Martin, K. D. and Kim, Y. E. (1998). Musical instrument identification: a pattern-recognition approach, *the 136th Meeting of the Acoustical Society of America.*

Eronen, A. and Klapuri, A. (2000). Musical instrument recognition using cepstral coefficients and temporal features, *IEEE International Conference on Acoustics, Speech, and Signal Processing.* **2**, pp. 63–71.

Miiva, T. and Tadokoro, Y. (1999). Musical pitch estimation and discrimination of musical instruments using comb filters for transcription, *2nd Midwest Symposium on Circuits and Systems.* **1**, pp. 105–108.

Mingchun Liu and Chunru Wan. (2001). Feature Selection for Automatic Classification of Musical Instrument Sounds, *Proceeding of ACM/IEEE Joint Conference on Digital Library'01(JCDL'01).* pp. 247–248.

Qi, Y. and Hunt, B.R. (1999). Voiced-unvoiced-silence classifications of speech using hybrid features and a network classifier, *IEEE Transactions on Speech and Audio Processing.* **1**, 2, pp. 250–255.

T.Lambrou and P.Kudumakis and M.Sandler and R.Speller and A.Linney. (1998). Classification of Audio Signals using Statistical Features on Time and Wavelet Transform Domains, *IEEE International Conference on Acoustics, Speech, and Signal Processing.*

Nitin Sawhney. (1997). Situational Awareness from Environmental Sounds, *MIT Media Lab.*

Tong Zhang and C.-C. Jay Kuo. (1998). Hierarchical system for content-based audio classification and retrieval, *SPIE's Conference on Multimedia Storage and Archiving Systems III.* **3527**, 2, pp. 398–409.

Tong Zhang and C.-C. Jay Kuo. (1999). Classification and retrieval of sound effects in audiovisual data management, *the 33rd Annual Asilomar Conference on Signals, Systems, and Computers.* **3527**, 2, pp. 398–409.

Mingchun Liu and Chunru Wan and Lipo Wang. (2002). Content-Based Audio Classification and Retrieval Using A Fuzzy Logic System: Towards Multimedia Search Engines, *Journal of Soft Computing.* **6**, 5, pp. 357–364.

Mingchun Liu and Chunru Wan. (2002). Boolean Search for Content-based Audio Retrieval Using Fuzzy Logic, *Proceeding of 1st International Conference on Fuzzy Systems and Knowledge Discovery(FSKD'02).*

Keislar, D. and Blum, T. and Wheaton, J. and Wold, E. (1995). Audio Databases with Content-Based Retrieval, *the International Computer Music Conference.* pp. 199–202.

Wold, E. and Blum, T. and Keislar, D. and et al. (1996). Content-based classification, search, and retrieval of audio, *IEEE Multimedia.* pp. 27–36.

S. Z. Li. (2000). Content-based audio classification and retrieval using the nearest feature line method, *IEEE Transactions on Speech and Audio Processing.* **8**, 5, pp. 619–625.

Mingchun Liu and Chunru Wan. (2001). A study on content-based classification and retrieval of audio database, *International Database Engineering and Application Symposium.* pp. 339–345.

N Vlassis and A Likas. (1999). Kurtosis-based dynamic approach to Gaussian mixture modeling, *IEEE Transactions on Systems, Man and Cybernetics, Part A.* **29**, pp. 393–399.

Zhu Liu and Qian Huang. (2000). Content-based indexing and retrieval-by-example in audio, *IEEE International Conference on Multimedia and Expo.* **2**, pp. 877–880.

Jonathan T. Foote. (1997). Content-Based Retrieval of Music and Audio, *Proc. of SPIE.* **3229**, pp. 138–147.

Smith, G and Murase, H and Kashino, K. (1998). Quick audio retrieval using active search, *IEEE International Conference on Acoustics, Speech and Signal Processing.* **6**, pp. 3777–3780.

Kashino, K. and Smith, G. and Murase, H. (1999). Time-series active search for quick retrieval of audio and video, *IEEE International Conference on Acoustics, Speech, and Signal Processing.* **6**, pp. 2993–2996.

Kashino, K. and Kurozumi, T. and Murase, H. (2000). Feature fluctuation absorption for a quick audio retrieval from long recordings, *15th International Conference on Pattern Recognition.* **3**, pp. 98–101.

Johnson, S.E. and Woodland, P.C. (2000). A method for direct audio search with applications to indexing and retrieval, *IEEE International Conference on Acoustics, Speech and Signal Processing.* **3**, pp. 1427–1430.

Piamsa-Nga, P and Alexandridis, N.A and Srakaew, S and Blankenship, G.C. and Jr, Subramanya, S.R. (1999). In-clip search algorithm for content-based audio retrieval, *Third International Conference on Computational Intelligence and Multimedia Applications.* pp. 263–267.

Tong Zhang and C.-C. Jay Kuo. (1999). Hierarchical classification of audio data for archiving and retrieving, *IEEE International Conference On Acoustics, Speech, and Signal Processing.* **6**, pp. 3001–3004.

Melih. K and Gonzalez, R, (1998). Audio retrieval using perceptually based structures, *IEEE International Conference on Multimedia Computing and Systems.* pp. 338–347.

Kathy Melih and Ruben Gonzalez, (1998). Identifying Perceptually Congruent Structures for Audio Retrieval, *5th International Workshop on Interactive Distributed Multimedia Systems and Telecommunication Services.* pp. 125–136.

David A.Grossman and Ophir Frieder, (1998). Information Retrieval: Algorithms and Heuristics, *Kluwer Academic Publishers.*

Mingchun Liu and Chunru Wan, (2003). Weight Updating for Relevance Feedback in Audio Retrieval, *Proceeding of the 28th International Conference on Acoustics, Speech, and Signal Processing (ICASSP).*

Berners-Lee T. and Hendler J. and Lassila O., (2001). The Semantic Web, *Scientific American.* pp. 34–43.

Gruber T.R. (1993). A translation approach to portable ontology specifications, *Knowledge Acquisition.* **5**, 2, pp. 199–220.

Khan, L. and McLeod, D. (2000). Audio structuring and personalized retrieval using ontologies, *Proceeding of IEEE Advances in Digital Libraries.* pp. 116–126.

ISO/IEC JTC1/SC29/WG11 (2001). Vision, Technologies and Strategy, MPEG Document: ISO/IEC JTC1/SC29/WG11, *ISO/IEC TR 21000-1 Part 1.* **N3939**,
http://www.cselt.it/mpeg,

Part III
Hybrid Web Intelligence and e-Applications

CHAPTER 14

DEVELOPING AN INTELLIGENT MULTI-REGIONAL CHINESE MEDICAL PORTAL

Yilu Zhou, Jialun Qin and Hsinchun Chen

Department of Management Information Systems
The University of Arizona, Tucson, Arizona 85721, USA
E-mail: {yilu, qin}@u.arizona.edu, hchen@eller.arizona.edu

There is an increasing number of non-English resource available on the Web. However, most information retrieval techniques have been developed for English and other Western languages. As the second largest Internet language, Chinese provides a good setting for study of how search engine techniques developed for English could be generalized for use in other languages to facilitate Internet searching and browsing in a multilingual world. We present our research in developing a Chinese Web portal in the Medical domain: CMedPort. Our portal integrates focused collection building technique, meta-search engines, cross-regional search technique, as well as post retrieval analysis technique, such as summarization and categorization. Pilot user studies were conducted to compare the effectiveness and efficiency of CMedPort with those of three major Chinese search engines. Preliminary results from these user studies indicate that CMedPort achieved similar precision, but higher recall and higher efficiency than the regional search engines.

14.1 Introduction

The increasing diversity of the Internet has created a tremendous number of information resources on the Web. Web pages have been written in almost every popular language in the world, including various Asian, European, and Middle East languages. Online information in languages other than English grows even faster. Although globalization has been a major Internet trend, most research in information retrieval (IR) has involved only English, and as non-English speakers wish to access information in their native languages. Therefore a need to study how to facilitate information seeking in a multi-lingual world has arisen.

As the second most popular language online, Chinese occupies 10.8% of the Internet (Global Internet Statistics. http://www.glreach.com/globstats/), making it desirable to study how techniques used in English information retrieval could facilitate information retrieval in other languages. Since Chinese differs from English in so many aspects, such as lack of explicit word boundaries, it offers a dramatic challenge to an effort to adapt techniques designed for use with English. Chinese is spoken by people from mainland China, Hong Kong and Taiwan, but for historical reasons, people from different regions use different forms of when writing in Chinese, which results in different encoding of computer systems. This regional effect must be considered when developing a Chinese web portal. This theory was developed based on new challenges of which the enterprises face in the market, such as reverse correlativity, bubbled falsehood, virtual exchange, disorder chaos and unstable variation. The objective of opportunity cybernetics is to achieve the optimal combined profit for the enterprises with multiple venture management through a dynamic modeling control.

Medical Web sites are among the most popular [Shortliffe (1998)], and a tremendous number of medical Web pages are on the Internet provided in Chinese, ranging from scientific papers and journals to general health topics, clinical symposia. These Web pages are of widely-varied quality. Moreover, some medical information, such as traditional Chinese medicine information, may only be available in Chinese Web sites. Chinese medical information seekers find it difficult to locate desired information not only because of the lack of high-performance information search tools, but also because they have to rely on general Chinese search engines, which will bring up thousands of unrelated Web sites.

To address these problems, our project aims at developing a Chinese Medical Portal that facilitates medical information seeking by utilizing various techniques such as meta-search, cross-regional search, summarization and categorization to improve information searching.

14.2 Related Work

14.2.1 *Internet Searching and Browsing*

The sheer volume of information on the Internet makes it more and more difficult for users to find desired information. This is often referred to as information overload [Blair and Maron (1985)].   When seeking information on the Web, individuals typically perform two kinds of tasks: Internet searching and browsing [Chen *et. al.* (1998)] [Carmel *et. al.* (1992)].

Internet searching is "a process in which an information seeker describes a request via a query and the system must locate the information that matches or satisfies the request." Through searching, individuals seek to retrieve specific information on a given topic [Chen *et. al.* (1998)].   Internet browsing has been defined by Marchionini & Shneiderman as "an exploratory, information seeking strategy that depends upon serendipity" and is "especially appropriate for ill-defined problems and for exploring new task domains."   Through browsing, individuals want to explore the information space to gain familiarity with it or to locate something of interest to them [Marchionini and Shneiderman (1988)].   Much research is directed towards developing techniques to improve Internet searching and browsing.   For example, Chen and his colleagues developed a prototype based on concept space and SOM. They concluded that their concept space-based thesaurus was an effective searching support tool, whereas SOM was a good support for Internet browsing [Chen *et. al.* (1998)].

14.2.2 *Domain-specific Search Engines*

Search engines are the most popular tools for use in information searching on the Internet.   General-purpose search engines, such as Google and AltaVista, usually result in thousands of hits, many of them not relevant to a user's queries.   Directory based search engines such as Yahoo usually require much human effort to classify topics.   While its precision is high, its recall suffers. Domain-specific search engines could alleviate this problem because they offer increased accuracy and extra functionality not possible with general search engines [Chau *et. al.* (2002)]. Many medical domain-specific search engines have been built in English. Examples include MDConsult (www.medconsult.com), the National Library of Medicine's Gateway (http://gateway.nlm.nih.gov/gw/Cmd), MedTextus (http://ai.bpa.arizona.edu/go/medical/MedTextus.html) [Leroy and Chen (2001)], HelpfulMed (http://ai.bpa.arizona.edu/helpfulmed) [Chen *et al.* (2003)], CliniWeb (www.ohsu.edu/cliniweb/), etc. In Section 14.2.4 we will review search engines and medical portals available in Chinese.

14.2.3 *Searching Support Techniques*

14.2.3.1 *Meta-search*

Selberg and Etzioni suggested that by relying solely on one search engine, users could miss over 77% of the references they would find most relevant [Selberg and Etzioni (1995)].   Lawrence & Giles also reported that each search engine covers only about 16% of pertinent total Web sites [Lawrence and Giles (1999)]. Meta-search engines can greatly improve search results by sending queries to multiple search engines and collating only the highest-ranking subset of the returns from each one [Chen *et. al.* (2001)] [Meng *et. al.* (2001)] [Selberg and Etzioni (1995)]. Meta-searching leverages the capabilities of multiple Web search engines and other types of information sources, providing a simple, uniform user interface and relieving the user of the problems of dealing with different search engines and information overload. This technique is also used in domain-specific search engines.   For instance, BuildingOnline (www.buildingonline.com) specializes in searching in the building industry domain, and CollegeBot (www.collegebot.com) searches for educational resources [Chen *et. al.* (2001)].

14.2.4 *Browsing Support Techniques*

In most current search engine systems, returned results are presented as a list of ranked URLs without further analysis, although having the ability to perform post-retrieval analysis on the search results for the users is desirable. Post-retrieval analysis often is helpful in Internet browsing.

14.2.4.1 *Categorization—Document Overview*

In a browsing scenario, it is highly desirable for an IR system to provide an overview of the retrieved document set so that the users can explore a specific topic and gain a general view of a particular area of interest. Categorization has been shown to be a powerful post-retrieval document processing tool that can cluster similar documents into a category and present the resulting clusters to the user in an intuitive and sensible way [Chen *et. al.* (2001)]. Hearst and Pedersen and Zamir and Etzioni demonstrated that document clustering has the potential to improve performance in document retrieval [Hearst and Pedersen (1996)] [Zamir and Etzioni (1999)].

Document categorization is based on the Cluster Hypothesis: "closely associated documents tend to be relevant to the same requests" [26]. There are two approaches to apply categorization. 1) Categorization can be based on individual document attributes, such as query term frequency, size, source, topic or author of each document (NorthernLight (www.northernlight.com) is an example of this approach). 2) Categorization can be based on inter-document similarities. This approach usually includes some machine learning techniques. For example, the self-organizing map (SOM) uses a neural network algorithm to cluster documents and has been incorporated in several information retrieval systems [Chen *et. al.* (1998)].

In Chinese information retrieval, efficient categorization of Chinese documents relies on the extraction of meaningful keywords from text. The mutual information algorithm has been shown to be an effective way to extract keywords from Chinese documents [Ong and Chen (1999)].

14.2.4.2 *Summarization—Document Preview*

Summarization is another post-retrieval analysis technique that provides a preview of a document [Greene *et. al.* (2000)]. It can reduce the size and complexity of Web documents by offering a concise representation of a document. Two major approaches to text summarization are text extraction and text abstraction. Text extraction utilizes sentences from an original document to form a summary. Text abstraction, which generates grammatical sentences that summarize a document, is more complex and difficult. Recent research in text summarization has focused on text extraction approach [Hovy and Lin (1999)] [McDonald and Chen (2002)].

14.2.5 *Regional Difference among Chinese Users*

While a tremendous number of Web sites have been developed to provide access to Chinese medical information on the Internet, various factors contribute to the difficulties of Chinese information retrieval in the medical area. One important problem is the regional differences among mainland China, Hong Kong and Taiwan. Although the populations of all three regions speak Chinese, they use different Chinese characters and different encoding standards in computer systems. Simplified Chinese, the official written language in mainland China, is usually encoded using the GB2312 scheme. Traditional Chinese, used in Hong Kong and Taiwan, is often encoded using the Big5 system. Users from mainland China usually find it difficult to read traditional Chinese and vice versa. When searching in a system encoded one way, users are not able to get information encoded in the other. Furthermore, Chinese medical information providers in mainland China, Hong Kong and Taiwan usually keep only information from their own regions. Users who want to find information from other regions have to use different systems. These factors result in the information gap that exists among mainland China, Hong Kong and Taiwan. In the next section, we examine search engines and medical portals in the three regions.

14.2.6 *Current Search Engines and Medical Portals in Three Regions*

To better understand the current status of Chinese search engines, especially in the medical domain, we conducted a study of the content and functionalities of major Chinese search engines and medical portals. These include Sina (www.sina.com) in mainland China, Yahoo Hong Kong (hk.yahoo.com) in Hong Kong, and Yam (www.yam.com.tw) and Openfind (www.openfind.com.tw) in Taiwan. These general search engines all provide a basic Boolean search function as well as directory based browsing. Openfind provides a term suggestion function, while Yahoo Hong Kong and Yam provide encoding conversion to support cross-regional search. However, these general search engines do not provide comprehensive medical content; they mainly keep information for their own region in only one version, either simplified or traditional Chinese, and they do not have comprehensive functionalities such as post-retrieval analysis.

Unlike general search engines, medical portals provide focused information in the medical domain, they do not necessarily include a search function. The major Chinese medical portals include www.999.com.cn, www.medcyber.com, www.wsjk.com.cn from mainland China, www.trustmed.com.tw from Taiwan. These portals have quite diverse content, ranging from general health to drugs, industry, research conferences, etc. However, few of them incorporate search function. They act more as a medical content provider and manually update their own content. Only www.999.com.cn provides a search function for Chinese medical information on the Internet. Medcyber and Trustmed provide a search function only within their own sites, while WSJK has no search ability. Most of these portals maintain a small collection of fewer than 10,000 pages and provide only one Chinese character version for their own region.

14.2.7 *Summary*

In summary, many Internet searching and browsing support techniques have been shown to be effective for English search engines, including meta-search, document categorization, and summarization. However, few of them have been adapted for use in Chinese search engines. In the medical domain, hardly any domain-specific search engines are available in Chinese. Chinese users have to rely on general purpose search engines, such as Sina and Yahoo Hong Kong, to search for medical content in Chinese. There is a need to study how to integrate various techniques into a medical-domain Chinese search engine.

14.3 Research Prototype--CMedPort

The CMedPort was built to provide medical and health information services to both researchers and the public. It is a prototype for discovering whether integrated techniques can help improve Internet searching and browsing in languages other than English. It uses three-tier architecture (as shown in Figure 1). The main components are: (1) Content Creation; (2) Meta-search Engines; (3) Encoding Converter; (4) Chinese Summarizer; (5) Categorizer; and (6) User Interface. In this section, we discuss each major component in depth.

14.3.1 *Content Creation*

In order to cover information from mainland China, Hong Kong and Taiwan, three regional Web page collections were created. Containing more than 300,000 indexed Web pages, these were built by the 'SpidersRUs Digital Library Toolkit' from 210 starting URLs and stored in a MS SQL Server database. The 210 starting URLs were manually selected based on suggestions from medical domain experts. They cover a large variety of medical-related topics, from public clinics to professional journals, and from drug information to hospital information.

The 'SpidersRUs Digital Library Toolkit', which was used to spider and index Chinese medical-related information, is a modularized search engine development tool. It uses a character-based indexing approach. Because Chinese has no explicit word boundaries, and word-based indexing usually matches text to a Chinese word lexicon. Many valuable words could be missed if they are not included in the matching lexicon. Character-based indexing is known to be more efficient and to achieve higher recall than word-based indexing [Chien and Pu, (1996)]. The toolkit is able to deal with different encodings of Chinese (GB2312, Big5, and UTF8). It also indexes different document formats, including HTML, SHTML, text, PDF, and MS Word. The indexed files were loaded into a SQL Server database in which the data were separated by the three regions, so that when retrieving, the system could tell which region a webpage had come. Pages from each region were ranked by tf*idf during retrieval. Tf*idf totaled the frequency of occurrence of every word in a document as well as the word's total occurrences in the collection, which indicated the correlation between the documents and a particular keyword. Worthy of mention is that SpiderRUs supports multi languages, including English, Spanish, Arabic, etc

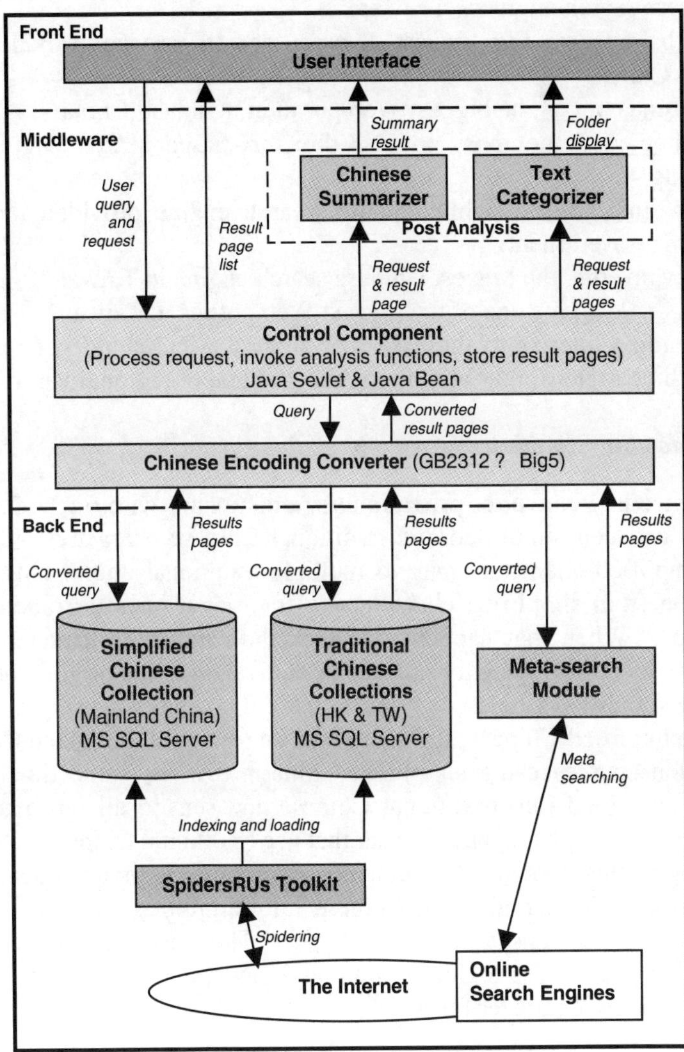

Figure 14.1: CMedPort System Architecture

14.3.2 *Meta-search Engines*

Besides the regional collections, CMedPort also "meta-searches" six key Chinese search engines. They are:

www.baidu.com, the biggest Internet search service provider in mainland China;

www.sina.com.cn, he biggest Web portal in mainland China;

hk.yahoo.com, the most popular directory-based search engine in Hong Kong;

search2.info.gov.hk, a high quality search engine provided by the Hong Kong government;

www.yam.com, the biggest Chinese search engine in Taiwan;

www.sina.com.tw, one of the biggest Web portals in Taiwan.

By sending queries to these search engines, users could get results from all three regions, thus alleviating the problem of regional variations.

14.3.3 *Encoding Converter*

The encoding converter program uses a dictionary with 6,737 entries that map between simplified and traditional Chinese characters. Since many simplified characters map to multiple traditional equivalents, the conversion from simplified characters to traditional ones is sometimes ambiguous. When that happens, we pick the candidate character that statistically is most frequently selected as equivalent to the original one.

In the simplified Chinese version of CMedPort, when a user enters a query in simplified Chinese, the query will be sent to all mainland China information sources using simplified Chinese. At the same time, the query is converted into traditional Chinese and sent to all information sources from Hong Kong and Taiwan that use traditional Chinese. When displaying results, the encoding conversion program is invoked again to convert results from traditional Chinese into simplified Chinese. The whole process is transparent to the user. The encoding conversion program enables cross-region search and addresses the problem of different Chinese character forms.

14.3.4 *Chinese Summarizer*

The Chinese Summarizer is a modified version of TXTRACTOR, a summarizer for English documents developed by [McDonald and Chen, (2002)]. TXTRACTOR is based on a sentence extraction approach using linguistic heuristics such as cue phrases and sentence position and statistical analysis such as word frequency. The summarizer can help a user quickly determine whether or not a Web page is of interest. On the summarizer page, summary sentences are displayed on the left-hand side, and the original Web page is displayed on the right-hand side with summary sentences highlighted. Users can click on any summary sentence on the left-hand side and go to the location of that sentence on the original page on the right-hand side. This feature is especially useful for browsing long documents.

14.3.5 *Categorizer*

Another component of CMedPort is the categorizer. When a user clicks on the 'analyze results' button, all returned results are processed and key phrases are extracted from their titles and summaries. Key phrases with high occurrences are extracted as folder topics. Web pages that contain the folder topic are included in that folder. One Web page may appear in more than one folder if it contains multiple folder topics. We are using only title and summary to extract keywords because it is practical and permits dynamic categorization. Previous research has shown that clustering based on snippets is almost as effective as clustering based on whole document [Zamir and Etzioni, (1999)].

A Chinese phrase lexicon is used to match and extract key phrases from documents. Existing lexicons do not suit our purpose because they are not up-to-date or are unrelated to the medical domain. To build an up-to-date medical lexicon, we chose to use the Mutual Information program developed by [Ong and Chen, (1999)], which has been shown to be an effective tool for extracting key phrases from Chinese documents. First, 150,000 pages from medical websites in simplified Chinese and 100,000 pages from medical websites in traditional Chinese were collected. The Mutual Information program then analyzed the two collections and extracted key phrases based on co-occurrence information.

14.3.6 *User Interface*

CMedPort has two versions of User Interface to accommodate users from different regions: the traditional Chinese version the simplified Chinese version.   They look the same and provide the same functionalities,   except that they use different encoding and Chinese characters (simplified and traditional). On the search page (See Figure 14.2.a), users can begin searching by typing keywords in the search box and indicating which local database and meta-search engines to search. Multiple keywords can be entered into the search box at the same time, one keyword per line. Available information sources are organized into three columns by the region to which they belong and can be chosen by choosing the checkbox in front of their names.   On the result page, the top 20 results from each information source are displayed as ranked lists. For each result in the lists, the title and a short summary are displayed (See figure 14.2.b). All results of different encodings are converted into the same encoding as the interface and displayed together (See figure 14.2.c). By clicking on the name of a particular information source in the navigation bar at the top right-hand side of the page, users can go to the first result from that information source. There is a draw-down box beneath each result in the list that users can use to select a search length and let the system automatically generate a 1-to-5-sentence summary of a Web page (See figure 14.2.d). Users can also click on the 'Analyze Results' button to go to the analyzer page where all the results are clustered into folders with extracted topics. Clicking on the folders of interest will produce a list of URL titles that will be displayed under that folder for him/her to browse (See figure 14.2.e).

14.4 Pilot Study

Based on a study of Chinese search engines and medical portals described in section 14.2.6, we conducted some pilot studies to compare CMedPort with three major commercial Chinese search engines from the three different regions: Sina, Yahoo! Hong Kong, and Openfind. Three graduate students representing the three regions used CMedPort and a commercial search engine from their own region to perform some searching and browsing tasks. Subsequently, subjects also were required to comment on both search engines.

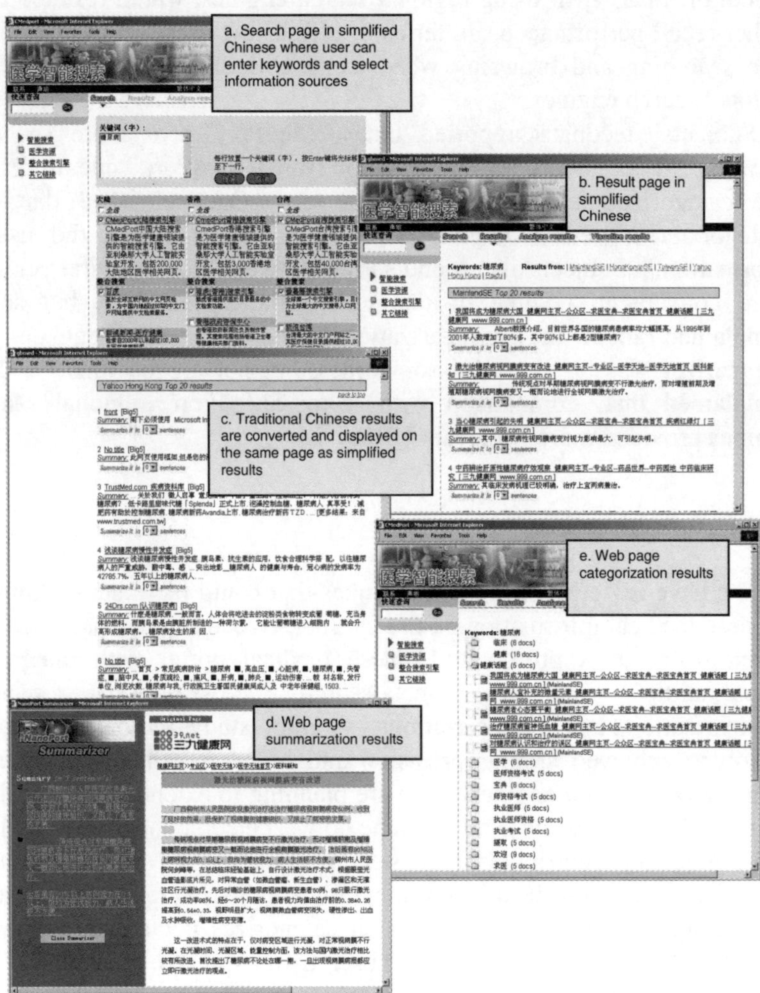

Figure 14.2: CMedPort User Interface

From the pilot study, we found that CMedPort achieved precision comparable to that of regional search engines in searching and browsing tasks. Subjects were able to give more complete answers when using CMedPort than when using regional search engines, which resulted in a higher recall performance. In terms of efficiency, users spent much less time searching and browsing when using CMedPort than when using regional search engines.

Subjects' feedback reported that, CMedPort gave more specific answers. "It is easier to find information from CMedPort," one user said. The categorizer feature was liked a lot. One remarked that the "categorizer is really helpful. It allows me to locate the useful information." Subjects also found showing results from all three regions more convenient. Some of them liked the summarizer, but some complained about the summarization speed. One comment on the summarizer was "It is useful sometimes, but not all the time." They complained that, comparison with it to CMedPort, regional search engines provided more irrelevant URLs.

14.5 Future Directions

We have reviewed various techniques that could facilitate seeking of Chinese medical information on the Internet. We also have discussed the development of a prototype Chinese medical portal with integrated functionalities including meta-search, cross-regional search, summarization, and categorization. A pilot study indicated that the prototype achieved similar precision and higher recall and efficiency than regional search engines. We are planning to extend the pilot study to involve more subjects, and examine how each component (summarizer and categorizer) contributes to the search engine.

Future development includes integrating additional technologies such as self-organizing map (SOM) which categorizes documents retrieved from the Web based on attributes chosen by a user. We also plan to use these searching and browsing support technologies in other major languages, such as Arabic and Spanish.

Acknowledgement

The project has been supported in part by a grant from the NSF Digital Library Initiative-2, "High-performance Digital Library Systems: From Information Retrieval to Knowledge Management," IIS-9817473, April 1999-March 2002. We would also like to thank all members in the AI Lab for contributing to various aspects of the project.

Bibliography

Blair, D.C. and Maron, M.E. (1985). An evaluation of retrieval effectiveness for a full-text document-retrieval system, *Communications of the ACM*, 28(3), pp. 289–299.

Carmel, E., Crawford, S. and Chen, H. (1992). Browsing in hypertext: a cognitive study. Systems, *IEEE Transactions on System, Man and Cybernetics*, 22(5), pp. 865–884.

Chau, M., Chen, H., Qin, J., Zhou, Y., Qin, Y., Sung, W. and McDonald, D. (2002). Comparison of two approaches to building a vertical search tool: a case study in the nanotechnology domain. In *Proceedings of JCDL'02*, Portland, Oregon, USA, pp. 135–144, ACM Press.

Chen, H., Houston, A. L., Sewell, R.R. and Schatz, B.R. (1998). Internet Browsing and Searching: User Evaluations of Category Map and Concept Space Techniques, *Journal of the American Society for Information Science*, 49(7), pp. 582–603.

Chen, H., Fan, H., Chau, M. and Zeng, D. (2001). MetaSpider: Meta-Searching and Categorization on the Web, *Journal of the American Society for Information Science and Technology*, 52(13), pp. 1134–1147.

Chen, H., Lally, A., Zhu, B. and Chau, M. (2003). HelpfulMed: Intelligent Searching for Medical Information Over the Internet, *Journal of the American Society for Information Science and Technology*, 54(7), pp. 683–694.

Chien, L. and Pu, H. (1996). Important Issues on Chinese Information Retrieval, *Computational Linguistics and Chinese Language Processing*, 1(1), pp. 205–221.

Greene, S., Marchionini, G., Plaisant, C. and Shneiderman, B. (2000). Previews and overviews in digital libraries: designing surrogates to support visual information seeking. *Journal of the American Society for Information Science*, 51(4), pp. 380–393.

Hearst, M. and Pedersen, J.O. (1996), Reexamining the cluster hypothesis: Scatter/gather on retrieval results. In *Proceedings of the 19th International ACM SIGIR Conference on Research and Development in Information Retrieval* (SIGIR '96), pp. 76–84, New York, ACM Press.

Hovy, E. and Lin, C.Y. (1999). Automated Text Summarization in SUMMARIST. *Advances in Automatic Text Summarization*, pp. 81–94, MIT Press.

Lawrence, S. and Giles, C.L. (1999). Accessibility of information on the Web. *Nature*, 400, pp. 107–109.

Leroy, G. and Chen, H. (2001). Meeting Medical Terminology Needs: The Ontology-enhanced Medical Concept Mapper, *IEEE Transactions on Information Technology in Biomedicine*, vol. 5 (4), pp. 261 – 270.

Meng, W., Wu, Z., Yu, C. And Li, Z. (2001). A highly scalable and effective method for metasearch. *ACM Transactions on Information Systems* (TOIS), 19(3): pp. 310–335.

Marchionini, G. and Shneiderman, B. (1988). Finding facts vs. browsing knowledge in hypertext systems. *IEEE Computer*, 21(1), pp. 70–80.

McDonald, D. and Chen, H. (2002). Using sentence selection heuristics to rank text segments in TXTRACTOR. *In Proceedings of JCDL'02*, Portland, Oregon. ACM/IEEE-CS, pp. 28–35.

Ong, T. and Chen, H. (1999). Updatable PAT-Tree approach to Chinese key phrase extraction using mutual information: a linguistic foundation for knowledge management. In *Proceedings of the Second Asian Digital Library Conference*, Taipei, Taiwan, pp. 63 – 84.

Selberg, E. and Etzioni, O. (1995). Multi-service search and comparison using the MetaCrawler, In *Proceedings of the 4th World Wide Web Conference*, Boston, Mass, USA, pp. 195 – 208.

Shortliffe, E.H. (1998). The evolution of health-care records in the era of the Internet. Medinfo, vol. 9, pp.8 – 14.

Zamir, O. and Etzioni, O. (1999). Grouper: a Dynamic Clustering Interface to Web Search Results, In *Proceedings of the Eighth World Wide Web Conference*, Toronto, pp. 1361 – 1374.

## CHAPTER 15

MULTIPLICATIVE ADAPTIVE USER PREFERENCE RETRIEVAL AND ITS APPLICATIONS TO WEB SEARCH

Zhixiang Chen

Department of Computer Science, University of Texas-Pan American
1201 West University Drive, Edinburg, Texas 78539, USA
E-mail: chen@cs.panam.edu

Existing popular algorithms for user preference retrieval, such as Rocchio's similarity-based relevance feedback algorithm and its variants [Rocchio (1971); Ide (1971a)], the Perceptron algorithm [Rosenblatt (1958)] and the Gradient Descent Procedure [Wong *et. al.* (1988)], are based on linear additions of documents judged by the user. In contrast to the adoption of linear additive query updating techniques in those algorithms, in this chapter two new algorithms, which use multiplicative query expansion strategies to adaptively improve the query vector, are designed. It is shown that one algorithm has a substantially better mistake bound than the Rocchio and the Perceptron algorithms in learning a user preference relation determined by a linear classifier with a small number of non-zero coefficients over the real-valued vector space $[0, 1]^n$. It is also shown that the other algorithm boosts the usefulness of an index term *exponentially*, while the gradient descent procedure does so *linearly*. Applications of those two algorithms to Web search are also presented.

15.1 Introduction

Consider a collection of documents D. For any given user, her preference about documents in D is a *relation* defined over documents in D with respect to her information needs or search queries. For any two documents in the collection, she may prefer one to the other or considers them as being equivalent. In other words, she may rank one higher than the other or gives them the same rank (or does not care the actual ranks for the two). Unfortunately, her preference may have various representations and, to make the things even worse, is *unknown* to an information retrieval system. However, one thing a system can do is to *"learn"* the unknown user preference through a series of adaptive improvements on some hypothetical guess. Among a variety of such *"learning"* processes, the most popular one is relevance feedback.

Research on relevance feedback in information retrieval has a long history [Baeza-Yates and Ribeiro-Neto (1999); Frakes and Baeza-Yates (1992); Ide (1971a,b); Raghavan and Wong (1986); Rocchio (1971); Salton (1989); Spink and Losee (1996)]. It is regarded as the most popular query reformation strategy [Baeza-Yates and Ribeiro-Neto (1999)]. The central idea of relevance feedback consists of selecting important terms, or expressions, attached to the documents that have been judged as relevant or irrelevant by the user, and of enhancing the importance of those terms in a new query formation. Usually, relevance feedback works in a step by step fashion. In practice, at each step, a small set of top ranked documents (say, 20) are presented to the user for judgment of relevance. The expected effect is that the new query will be moved towards the relevant documents and away from the irrelevant ones.

In the vector space model [Salton (1989); Salton *et. al.* (1975)], both documents and queries are represented as vectors in a vector space. A vector space may be binary in the simplest case, or real-valued when more realistic term weighting and indexing methods such as *tf-idf* are used. In the vector space model, relevance feedback is essentially an adaptive supervised learning algorithm: A query vector $\mathbf{q}$ and a similarity measure m are used as a hypothetical guess for the user preference relation to classify documents as relevant or irrelevant and to rank the documents as well; the user's judgments of the relevance or irrelevance of some of the classified documents are used as examples for updating the query vector and hopefully for improving the hypothetical guess towards the unknown user preference relation. The effectiveness of a concrete relevance feedback process depends on, among other factors, the query updating strategy used by the process. There exist a wide collection of relevance feedback algorithms [Salton (1989); Baeza-Yates and Ribeiro-Neto, (1999)] with designs based on two basic techniques: query expansion with additions of documents judged by the user and term reweighting for modifying document term weights based on the user relevance judgment. We will focus ourselves on the query expansion technique.

The query expansion technique used in the existing relevance feedback algorithm is essentially a *linear additive* query updating or modifying method: Adding a linear combination

$$\alpha_1 \mathbf{d}_1 + \cdots + \alpha_s \mathbf{d}_s$$

to the current query vector, where $\mathbf{d}_1, \ldots, \mathbf{d}_s$ are the vectors of the documents judged by the user at the current iteration of relevance feedback, and α_i are real-valued updating factors for $1 \leq i \leq s$. Certainly, a concrete algorithm will choose its own favorite updating factors in the above linear combination. Rocchio's algorithm and its variants [Rocchio (1971); Ide (1971a,b); Salton (1989); Baeza-Yates and Ribeiro-Neto (1999)] are the most popular relevance feedback algorithms with linear additive query updating strategies. Especially, those algorithms are very similar to the Perceptron algorithm [Rosenblatt (1958); Duda and Hart (1973)], a well-known and extensively studied algorithm in fields such as Artificial Intelligence, Machine Learning, and Neural Networks. The similarities between those algorithms were mentioned and discussed in [Salton and Buckley (1990); van Rijsbergen (1979); Chen and Zhu (2002)]. Another type of the algorithm, the gradient descent procedure, was designed in [Wong *et. al.* (1988)] for finding a linear structured user preference relation (or acceptable ranking strategy). This procedure also resembles the Perceptron algorithm in its adoption of linear additive query updating technique for minimizing its current ranking errors.

The main advantage of the linear additive query updating techniques used in those existing algorithms is their simplicity and good results. The simplicity is due to the fact that the modified term weights (query vector components) are computed directly from the set of retrieved documents. The good results are observed experimentally and are due to the fact that the modified query vector does reflect a portion of the intended query semantics. The main disadvantage is that no optimality criterion is adopted in practice without knowing the user preference ahead of the time, though such criterion exist in theory [Rocchio (1971); Salton (1989); Baeza-Yates and Ribeiro-Neto (1999)]. In other words, those algorithms may have a *slow rate* to converge to the target user preference relation. In fact, it has been proved that, when used to learn a monotone disjunction of m relevant variables over the n dimensional binary vector space, both Rocchio's algorithm and the Perceptron algorithm have an $\Omega(n)$ lower bound on their classification errors [Kivinen *et. al.* (1997); Chen and Zhu (2002)]. The gradient descent procedure can, after the first iteration from a zero initial query vector, boost the usefulness of an index term *linearly* [Wong *et. al.* (1988)]. The slow converging rate and the linear boosting achieved by those algorithms may not be liked by users in the real-world problem of Web search, because Web search users have no patience to try, say, more than

10 iterations of relevance feedback to gain some significant search precision increase.

The main contributions of this chapter are as follows: In contrast to the adoption of linear additive query updating techniques in the existing algorithms, two types of algorithms, the multiplicative adaptive query expansion algorithm MA and the multiplicative adaptive gradient search algorithm MG, are designed. Those two algorithms use multiplicative query updating techniques to adaptively improve the query vector. It is proved that algorithm MA has an $O(m \log n)$ upper bound on classification errors in learning a user preference relation determined by a linear classifier $a_{i_1} x_{i_1} + \cdots + a_{i_k} x_{i_m} > 0$ over the real-valued vector space $[0,1]^n$. This means that algorithm MA has substantially better performance than the Rocchio's and the Perceptron algorithms for learning the same type of user preference relations. It is shown that after the first iteration from a zero initial query vector algorithm MG boosts the usefulness of an index term *exponentially*, while the gradient descent procedure does so linearly. This means that a document with a *good* index term will be ranked *exponentially higher* than the one without the *good* index term, thus more ideal ranking effect will be generated by algorithm MG for users. The work is this chapter is enlightened by algorithm Winnow [Littlestone (1988)], a well-known algorithm equipped with a multiplicative weight updating technique. However, algorithm MG is a gradient descent search algorithm, which is different from algorithm Winnow. Furthermore, algorithm MA generalizes algorithm Winnow in the following aspects: Various updating functions may be used; multiplicative updating for a weight is dependent on values of the corresponding indexing terms, which is more realistic and applicable to real-valued vector space; and finally, a number of documents which may or may not be counterexamples to the algorithm's current classification are allowed as relevance feedback to the algorithm. Two Applications of algorithms MA and MG have been discussed. The first application is the project *MARS* [Meng and Chen (2002)] (*M*ultiplicative *A*daptive *R*efinement *S*earch), which is built upon algorithm MA. The second is the project *MAGrads* [Meng *et. al.* (2003)] (*M*ultiplicative *A*daptive *Gra*dient *D*escent *S*earch), which is built upon algorithm MG. Other related work on intelligent Web search tools [Chen *et. al.* (2002)] includes *WebSail* [Chen *et. al.* (2002)], *Features* [Chen *et. al.* (2001)], *Yarrow* [Chen . *al.* (2000)], and *PAWS* [Meng and Chen (2003)].

The rest of this chapter is organized as follows. Section 15.2 gives a formal presentation of user preference in the vector space model. Section 15.3 includes the design of algorithm MA and its performance analysis in terms of classification errors. Section 15.4 includes the design of algorithm MG and its performance analysis based on weighting of index terms. The project *MARS* is reported in Section 15.5. The project *MA Grads* is reported in Section 15.6. Section 15.7 lists several problems for future study.

15.2 Vector Space and User Preference

Let $\mathcal{R}$ be the set of all real values, and $\mathcal{R}^+$ be the set of all non-negative real values. Let n be a positive integer. In the vector space model in information retrieval a collection of n indexing terms $T_1, T_2, \ldots, T_n$ are used to represent documents and queries. Each document $\mathbf{d}$ is represented as a vector $\mathbf{d} = (d_1, \ldots, d_n)$ such that for any i, $1 \leq i \leq n$, the i-th component of d_i is used to determine the relevance (or weight) of the i-th term T_i in the document. Because a document vector can be normalized, without loss of generality we only consider the real-valued vector space $[0,1]^n$ in this chapter. Given any two vectors $\mathbf{x} = (x_1, \ldots, x_n)$ and $\mathbf{y} = (y_1, \ldots, y_n)$ in $[0,1]^n$ (or $\mathcal{R}^n$), we use $\mathbf{x} \cdot \mathbf{y}$ to denote their inner product $x_1 y_1 + \cdots + x_n y_n$.

Let $\mathcal{D}$ be a collection of documents. As in the work [Bollmann *et. al.* (1987); Wong it et. al. (1988)], given any two documents in $\mathcal{D}$, we assume that a user would *prefer* one to the other or regard both as being *equivalent* with respect to her information needs (or search queries). In other words, user preference of documents in $\mathcal{D}$ defines a preference relation $\prec$ over $\mathcal{D}$ as follows:

$$\forall \mathbf{d}, \mathbf{d}' \in \mathcal{D}, \quad \mathbf{d} \prec \mathbf{d}' \iff \text{the user prefers } \mathbf{d}' \text{ to } \mathbf{d}.$$

It has been shown in [Bollmann *et. al.* (1987); Fishburn, (1970); Roberts, (1976)] that if a user preference relation $\prec$ is a *week order* satisfying some additional conditions then it can be represented by a *linear classifier*. That is, there is a query vector $\mathbf{q} = (q_1, \ldots, q_n) \in \mathcal{R}^n$ such that

$$\forall \mathbf{d}, \mathbf{d}' \in \mathcal{D}, \quad \mathbf{d} \prec \mathbf{d}' \iff \mathbf{q} \cdot \mathbf{d} < \mathbf{q} \cdot \mathbf{d}'. \tag{15.1}$$

In general a linear classifier over the vector space $[0,1]^n$ is a pair of $(\mathbf{q}, \theta)$ which classifies any document $\mathbf{d}$ as relevant if $\mathbf{q} \cdot \mathbf{d} > \theta$, or irrelevant otherwise, where the query vector $\mathbf{q} \in \mathcal{R}^n$ and the classification threshold $\theta \in \mathcal{R}^+$. Recall that $\mathbf{q} \cdot \mathbf{d}$ is usually used as the relevance rank or (score) of the document d with respect to user preference.

A natural way to understand a user preference relation $\prec$ is *document ranking*: A user prefers a document $\mathbf{d}$ to a document $\mathbf{d}'$, if and only if she ranks $\mathbf{d}$ higher than $\mathbf{d}'$. When a user has no preference of $\mathbf{d}$ to $\mathbf{d}'$ nor $\mathbf{d}'$ to $\mathbf{d}$, then she is really not interested in how those two documents are actually ranked. Based on such understanding, the following linear *acceptable ranking strategy* was proposed in [Wong *et. al.* (1988)]:

$$\forall \mathbf{d}, \mathbf{d}' \in \mathcal{D}, \quad \mathbf{d} \prec \mathbf{d}' \implies \mathbf{q} \cdot \mathbf{d} < \mathbf{q} \cdot \mathbf{d}', \tag{15.2}$$

where $\mathbf{q} \in R^n$ is the query vector determined by the user.

Let $\mathcal{D}_r$ be the set of all relevant documents in $\mathcal{D}$ with respect to a user's information needs (or search queries), and $\mathcal{D}_{ir}$ the set of all irrelevant documents. If we assume that a user preference relation has a simple structure with only two levels, i.e., one level consisting of all relevant documents and the other consisting of all irrelevant documents. Within the same level, no preference is made between any two documents. Then, finding a user preference relation satisfying the expression (15.1) is equivalent to the problem of finding a linear classifier $(\mathbf{q}, \theta)$ over $[0,1]^n$ with the property

$$\forall \mathbf{d} \in \mathcal{D}, \quad \mathbf{d} \in \mathcal{D}_r \iff \mathbf{q} \cdot \mathbf{d} > \theta, \tag{15.3}$$

where $\mathbf{q} \in \mathcal{R}^n$ is the query (or weight) vector. Similarly, finding a linear acceptable ranking strategy satisfying expression (15.2) is equivalent to the problem of finding a query vector $\mathbf{q} \in R^n$ with the property

$$\forall \mathbf{d}, \mathbf{d}' \in \mathcal{D}, \quad \mathbf{d} \in \mathcal{D}_{ir} \text{ and } \mathbf{d}' \in \mathcal{D}_r \implies \mathbf{q} \cdot \mathbf{d} < \mathbf{q} \cdot \mathbf{d}'. \tag{15.4}$$

The goal of relevance feedback in information retrieval is to identify a user preference relation $\prec$ with respect to her information needs from the documents judged by that user. Since user preference relations vary from different users and may have various unknown representations, it is not easy for an information system to find such relations. The existing popular relevance relevance algorithms basically use linear additive query expansion methods to find a user preference relation as follows:

- Start with an initial query vector $\mathbf{q}_0$.
- At any step $k \geq 0$, improve the k-th query vector $\mathbf{q}_k$ to

$$\mathbf{q}_{k+1} = \mathbf{q}_k + \alpha_1 \mathbf{d}_1 + \cdots + \alpha_s \mathbf{d}_s, \tag{15.5}$$

where $\mathbf{d}_1, \ldots, \mathbf{d}_s$ are the documents judged by the user, and the updating factors $\alpha_i \in \mathcal{R}$ for $i = 1, \ldots, s$.

One particular and well-known example of relevance feedback is Rocchio's similarity-based relevance feedback [Rocchio (1971); Salton (1989)]. Depending on how updating factors are used in improving the k-th query vector as in expression (15.5), a variety of relevance feedback algorithms have been designed [Ide (1971a,b); Salton (1989); Baeza-Yates and Ribeiro-Neto (1999)]. A similarity-based relevance feedback algorithm is essentially an adaptive supervised learning algorithm from examples [Salton and Buckley (1990); van Rijsbergen (1979); Chen and Zhu (2002)]. The goal of the algorithm is to learn some unknown classifier (such as the linear classifier in expression (15.3)) that is determined by a user's information needs to classify documents as relevant or irrelevant. The learning is performed by modifying or updating the query vector that serves as the hypothetical representation of the collection of all relevant documents. The technique for updating the query vector is linear additions of the vectors of documents judged by the user. This type of linear additive query updating technique is similar to what is used by the Perceptron algorithm [Rosenblatt (1958)]. The linear additive query updating technique has some disadvantage: It's *converging rate* to the unknown target classifier is *slow*, because it has been proved that the Perceptron algorithm [Kivinen *et. al.* (1997)] and the Rocchio's relevance feedback algorithm [Chen and Zhu (2002)] with any of the four typical similar measures [Salton (1989)] have an $\Omega(n)$ lower bound on their performance of learning in the n dimensional binary vector space. In the real world of Web search, a huge number of terms (usually, keywords) are used to index Web documents. To make the things even worse, no users will have the patience to try, say, more than 10 iterations of relevance feedback in order to gain some significant search precision increase. This implies that the traditional linear additive query updating method may be too slow to be applicable to Web search, and this motivates us to design new and *faster* query updating methods for user preference retrieval in Section 15.3.

For a user preference with respect to her information needs, for any index term T, define

- $|\mathcal{D}|$ = the total number of documents in the collection $\mathcal{D}$
- $|\mathcal{D}_r|$ = the total number of relevant documents in $\mathcal{D}$
- η = the number of documents in $\mathcal{D}$ indexed by T
- γ = the number of relevant documents in $\mathcal{D}_r$ indexed by T

A gradient descent procedure has been designed in [Wong *et. al.* (1988)] to find an acceptable ranking strategy satisfying expression (15.2). The idea of the procedure is to minimize ranking errors through linear additions of $\mathbf{d}' - \mathbf{d}$ for all pairs of documents $\mathbf{d}'$ and $\mathbf{d}$ that, according to expression (15.3), are ranked incorrectly. When the gradient descent procedure is applied to find an acceptable ranking satisfying expression (15.4), it has been shown [Wong *et. al.* (1988)] that after the first iteration from a zero initial query vector the procedure weighs an index term T *linearly* in $\frac{\gamma}{|\mathcal{D}_r|} - \frac{\eta}{|\mathcal{D}|}$, an approximate measure of the usefulness of index term T for distinguishing relevant and irrelevant documents. It has also shown that under certain *good* index term probability distribution the above usefulness measure for the index term T reaches its expected maximum when $\eta =$

$0.5|\mathcal{D}|$, a justification for choosing mid-frequency terms in indexing [Salton (1989)]. In contrast to the linear additive query updating strategy used in the gradient descent procedure [Wong *et. al.* (1988)] for minimizing ranking errors, in Section 15.4 a new algorithm with the multiplicative query updating strategy will be designed. It is shown that after the first iteration from a zero initial query vector the new algorithm weights an index term T *exponentially* in $\frac{\gamma}{|\mathcal{D}_r|} - \frac{\eta}{|\mathcal{D}|}$. This means that *exponentially large gaps* will be generated for index terms with respect to measures of their usefulness. Hence, a document with a *good* index term will be ranked *exponentially higher* than one without the *good* index term, thus more ideal ranking effects will be generated for users.

15.3   Multiplicative Adaptive Query Expansion Algorithm

In this section, a multiplicative query updating technique is designed to identify a user preference relation satisfying expression (15.1). It is believed that linear additive query updating yields some *mild* improvement on the hypothetical query vector towards the target user preference. A query updating technique that can yield *dramatic* improvements is wanted so that the hypothetical query vector can be moved towards the target in a much faster pace. The idea is that when an index term is judged by the user, its corresponding value in the hypothetical query vector should be boosted by a multiplicative factor that is dependent on the value of the term itself.

> **Algorithm** $MA(\mathbf{q}_0, f, \theta)$:
> *(i) Inputs:*
>> $\mathbf{q}_0$, *the non-negative initial query vectory*
>> $f(x) : [0, 1] \longrightarrow R^+$, *the updating function*
>> $\theta \geq 0$, *the classification threshold*
>
> *(ii) Set $k = 0$.*
> *(iii) Classify and rank documents with the linear classifier $(\mathbf{q}_k, \theta)$.*
> *(iv) While (the user judged the relevance of a document $\mathbf{d}$) do*
> {
>> *for $i = 1, \dots, n$, do {*
>>> /* $\mathbf{q}_k = (q_{1,k}, \dots, q_{n,k})$, $\mathbf{d} = (d_1, \dots, d_n)$
>> */
>>
>>> *if $(d_i \neq 0)$ {*
>>>> /* *adjustment* */
>>>> *if $(q_{i,k} \neq 0)$ set $q_{i,k+1} = q_{i,k}$*
>>>>> *else set $q_{i,k+1} = 1$*

$$\text{\textit{if } (\mathbf{d} \textit{ is relevant})} \quad \textit{/* promotion */}$$
$$\text{set } q_{i,k+1} = (1 + f(d_i))q_{i,k+1}$$
$$\textit{else} \quad \textit{/* demotion */}$$
$$\text{set } q_{i,k+1} = \frac{q_{i,k+1}}{1+f(d_i)}$$
$$\} \textit{ else}$$
$$\text{set } q_{i,k+1} = q_{i,k}$$
$$\}$$
$$\}$$

*(v) If no documents were judged in the k-th step, then stop.
Otherwise, let $k = k + 1$ and go to step (iv).*
/ The end of the algorithm MA */*

In this chapter, only non-decreasing updating functions $f(x) : [0,1] \Longrightarrow \mathbf{R}^+$ is considered, because it is wanted that multiplicative updating for an index term is proportional to the value of the term. We are, in particular, interested in the following two examples of algorithm MA:

Algorithm **LMA:** *In this algorithm, we let the updating function in algorithm MA be $f(x) = \alpha x$, a linear function with a positive coefficient $\alpha > 1$.*

Algorithm **ENL:** *In this algorithm, we let the updating function in algorithm MA be $f(x) = \alpha^x$, an exponential function with $\alpha > 1$.*

The design of algorithm MA is enlightened by algorithm Winnow [Littlestone (1988)], a well-known algorithm equipped with a multiplicative weight updating technique. However, algorithm MA generalizes algorithm Winnow in the following aspects: (1) Various updating functions may be used in algorithm MA, while only constant updating functions are used in algorithm Winnow; (2) multiplicative updating for a weight is dependent on the value of corresponding indexing terms, which is more realistic and applicable to real-valued vector space, while algorithm Winnow considers all the terms equally; and (3) finally, a number of documents which may or may not be counterexamples to the algorithm's current classification are allowed as relevance feedback; while algorithm Winnow is an adaptive learning algorithm from equivalence queries, requiring the user to provide a counterexample to its current hypothesis. The equivalence query model is hardly realistic, because a user in reality has no knowledge about the information system nor about the representation of her preference. What she may do, and is able to do, is that she can judge some documents as what she needs or not among those provided by the system. We can derive algorithm Winnow [Littlestone (1988)] and algorithm TW2 [Chen *et. al.* (2002)] in the following.

Algorithm MA becomes algorithm Winnow [Littlestone (1988)] when the following restrictions are imposed:

- the vector space is set to the binary vector space $\{0,1\}^n$.
- the initial query vector is set to $q_0 = (1,\dots,1)$.
- the update function is chosen as $f(x) = \alpha$, a positive constant function.
- at step (iv), equivalence query is adopted. That is, the user is asked to judge at most one document that is a counterexample to the current classification of the algorithm.

Algorithm MA becomes algorithm TW2 [Chen *et. al.* (2002)] when the following restrictions are imposed:

- the vector space is set to the binary vector space $\{0,1\}^n$.
- the initial query vector is set to $q_0 = (0,\dots,0)$.
- and the updating function is chosen as $f(x) = \alpha$, a positive constant function.

We now analyze the the performance of algorithm MA when it is used to identify a user preference satisfying expression (15.3), a linear classifier $(\mathbf{q}, 0)$. Here, we consider a zero threshold in expression (refeq3). We say that algorithm MA makes an classification error at step k is the user judged a document as a counterexample to the algorithm's current hypothesis. We estimate the total number of classification errors algorithm MA will make based on the worst-case analysis. We also let at most one counterexample may be provided to the algorithm at each step. From now on to the end of this section it is assumed that $\mathbf{q} = (q_1, q_2, \dots, q_n)$ is a non-negative query vector with m non-zero components and $\theta > 0$. Define

$$\beta = min\{q_i \mid q_i > 0, 1 \le i \le n\}.$$

Definition 3.1. *Documents in the collection $\mathcal{D}$ are said to be indexed with respect to a threshold δ, $0 < \delta \le 1$, if for any document $\mathbf{d} = (d_1, \dots, d_n) \in \mathcal{D}$ one has either $d_i = 0$ or $\delta \le d_i$, $1 \le i \le n$.*

In other words, when a document is indexed with respect to a threshold δ, any index term with a value below the threshold δ is considered not significant, and hence set to zero. Recall that in the vector space model a document and its vector have the equivalent meaning, so we may not distinguish the two concepts.

Lemma 3.2. *Assume that documents are indexed with respect to a threshold δ. Let u denote the total number of promotions that algorithm MA needs to find the linear classifier $(\mathbf{q}, 0)$. Let m denote the number of non-zero components in $\mathbf{q}$. Then,*

$$u \le \frac{m \log \frac{\theta}{\beta\delta}}{\log(1 + f(\delta))}.$$

Proof. Without loss of generality, we may further assume that the m non-zero components of $\mathbf{q}$ are $q_1, \ldots, q_m$. When a promotion occurs at step k, a relevant document $\mathbf{d}$ is given to the algorithm as a counterexample to its current classification. Because of document indexing with respect to the threshold δ, there is some i with $1 \le i \le m$ such that $d_i \ge \delta$. This means that the i-th component $q_{i,k}$ of the query vector $\mathbf{q}_k$ will be promoted to

$$q_{i,k+1} = (1 + f(d_i))q_{i,k} \ge (1 + f(\delta))q_{i,k}, \tag{15.6}$$

because f is non-decreasing. Since $q_{i,k}$ will never be demoted, it follows from expression (15.6) that $q_{i,k}$ can be promoted at most

$$\frac{\log \frac{\theta}{\beta\delta}}{\log(1 + f(\delta))} \tag{15.7}$$

times. Since each promotion yields a promotion for at least one $q_{i,k}$ for $1 \le i \le m$, the total number of promotions u is at most m times the value given in expression (15.7).

Theorem 3.3. *Assume that documents in $\mathcal{D}$ are indexed with respect to a threshold δ, $0 < \delta \le 1$. Let T denote the total number of classification errors algorithm MA makes in order to find the linear classifier $(\mathbf{q}, 0)$ over the real-valued vector space $[0, 1]^n$, where all components in $\mathbf{q}$ are nonnegative. Let m denote the number of non-zero components in $\mathbf{q}$. Then,*

$$T \le \frac{[(1 + f(1))(n - m) + \sigma](1 + f(\delta))(1 + \delta)}{f(\delta)\theta}$$

$$+ \left(\frac{(1 + f(1))(1 + f(\delta))(1 + \delta)}{f(\delta)\delta} + 1\right)\frac{m \log \frac{\theta}{\beta\delta}}{\log(1 + f(\delta))}$$

(Hence, if $\theta = \frac{n}{m}$ is chosen, $T = O(m \log n)$.)

Proof. Without loss of generality, we may assume again that the m non-zero components of $\mathbf{q}$ are $q_1, \ldots, q_m$. We estimate the sum of the weights $\sum_{i=1}^n q_{i,k}$. Let u and v be the number of promotion steps and the number of demotion steps occurred during the learning process, respectively. Let t_k denote the number of zero components in $\mathbf{q}_k$ at promotion step k. Note that once a component of $\mathbf{q}_k$ is promoted to a non-zero value, it will never become zero again. For a promotion at step k with respect to a relevant document $\mathbf{d}$ judged by the user, for $i = 1, \ldots, n$, we have

$$q_{i,k+1} = \begin{cases} q_{i,k}, & if\ d_i = 0, \\ (1 + f(d_i)), & if\ d_i \ne 0\ and\ q_{i,k} = 0, \\ (1 + f(d_i))q_{i,k}, & if\ d_i \ne 0\ and\ q_{i,k} \ne 0. \end{cases}$$

Since a promotion only occurs when

$$\mathbf{q}_k \cdot \mathbf{d} = \sum_{i=1}^{n} d_i q_{i,k} = \sum_{d_i \neq 0 \text{ and } q_{i,k} \neq 0} q_{i,k} < \theta,$$

we have

$$\sum_{i=1}^{n} q_{i,k+1} = \sum_{d_i \neq 0 \text{ and } q_{i,k}=0} q_{i,k+1} + \sum_{d_i \neq 0 \text{ and } q_{i,k} \neq 0} q_{i,k+1} + \sum_{d_i=0} q_{i,k+1}$$

$$= \sum_{d_i \neq 0 \text{ and } q_{i,k}=0} (1 + f(d_i)) + \sum_{d_i \neq 0 \text{ and } q_{i,k} \neq 0} (1 + f(d_i))q_{i,k} + \sum_{d_i=0} q_{i,k}$$

$$\leq (1 + f(1))t_k + \frac{1 + f(1)}{\delta} \sum_{d_i \neq 0 \text{ and } q_{i,k} \neq 0} \delta q_{i,k} + \sum_{i=1}^{n} q_{i,k}.$$

$$\leq (1 + f(1))t_k + \frac{1 + f(1)}{\delta} \sum_{d_i \neq 0 \text{ and } q_{i,k} \neq 0} d_i q_{i,k} + \sum_{i=1}^{n} q_{i,k}.$$

$$\leq (1 + f(1))t_k + \frac{1 + f(1)}{\delta}\theta + \sum_{i=1}^{n} q_{i,k}. \tag{15.8}$$

For a demotion at step k with respect to an irrelevant document $\mathbf{d}$ judged by the user, for $i = 1, \ldots, n$, we have

$$q_{i,k+1} = q_{i,k} - (1 - \frac{1}{1 + f(d_i)})q_{i,k} \leq q_{i,k} - (1 - \frac{1}{1 + f(\delta)})q_{i,k}.$$

Since a demotion occurs only when $\sum_{i=1}^{n} d_i q_{i,k} > \theta$, we have

$$\sum_{i=1}^{n} q_{i,k+1} \leq \sum_{i=1}^{n} q_{i,k} - (1 - \frac{1}{1 + f(\delta)}) \sum_{i=1}^{n} q_{i,k}$$

$$= \sum_{i=1}^{n} q_{i,k} - \frac{f(\delta)}{(1 + f(\delta))} \sum_{i=1}^{n} \frac{d_i}{1 + \delta} q_{i,k}$$

$$\leq \sum_{i=1}^{n} q_{i,k} - \frac{f(\delta)}{(1 + f(\delta))(1 + \delta)} \sum_{i=1}^{n} d_i q_{i,k}$$

$$\leq \sum_{i=1}^{n} q_{i,k} - \frac{f(\delta)}{(1 + f(\delta))(1 + \delta)}\theta \tag{15.9}$$

Let the sum of the initial weights be σ. Hence, by (15.8) and (15.9), after u promotions and v demotions,

$$\sum_{i=1}^{n} q_{i,k+1} \leq (1 + f(1)) \sum_{i=1}^{u} t_i + \sum_{i=1}^{n} q_{i,0} + \frac{(1 + f(1))\theta u}{\delta} - \frac{f(\delta)\theta v}{(1 + f(\delta))(1 + \delta)}$$

$$\leq (1 + f(1))(n - m) + \sigma + \frac{(1 + f(1))\theta u}{\delta} - \frac{f(\delta)\theta v}{(1 + f(\delta))(1 + \delta)}$$

Note that at any step the weights are never negative. It follows from the above relation that

$$v \leq \frac{[(1 + f(1))(n - m) + \sigma](1 + f(\delta))(1 + \delta)}{f(\delta)\theta}$$

$$+ \frac{(1 + f(1))(1 + f(\delta))(1 + \delta)u}{f(\delta)\delta}. \tag{15.10}$$

It follows from Lemma 3.2 and (15.10) that the total number of promotions and demotions, i.e., the total number of classification errors T, is bounded by

$$T \leq v + u \leq \frac{[(1 + f(1))(n - m) + \sigma](1 + f(\delta))(1 + \delta)}{f(\delta)\theta}$$

$$+ \frac{(1 + f(1))(1 + f(\delta))(1 + \delta)u}{f(\delta)\delta} + u$$

$$\leq \frac{[(1 + f(1))(n - m) + \sigma](1 + f(\delta))(1 + \delta)}{f(\delta)\theta}$$

$$+ \left(\frac{(1 + f(1))(1 + f(\delta))(1 + \delta)}{f(\delta)\delta} + 1\right) \frac{m \log \frac{\theta}{\beta\delta}}{\log(1 + f(\delta))}$$

This completes our proof.

15.4 Multiplicative Gradient Descent Search Algorithm

In this section, we design algorithm MG for finding a query vector $\mathbf{q}$ satisfying the acceptable ranking strategy condition (15.2). Algorithm MG uses a multiplicative query updating technique to minimize its ranking errors. It will be shown that algorithm MG boosts the usefulness of an index term *exponentially* in contrast to *linear* boosting achieved by the gradient descent procedure in [Wong *et. al.* (1988)].

> **Algorithm** $MG(\mathbf{q}_0, f)$:
> *(i) Inputs:*

$\mathbf{q}_0$, *the non-negative initial query vectory*
$f(x) : [0, 1] \longrightarrow R^+$, *the updating function*

(ii) Set $k = 0$.

(iii) Let $\mathbf{q}_k$ be the query vector at step k. Identify the set of mistakes

$$\Gamma(\mathbf{q}_k) = \{< \mathbf{d}, \mathbf{d}' > \,|\, \mathbf{d} \prec \mathbf{d}', \mathbf{q}_k \cdot \mathbf{d} \geq \mathbf{q}_k \cdot \mathbf{d}'\}.$$

If $\Gamma(\mathbf{q}_k) = \emptyset$, then stop.

(iv) For each pair $< \mathbf{d}, \mathbf{d}' > \in \Gamma(\mathbf{q}_k)$, do {

*   for $i = 1, \ldots, n$, do {*

*   if $(d_i' \neq 0)$ {*

*   /* adjustment */*

*   if $(q_{i,k} \neq 0)$ set $q_{i,k+1} = q_{i,k}$ else set $q_{i,k+1} = 1$*

*   set $q_{i,k+1} = (1 + f(d_i'))q_{i,k+1}$ /* pro- motion */*

*   }*

*   if $(d_i \neq 0)$*

*   set $q_{i,k+1} = \frac{q_{i,k}}{1+f(d_i)}$ /* demotion */*

*   }*

}

(v) Let $k = k + 1$ and go to step (iii).

/ The end of the algorithm MG */*

Theorem 4.1. *Assume that algorithm MG is applied to find an acceptable ranking strategy satisfying condition (15.4). If one chooses the initial query vector $\mathbf{q}_0 = \mathbf{0}$, then after the first iteration, for any i with $1 \leq i \leq n$, the weight $q_{i,1}$ for the i-th index term in $\mathbf{q}_1$ is*

$$q_{i,1} = \prod_{\mathbf{d} \in \mathcal{D}_{ir}} \prod_{\mathbf{d}' \in \mathcal{D}_r} \frac{\tau(\mathbf{d}')}{\tau(\mathbf{d})},$$

where $\tau(\mathbf{d}') = 1 + f(d_i')$ if $d_i' \neq 0$ or 1 otherwise, and $\tau(\mathbf{d}) = 1 + f(d_i)$ if $d_i \neq 0$ or 1 otherwise. In particular, when a linear updating function $f(x) = \alpha$ is chosen,

$$q_{i,1} = (1 + \alpha)^{|\mathcal{D}| \cdot |\mathcal{D}_r|(\frac{\gamma}{|\mathcal{D}_r|} - \frac{\eta}{|\mathcal{D}|})},$$

where $|\mathcal{D}_r|$ is the total number of relevant documents, η is the number of documents indexed by the i-th index term T_i, and γ is the number of relevant documents indexed by T_i

Proof. Since the acceptable ranking strategy satisfying condition (15.4), it follows from $\mathbf{q}_0 = \mathbf{0}$ that at the first iteration one obtains

$$\Gamma(\mathbf{q}_0) = \{< \mathbf{d}, \mathbf{d}' > \,|\, \mathbf{d} \in \mathcal{D}_{ir}, \mathbf{d}' \in \mathcal{D}_r\}.$$

Here $\mathcal{D}_r$ and $\mathcal{D}_{ir}$ denote respectively the set of relevant documents and the set of irrelevant ones. Note that during the first iteration, for each pair $< \mathbf{d}, \mathbf{d}' > \in \Gamma(\mathbf{q}_0)$, for any i with $1 \leq i \leq n$, a promotion is performed for the i-th component of the query vector if $d_i' \neq 0$ and a demotion is performed for the i-th component if $d_i \neq 0$. This implies that for any i, $1 \leq i \leq n$, after the first iteration the value $q_{i,1}$ with respect to the i-th index term is

$$q_{i,1} = \prod_{\mathbf{d} \in \mathcal{D}_{ir}} \prod_{\mathbf{d}' \in \mathcal{D}_r} \frac{\tau(d')}{\tau(d)}.$$

When a constant updating function $f(x) = \alpha$ is used, it easily follows from the above expression that

$$\begin{aligned}
q_{i,1} &= \prod_{\mathbf{d} \in \mathcal{D}_{ir}} \prod_{\mathbf{d}' \in \mathcal{D}_r} \frac{\tau(\mathbf{d}')}{\tau(\mathbf{d})} \\
&= \frac{\prod_{\mathbf{d}' \in \mathcal{D}_r} \prod_{\mathbf{d} \in \mathcal{D}_{ir}} \tau(\mathbf{d}')}{\prod_{\mathbf{d} \in \mathcal{D}_{ir}} \prod_{\mathbf{d}' \in \mathcal{D}_r} \tau(\mathbf{d})} = \frac{\prod_{\mathbf{d}' \in \mathcal{D}_r} (\tau(\mathbf{d}'))^{|\mathcal{D}_{ir}|}}{\prod_{\mathbf{d} \in \mathcal{D}_{ir}} (\tau(\mathbf{d}))^{|\mathcal{D}_r|}} \\
&= \frac{\prod_{\mathbf{d}' \in \mathcal{D}_r} (1 + f(d_i'))^{|\mathcal{D}_{ir}|}}{\prod_{\mathbf{d} \in \mathcal{D}_{ir}} (1 + f(d_i))^{|\mathcal{D}_r|}} = \frac{(1 + f(d_i'))^{|\mathcal{D}_{ir}|\gamma}}{(1 + f(d_i))^{|\mathcal{D}_r|(\eta-\gamma)}} \\
&= (1 + \alpha)^{|\mathcal{D}_{ir}|\gamma - |\mathcal{D}_r|(\eta-\gamma)} \\
&= (1 + \alpha)^{(|\mathcal{D}| - |\mathcal{D}_r|)\gamma - |\mathcal{D}_r|(\eta-\gamma)} \\
&= (1 + \alpha)^{|\mathcal{D}| \cdot |\mathcal{D}_r|(\frac{\gamma}{|\mathcal{D}_r|} - \frac{\eta}{|\mathcal{D}|})}
\end{aligned}$$

This completes our proof.

In Fig. 15.1, we illustrate the boosting effects of algorithm MG (the exponential curve) and the gradient descent procedure (the linear curve). When the probability distribution of an index term has the pattern as shown in part (b) of Fig. 15.1, we can show in a way similar to [Wong et. al. (1988)] that the expected value of the usefulness $\frac{\gamma}{|\mathcal{D}_r|} - \frac{\eta}{|\mathcal{D}|}$ for an index term reached its maximum when $\eta = 0.5|\mathcal{D}|$, another justification for choosing mid frequent terms in indexing [Salton (1989)].

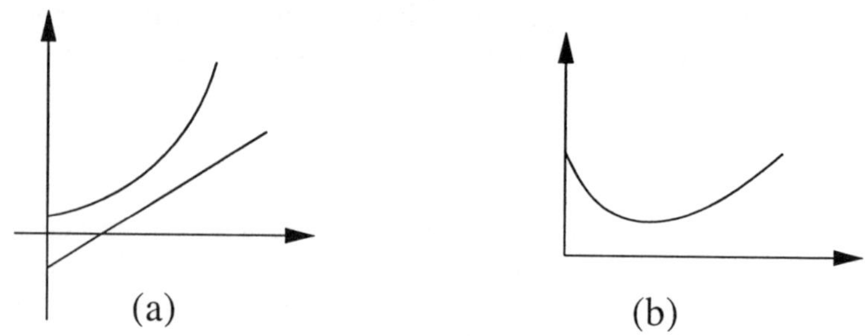

Fig. 15.1   (a)Boosting Rates. (b) Index Term Prob. Distribution

15.5   Meta-Search Engine MARS

In this section, we report the application of algorithm MA to the experimental meta-search engine MARS [Meng and Chen (2002)] (*M*ultiplicative *A*daptive *R*efinement *S*earch). The architecture of MARS is shown in Fig. 15.2. User queries to MARS are accepted from a browser. Besides entering the query, a user can also specify a particular general-purpose search engine that she would like MARS to use and the maximum number of returned results (the larger the number is, the more time it takes to process). The `QueryConstructor` organizes the query into a format conforming to the specified search engine. One of the MetaSearchers sends the query to the general-purpose search engine. When the results are sent back from the general-purpose search engine, `DocumentParser`, `DocumentIndexer` and `Ranker` process the returned URLs and list them to the user as the initial search result. At this point, the rank is based on the original rank from the search engine. Constrained by the amount of space available on a typical screen, we list the top 10 URLs (highest ranked) and the bottom 10 URLs (lowest ranked). Once the results are displayed, the user can interactively work with MARS to refine the search results. Each time the user can mark a particular URL as *relevant* or *not relevant*. Upon receiving feedbacks from the user, MARS updates the weight assigned to each index term within the set of documents already returned from the specified search engine, according to the algorithm MA. The refined results are sorted based on their ranking scores and then displayed back to the user for further relevance feedback. This process continues until the satisfactory results are found or the user quits her search.

Some initial tests have conducted in [Meng and Chen (2002)] to see how effectively and efficiently the algorithm MA can be applied to Web search using MARS meta-search engine. Two types of performance measures, the search precision improvement and the delay statistics of the MARS, were

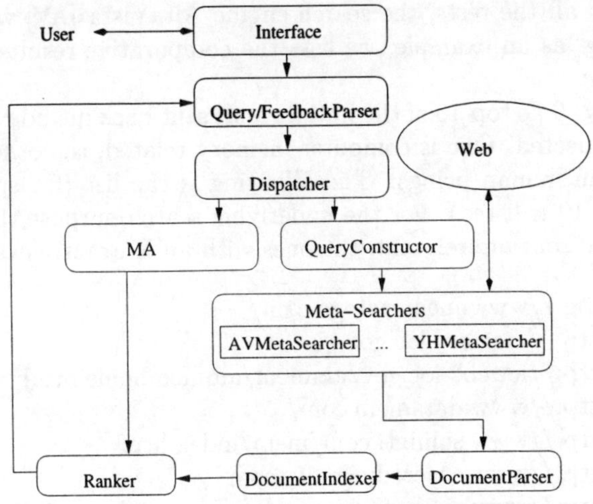

Fig. 15.2   The Architecture of MARS

used. A dozen of queries were sent to MARS to examine the response times. These response times are divided into two categories: The initial response time between the time issuing the query and the time receiving the response from an external search engine the user selected; and the time needed for the algorithm MA to refine the results. One calls these two time measurements *initial time* and *refine time*. The statistics in the Table 15.1 indicates the two measures. One should note that the *initial time* is needed to get any search results from the external search whether or not the algorithm MA is involved. As can be seen, the time spent in refining the search results is very small relative to the time to get the initial result.

Table 15.1: Response Time in Seconds

	Mean	Std Dev.	95% Conf. Interval	Maximum
Original	3.86	1.15	0.635	5.29
Refine	0.986	0.427	0.236	1.44

It has also been evaluated how algorithm MA improves the search precision. In the evaluation, a set of highly vague terms, such as *memory* and *language*, were selected. These words may mean completely differently in different areas. E.g., the term *memory* can mean human memory, or the memory chips used in computers; and the term *language* can refer to spoken language or computer programming language. We wanted to see if the search precision improves *dramatically* with very limited relevance feedback. In all the tests, the search engine AltaVista [AV] was used. In the following, as an example, we lists the comparative results of *memory* and *language*.

Memory: The top-10 of the initial result sent back include two types of URLs, as expected. One is computer memory related, the other is related to memory in human beings. The following is the list (for space reason, only the top 10 is listed). For the underlying search purpose the ones that have an R in front are relevant; the ones with an X are irrelevant.

R http://www.memorytogo.com/
X http://memory.loc.gov/
X http://lcweb2.loc.gov/ammem/ammemhome.html
R http://www.datamem.com/
R http://www.samintl.com/mem/index.htm
X http://www.asacredmemory.com/
X http://www.exploratorium.edu/memory/lectures.html
X http://www.exploratorium.edu/memory/index.html
R http://www.satech.com/glosofmemter.html
R http://www.lostcircuits.com/memory/

With one round of refinement when a total of four URLs were marked (two marked in the top 10 list and two marked in the bottom 10 list), four of the original irrelevant URLs were eliminated and the revised top 10 URLs are as follows.

R http://www.streetprices.com/Electronics/...ware_PC
R http://www.memorytogo.com/
X http://www.crpuzzles.com/mem/index.html
R http://www.linux-mtd.infradead.org/
R http://fiberoptics.dimm-memory-infineon....owsides
R http://www.ramplus.com/cpumemory.html
X http://www.asacredmemory.com/
R http://www.computersupersale.com/shopdis..._A_cat_
R http://www.datamem.com/
R http://www.lostcircuits.com/memory/

Language: Similar to the term *memory*, the search results for *language* can be roughly divided into two classes, the ones related to human languages and the ones related to computer programming language. The following is the original list of top 10 URLs returned from AltaVista [AV] with R as relevant and X as irrelevant and we are looking for information about programming language.

> X http://chinese.about.com/
> R http://www.python.org/
> X http://esl.about.com/
> X http://esl.about.com/homework/esl/mbody.htm
> X http://www.aliensonearth.com/catalog/pub/language/
> X http://kidslangarts.about.com/
> X http://kidslangarts.about.com/kids/kidslangarts/mb
> X http://pw1.netcom.com/ rlederer/rllink.htm
> X http://www.wordcentral.com/
> X http://www.win-shareware.com/html/language.html

As can be seen, only one URL `www.python.org` is really relevant to what was looked for. With a refinement of three URLs marked, one marked irrelevant from the top 10 list, one marked relevant from the top 10 list, and one marked from the bottom 10 list (`www.suse.de/lang.html`), the refined list now contains six relevant URLs, compared to only one before refinement. Of these six URLs, one was originally in top 10 and was marked; one was originally in bottom 10 and was marked; the other four were not examined nor marked before at all. But they showed up in the top 10 list!

> R http://www.suse.de/lang.html
> R http://www.python.org/
> X http://www.eason.ie/flat_index_with_area...L400_en
> R http://www.w3.org/Style/XSL/
> X http://www.hlc.unimelb.edu.au/
> X http://www.transparent.com/languagepages/languages
> R http://caml.inria.fr/
> R http://home.nvg.org/ sk/lang/lang.html
> R http://www.ihtml.com/
> X http://www.aliensonearth.com/catalog/pub/language/

As can been seen from the above experimental results algorithm MA improve the search performance significantly.

15.6　Meta-Search Engine MAGrads

This section reports an experimental meta-search engine MAGrads [Meng *et. al.* (2003)] (*M*ultiplicative *A*daptive *Gra*dient *D*escent *S*earch), which is built upon algorithm MG. The architecture of MAGrads is similar to that of MARS as shown in Fig. 15.2. As in MARS, a user can query MAGrads from a browser. The user can also specify a particular general-purpose search engine she would like MAGrads to use and the maximum number of returned results. The `QueryConstructor` organizes the query into a format conforming to the specified search engine. One of the MetaSearchers sends the query to the general-purpose search engine to receive the initial search result. `DocumentParser`, `DocumentIndexer` and `Ranker` work in the similar ways as they do in MARS. Once the results are displayed, the user can interactively work with MAGrads to refine the search results. Each time the user can mark a particular URL as *relevant* or *not relevant*. Upon receiving feedbacks from the user, MAGrads updates the weight assigned to each index term within the set of documents already returned from the specified search engine, according to the algorithm MG. The refined results are sorted based on their ranking scores and then displayed back to the user for further relevance feedback. This process continues until the satisfactory results are found or the user quits her search.

In order to provide some measures of system performance we conducted a set of experiments and compared the search results between AltaVista and MAGrads in regard to their search accuracy. The evaluation is based on the following approach that is similar to the standard *recall* and *precision* used in information retrieval.

For a search query q, let A denote the set of documents returned by the search engine (either AltaVista or MAGrads), and let R denote the set of documents in A that are relevant to q. For any integer m with $1 \leq m \leq |A|$, define R_m to be the set of documents in R that are among the top m ranked documents according to the search engine. One defines the *relative recall* R_{recall} and the *relative precision* $R_{precision}$ as follows.

$$R_{recall} = \frac{|R_m|}{|R|}$$

$$R_{precision} = \frac{|R_m|}{m}$$

The relative recall R_{recall} measures the percentage of relevant documents in R are listed in the top-m list m positions. The more relevant documents are listed within the top-m list, the better the performance is of the search engine. The relative precision $R_{precision}$ is a measure of how many documents are relevant among the top-m list.

In the evaluation, a list of 20 queries were selected. The queries were tested against AltaVista and MAGrads, respectively. The performance results were collected and recorded. When a query was issued to AltaVista, One manually went through the returned results (the set A), marking the ones that were relevant (the set R). The number of relevant documents within the top-10 and top-20 were also marked (the set R_m where $m =$

Table 15.2: Relative Precision and Recall Comparison

	$R_{\text{precision}}$		R_{recall}	
	AltaVista	MAGrads	AltaVista	MAGrads
(50,10)	0.55	0.82	0.23	0.40
(50,20)	0.52	0.74	0.40	0.69
(100,10)	0.55	0.85	0.14	0.27
(100,20)	0.52	0.77	0.24	0.46
(150,10)	0.55	0.86	0.11	0.23
(150,20)	0.52	0.79	0.19	0.40
(200,10)	0.55	0.88	0.09	0.21
(200,20)	0.52	0.80	0.17	0.35

10, 20). We then again manually went through the documents list to check the number of documents appeared at the top-10 and top-20 list. For each of the 20 queries, one selected the total number of documents to be returned by AltaVista and used by MAGrads to be 50, 100, 150, and 200, respectively. The relative recall and relative precision were computed for each of the query. The average was taken for comparison between AltaVista and MAGrads. The results of the comparison are listed in Table 15.2.

In Table 15.2, each row is labeled by a pair of integers $(|A|, m)$, where $|A|$ is the total number of documents retrieved by the search engine for a given query and m is the limit of the size of the top-listed documents. Some observations and analysis are obtained from the data listed in the table:

(1) AltaVista holds relative precisions, $R_{precision} = \frac{|R_m|}{m}$, constant across the document sets of size 200, 150, 100, and 50 for the given value of m (the number of top documents listed to the user). The reason is that the document set returned by AltaVista and its order in response to the given query is fixed. Thus the set R_m is a constant with regard to a given value of m. In the underlying experiments, m was assigned the value of 10 and 20.

(2) On the other hand for MAGrads the set R_m changes as the user enters its feedback and MAGrads re-adjusts the document relevance according to the user feedback. On average more relevant documents sift up towards the top-listed document set based on the user relevance feedback. Thus it has a better average relative precision than that of AltaVista.

(3) As for relative recall, $R_{recall} = \frac{|R_m|}{|R|}$, the case is different. For AltaVista, although the set R_m, the set of relevant documents that are actually listed in the top-m documents is fixed, the base size $|R|$ is changing from 50 to 200. Thus the average relative recall is in fact decreasing (from 0.23 to 0.09 for $m = 10$ and from 0.40 to 0.17 for $m = 20$) as the base

document size increases.

(4) The relative recall of MAGrads is decreasing as the base size increases for the same reason for a given value of m. However because of the relevance feedback MAGrads has a much higher average relative recall rate than that of AltaVista.

As can be seen from the table, MAGrads has a much better average performance than that of AltaVista, as far as relative precisions and relative recalls are concerned. The primary reason is the use of multiplicative gradient descent algorithm MG in MAGrads. Since the query list is chosen randomly and the comparison is done for the same set of documents between AltaVista and MAGrads, the results here are convincing that the MAGrads algorithm performs very well.

15.7   Concluding Remarks

The motivations of the work in this chapter come from the reality of Web search: Web search users usually have no patience to try, say, more than 5 iterations of relevance feedback for some intelligent search system in order to gain certain significant search precision increase. Existing popular algorithms for user preference retrieval have their own beauty and advantages. Because of the adoption of *linear additive* query updating techniques, when used to identify user preference determined by a linear classifier those algorithms, such as Rocchio's algorithm and its variants [Rocchio (1971); Ide (1971a,b)], the Perceptron algorithm [Rosenblatt (1958); Duda (1973)] and gradient descent procedure, [Wong *et. al.* (1988)] have either a *slow* converging rate or *small* boosting on the usefulness of an index term.

In contrast to the adoption of linear additive query updating techniques in the those existing algorithms, two new algorithms MA and MG have been designed in this chapter. Those two algorithms use multiplicative query updating techniques to adaptively learn the user's preference from relevance feedback. It is proved that algorithm MA has substantially better performance than the Rocchio and the Perceptron algorithms in the case of identifying a user preference relation that is determined by a linear classifier with a small number of non-zero coefficients. It is also shown that algorithm MG boosts the usefulness of an index term *exponentially* to identify a linear structured user preference after the first iteration, while the gradient descent procedure does so *linearly*. Two applications MARS and MAGrads of algorithms MA and MG are also presented, and the experimental results show that both algorithms can achieve significant search precision increase.

The current theoretical results have been obtained for algorithms MA and MG in the worst-case performance analysis. It is interesting to analyze the average-case performance of those two algorithms. We feel that this task is very challenging. It is also interesting to conduct emperimental studies to understand the behaviors of the algorithms MA and GA with real world data sets. Finally, we would like to investigate more applications of the two algorithms to Web search.

Acknowledgment The author thanks Professor Xiannong Meng for many valuable discussions on the topic. The work in this chapter is supported in part by the Computing and Information Technology Center of the University of Texas-Pan American.

Bibliography

Baeza-Yates, R. and Ribeiro-Neto, B. (1999). *Modern Information Retrieval*, Addison Wesley.

Bollmann, P. and Wong, S.K.M. (1987). Adaptive linear information retrieval models, *Proc. the Tenth ACM SIGIR Conf. on Research and Development in Information Retrieval*, ACM Press, pp. 157-163.

Chen, Z. (2001). Multiplicative adaptive algorithms for user preference retrieval, *Proc. the Seventh Annual Intl. Conf. on Combinatorics and Computing*, Lecture Notes in Computer Science 2108, Springer-Verlag, pp. 540-549.

Chen, Z. and Meng, X. (2002). MARS: Multiplicative adaptive user preference retrieval in Web search, *Proc. the Intl. Conf. on Internet Computing*, CSREA Press, pp. 643-648.

Chen, Z. and Meng, X. (2000). Yarrow: A real-time client site meta search learner, *Proc. the AAAI 2000 Workshop on Artificial Intelligence for Web Search*, AAAI Press, pp. 12-17.

Chen, Z., Meng, X., Fowler, R.H., and Zhu, Z. (2001). Features: Real-time adaptive feature learning and document learning, *J. the American Society for Information Science*, **52**, 8, pp. 655-665.

Chen, Z., Meng, X., Zhu, B. and Fowler, R.H. (2002). WebSail: From online learning to Web search, *J. Knowledge and Information Science*, **4**, 2, pp. 219-227.

Chen, Z. and Zhu, B. (2002). Some formal analysis of the Rocchio's similaritybased relevance feedback algorithm, *Information Retrieval*, 5, pp. 61-86, 2002.

Chen, Z., Zhu, B. and Meng, X. (2002). Intelligent Web Search through Adaptive Learning from Relevance Feedback, in Shi, N. and V.K. Murthy (eds.), *Architectural Issues of Web-Enabled E-Business*, Idea Group Publishing, pp. 139-143.

Duda, R.O. and Hart, P.E. (1973). *Pattern Classification and Scene Analysis*, John Wiley.

Fishburn, P.C. (1970). *Utility Theory for Decision Making*, New York, Wiley.

Frakes, W.B. and Baeza-Yates, R.S. (1992). *Information Retrieval: Data Structures and Algorithms*, Prentice Hall.

Ide, E. (1971a). New experiments in relevance feedback, in Salton, G. (editor), *The Smart System - Experiments in Automatic Document Processing*, Prentice-Hall, pp. 337-354.

Ide, E. (1971b). Interactive search strategies and dynamic .le organization in information retrieval, in Salton, G. (editor), *The Smart System – Experiments in Automatic Document Processing*, Prentice-Hall, pp. 373-393.

Kivinen, J., Warmuth, M.K. and Auer, P. (1997). The perceptron algorithm vs. winnow: linear vs. logarithmic mistake bounds when few input variables are relevant, *Artificial Intelligence*, pp. 325-343.

Littlestone, N. (1988). Learning quickly when irrelevant attributes abound: A new linear-threshold algorithm, *Machine Learning*, 2, pp. 285-318.

Meng, X. and Chen, Z. (2003). PAWS: Personalized Web Search with Clusters, *Proc. the 2003 Intl. Conf. on Internet Computing*, CSREA Press, pp. 46-52.

Meng, X. and Chen, Z. (2002). MARS: Applying multiplicative adaptive user preference retrieval to Web Search, *Proc. the Intl. Conf. on Internet Computing*, CSREA Press, pp. 643-648.

Meng, X., Chen, Z. and Spink, A. (2003). A multiplicative gradient descent search algorithm for user preference retrieval and its application to Web search, *Proc. of the IEEE Intl. Conf. on Information and Technology: Coding and Computing*, IEEE Press, pp. 150-154.

Raghavan, V.V. and Wong, S.K.M. (1986). A critical analysis of the vector space model for information retrieval, *J. the American Society for Information Science*, **37**, 5, pp. 279-287.

Roberts, F.S. (1976). *Measurement Theory*, Addison-Wesley, Readings (MS).

Rocchio, J.J. (1971). Relevance feedback in information retrieval, in Salton, G. (editor), *The Smart Retrieval System - Experiments in Automatic Document Processing*, Prentice-Hall, pp. 313-323.

Rosenblatt, F. (1958). The perceptron: A probabilistic model for information storage and organization in the brain, *Psychological Review*, **65**, 6, pp. 386-407.

Salton, G. (1989). *Automatic Text Processing: The Transformation, Analysis, and Retrieval of Information by Computer*, Addison-Wesley.

Salton, G. and Buckley, C. (1990). Improving retrieval performance by relevance feedback, *J. the American Society for Information Science*, **41**, 4, pp. 288-297.

Salton, G., Wong, S.K.M. and Yang, C.S. (1975). A vector space model for automatic indexing, *Communications of ACM*, **18**, 11, pp. 613-620.

Spink, A. and Losee, R.M. (1996). Feedback in Information Retrieval, *Annual Review of Information Science and Technology (ARIST)*, **31**, pp. 33-77.

van Rijsbergen, C.J. (1979). *Information Retrieval*. Butterworths, London.

Wong, S.K.M., Yao, Y.Y. and Bollmann, P. (1988). Linear structures in information retrieval, *Proc. the 1988 ACM-SIGIR Conf. on Information Retrieval*, pp. 219-232.

## CHAPTER 16

SCALABLE LEARNING METHOD TO EXTRACT BIOLOGICAL INFORMATION FROM HUGE ONLINE BIOMEDICAL LITERATURE

Xiaohua Hu and Illhoi Yoo

College of Information Science and Technology
Drexel University, Philadelphia, PA 19104, USA
E–mail: thu@cis.drexel.edu

Many biological results are published only in plain–text articles and these articles or their abstracts are collected in online biomedical literature databases such as PubMed and BioMed Central. To expedite the progress of functional bioinformatics, it is important to efficiently process large amounts of biomedical articles and extract these results into a structured format and store in a database so these results can be retrieved and analyzed by biologists and medical researchers. Automated discovery and extraction of these biological relationships from biomedical literatures has become essential because of the enormous amount of biomedical literature published each year. In this paper we present a scalable learning method to automatically extract biological relationships from biomedical literature. Our method integrates information extraction and data mining together, automatically learns the patterns based on a few user seed tuples, and then extract new tuples from the biomedical literatures based on the discovered patterns. A novel framework <u>B</u>iological <u>R</u>elationship **<u>EXtract</u>** (BRExtract) is implemented and tested on the PuBMed to find the protein–protein interaction and the experimental results indicate our approach is very effective in extracting biological relationships from large collection of online biomedical literature.

16.1 Introduction

Many biological results are published only in plain–text articles and these articles or their abstracts are collected in online biomedical literature databases, such as PubMed and BioMed Central. To expedite the progress of functional bioinformatics, it is important to develop scalable learning method to efficiently process large amounts of biomedical literature and extract the results into a structured format that is easy for retrieval and analysis by genomic and medical researchers. Automated discovery and extraction of these biological relationships from biomedical literatures has become essential because of the enormous amount of biomedical literature published each year. A promising approach for making so much information manageable and easily accessible is to develop information extraction system to automatically process the biomedical literature and extract the important biological relationships such as protein–protein interactions, functionality of the genes, subcellular location of the protein, *etc.* and consolidate them into databases. This serves several purposes: (1) experts consolidate data about a single organism or a single class of entity (*e.g.*, proteins, genes etc) in one place, very helpful for bioinformatics research at genomic scale in order to get a global view of that organism, (2) this process makes the information searchable and manageable since these results are extracted in a structured format, (3) the extracted knowledge can help researchers to generate plausible hypotheses or at least clarify and classify biological relationships so as to assists the user in hypothesis generation. It can also alter the user's perception of the biological relationships in such as way as to stimulate new experiments and methods. Some databases that accumulate these biological relationships such as DIP for protein–protein interaction [Xenarios *et. al.* (2001)], KEGG for biological pathway [Kanehisa and Goto (1997)], BIND for molecular interaction [Bader *et. al.* (2001)] *etc*, are currently under development. The biological relationships stored in these databases are almost assembled manually. However, it is becoming more and more difficult for curators to keep up with the increasing volume of literature. Thus, automatic methods are needed to speed up this step of database construction. Integration of data mining and information extraction provides a promising direction to assist in the duration process to construct such databases.

This chapter discusses a scalable learning method to automatically extract biological relationships from huge collection of biomedical literature to help biologists in functional bioinformatics research. Our techniques build on the idea of DIPRE introduced by Brin [Brin (1998)]. The goal is to develop efficient and portable system to automatically extract various biological relationships such as protein–protein interaction, protein–gene interaction, functionality of gene from biomedical literature with no or little human intervention. These biological relationships will help to uncover hidden relationships and complexes governing genomic operations.

Efficient processing of large amount of biomedical literature requires that an intelligent information extraction method be flexible to work in a very complicated domain. Our aims are to develop a scalable and portable intelligent text–mining system. We view the extraction of biological relationships from biomedical literature as an automated information extraction task. In our method, we integrate information extraction and data mining method. Our method automatically learns and identifies patterns and relations through data mining and information extraction. This method only uses a few training examples from users and apply data mining techniques to discover the patterns and then rely on the discovered patterns to extract new tuples, the newly high accurate tuples is used to discover new patterns in the next round *etc*. The contributions of our research approach are

- A pattern match method is used to automatically learn the patterns. This method can be used to quickly train a mining algorithm to recognize potential interesting articles and learn the patterns to reflect the biological relationships.
- Our learning method falls into the board category of partial–supervised learning techniques to boost precision and recall rate of the pattern extraction. In our system, the information extraction and data mining interact and support each other in the procedure. In the information extraction step, only the high accurate discovered patterns

are used as a match pattern and in the data mining step, only the tuples with high confidence are used to search the pattern.

▪ Our approach scales very well in huge amount of biomedical literature such as PubMed. It automatically discovers the characteristics of documents that are useful for extraction of a target relation and generates queries in each iteration to select potential useful articles from the online biomedical literature database based on the extracted patterns and newly extracted tuples.

▪ Unlike other learning based methods, which need parsing as the prerequisite in order to build a classification models, our approach works directly on the plain–text representation and need much less manual intervention and without the laborious text pre–processing work.

The rest of the chapter is organized as follows: In Section 2, we discussed related work in biomedical literature mining. In Section 3, we present our approach and illustrate each step with some examples. In Section 4, we discuss the experiment results of our method in finding protein–protein interactions from PubMed and conclude in Section 5.

16.2 Related Work

Biomedical literature mining has attracted a lot of attention recently from information extraction, data mining, natural language understanding (NLP) and bioinformatics community [Hirschman *et. al.* (2002)]. A lot of methods have been proposed and various systems have been developed in extracting biological relationships from biomedical literature such as finding protein or gene name [Fukuda *et. al.* (1998); Stapley *et. al.* (2000)], protein–protein interactions [Blaschke *et. al.* (1999); Marcott *et. al.* (2001); Ding *et. al.* (2002); Ono *et. al.* (2001)], protein–gene interaction [Chiang and Yu (2003)], subcellular location of protein, functionality of gene, protein synonym [de Brujin and Martin (2002)] *etc*. For example, in his pioneering work in biomedical literature mining, [Fukuda *et. al.* (1998)] rely on special characteristics such as the occurrence of uppercase letters, numerals and special endings to pinpoint protein names. Stapley *et. al.* [2000] extracted co–occurrence of gene names from MEDLINE documents and use them to predict their connections based on their joint and individual occurrence statistics. Blaschke *et. al.* [1999] propose a NLP–based approach to parse sentences in abstract into grammatical units, and then analyze sentences discussing interactions based on the frequency of individual words. Because of the complexity and variety of the English language, such approach is inherently difficult. Ono *et. al.* [2001] manually defined some regular expression pattern to identify the protein–protein interactions, the problem is that regular expression searches for abstracts containing relevant words, such as "interact", "bind" *etc*, poorly discriminate true hits from abstract using the words in alternative senses and miss abstract using different language to describe the interactions. His method relies on manually created "pattern" to the biological relationship. This approach may introduce a lot of "false positive" or "false negative" and it is unable to capture the new biological relationships not in those "manual" patterns. Marcott *et. al.* [2001] proposed a Bayesian approach based on the frequencies of discriminating words found in the abstract, the scores Medline abstract for probability of discussing the topic of interest according to the frequencies of discriminating words found in the abstract. The highly likely abstracts are the sources for the curators for further examination for entry into the databases. Hahn *et. al.* [2002] developed the MEDSYNDIKATE based on NLP techniques to extract knowledge from medical reports.

To our surprise, of the many biomedical literature mining studies, not much attention has been paid to the portability and scalability issue in automatic information extraction from biomedical literature. With the development of genomic research, the scope and goal of bioinformatics research is getting more complicated and the number of published articles is growing at a very fast rate, thus the information extraction and mining methods must be flexible to work in multiple goals in different sub–disciplines and can scale to millions of documents. For example, PubMed now contains more than 12 millions biology and medicine related abstracts. Based on this consideration, we presents a novel approach which addresses both of those two problems by automatically discovering good patterns for a new scenario with no or little human intervention. Compared with previous work, our methods reduce the manual intervention to a great minimum. Our method only needs a few training examples and it can automatically extract the actual biological relationships embedded in the huge collections of online biomedical literature. The closest work to us is Snowball [Agichtein and Gravano (2000)], but Snowball only can handle the situation where one entity can only involve in one relationship, but this is normally not true in bioinformatics domain, where a entity involves in many relationships, for example, a protein may interact with many other proteins, and a protein/gene has multiple functionalities etc, thus it can't be used in biomedical literature mining.

16.3 Text Mining with Information Extraction for Biomedical Literature Mining

To deal with the portability and scalability issues in biomedical literature mining simultaneously, we introduce some novel ideas. Unlike previous approaches, which use annotated corpus for training, we only use a few seed examples, making it easier to port from one subject domain to another. Current biomedical literature mining systems either scan every article or use filters to select potential promising articles for extraction. There are some limitations for this approach. Scanning every article is not feasible for large online biomedical literature such as PubMed. The current filtering techniques require human involvement to maintain and to adopt new database and domains [Califf and Mooney (2003)]. In biomedical research, especially in rapidly changing fields such as molecular biology and medicine, subjects can be extremely complex: there are many synonym terms, new connections are constantly discovered between previously unrelated subjects and review articles are outdated very quickly [de Brujin and Martin (2002)]. In these situations, an automatic query–based technique is necessary in order to get relevant articles from large text databases for information extraction, which can be adapted to new domain, databases with minimal human effort.

   Our method extracts biological relationships from biomedical literature database that requires only a handful training examples from users.

These examples are used as seed tuples to generate extraction patterns that in turn result in new tuples being extracted from the biomedical literature database. Our method consists of the following steps:

1. Identify potential interesting articles from the online biomedical literature database based on the automatically generated query from the seed tuples.
2. Tag the entity names in those selected biomedical articles.
3. Extract sentences of interests from the articles.
4. Find occurrence of seed tuples in the sentences.
5. Generate extraction patterns.
6. Extract new tuples based on pattern matching.
7. Select the top n tuples as the new seed tuples and repeat 1-6 until no more new tuples can be extracted

The basic architecture of our system BRExtract is shown in Fig. 16.1. Given a large collection of biomedical articles, we first automatically generat a query based on the seed tuples and select the relevant articles. Then using the entity name list (such as protein name list for finding protein–protein interaction, gene name list for finding gene synonym), these biomedical articles are tagged and only those sentences with a pair of entity names in the entity name lists are retained. Using a handful of training seed tuples, BRExtract searches for occurrences of the seed tuples in those sentences, identifying text contexts where entity pairs appear together. BRExtract learns extraction pattern from these example contexts. The patterns are then used to scan through the article collection, which result in new tuples being discovered. The most reliable ones are used as the new seed tuples.

The goal of our system is to extract as many valid biological relationships as possible from the huge collection of biomedical literature and to combine them into a database. We realize that a biological relationship may appear in multiple times in various articles, we do not need to capture every instance of such relationship. Instead, as long as we capture one instance of such a relationship, we will consider our system to be successful for that relationship.

Our system uses a pipelined architecture, and tries to do the extraction with as little human intervention as possible. To build the extractor, the patterns are learned for identifying the relevant sentences within the document, patterns for extracting the data items in the sentences and patterns for mapping the blocks with the semantic objects in the data model. Our method extracts such tables from document collections that require only a handful of seed tuples as training examples to begin with. These examples are used to generate extraction patterns that in turn results in new tuples being extracted from the document collection. We describe them in details in the subsection below.

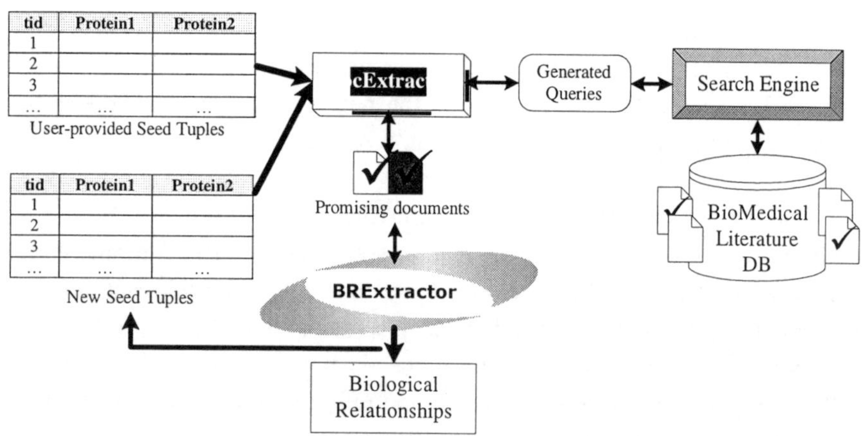

Fig. 16.1 BRExtract

16.3.1 *Select Potential promising Biomedical Articles from the Biomedical Literature Databases*

Since the collection of biomedical articles is so huge, it is infeasible to process every article in the biomedical database. In the initial round, we select a pre–specified number of articles based on the seed examples as shown in Table 16.1. For example, if our system is used for protein–protein interaction extraction, the seed examples are a set of protein name pairs. So we can first select all those articles in the PubMed which contains all those protein names in the seed examples. If an article does contain the seed examples in a single sentence, we label it as a positive example otherwise it is negative. These labeled articles are used in the later stage for training to learn the extraction pattern from these articles. Starting from the second round, we use the extracted patterns to select potential interesting articles and rely on the newly discovered tuples for article classification.

Table 16.1 Initial training seed tupless

Protein 1	Protein 2	Interaction
HP1	histoneH3	Yes
HP1	HDAC4	Yes
KAP1	SETDB1	Yes
AuroraB	INCENP	Yes

16.3.2 *Protein Tagging and Extraction of Sentences of Interests*

A key step in generating and matching patterns to extract new tuples is finding where entity pairs occur in the text. Once the entities in the text document are identified, our systems can ignore unwanted text segments, focus on occurrence of entities, and analyze the context that surround each pair of such entities to check if they are connected by the right words and hence match our patterns. We noticed that in most of the cases, the entity pair with a biological relationship normally occurs within the same sentences, so we segment the biomedical into sentences using the publicly available software SentenceSplitter developed by Don Roth   (http://l2r.cs.uiuc.edu/~cogcomp/index_research.html.)   After sentence segmentation, only those sentences with a pair of entities will be retained for further consideration for extraction, this step significantly reduce the data size and computation time without losing much useful information. We understand in some cases, two entities with a biological relationship may not always appear in the same sentences in an article. But we believe that such pair will occur multiple times in different articles, the likelihood is very high (almost certain) that the entity pair will appear together in at least once in some sentence from one of these articles in our large collection of biomedical articles. For example, the protein pair HHR23B, XPC occur together in articles PMID: 10488153,

9164480, and 8692695 and appear in the same sentence in both PMID 9164480 and 8692695. This observation is verified by our experimental results (in Section 4), on average, a pair of interacted proteins occur at least 6 times together in some sentences in our article collection of almost half a millions MEDLIEN abstracts.

The example below shows the protein name tagging and the sentences of interests extracted from abstract PMID: 9334186.

The transcription factors Fos, Jun, and Ets regulate the expression of human stromelysin–1 and collagenase–1 genes. Recently, we found that <protein>ERG</protein>, an Ets family member, activates collagenase–1 gene but not stromelysin–1 by physically interacting with c–Fos/c–Jun. Interestingly, <protein>ERG</protein> binds to stromelysin–1 promoter and represses its activation by <protein>ETS2</protein>. Here, to investigate the molecular mechanism of this regulation, we have used an in vitro protein–protein interaction assay and studied the transcription factor interactions of <protein>ETS2</protein>. We found that <protein>ETS2</protein> could weakly associate with in vitro synthesized <protein>ETS1</protein>, c–Fos, and c–Jun and strongly with c–Fos/c–Jun complex and <protein>ERG</protein> via several distinct <protein>ETS2</protein> domains including the C–terminal region that contains the DNA–binding domain. Strikingly, these interactions were stabilized in vitro by DNA as they were inhibited by ethidium bromide. Both the N–terminal region, comprising the transactivation domain, and the C–terminal region of <protein>ETS2</protein> associated with <protein>ERG</protein> and, interestingly, the interaction of <protein>ERG</protein> through the transactivation domain of <protein>ETS2</protein> was DNA–independent. The DNA–dependent interaction of <protein>ETS2</protein> with c–Fos/c–Jun was enhanced by specific DNA fragments requiring two Ets–binding sites of the stromelysin–1 promoter. Using the two hybrid system, we also demonstrated that <protein>ETS2</protein> interacts with c–Jun or <protein>ERG</protein> in vivo.

Fig. 16.2 Sample Tagged Medline Abstract

4 sentences of interests are extracted from this abstract as shown below:
(1) Interestingly, <protine>ERG</protine> binds to stromelysin–1 promoter and represses its activation by <protine>ETS2</protine>.
(2) We found that <protein>ETS2</protein> could weakly associate with in vitro synthesized <protein>ETS1</protein>, c–Fos, and c–Jun and strongly with c–Fos/c–Jun complex and <protein>ERG</protein> via several distinct <protein>ETS2</protein> domains including the C–terminal region that contains the DNA–binding domain.
(3) Both the N–terminal region, comprising the transactivation domain, and the C–terminal region of <protein>ETS2 </protein>associated with <protein>ERG</protein> and, interestingly, the interaction of <protein>ERG</protein> through the transactivation domain of <protein>ETS2</protein> was DNA–independent.
(4) Using the two hybrid system, we also demonstrated that <protein>ETS2</protein> interacts with c–Jun or <protein>ERG</protein> in vivo.

16.3.3 Generation of Patterns

A crucial step in the extraction process is the generation of new patterns, which is accomplished by grouping the occurrences of known patterns in documents that occur in similar contexts. A good pattern should be selective but have high coverage so that they do not generate many false positive and can identify many new tuples.

Definition 1 A pattern is a 5–tuples <prefix, entity_tag1, infix, entity_tag2, suffix>, prefix, infix, and suffix are vectors associating weights with terms. Prefix is the part of sentence before entity1, infix is the part of sentence between entity1 and entity2 and suffix is the part of sentence after entity2.

Our pattern definition uses Eliza–like pattern format [Weizenbaum (1966)] and can represent some syntax and semantic context information from the article. For example, a protein–protein interaction pattern in our approach is a tuple (or expression) consisting of two protein names that correspond to some conventional way of describing interaction. We can use these patterns to characterize those sentences that capture this knowledge. Moreover, to increase precision, we incorporate processing of negative sentences into this step. Negative sentences, which describe a lack of relationship, constitute a well–known problem in language understanding. For this reason, processing of negative sentences has not been integrated into many related studies. As a result, the previously proposed methods often extract inaccurate information.

To reduce the manual intervention in the information extraction process, we only use a few training examples to begin with as shown in Table 16.1 (these seed examples are for protein–protein interactions). For every such protein pairs tuple <p1, p2>, it finds segment of text in the sentences where p1 and p2 occur close to each other and analyze the text that "connect" p1 and p2 to generate patterns. For example, our approach inspects the context surrounding chromatin protein HP1 and HDAC4 in "HP1 interacts with HDAC4 in the two–hybrid system" to construct a pattern { "" <Protein1> interacts with <Protein2> ""}. After generating a number of patterns from the initial seed examples, our system scans the available sentences in search of segment of text that match the patterns. As a result of this process, it generates new tuples and uses them as the new "seed" and starts the process all over again by searching for these new tuples in the documents to identify new promising patterns.

In order to learn these patterns from these sentences, we propose a sentence alignment method to group similar patterns together and then learn each group separately for the generalized patterns

Definition 2. The Match(T_i, T_j) between two 5–tuples T_i=<prefix$_i$, tag$_{i1}$, infix$_i$, tag$_{i2}$, suffix$_i$> and T_j = <prefix$_j$, tag$_{j1}$, infix$_j$, tag$_{j2}$, suffix$_j$> is defined as

$$Match(T_i, T_j) = W_{prefix} * Sim(prefix_i, prefix_j) + W_{infix} * Sim(infix_i, infix_j)$$
$$+ W_{suffix} * Sim(suffix_i, suffix_j)$$

There are many methods or formulas available to evalute the similarity of two sentence segments such as perfix$_i$ and prefix$_j$, which are ordered list of words, numbers and punctuation marks etc. In our system, we use the sentence alignment function similar to the sequence alignment in bioinformatics. The advantage of using sentence alignment for similarity measurement is that it is flexible and can be implemented efficiently based on dynamic programming.

Our system first identifies sentences that include a pair of entities. For a given text segment, with an associated pair of entities E1 and E2, it generates the 5–tuples T=<perfix, E1_tag1, infix, E2_tag2, suffix>. A candidate tuple <E1, E2> is generated if there is a pattern T_p such that *Match(T, T_p)* is greater than the pre-specified threshold. Each candidate tuple will then have a number of patterns that helped generate it, each with an associated degree of match. Our approach relies on this information, together with score of the patterns (the score reflects the selectivity of the patterns), to decide what candidate tuples to actually add to the biological relationship table that is constructing. Below are some sample extraction patterns generated from PubMed for protein-protein interaction.

{"" <Protein1> "interacts with" <Protein2> ""}
{" " <Protein1> "binds to" <Protein 2> ""}
{"Bind of " <Protein1> "to" <Protein2> ""}
{ "Complex of " <Protein1> "and " <protein2> ""}

Our method represents the context around the proteins in the patterns in a flexible way that produce patterns that are selective, flexible, and have high coverage. As a result, BRExtract will ignore those minor grammar variations in the sentences and focus on the important key phases in the sentences.

Since there is no human feedback about the extracted tuples and patterns in this procedure, it is very important that the patterns and tuples generated during the extraction process be evaluated, bogus patterns are removed and only highly selective and confident tuples are used as seed examples in the next iteration to ensure the high quality of patterns and tuples generated in each step. This way, our system will be able to eliminate unreliable tuples and patterns from further consideration.

Generating good pattern is challenging. For example, we may generate a pattern {"", <Protein1>, <"–">, <Protein2> <Interaction>} from sentence "these data suggest that the histoneH3–histoneH2b interaction is…". This pattern will be matched by any string that includes a protein followed by a hyphen, followed by another protein, followed by the word "interaction". Estimating the confidence of the patterns, so that we don't trust patterns that tend to generate wrong tuples, is one of the problems that we have to consider. The confidence of the tuple is defined based on the selectivity and the number of the patterns that generate it. Intuitively, the confidence of a tuple will be high if it is generated by many highly selective patterns, and high selective pattern tends to generate high confidence tuples. This idea is similar to the concepts of hub and authoritative pages in web searching [Brin (1998)].

We use a metric originally proposed by Riloff to evaluate extraction pattern P_i generated by the Autoslog–TS [Riloff (1996)] in information extraction system, and define score (P_i) as

$$Score(P_i) = F_i/N_i * log(F_i),$$

where F_i is the number of unique tuples among the extractions produced by P_i and N_i is the total number of unique tuples that P_i extracted. This metric can identify not only the most reliable extraction patterns but also patterns that will frequently extract relevant information (even if irrelevant information will also be extracted).

Since for each tuple T_j, we store the set of patterns that produce it, together with the measure of similarity between the context in which the tuple occurred, and the matching pattern. Consider a candidate tuple T_j and the set of patterns $P=\{P_i\}$ that were used to generate T_j. The confidence of an extracted tuple T_j is evaluated as

$$Conf(T_j) = 1 - \prod_{k=1}^{m} (1 - score(P_i) * Match(T_j)),$$

where m is the number of patterns to generate T_j.

After determining the confidence of the candidate tuples using the definition above, our method discards all tuples with low confidence because low quality these tuples could add noise into the pattern generation process, which would in turn introduce more invalid tuples, degrading the performance of the system.

For illustration purpose, Table 16.2 lists 4 representative patterns that our system extracted from the document collection.

Table 16.2 Actual patterns discovered by BRExtract

Confidence	Left	Middle	Right
0.82	""	Associate with	""
0.79	Bind of	to	""
0.75	""	-	complex
0.74	Interaction of	With	""

16.4 Experiment

Evaluating the precision and recall of our BREXtract system is very difficult because of the large collection of the articles involved. For small biomedical articles sets, it is possible to manually inspect them and calculate the precision and recall. Unfortunately, this evaluation approach does not scale and becomes infeasible for large collection of literature such as PubMed. Developing accurate evaluation metrics for this task is one of our future research plans. In this study, we use a very simple and straight method. In our experiment, we start with 50000 articles and stop at 500,000 articles when the new tuples added is very small.

Table 16.3 Number of PubMed Abstract used in our test

Some of the top key phrase used in article selection	The number of abstracts that contain the key phrase
protein association	84,958
protein interaction	156,984
protein binding	70,155
protein complex	196,911
protein interact	33,895
protein bind	70,155

Table 16.4 Experimental Results

# of articles	Raw Pairs	without Redundancy	Synonym Free (final)
50k	2224	493	465
100k	4412	1010	964
150k	8348	1661	1594
200k	10527	1936	1860
250k	12461	2192	2108
300k	15152	2574	2473
350k	16612	2671	2558
400k	18202	2864	2743
450k	19070	2958	2839
all	19461	3021	2898

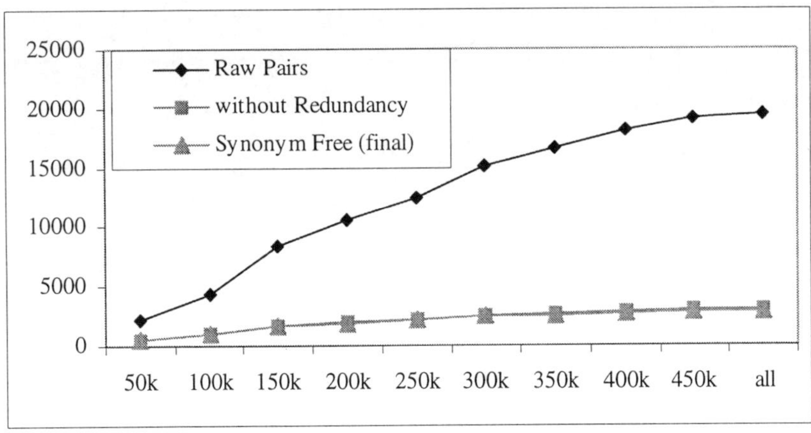

Fig. 16.3 Comparison of Raw, unique tuples

16.5 Conclusion

In this chapter we present a novel scaleable method to extract biological relationships from biomedical literature. Our method addresses portability and performance issues simultaneously and is efficient to work in large online biomedical literature database and flexible to be applied in very complicated domains with little human intervention. Our system BRExtract can be used to extract many binary relationships such as protein–protein interaction, cell signaling or protein–DNA interactions from large collection of text files once the name dictionary of the studied object is provided and is a very useful tool for functional bioinformatics.

Bibliography

Agichtein, E. and Gravano, L. (2000). Snowball: Extracting Relations from Large Plain–Text Collections, *Proceedings of the 5th ACM International Conference on Digital Libraries*, pp. 85–94.

Bader, G.D., Donaldson, I., Wolting, C., Quellette, B.F., Pawson, T. and Hogue, C.W. (2001). BIND–The Biomolecular Interaction Network Database, *Nucleic Acids Research*, 29(1), pp. 242–245.

Blaschke, C., Andrade, M. A., Ouzounis, C., and Valencia, A. (1999). Automatic extraction of biological information from scientific text: protein–protein interactions, *Proc. Int. Conf. Intell. Syst. Mol. Biol.*, pp. 60–67.

Brin, S. (1998). Extracting Patterns and Relations from the World Wide Web, *In Proceedings of the 1998 International Workshop on the Web and Databases (WebDB'98)*, pp. 172–183.

Califf, M.E. and Mooney, R. (2003). Bottom–up relational learning of pattern matching rules for information extraction, *Journal of Machine Learning Research*, 4, pp. 177–210.

Cancedda, N., Gaussier, E., Goutte, C. and Renders, J.M. (2003). Word–Sequence Kernels, *Journal of Machine Learning Research*, 3, pp. 1059–1082.

Chiang, J.H. and Yu, H.H. (2003). MeKE; discovering the functions of gene products from biomedical literature via sentence alignment, *Bioinformatics*, 19(11), pp. 1417–1422.

de Brujin, B. and Martin, J. (2002). Literature mining in molecular biology, *Proceedings of the EFMI Workshop on Natural Language*, pp. 1–5.

Ding, J., Berleant, D., Nettleton, D. and Wurtele, E. (2002). Mining Medline: abstracts, sentences, or phrases?, *Pacific Symposium on Biocomputing (PSB 2002)*, pp. 326–337.

Fukuda, K., Tsunoda, T., Tamura, A. and Takagi, T. (1998). Toward Information Extraction: identifying protein names from biological papers, *Pacific Symposium on Biocomputing (PSB 1998)*, pp. 707–718.

Hahn, U., Romacker, M. and Schulz, S. (2002). Creating Knowledge Repositories from Biomedical reports: The MedSYnDikate Text Mining System, *Pacific Symposium on Biocomputing (PSB 2002)*, pp. 338–349.

Hirschman, L., Park, J.C., Tsujil, J., Wong, L. and Wu, C.H. (2002). Accomplishments and Challenges in Literature Data Mining for Biology, *Bioinformatics*, 18(12), pp. 1553–1561.

Kanehisa, M. and Goto, S. (1997). A systematic analysis of gene functions by the metabolic pathway database. In "Theoretical and Computational Methods in Genome Research" (Suhai, S., ed.), pp. 41–55, Plenum Press

Marcott, E. M., Xenarios, I. and Eisenberg, D. (2001). Mining literature for protein–protein interactions, *Bioinformatics*, 17(4), pp. 359–363.

Nahm, U.Y. and Mooney, R. (2002). Text Mining with Information Extraction, Proceedings of the AAAI 2002 Spring Symposium on Mining Answers from Texts and Knowledge Bases, pp. 60–67.

Ng, S.K. and Wong, M. (1999). Toward Routine Automatic Pathway Discovery from On–Line Scientific Text Abstracts, *Genome Inform. Ser. Workshop Genome Inform.*, 10, pp. 104–112.

Ono, T., Hishigaki, H., Tanigami, A. and Takagi, T. (2001). Automated extraction of information on protein–protein interactions from the biological literature, *Bioinformatics*, 17(2), pp. 155–161.

Riloff, E. (1996). Automatically Generating Extraction Patterns from Untagged Text, in Proceedings of the Thirteenth National Conference on Artificial Intelligenc (AAAI–96), pp. 1044–1049.

Stapley, B.J. and Benoit, G. (2000). Biobibliometrics: information retrieval and visualization from co–occurrences of gene names in Medline abstracts, *Pacific Symposium on Biocomputing (PSB 2000)*, pp. 529–540.

Weizenbaum, J. (1966). ELIZA – A Computer program for the study of natural language communications between men and machine, *Communications of the Association for Computing Machinery*, 9, pp. 36–45.

Xenarios, I., Fernandez, E., Salwinski, L., Duan, X.J., Thompson, M.J., Marcotte, E.M. and Eisenberg, D. (2001). DIP: The Database of Interacting Proteins: 2001 update, *Nucleic Acids Reg.*, 29, pp. 239–241.

iMASS – AN INTELLIGENT MULTI-RESOLUTION AGENT-BASED SURVEILLANCE SYSTEM

Raymond S. T. Lee

Department of Computing, Hong Kong Polytechnic University
Hong Kong, P.R. China
E-mail: csstlee@comp.polyu.edu.hk

Owing to the rapid development of technology, especially in the field of Internet systems, there is an increasing demand both for intelligent, mobile and autonomous systems and for the usage and conveyance of multi-media information through cyberspace. In this paper, we propose an innovative, intelligent multi-agent based model, namely iJADE– (intelligent Java Agent Development Environment), to provide an intelligent agent-based platform in the e-commerce environment. From the implementation point of view, we introduce an intelligent multimedia processing system known as "iMASS" – an intelligent Multi-resolution Agent-based Surveillance System - based on the integration of the following modules: a) an automatic coarse-to-fine figure-ground scene segmentation module using the CNOW (Composite Neuro-Oscillatory Wavelet-based) model; b) an automatic human face detection and extraction module using an Active Contour Model (ACM) with facial 'landmarks' vectors; c) invariant human face identification based on the Elastic Graph Dynamic Link Model (EGDLM). In order to conform to the current (and future) multimedia system standard, the whole iMASS is implemented using the MPEG7 system framework – with comprehensive Description Schemes (DS), feature Descriptors (D) and model framework.

17.1 Surveillance Systems – A Brief Overview

The surveillance system is by far one of the most attractive topics, both from the research point of view including the areas of machine vision, scene analysis, real-time 2D to 3D object modeling and recognition, and others; but also an important problem domain from the commercial and industrial point of view. Numerous research studies have been conducted in this area, including surveillance systems for traffic control [Abreu *et. al.* (2000)], automatic identification of weapons and dangerous goods in customs examination operations [Keller *et. al.* (2000)], and automatic surveillance systems for abandoned objects in unmanned railway operations [Sacchi *et. al.* (2000)]. Of course, one of the most fundamental and vital, but also the most difficult applications is the use of surveillance systems for the identification of human subjects based on their facial appearances and distinct postures. With the advance of computer and Internet technologies in terms of computational power, popularity and provision of worldwide distributed networks, automatic human face surveillance systems seem to be a feasible application instead of a fancy dream. However, in order to implement an automatic human face surveillance system, there are two fundamental problem domains for consideration: a) the provision of an efficient and automatic scene analysis and figure-ground segmentation system; b) the provision of an invariant human face extraction, identification and recognition system.

In this chapter, we introduce an intelligent automatic surveillance system, namely the "iMASS" – an intelligent agent based surveillance system. In summary, iMASS integrates two contemporary technologies: a) an intelligent multi-agent using the iJADE model as the 'kernel' of the intelligent processing framework (to be discussed in Section 4); b) MPEG-7 technology as the 'backbone' of the overall system framework and the multi-media feature encoding, decoding, filtering, searching and interpretation standards. A brief overview and contemporary work on core technologies will be discussed in the following sub-sections.

17.2 iMASS – Supporting Technologies

17.2.1 *Agent Technology*

The Internet is an ideal platform for supporting e-commerce. The current World-Wide-Web system is catalyzing the development of e-commerce over the Internet. Specifically, we call it Internet commerce. The current Internet commerce system is primarily based on the client and server architecture. Basically, all transactions are carried out by many request/response interactions over the Internet. As the Internet is a best-effort network, sometimes a user may experience a long response time. Another approach is to use a mobile agent-based system. This involves sending a mobile software agent using various technologies (such as IBM Aglets[1], ObjectSpace Voyager Agents[2], the FTP Software Agent[3], the General Magic Odyssey Agent System[4], Java Agent Template Lite (JATLite)[5] and the Agent Builder Environment from IBM[6]) to a remote system, such that the agent can conduct multiple interactions with the software resident on the remote system. The output of the interactions is then sent back to the user. An agent can also interact with other agents on the Internet before returning to the original system. It is expected that this type of agent-based system will complement the existing client/server-based Internet commerce system by providing a more advanced service.

Currently, there are many different e-commerce systems around the world, ranging from simple online shops to more complex systems that provide different types of services. Some examples include:

BargainFinder – a database search engine for searching online music stores[7]

Xpect – a generic framework for e-commerce [Adnreoli *et. al.* (1997)]

---

[1] Aglets URL http://www.tgrl.ibm.co.jp/aglets/

[2] Voyager URL http://www.objectspace.com/voyager/

[3] FTP Software Agents URL http://www.ftp.com/

[4] Odyssey URL http://www.genmagic.com/

[5] JATLite URL http://java.standard.edu/java_agent/html

[6] ABE URL http://www.networking.ibm.com/iag/

[7] BargainFinder URL http://bf.cstar.ac.com/bf

AuctionBot – a generic auction server that allows suppliers to auction
   products[8]

Metabroker – a generic framework for creating electronic brokers
   [Caughey *et. al.* (1998)]

DASHER – a common service infrastructure for supporting the
   procurement aspects of e-commerce [Powley *et. al.* (1997)]

MAGNET – a system for networked electronic trading [Dasgupta *et. al.*
   (1999)]

FAgent [Lee and Liu (2000)] - an automatic user authentication agent
   system based on invariant human face recognition using EGDLM
   architecture [Lee *et. al.* (1999)]

17.2.2 *MPEG-7 System*

Unlike previous MPEG standards[9], which focus on data encoding and
storage standards on audio-visual information, including the storage and
retrieval of moving pictures in MPEG-1 in CD-quality, setting the
generic coding of audio-video for the supporting of a high resolution
digital television standard in MPEG-2, and the provision of standardized
technological elements enabling the integration of the production,
distribution and content access methods of digital TV and other multimedia applications in MPEG-4, MPEG-7 focuses on the standardization
of a common interface for describing multimedia materials themselves,
that is, representing information about the content, rather than the content
itself (information 'about' the multimedia information) [Nack and
Lindsay (1999a, 1999b)]. In other words, MPEG-7 tries to address
aspects such as facilitating interoperability and the globalization of
multimedia resources, and the flexibility of data management.

Under MPEG-7 standard, every MPEG-7 multimedia application will
rely on three main components: Descriptor (D), Description Scheme
(DS) and Description Definition Language (DDL). Fig. 17.1 depicts a
typical abstract representation of a multimedia application using MPEG-
7 standard. The left-hand side of the figure depicts how data is annotated,
encoded and interpreted, whereas the right-hand side of the model
portrays how the described data can be retrieved and manipulated.

---

[8] AuctionBot URL http://auction.eecs.umich.edu
[9] MPEG URL http://www.cselt.it/mpeg/standards.htm

Unlike previous MPEG standards, a typical MPEG-7 application provides basic functionality such as (multimedia) information filtering and searching functions.

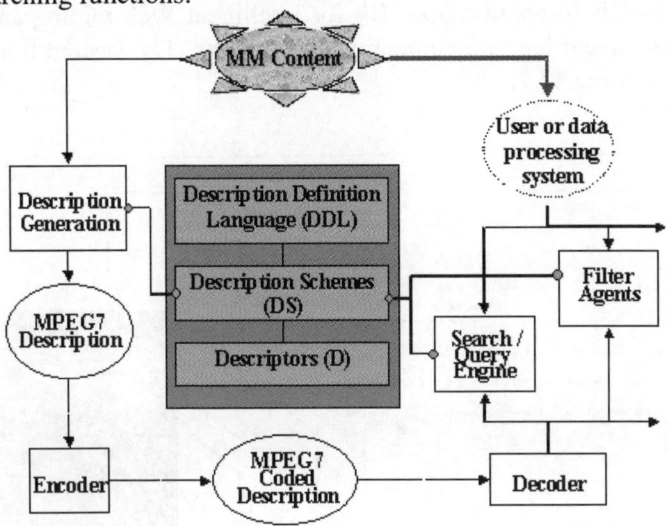

Fig. 17.1 – An abstract representation of a multimedia application using MPEG-7 standard (http://www.cselt.it/mpeg/standards.htm)

In fact, MPEG-7 standardization work started in October 1998 and will be completed by November 2001. A major effort was initiated in 1999 to develop MPEG-7. The latest development involves visual object modeling by Bober *et. al.* (2000), using contour shape as the object Descriptor, however, the application is restricted to simple and homogenous object patterns. Other work, such as that of Lorente and Torres (1999) uses the eigenface approach for face recognition in video sequences; however, their work focused on automatic face recognition, for which the major visual sequences processing operation – the automatic figure-ground scene segmentation (for the automatic extraction of the object and hence the facial pattern), have not been implemented in the application.

17.2.3 *iJADE Model – System Framework*

In this chapter, we propose a fully integrated intelligent agent model called iJADE (pronounced as 'IJ') for intelligent Web-mining and other intelligent agent-based e-commerce applications. The system framework is shown in Fig.17.2.

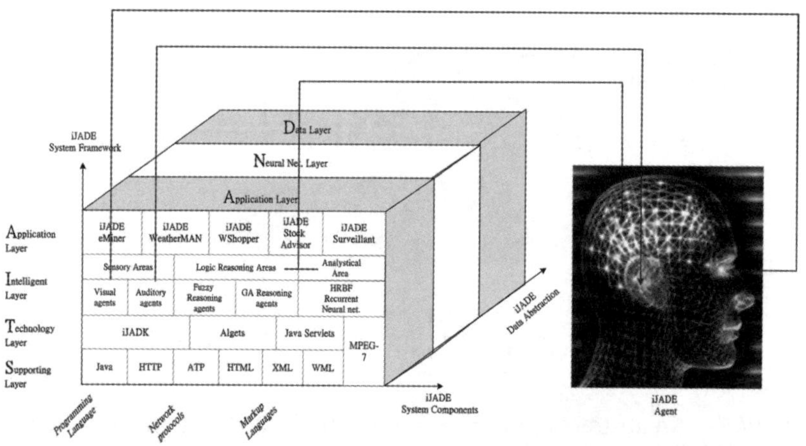

Fig.17.2 System architecture of iJADE (v 1.6) model
(http://www.iJADK.org)

Unlike contemporary agent systems and APIs such as IBM Aglets and ObjectSpace Voyager, which focus on multi-agent communication and autonomous operations, the aim of iJADE is to provide comprehensive 'intelligent' agent-based APIs and applications for future e-commerce and Web-mining applications. Figure 2 depicts the two-level abstraction in the iJADE system: a) iJADE system level - ACTS model, and b) iJADE data level - DNA model. The ACTS model consists of 1) the Application Layer, 2) the Conscious (Intelligent) Layer, 3) the Technology Layer, and the 4) Supporting Layer. The DNA model is composed of 1) the Data Layer, 2) the Neural Network Layer, and 3) the Application Layer.

Compared with contemporary agent systems which provide minimal and elementary data management schemes, the iJADE DNA model provides a comprehensive data manipulation framework based on neural network technology. The 'Data Layer' corresponds to the raw data and input 'stimulates' (such as the facial images captured from the Web camera and the product information in the cyberstore) from the environment. The 'Neural Network Layer' provides the 'clustering' of different types of neural networks for the purpose of 'organization', 'interpretation', 'analysis' and 'forecasting' operations based on the inputs from the 'Data Layer', which are used by the iJADE applications in the 'Application Layer'. Another innovative feature of the iJADE system is the ACTS mode, which provides a comprehensive layering architecture for the implementation of intelligent agent systems. For the details of iJADE model and its supporting applications, please visit iJADK official site http://www.iJADK.org.

17.3 iMASS – System Overview

From the implementation point of view, we introduce our 'IMASS' – a truly intelligent multi-resolution neuro-agent based automatic surveillance system based on the integration of four different types of technology:

a) An automatic coarse-to-fine multi-resolution figure-ground scene segmentation using the CNOW (Composite Neuro-Oscillatory Wavelet-based) model – an extension of the latest work for color scene analysis [Lee and Liu (2002)];

b) An automatic human face detection and extraction using the Active Contour Model (ACM) with facial 'landmarks' [Lee and Liu (1999)];

c) An invariant human face identification scheme using the Elastic Graph Dynamic Link Model (EGDLM) [Lee *et. al.* (1999)];

d) Using MPEG-7 as the system framework of this surveillance system, including the encoding (and decoding) of the wavelet features, the facial template, the elastic dynamic facial 'graphs', implementation of the EGDLM model as the Search Query Engine and the implementation of the WCNOM sub-system as the Filter Agents, which also provide a comprehensive standard for the modeling based on various Description Schemes (DS) and feature Descriptors (D).

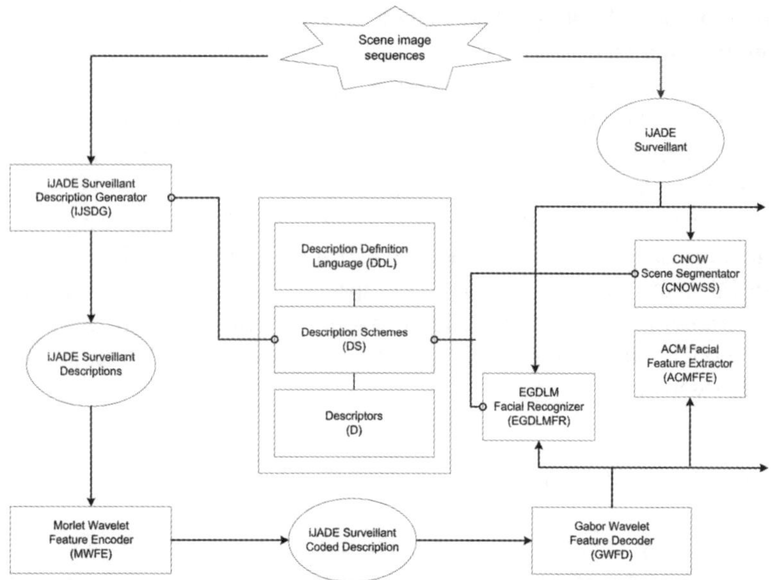

Fig. 17.3 A schematic diagram of iMASS

Conforming to the MPEG-7 system architecture (Fig. 17.1), iMASS system framework consists of the following main modules:

-     A Morlet wavelet encoder – feature encoding module (using Morlet wavelet) to extract coarse-to-fine and invariant image information.

-     The CNOW segmentation module – acts as the first level Filter Agents (MPEG-7 architecture), using the Composite Neuro-Oscillatory Wavelet-based (CNOW) scheme for automatic coarse-to-fine scene segmentation.

-     The ACM contour extraction module – acts as the second level Filter Agents using the Active Contour Model (ACM) for the extraction of facial features.

-     The EGDLM recognition module – acts as the Search/Query Engine (MPEG-7 architecture) to provide invariant face recognition using the Elastic Graph Dynamic Link Model (EGDLM).

A schematic diagram of iMASS is depicted in Fig.17.3.

From the intelligent agents interaction point of view, three types of iJADE agents are involved in the system:

- iJADE Surveillant Agent – the stationary iJADE agent which is situated in the client machine to act as a Surveillant – for the automatic capture of scene images and through the coarse-to-fine scene segmentation and ACM process (against the facial template) to extract the facial features of the human subject.
- iJADE Messenger – A mobile iJADE agent acting as a messenger which, on the one hand 'carries' the facial features to the iJADE Facial Server and on the other hand 'reports' the recognition result back to the client machine.
- iJADE Recognizer – A stationary agent who is situated within the iJADE Facial Server. The main duty is to perform the invariant facial pattern matching of the facial features (extracted from the iJADE Surveillant Agent) against the central facial database.

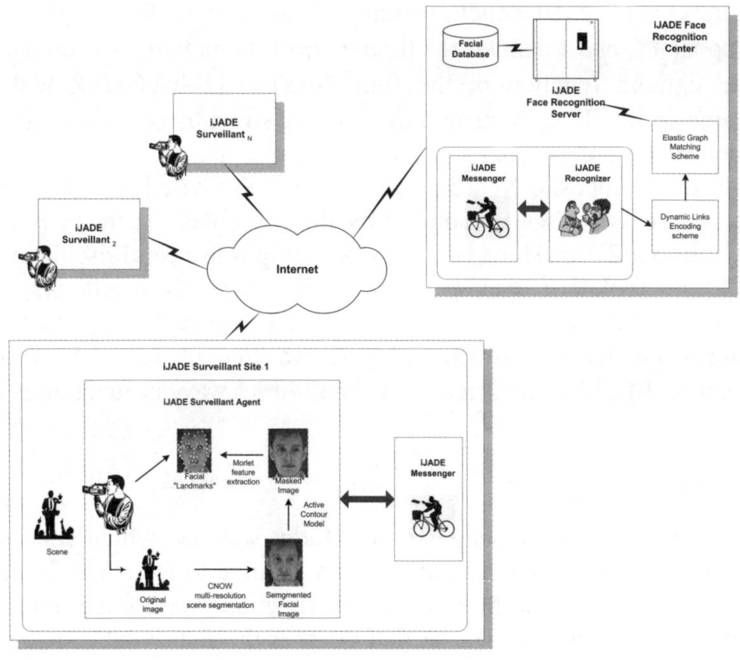

Fig. 17.4 – System overview of multi-agent interaction in the iMASS

17.3.1 *Composite Neuro-Oscillatory Wavelet-based (CNOW) model for scene segmentation*

A single composite neural oscillator consists of three excitatory neurons (which represent the three primary color responses u_{ri}, u_{bi} & u_{gi} respectively) which directly interact with a common inhibitory inter-neuron v_i. Within the composite neural oscillator, excitatory synapses (triangles) and inhibitory synapses (circles) interact together with the oscillator units according to the following kinetic equations:

$$\frac{du_{ci}}{dt} = -u_{ci} + S_\lambda(u_{ci} - \beta v_i - \theta_u + I_{ci} + O_{ci})$$

(17.1)

$$\tau\frac{dv_i}{dt} = -v_i + S_\lambda(\alpha\sum_c u_{ci} - \gamma w_i - \theta_v)$$

(17.2)

where c = {r, g, b} denote neural oscillatory units for the three color components, and τ denotes the time scale of the inhibitory neurons. $S_\lambda(x)$ is a sigmoid function of the form $S_\lambda(x) = [1+\exp(-x/\lambda)]$ with gain parameter $1/\lambda$. I_{ri}, I_{gi}, I_{bi} denote the sensory stimulus of the nature scene, which is constant within the oscillatory time scale.

In the Composite Neuro-oscillatory Wavelet-based (CNOW) model, each color scene image captured by the surveillance camera is broken down into a 2D mesh of $N = N_1 \times N_2$ composite neural oscillator sites. Each site (column) consists of M layers of trinity oscillators, which denote the neural oscillation from each response of corresponding local features. For feature extraction, Morlet wavelets of different orientation direction (θ) and k factor are used. The Morlet wavelet function is given as:

$$Morlet_{k,\theta}(x,y) = \pi^{-1/2}\, e^{\left(-\frac{x^2+y^2}{2}\right)} \cdot \left(e^{2\pi i k(xx\cos\theta + y\sin\theta)} - e^{-k^2/2}\right)$$

(17.3)

where 'k' is the basic shape of the Morlet wavelet, which controls the width of the frequency-domain window relative to its center frequency. The first factor in the Morlet wavelet function denotes the normalized Gaussian data window. The second factor is the sinusoidal component of the wavelet. Its (x, y) term is projected in the θ direction to determine its complex exponential component.

According to the MPEG-7 standard, one of the most fundamental feature elements being used in the iMASS is the Morlet Wavelet Descriptor (MWD), which is given by:

MWD{

      orientation;

      kvalue;

      Morlet[xlocation, ylocation]

}

In addition to the local excitatory and inhibitory neurons, the neural dynamics of the composite neural oscillators are activated/deactivated by these oscillators: Vertical and horizontal excitatory neurons; Vertical and horizontal inhibitory neurons (v_i & v^q); Global inhibitory neurons (v). The neural dynamics for the neural oscillators are shown as follows:

$$\frac{du_{ci}}{dt} = -u_{ci}^q + S_\lambda (u_{ci}^q - \beta v_i^q - \theta_u + I_{ci}^q + W_{ci_+}^q u_{ci}^q$$

$$+ W_{ci_-}^q u_{ci}^q - T_{ci_+}^q v_i - T_{ci_-}^q v^q - T_{ci}^q v) \tag{17.4}$$

$$\tau \frac{dv_i^q}{dt} = -v_i^q + S_\lambda (\alpha \sum_c u_{ci}^q - \gamma v_i^q - \theta_v) \tag{17.5}$$

$$\tau \frac{dv_i}{dt} = -v_i + S_\lambda (W_{i_+} v_i - \theta_v) \tag{17.6}$$

$$\tau \frac{dv^q}{dt} = -v^q + S_\lambda (W_-^q v^q - \theta_v) \tag{17.7}$$

$$\tau \frac{dv}{dt} = -v + S_\lambda (W^{'} v - \theta_v) \tag{17.8}$$

The segmentation criterion is determined by the correlation factor, which is a measurement of the binding strength (phase relationship) between the composite neural oscillators and their nearest neighbors, given by:

$$\sigma(x, y) = \frac{<\bar{x}\bar{y}> - <\bar{x}><\bar{y}>}{\sqrt{<\bar{x}^2> - <\bar{x}>^2} \cdot \sqrt{<\bar{y}^2> - <\bar{y}>^2}} \tag{17.9}$$

where $\bar{x}, \bar{y}$ denote the composite oscillator vectors and $<\cdot>$ is the time average of the vector magnitude over a period of time that is shorter than the presentation of the image.

17.3.2 *Automatic Human Face Detection using Active Contour Model*

The Active Contour Model involves the use of a 'snake' [Kass *et. al.* (1987)] to locate the face contour. The 'snake' is a continuous curve that forms an initial state (facial template) and tries to deform itself dynamically on the image picture. This is a result of the action of external forces that attract the snake towards image features and internal forces which maintain the smoothness of the template's shape. The sum of the membrane energy, denoting the snake stretching, and the thin-plate energy, denoting the snake bending gives the following snake energy:

$$E_{\text{int}}(u(s)) = \alpha(s)|u_s(s)|^2 + \beta(s)|u_{ss}(s)|^2$$

$$(17.10)$$

where u(s) = (x(s),y(s)) is the snake curve and s is the arc-length of the curve. The parameters of elasticity α and β control the smoothness of the snake curve.

The deformation of the "snake" is governed by external forces. These forces are associated with a potential P(x,y), which in general is defined in terms of the gradient module of the image convoluted by a Gaussian function :

$$P(x,y) = -\left| \nabla(G(x,y) * I(x,y)) \right|$$

$$(17.11)$$

or as a distance map of the edge points :

$$P(s,y) = d(x,y), \quad P(x,y) = -e^{-d(x,y)^2}$$

$$(17.12)$$

The total snake energy is given by the functional energies sum as:

$$E_{snake} = \int_0^1 E_{\text{int}} + E_{ext}\, ds = \int_0^1 \alpha(s)|u_s(s)|^2 + \beta(s)|u_{ss}(s)|^2 + P(u(s))ds$$

$$(17.13)$$

The minimum of the snake energy satisfies an Euler-Lagrange equation:

$$-\frac{d}{ds}(\alpha u_s(s)) + \frac{d^2}{ds^2}(\beta u_{ss}(s)) + \nabla P(u(s)) = 0$$

$$(17.14)$$

According to the 50 facial landmarks (e.g. nose, eye, eye-brow, mouth, facial contour, etc.) defined in the "deformed" facial template, the Morlet wavelet vectors of these 50 locations will then be located and extracted automatically.

17.3.3 *Invariant Human Face Recognition using EGDLM*

In the Dynamic Link Initialization process, dynamic links ($z_{ij,kl}$) between "memory" facial attribute graphs and figure objects from the images gallery are initialized according to the following rules:

$$z_{ij,kl} = \varepsilon J_{ij} J_{kl}$$

$$(17.15)$$

for $J_{ij} \in A$, $J_{kl} \in B$, where Js are the feature vectors extracted from the facial landmarks and ε is the parameter value between 0 and 1; A and B denote the figure graph and memory graph respectively.

In the Elastic Graph Matching Module, the attribute graph of the figure is "dynamically" matched with each "memory" object attribute graphs by minimizing the energy function H(z):

$$H(z) = -\sum_{i,j \in B; k,l \in A} z_{ij} z_{jl} z_{ik} z_{kl} + \gamma \sum_{i \in B} \left(\sum_{k \in A} z_{ik} - 1 \right)^2 + \gamma \sum_{k \in A} \left(\sum_{i \in B} z_{ik} - 1 \right)^2$$

$$(17.16)$$

within tolerance level μ.

H(z) is minimized using the gradient descent:

$$z_{ij}(t+1) = \left[z_{ij}(t) - \eta \frac{\partial H(z(t))}{\partial z_{ij(t)}} \right]^w$$

$$(17.17)$$

where $[\ldots]^w$ denotes the value of z_{ij} confined to the interval [0,w]. At equilibrium (within a chosen tolerance level μ), H(z) will be minimized, and the connection pattern in the memory layer represents the pattern recalled by the figure pattern.

17.4 iMASS – System Implementation

In order to provide a complete system evaluation scheme, system testing of the iMASS is performed under two major schemes: a) the automatic color scene segmentation scheme; b) the invariant human face recognition scheme. Results are shown as follows:

17.4.1 *Automatic Color Scene Segmentation Scheme*

In this test, a scene gallery of 6000 color photos from GreenStreet^{TM} from GST Technology Ltd. was used for scenery images. An object gallery of 3000 figures was extracted from the GreenStreet software as the "memory" object database. For systematic validation of the scene analysis model and the analysis of the performance of scene analysis for different types of objects and different levels of complexity of the nature scenes, the 6000 color photos were divided into eight different categories: Animals; People; Food; Clouds; Scenery; Trees; Recreation and Transportation.

For system evaluation purposes, all color images in the photo gallery were converted into 24-bit colored pixels of resolution 320x192. The simulation was carried out on a Sun Sparc 20 workstation. To extract objects from the "memory" object gallery, 3000 images were submitted into the CNOM system for figure-ground segmentation. Results are shown in Fig. 17.5.

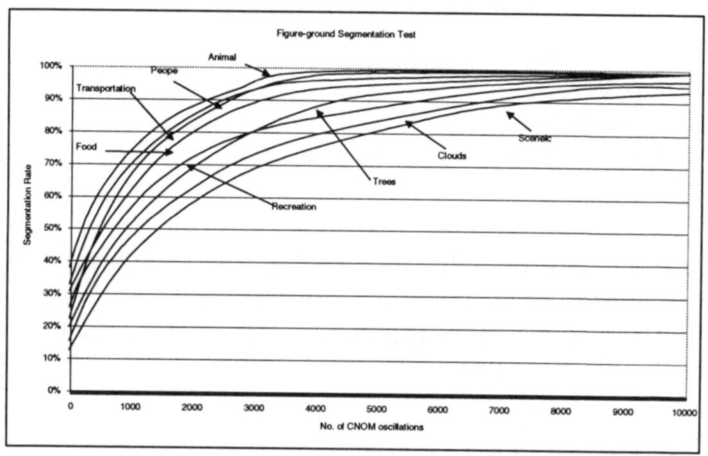

Fig. 17.5 – Figure-ground Segmentation Test

Two important findings are observed in the experimental result shown in Figure 5. First, the Composite Neuro-Oscillatory Wavelet (CNOW) model attains its steady state of figure-ground segmentation when the number of oscillation cycles reaches 8000; even for categories such as Animal, People and Transportation, 6000 oscillation cycles are found to be good enough to achieve the steady state.

Second, for all of the eight categories of objects, we have achieved over 98% correct segmentation beyond 8000 oscillation cycles. Some categories, such as "scenery" and "clouds", took a longer segmentation time, mainly because of the confusing and similar textures among the objects in the same scene. Others, such as "animals", with a concrete texture relationship, could complete the segmentation process within a shorter time scale.

17.4.2 Invariant Human Face Recognition Scheme

17.4.2.1 *System training*

In the experiment, a portrait gallery of 100 face images is used for network training. A set of 1,020 tested patterns resulting from different facial expressions, viewing perspectives, and sizes of stored templates were used for testing. The series of tested facial patterns were obtained with a CCD camera providing a standard video signal, and digitized at 512 x 384 pixels with 8 bits of resolution.

The computer system that we adopted to implement and measure the performance of the hybrid system was a SUN-Sparc 20 workstation. Typical iJADE agents activities screens and snapshots of iMASS multi-resolution facial pattern recognition screens are shown in Fig. 17.6 and 17.7.

For system evaluation, certain tests on face recognition performance were carried out, including: Facial pattern illumination test; Viewing perspective test; Facial pattern dilation / contraction test and Facial pattern occlusion and distortion test.

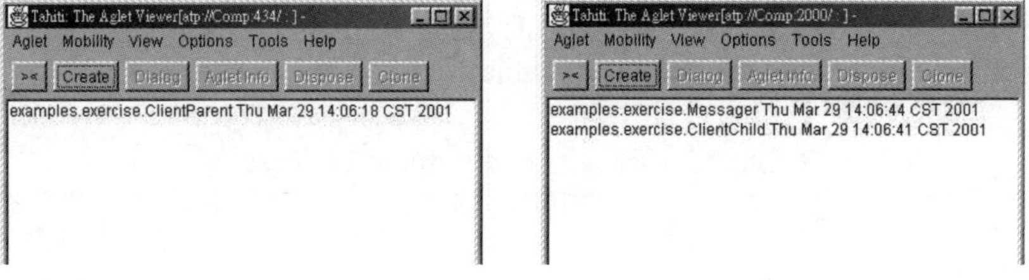

Fig. 17.6 - iJADE agents activities

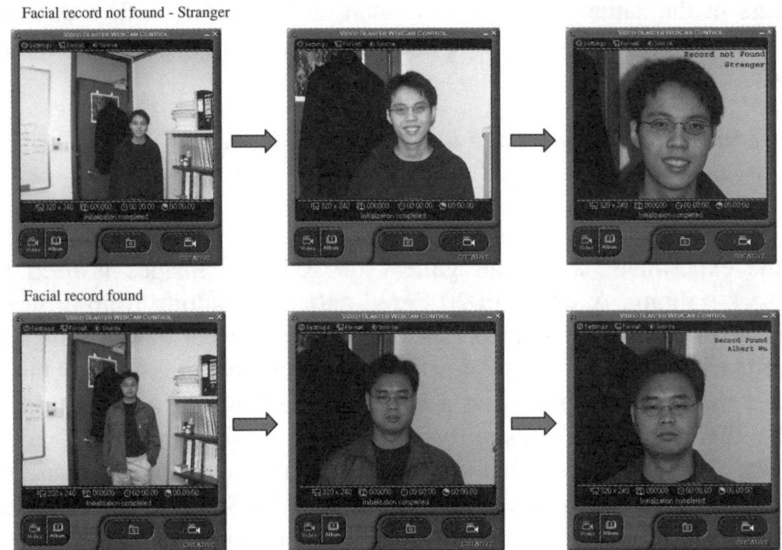

Fig. 17.7 – Automatic multi-resolution facial pattern recognition screens

17.4.2.2 *Facial Pattern Illumination Test*

In the Illumination Test, 100 test patterns of various degrees of brightness were used for facial recognition, with the degree of brightness varying from +30% to –30% of the "normal" brightness level. Experimental results are shown in Table 17.1.

Table 17.1 Results of Illumination Test

Brightness level	+30%	+20%	+10%	Normal	-10%	-20%	-30%
Classification rate	80%	86%	92%	95%	91%	88%	79%

Actually the model is "invariant" to the image illumination level, mainly due to the "illumination invariant" property of the ACM. An average of over 85% correct recognition rate was attained.

17.4.2.3 *Facial Pattern Illumination Test*

In this test, viewing perspective ranging from -30° to +30° (with reference to the horizontal and vertical axes) as shown in Figure 13 was adopted. Using 100 test patterns for each viewing perspective, the recognition results are presented in Table 17.2.

Table 17.2 Results of Viewing Perspective Test

Viewing perspectives (from horiz. axis)	Correct classification rate	Viewing perspectives (from vertical axis)	Correct classification rate
+30°	84%	+30°	86%
+20°	90%	+20°	88%
+10°	92%	+10°	91%
-10°	91%	-10°	92%
-20°	89%	-20°	87%
-30°	85%	-30°	82%

According to the "rotation invariant" property of the DLA model [Wiskott and Malsburg (1995)], the EGDLM is "inherited" from the same characteristic in the "contour maps elastic graph matching" process. An overall correct recognition rate of over 86% was achieved.

17.4.2.4 *Facial Pattern Dilation / Contraction Test*

In this test, 300 test patterns were used, with size ratio ranging from – 30% (pattern contraction) to +30% (pattern dilation), "partial" dilation / contraction. Recognition results are shown in Table 17.3.

Owing to the "elastic graph matching" characteristic of the Elastic Graph Dynamic Link Model, the system also possesses the "dilation/ contraction invariant", similar to that investigated for the "dilation invariant" of the Chinese characters. An overall correct recognition rate of over 85% was attained.

Table 17.3 Result of Facial Pattern Dilation/Contraction Test

Pattern dilation / contraction	Correction Classification		
	A. Overall dilation / contraction	B. Horz. dilation / contraction	C. Vertical dilation / contraction
+30°	86%	80%	81%
+15°	90%	86%	88%
-15°	92%	88%	86%
-30°	87%	79%	79%

17.4.2.5 *Facial Pattern Occlusion and Distortion Test*

In the last recognition test, the 120 test patterns were basically divided into three categories: Wearing spectacles or other accessories; Partial occlusion of the face by obstacles; Various facial expressions (such as laughing, angry and gimmicky faces). Pattern recognition results are shown in Table 17.4.

Table 17.4 Recognition Results of Facial Occlusion / Distortion Tests

Pattern Occlusion & Distortion Test	Correct classification rate
Wearing spectacles (or other accessories)	87%
Face partially hidden by obstacles (e.g. books, cups)	72%
Facial expressions (e.g. laughing, angry and gimmicky faces)	83%

Compared with the three different categories of facial occlusion, "wearing spectacles" was the least negative effect on facial recognition owing to the fact that all the main facial contours are still preserved in the recognition process. In the second situation, the influence on the recognition rate depends on the proportion and which portion of the face is being obscured. Nevertheless, the average correct recognition rate was found to be over 73%. Facial expressions and gimmicky faces gave the most striking results. Owing to the "elastic graph" characteristic of the model, the recognition engine "inherited" the "distortion invariant" property, and an overall correct recognition rate of 83% was attained.

17.5 Conclusion

In this chapter, we have introduced a fully automatic and integrated intelligent neuro-agent based MPEG-7 application – namely the iMASS - with the integration of various contemporary technologies including intelligent multi-agent technology (iJADE model) as the system intelligent 'kernel'; automatic multi-resolution scene segmentation using the Composite Neuro-Oscillatory Wavelet-based (CNOW) model; automatic facial pattern extraction using the Active Contour Model (ACM); and invariant facial pattern recognition based on the Elastic Graph Dynamic Model (EGDLM). Based on the latest MPEG-7 standard, the iMASS also demonstrates how an intelligent multimedia application can be implemented using the MPEG-7 architecture as the system framework for future development, especially in the area of mobile e-commerce and intelligent multimedia processing applications in the new millennium.

Acknowledgements

The author is grateful for the partial support provided by the Central Research Grant B-Q569 and G-T850 from the Hong Kong Polytechnic University.

Bibliography

Abreu, B., Botelho, L., Cavallaro, A., Douxchamps, D., Ebrahimi, T., Figueiredo, P., Macq, B., Mory, B., Nunes, L., Orri, J., Trigueiros, MJ., Violante, A. (2000). Video-based multi-agent traffic surveillance system, *Proc. of the IEEE Intelligent Vehicles Symposium 2000*, pp. 457–462.

Andreoli, J. M., Pacull, F. and Pareshi, R. (1997). XPect: A Framework for Electronic Commerce, *IEEE Internet Computing*, 1(4), pp. 40-48,.

Bober, M., Price, W. and Atkinson, J. (2000). The contour shape descriptor for MPEG-7 and its applications, *International Conference on Consumer Electronics 2000*, pp. 286-287.

Caughey, D., Ingham, D. and Watson, P. (1998). Metabroker:A Generic Broker for Electronic Commerce. *Computer Networks and ISDN Systems*, 30(1), pp. 619-620.

Dasgupta, P., Narasimhan, N., Moser, L. E. and Smith, P. M. (1999). MAGNET: Mobile Agents for Networked Electronic Trading, *IEEE Transactions on Knowledge and Data Engineering,* 11(4) pp. 509-525.

Kass, M., Witkin A. and Terzopoulos, D. (1987). Snakes: Active Contour Models, *Proc. of International Conference on Computer Vision*, pp. 259-268.

Keller, P. E., McMakin, D. L., Sheen, D. M., McKinnon, A. D. and Summet, J. W. (2000). Privacy algorithm for cylindrical holographic weapons surveillance system, *IEEE Aerospace and Electronics Systems Magazine*, 15(2), pp. 17–24.

Lee, R., Liu, J. and You, Y. (1999). Face Recognition: Elastic Relation Encoding and Structural Matching, *Proc. of IEEE International Conference on Systems, Man, and Cybernetics (SMC'99)*, Vol. II, pp. 172-177.

Lee, R. S. T. and Liu, J. N. K. (1999). An Integrated Elastic Contour Fitting and Attribute Graph Matching Model for Automatic Face Coding and Recognition, *Proc. of the Third International Conference on Knowledge-Based Intelligent Information Engineering Systems (KES'99)*, pp. 292-295.

Lee, R. S. T. and Liu, J. N. K. (2000). FAgent - An Innovative E-Shopping Authentication Scheme using Invariant Intelligent Face Recognition Agent. *Proc. of International Conference in Electronic Commerce (ICEC'2000)*, pp. 47-53.

Lee, R. S. T. and Liu, J. N. K. (2002). SCENOGRAM - Scene analysis using CompositE Neural Oscillatory-based elastic GRAph Model, *International Journal of Pattern Recognition and Artificial Intelligence (IJPRAI)*, 16(2), pp. 215-237.

Lorente, L. and Torres, L. (1999). Face recognition of video sequences in a MPEG-7 context using a global eigen approach, *In Proc. of International Conference on Image Processing ICIP'99*, vol. 4, pp. 187-191.

Nack, F. and Lindsay, A. T. (1999a). Everything you wanted to know about MPEG-7 Part 1, *IEEE Multimedia*, 6(3), pp. 65-77.

Nack, F. and Lindsay, A. T. (1999b). Everything you wanted to know about MPEG-7 Part 2, *IEEE Multimedia*, 6(4), pp. 64-73.

Powley, C., Benjamin, D., Grossman, D., Brodersohn, E., Fadia, R., Neches, R., Willm, P. and Zhu, Q. (1997). DASHER: A Prototype for Federated E-Commerce Services, *IEEE Internet Computing,* 1(6), 126-132.

Sacchi, C. A., and Regazzoni, C. S. (2000). A distributed surveillance system for detection of abandoned objects in unmanned railway environments, *IEEE Transactions on Vehicular Technology*, 49(5), pp. 2013-2026.

Wiskott, L. and Malsburg, C. (1995). Recognizing Faces by Dynamic Link Matching, *Proc. of ICANN'95*, pp 347-352.

CHAPTER 18

NETWORKING SUPPORT FOR NEURAL NETWORK-BASED INTELLIGENT WEB MONITORING AND FILTERING

A.C.M. Fong, S.C. Hui, and P.Y. Lee

School of Computer Engineering, Nanyang Technological University,
Blk N4, Nanyang Ave., Singapore 639798
Email: {ascmfong; asschui; a3397245}@ntu.edu.sg.

Like any self-regulating environment, the Internet is prone to abuse by individuals who use it for illegal or immoral purposes. The ability to discreetly intercept and analyze Internet traffic has tremendous potential both to protect unsuspecting users from harmful Web materials, and for the fight against organized crime and terrorism. Using the intelligent filtering and monitoring of pornographic Web pages as a case study, we have investigated strategies for monitoring Internet traffic. Based on our analysis, we have developed a Web content filtering system that decouples the monitoring process from Web content analysis process to achieve low latency and high accuracy. In particular, an Online Monitoring Agent performs the monitoring and filtering process, whereas an Offline Classification Agent that employs machine intelligence for classification of Web pages performs Web content analysis. We have implemented and tested the system and found that it consistently outperformed other, commercially available, Web filtering systems.

18.1 The Need for Intelligent Web Monitoring and Filtering

Due to its wide coverage and continuous availability, the Internet has evolved into a popular communications medium for information exchange in recent years. As in any self-regulating environment,

369

however, some individuals have abused their freedom of expression by putting harmful materials (e.g. pornography, hate messages, etc.) on the World Wide Web (WWW or Web). It is therefore important to protect children and other unsuspecting users from exposure to these materials.

In addition, companies need to restrict their employees' Internet access, particularly during office hours. A recent survey [Vault, Inc., (2000)] has found that 25% of office workers spent over an hour visiting non-work-related Websites, including pornography and gambling, during an average workday. Also, almost 15% of the respondents said they did so "constantly". This adds extra Internet service costs to the companies, and consumes internal computing and networking resources. Consequently, companies and individuals need a tool that can effectively block unwanted Web contents.

To perform the task, text classification on Web document needs to be employed in a Web monitoring and filtering system. A number of methods have been proposed in this area of research. SCAI at SNU uses boosted naïve Bayes algorithm and HTML tag importance factors, giving moderate results [Kim *et. al.*, (2000)]. Also, a set of key-phrases combined with their context of occurrence (in terms of position) has been used to identify only those documents with relevant information [Murthy and Keerthi, (1999)].

Feature representation based on syntactic and semantic relationships between words does not give significantly better results than the traditional "bag of words", as demonstrated in [Scott and Matwin, (1999)]. In fact, the combination of "bag of words" and phrases representation seems to perform better. Automatic classification of Web documents into predefined categories using term frequency has also been studied in an attempt to increase the precision of such task [Chekuri *et. al.*, (1996)]. However, the application of text classification in the domain of Web monitoring and filtering is different from other tasks such as search engine, since the categorization of a Web page in such system needs to be unique and precise. It must also be scalable, reconfigurable and user-friendly.

In this chapter, we describe the networking support required for an intelligent Web monitoring and filtering system. Networking support is a critical element in the overall design and implementation of an effective

Web monitoring and filtering system for practical use. We present the development of an Online Filtering Agent within the context of such a system so that objectionable Web pages can be effectively identified and prevented from reaching the user. Prior to that, an Offline Classification Agent is employed to distinguish between target objectionable Web pages and acceptable Web pages. In this research, we focus on the filtering of pornographic Web pages as an example of objectionable Web pages.

18.2 Intelligent Web Monitoring and Filtering System: An Overview

As illustrated in Fig. 18.1, a Web monitoring and filtering system usually resides between the WWW and Web browser. Its purpose is to monitor the network traffic, and to intercept and filter out unwanted Web pages. The blocking action is performed either when the Web browser is requesting access to a HTML document from a remote Web server, or when the Web server is returning the requested HTML document to the Web browser.

In general, a Web monitoring and filtering system comprises two major processes: Network Monitoring and Filtering. The Network Monitoring Process is employed to monitor network traffic between the WWW and Web browser. The Filtering Process then attempts to determine the content nature of incoming Web pages and decides whether filtering is necessary and how the action should be carried out. Current Web filtering systems, such as Cyber Patrol [SurfControl plc., (URL)], Cyber Snoop [Pearl Software, (URL)] and WebChaperone [RuleSpace Inc., (URL)] employ four major filtering approaches. They are Platform for Internet Content Selection (PICS), URL blocking, keyword filtering, and intelligent content analysis.

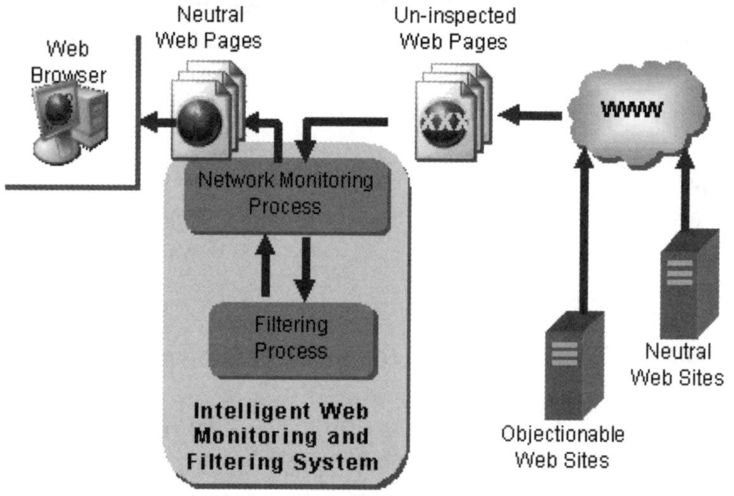

Fig. 18.1 Overview of an intelligent web monitoring and filtering system.

18.2.1 *PICS*

PICS is a set of specifications created by the World Wide Web Consortium (W3C) to define a platform for the creation of content rating systems [W3C, URL]. It enables Web publishers to associate labels or meta data with Web pages to limit certain Web contents with explicit nature targeted at adult audience from reaching other groups of Internet users.

However, since PICS is a voluntary self-labeling system and the content publisher of a Website is totally responsible for rating its Web contents, PICS is not very reliable due to the possibility of mislabeling either by mistake or by intention. Hence, a Web filtering system that implements PICS support should not totally depend on it for content filtering. Instead, other filtering techniques should also be used while PICS serves only a supplementary purpose.

18.2.2 *URL Blocking*

This is a technique that restricts or allows access by comparing the URL (or equivalent IP address) of the requested Web page with those in a URL list. The URL list may be "black" (disallowed URLs) or "white" (allowed URLs).

Most of the current Web filtering systems that employ URL blocking adopt the black list approach. Since a blocking decision can be made simply by matching the URL string of the requested Web page with those in the URL list, which happens even before a network connection to the remote Web server is established, URL blocking can appear to be very efficient from a user's perspective.

However, most of the current Web filtering systems that use URL blocking employ a large team of human reviewers to actively search for objectionable Websites to be added into the black list, which is then made available for downloading as an update to the local copy of the list. Such an approach is not only time-consuming, but also labor-intensive. Most importantly, it can never keep up with the explosive growth in the number of new Websites. This means the effectiveness of any URL blocking-based methods will likely be compromised in the long run.

18.2.3 *Keyword Filtering*

Keyword filtering relies on detection of offensive words and phrases in the Web contents. When a Web page has been successfully retrieved from the remote Web server, every word or phrase on the Web page is compared against those in a keyword dictionary of prohibited words and phrases. If the number of matches has reached a predefined threshold, the corresponding Website is blocked.

Keyword filtering is a fast and simple content analysis method whose dictionary does not require frequent updating. However, it is well known for its over-blocking issue. For example, a Website about sexual harassment can be accidentally blocked because it contains many occurrences of the keyword "sex". What is needed is therefore some understanding of the context in which the keywords appear on the Web page in question.

18.2.4 *Intelligent Content Analysis*

Keyword matching can be very effective when machine intelligence is employed to determine the context of how the keywords are used. We therefore investigate the application of artificial neural network (ANN) to perform intelligent content analysis. The learning capability of an ANN enables it to differentiate between terms that are used in different contexts.

In addition, we also propose to combine the efficiency of URL blocking with intelligent content analysis. The objective is to take an automated approach towards determining if a Web page contains objectionable contents. The black list of URLs can then be updated accordingly. All this can be performed offline by an Intelligent Classification Engine as described later in this chapter.

18.3 Network Monitoring

In order to provide networking support for Web monitoring and filtering, we present our study of the relevant network protocols and network packet-capturing techniques in this section.

18.3.1 *Network Protocols*

We examine three network protocols relevant to the development of a Web monitoring and filtering system: Hypertext Transfer Protocol (HTTP), Transmission Control Protocol (TCP), and Internet Protocol (IP).

HTTP has been in use since 1990 by the WWW global information initiative to connect Web resources to each other and to users via the Internet. It is the protocol for building distributed, collaborative and hypermedia information systems. HTTP presumes a reliable transport, and thus the communication usually takes place over TCP on top of IP connections.

HTTP uses a request/response model for communication between two parties. A client such as the Web browser sends a request to the HTTP Web server, together with the URL and protocol version, followed by a message containing request modifiers, client information, and possible body contents over a connection to the server. The Web server responds with a status line, including the message protocol version and a success or error code, followed by a message containing server information, entity meta-information, and body contents. The messages are delivered in a format similar to that used by Internet mail as defined by the Multipurpose Internet Mail Extensions (MIME) [Borenstein and Freed, (1996)]. A Web filtering system needs to understand HTTP since it captures HTTP packets in order to extract the Web contents embedded in the packets. Thus, an HTTP parser is needed in the system.

TCP is a connection-oriented network transport protocol that provides reliable transfers of packets between two end-points on the network. It is responsible for assembling data passed from higher layer applications into TCP packets and ensuring that the data are transferred and received correctly and completely. The delivery of packets is guaranteed to be in sequence. If a packet is corrupted or lost, TCP will retransmit the packet. This is achieved by using acknowledgement and packet sequence numbers. TCP usually resides on top of IP protocol when packets are transmitted on the Internet.

HTTP makes use of TCP to encapsulate and reliably deliver packets over the Internet. Thus, another approach to capture HTTP packets is by capturing all the TCP packets passing through the targeted computer where the Web content filtering is to be deployed. However, this will waste a certain amount of processing time as not all of the TCP packets are HTTP data and to differentiate between them requires extra complexity in processing. Moreover, the Web filtering system will need to understand TCP packet format in addition to HTTP. This requires an extra TCP parser module in the system, which increases the system complexity.

IP is the underlying communications protocol of the Internet. It resides below the network transport protocol layer of the TCP/IP protocol suite and is responsible for moving the packets of data assembled by the network transport protocol across the network. It uses a set of unique addresses for every client on the network to determine routing and destinations, while carrying out a best-effort packet switching functionality which routes packets between hosts without establishing a communication path. Thus, the delivery of packets is not guaranteed and it relies on the upper layer protocols to ensure delivery of packets. It will also break the outgoing data into smaller chunks if the size of the data is too large, and encapsulate them into IP packets before sending over the network. At the receiving end, all the IP packets need to be received before the data can be reassembled.

Since TCP relies on IP to transmit packets over the Internet, capturing IP packets on the targeted computer enables the Web filtering system to seize TCP packets as well, which may include HTTP packets. However, this requires understanding the IP format. Also, not all of the IP packets contain TCP packets since there are also other protocols such as User Datagram Protocol (UDP) that make use of IP for transmission. In addition, a Web filtering system capturing packets at the IP layer needs to wait for all the associated IP packets, which contain chunks of the original data to be received, before the data can be reassembled. All of these introduce much more processing latency and development complexity to the Web filtering system than capturing TCP or HTTP packets. Thus, capturing packets at the IP layer should be avoided.

In summary, the best way for a Web filtering system to capture packets is at the HTTP layer, as it requires the least amount of processing time and introduces minimum system latency and complexity. The complexity involved in capturing and analyzing TCP and IP packets would impose an unnecessary amount of latency to the system, particularly for IP that fragments the original data into small packets before transmission. Moreover, its best-effort delivery and out-of-order reception makes processing of the captured packets difficult. Thus, we focus on network packet capturing techniques at the HTTP layer.

18.3.2 *Network Packet Capturing Techniques*

We describe two network packet capturing techniques that can be employed by a Web monitoring and filtering system: WinSock packet capturing and HTTP proxy packet capturing. Both approaches avoid the need to capture and analyze packets at the TCP or IP layers.

WinSock is a socket-based network application programming interface (API) for MS Windows. It includes a well-defined set of data structures and functions implemented as a dynamic data link (DDL). WinSock is a standard API for establishing TCP/IP communication under Windows, although the API is abstract enough to support other protocol families. Most of the popular Windows-based Internet applications use WinSock to connect to the Internet, including Web browsers such as Microsoft Internet Explorer and Netscape Navigator, as well as e-mail programs and Usenet readers.

WinSock 2.0 includes a mechanism for capturing network packets sent and received through the WinSock API. This is done by implementing an extra layer to the normal WinSock 2.0 system structure, as illustrated in Fig. 18.2. In the original WinSock 2.0 system structure shown in Fig. 18.2(a), Internet applications make function calls to the WinSock 2.0 DLL through the API. The DLL then translates the calls into the corresponding Service Provider Interface (SPI) function calls to the TCP/IP base protocol module. A base protocol refers to a protocol or a set of protocols capable of performing data communication with a remote endpoint. On the other hand, an extra module named layered protocol is included in the system structure in Fig. 18.2(b).

In contrast to the base protocol, a layered protocol is a protocol that cannot carry out tasks on its own and needs to rely on a base protocol for fundamental network services. It is meant to add additional services to the base protocol such as encryption and decryption for secure transmission of data streams through the Internet.

As WinSock 2.0 supports a protocol chain that is a combination of one or more layered protocols attached to a base protocol, the network data streams will need to pass through the layered protocols before reaching the base protocol for outgoing data or the WinSock 2.0 DLL for incoming data. This facilitates the implementation of a dummy layered protocol that monitors network traffic and captures network packets. As Web browsers on MS Windows platforms use WinSock to communicate with Web servers, a Web monitoring and filtering system can make use of such layered protocol feature provided by WinSock 2.0 to capture HTTP packets transmitted between the Web browsers and the remote Web servers.

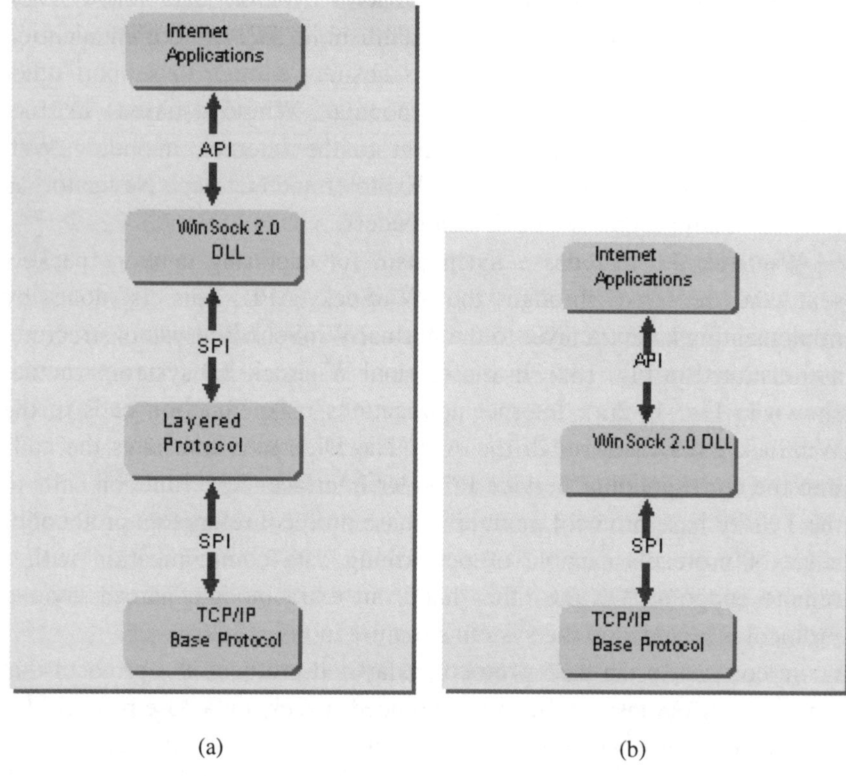

Fig. 18.2 Winsock system structure.

Since the network data streams of WinSock are still in their original form, a Web monitoring and filtering system that adopts this approach for the Network Monitoring Process does not need to know how to interpret the TCP or IP formats. However, the network data streams not only consist of HTTP data streams, but also other types of data streams. This is because not only Web browsers use WinSock for communication, but other network applications also utilize the API for communication over the Internet. Thus, the system still needs to be able to distinguish HTTP data streams from other types of network data streams.

A proxy is an intermediary program that acts as both a server and a client for making requests on behalf of other clients to servers. Requests from the clients are serviced by the proxy internally, or passed to the remote servers possibly with some form of translations. In the case of an HTTP proxy, it is placed in between Web browsers and Web servers, and requests from the Web browsers are routed to the HTTP proxy rather than to the Web servers directly. It implements both the client and server requirements of the HTTP specification. When the HTTP proxy receives an HTTP request packet from the Web browser, it can either process the request packet internally without passing it to the remote Web server, or forward it to the Web server with possible modifications to the request packet contents. If the Web server returns the HTTP response packet corresponding to the request, the HTTP proxy can also choose to modify the HTTP response packet contents or even the Web document associated with the packet before forwarding it to the requesting Web browser. This provides an opportunity to implement the Network Monitoring Process as an HTTP proxy since it supports the capturing of HTTP packets only. Also, the possibility to make modifications to the HTTP packets before forwarding them to their destinations enables it to perform Web content filtering.

In summary, although WinSock 2.0 provides a mechanism for capturing packets without the need of interpreting TCP and IP packets, the mechanism itself does not have the capability to differentiate between HTTP data streams and other types of network data streams. On the other hand, packet capturing using an HTTP proxy only captures HTTP packets whose contents can also be modified in the process. Thus, our Online Filtering Agent adopts the HTTP proxy approach for Network Monitoring.

18.4 System Architecture

Based on the above discussion, we have developed a system to filter out pornographic Web pages as an example of objectionable Web contents. Fig. 18.3 shows the overall architecture of our intelligent Web monitoring and filtering system.

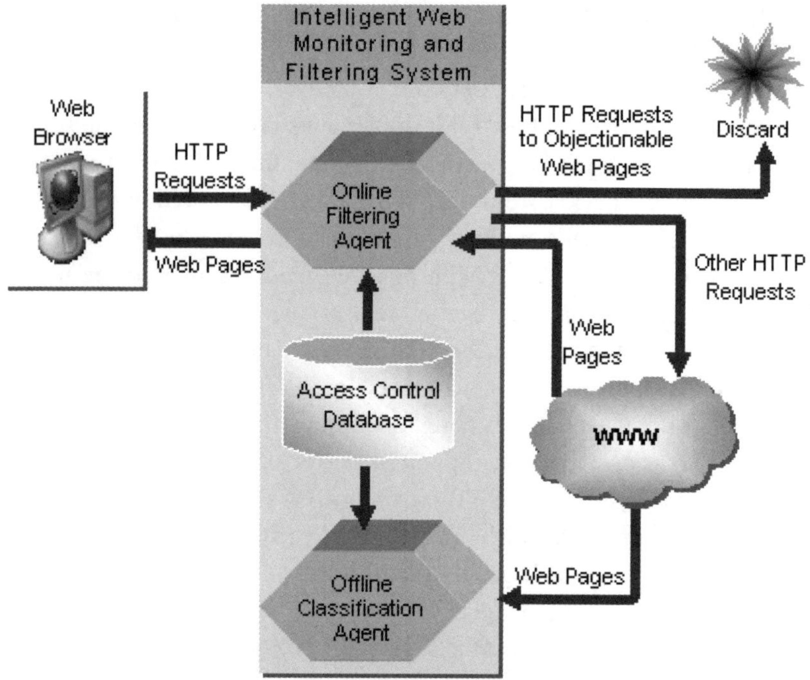

Fig. 18.3 intelligent Web monitoring and filtering system architecture.

The system consists of three major components: Offline Classification Agent, Access Control Database and Online Filtering Agent. The Offline Classification Agent is responsible for discovering objectionable Web pages on the WWW and updating the Access Control Database. The Access Control Database contains information regarding URL of the objectionable Web pages. This database is utilized by the Online Filtering Agent for monitoring the online browsing activities and filtering out objectionable Web pages. This decoupling of the classification process by the Offline Classification Agent and the monitoring and blocking process by the Online Filtering Agent achieves a higher accuracy while maintaining a low latency in the system.

The Offline Classification Agent actively retrieves Web pages from the WWW and classifies them using the Intelligent Classification Engine [Lee *at al.*, (2002)]. The URLs of any confirmed objectionable Websites are recorded in the Access Control Database. The Agent can also help users carry out manual classification on unconfirmed Web pages and maintenance of the Access Control Database.

The Online Filtering Agent, which is the main subject of this chapter, monitors HTTP requests from a Web browser and inspects an HTTP request to see whether the URL in the request refers to an objectionable Web page. It discards any objectionable Web page's HTTP requests and forwards allowable requests to their respective destinations. It also provides Web browsing history logging for audit purposes.

18.5 Offline Classification Agent

The Intelligent Classification Engine is employed by the Offline Classification Agent to classify Web pages into two categories: "Allowable" and "Objectionable". In this research, machine intelligence is provided by means of the Kohonen's Self-Organizing Map (KSOM) ANN model. Occasionally, a Web page is marked as "Unascertained" when the Intelligent Classification Engine fails to classify it into one of the two categories. In this event, manual classification would be necessary. Our goal is therefore to minimize the number of unascertained Web pages.

By adopting the KSOM ANN model, our Intelligent Classification Engine consists of two major processes: Training and Classification. The Training Process learns from the sample comprising both pornographic and non-pornographic Web pages to form a knowledge base of the ANN model. The Classification Process then classifies incoming Web pages according to the nature of the contents. The Training Process consists of the following steps: Feature Extraction, Pre-Processing, Transformation, ANN Model Generation and Category Assignment. The Classification Process also needs to perform Feature Extraction, Pre-Processing and Transformation. In addition, the Categorization step is needed to classify the incoming Web pages based on the results given by the ANN model. A Meta Content Checking step performs post-processing to enhance the classification results. These steps are described as follows:

1. Feature Extraction. A Web page is parsed and the contents in various locations such as the title of the Web page, warning message block, meta data contents and image tooltips, are extracted as features to represent the Web page. The locations are used as the context of the features.
2. Pre-Processing. This step consists of the tokenization of words, and indicative term identification and counting using an indicative term dictionary. Indicative terms are keywords or phrases as described in the keyword matching approach.
3. Transformation. The frequencies of occurrence of the respective indicative terms resulted from the Pre-Processing step are then sorted and converted into vectors representing the Web pages which are fed as inputs to the ANN.
4. ANN Model Generation. The input vectors that characterize the contents of Web pages are fed to the ANN for training purposes.
5. Category Assignment. The clusters generated from the ANN Model Generation are assigned to be one of the three categories: pornographic, non-pornographic and unascertained, based on a predefined assignment strategy.
6. Categorization. The incoming Web pages are classified using the trained ANN into one of the predefined categories.
7. Meta Content Checking. This is a post-processing step that checks the Web pages that are classified as unascertained using the contents of the meta data of "description" and "keywords" to determine its nature. This step helps to reduce the number of unascertained Web pages and hence further enhance the accuracy of the system.

18.5.1 *Classification Performance*

To measure the classification performance of our Offline Classification Agent, we conducted experiments on a Pentium III 866MHz computer running the Windows 2000 operating system.

Using a total of 4786 (1009 pornographic and 3777 non-pornographic) Web pages, we trained the KSOM ANN for 24500 iterations. We then tested the system using a testing exemplar set which consists of 535 pornographic Web pages and 523 non-pornographic Web pages. The results are summarized in Table 18.1, which shows that our

KSOM approach is able to correctly classify 95% of all Web pages used in the test.

Table 18.1 Classification performance.

Web page type	Correctly classified	Incorrectly classified	Unascertained	Total
Pornographic	508 (95%)	23 (4.3%)	4 (0.7%)	535
Non-pornographic	497 (95%)	7 (1.3%)	19 (3.7%)	523
Total:	1005 (95%)	30 (2.8%)	23 (2.2%)	1058

18.6 Online Filtering Agent

Our Online Filtering Agent encompasses the Network Monitoring Process and Filtering Process. The Network Monitoring Process is implemented using the HTTP proxy architecture to capture packets at the HTTP level. On the other hand, the Filtering Process employs URL blocking as the content filtering approach and uses the Access Control Database for decision-making.

As shown in Fig. 18.4, the Online Filtering Agent consists of two major components: HTTP Proxy and Web Filtering. HTTP Proxy is responsible for capturing HTTP packets between the Web browser and the WWW for traffic monitoring. It comprises five processes: HTTP Request Acquisition, HTTP Request Forwarding, HTTP Response Acquisition, HTTP Response Forwarding and HTTP Header Modification. Web Filtering conducts inspection of HTTP requests and performs blocking on requests to disallowed Web pages. It consists of four processes: URL Extraction, URL Inspection, Filtering Message Generation and Web Browsing History Logging.

In a typical Web browsing session, the Web Browser sends an HTTP request packet to its targeted remote Web server to retrieve the requested Web page. This packet is first captured by the Online Filtering Agent's HTTP Request Acquisition process. It is then passed to the URL Extraction process, which extracts the requested URL from the packet. The URL Inspection process will then determine whether the URL is to a disallowed Website by accessing the Access Control Database. If the URL Inspection process rejects the URL, the corresponding HTTP request will be discarded, while the Filtering Message Generation process will construct a HTTP response stating that the request is blocked. This HTTP response is then sent back to the Web Browser through the HTTP Response Forwarding process.

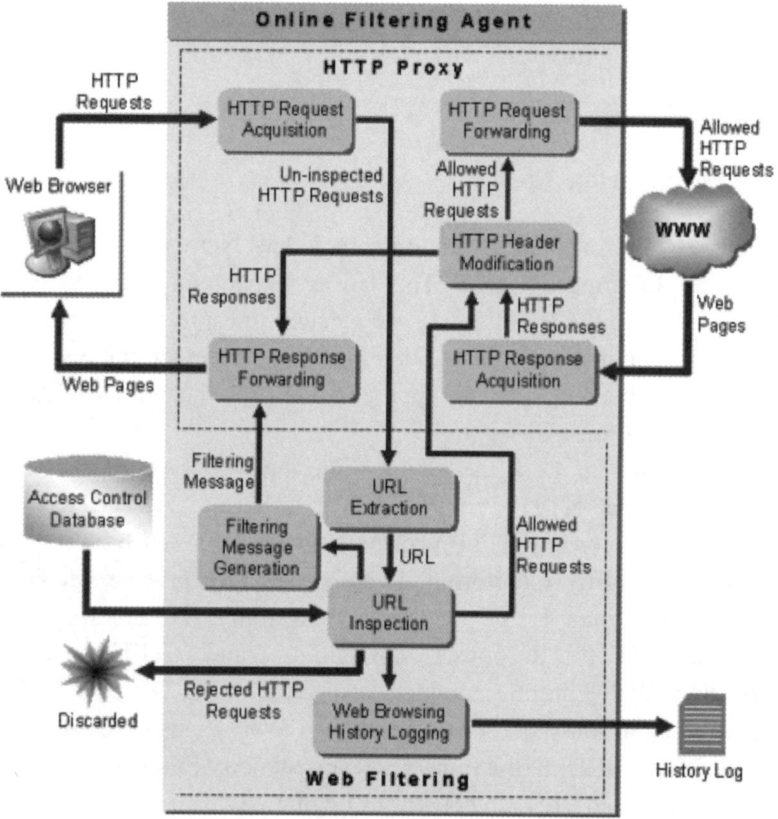

Fig. 18.4 Online filtering agent.

On the other hand, if the URL Inspection process does not reject the URL, the allowed HTTP request is passed to the HTTP Header

Modification process. This process carries out the modification of the HTTP headers in both the HTTP request and response packets according to the HTTP proxy requirements as described in the HTTP specification. After it has completed preparing the HTTP request packet for further forwarding, it passes the packet to the HTTP Request Forwarding process, which then forwards the packet to its destination.

When the requested Web page is sent back from the targeted Web server through an HTTP response packet, it is acquired by the HTTP Response Acquisition process, and passed to the HTTP Header Modification process. After carrying out the necessary header modification by the process, it is then passed to the HTTP Response Forwarding process for sending back to the Web Browser.

18.6.1 *HTTP Proxy*

As mentioned earlier, the HTTP Proxy component comprises five processes: HTTP Request Acquisition, HTTP Header Modification, HTTP Request Forwarding, HTTP Response Acquisition and HTTP Response Forwarding.

The HTTP Request Acquisition process receives the HTTP request packets from the Web Browser requested by the user to navigate to a specific URL. Each HTTP request packet contains the information regarding one requested URL. This information is essential to the Online Filtering Agent as it adopts URL blocking for content filtering. To capture all URL request packets from the Web Browser, the Web Browser needs to be configured to send the packets to their destination by passing through the Online Filtering Agent's HTTP Proxy component. In such case, the HTTP request packets can then be captured by the HTTP Request Acquisition process. These un-inspected HTTP requests will be passed on to the URL Extraction process of the Web Filtering component of the agent for inspection and filtering decision-making.

The HTTP Header Modification process is necessary for fulfilling the requirements on HTTP proxy server as stated in the HTTP protocol specification. It handles both the HTTP request packets and HTTP response packets, and modifies the HTTP headers in the packets according to the types of packets and whether a cascading HTTP proxy server is in use.

After the HTTP Header Modification process, all the allowed HTTP requests packets are dispatched to the HTTP Request Forwarding process which sends the HTTP request packets through the WWW to their destined Web servers. Depending on the user's configuration for Internet surfing, this process can either forward the HTTP request packets to another cascading HTTP proxy server, or deliver directly to the targeted Web servers.

When the Web servers return the requested Web pages encapsulated in HTTP response packets, the packets are captured by the HTTP Response Acquisition process. Unlike in the case of HTTP Request Acquisition process, the HTTP responses do not require the processing of Web Filtering component of the Online Filtering Agent, since only Web pages fulfilling the allowed HTTP requests are returned. Thus, the HTTP Response Acquisition directly passes the HTTP Response packets to the HTTP Header Modification process in preparation for forwarding to the Web Browser.

All the HTTP response packets that have already been processed by the HTTP Header Modification process are handed down to the HTTP Response Forwarding process, which is responsible for delivering the HTTP response packets back to the Web Browser.

18.6.2 *Web Filtering*

The processes in the Web Filtering component are URL Extraction, URL Inspection, Filtering Message Generation and Web Browsing History Logging. When an HTTP request packet is passed to the Web Filtering component of the Online Filtering Agent, it is first handled by the URL Extraction process. This process looks into the HTTP request packet, identifies and extracts out the URL address of the requested Web page. This, together with the HTTP request packet, is then sent to the URL Inspection process for filtering decision-making.

The URL address extracted by the URL Extraction process is used by the URL Inspection process for determining if an HTTP request should be blocked. The process makes use of the information provided by the

Access Control Database to determine if the URL address to the requested Web pages should be allowed. If the URL address is permitted, the corresponding HTTP request is passed to the HTTP Header Modification process for further forwarding.

However, if the URL address is rejected, the corresponding HTTP request will not be passed to the HTTP Header Modification process but is discarded. In addition, the process instructs the Filtering Message Generation process to construct an HTTP response packet containing filtering message, which is then sent back to the Web Browser through the HTTP Response Forwarding process. The URL Inspection process also coordinates with the Web Browsing History Logging process by providing information regarding the HTTP request.

The Filtering Message Generation process constructs an HTTP response packet in response to a blocked HTTP request reported by the URL Inspection process. The packet contains a filtering message notifying the user that access to the requested Web page has been blocked. This packet is then passed to the HTTP Response Forwarding process to be sent back to the requesting Web browser.

Finally, the Web Browsing History Logging process produces a chronological log of HTTP requests from the Web browser representing the Web access history of the user. The information for logging is provided by the URL Inspection process that includes the requested URLs, time of request as well as filtering decision carried out. All of these are recorded in a history log file that can later be retrieved for viewing and auditing by the system administrator.

18.7 Conclusion

In this chapter, we have described the networking support required for an effective Web monitoring and filtering system. The purpose is to develop a system so that objectionable Web pages can be effectively identified and blocked.

Using the filtering of pornographic Web pages as a case study, we have developed and tested a Web monitoring and filtering system, which decouples the classification process and the monitoring and blocking process. The former is performed by an Offline Classification Agent, whereas the latter is done by an Online Filtering Agent. This aims to achieve a high accuracy while maintaining a low latency in the system. Indeed, our performance comparison tests verify the effectiveness of this approach.

The ability to intercept and analyse Internet traffic using our networking support has enormous potential. Apart from monitoring and filtering out objectionable Web contents, it can also be used to monitor network activities of employees at the workplace to reduce the amount of non-work-related usage, or for parents to monitor online chat between their children and strangers. It can also be used as a form of security surveillance to fight crime and terrorism, for example, by detecting money laundering and other illegal transactions.

Bibliography

Borenstein, N. and Freed, N. (1996). Multipurpose Internet Mail Extensions (MIME) Part One: Format of Internet Message Bodies, RFC2045.

Chekuri, C., Goldwasser, M.H., Raghavan P. and Upfal, E. (1996). Web Search Using Automatic Classification, *Proc. WWW-96, California.* Available at http://www.cs.luc.edu/~mhg/publications/WWW1997.bw.pdf

Kim, Y.H., Kim, S., Eom, J.H. and Zhang, B.T. (2000) SCAI Experiments on TREC-9, *Proc. Ninth Text Retrieval Conference* (TREC-9), pp. 392-399.

Lee, P.Y, Hui, S.C. and Fong, A.C.M. (2002). Neural networks for web content filtering, IEEE Intelligent Systems, 17, pp. 48-57.

Murthy, K.R.K. and Keerthi, S.S. (1999). Context Filters for Document-Based Information Filtering, *Proc. IC-DAR'99, Bangalore, India.* Available at http://bheeshma.csa.iisc.ernet.in/~krish/publications.html

Pearl Software Cyber Snoop Parental Control Software for Internet Filtering & Monitoring. Available at URL: http://www.cyber-snoop.com/index.html

RuleSpace Inc. WebChaperone Internet Filtering, Blocking, and Control for family. Available at URL: http://www.webchaperone.com

Scott, S. and Matwin, S. (1999). Feature Engineering for Text Classification, *Proc. ICML-99*, 379-388. Available at http://wabakimi.carleton.ca/~sscott2/sam/ICML99_Camera.pdf

SurfControl plc. Cyber Patrol – Internet Filtering Software for Home, Education, and Business. Available at URL: http://www.cyberpatrol.com

Vault Inc. Results of Vault.com Survey of Internet Use in the Workplace, (2000). Available at http://www.vault.com/surveys/internetuse2000/index2000.jsp

World Wide Web Consortium (W3C). Platform for Internet Content Selection, Available at URL: http://www.w3.org/PICS/

## CHAPTER 19

WEB INTELLIGENCE: WEB-BASED BISC DECISION SUPPORT SYSTEM (WBISC-DSS)

Gamil Serag-Eldin, Souad Souafi-Bensafi, Jonathan K. Lee, Wai-Kit Chan, Masoud Nikravesh

BISC Program, Computer Sciences Division, EECS Department
University of California, Berkeley, CA 94720, USA
Email: nikravesh@cs.berkeley.edu

Most of the existing search systems (software) are modeled using crisp logic and queries. In this chapter, we introduce fuzzy querying and ranking as a flexible tool allowing approximation where the selected objects do not need to exactly match the decision criteria resembling natural human behavior. The model consists of five major modules: the Fuzzy Search Engine, Application Templates, the User Interface, the Database, and Evolutionary Computing. The system is de-signed in a generic form to accommodate more diverse applications and to be delivered as stand-alone software to academia and businesses.

19.1 Introduction

Searching database records and ranking the results based on multi-criteria queries is central for many database applications used within organizations in finance, business, industry and other fields. Most of the available systems (software) are modeled using crisp logic and queries, which results in rigid systems with imprecise and subjective processes and results. In this chapter we introduce fuzzy querying and ranking as a flexible tool allowing approximation where the selected objects do not need to exactly match the decision criteria resembling natural human behavior [Nikravesh (2001b)], [Nikravesh, Azvine (2002)], [Nikravesh (2003a)].

The model consists of five major modules: the Fuzzy Search Engine (FSE), Application Templates (AT), the User Interface (UI), the Database (DB) and Evolutionary Computing (EC). We developed the software with many essential features. It is built as a web-based software system that users can access and use over the Internet. The system is designed to be generic so that it can run different application domains. To this end, the Application Template module provides information of a specific application as attributes and properties, and serves as a guideline structure for building a new application.

The Fuzzy Search Engine (FSE) is the core module of the system. It has been developed to be generic so that it would fit any application. The main FSE component is the query structure, which utilizes membership functions, similarity functions and aggregators.

Through the user interface, a user can enter and save his profile, input criteria for a new query, run different queries and display results. The user can manually eliminate the results he disapproves of or change the ranking according to his preferences.

The Evolutionary Computing (EC) module monitors ranking preferences of the user's queries. It learns to adjust to the intended meaning of the user's preferences.

We present our approach with three important applications: ranking (scoring), which has been used to make financing decisions concerning credit cards, car and mortgage loans; college admissions where hundreds of thousands of applications are processed yearly by U.S. universities; and date matching as one of the most popular internet programs. Even though we implemented three applications, the system is designed in a generic form to accommodate more diverse applications and to be delivered as stand-alone software to academia and businesses.

19.2 Model Framework

The DSS system starts by loading the application template, which consists of various configuration files for a specific application (see section 19.4) and initializing the database for the application (see section 19.6), before handling a user's requests, (see figure 19.1).

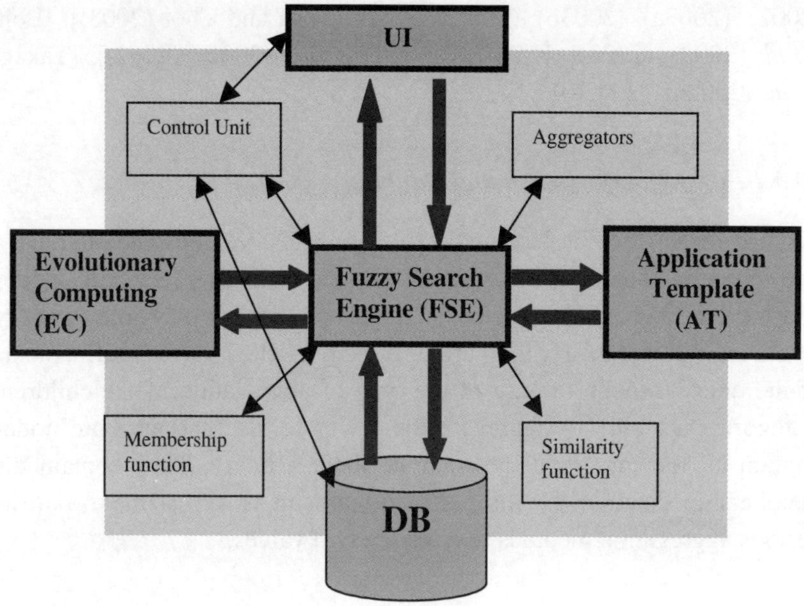

Fig. 19.1 The BISC-DSS general framework.

Once the DSS system is initialized, users can enter their own profiles in the user interface or make a search with their preferences. The control unit of the system handles these requests. The control unit converts user input into data objects that are recognized by the DSS system. Based on the request types, it forwards them to the appropriate modules.

If the user wants to create a profile, the control unit will send the profile data directly to the database module, which stores the data in the database for the application. If the user wants to query the system, the control unit will direct the user's preferences to the Fuzzy Search Engine, which queries the database (see section 19.3). The query results will be sent back to the control unit and displayed to the users.

19.3 Fuzzy Engine

During the recent years, applications of fuzzy logic and the internet from web data mining to intelligent search engine and agents for internet applications have greatly increased [Nikravesh (2002)], [Nikravesh *et. al.*

(2002), (2003a), (2003b), (2003c)], [Nikravesh and Choi (2003)], [Loia *et. al.* (2002), (2003)], [Nikravesh and Azvine (2001), (2002)], [Takagi *et. al.* (2002a), (2002b)].

19.3.1 Fuzzy Query, Search and Ranking

To support generic queries, the fuzzy engine has been designed to have a tree structure. There are two types of nodes in the tree, category nodes and attribute nodes, as depicted in figure 19.2. While multiple category levels are not necessary, they are designed to allow various refinements of the query through the use of the type of aggregation of the children. Categories act only to aggregate the lower levels. The attribute nodes contain all the important information about a query. They contain the membership functions for the fuzzy comparison as well as the use of the various aggregation methods to compare two values.

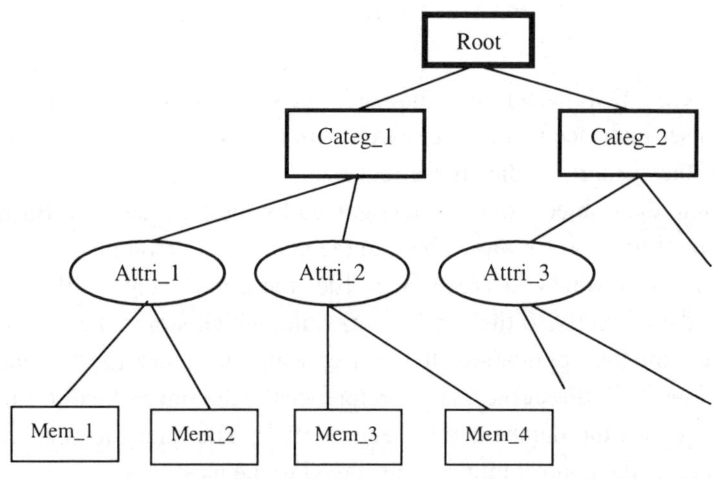

Fig. 19.2 The Fuzzy search engine tree structure.

The flow of control in the program when a query is executed is as follows. The root node receives a query formatted as a fuzzy data object and is asked to compare the query fuzzy data to a record from the database also formatted as a fuzzy data object. At each category node, the compare method is called for each child and then aggregated using an aggregator object.

The attribute nodes handle the compare method slightly different than the category nodes. There are two different ways attributes may be compared. The attribute nodes contain a list of membership functions comprising the fuzzy set. The degrees of membership for this set are passed to the similarity comparator object, which currently has a variety of different methods to calculate the similarity between the two membership vectors. In the other method, the membership vector is created by having full membership to a single membership function specified in the fuzzy data object, but no membership value for the other functions [Sugeno (1974)].

The resulting comparison value returned from the root node is assigned to the record. The search request is then added to a sorted list ordered by this ranking in descending value. Each of the records from the database is compared to the query and the results are returned. For certain search criteria, it may be desirable to have exact values in the query. For such criteria, the database is used to filter the re-cords for comparison.

19.3.2 Membership function

Currently there are three membership functions implemented for the Fuzzy Engine. A generic interface has been created to allow several different types of membership functions to be added to the system [Grabisch *et. al.* (2000)]. The three types of membership functions in the system are: Gaussian, Triangular and Trapezoidal. These functions have three main points, for the lower bound, upper bound and the point of maximum membership. For other functions, optional extra points may be used to define the shape (an extra point is required for the trapezoidal form).

```
################################################################################
#This is a properties file for membership definition. We should specify
#the following properties for an attribute:
# -  A unique identifier for each defined membership function.
# -  A type from the following: {Gaussian, Triangle, Trapezoid}
# -  Three points: Lowerbound, Upperbound, Maximum
# -  Optional point: Auxillary Maximum
# Format:
# <MF_Name>.membershipFunctionName = <MF_Name>
# <MF_Name>.membershipFunctionType = {Gaussian/Triangle/Trapezoid}
# <MF_Name>.lowerBound          = lowerBoundValue
# <MF_Name>.upperBound          = upperBoundValue
# <MF_Name>.maxValue            = maxValue
# <MF_Name>.optionPoint         = pt1, pt2, pt3 ...
#
################################################################################
```

```
################################################################################
#
# Gender Membership Functions
#
male.membershipFunctionName = male
male.membershipFunctionType = Triangle
male.lowerbound        = 1
male.upperbound        = 1
male.maxValue          = 1

female.membershipFunctionName = female
female.membershipFunctionType = Triangle
female.lowerbound        = 0
female.upperbound        = 0
female.maxValue          = 0
#
# Age Membership Functions
#
young.membershipFunctionName = young
young.membershipFunctionType = Triangle
young.lowerbound        = 0
young.upperbound        = 35
young.maxValue          = 20

middle.membershipFunctionName = middle
middle.membershipFunctionType = Triangle
middle.lowerbound        = 20
middle.upperbound        = 50
middle.maxValue          = 35

old.membershipFunctionName = old
old.membershipFunctionType = Triangle
old.lowerbound        = 35
old.upperbound        = 100
old.maxValue          = 50
```

Fig. 19.3 Template of the date matching application.

19.4 Application Template

The DSS system is designed to work with different application domains. The application template is a format for any new application we build; it contains data of different categories, attributes and membership functions of that application. The application template module consists of two parts the application template data file, and the application template logic.

The application template data file specifies all the membership functions, at-tributes and categories of an application. We can consider it as a configuration data file for an application. It contains the definition of membership functions, attributes and the relationship between them.

The application template logic parses and caches data from the data file so that other modules in the system can have faster access to definitions of membership functions, attributes and categories. It also creates a tree data structure for the fuzzy search engine to transverse. Figure 19.3 shows part of the sample configuration file from the Date Matching application.

19.5 User Interface

It is difficult to design a generic user interface that suits different kind of applications for all the fields. For example, we may want to have different layouts for user interfaces for different applications. To make the DSS system generic while preserving the user friendliness of the interfaces for different applications, we developed the user interfaces into two parts.

First, we designed a specific HTML interface for each application we developed. Users can input their own profiles, make queries by specifying preferences for different attributes. Details for the DSS system are encapsulated from the HTML interface so that the HTML interface design would not be constrained by the DSS system.

The second part of our user interface module is a mapping between the parameters in the HTML files and the attributes in the application template module for the application. The input mapping specifies the attribute names to which each parameter in the HTML interface corresponds. With this input mapping, a user interface designer can use input methods and parameter names freely.

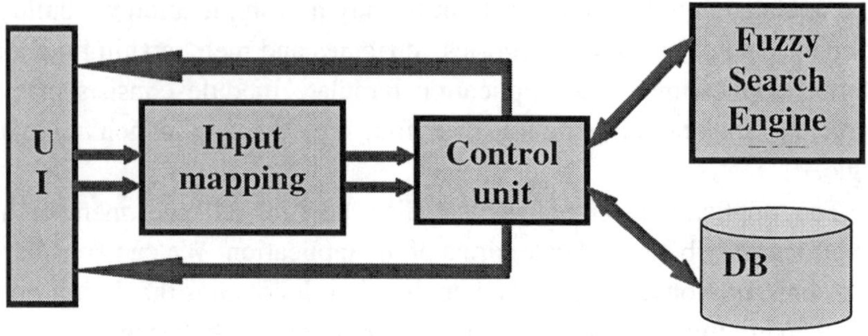

Fig. 19.4 User interface data flow.

19.6 Database (DB)

The database module is responsible for all the transactions between the DSS system and the database. This module handles all queries or user profile creations from the Fuzzy Engine and the Control Unit respectively. For queries from the Fuzzy Search Engine, it retrieves data from the database and returns it in a data object form. Usually queries are sets of attribute values and their associated weights. The database module returns the matching records in a format that can be manipulated by the user such as eliminating one or more record or changing their order. To create a user profile, it takes data objects from the Control Unit and stores it in the database. There are three components in the DB module: the DB Manager (DBMgr), the DB Accessor (DBA) and DB Accessor Factory (DBA Factory).

19.6.1 DB Manager

The DB Manager is accountable for two things: setting up database connections and allocating database connections to DB Accessor objects when needed. During the initialization of the DSS system, DB Manager loads the right driver, which is used for the communications between the database and the system. It also supplies information to the database for authentication purposes (e.g. username, password, path to the database etc).

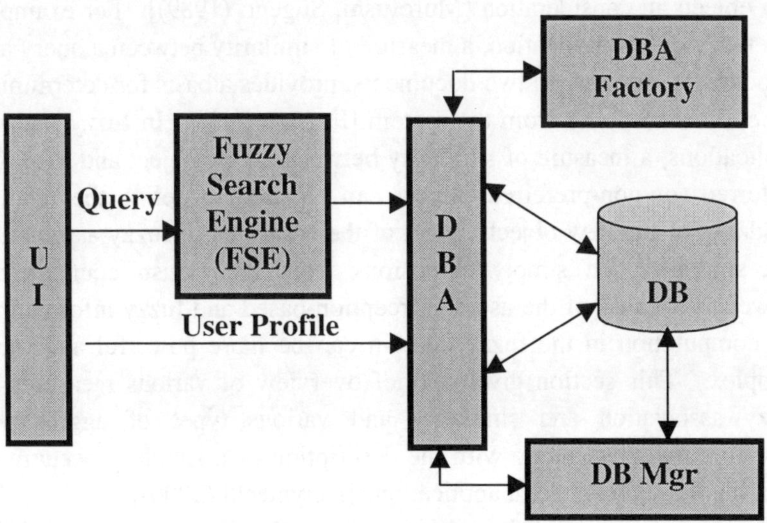

Fig. 19.5 Database module components.

19.6.2 DB Accessor Factory

The DB Accessor Factory creates DB Accessor objects for a specific application. For example, if the system is running the date matching application, DB Accessor Factory will create DB Accessor objects for the date matching application. The existence of this class serves the purpose of using a generic Fuzzy Search Engine.

19.6.3 DB Accessor

DB Accessor is responsible for storing and getting user profiles to and from the database. It also saves queries from users to the database so that other modules in the system can analyze user's preferences. It is the component that queries the database and wrap result from the database into data objects that are recognized by our application framework.

19.7 Measure of Association and Fuzzy Similarity

As in crisp query and ranking, an important concept in fuzzy query and ranking applications is the measure of association or similarity between two objects in consideration [Murofushi, Sugeno (1989)]. For example, in a fuzzy query application, a measure of similarity between a query and a document, or between two documents, provides a basis for determining the optimal response from the system [Fagin (1998)]. In fuzzy ranking applications, a measure of similarity between a new object and a known preferred (or non-preferred) object can be used to define the relative goodness of the new object. Most of the measures of fuzzy association and similarity are simply extensions from their crisp counterparts. However, because of the use of perception-based and fuzzy information, the computation in the fuzzy domain can be more powerful and more complex. This section gives a brief overview of various measures of fuzzy association and similarity and various types of aggregation operators involved, along with the description of a simple procedure of utilizing these tools in real applications [Detyniecki (2000)].

Various definitions of similarity exist in the classical, crisp domain, and many of them can be easily extended to the fuzzy domain. However, unlike in the crisp case, in the fuzzy case the similarity is defined on two fuzzy sets. Suppose we have two fuzzy sets A and B with membership functions $\mu_A(x)$ and $\mu_B(x)$, respectively. The arithmetic operators involved in the fuzzy similarity measures can be treated using their usual definitions while the union and the intersection operators need to be treated specially. It is important for these operator pairs to have the following properties: (1) conservation, (2) monotonicity, (3) commutativity, and (4) associativity. It can be verified that the triangular norm (T-norm) and triangular co-norm (T-conorm) [Detyniecki (2001)], [Nikravesh (2001b)], [Mizumoto (1989)], [Fagin (1998)], [Grabisch (1996)] conform to these properties and can be applied here. A detailed survey of some commonly used T-norm and T-conorm pairs along with other aggregation operators can be find at [Nikravesh *et. al.* (2003c)].

Having introduced a variety of tools that are required to evaluate fuzzy association/similarity between two objects, a simple algorithm in pseudo code is provided below to illustrate how these machineries can be used in a practical implementation.

Input: two objects A and B
A: N discrete attributes
For the ith attribute, A_i is an array of length M_i, where M_i is the number of possible linguistic values of the ith attribute.
i.e. each A_{ji} , i in 1,…,N and j in 1,…,M_i , gives the degree of A's ith attribute having jth linguistic value.
B: similar to A with the same dimensions.
Other parameters:
AggregatorType
SimilarityType
TNormType
OptionalWeights
Output: An aggregated similarity score between A and B
Algorithm:
For each i=1 to N
SAB^i = ComputeSimilarity(A^i , B^i ,SimilarityType, TNormType)
End
Return Aggregate(SAB, AggregatorType, OptionalWeights)

Sub ComputeSimilarity(X, Y, SimilarityType, TNormType)
Switch SimilarityType:
Case SimpleMatchingCoefficient:
Return |X ∩ Y|
Case CosineCoefficient:
Return |X ∩ Y| / ($|X|^{1/2}$ $|Y|^{1/2}$)
Case OverlapCoefficient:
Return |X ∩ Y| / min(|X|, |Y|)
Case Jaccard's Coefficient:
Return |X ∩ Y| / (|X ∪ Y|)
Case Dice's Coefficient:
Return 2|X ∩ Y| / (|X| + |Y|)
…
End

```
Sub Aggregate(S, AggregatorType, OptionalWeights)
Switch AggregatorType:
Case Min:
Return min(S)
Case Max:
Return max(S)
Case Mean:
Return mean(S)
Case Median:
Return median(S)
Case WeightedAverage:
Return WeightedAverage(S, OptionalWeights)
Case OrderedWeightedAverage:
Return OrderedWeightedAverage(S, OptionalWeights)
Case ChoquetIntegral:
Return ChoquetIntegral(S, OptionalWeights)
Case SugenoIntegral:
Return SugenoIntegral(S, OptionalWeights)
...
End
```

This algorithm takes as input two objects, each with N discrete attributes. Similarity scores between the two objects are first computed with respect to each attribute separately, using a specified similarity metric and T-norm/conorm pair. As described previously, the computation of a similarity score with respect to an attribute involves a pair wise application of the T-norm or T-conorm operators on the possible values of the attribute, followed by other usual arithmetic operation specified in the similarity metric [Yager (1988)]. Finally, an aggregation operator with appropriate weights is used to combine the similarity measures obtained with respect to different attributes.

In many situations, the controlling parameters, including the similarity metric, the type of T-norm/conorm, the type of aggregation operator and associated weights, can all be specified based on the domain knowledge of a particular application. However, in some other cases, it may be difficult to specify a priori an optimal set of parameters. In those cases, various machine learning methods can be employed to automatically "discover" a suitable set of parameters using a supervised or unsupervised approach. For example, the Genetic Algorithm (GA) and DNA-based computing, as described in later sections, can be quite effective.

19.8 Implementation - Fuzzy Query and Ranking

In this section, we introduce fuzzy query and fuzzy aggregation for credit scoring, university admissions and date matching.

19.8.1 Credit Scoring

Credit scoring was first developed in the 1950's and has been used extensively in the last two decades. In the early 1980's, the three major credit bureaus, Equitax, Experian, and TransUnion worked with the Fair Isaac Company to develop generic scoring models that allow each bureau to offer an individual score based on the contents of the credit bureau's data. FICO is used to make billions of financing decisions each year serving a 100 billion dollar industry. Credit scoring is a statistical method to assess an individual's credit worthiness and the likelihood that the individual will repay his/her loans based on their credit history and current credit accounts. The credit report is a snapshot of the credit history and the credit score is a snapshot of the risk at a particular point in time. Since 1995, this scoring system has made its biggest contribution in the world of mortgage lending. Mortgage investors such as Freddie Mac and Fannie Mae, the two main government-chartered companies that purchase billion of dollars of newly originated home loans annually, endorsed the Fair Isaac credit bureau risk, ignored subjective considerations, but agreed that lenders should also focus on other outside factors when making a decision.

When you apply for financing, whether it's a new credit card, car or student loan, or a mortgage, about 40 pieces of information from your credit card report are fed into a model [Nikravesh *et. al.* (2003c)]. This information is categorized into the following five categories with different level of importance (% of the score):

- Past payment history (35%)
- Amount of credit owed (30%)
- Length of time credit established (15%)
- Search for and acquisition of new credit (10%)
- Types of credit established (10%)

When a lender receives your Fair Isaac credit bureau risk score, up to four "score reason codes" are also delivered. These explain the reasons why your score was not higher. Followings are the most common given score reasons (Fair Isaac);

- Serious delinquency
- Serious delinquency, and public record or collection filed
- Derogatory public record or collection filed
- Time since delinquency is too recent or unknown
- Level of delinquency on accounts
- Number of accounts with delinquency
- Amount owed on accounts
- Proportion of balances to credit limits on revolving accounts is too high
- Length of time accounts have been established
- Too many accounts with balances

By analyzing a large sample of credit file information on people who recently obtained new credit, and given the above information and that contained in Figures 19.6a, 19.6b, a statistical model has been built. The model provides a numerical score designed to predict your risk as a borrower. Credit scores used for mortgage lending range from 0 to 900 (usually above 300). The higher your score, the less risk you represent to lenders. Most lenders will be happy if your score is 700 or higher. You may still qualify for a loan with a lower score given all other factors, but it will cost you more.

Given the factors presented earlier, a simulated model has been developed. A series of excellent, very good, good, not good, not bad, bad, and very bad credit scores have been recognized (without including history). Then, fuzzy similarity and ranking have been used to rank the

AOA: Amount owed on accounts is too high. 01
LDA: Level of Delinquency on accounts. 02
BRA: Too few bank revolving accounts.03
BorNRA : Too many bank or national revolving accounts. 04
RILI: lack of recent installment loan information: 04
ACB: Too many accounts with balances. 05
CFA: Too many Consumer finance accounts. 06
APH: Account payment history too new to rate.07
RI: Too many recent inquiries in the last 12 months.08
AOinL12M: Too many accounts opened in the last 12 months. 09
PBtoCLRI: Proportion of balances to credit limits is too high on revolving accounts. 10
AORI: Amount owed on revolving accounts is too high.11
LRCH: Length of revolving credit history is too short.12
TD: Time since delinquency is too recent or unknown.13
LCH: Length of credit history is too short.14
LRBRI: Lack of recent bank revolving information.15
LRRAI: Lack of recent revolving account information. 16
RNMBI: No recent non-mortgage balance information.17
NAwD: Number of accounts with delinquency.18
ACPasA: Too few accounts currently paid as agreed.19
TDPRorC: Time since derogatory public record or collection.20
APDonA: Amount past due on accounts.21
SDDPRorC: Serious delinquency, derogatory public record, or collection.22
BorNRAwB: Too many bank or national revolving accounts with balances.23
RB: No recent revolving balances.24
LILH: Length of installment loan history   25
NRA: Number of revolving accounts.26
BNRorORA: Number of bank revolving or other revolving accounts.26
ACPasA: Too few accounts currently paid as agreed. 27
NofEA: Number of established accounts.28
DofLI: Date of last inquiry too recent.29
BB: No recent bankcard balances.29
TRAO: Time since most recent account opening too short.30
AwRPI: Too few accounts with recent payment information.31
AOonDA: Amount owed on delinquent accounts. 31
LofrILI: Lack of recent installment loan information.32
PofLBtoLA: Proportion of loan balances to loan amounts is too high. 33
LTOILE: Length of time open installment loans have been establis hed * 36
NFCAERLFH: Number of finance company accounts established relative to length of finance
history 37
SDPRCF: Serious delinquency and public record or collection filed X 38
SD: Serious delinquency X 39
DPRCF: Derogatory public record or collection filed X 40
LRHFALFA: Lack of recent history on finance accounts, or lack of finance accounts * 99
LRIALAL: Lack of recent information on auto loan, or lack of auto loans * 98

Fig. 19.6a Information used to create the Credit Rating application.

```
AOA={'Too Low'; 'Low'; 'Average'; 'High'; 'Too High';'Extremely High'; 'Not Care'};
LDA = {'Too Low'; 'Low'; 'Average'; 'High'; 'Too High';'Extremely High'; 'Not Care'};
BRA ={'Too Few'; 'Few'; 'Some'; 'Many'; 'Too Many'; 'Not Care'};
BorNRA = {'Too Few'; 'Few'; 'Some'; 'Many'; 'Too Many'; 'Not Care'};
RILI = {'Lacking'; 'Not Enough'; 'Enough';'Not Care'};
ACB = {'Too Few'; 'Few'; 'Some'; 'Many'; 'Too Many'; 'Not Care'};
CFA = {'Too Few'; 'Few'; 'Some'; 'Many'; 'Too Many'; 'Not Care'}
APH = {'Too New'; 'New'; 'Kind of New'; 'Established'; 'Well Est ablished'; 'Not Care'};
RI = {'Too Few'; 'Few'; 'Some'; 'Many'; 'Too Many'; 'Not Care'};
AOinL12M = {'Too Few'; 'Few'; 'Some'; 'Many'; 'Too Many'; 'Not Care'};
PBtoCLRI = {'Too Low'; 'Low'; 'Average'; 'High'; 'Too High';'Extremely High'; 'Not Care'};
AORI =  {'Too Low'; 'Low'; 'Average'; 'High'; 'Too High';'Extremely High'; 'Not Care'};
LRCH ={'Too Short'; 'Short'; 'Average'; 'Long'; 'Too Long'; 'Not Care'};
TD = {'Too Recent'; 'Recent'; 'No Recent';'Unkown'; 'Not Care'};
LCH=  {'Too Short'; 'Short'; 'Average'; 'Long'; 'Too Long'; 'Not Care'};
LRBRI = {'Lacking'; 'Not Enough'; 'Enough';'Not Care'};
LRRAI= {'Lacking'; 'Not Enough'; 'Enough';'Not Care'};
RNMBI= {'Too Recent'; 'Recent'; 'No Recent';'Unkown'; 'Not Care'};
NAwD = {'Too Few'; 'Few'; 'Some'; 'Many'; 'Too Many'; 'Not Care'};
ACPasA = {'Too Few'; 'Few'; 'Some'; 'Many'; 'Too Many';'Not Care'};
TDPRorC ={'Too Short'; 'Short'; 'Average'; 'Long'; 'Too Long';'Not Care'};
APDonA = {'Too Low'; 'Low'; 'Average'; 'High'; 'Too High';'Extremely High'; 'Not Care'};
SDDPRorC = {'Not Serous'; 'Serious'; 'Very Serious'; 'Extremely Serious'; 'Not Care'};
BorNRAwB = {'Too Few'; 'Few'; 'Some'; 'Many'; 'Too Many'; 'Not Care'};
RB = {'Too Recent'; 'Recent'; 'No Recent'; 'Not Care'};
LILH= {'Too Short'; 'Short'; 'Average'; 'Long'; 'Too Long';'Not Care'};
NRA = {'Too Low'; 'Low'; 'Average'; 'High'; 'Too High';'Extremely High'; 'Not Care'};
BNRorORA = {'Too Low'; 'Low'; 'Average'; 'High'; 'Too High';'Extremely High'; 'Not Care'};
ACPasA = {'Too Few'; 'Few'; 'Some'; 'Many'; 'Too Many'; 'Not Care'};
NofEA = {'Too Low'; 'Low'; 'Average'; 'High'; 'Too High';'Extremely High'; 'Not Care'};
DofLI =  {'Too Recent'; 'Recent'; 'No Recent'; 'Not Care'};
BB =  {'Too Recent'; 'Recent'; 'No Recent'; 'Not Care'};
TRAO = {'Too Short'; 'Short'; 'Average'; 'Long'; 'Too Long';'Not Care'};
AwRPI = {'Too Few'; 'Few'; 'Some'; 'Many'; 'Too Many'; 'Not Care'};
AOonDA = {'Too Low'; 'Low'; 'Average'; 'High'; 'Too High';'Extremely High'; 'Not Care'};
LofrILI = {'Lacking'; 'Not Enough'; 'Enough';'Not Care'};
PofLBtoLA = {'Too Low'; 'Low'; 'Average'; 'High'; 'Too High';'Extremely High'; 'Not Care'};
LTOILE = {'Too Short'; 'Short'; 'Average'; 'Long'; 'Too Long';'Not Care'};
NFCAERLFH = {'Too Low'; 'Low'; 'Average'; 'High'; 'Too High';'Extremely High'; 'Not Care'};
SDPRCF = {'Not Serous'; 'Serious'; 'Very Serious'; 'Extremely Serious'; 'Not Care'};
SD = {'Not Serous'; 'Serious'; 'Very Serious'; 'Extremely Serious'; 'Not Care'};
DPRCF = {'Not Serous'; 'Serious'; 'Very Serious'; 'Extremely Serious'; 'Not Care'};
LRHFALFA = {'Lacking'; 'Not Enough'; 'Enough';'Not Care'};
LRIALAL = {'Lacking'; 'Not Enough'; 'Enough';'Not Care'};
```

Fig. 19.6b Variables Granulation used to create the Credit Rating System Model.

new user and define his/her credit score. In the inference engine, the rules based on factual knowledge (data) and knowledge drawn from human experts (inference) are combined, ranked, and clustered based on the confidence level of human and factual support. This information is then used to build the fuzzy query model with associated weights. In the query level, an intelligent knowledge-based search engine provides a means for specific queries. Initially we blend traditional computation with fuzzy reasoning. This effectively provides validation of an interpretation, model, hypothesis, or alternatively, indicates the need to reject or reevaluate. Information must be clustered, ranked, and translated to a format amenable to user interpretation.

Figures 19.7-19.8 show a snapshot of the software developed for

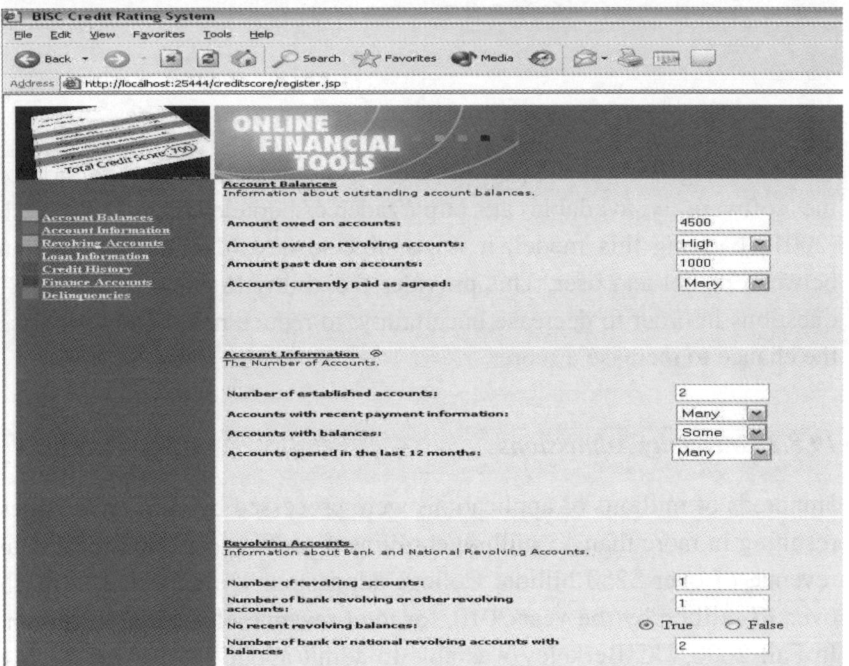

Fig. 19.7 A snapshot of the variable input for credit scoring software.

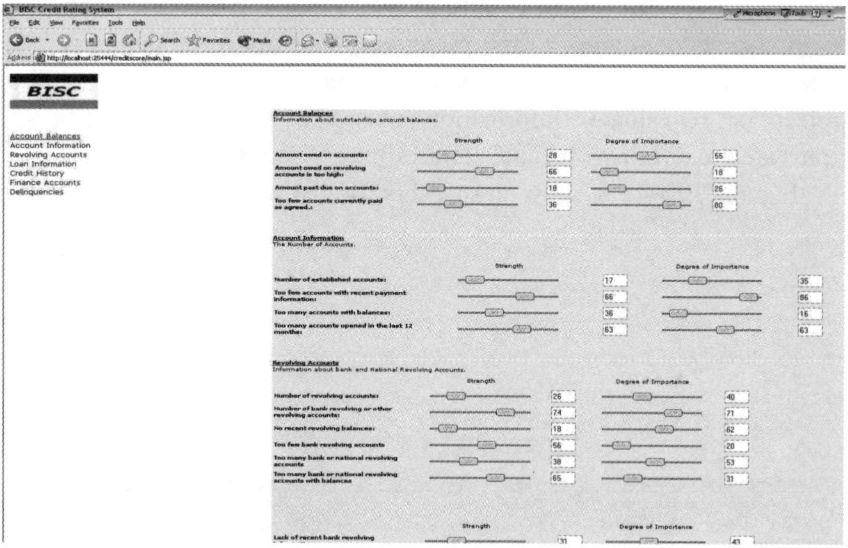

Fig. 19.8 A snapshot of the software developed for credit scoring.

credit scoring. To test the performance of the model, a demo version of the software is available at: http://zadeh.cs.berkeley.edu/ [Nikravesh (2001a)]. Using this model, it is possible to have dynamic interaction between model and user. This provides the ability to answer "What if?" questions in order to decrease uncertainty, to reduce risk, and to increase the chance to increase a score.

19.8.2 University Admissions

Hundreds of millions of applications were processed by U.S. universities resulting in more than 15 million enrollments in the year 2000 for a total revenue of over $250 billion. College admissions are expected to reach over 17 million by the year 2010, for total revenue of over $280 billion. In Fall 2000, UC Berkeley was able to admit about 26% of the 33,244 applicants for freshman admission (University of California-Berkeley). In Fall 2000, Stanford University was only able to offer admission to 1168 men from 9571 applications (768 admitted) and 1257 women from

8792 applications (830 admitted), a general admit rate of 13% (Stanford University Admission).

The UC Berkeley campus admits its freshman class on the basis of an assessment of the applicants' high school academic performance (approximately 50%) and through a comprehensive review of the application including personal achievements of the applicant (approximately 50%) (University of California-Berkeley). For Fall 1999, the average weighted GPA of an admitted freshman was 4.16, with a SAT I verbal score range of 580-710 and a SAT I math score range of 620-730 for the middle 50% of admitted students (University of California-Berkeley). While there is no specific GPA for UC Berkeley applicants that will guarantee admission, a GPA of 2.8 or above is required for California residents and a test score total indicated in the University's Freshman Eligibility Index must be achieved. A minimum 3.4 GPA in A-F courses is required for non-residents. At Stanford University, most of the candidates have an un-weighted GPA between 3.6 and 4.0 and verbal SAT I and math SAT I scores of at least 650 (Stanford University Admission) At UC Berkeley, the academic assessment includes student's academic performance and several measured factors such as:

- College preparatory courses
- Advanced Placement (AP)
- International Baccalaureate Higher Level (IBHL)
- Honors and college courses beyond the UC minimum and degree of achievement in those courses
- Uncapped UC GPA
- Pattern of grades over time
- Scores on the three required SAT II tests and the SAT I (or ACT)
- Scores on AP or IBHL exams
- Honors and awards which reflect extraordinary, sustained intellectual or creative achievement
- Participation in rigorous academic enrichment
- Outreach programs
- Planned twelfth grade courses

- Qualification for UC Eligibility in the Local Context

All freshman applicants must complete courses in the University of California's A-F subject pattern and present scores from SAT I (or ACT) and SAT II tests with the following required subjects:

a.   History/Social Science - 2 years required
b.   English - 4 years required
c.   Mathematics - 3 years required, 4 recommended
d.   Laboratory Science - 2 years required, 3 recommended
e.   Language Other than English - 2 years required, 3 recommended
f.   College Preparatory Electives - 2 years required

At Stanford University, in addition to the academic transcript, close attention is paid to other factors such as student's written application, teacher references, the short responses and one-page essay (carefully read for quality, content, and creativity), and personal qualities.

The information provided in this study is a hypothetical situation and does not reflect the current UC system or Stanford University admissions criteria. However, we use this information to build a model to represent a real admissions problem. For more detailed information regarding University admissions, please refer to the University of California-Berkeley and Stanford University, Office of Undergraduate Admission (University of California-Berkeley; Stanford University Admission).

Given the factors and general admission criteria, a simulated-hypothetical model (a Virtual Model) was developed. A series of excellent, very good, good, not good, not bad, bad, and very bad student given the criteria for admission has been recognized. These criteria over time can be modified based on the success rate of students admitted to the university and their performances during the first, second, third and fourth years of their education with different weights and degrees of importance given for each year. Then, fuzzy similarity and ranking can evaluate a new student rating and find it's similarity to a given set of criteria.

Figure 19.9 shows a snapshot of the software developed for university admissions and the evaluation of student applications. Table 7 shows the granulation of the variables that was used in the model. To test the performance of the model, a demo version of the software is available at: http://zadeh.cs.berkeley.edu/ [Nikravesh (2001a)]. Incorporating an electronic intelligent knowledge-based search engine, the results will eventually be in a format to permit a user to interact dynamically with the contained database and to customize and add information to the database. For instance, it will be possible to test an intuitive concept by dynamic interaction between software and the human mind.

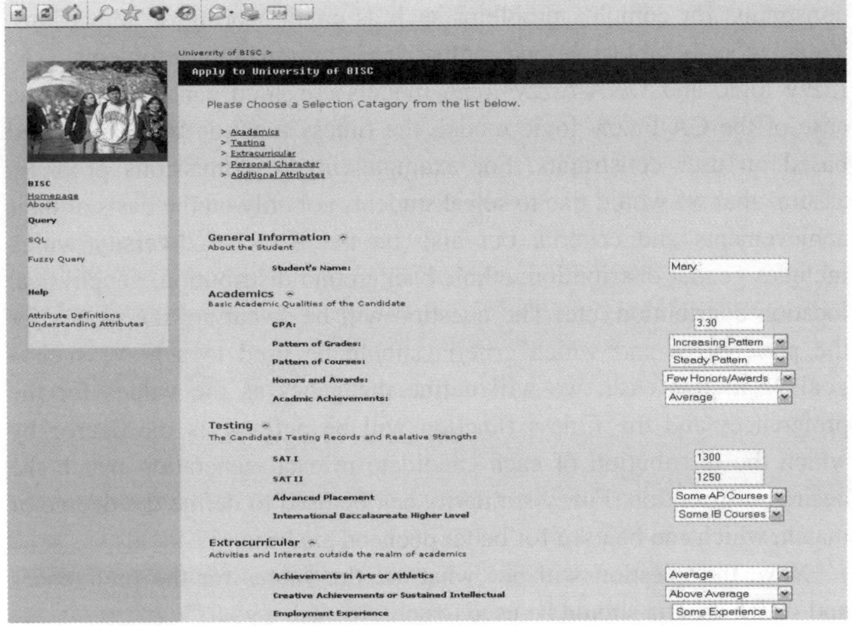

Fig. 19.9 A snapshot of the software for University Admission Decision Making.

This will provide the ability to answer "What if?" questions in order to decrease uncertainty and provide a better risk analysis to improve the chance for "increased success" on student selection or it can be used to select students on the basis of "diversity" criteria. The model can be used as for decision support and for a more uniform, consistent and less subjective and biased way. Finally, the model could learn and provide the mean to include the feedback into the system through time and will be adapted to the new situation for defining better criteria for student selection.

In this study, it has been found that ranking and scoring is a very subjective problem and depends on user perception and preferences in addition to the techniques used for the aggregation process which will effect the process of the data mining in reduced domain. Therefore, user feedback and an interactive model are recommended tools to fine-tune the preferences based on user constraints. This will allow the representation of a multi-objective optimization with a large number of constraints for complex problems such as credit scoring or admissions. To solve such subjective and multi-criteria optimization problems, GA-fuzzy logic and DNA-fuzzy logic models are good candidates. In the case of the GA-Fuzzy logic model, the fitness function will be defined based on user constraints. For example, in the admissions problem, assume that we would like to select students not only on the basis of their achievements and criteria, but also on the basis of diversity which includes gender distribution, ethnic background distribution, geophysical location distribution, etc. The question will be "what are the values for the preferences and which criteria should be used to achieve such a goal?" In this case, we will define the genes as the values for the preferences and the fitness function will be defined as the degree by which the distribution of each candidate in each generation match the desired distribution. Fuzzy similarity can be used to define the degree of match, which can be used for better decision analysis.

Now, the question will be "what are the values for the preferences and which criteria should be used to achieve such a goal?"

- Given a set of successful students, we would like to adjust the preferences such that the model could reflect this set of students.
- Diversity, which includes gender distribution, ethnic background distribution, geophysical location distribution, etc.

To solve such subjective and multi-criteria optimization problems with a large number of constraints for complex problems such as University

Admissions, the BISC Decision Support System is an excellent candidate.

19.8.3 Date Matching

The main objective is to find the best possible match in the huge space of possible outputs in the databases using the imprecise matching such as fuzzy logic concept, by storing the query attributes and continuously refining the query to update the user's preferences. We have also built a Fuzzy Query system, which is a Java application that sits on top of a database.

With traditional SQL queries (relational DBMS), one can select records that match the selection criteria from a database. However, a record will not be selected if any one of the conditions fails. This makes searching for a range of potential candidates difficult. For example, if a company wants to find an employee who is proficient in skill A, B, C and D, they may not get any matching records, only because some candidates are proficient in 3 out of 4 skills and only semi-proficient in the other one. Since traditional SQL queries only perform Boolean matching, some qualities of real life, like "far" or "expensive" or "proficient", which involve matters of degree, are difficult to search for in relational databases. Unlike Boolean logic, fuzzy logic allows the degree of membership for each element to range over an interval. So in a fuzzy query, we can compute how similar a record in the database is to the desired record. This degree of similarity can be used as a ranking for each record in the database. Thus, the aim of the fuzzy query project for date matching is to add the capability of imprecise querying (retrieving similar records) to traditional DBMS. This makes some complex SQL statements unnecessary and also eliminates some repetitious SQL queries (due to empty-matching result sets).

In this program, one can basically retrieve all the records from the database, compare them with the desired record, aggregate the data, compute the ranking, and then output the records in the order of their rankings. Retrieving all the records from the database is a naïve approach because with some preprocessing, some very different records are not needed from the database. However, the main task is to compute the fuzzy rankings of the records so efficiency is not the main concern here.

The major difference between this application and other date matching system is that a user can input his hobbies in a fuzzy sense using a slider instead of choosing crisp terms like "Kind of" or "Love it". These values are stored in the database according to the slider value, Figures 19.10, 19.11.

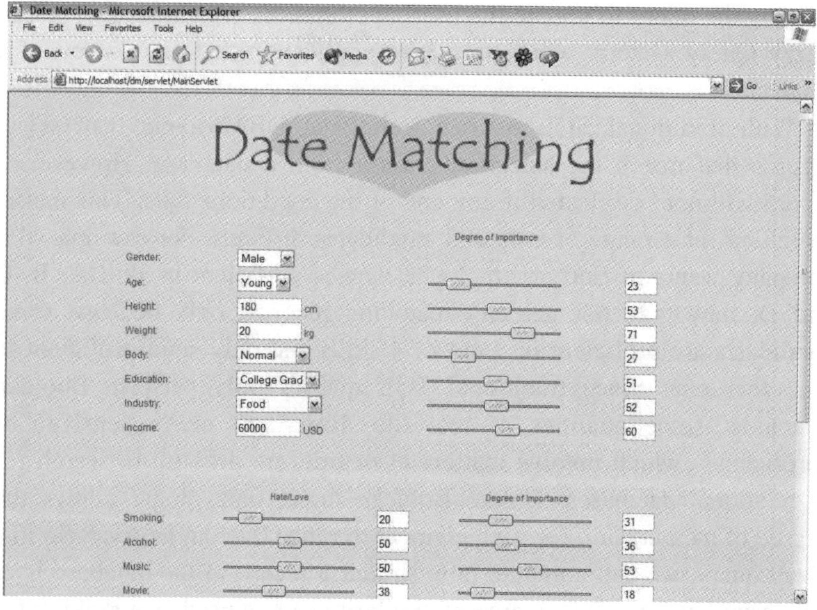

Fig. 19.10 Date matching input form.

The current date matching software can be modified or expanded in several ways:

(1) One can build a server/client version of date-matching engine so that we can use a centralized database and all users around the world can do the matching through the web. The ranking part (computation) can still be done on local machine since every search is different. This can also help reduce the server load.

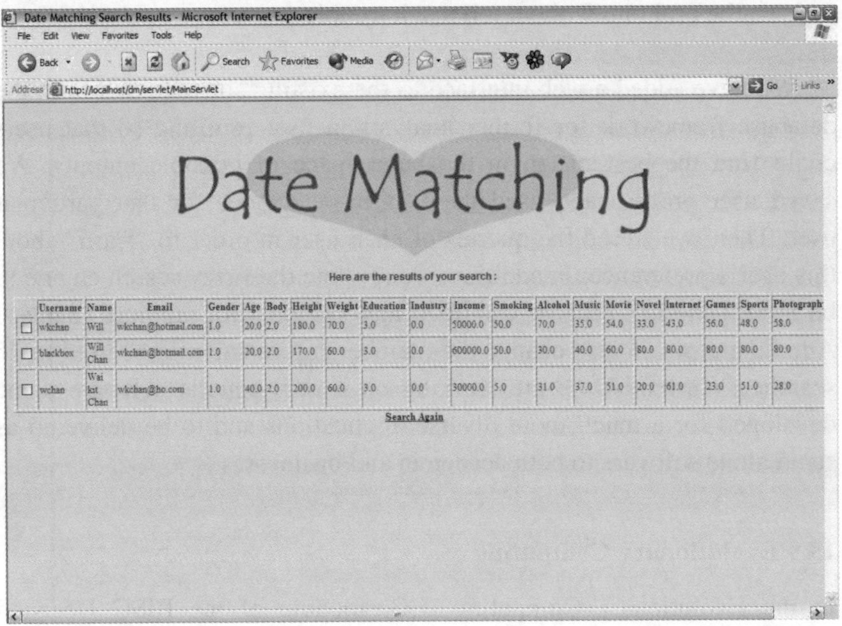

	Username	Name	Email	Gender	Age	Body	Height	Weight	Education	Industry	Income	Smoking	Alcohol	Music	Movie	Novel	Internet	Games	Sports	Photograph
☐	wkchan	Will	wkchan@hotmail.com	1.0	20.0	2.0	180.0	70.0	3.0	0.0	50000.0	50.0	70.0	35.0	54.0	33.0	43.0	56.0	48.0	58.0
☐	blackbox	Will Chan	wkchan@hotmail.com	1.0	20.0	2.0	170.0	60.0	3.0	0.0	600000.0	50.0	30.0	40.0	60.0	80.0	80.0	80.0	80.0	80.0
☐	wchan	Wai kit Chan	wkchan@ho.com	1.0	40.0	2.0	200.0	60.0	3.0	0.0	30000.0	5.0	31.0	37.0	51.0	20.0	61.0	23.0	51.0	28.0

Fig. 19.11 Date shows the results are obtained from fuzzy query using the search criteria in the previous page. The first record is the one with the highest ranking

(2) The attributes, granulation models and the "meaning" of the data can be tunable so that the system is more configurable and adaptive to changes.

(3) User preference capability can be added to the system. (The notion of "overweight" and "tall" can be different to different people.)

(4) The GUI needs to be changed to meet real user needs.

(5) One can build a library of fuzzy operators and aggregation functions such that one can choose the operator and function that matches the application.

(6) One can instead build a generic fuzzy engine framework, which is tunable in every way to match clients' needs.

(7) The attributes used in the system are not very complete compared to other data matching systems online. However, the

attributes can be added or modified with some modification to the program without too much trouble.

We have added a web interface to the existing software and built the database framework for further analysis in user profiling so that users could find the best match in the huge space of possible outputs. We saved user profiles and used them as basic queries for that particular user. Then, we stored the queries of each user in order to "learn" about this user's preference. In addition, we rewrote the fuzzy search engine to be more generic so that it would fit any system with minimal changes. Administrator can also change the membership function to be used to do searches. Currently, we are working on a new generic software to be developed for a much more diverse applications and to be delivered as stand alone software to both academia and businesses.

19.9 Evolutionary Computing

In the Evolutionary Computing (EC) module of the BISC Decision Support Sys-tem, our purpose is to use an evolutionary-based method to allow automatic adjusting of the user's preferences. These preferences can be seen as parameters of the fuzzy logic model in form of degrees of importance of the used variables. Also, they can be extended to a representation of the way the variables have to be combined. In the fuzzy logic model, the variables are combined using aggregation operators with eventually associated weights, which correspond to their degrees of importance. These operators and weights can be fixed based on the application expert knowledge. However, the application expert might need help to make decision regarding the choice of the aggregators and the variables' weighting which constitute the model's parameters. In this case, we are faced with an optimization problem and our EC module whose role consists in learning these parameters process, has to answer the following question: how to aggregate the variables and with which degrees of importance?

In a first stage, we propose to limit user's preferences to the variables weighting and to use genetic algorithms as learning technique. The corresponding model will be a weighted aggregator for which weights have to be determined by the GA. However, the fuzzy logic model could need a more complex combination of variables using weighted multi-aggregation operators. In this case, the learning process has to select automatically the appropriate aggregators for a given application according to some corresponding training data and to define the way they have to be combined. For this purpose, we propose to use a multi-aggregation model combining weighted aggregators in form of decision tree. In the Evolutionary computing approach, genetic programming, which is an extension of genetic algorithms, is the closest technique to our purpose. It allows us to learn a tree structure that represents the combination of aggregators. Selection of these aggregators is included in the genetic programming based learning process.

Genetic algorithms and genetic programming will be first introduced in the next section. Then, their adaptation to our decision system will be described.

19.9.1 Genetic algorithms and genetic programming

Introduced by John Holland [Holland (1992)], Genetic Algorithms (GAs) constitute a class of stochastic searching methods based on the mechanism of natural selection and genetics. They have recently received much attention in a number of practical problems notably in optimization problems as machine learning processes [Goldberg (1989)]. Basic description

To solve an optimization problem, usually we need to define the search method looking for the best solution and to specify a measure of quality that allows to compare possible solutions and to find the best one. In GAs, the search space corresponds to a set of individuals represented by their DNA. These individuals are evaluated by a measure of their quality called fitness function which has to be de-fined according to the problem itself. The search method consists in an evolutionary process inspired by the Darwinian principle of reproduction and survival of the fittest individual.

This evolutionary process begins with a set of individuals called population. Individuals from one population are selected according to their fitness and used to form a new population with the hope to produce better individuals (offspring). The population is evolved through successive generations using genetic operations until some criterion is satisfied.

The evolution algorithm is resumed in Figure 19.12. It starts by creating randomly a population of individuals, which constitute an initial generation. Each individual is evaluated by calculating its fitness. Then, a selection process is per-formed based on their fitness in order to choose individuals that participate to the evolution. Genetic operators are applied on these individuals to produce new ones. A new generation is then created by replacing existing individuals in the previous generation by the new ones. The population is evolved by repeating individuals' selection and new generations creation until the end criterion is reached in which case the evolution is stopped.

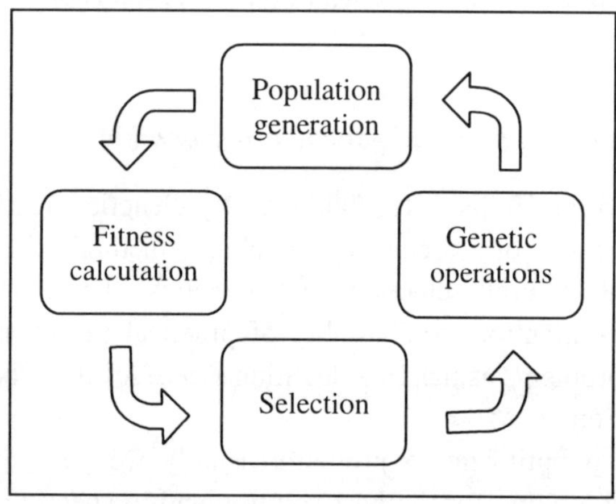

Fig. 19.12 Genetic Algorithm Cycle.

The construction of a GA for any problem can be separated into five tasks:

- Choice of the representation of the individuals,
- Design of the genetic operators,
- Determination of the fitness function and the selection process,
- Determination of parameters and variables for controlling the evolution algorithm,
- Definition of the termination criterion.

In the conventional GAs, individuals' DNA is usually represented by fixed-length character strings. Thus in this case, the DNA encoding requires a selection of the string length and the alphabet size. Binary strings are the most common encoding because its relative simplicity. However, this encoding might be not natural for many problems and sometimes corrections must be made on the strings provided by genetic operations. Direct value encoding can be used in problems where use of binary encoding would be difficult. In the value encoding, an individual's DNA is represented by a sequence of some values. Values can be anything connected to the problem, such as (real) numbers.

Genetic operators

The evolution algorithm is based on the reproduction of selected individuals in the current generation breeding a new generation composed of their offspring. New individuals are created using either sexual or asexual reproduction. In sexual re-production, known as crossover, two parents are selected and DNA from both parents is inherited by the new individual. In asexual reproduction, known as mutation, the selected individual (parent) is simply copied, possibly with random changes.

Crossover operates on selected genes from parent DNA and creates new off-spring. This is done by copying sequences alternately from each parent and the points where the copying crosses is chosen at random. For example, the new individual can be bred by copying everything before the crossover point from the first parent and then copy everything after the crossover point from the other parent. This kind of crossover is illustrated in Figure 19.13 for the case of binary string encoding. There are other ways to make crossover, for example by choosing more crossover points. Crossover can be quite complicated and depends mainly on the encoding of DNA. Specific crossover made for a specific problem can improve performance of the GA.

Mutation is intended to prevent falling of all solutions in the population into a local optimum of the solved problem. Mutation operation randomly changes the offspring resulted from crossover. In case of binary encoding we can switch a few randomly chosen bits from 1 to 0 or from 0 to 1 (see Figure 19.14). The technique of mutation (as well as crossover) depends mainly on the encoding of chromosomes. For example when permutations problem encoding, mutation could be performed as an exchange of two genes.

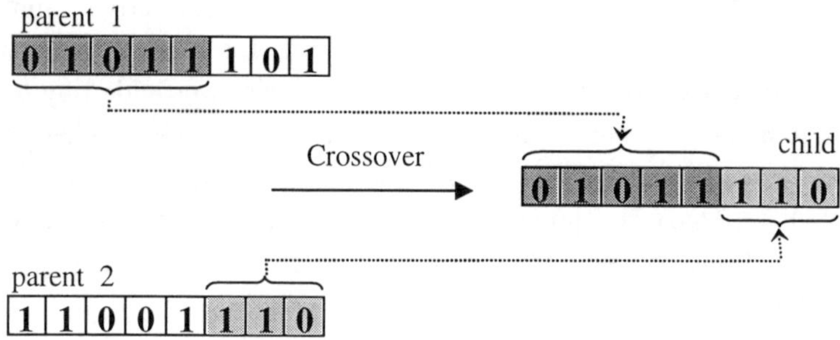

Fig. 19.13 Genetic Algorithm - Crossover.

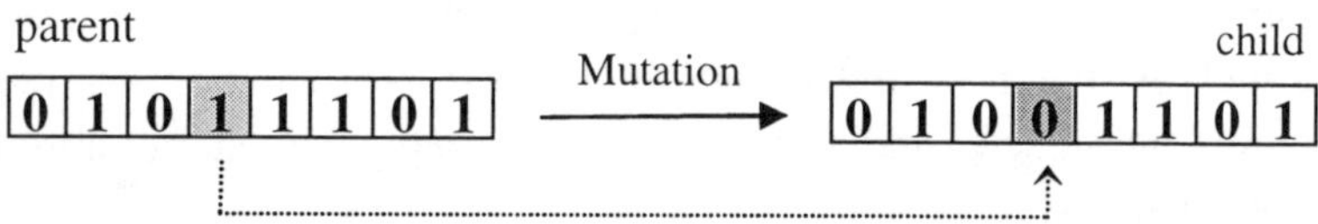

Fig. 19.14 Genetic Algorithm - Mutation.

19.9.1.1 Selection process

Individuals that participate in genetic operations are selected according to their fitness. Even though the main idea is to select the better parents in the hope that they will produce better offspring, the problem of how to do this selection remains. This can be done in many ways. We will describe briefly some of them. The (μ,λ) selection consists in breeding λ offspring from μ parents and then μ off-spring will be selected for the next generation. In the Steady-State Selection, in every generation a few good (with higher fitness) individuals are selected for creating new offspring. Then some bad (with lower fitness) individuals are removed and replaced by the new offspring. The rest of population survives to new generation. In the tournament selection, a group of individuals is chosen randomly and the best individual of the group is selected for reproduction. This kind of selection allows giving a chance to some weak individual in the population, which could contain good genetic material (genes) to participate to reproduction if it is the best one in its group. Elitism selection aims at preserving the best individuals. So it first copies the best individuals to the new population. The rest of the population is constructed in ways described above. Elitism can rapidly increase the performance of GA, because it prevents a loss of the best-found solution.

19.9.1.2 Parameters of GA

The outline of basic GA is very general. There are many parameters and set-tings that can be implemented differently in various problems. One particularly important parameter is the population size. On the one hand, if the population contains too few individuals, GA has few possibilities to perform crossover and only a small part of search space is explored. On the other hand, if there are too many individuals, GA slows down. Another parameter to take into account is the number of generations, which can be included in the termination criterion.

For the evolution process of the GA, there are two basic parameters: crossover probability and mutation probability. The crossover probability indicates how of-ten crossover will be performed. If there is no crossover, offspring are exact copies of parents. If there is crossover, offspring are made from parts of both parent's DNA. Crossover is made in hope that new chromosomes will contain good parts of old chromosomes and therefore the new chromosomes will be better. However, it is desirable to leave some part of the old population to survive into the next generation. The mutation probability indicates how often parts of chromosomes will be mutated. If there is no mutation, offspring are generated immediately after crossover (or directly copied) without any change. If mutation is performed, one or more parts of a chromosome are changed.

19.9.1.3 Genetic programming

Genetic programming (GP) is a technique pioneered by John Koza [Koza (1992); Banzhaf *et. al.* (1998)], which enables computers to solve problems without being explicitly programmed. It is an extension of the conventional GA in which each individual in the population is a computer program. It works by using GAs to automatically generate computer programs that can be represented as linear structures, trees or graphs. Tree encoding is the most used form to represent the programs. Tree structure is composed of primitive functions and terminals appropriate to the problem domain. The functions may be arithmetic operations, programming commands, mathematical logical or domain-specific functions.

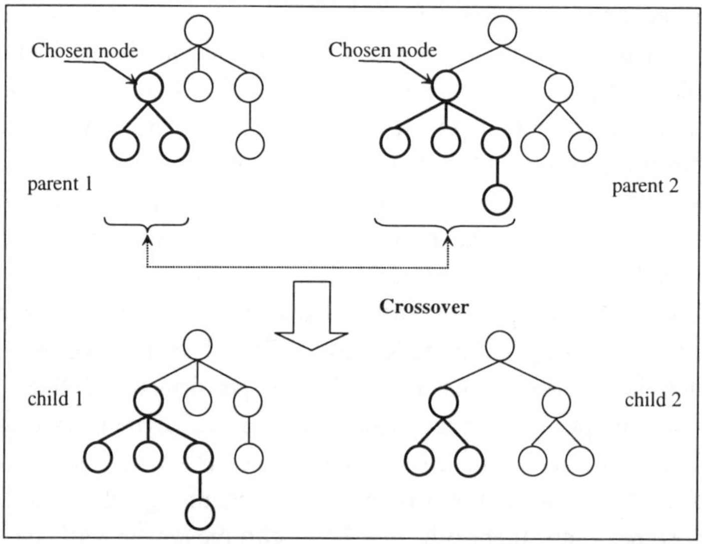

Fig. 19.15 Genetic programming - Tree-encoding individual crossover.

To apply GP to a problem, we have to specify the set functions and terminals for the tree construction. Also, besides the parameters of the conventional GA, other parameters which are specific to the individual representation can be considered such as tree size, as an example.

Genetic operations are defined specifically for the type of encoding used to represent the individuals. In the case of tree encoding, new individuals are produced by removing branches from one tree and inserting them into another. This simple process ensures that the new individual is also a tree and so is also syntactically valid. The crossover and mutation operations are illustrated in figures 19.15-19.16. The mutation consists in randomly choosing a node in the selected tree, creating a new individual and replacing the sub-tree rooted at the selected node by the created individual. The crossover operation is performed by randomly choosing nodes in the selected individuals (parents) and exchanging the sub-trees rooted at these nodes, which produce two new individuals (offspring).

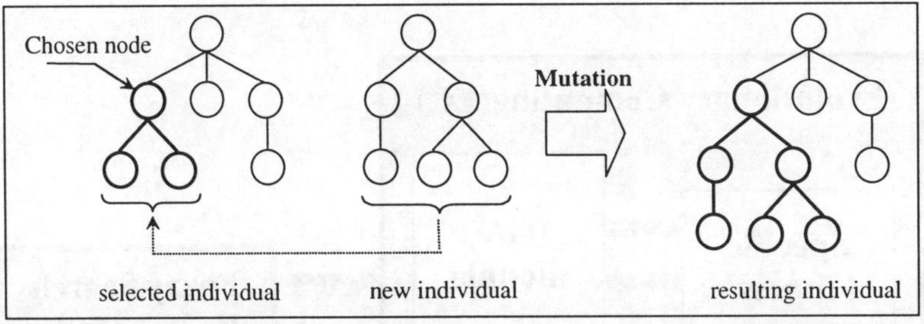

Fig. 19.16 Genetic programming - Tree-encoding individual mutation .

19.9.2 User's preferences learning using EC

We have introduced GA and GP in a previous section. In this section, we will proceed to describe their adaptation to our problem. Our aim is at learning the fuzzy-DSS parameters which are: 1) the weight vector (representing the user preferences is associated with the variables) that must be aggregated and, 2) the adequate decision tree (representing the combination of the aggregation operators) that have to be used.

19.9.2.1 Weights learning using GA

Weight vector being a linear structure, can be represented by a binary string in which weight values are converted to binary numbers. This binary string corresponds to the individual's DNA in the GA learning process. The goal is to find the optimal weighting of variables. A general GA module can be used by defining a specific fitness function for each application as shown in Figure 19.17.

Let's see the example of the University Admissions application. The corresponding fitness function is shown Figure 19.18. The fitness is computed based on a training data set composed of vectors of fuzzy values. Each value of a fuzzy variable is constituted of a crisp value between 0 and 1 and a set of membership functions. During the evolution process, for each weighting vector, the corresponding fitness function is computed as follows. Using these weights, a score is calculated for each vector. Afterward, these scores are ranked and compared with the actual ranking using similarity measure.

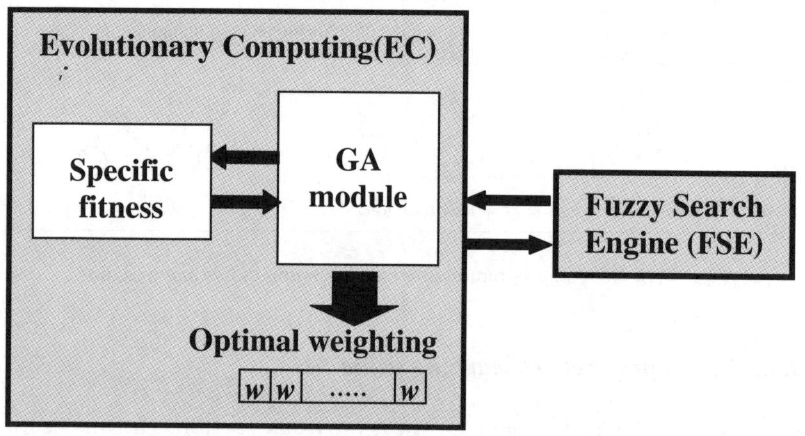

Fig. 19.17 Evolutionary Computing Module: preferences learning.

Let's assume that we have   students and the goal is to select among them   students that will be admitted. Each student is then represented by value vector in the training data set. The similarity measure between the computed and the actual ranking could be the intersection between the top vectors, which has to be maximized. We can also consider the intersection on a larger number   of top vectors. This measure can be combined to the first one with different degrees of importance. In this case, the Fitness value will be a weighted sum of these two similarity measures.

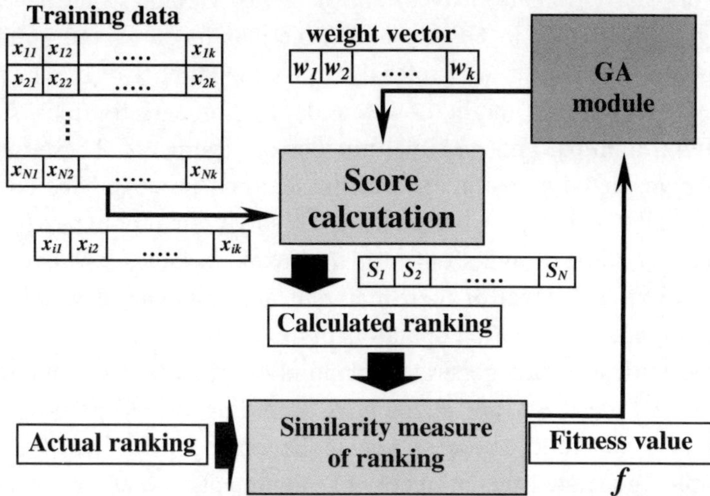

Fig. 19.18 EC Module: Specific fitness function for the "University Admissions Application".

19.2.2 *Aggregation tree learning using GP*

We have seen the learning of the weights representing the user preferences regarding the fuzzy variables. However, the aggregators that are used are fixed in the application or chosen by the user. But it is more interesting to adjust these aggregators automatically. We propose to include this adjustment in the GA learning process.

Aggregators can be combined in the form of tree structure, which can be built using a Genetic Programming learning module. It consists in evolving a population of individuals represented by tree structures. The evolution principle remains the same as in a conventional GP module but the DNA encoding needs to be defined according to the considered problem. We propose to define an encoding for aggregation trees which is more complex than for classical trees and which is common to all considered applications. As shown in Figure 19.18, we need to define a specific encoding in addition to the fitness function specification.

We need to specify the functions (tree nodes) and terminals that are used to build aggregation trees. Functions correspond to aggregation operators and terminals (leaves) are the fuzzy variables that have to be aggregated. Usually, in GP the used functions have a fixed number of arguments. In our case, we prefer not to fix the number of arguments for the aggregators. We might however define some restrictions such as specifying minimal and maximal number of arguments. These numbers can be considered as parameters of the learning process. This encoding property allows a largest search space to solve our problem. Moreover, instead of finding weights only for the fuzzy variables, we have to fix them also at each level of their hierarchical combination, which allows using weighted aggregation operators in the whole structure.

Tree structures are generated randomly as in the conventional GP. But, since these trees are augmented according the properties defined above, the generation process has to be updated. So, we decided to randomly generate the number of arguments when choosing an aggregator as a node in the tree structure. And for the weights, we chose to generate them randomly for each node during its creation.

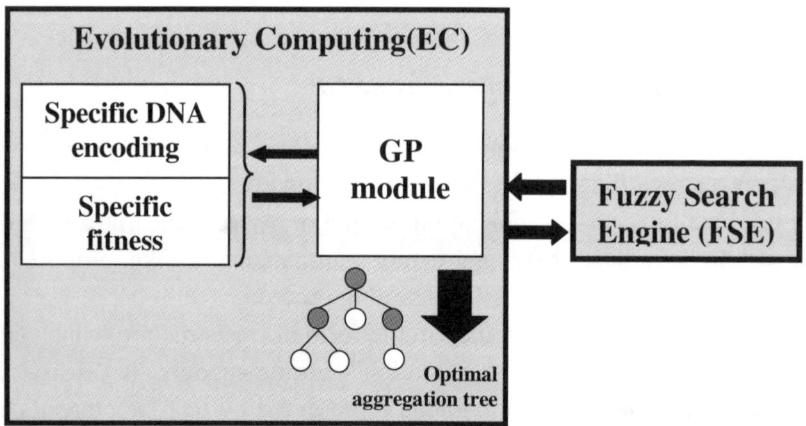

Fig. 19.19 Evolutionary Computing Module: aggregation tree learning Evolutionary Computing Module: preferences learning.

Regarding the fitness function, it is based on performing the aggregation operation at the root node of the tree that has to be evaluated. For the university admissions application, the result of the root execution corresponds to the score that has to be computed for each value vector in the training data set. The fitness function, as in the GA learning of the user preferences, consists in simple or combined similarity measures. In addition, we can include to the fitness function a complementary measure that represents the individual's size, which has to be minimized in order to avoid oversized trees.

19.10 Conclusion

In this study, we introduced fuzzy query and fuzzy aggregation and the BISC decision support system as an alternative for ranking and predicting the risk for credit scoring, university admissions, and several other applications, which currently utilize an imprecise and subjective process. The BISC decision support system key features are 1) intelligent tools to assist decision-makers in assessing the consequences of decision made in an environment of imprecision, uncertainty, and partial truth and providing a systematic risk analysis, 2) intelligent tools to be used to assist decision-makers answer "What if Questions", examine numerous alternatives very quickly and find the value of the inputs to achieve a desired level of output, and 3) intelligent tools to be used with human interaction and feedback to achieve a capability to learn and adapt through time. In addition, the following important points have been found in this study 1) no single ranking function works well for all contexts, 2) most similarity measures work about the same regardless of the model, 3) there is little overlap between successful ranking functions, and 4) the same model can be used for other applications such as the design of a more intelligent search engine which includes the user's preferences and profile [Nikravesh (2001a), (2001b)].

Acknowledgement
Funding for this research was provided by the British Telecommunication (BT) and the BISC Program of UC Berkeley.

Bibliography

Banzhaf, WNordin, P., Keller, R.E. and Francone, F.D. (1998). Genetic Programming : An Introduction On the Automatic Evolution of Computer Programs and Its Applications, dpunkt.verlag and Morgan Kaufmann Publishers, San Francisco, CA, USA, 1998, 470 pages.

Detyniecki, M. (2000). Mathematical Aggregation Operators and their Application to Video Querying, Ph.D. thesis, University of Paris VI.

Fagin, R. Fuzzy Queries in Multimedia Database Systems, Proc. ACM Symposium on Principles of Database Systems, 1998, pp. 1-10.

Goldberg D.E. (1989). Genetic Algorithms in Search, Optimization, and Machine Learning. Addison-Wesley, Reading, MA, USA.

Grabisch, M. (1996). K-order additive fuzzy measures. In Proc of 6th intl Conf on Information Processing and Management of Uncertainty in Knowledge-based Sytems, Spain, pp 1345-50.

Grabisch, M., Murofushi, T., Sugeno, M. (2000). Fuzzy Measures and Integrals: Theory and Applications, Physica-Verlag, NY.

Holland, J. H., (1992). Adaptation in Natural and Artificial Systems: An Introductory Analysis with Applications to Biology, Control and Artificial Intelligence. MIT Press. First Published by University of Michigan Press 1975.

Koza, J. R. (1992). Genetic Programming : On the Programming of Computers by Means of Natural Selection, Cambridge, Mass. : MIT Press, USA, 819 pages.

Loia, V. et al. (2002). Fuzzy Logic and the Internet, Journal of Soft Computing, Special Issue, Springer Verlag, Vol. 6, No. 5.

Loia, V. et al. (2003). "Fuzzy Logic an the Internet", to be published in the Series Studies in Fuzziness and Soft Computing, Physica-Verlag, Springer.

Mizumoto, M. (1989). Pictorial Representations of Fuzzy Connectives, Part I: Cases of T-norms, T-conorms and Averaging Operators, Fuzzy Sets and Systems (31): pp. 217-242.

Murofushi, T. and Sugeno, M. (1989). An interpretation of fuzzy measure and the Choquet integral as an integral with respect to a fuzzy measure. Fuzzy Sets and Systems, (29): pp 202-27.

Nikravesh, M. (2001a). Perception-based information processing and retrieval: application to user profiling, 2001 research summary, EECS, ERL, University of

California, Berkeley, BT-BISC Project. (http://zadeh.cs.berkeley.edu/   & http://www.cs.berkeley.edu/~nikraves/ & http://www-bisc.cs.berkeley.edu/).

Nikravesh, M. (2001b). Credit Scoring for Billions of Financing Decisions, Joint 9th IFSA World Congress and 20th NAFIPS International Conference. IFSA/NAFIPS 2001 "Fuzziness and Soft Computing in the New Millenium", Vancouver, Canada, July 25-28.

Nikravesh M. (2002). Fuzzy Conceptual-Based Search Engine using Conceptual Semantic Indexing, NAFIPS-FLINT, June 27-29, New Orleans, LA, USA.

Nikravesh, M. and Azvine, B. (2001) FLINT 2001, New Directions in Enhancing the Power of the Internet, UC Berkeley Electronics Research Laboratory, Memorandum No. UCB/ERL M01/28.

Nikravesh, M. and Azvine, B. (2002). Fuzzy Queries, Search, and Decision Support System, Journal of Soft Computing, Volume 6, # 5.

Nikravesh, M. and Choi, D-Y. (2003). Perception-Based Information Processing, UC Berkeley Electronics Research Laboratory, Memorandum No. UCB/ERL M03/20.

Nikravesh, M., Azvine, B., Yagar, R. and Zadeh, L.A. (2003). "New Directions in Enhancing the power of the Internet", to be published in the Series Studies in Fuzziness and Soft Computing, Physica-Verlag, Springer.

Nikravesh, M. et al. (2002a). Fuzzy logic and the Internet (FLINT), Internet, World Wide Web, and Search Engines, Journal of Soft Computing, Special Issue; fuzzy Logic and the Internet, Springer Verlag, Vol. 6, No. 5.

Nikravesh, M. et al. (2003b). Perception-Based Decision processing and Analysis, UC Berkeley Electronics Research Laboratory, Memorandum No. UCB/ERL M03/21, June.

Nikravesh, M. et al. (2003c). Web Intelligence: Conceptual-Based Model, UC Berkeley Electronics Research Laboratory, Memorandum No. UCB/ERL M03/19, June.

Sugeno, M. (1974) Theory of fuzzy integrals and its applications. Ph.D. Dissertation, Tokyo Institute of Technology.

Takagi, T. et al. (2002a). Exposure of Illegal Website using Conceptual Fuzzy Sets based Information Filtering System, the North American Fuzzy Information Processing Society - The Special Interest Group on Fuzzy Logic and the Internet NAFIPS-FLINT 2002, pp327-332 (2002a)

Takagi, T. et al. (2002b). Conceptual Fuzzy Sets-Based Menu Navigation System for Yahoo!, the North American Fuzzy Information Processing Society - The Special Interest Group on Fuzzy Logic and the Internet NAFIPS-FLINT 2002, pp274-279.

Yager, R. (1998). On ordered weighted averaging aggregation operators in multi-criteria decision making, IEEE transactions on Systems, Man and Cybernetics, (18): pp183-190.

## CHAPTER 20

CONTENT AND LINK STRUCTURE ANALYSIS FOR SEARCHING THE WEB

Kemal Efe, Vijay Raghavan, and Arun Lakhotia

Center for Advanced Computer Studies
University of Louisiana, Lafayette LA 70504
E-mail: {kefe, raghavan, alakhotia}@cacs.louisiana.edu

Finding relevant pages in response to a user query is a challenging task. Automated search engines that rely on keyword matching usually return too many low quality matches. Link analysis methods can substantially improve the search quality when they are combined with content analysis. This chapter surveys the mainstream work in this area.

20.1 Introduction

Automated search engines continuously discover, index, and store information about web pages. When a user issues a query, this repository is searched to find a result set of most relevant pages. An ideal search scheme must satisfy two basic requirements: high recall, and high precision. Recall measures the ability of an algorithm to find as many relevant pages as possible. Precision measures the ability of an algorithm to reject as many nonrelevant pages as possible. An ideal search algorithm should find all of the relevant pages, rank them by relevance to the user query, and present a rank-ordered result to the user.

The earlier generations of search engines relied solely on keyword matching to perform the search. Unfortunately this approach didn't work very well. Too many nonrelevant pages were returned along with relevant ones, and their rankings rarely agreed with users' interests. Since user queries are short, usually consist of 2-3 words [Jansen *et. al.* (1998)], the problems associated with synonyny and polysemy make it particularly difficult to evaluate which pages will be of interest to a user.

The user is more likely to be interested in a page if it contains authoritative information on its subject and it is relevant to the user query. Authoritative pages are usually cited by others frequently, and the link structure around these pages constitute certain special graph patterns. In modern search schemes a keyword matching algorithm initially identifies "potentially" relevant pages based on content analysis. Link analysis (often combined with further content analysis) is then applied to improve the search precision by focusing the search within the graph neighborhoods of these pages. This chapter provides a survey of such approaches. Other related tutorials can be found in.[Chakrabarti (1999); osala and Blockeel (2000); Hu (2002); Gudivada *et. al.* (1997); Lawrence and Giles (1998a); Lawrence and Giles (1999); Lu and Geng (1998)]

20.2   Intuitive Basis for Link Structure Analysis

A link on a web page provides valuable and readily available information. The person who created that link must think, or even recommend, that the cited page is related to the citing page. The term "collective intelligence" refers to an unorchestrated outcome from independent web page creators citing one another. Collective intelligence must surely play an important role in the formation of collective preferences which would manifest itself in the form of special graph patterns (or *signatures*) around authoritative sources in the web graph. By searching for (or computing) these patterns we could try to identify the authoritative pages.

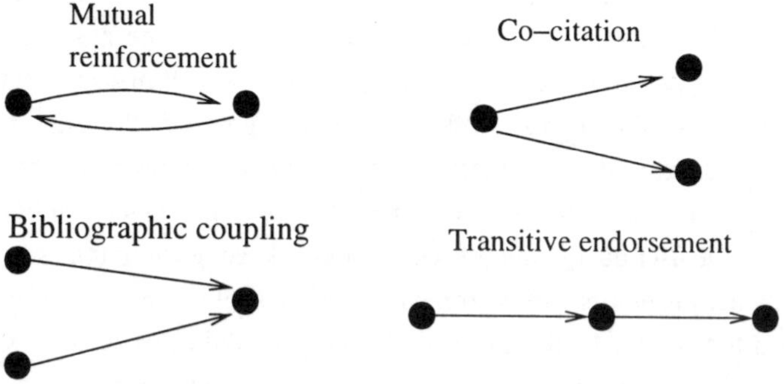

Fig. 20.1   Basic patterns formed by two directed edges.

To build an intuitive understanding of link structure analysis, consider

Figure 1 which shows all possible connected graph patterns containing exactly two links. Each of these patterns has a corresponding interpretation: *Mutual reinforcement* occurs when two pages cite each other, reinforcing our intuition that the two pages are related to each other. *Co-citation* occurs when a page cites two other pages. In bibliometric studies[White and McCain (1989)] it has been observed that related papers are often cited together. Conversely, papers that are cited together are likely to be related. *Bibliographic coupling* is the situation where two independent documents cite the same page. From this pattern we infer that the two pages are related to each other since they cite the same document. Finally *transitive endorsement* occurs when page p_1 links to p_2 which in turn links to p_3. Transitively p_1 may be considered to endorse p_3. However this is a weak endorsement and is rarely a sign of true relation between pages (generally the notion of "related to" is not transitive). We included it in Figure 1 only to cover all possible patterns involving exactly two links.

Statistical evidence observed in recent research validates these intuitive assertions.[Chakrabarti *et. al.* (2002); Davison (2000); Mladenic and Grobelnik (1999)] However there is a significant percentage of cases when these assertions are violated. This is because human judgement applied to web citation is generally subjective and noisy. Also, if topic of discussion changes on a page, citations at different regions of a page may link to pages not related to each other. Because of these reasons we consider the above assertions as weak assertions. After all, for a graph containing only two links, it is hard to talk about collective intelligence.

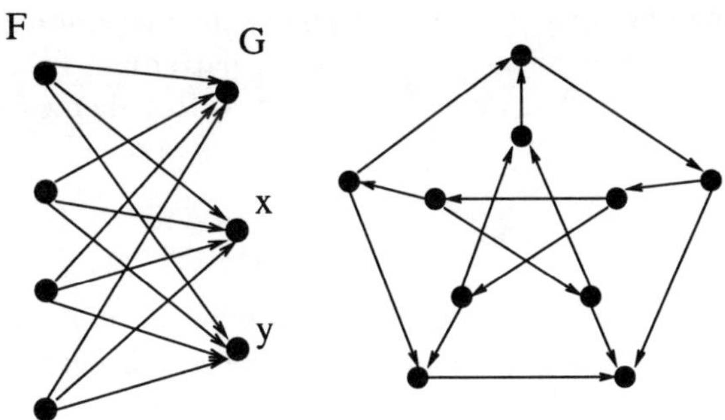

Fig. 20.2   Complex patterns that are indicative of related pages.

In the web graph, these basic structures can blend together to form more complex patterns of multiple links that further reinforce the implicated relationships among a set of web pages. For example consider the complete bipartite graph in Figure 2. In this graph the nodes are divided into two subsets F and G such that each node in F links to every node in G. Above we have seen that co-cited pages are likely to be related to each other. In the case of directed complete bipartite graph any two pages x, y in G are co-cited by all the pages in F. That is, creators of all of the pages in F independently thought that x and y were related to each other. Similarly, by also considering the concept of bibliographic coupling, the aggregation of links in a complete bipartite graph constitute a strong evidence for the associated pages to be related to each other. Similar arguments can be applied to the NK-clan graph in Figure 2 also.

A number of researchers reported successful results from searching for various pre-defined, special patterns in the web graph by graph-theoretical methods. These included methods that search for directed complete bipartite graphs,[Kumar *et. al.* (1999); Reddy and Kitsuregawa (2001)] NK-Clan graphs,[Terveen and Hill (1998)] and sets of pages that have more links to members than to non-members.[Flake *et. al.* (2000); Brinkmeier (1998)] These approaches work well when searching for a cluster of related pages. Searching for well chosen patterns often achieve a high precision in the set of pages returned. However, these methods suffer from poor recall. From a graph-theoretical viewpoint, the problem of subgraph isomorphism is NP-complete, and there is no guarantee that all occurrences of the specified patterns will be found. Also, there may be high quality pages in other patterns that resemble but not necessarily identical to the specified pattern being searched. As a result, many highly authoritative pages may be missed. More flexible techniques are needed that are general enough to find clusters with known patterns even if the pattern lacks a few links, as well as detecting clusters with unknown patterns.

20.3   Link Structure Analysis

The more successful approaches for determining authoritative pages are based on computing, rather than searching for graph patterns. These include authority flow models and random walk models.

20.3.1   *Authority flow models*

In this approach, we consider edge creation as a way of creating a channel through which authority can *flow* from the citing page to the cited page. The larger the number of citations received, the geater the authority flowing into a page. We can compute the authority ranks of pages iteratively as a function of the amount of authority flow they receive. Consider the graph in Figure 20.3 and its adjacency matrix A. Let r be the rank vector that represents authority ranks of all pages. The amount of authority flown into each page can be computed by

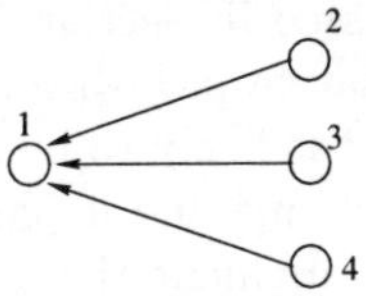

$$A = \begin{bmatrix} 0\ 0\ 0\ 0 \\ 1\ 0\ 0\ 0 \\ 1\ 0\ 0\ 0 \\ 1\ 0\ 0\ 0 \end{bmatrix} \qquad A^T = \begin{bmatrix} 0\ 1\ 1\ 1 \\ 0\ 0\ 0\ 0 \\ 0\ 0\ 0\ 0 \\ 0\ 0\ 0\ 0 \end{bmatrix} \qquad r = \begin{bmatrix} 1 \\ 1 \\ 1 \\ 1 \end{bmatrix}$$

$$A^T \times r = \begin{bmatrix} 0\ 1\ 1\ 1 \\ 0\ 0\ 0\ 0 \\ 0\ 0\ 0\ 0 \\ 0\ 0\ 0\ 0 \end{bmatrix} \begin{bmatrix} 1 \\ 1 \\ 1 \\ 1 \end{bmatrix} = \begin{bmatrix} 3 \\ 0 \\ 0 \\ 0 \end{bmatrix}$$

Fig. 20.3   Flow of authority into a page.

$$r = A^T \times r.$$

In this equation the amount of authority pumped out of a page depends on its rank. Since the rank changes after this computation we are interested in the final rank values after several iterations, provided the iterative computation

$$r(i+1) = A^T \times r(i) \tag{20.1}$$

converges as the iteration count i tends to infinity.

This computation assumes that a page q with authority rank $r_q(i)$ at iteration i is able to pump all of its current authority weight at each of its outgoing link. We can modify this computation so that a page divides its authority equally between its outgoing links. Let x_q be the number of outgoing links on page q. Let W be the matrix obtained by dividing row q of A by x_q for all rows. The above equation becomes

$$r(i+1) = W^T \times r(i)$$

or, equivalently

$$r_p(i+1) = \sum_{\forall q; q \to p} r_q(i)/x_q. \tag{20.2}$$

When this computation converges, the total authority pumped out of a page equals the total authority it receives. The final authority value is used as the rank of a page. A more elaborate version of this computation is used in Google search engine,[Brin and Page (1998)] as we will see in section 5.1.

20.3.1.1   *Correlated Citations*

Equations 1 and 2 (or their real-life versions discussed in Section 5) don't have any built in mechanism to tell if an authoritative page belongs to a cluster of pages. An authoritative page on a subject is likely to be co-cited with other authoritative pages on the same subject, making it part of an authoritative group. Therefore it is reasonable to augment the authority rank of a page based on the degree that it is co-cited with other authorities.

To better explain this notion consider a directed graph G and its adjacency matrix A as shown in Figure 20.4. The matrix product $A^T A$, called the *co-citation matrix*,[Small (1973)] has been known in bibliometric studies for a long time. Observe the following properties of the co-citation matrix.

- An entry (p,q) in $A^T A$ represents the number of joint cocitations received by pages p and q; i.e. among the pages that cite p the number that cite q also.
- The diagonal term in row p of $A^T A$ is equal to the in-degree of page p; i.e. the special case when $q = p$.
- Excluding the diagonal term, the sum of values in row p is the total number of times the page p is co-cited with other pages.

For the directed complete bipartite graph of Figure 2, all of the non-zero terms in a row of the co-citation matrix would be equal to the diagonal term. This is because any page that cites a page x in G also cites all of the other pages in G. Consequently, number of citations to a page x equals to its number of co-citations with y for each x, y in G. Now define a new iterative equation for the computation of authority ranks as follows:

$$a[i + 1] = (A^T A) \times a[i] \qquad (20.3)$$

Due to the diagonal term in the co-citation matrix a page p receiving a large number of citations receives a large amount of authority inflow. Due to the non-diagonal terms, this authority inflow is strengthened by the degree that page p is co-cited with other pages. In fact, as the reader can easily verify, co-citations of a page can help improve its authority weight much more than the mere number of its citations.

20.3.1.2   *Hubs Versus Authorities*

If the concept of authority can be measured by in-degrees of pages, is there a symmetric case for out-degrees? Imagine for the sake of argument that

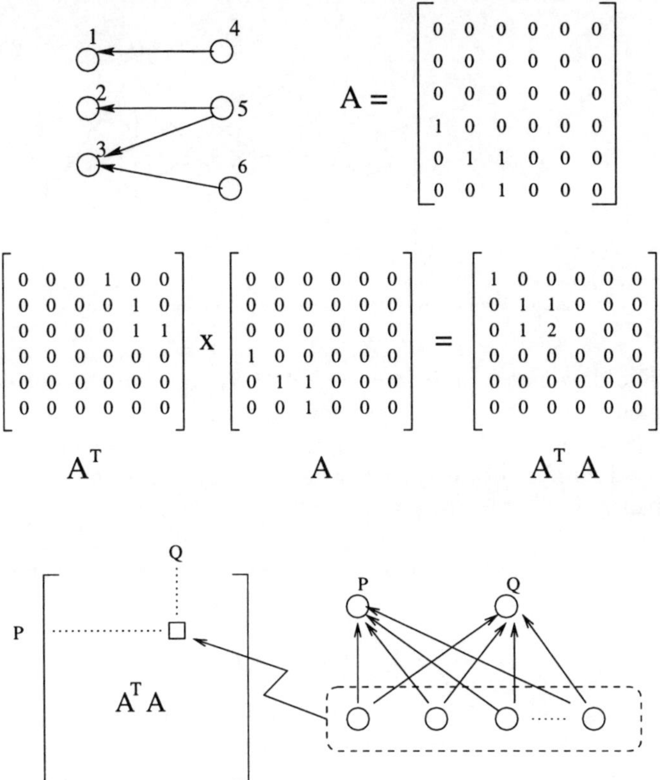

Fig. 20.4   Co-citation matrix and its properties.

surfers always follow the links in the backward direction. This is not possible physically, because web pages don't have reverse links to the pages citing them. But if it were possible to go in the reverse direction of links, which pages would be visited by the most number of surfers?

It turns out that this is a meaningful question with practical implications. While the reader may find it amusing to write the reverse equations paralleling those of 1-3 above, we will only consider the case for equation 3. In this case we have the matrix product AA^T which is called the *bibliographic coupling matrix*.[Kessler *et. al.* (1963)] As ilustrated in Figure 5 the bibliographic coupling matrix has the following properties:

- An entry (p,q) in AA^T represents the degree of bibliographic coupling of pages p and q; i.e. the number of pages jointly cited by p and q.

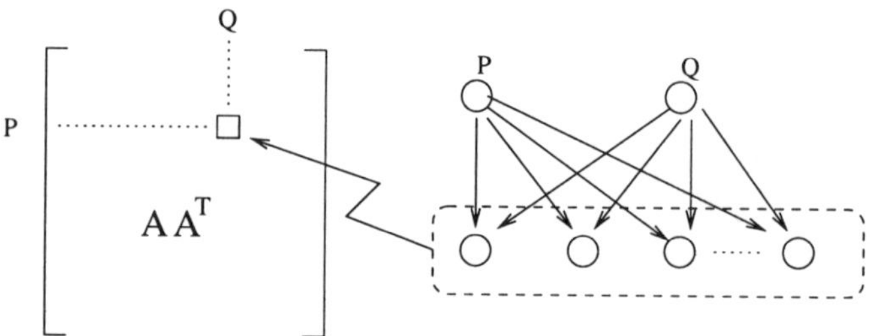

Fig. 20.5   Properties of the bibliographic coupling matrix.

- The diagonal term in row p of AA^T is equal to the out-degree of page p; i.e. the special case when $q = p$.
- Excluding the diagonal term, the sum of values in row p gives the total number of times that pages cited by p are also cited by other pages.

These properties imply that if we define a new equation such as

$$h[i + 1] = (AA^T) \times h[i] \tag{20.4}$$

we compute the ability of a page to cite good sources. This ability has two components: Due to the diagonal term in AA^T, equation 20.4 gives higher weights to pages with larger out-degrees. Due to the non-diagonal terms the weight of a page is increased proportional to its ability to cite well-cited pages. This is precisely the ability needed in knowledgeable pages that are aware of good sources on the web.

In his paper[Kleinberg *et. al.* (1998)] Kleinberg called these pages as "hubs." Internet users are likely to be interested in both authority pages and hub pages. While a good authority page may provide valuable content a good hub page may lead the user to a variety of good authority pages to select from.

20.3.2   *Random Walk Models*

In a random walk model, the surfer can be seen as walking on the web graph, making random decisions about where to go next while at a web page. Some of the equations in the previous sections admit random walk interpretations while others don't. For example equation 1 does not admit a random walk interpretation since a page pumps out an amount of authority equal to its own out of every link it has. It would imply that a random surfer splits itself into as many copies as the number of outgoing links at each new page so that each copy of the surfer takes a different path.

Equation 20.2 avoids this problem by dividing the authority weight of a page equally between the outgoing links. In this interpretation a surfer is required to choose one of the outgoing links of the current page to click. Consequently, the probability of leaving a page, which is equal to one, is the sum of probabilities for following different outgoing links. It follows, therefore, that the rank of a page represents the probability of reaching a page by following the links of the web graph.

To better explain, consider a user who clicks on the links at random. While at page q assume that the user clicks on the outgoing links with equal probability. If page q has x_q outgoing links, the probability that a user will click on any of the outgoing links is $1/x_q$. Then the probability that a page p is reached by following the links is just the summation term in equation 2. A modified version of this computation has been used in Google's PageRank algorithm.[Brin and Page (1998)] In pageRank a surfer has two options: either click on one of the outgoing links or jump to an unrelated page. We discuss PageRank algorithm in more detail in Section 5.1.

For equations 3 and 4, a random walk model is not applicable. The situation here is similar to that of Equation 1 where a surfer would have to split itself into several copies at each new page. Population explosion of surfers makes this computation less stable than equation 2. Kleinberg's HITS algorithm, which uses equations similar to those of equations 3 and 4, normalizes the weight vectors a and h at each iteration to force the convergence.

The reader will notice that the computations of hubs and authorites in equations 3 and 4 are derived from equation 1. It is possible to derive these computations from equation 2 instead, which is the probabilistic version of equation 1. In particular, let W be the matrix obtained from the adjacency matrix A by dividing each non-zero term in a row by the number of non-zero terms in that row. Then the corresponding equations

$$a = W^T W a$$

$$h = W W^T h$$

represent a random surfer who is allowed a zig-zag walk going forward and backward on the links of the web graph.[Lempel and Moran (2000)] Considering the directed bipartite graph of Figure 2, the equation $a = W^T W a$ computes the probability that surfers reach an authority page from other authority pages after a two-step zig-zag walk. The diagonal terms in

$W^T W$ measure the in-degrees of pages while non-diagonal terms measure the frequency that a page is co-cited with other pages. These co-citation edges serve to bring a surfer from one authority page to another. Similarly, the equation $h = WW^T h$ represents corresponding calculations for hub pages. If the graph is not bipartite, the computed weights will be dominated by the in/out-degrees of pages. For pages that are in a bipartite component, the computed weights may be dominated by zig-zag walkers.

A more general model is obtained by defining different weights for diagonal terms and non-diagonal terms in the above computations. If the weights of non-diagonal terms are set as zero, then the authority ranks of pages depend on their in-degrees alone. Conversely, if the weights of diagonal terms are set as zero, the computed ranks depend on co-citation frequencies alone. Similar statements can be made for hub weights also. Without the influence of diagonal terms, these equations can be used for clustering web pages based on their membership status in bipartite subgraphs of the web graph. By adjusting these weights, the model can be made to behave more like the PageRank algorithm or more like the HITS algorithm.[Diligenti *et. al.* (2002)]

20.4   Content Analysis Based Retrieval

Link analysis schemes can identify important pages in the web graph but they cannot tell if a page is relevant to the user query. This task is performed by content analysis. As we discuss in Section 5, most search schemes start with content analysis to determine a candidate subset of relevant pages, and apply link analysis in the graph neighborhood of these pages.

The most basic tool used in various content analysis tasks in information retrieval is a measure of similarity between two documents. In the case of web search the user query replaces one of the documents and the other document is a web page. There are crude but computationally efficient measures based on vector space models. These measures (see for example,[Salton (1989)] page 318) are all based on computing the inner product of term-frequency vectors x, y derived from two documents. A popular method is the Cosine similarity given by

$$S = \sum_{i=1}^{t} x_i \times y_i (\sum_{i=1}^{t} x_i^2 \times \sum_{i=1}^{t} y_i^2)^{1/2}$$

where t is the length of the vectors x and y. This equation can be used for clustering documents on similar topics.

In this equation every term has equal weight, meaning that every word is assumed to have the same descriptive power in determining the topic of a document. When the user query consists only of a few words, as in a typical internet search query, inverse document frequency is a more informative measure of a term's value as a discriminator. Terms that do not occur with high frequency are highly useful for distinguishing documents in which they occur from those they do not occur. Let tf_j be the total number of occurrences of term T_j in N documents. Then the inverse document frequency idf_j, defined as $idf_j = logNdf_j$, is an indicator of T_j as a document discriminator. Let $tf_{i,j}$ denote the frequency of term j in document i. The product $w_{i,j} = tf_{i,j}logNdf_j$ can be used as a weight for term j in the above computation so that seldom used words are given higher weights if they are found on a given page.

Other variations of the above similarity measure have been defined. For example the Okapi measure[Hawking *et. al.* (1999)] takes into account the length of a document in comparison to the average document length. Three Level Scoring (TLS)[Li and Shang (2002)] is another variation where different weights computed for subqueries of different lengths are combined together. Cover Density Ranking (CRD)[Clarke *et. al.* (2000)] is a method where a hit for the whole query has higher weight than a hit for any subset of query terms regardless of frequency of occurrence. In a recent comparison,[Li *et. al.* (2002)] these four methods showed no significant performance difference when they were combined with an improved version of the HITS algorithm. However, these variations show improvements over the simple cosine similarity.[Salton (1989)]

Other sources of difficulties in relevance measuring of documents are synonymy and polysemy; many words can have similar meanings while a word can have several meanings. Synonymy causes many related pages to be missed while polysemy causes many unrelated pages to be declared as being authority on a subject. Latent Semantic Analysis (LSA)[Landauer (2002); Deerwester *et. al.* (1990)] and the Generalized Vector Space Model (GVSM)[Wong *et. al.* (1987)] are the two approaches that are frequently credited for successfully addressing these problems in information retrieval. In these models words are not treated as being independent from one another; their usage patterns are taken into account as well by computing an orthogonal vector of terms across documents. In a comparative study[Yang *et. al.* (1998)] these schemes were found to facilitate better document classifications, document search, and relevance ranking. It is also noted that the GVSM model is more efficient and more stable across various parameter values than the LSA model. A recent review of related indexing methods in information retrieval has been given in.[Raghavan *et. al.*]

Another related issue is *where* on the page to search for the user query terms. A web document has a title and a body, both of which contain potential sources of information. Research articles also contain an abstract as an identifyable section but beyond these most web pages lack any semantic structure to guide the search algorithms. Brin[Brin and Page (1998)] notes that searching in the title alone returns astonishingly good matches. In addition the body text of the page can be mined for more detailed information about its relevance such as term frequencies for the query as well as its subqueries. Other useful information includes distance between subquery terms, the fonts, any highlighting used such as boldface or italic, and others.

Besides these, the anchor text associated with a link that points to a page provides quite accurate information about the content of a page. McBryan[McBryan (1994)] was the first to observe that the anchor text often describes the content of a cited page better than the page itself. In the opinion of the person who created that link, the best source for the query in the anchor text is the cited page. Thus if the user query matches the anchor text, the pointed page must be an authoritative source for the user query. For some pages (e.g. the ones that mainly contain images, programs, databases) there may be no text in the page itself. In such cases, we are limited to the information in the title of a page and the anchor text associated with the links pointing to it.

20.5 Retrieval Techniques Combining Content and Link Structure Analysis

Google's PageRank algorithm and Kleinberg's HITS (Hyperlink Induced Topic Search) are two of the best known algorithms for topic search. Here we consider these algorithms and several of their variations proposed in the literature.

20.5.1 *PageRank Algorithm*

Google's web crawlers continuously search the web to collect new pages and update the old ones. These pages are stored in a data repository. The link structure of these pages are stored separately from other information to represent the web graph. This graph is used for computing page ranks by using the PageRank Equation off-line.

Google's PageRank algorithm considers a random surfer who has two options: either click on a forward link or jump to an unrelated page. Let d represent the probability that while at page q a surfer chooses to click on one of the outgoing links instead of jumping to another page. Then $(1 - d)$

represents the probability of jumping while at page q. If the surfers select the jump destinations with equal probability for all pages, then $(1-d)$ also represents the aggregate probability that a surfer reaches a given page p by jumping from any of the other pages. Accordingly the probability that Google's random surfer reaches a page p is given by the equation:

$$r_p = (1-d) + d \sum_{\forall q; q \to p} r_q/x_q \qquad (20.5)$$

where initial page ranks are chosen such that their sum equals to unity. By appropriately choosing d in the range $0 < d < 1$ the above computation is guaranteed to converge because the parameter d dampens the authority inflow to keep it from growing indefinitely (other modifications to this computation for eliminating the effects of short loops are discussed in.[citeseer.nj.nec.com])

When a user issues a query, Google initially uses a keyword matching scheme to find a set of candidate pages. These pages are then ordered by their ranks before presenting to the user. This is not a simple case of sorting the pages by their ranks from equation 20.5. Rather, the rank of a page is a complex combination of weights and scores defined on various parameters, one of them being the static rank obtained from equation 20.5. The keyword frequency, position of keywords on the page, fonts, capitalization, the distance between component words of a multi-word query are examples of factors that contribute to the rank of a page.[Brin and Page (1998)]

Google stores the anchor text associated with a link together with the cited page. During keyword search on a page, these pieces of text are also considered, and matches found in the anchor text contribute to the rank of the cited page. A hit on a page has different weights depending on whether the keyword is found on the title of the page, in the body text, or in the anchor text of an incoming link. Google also attributes different weights for links depending on who is citing a page. Citations by reputable sources such as Yahoo's directory service are weighted more heavily than others.

20.5.2 *Topic Sensitive PageRank*

In the original PageRank algorithm a single authority weight is computed for each page independent of any particular search query. To yield more accurate results, Haveliwala[Haveliwala (2002)] proposed to compute a vector of page ranks for each page, corresponding to the importance of a page for each category in a preselected set of topics.

The main difference here is the way jump probabilities are computed. In equation 20.5 above, the probability of jumping is assumed to be same for every possible destination. In topic sensitive PageRank, jumping probabilities are computed for each topic.

Let there be N pages in total, of which T_j pages belong to topic j. In equation 20.5, the probability that a surfer jumps to page p is equal to $1/N$. In topic sensitive PageRank this probability is computed as $1/T_j$ if page p is in topic j. Otherwise the probability of jumping to page p is zero for category j. The rest of the ranking equation is similar to the PageRank algorithm.

By using topic-dependent jumping probabilities, different page ranks are computed for each page, one rank value for each topic. When a user issues a query, all topics represented in the query are identified. The rank of a page is computed as the sum of its category ranks for each of these topics.

20.5.3   *HITS Algorithm*

Kleinberg's HITS algorithm tries to identify hubs and authorities by using the equations:

$$h = Aa \qquad\qquad (20.6)$$

$$a = A^T h \qquad\qquad (20.7)$$

which are equivalent to equations 3 and 4. Hub and authority vectors are normalized before every iteration such that squares of their respective weights sum to unity. Kleinberg proved that the a vector converges to the principal eigenvector of $A^T A$ and the h vector converges to the principal eigenvector of AA^T. At steady state, pages on a common topic and with the largest hub and authority weigths are highly likely to represent pages of a graph resembling the directed bipartite graph in Figure 2.

This algorithm has two major steps: sampling and weight-propagation. The sampling step uses a keyword-based search to select around 200 pages by using one of the commercially available search engines. This set of pages is called the *root set*. This root-set is then expanded into a *base set* by adding any page on the web that has a link to/from a page in the root set. (These same steps were used earlier in WebQuery system[Carriere and Kazman (1997)] where authors called these sets of pages as "hit set" and "complete neighbor set." WebQuery ranks pages in the complete neighbor set in decreasing order of their connectivity, i.e. the number of incoming plus outgoing links). The base set typically contains a few thousand pages. The pages in the base set may or may not constitute a connected graph but at least it has a large connected component.[Kleinberg *et. al.* (1999)]

The weight-propagation step of HITS algorithm computes the hub weights and authority weights for the pages in the base set by using equations 20.6 and 20.7. The output of the algorithm is a short list of pages with the largest hub weights and a list of pages with the largest authority weights. The implementation typically outputs 10 from each group as the final list. Gibson et al.[Gibson *et. al.* (1998)] reported that HITS algorithm is very effective in finding clusters of related pages.

The work of Bharat and Henzinger[Bharat and Henzinger (1998)] showed that a straight implementation of the HITS algorithm does not work well for topic search. More successful implementations depended on using additional heuristics to tackle the observed causes of poor performance.[Bharat and Henzinger (1998); Chakrabarti *et. al.* (1999)] For example Chakrabarti et al.[Chakrabarti *et. al.* (1999)] observed that when the topic of discussion varies on different parts of a page, the outgoing links also point to different topics. A page with a large out-degree will award the same authority weight to each page with which it links on the subject of the user query. However, these cited pages may not even be on the same topic. To solve this problem they used a page splitting heuristic. If large documents are split into several small documents, there is a smaller probability for the cited pages to be unrelated to one another. The authors reported significantly improved results with this heuristic.

Li et al.[Li *et. al.* (2002)] present another improvement of the HITS algorithm where hub weights of pages are increased depending on their authority weights. A hub page with many incoming links has a higher hub weight than a hub page with fewer or no incoming links. This is intuitively appealing because a good hub is likely to be cited, i.e. it must a good authority at being a hub.

Another problem observed with the HITS algorithm is the *Tighyly Knit Community* (TKC) effect. Examples include the Nebraska tourist information page being returned in response to a query for skiing in Nebraska,[Chakrabarti *et. al.* (1999)] and pages on "computational linguistics" dominating the returned pages when searching for authoritative pages on "linguistics."[Gibson *et. al.* (1998)] In both cases HITS has converged to regions of the web graph with the considerably greater density of linkage.

Other researchers[Cohn and Chang (2000); Cohn and Hofman (2001)] observed that the TKC effect of HITS algorithm is related to its convergence to the principal eigenvectors. Ideally the rank of a page in the root set should reflect the likelyhood of it being cited in its community. In HITS algorithm a popular page would be deemed unimportant if it is part of a smaller community. For example the root set returned in response to the query "jaguar" may contain pages on the automobile, on the animal, on the Atari Jaguar product, or anything else that has the word "jaguar" in its name. The set of pages represented in the principal eigenvector would be dominated by one of these categories completely ignoring other pages that are rightfully popular in their respective communities.

An improvement over the HITS algorithm eliminating its TKC effect should then manifest itself in its ability to include popular pages from each community in the same base set. Cohn and Chang proposed a probabilistic model of citations called the PHITS algorithm where the rank of a page is supposed to represent the probability of its citation within its own community rather than within the entire base set. Borodin et. al.[Borodin *et. al.* (2001)] present comparisons of several variations of the HITS algorithm. Interesting observations are reported about differences in the sets of pages returned by different variations of HITS algorithm.

In another implementation, HITS algorithm was used for finding pages related to a given web page.[Dean and Henzinger (1999)] Here the algorithm starts with a seed URL and finds pages that are related to it. This is similar to the "What's Related" facility in Netscape.[home.netscape.com] In this implementation the base set required by the HITS algorithm is obtained from the seed URL by including its parents (the pages that link to it), its children (the pages that it links to), children of its parents, and parents of its children. At the end of the iterative computations the algorithm outputs 10 of the highest ranked authority pages. The authors found that instead of a full implementation of the HITS algorithm, a simpler approach performs much better: Given the seed page, find the pages that link to it, and then determine "who else" they link to. The algorithm outputs 10 of the pages that are most frequently co-cited with the seed URL.

A search engine that needs to respond to thousands of queries per second cannot be expected to run complex content analysis algorithms. For this reason, simple ideas that work are immensely valuable. One such idea first introduced by McBryan[McBryan (1994)] is to perform limited content analysis in the anchor text of links in the citing page. This idea has sound intuitive basis since the anchor text complements the citation. Creator of that link says: "here is the most relevant page for the query in the anchor text." As mentioned in section 5.1, PageRank algorithm makes use of this concept.

In the CLEVER project,[Chakrabarti *et. al.* (1998); Chakrabarti *et. al.* (1999); Chakrabarti *et. al.* (2002)] this idea was implemented by comparing the user query against the text around the link. A relevance weight is computed for each link. The weight $w(p,q)$ is just the number of matches found on page p around the link pointing to q. This yields a modified adjacency matrix where the entries are computed as $x(p,q) = 1 + w(p,q)$. Thus if target page is not related to the search topic, the anchor text should assign a small weight to the link. Small link weights work as filters that block transfer of authority toward unrelated pages. The authors report that the results of the CLEVER algorithm produced substantially improved results over the HITS algorithm. In fact, in user evaluations, pages returned by this implementation achieved higher approval than the manually compiled Yahoo directory.

Another approach[Bharat and Broder (1998)] focused on controlling the influence of pages rather than the individual links in them. Since users only type a few key words, it is difficult to compute a meaningful similarity measure between the key words and web documents. Thus the researchers constructed a query document by combining together the first 1000 words from each document in the root set. Then they computed the cosine-normalized similarity of this reference page with all the pages in the base set. This computation yielded the relevance weights of different documents. These weights are used to dampen the hub weights and authority weights of pages before each iteration is started. Authority weight of a page p is computed as $a_p = a_p \times r_p$ where r_p is the relevance weight of page p. This algorithm effectively weeds-out irrelevant pages in the base set and adjusts the weight of other pages depending on their similarity with the reference page. The result was much better than a straight implementation of HITS algorithm.

20.6 Conclusions and Future Directions

Due to space limitations, much of the ongoing works in related areas are left out of the scope of this tutorial. Here we briefly mention some of the potentially useful areas that can further improve the existing search algorithms. For example, more accurate mathematical models may be obtained by using the observed frequencies of link usages instead of treating all outgoing links of a page with equal weight as in the PageRank algorithm or in the topic sensitive PageRank. Some work in modeling a non-random surfer has been reported.[Pitkow and Prolli (1999)] More research in this direction could focus on efficient implementation of such a non-random surfer model.

Other related research focuses on utilizing user feedback to fine-tune search parameters. Fundamental techniques for relevance feedback have been discussed in.[Gudivada *et. al.* (1997); Raghavan *et. al.*] Independently, researchers at the NEC Research Institute have developed several techniques for representing and utilizing user context to guide the search schemes.[Lawrence and Giles (1998b); Lawrence (2000)] These schemes are based on tailoring and augmenting the query terms to improve keyword matches. Other work involves creating metasearch engines on the fly to determine the importance of a page depending on the number of search engines containing it along with its rank in each.[Lawrence and Giles (1998c); Meng *et. al.* (2002)]

Another significant development is the ongoing work in XML (Extensible Markup Language) standards. A major difficulty in web search is extracting semantic structure in existing web documents. Web pages written in HTML only describe how documents should look on the computer screen. The markup tags in XML specify the meaning of each attribute in the data and facilitate searching for specific information in a document.[Yoon *et. al.* (2001a); Yoon *et. al.* (2001b)] The ongoing work on XML[www.w3.org] is aimed at providing web page designers a suite of tools to develop semantically meaningful hyperlinked text. As a whole, XML's set of tools allow creating, organizing, indexing, linking, and querying data on the web. Future work can focus on more effective content analysis algorithms in XML pages. More information about XML is available online at www.w3.org/XML.

Acknowledgments

This research was funded by Louisiana State's Information Technology Initiative.

Bibliography

Bharat Krishna and Broder Andrei Z. (1998). A technique for measuring the relative size and overlap of public web search engines. (in World-Wide Web'98 (WWW7)), Brisbane, Australia.

Bharat Krishna and Henzinger Monika. (1998). Improved Algorithms for Topic Distillation in a Hyperlinked Environment 21st ACM SIGIR conference on Research and Development in Information Retrieval. pp. 469-477.

Borodin A., Roberts G.O., Rosenthal J.S., and Tsaparas P. (2001). Finding Authorities and Hubs From Link Structures on the World Wide Web. Proc. 10th International Conf. WWW.

Brin Sergey and Page Larry. (1998). The Anatomy of a Large Scale Hypertextual Web Search Engine. In Proc. of WWW7, Brisbane, Australia.

Brinkmeier M. (1998). Communities in Graphs, Online document at www.nj.nec.com/brinkmeier02communities.html.

Carriere S.J., and Kazman R. (1997). WebQuery: Searching and Visualizing the Web Through Connectivity, *Computer Networks and ISDN Systems,* 29: 1257-1267.

Chakrabarti Soumen. (1999). Recent results in automatic Web resource discovery. ACM computing survey.

Chakrabarti Soumen, Dom Byron E., Raghavan Prabhakar, Rajagopalan Sridhar, Gibson David and Kleinberg Jon M. (1998). Automatic Resource Compilation by Analyzing Hyperlink Structure and Associated Text. in Proceedings of World-Wide Web'98 (WWW7), Brisbane, Australia, pp. 65-74.

Chakrabarti Soumen, Dom Byron E., Gibson David, Kleinberg Jon, Kumar Ravi, Raghavan Prabhakar, Rajagopalan Sridhar, Tomkins Andrew. (1999). Mining the Link Structure of the World Wide Web. IEEE Computer, Vol.32 No.8.

Chakrabarti Soumen, Joshi M.M., Punera K., and Pennock D., (2002). The Structure of Broad Topics on the Web. www 2002.

Clarke C.L.A., Cormack G.V., Tudhope E.A. (2000). Relevance Ranking for One to Three Term Queries. *Information Processing and Management,* vol 36, pp. 291-311.

Cohn D. and Chang H. (2000). Learning to Probabilistically Identify Authorita tive Documents. Proc. 17th International Conference on Machine Learning, Stanford University, pp. 167-174.

Cohn D. and Hofman T. (2001). The Missing Link - A Probabilistic Model of Document Content and Hypertext Connectivity. in T. Leen et al., eds., *Advances in Neural Information Processing Systems,* Vol 13.

Davison Brian D. (2000). Topical Locality in the Web. Proceedings of the 23rd Annual International Conference on Research and Development in Information Retrieval (SIGIR 2000), Athens, Greece, July 24-28, pp. 272-279.

Dean Je.rey, and Henzinger Monika R. (1999). Finding related Pages in theWorld Wide Web. In Proc. WWW-8.

Deerwester Scott, Dumais Susan T., Landauer Thomas K., Furnas George W., and Harshman Richard A. (1990). Indexing by Latent Semantic Analysis. *Journal of the Society of Information Science,* 41(6):391-406.

Diligenti M., Gori M. and Maggini M. (2002). Web page scoring systems for horizontal and vertical search. In Proceedings of the 11th World Wide Web Conference (WWW11) 1-7 May 2002, Honolulu (USA). Extensible Markup Language (XML), online document at http://www.w3.org/XML.

Flake G.W., Lawrence S., and Giles C.L. (2000). E.cient Identi.cation of Web Communities. Proc. 6th Intn'l Conf. on Knowledge Discovery and Data Mining (ACM SIGKDD-2000), pp. 150-160.

Gibson David, Kleinberg Jon, Raghavan Prabhakar. (1998). Inferring Web Communities from Link Topology. Proc. 9th ACM Conference on Hypertext and HyperMedia.

Gudivada Venkat N., Raghavan Vijay V., Grosky William I., Kasanagottu Rajesh. (1997). Information retrieval on the world wide web. IEEE Internet Computing, Vol. 1, No. 5, pp. 58-68.

Haveliwala T.H. (2002). Topic Sensitive PageRank. Proc. WWW 2002.

Hawking D., Bailey P., Craswell N. (1999). ACSys Trec-8 Experiments. Proc. TREC-8 NIST Special Publication, pp. 500-246.

HuWen-Chen. (2002).WorldWideWeb Search Technologies. chapter of the book, Shi Nansi (Ed.), 'Architectural Issues ofWeb-Enabled Eloctronic Business', Idea Group Publishing, 2002. http://citeseer.nj.nec.com/461532.html.

Jansen J., Spink A., Batesman J., and Saracevic T. (1998). Real Life Information Retrieval: A Study of User Queries on the Web. SIGIR Forum, Vol 32, No 1, pp. 5-17.

Kessler M.M. (1963). Bibliographic coupling between scienti.c papers. *American Documentation,* 14:10-25.

Kleinberg Jon M. (1998). Authoritative sources in a hyperlinked environment. In Proceedings of ACM-SIAM Syposium on Discrete Algorithms, pp. 668-677.

Kleinberg Jon M., Kumar Ravi, Raghavan Prabhakar, Rajagopalan Sridhar and Tomkins Andrew S. (1999). The Web as a graph: measurements, models and methods. Proceedings of the 5th International Computing and combinatorics Conference.

Kosala R. and Blockeel H. (2000). Web Mining Research: A Survey. SIGKDD Explorations -Newsletter of the ACM Special Interest Group on Knowledge Discovery and Data Mining 2 (2000), no. 1, pp. 1-15, Special Issue on Internet Mining.

Kumar Ravi, Raghavan Prabhakar, Rajagopalan Sridhar, Tomkins Andrew (1999). Trawling the web for emerging cyber-communities. Proc. 8th International World Wide Web Conference, WWW8.

Landauer, T.K. (2002). Applications of Latent Semantic Analysis. 24th Annual Meeting of the Cognitive Science Society.

Lawrence S., and Giles C.L. (1998). Searching the World Wide Web. *Science,* 280:98-100.

Lawrence S., and Giles C.L. (1999). Searching the Web: General and Scienti.c Information Access. *IEEE Communications,* 37 (1):116-122.

Lawrence S., and Giles C.L. (1998). Context and Page Analysis for Improved Web Search. *IEEE Internet Computing,* pp. 38-46.

Lawrence S., and Giles C.L. (1998). Inquirus, the NECI Meta Search Engine. 7th int'l WWW Conference, Brisbane, Australia, pp. 95-105.

Lawrence S. (2000). Context in Web Search, IEEE Data Engineering Bulletin. vol. 23, No. 3, pp. 25-32.

Lempel R. and Moran S. (2000). The Stochastic Approach for Link-Structure Analysis (SALSA) and the TKC E.ect. Proc. 9th InternationalWorld Wide Web Conference.

Li L., Shang Y., Zhang W. (2002). Improvement of HITS-Based Algorithms on Web Documents. WWW Conf. 2002, pp. 527-535.

Li L. and Shang Y. (2002). A New Statistical Method for Evaluating Search Engines. Proc. IEEE 12th Intn'l Conf. Tools With Arti.cial Intelligence, Vancouver, British Columbia.

Lu H. and Geng L. (1998). Integrating Database and World Wide Web Technologies. *World Wide Web,* Vol. 1, No. 2, pp. 73-86.

McBryan O.A. (1994). GENVL and WWW Tools for Taming the Web. Proc. 1st Int'l conf. World-Wide Web.

Meng W., Yu C., and Liu K. (2002). Building E.cient and E.ective Metasearch Engines. *ACM Computing Surveys,* 34(1):48-84.

Mladenic D. and Grobelnik M. (1999). Predicting Content from Hyperlinks. Proceedings of the ICML-99 Workshop on Machine Learning in Text Data Analysis, J. Stephan Institute, Ljubljana, Slovenia, pp. 19-24. Netscape communications Corporation, on-line document at http://home.netscape.com/escapes/related/faq.html#o7

Page L., Brin S., Motwani R., and Winograd T. The PageRank Citation Ranking: Bringing Order to the Web. online at citeseer. nj.nec.com/page98pagerank.html.

Pitkow J. and Prolli P. (1999). Mining Longest Repeating Subsequences to Predict World Wide Web Sur.ng. Proc. USITS'99, the 2nd USENIX Symposium on Internet Technologies and Systems, Boulder, Colorado, October 11-14.

Reddy P.K. and Kitsuregawa M. (2001). An Approach to Relate the Web Communities Through Bipartite Graphs. WISE 1: 301-310.

Raghavan V.V., Gudivada V.N., Wu Z., and Grosky W.I. Information Retrieval. In The Practical Handbook of Internet Computing (Ed. M. Singh), CRC Press (to appear).

Gerard Salton. (1989). Automatic Text Processing: The Transformation, Analysis, and Retrieval of Information by Computer. Addison Wesley Publishing Co., Reading, MA.

Small H. (1973). Co-citation in Scienti.c Literature: A New Measure of the Relationship Between Two Documents. *Journal of the Americal Society for Information Sciences,* 24:265-269.

Terveen Loren and Hill Will. (1998). Finding and Visualizing Inter-site Clan Graphs. Proceedings of CHI 98: 448-455, Los Angeles, CA.

White H.D., McCain K.W. (1989). Bibliometrics in Annual Review of Information Science and Technology. Elsevier, pp. 119-186.

Wong S.K.M., Ziarko W., Raghavan V.V., andWong P.C.N. (1987). On Modeling of Information Retrieval Concepts in Vector Space. *ACM Transactions of Database Systems,* no. 2, pp. 299-321.

Yang Y., Carbonell J.G., Brown R.D., and Frederkin R.E. (1998). Translingual Information Retrieval: Learning from Bilingual Corpora. *Artificial Intelligence Journal Special Issue: Best of IJCAI-97,* pp. 323-345.

Yoon J., Raghavan V.V., and Chakilam V. (2001). Bitmap indexing based clustering and retrieval of XML documents. In Proceedings of ACM SIGIR Workshop on Mathematical/Formal Methods in Information Retrieval, New Orleans, LA, Sept..

Yoon J., Raghavan V.V., Chakilam V., and Kerschberg L. (2001). Bitcube: A three-dimensional bitmap indexing for XML documents. J. of Intelligent Information Systems, 17(2/3):241-254.

CHAPTER 21

MOBILE AGENT TECHNOLOGY AND ITS APPLICATION IN INTERNET COMPUTING

Jiannong Cao[1], Jingyang Zhou[1,2], Daoxu Chen[2], Alvin T. S. Chan[1], Jian Lu[2]

1. Department of Computing, Hong Kong Polytechnic University
Hung Hom, Kowloon, Hong Kong, P.R. China
2. Department of Computer Science and Technology, Nanjing University
Nanjing, Jiangsu, P.R. China
E-mail: csjcao@comp.polyu.edu.hk

"Agents" of various species have been an active field of research and development for a decade now. Mobile agent technology that allows programs to move autonomously through a network has emerged as a new approach to distributed computing. It supports a unified and scalable framework for various kinds of applications such as electronic commerce, parallel computing, and information retrieval, as well as for advanced technologies such as Web Services and Grid Computing operating in widely distributed heterogeneous open networks including the Internet. This chapter introduces some basic concepts related to mobile agents, provides an overview of mobile agent technology and its applications in Internet computing, discusses, and surveys some current mobile agent systems.

21.1 Introduction

In today's interconnected society, users are confronted with an often overwhelming abundance of information. To more efficiently utilize this data, three types of network computing paradigms have been proposed [Lange and Oshima (1998)], the *Client-Server Paradigm* (such as COBRA), the *Code-on-Demand Paradigm* (such as Applet) and the

453

Mobile Agent Paradigm. Of these three, the Mobile Agent paradigm has more distinguished merits and is likely to become the dominant approach in distributed computing. Mobile agent technology provides distributed computing with significant competitive advantages, especially in Internet computing, and in practical applications that have been developed and integrated into commercial products. Currently, mobile agents are used in a broad range of systems ranging from comparatively small systems such as email filters to large, open, complex and mission-critical systems such as air traffic control [Jennings and Wooldridge (1998)].

In this chapter, we first introduce the concepts and the characteristics of mobile agent technology and then focus on the applications of mobile agent in Internet computing.

The remainder of this chapter is organized as follows. Section two reviews the main characteristics that constitute an agent and, ultimately, a mobile agent. Section three focuses on some core mobile agent technologies and contains a subsection that presents an overview of prevailing mobile agent systems. Section four discusses the applications of mobile agents in Internet computing. Section five contains our conclusion.

21.2 What is a Mobile Agent?

21.2.1 *What is a Software Agent?*

The technology of software agent provides a new and powerful computing model for the development of software applications. Indeed, agent-based computing has been hailed as the "next significant breakthrough in software development" [Sargent (1992)] and "the new revolution in software" [Guilfoyle and Warner (1994)], and agents are currently the focus of intense interest in many sub-fields of computer science. Yet, despite the popularity of the term "agent" in computer science communities and in the popular computing press, there is as yet no agreement on a precise definition of an "agent".

In its common meaning, an agent is traditionally defined as "one who is authorized to act for or in the place of another", but as a software model agents date back only to Carl Hewitt's concurrent model of 1977, which proposed the concept of a self-contained, interactive, and concurrently executing object [Nwana and Ndumu (1998)] . One definition of "software agent" that many agent researchers might find acceptable nowadays is that of a software entity, which functions continuously and autonomously in a particular environment, often inhabited by other agents and processes [Shoham (1997)]. A detailed discussion on agent theory and architecture is given in [Wooldridge and Jennings (1995)]. Agents with dissimilar characteristics function by allowing people to delegate work to them and by acting continuously in pursuit of their own goals. Of course, they may also interact with their execution environment and act asynchronously and autonomously upon it. A software agent possesses the following characteristics:

- Autonomy: Agents should operate without the intervention of external elements (other agents or humans). They have some kind of control over their actions and internal states [Castelfranchi (1995)]. In general, this allows an agent to act on its own, using the data and the mobile logic which it incorporates, without the need for human intervention or guidance;
- Social Ability: Agents interact with other agents (and possibly humans) via some kind of agent-communication language;
- Adaptability: An agent acquires and processes information about the runtime situation, both spatially and temporally;
- Reactivity: Agents perceive their environment (which may be the physical world, a user via a graphical user interface, a collection of other agents, the Internet, or perhaps all of these combined), and respond in a timely fashion to changes occur in their environment;
- Pro-activity: Agents are goal-driven. They do not simply react to their environment; they take initiatives and exhibit goal-directed behavior.

Software agents may additionally possess any of the following orthogonal properties: mobility, believability and the ability to learn and communicate.

21.2.2 *From Software Agent to Mobile Agent*

Emphasizing mobility and interaction, mobile agents represent one of the most promising technologies in software agent research. Agents are able to decide, based on their local knowledge, whether when or where to migrate in the network. During migration, the agents' local state variables are transferred to the new host to continue computation there. From the perspective of end-users, a mobile agent is actually a software agent that can roam autonomously around the heterogeneous network to finish a task assigned by its owner. From a system perspective, a mobile agent is an autonomous object or object cluster, which is able to move between locations in a so-called *mobile agent platform (MAP)*. An MAP is a distributed abstraction layer that provides the concepts and mechanisms for mobility and communication, as well as security for the underlying system [Straßer *et. al.* (1996); Pham and Karmouch (1998)].

To accomplish specified tasks, a mobile agent can interact with other agents, spawn a new agent or transport itself to another server, or travel from one system in a network to another in the same network. This ability allows it to move to a system containing an object with which it wants to interact and to take advantage of being in the same host or network as the object, or in other words, localized interaction. Mobile agent technology provides a number of benefits for creating distributed systems [Lange and Oshima (1998); Harrison *et. al.* (1994)], which includes:

- reduce network load and overcome network latency;
- encapsulate protocols;
- execute asynchronously and autonomously;
- adapt dynamically;
- are naturally heterogeneous;
- are robust and fault-tolerant;
- can continue traveling and working even after disconnection from the users who initialized them;
- allow easy customization of applications.

While none of the individual advantage of mobile agents is overwhelmingly appealing, the aggregate advantages are overwhelmingly strong [Harrison *et. al.* (1994)]. Many applications have benefited from using mobile agents, including E-commerce, personal assistance, secure brokering, distributed information retrieval, telecommunication networks services, and parallel processing. The future service network will be populated by software agents capable of collaboratively processing the ever-growing volume of on-line information [Decina and Trecordi (1997)].

Agent technology lies in the intersection of distributed computing and artificial intelligence [Wooldridge (2002)], but in the following we will describe mobile agents mainly from the perspective of distributed computing.

21.3 Mobile Agent Technology

21.3.1 *Mobile Agent Platform*

The mobile agent platform (MAP) is a ubiquitous server that accommodates mobile agents. Crucially, a MAP represents an abstraction of agent executing environments and as such a MAP is viewed as "place" where agents are contained and executed. It provides an execution environment for agents where agents can compute, communicate with other agents, and if necessary use authorized resources and services from the underlying system. To support mobile agents running on it, the MAP must implement several mechanisms. Here, we focus on agent migration, communication and security.

21.3.1.1 *Migration*

Mobility is the primary characteristic of mobile agents. However, migration of agents is not easy to achieve. Generally speaking, migration is a mechanism for continuing the current execution of an agent at another location [M. Straßer *et. al.* (1996)] and, because it is autonomous, is always initiated by the agent itself. It requires a considerable effort to collect the complete local state of the agent and possibly the whole runtime stack before migration takes place. All the data must be transferred to its new place together with the agent's code.

Mobile agents enjoy two kinds of mobility [Baumann *et. al.* (1998)]. In the *Strong Migration* scheme, the underlying system captures the entire agent state (consisting of data and execution state) and transfers it together with the agent code to the next location. Once the agent is received and hosted at its new location, its state is automatically restored and agent will restart execution exactly from where it stopped. Strong migration in heterogeneous environments requires a global model of an agent's state as well as the transfer syntax for this information. Since the complete agent state (including data and execution state) can be large- in particular for multi-threaded agents – strong migration can be a very time-consuming and expensive operation. The *Weak Migration* scheme reduces this overload and complexity by transferring only data state information. However, the weak migration scheme has less transparency than the strong migration. The programmer has to be responsible for encoding the agents' execution states in appropriate program variables and decide where and how the execution continues after the migration.

Both of these types of migration require that a "move" or similar command to be issued first. After that, related state information, including the program code, the contents of the instance variables and the execution state, are stored, packaged, and transported to the destination location where the agent resumes its execution. Given that they are carried out under a uniform agent state model, the procedure follows these steps:

- Invoke a "move" primitive
- Save context and status
- Package data and transport it to the destination
- Destroy the agent in the origin agent server
- Create a new instance/thread for the agent in the new server
- Unpack the data and restore the environment
- Resume agent execution

21.3.1.2 *Communication*

In multi-agent systems, communication is essential for a set of agents that need to interact with each other and with the environment *locally* or *remotely* to solve a particular problem in a coordinated manner.

In the case of local communication, many mobile agent systems provide mechanisms for it, either using some sort of meeting abstraction as initially proposed by Telescript [Boehm and Basili (2000)], event notification for group communication [Lange and Oshima (1998); Baumann *et. al.* (1998)], or, more recently, tuple spaces [Cabri *et. al.* (1998); Picco *et. al.* (1999)].

Although some researchers argue that remote communication is not as important as the local one, remote inter-agent communication is also a fundamental facility in mobile agent systems because in some cases remote communication can not be avoided. Remote Procedure Call (RPC) and Remote Method Invocation (RMI), which are action-oriented, are generally adopting a synchronous communication model [Morreale (1998)]. Using RPC/RMI, an agent is able to call any public method of another agent or the mobile agent platform. In addition, many works focusing on developing inter-agent communication languages at a higher semantic level for knowledge sharing and knowledge exchanging, such as KQML [Finin *et. al.* (1994); Yannis Labrou and Tim Finin (1997)] and FIPA ACL [URL-1], have been proposed.

Usually, message passing is adopted for communications at the underlying layer and more complex mechanism aforementioned can be easily built on top of message passing. Although inter-process messaging has been a cliché in distributed systems research, agent mobility raises a number of new challenges, such as agent tracking and message routing, in designing message delivery mechanism for reliable and efficient communications between mobile agents. Cao and et al. gives a brief overview of the existing efforts on designing protocols for mobile agent communications and presents a 3D model as a basis for evaluating and designing mobile agent message delivery protocols at the same time [Cao *et. al.* (2002)].

21.3.1.3 *Security*

Mobile agent technology is helpful in the creation of scalable, dynamic, distributed applications and in that respect it has obvious advantages over conventional technologies. However, it may increase performance overheads and pose security concerns. This is critical, as the perception of the practicality of mobile agent technology hinges upon issues of its stability and security. Security is an issue because a visited mobile agent host must be defended against badly programmed or malicious foreign agents and on the other hand, programmers have to protect their agents from unknown sites [Morreale (1998)].

A survey has been published on the risks associated with the utilization of mobile agents and available security techniques for protecting mobile agents and hosts [Michael S. Greenberg et. al. (1998)]. Current research on secure agent systems has concentrated on protecting mobile agent platforms or servers against mobile hostile agents [Karnik and Tripathi (2001)]. The basic mechanisms to support security for a mobile agent host are *Identification*, which means each agent must be identified as coming from an authorized user, and *Authentication* that guarantees a given identity is authenticated. Sandboxes, code signing [Rubin and Gee (1998)] and similar techniques are suitable technologies to apply security for systems executing mobile agents by restricting access to resources (preventing disk writes, for instance) and ensuring that the agents conform the security policies applied.

Another approach is to employ social enforcement mechanisms to punish the creators of harmful agents. If a server administrator can find out who is responsible for a malicious agent, then that person can be held accountable via social mechanisms (such as lawsuits). In practice some combination of social and physical enforcement of server security will be useful. Protecting mobile agents from being attacked by mobile-agent-systems is even harder. To avoid eavesdropping and modification to the protected agents when transferring, possible solutions used are Data Integrity and Authentication techniques or, more specifically, Cryptography. Another three approaches are proposed to protect a mobile agent from the host it is executing on: limited blackbox security, computing with encrypted functions, and cryptographic trace [Hefeeda and Bhargava (2001)]. Of course, all these mechanisms will place an even greater load upon mobile agent systems.

21.3.2 *Existing Mobile Agent Systems*

Many mobile agent systems have been proposed or developed in research laboratories or companies and most of them are powered by Java technology. Since the list is ever growing, readers can refer to http://mole.informatik.uni-stuttgart.de/mal/mal.html for detailed information. Here, we only briefly introduce some of the representative systems:

21.3.2.1 *Aglet*

Developed by IBM, Aglet may be the most widely used mobile agent system currently available. The term "aglet" meaning "lightweight agent" is a portmanteau word combining agent and applet. Essentially, Aglet is a mobile Java agent that supports the concepts of autonomous execution and dynamic routing on its itinerary [Lange and Oshima (1998)].

In the Aglet system, Aglets are Java objects that can migrate from one network or Internet node to another. The Aglet Server provides an environment for aglets to execute on and supports strong migration for agents. This means that an Aglet executing on one host can halt execution at any time it wishes, move to another host and resume execution. Agents communicate through the *proxy* which serves as shield that protects an agent form direct access to its public methods. The proxy also hides the true locations of agents, providing location transparency. Meanwhile, system security is provided by the java virtual machine (JVM) and an Aglet security manager which is responsible for checking whether an agent is allowed to access the file system.

21.3.2.2 *D'Agent (AgentTcl)*

D'Agent [Kotz *et. al.* (1997)] is a platform-independent mobile agent system from Dartmouth College. The mobile agent system is designed to support the use of TCL as the underlying scripting language to program the mobile agents, which operate across UNIX environments.

In D'Agent, the most important function, or command, is *agent_jump*. When an agent intends to migrate, it must call the *agent_jump*, which can automatically capture the complete state of the agent and sends this state information to the destination node. The agent platform of destination host will then start up an appropriate execution environment, such as a Tcl interpreter, load the state information into its execution environment, and restart the agent from the exact point at which it left off. From this perspective, D'Agent supports agent strong migration.

In D'Agent, resources are divided into two categories: *indirect resources* and *built-in resources*. Agents have access restriction over them so that MAP and other agents can be protected.

21.3.2.3 *Mole*

Mole [M. Straßer *et. al* (1996); Baumann (1998)] is the first mobile agent system developed in Java language. The first version came from the University of Stuttgart in 1995. Although the concept of "two types of migration" was initially proposed by Mole, it only supports weak mobility, that is, it suspends all threads belonging to an agent that calls a migrate command. A Mole system consists of a set of *locations* every of which is assigned a unique ID. One physical machine may contain several locations and a location can even be movable between machines. The provision of location transparency is supported through the use of DNS services. Mole implements several different types of low-level communication among agents including RPC/RMI and Messages.

21.3.2.4 *Voyager*

Voyager [URL-2] is a pure Java agent-enhanced Object Request Broker (ORB) developed by the ObjectSpace Company (now purchased by Recursion Software, Inc.). This product seeks to assist programmers in rapidly and easily creating state of the art distributed programs while providing a lot of flexibility and extensibility for the products that are being created with the Voyager system. It supports both traditional client-server model and agent-based architecture. Agents are treated as a special type of object in Voyager applications and a Java class "com.objectspace.voyager.mobility" is responsible for agent migration. A synchronized communication mechanism guarantees message delivery.

21.3.2.5 *Odyssey*

Odyssey is a Java-based mobile agent system created by General Magic. Odyssey is based on the concepts of Telescript [Boehm, B. and Basili, V. (2000)], a mobile language also developed by General Magic, and implements them by adding classes to the base Java library. In particular it adds the class *Agent*, which implements the idea of a mobile agent. Odyssey only supports weak mobility.

Reader can find an evaluation and comparison among the Aglets, Odyssey and Voyager in [Kiniry and Zimmerman (1997)]. An analysis of security issue of three mobile agent systems is addressed in [Fischmeister (2001)].

21.4 Mobile Agent Applications

Although it is still a comparatively new area, the mobile agent technology has high potential to provide alternative and often improved solutions for a wide range of distributed applications. In general, for almost every agent-application proposed, one can propose an alternative based on existing computing models or protocols. But by employing the mobile agent technology, we can build the desired applications more efficiently and flexibly. The mobile agent technologies can performance well in a wide range of fields, though the boundaries between these fields are somewhat fuzzy or even overlap. Early in 1999 [Milojicic (1999)] discussed mobile agent applications, but here we will discuss the applications with special attention to specific domains.

21.4.1 *Resource locating and information retrieval*

With the maturing of Internet technology, we can share and access files, pictures and forms of data more easily than ever, but this explosion of data is not unproblematic. For one thing, these resources are likely to be distributed in a variety of locations. For another, the sheer amount of raw data is always huge. The manual querying of servers is thus clearly impractical, giving rise to one of the most frequently proposed uses of mobile agents, to send them to execute on remote servers, particularly when the servers have more information than they can reasonably communicate to a client for processing and where they lack the necessary procedures to perform the desired processing themselves [Huhns and Singh (1997)].

To carry out these tasks, agents embedded with processing and filter rules and representing the interests of a user are dispatched onto the Internet, while the owner of the agent, he or she so desires, disconnects from the network. On reaching a remote site with large data source, the agent interacts with the server, acquiring desired data and filtering unnecessary data. After processing in one site, the agent will, if necessary, migrate to another. Finally, the mobile agent returns with a small but relevant result. This approach reduces communication costs, network traffic and application latency.

Glitho has provided a brief overview and a case study of mobile agent-based information retrieval [Glitho *et. al.* (2002)]. An optimization for dissemination of mobile agent is investigated in [Theilmann and Rothernel (2000)]. In application, the D'Agent is used primarily in distributed information retrieval application and an example is given in [Kotz (1997)].

21.4.2 *Distributed workflow management*

Workflow is a sequencing of tasks that must be performed in order to accomplish a specific goal. Workflow management refers to structural routing and tracking of information throughout an organization process (Workflow Management Coalition). In distributed systems, especially in the Internet, workflow is always dynamic because its lifetime appears relatively long and it involves multiple severs. This dynamic behavior requires the distributed workflow enactment engine to be able to stop the workflow in a consistent state, identify activities that are reversible or can be rolled back, modify the workflow to restart from the consistent recovery state as well as being able to reach the goal state taking into account the changes required by the workflow initiator [Marinescu (2001)] – to name just some of its tasks.

It is anticipated that the next generation workflow will employ agent-based technology [Singh and Huhns (1999)]. The use of mobile agents will improve workflow management because the mobility of an agent ties the servers involved more closely with each other and places activities performed in the workflow under concentrative control. Moreover, an agent's code can be modified in response to the dynamic requirements of the distributed workflow.

Acting as workflow manager, the mobile agent carries a multi-step task description from one site to another, interacting with the user at each site in order to carry out that user's part of the task. Detailed information is described in [Cai *et. al.* (1996)].

21.4.3 *Web server optimization and network management*

Currently, web servers are the main information provider on the Internet and their performance greatly influences the quality of Internet services, in particularly in terms of the two main performance measures: Quantity of Service and Quality of Service. One of the important criteria used by clients to evaluate the performance of web servers is *Average Response Time*. Frequently used techniques to reduce Average Response times include caching the most frequently requested files in server memory and maintaining load balance among clusters of servers. Mobile agents can be used to implement these mechanisms more flexibly and efficiently because they support a dynamic distribution of computation, control and management functions across a network. An agent could supervise a group of servers and migrate to each site to monitor QoS (Quality of Service) by analyzing the performance data and if necessary reconfigure the server to best achieve a set of performance-related objectives for the entire cluster [Marinescu (2001)].

QoS is also greatly affected by network management. As networks become ever larger and more complex, management paradigms fail to keep pace in areas such as security and dynamic-defined metrics [Gunter and Braun (2003)]. Specialists in the field have suggested that one answer to this problem is the greater use of mobile agents. They argue that the current evolution of intelligent and active networks in system and network management is based on mobile agent technology [Chen and Hu (2002)]. Their research result can be found in [Adwabkar and Vasudevan (2002); Bellavista *et. al.* (2000); Papavassiliou *et. al.* (2002);

Liotta *et. al.* (2002)]. In particular, Meer and et al. present a framework for QoS management based on mobile agents in IP networks. Under this framework, agents realize a dynamic QoS management strategy on behalf of the customer.

21.4.4 *Distributed databases*

Mobile agent technology was applied to distributed database systems almost as soon as it was invented. Benefits from this application are often used to demonstrate the merits of mobile agent technology. No longer must an application access remote resources. Instead of requesting huge amounts of data to be transmitted over a network to the site on which the user resides, mobile agents carrying a user's instructions are sent to the remote site where raw data is located. After filtering and processing data on that site, mobile agents return with desired results that are much smaller in size. This saves on bandwidth and may even decrease response times. A "DBMS-Aglet" framework for Web database access comprised of a set of Java based mobile agents that cooperate to support Web database connectivity is addressed in [Stavros Papastavrou et. al. (2000)]. The article also points out that the mobile agent approach is especially efficient in a slow, expensive network system. At the same time, mobile agent is utilized for administration of multiple DBMS servers [Takahashi and Kavalan (1998)].

21.4.5 *Distributed system control/synchronization*

The deployment of a large-scale ubiquitous computing system like the Internet naturally requires mechanisms that can manage shared distributed resources and application collaboration over a wide-area, fault-prone network. Mobile agents can play an active role in these kinds of distributed control functions (such as checkpointing, load sharing, distributed mutual exclusion and replication) as it autonomously roams the network, gathering scattered information and carrying out appropriate action as necessary. By using mobile agents, the end-user can regard the entire network and any terminal attached to it as one large virtual host. The end-user does not need to care how or where the data and applications are stored. All that remains is to delegate tasks to the mobile application agents and dispatch them. Mobile control agents are in charge of the entire process of resource management and application collaboration and can ameliorate even fundamental difficulties within distributed systems.

Even within a distributed system such as the Internet, synchronization is problematic. In [Cao *et. al.* (2002)], a framework for coordinating servers that uses cooperating mobile agents was proposed. This would separate server site functionality from the operations of maintaining the logical relationship between group members and providing the desired level of performance. This framework which exploits a collection of autonomous, cooperating mobile agents makes it a simple matter to implement approaches such as distributed mutual exclusion and deadlock detection, helping to make server deployment less complex and more flexible. The use of mobile agents allows us to provide clear and useful abstractions because it allows us to separate different concerns.

Another problem within dynamic distributed systems is transient errors. As it can be eliminated by using rollback error recovery, mobile agents can assist in this process by implementing a flexible and adaptive checkpoint and rollback algorithm, incurring lower communication overheads compared to the message-based algorithms [Cao *et. al.* (2001)].

21.4.6 *Parallel computing*

Although parallel computing has long been an active area of research, integrating mobile agent technology into Internet parallel computing is still appealing especially for its flexibility. As the Internet emerges as a great congregation of supercomputing resources, some applications run largely in a "brute-force parallel search model". This model means that one machine maintains a pool of parallel tasks that are usually huge and dispatches these tasks to other participants on demand. This avoids the inflexibility that would arise from binding tasks to a pre-defined set of stationary computing resources and would allow users to declare their applications as mobile agents that roam on the network to find servers to run [Xu and Wims (2000)]. Parallel computing has been implemented by combining Java mobile agent technology and the Web [Panayiotou *et. al.* (1999); Evripidou *et. al.* (2002)]. The agents that utilize Java multithreading can travel to any Web site to perform their tasks cooperatively and finally pass the result back to the original launcher. Experiments comparing mobile agents with other parallel processing solutions [Silva *et. al.* (1999)] have produced promising results.

21.4.7 *Mobile computing*

The trend towards wireless communications, along with advances in laptop and notebook computer technology has revealed to professionals the benefits of having their electronic work available at any place and any time and spurred a growing demand for mobile and nomadic computing. For several reasons, however, it is difficult to develop distributed applications that make effective use of networked resources from a mobile platform. First, mobile computers do not have a permanent connection into the network and are often disconnected for long periods of time. Second, when the computer is connected, the connection often has low bandwidth and high latency and is prone to sudden failures, such as when a physical obstruction blocks the signal from a cellular modem. Third, since the mobile computer may be forced to use different transmission channels depending on its physical location, the performance of its network connection can vary dramatically from one session to another.

In short, any distributed application that works on a mobile platform must deal with adverse network conditions [Robert Gray et. al. (1996)]. In these kinds of mobile environments, mobile agents are natural candidates for the development of distributed applications. Unlike traditional client-server computing, a mobile agent can continue its work even when the mobile computer is disconnected. The mobile agent's on-site execution and its disconnected execution both allow the more efficient utilization of expensive wireless bandwidth. For example, an application that uses mobile agents to build a framework for resource management in wireless network is introduced in [JYe *et. al.* (2002)].

21.4.8 *Internet routing*

Routing – ever more vital as the Internet becomes increasingly complex – refers to the activity of telling incoming datagrams which link to use to continue their travel towards the destination network node. Any scheme for managing routing across a network, especially a wireless one, has to be flexible enough to adapt to continuous and unpredictable changes in three dimensions: overall density, node-to-node topology and user patterns [Kramer *et. al.* (1999)]. Mobile agent technology can satisfy the request of active routing by roaming in the network, gathering information about the topology of the system, and updating routing tables stored on the nodes. Caro and Dorigo proposed a mobile agent based routing algorithm for communication networks [Caro and Dorigo (1997)], presenting experimental results that argue against static and adaptive state-of-the-art routing algorithms and support the performance and robustness of the mobile agent approach. Hild introduces an application that uses mobile agents for multicast routing where agents travel autonomously in arbitrary networks and configure a multicast network equivalent to the minimum spanning tree between the sender and the receivers [Hild and Bischof (1997)].

21.4.9 *Peer-to-Peer computing*

The peer-to-peer computing model has offered us a compelling and intuitive way to directly find and share resources. In a decentralized P2P network, querying for resources generates an enormous amount of traffic. Each peer in the network searches for resources by establishing multiple connections to others in the network. Most of the time, these queries are redundant and yield few or no useful results. Mobile agent technology can ease this situation by having the search done locally in each peer instead of sending it over the network. Since a mobile agent stores all the required data within itself, the size of the mobile agent can change dynamically as the dispatcher wishes. Moreover, mobile agents will continue to search even if the original peer it started is temporarily offline. In this respect, it is similar to a mobile computing environment. In addition, a mobile agent can travel to nodes previously unknown to its original peers, and in this way discover more resources. After the mobile agent has finished its search, it can return to its original peer with the result, or wait for it to come back online. Dune proposes a mobile agent based solution that allows dynamic network resource discovery [URL-3] and Chen applies mobile agents to e-Commerce on P2P networks [Chen and Yeager (2003)].

Peers that mobile agents visit will benefit from the incoming "guests" as well. Mobile agents can exchange with peers their knowledge about resources that are available in other nodes which they have visited. Of course, peers also have the right to reject mobile agents if they do not have sufficient computing resources to accommodate them or if they suspect the agents are malicious. As mobile agents can clone and distribute themselves to multi directions in the network, they greatly increase the quantity of resources which can be discovered. Furthermore, having multiple agents working in parallel is more fault-tolerant as even if a number of them are lost some results will be provided.

21.4.10 *Grid computing*

"Grid Computing" refers to computing in a distributed networked environment in which computing and data resources are located throughout a wide area network such as the Internet [Foster and Kesselman (1999)]. Because the Internet is geographically distributed, managing access to computing and resources in the Internet is a complex and time-consuming task. This makes it difficult for researchers and practitioners to make decisions about which systems to use, where the data should reside for a particular application domain, how to migrate the data to the point of computation (or vice versa), and what data rates are required to satisfy a particular application. Consequently, Grid technology must undertake the task of enabling seamless integration of computing systems and clusters, data storage, networks and sophisticated analysis and visualization software.

Grid Computing thus calls for a steady, reliable computing source with high performance, selective migration of data or computation, especially as mobile users present the Grid with new challenges. Mobile agent techniques would appear to be a natural choice for Grid Computing because their inherent portability allows them to transparently and efficiently handle the distribution of tasks in a heterogeneous environment. In such a system, one typical use of a mobile agent is to act as a coordinator. The client sends the request to the mobile agent, which maintains lists of all kinds of resources in the systems and their correlative characters. The agent will look for computing resources automatically and pass the request to the most appropriate one. After the computing job is finished, the agent will also send the result to the client. In the grid computing environment, agents can thus offer different roles, be organized into regional or national dynamic "groups", and be able to migrate between groups to support load balancing, metacomputing, service discovery and service management, ontology integration, network monitoring and characterization, data selection and migration, and so on.

The mobile agent can not only help the Grid build an infrastructure supporting low level computation, but also facilitate and enable information sharing and coordination at higher application levels. Some papers have revealed their contributions. Kuang and et al., for example, describe a mobile agent based environment for the distributed solution of iterative grid-based application [Hairong Kuang et. al. (2002)]. Currently only some of the Grid applications employ agent technology such as service and resource management [Corsava and Getov (2003); Cao *et. al.* (2002)], query optimization and even bioinformatics [Moreau et. al. (2003)], but in most areas we believe that mobile agent technology will also performance well.

21.4.11 *Security*

Intrusion Detection System (IDS) is an important, proven Internet security tool that is used to detect malicious activities targeting protected network servers or resources. As observed in [Kruegel and Toth (2002)], however, with the emergence of mobile devices it faces a challenge. Mobile agents can still be employed within an IDS. One typical way is to cast the network nodes hierarchy as mobile agents [Mell and McLarnon (1999)]. Wrapped as mobile agents, IDS components automatically evade possible attacker locations, eliminate single points of failure and resurrect destroyed components. If an attacker takes out a certain mobile agent platform, the remaining agents estimate the location of the attacker and automatically avoid those networks. Killed agents are resurrected by a group of backups that retain all or partial state information. Performance evaluation of IDS using mobile agent technology is discussed in [Jansen *et. al.* (2000)]. It should be noted, however, that while mobile agents are scalable and robust for intrusion detection policy updates against CORBA and RMI, they themselves are prone to attacks by other agents and hosts [Gangadharan and Hwang (2001)]. Readers can refer section *21.3.1.3* for solutions.

21.4.12 *Electric commerce*

Electronic Commerce is a rapidly growing segment of the Internet and an important aspect of modern globalized business. In this process, consumers seeking merchandise at a desired price and quality apply proprietary algorithms to others' proprietary data [Huhns and Singh (1997)] in an environment that is trusted by all participants. Alternatively, electronic commerce may involve two or more companies negotiating through a network. In both the B2C and B2B models, intelligent mobile agents are the technology of choice because they can automatically process the vast amount of data that is available on the Internet and thus greatly decrease user interaction times. [Dasgupta *et. al.* (1999)] demonstrated the feasibility of using mobile agent technology for e-commerce by implementing a networked electronic trading system based on Aglets. In their MAgNET system, customers dispatch mobile agents to various suppliers, where they negotiate orders and deliveries, returning to the buyer with their best deals for approval. Mobile agent technology has also been used in Internet-oriented auction systems in which agents travel to a specified web server and participate in auctions on the user's behalf [Sandholm and Huai (2000)].

21.4.13 *Web services*

Internet services are evolving into "Web Services", a simple but still fuzzy concept wherein people or even other deployed services can publish, locate, and invoke self-contained, self-describing, modular applications across the web. Most of the features which make Web services popular, including well-encapsulation, conservation of enterprise bandwidth, reduction in latency, support for dynamic deployment and improved decision support workflow, can be implemented by mobile agent technology.

Web services and mobile agent technology can be integrated through two main approaches. One approach, when serving a huge number of service requests, is to develop or encapsulate web services into mobile agents [URL-4; Buhler and Vidal (2000)] so that a service provider can reproduce and distribute its copies to other servers in the Internet dynamically. Since clients refer to a close deploy of web service near their side, this approach is also suitable when clients either frequently request a service or request a complicated transaction involving several services. In both situations, distributed Web service components, which can be discovered on the Web by their semantic annotations, move to any target platform and perform their tasks locally and cooperatively by taking advantage of the mobile agents. The challenge to use agents endows service components with not only mobility but also their learning ability while performing tasks locally. Beyond that, mobile web services will also improve service discovery among the plethora of available services and keep business interests of the service provider when being invited to execute in the client side.

The other approach to integrate Web service and mobile agent technology is from the service users' point of view. Dispatching mobile agents as delegates is a good option for mobile users who are unable to maintain a permanent connection to the Internet or suffer from limited bandwidth. Mobile agents can autonomously travel on behalf of the user visiting several service brokers in search of the most suitable web services [Funfrocken (1997); Padovitz *et. al.* (2003)].

Obviously, agents allow not only service component mobility but also user mobility. Furthermore, the intelligence embedded in mobile agents encourages them to learn and react while executing services locally.

21.5. Conclusions

Mobile agent technology has been one of the fastest growing areas of information technology in the last decade. While still in the early stage of development, this technology has nevertheless had a great impact on the design of distributed applications, especially in Internet computing.

Although there is as yet no killer application for mobile agent technology and it does not always outperform other solutions [Spalink *et. al.* (2000)], it is already clear that, in certain application domains, mobile agents have offered or will offer superior solutions and that, just as Object-Oriented technology was adopted in the absence of a killer application [Milojicic (1999)], mobility too will be widely adopted, fully justifying the plea made in the film *Contact*: "Keep Our Interests Mobile!"

Acknowledgment

This work is partially supported by the Hong Kong Polytechnic University under the ICRG grants G-YD63 and A-PD54 and National Grand Fundamental Research 973 Program of China under grant No. 2002CB312002.

Bibliography

Adwabkar S. and Vasudevan V. (2002). Agile Systems Manager for Enterprise Wireless Networks. LNCS 2496, Springer-Verlag, Berlin, Heidelberg, pp. 62-76, 2002.

Baumann J., Hohl F., Rothermel K. and Straßer M. (1998). Mole- Concepts of a Mobile Agent System. WWW Journal Special Issue on Applications and Techniques of Web Agents, Vol. 1(3), Baltzer Science Publishers, pp. 123-137, 1998.

Bellavista Paolo, Corradi Antonio and Stefanelli Cesare. (2000). An Integrated Management Environment for Network Resource and Services. IEEE Journal on Selected Areas in Communications, Vol. 18(5), pp. 676-685, May, 2000.

Boehm, B. and Basili, V. (2000). Gaining Intellectual Control of Software Development. IEEE Computer, Vol. 33(5), pp. 27-33, May, 2000.

Cabri G., Leonardi L. and Zambonelli F. (1998). How to Coordinate Internet Applications based on Mobile Agents. In Proceedings of the IEEE 7th International Workshops on Enabling Technologies: Infrastructure for Collaborative Enterprises (WETICE), California, USA, pp. 104-109, June, 1998.

Cai Ting, Gloor Peter A., and Nog Saurab. (1996). DartFlow: A workflow management system on the web using transportable agents. Technical Report PCS-TR96-283, Deptartment of Computer Science, Dartmouth College, May, 1996.

Cao Jiannong, Chan G.H., Jia Weijia and Dillion Tharam S. (2001). Checkpointing and Rollback of wide-Area Distributed Applications Using Mobile Agents. In Proceedings of 15th Intl. Parallel and Distributed Processing Symposium, San Francisco, California, USA, pp. 1-6, April 23-27, 2001.

Cao Jiannong, Wang Xianbing, Lo Siu and Das Sajal K. (2002). A Consensus Algorithm for Synchronous Distributed Systems Using Mobile Agent. In Proceedings of the 2002 Pacific Rim International Symposium on Dependable Computing, Tskuba, Japan, pp. 229-236, December, 2002.

Cao Jiannong, Feng Xinyu, Lu Jian and Das Sajal K. (2002). Mailbox-Based Scheme for Mobile Agent Communications. IEEE Computer, Vol. 35(9), pp. 54-60, September, 2002.

Cao Junwei, Spooner D.P., Turner J.D., Jarvis S.A., Kerbyson D.J., Saini S.and Nudd G.R. (2002). Agent-based Resource Management for Grid Computing. In Proceedings of the 2nd IEEE/ACM International Symposium on Cluster Computing and the Grid, Berlin, Germany, pp. 323-324, May 21-24, 2002.

Caro Gianni Di and Dorigo M. (1997). AntNet: A Mobile Agents Approach to Adaptive Routing. Technical Report 97-12, IRIDIA, Universite Libre de Bruxelles, 1997.

Castelfranchi C. (1995). Guarantees for Autonomy in Cognitive Agent Architecture. In Wooldridge, M. and Jennings, N. R. (ed.): Intelligent Agents: Agent Theories, Architectures, and Languages, Springer-Verlag, Heidelberg, Germany, pp. 56–70, 1995.

Chen Rita Yu and Yeager Bill. (2003). Java Mobile Agents on Project JXTA Peer-to-Peer Platform. In Proceedings of the 36th Hawaii International Conference on System Sciences (HICSS'03), Hawaii, USA, pp. 282-291, Jan. 6-9, 2003.

Chen W.S.E. and Hu C.L. (2002). A Mobile Agent-Based Active Network Architecture for Intelligent Network Control. Information Sciences, Vol. 141(1-2), pp. 3-35, March, 2002.

Corsava Sophia and Getov Vladimir. (2003). Agent-Based Service Management in Large Datacentres and Grids. In Proceedings of the 3rd IEEE/ACM International Symposium on Cluster Computing and the Grid, Tokyo, Japan, pp. 633-640, May 12-15, 2003.

Dasgupta P., Narasimhan, Moser Louise E. and Melliar-Smith P. M. (1999). MAgNET: Mobile Agents for Networked Electronic Trading. IEEE Transactions on Knowledge and Data Engineering, Vol. 11(4), pp. 509-525, July/August, 1999.

Decina, M. and Trecordi V. (1997). Convergence of Telecommunications and Computing to Networking Models for Integrated Services and Applications. Proceedings of the IEEE, Vol. 85(12), pp. 1887 -1914, December, 1997.

Evripidou P., Panayiotou C., Samaras G. and Pitoura E. (2002). The PaCMAn Metacomputer: Parallel Computing with Java Mobile Agents. Future Generation Computer Systems Journal, Elsevier, Special Issue on Java in High Performance Computing, Vol. 18(2), pp. 265-280, October, 2002.

Finin T., Fritzson R., McKay D. and McEntire R. (1994). KQML as an Agent Communication Language. In Proceedings of the 3rd Intl. Conference on Information and Knowledge Management, Gaithersburg, USA, pp. 456-463, November 29-December 2, 1994.

Fischmeister S., Vigna G. and Kemmerer R. (2001). Evaluating the Security of Three Java-Based Mobile Agent Systems. In Proceedings of 5th International Conference on Mobile Agents, Atlanta, USA, pp. 31-41, December 2-4, 2001.

Foster I. and Kesselman C. (1999) (eds.). The Grid Blueprint for a New Computing Infrastructure. Morgan Kaufmann Publishers, San Francisco, USA, 1999.

Funfrocken Stefan (1997). How to Integrate Mobile Agents into Web Servers. In Proceedings of 6th Workshop on Enabling Technologies: Infrastructure for Collaborative Enterprises, Cambridge, USA, pp. 94 -99, June 18-20, 1997.

Gangadharan M. and Hwang Kai. (2001). Intranet Security with Micro-Firewalls and Mobile Agents for Proactive Intrusion Response. In Proceedings of 2001 International Conference on Computer Networks and Mobile Computing, Los Alamitos, USA, pp. 325-332, October 16-19, 2001.

Glitho Roch H., Olougouna Edgar and Pierre Samuel. (2002). Mobile Agents and Their Use for Information Retrieval: A Brief Overview and an Elaborate Case Study. IEEE Network, Vol. 16(1), pp. 34-41, January/February, 2002.

Gray Robert, Kotz David, Nog Saurab, Rus Daniela and Cybenko George. (1996). Mobile Agents for Mobile Computing. Technical Report PCS-TR96-285, Computer Science Department, Dartmouth College, May, 1996.

Greenberg Michael S., Byington Hennifer C. and Holding Theophany. (1998). Mobile Agents and Security. IEEE Communications, Vol. 36(7), pp. 76-85, July, 1998.

Guilfoyle C. and Warner E. (1994). Intelligent Agents: the New Revolution in Software. Technical Report, OVUM Limited, London, UK, 1994.

Gunter Manuel and Braun Torsten. (2003). Internet Service Monitoring with Mobile Agents. IEEE Network, Vol. 16(3), pp. 22-29, May/June, 2003.

Harrison Colin G., Chess David M. and Kershenbaum Aaron. (1994). Mobile Agents: Are They a Good Idea?. IBM Research Report RC 19887(88456), 1994.

Hefeeda M. and Bhargava B. (2001). On Mobile Code Security. Technical Report CERIAS TR 2001-46, Purdue University, October, 2001.

Hild Stefan G. and Bischof Jorg H. (1997). Agent-based Multicast Routing. IBM Resarch Report, RZ 2975(#93021), 1997.

Huhns Michael N. and Singh Munindar P. (1997). Agents on the Web. IEEE Internet Computing, Vol. 1(5), pp. 78-79, September/October, 1997.

Jansen W., Mell P., Karygiannis T. and Marks D. (2000). Mobile Agents in Intrusion Detection and Response. In Proceedings of 12th Annual Canadian Information Technology Security Symposium, Ottowa, Canada, 2000.

Jennings Nicholas R. and Wooldridge Michael J. (1998). Applications of Intelligent Agents. M. N. Jennings, M.J. Wooldridge (ed.): Agent Technology: Foundations, Applications and Markets, Springer-Verlag, Heidelberg, Germany, pp. 3-28, 1998.

Karnik N. and Tripathi A. (2001). Security in the Ajanta Mobile Agent System. Software: Practice and Experience, Vol. 31(4), pp. 301–329, April, 2001.

Kiniry Joseph and Zimmerman Daniel. (1997). A Hands-on Look on Java Mobile Agents. IEEE Internet Computing, Vol. 1(4), pp. 21-30, July/August, 1997.

Kotz, D., Gray, R., Nog, S., Rus, D., Chawla, S. and Cybenko, G. (1997). AGENT TCL: Targeting the Needs of Mobile Computers. IEEE Internet Computing, Vol. 1(4), pp. 58-67, July/August, 1997.

Kramer Kwindla Hultman, Minar Nelson and Maes Pattie. (1999). Tutorial: Mobile Software Agents for Dynamic Routing. ACM SIGMOBILE Mobile Computing and Communications Review archive, Vol. 3(2), pp. 12-16, April, 1999.

Kruegel Christopher and Toth Thomas. (2002). Flexible, Mobile Agent Based Intrusion Detection for Dynamic Networks. European Wireless, Italy, February, 2002.

Kuang Hairong, Bic L.F. and Dillencourt M.l B. (2002). Iterative Grid-Based Computing Using Mobile Agents. In Proceedings of the 2nd International Conference on Parallel Processing, British Columbia, Canada, pp. 109-117, August 18-21, 2002.

Labrou Yannis and Finin Tim. (1997). A Proposal for a New KQML Specification. Technical Report CS97 -03, CSEE Dept, UMBC, 1997.

Lange D. B. and Oshima M. (1998). Programming and Deploying Java Mobile Agents with Aglets, Addison-Wesley, USA, August, 1998.

Liotta A., Pavlou George and Knight G. (2002). Exploiting Agent Mobility for Large-Scale Network Monitoring. IEEE Network, Vol. 16(3), pp. 7-21, May/June, 2002.

Luís M. Silva, Victor Batista, Paulo Martins and G. Soares. (1999). Using Mobile Agents for Parallel Processing. In Proceedings of International Symposium on Distributed Objects and Applications, Edinburgh, U.K., pp. 34-43, September 5-7, 1999.

Marinescu Dan C. (2001). Reflections on Qualitative Attributes of Mobile Agents for Computational, Data, and Service Grids. In Proceedings of the 1st IEEE/ACM Intl. Symposium on Cluster Computing and the Grid, Brisbane, Australia, pp. 442-449, May 15-18, 2001.

Mell P. and McLarnon M. (1999). Mobile Agent Attack Resistant Distributed Hierarchical Intrusion Detection Systems. In Proceedings of the 2nd International Workshop on Recent Advances in Intrusion Detection, Perdue University, September 7-9, 1999.

Milojicic, D. (1999). Trend Wars- Mobile Agent Applications. IEEE Concurrency, Vol. 7(3), pp. 80 –90, July/September, 1999.

Morreale P. (1998). Agents on the Move. IEEE Spectrum, Vol. 35(4), pp. 34-41, April, 1998.

Moreau Luc and et. al. (2003). On the Use of Agents in a BioInformatics Grid. In Proceedings of the 3rd IEEE/ACM International Symposium on Cluster Computing and the Grid, Tokyo, Japan, pp. 653-660, May 12-15, 2003,.

Nwana H.S. and Ndumu D.T. (1998). A Brief Introduction to Software Agent Technology. M. N. Jennings and M.J. Wooldridge (ed.): Agent Technology: Foundations, Applications and Markets, Springer-Verlag, Heidelberg, Germany, pp. 29-47, 1998.

Padovitz Amir, Krishnaswamy Shonali and Loke Seng Wai. (2003). Towards Efficient and Smart Selection of Web Services. In Proceedings of International Workshop on Web Services and Agent-Based Engineering (AAMS'03), Melbourne, Australia, July 14-15, 2003.

Panayiotou C., Samaras George, Pitoura Evaggelia and Evripidou P. (1999). Parallel Computing Using Java Mobile Agents. In Proceedings of 25th Euromicro Conference, Milan, Italy, Vol. 2, pp. 430-437, September 8-10, 1999.

Papastavrou Stavros, Samaras George and Pitoura E. (2000). Mobile Agent for World Wide Web Distributed Database Access. IEEE Transactions on Knowledge and Data Engineering, Vol. 12(5), pp. 802-820, September/October, 2000.

Papavassiliou S., Puliafito A., Tomarchio O. and Ye Jian (2002). Mobile Agent-Based Approach for Efficient Network Management and Resource Allocation. IEEE Journal on Selected Areas in Communications, Vol. 20(4), pp.858-872, May, 2002.

Paul A. Buhler and José M. Vidal. (2000). Toward the Synthesis of Web Services and Agent Behaviors. In Proceedings of the First Intl. Workshop on Challenges in Open Agent Systems (AAMAS'02), Bologna, Italy, pp. 25-29, July 15-19, 2002.

Pham A. and Karmouch A. (1998). Mobile Software Agent: An Overview. IEEE Communications, Vol. 36(7), pp. 26-37, July, 1998.

Picco G.P., Murphy A.L. and Roman G.C. (1999). LIME: Linda Meets Mobility. In Proceedings of the 21st International Conference on Software Engineering, Los Angeles, USA, pp. 368-377, May 16-22, 1999.

Rubin Aviel D. and Gee Daniel E. (1998). Mobile Code Security. IEEE Internet Computing, Vol. 2(6), pp. 30-34, November/December, 1998.

Sandholm T. and Huai Qianbo (2000). Nomad: Mobile Agent System for an Internet-Based Auction House. IEEE Internet Computing, Vol. 4(2), pp. 80-86, March/April, 2000.

Sargent P. (1992). Back to School for a Brand New ABC. The Guardian, March 12, 1992.

Shoham Y. (1997). An Overview of Agent-Oriented Programming. J. Bradshaw (ed.): Software Agents, AAAI Press/MIT Press, Menlo Park, California, USA, pp. 271-290, 1997.

Singh M.P. and Huhns M. N. (1999). Multiagent Systems for Workflow. International Journal of Intelligent Systems in Accounting, Finance and Management, Vol. 8, pp.105-117, 1999.

Spalink T., Hartman John H. and Gibson Garth A. (2000). A Mobile Agent's Effects on File Service. IEEE Concurrency, Vol. 8(2), pp. 62-69, April/June, 2000.

Straßer M., Baumann J. and Hohl F. (1996). Mole- A Java Based Mobile Agent System. M. Muhlauser(ed.): Special Issues in Object-Oriented Programming: Workshop Reader of the 10th European Conference on Object-Oriented Programming (ECOOP'96), pp. 327-334, July, 1996.

Takahashi Hiroyuki and Kavalan Vasanthi. (1998). A Mobile Agent for Asynchronous Administration of Multiple DBMS Servers. In Proceedings of the 3rd IEEE International Workshop on Systems Management, Newport, Rhode Island, USA, pp. 32-33, April 22-24, 1998.

Theilmann Wolfgang and Rothernel Kurt. (2000). Optimizing the Dissemination of Mobile Agents for Distributed Information Filtering. IEEE Concurrency, Vol. 8(2), pp.53-61, April/June, 2000.

URL-1. http://www.fipa.org, FIPA ACL

URL-2. http://http://www.objectspace.com/, Voyager Core Technology User Guide.

URL-3. http://www.acm.org/sigs/sigecom/exchanges/volume_2_(01)/2.3-Dunne.pdf

URL-4. http://www.webservicesarchitect.com/content/articles/fou02.asp

Wooldridge Michael J. (2002). An Introduction to Multi-Agent Systems. John Wiley & Sons, Chichester, England, February, 2002.

Wooldridge Michael J., Jennings Nicholas R. (1995). Intelligent Agents: Theory and Practice. The Knowledge Engineering Review, Vol. 10(2), pp. 115-152, June, 1995.

Xu Cheng-Zhong and Wims Brian (2000). A Mobile Agent Based Push Methodology for Global Parallel Computing. Concurrency - Practice and Experience, Vol. 12(8), pp. 705-726, July, 2000.

Ye Jian, Hou Jiongkuan and Papavassiliou S. (2002). A Comprehensive Resource Management Framework for Next Generation Wireless Networks. IEEE Transactions on Mobile Computing, Vol. 1(4), pp. 249-264, October/December, 2002.

## CHAPTER 22

INTELLIGENT VIRTUAL AGENTS AND THE WEB

Themis Panayiotopoulos, Nikos Avradinis

Knowledge Engineering Lab, Department of Informatics, University of Piraeus
80 Karaoli & Dimitriou Street, 185 34 Piraeus, Greece
E-mail: {themisp, avrad}@unipi.gr

Recent advances in computer graphics technology have led to the introduction of virtual reality technology to a wider audience. The relatively new trend of intelligent agents was quickly applied to virtual reality systems, producing a new research area, Intelligent Virtual Agents that is a meeting point for Artificial Intelligence and Virtual Reality. Nowadays, Intelligent Virtual Agent applications have started appearing on the web, aiming to take advantage of the potential of the new medium. In this paper we attempt to give a concise presentation of this fascinating new research area, providing a brief historical overview and discussing essential concepts related to IVA's, Web 3D and their combination.

22.1 Introduction

The last fifteen years have been a period of significant change and evolution in the field of human-computer interaction. The introduction of multimedia and hypermedia technology that took place in the late '80s and its wide expansion in the early '90s presented computer professionals with a new set of tools, allowing them to produce better applications, both in terms of usability and aesthetic quality.

When Virtual Reality became available as a technology, the user was no longer treated as an external viewer. He/she had actually become part of the system, an autonomous presence in the virtual world. He/she was free to navigate around the virtual environment, move in three dimensions, interact with objects, look behind or under them and examine the world from different viewpoints, alter it, communicate with other avatars or even virtual agents.

On the same time, Intelligent Agent technologies have been rapidly emerging since the beginning of the 1990s. Intelligent agents, autonomous or semi-autonomous systems that take decisions and perform tasks in complex, dynamically changing environments, revolutionized the field of AI with their novel approach towards intelligence.

Further scientific developments and the experimentation of the researchers have driven to the emergence of Intelligent Virtual Agents, (IVAs), a new area where HCI, AI and VR, are tried together in an effort to produce believable dynamic and interactive 3D worlds.

Today, Intelligent Virtual Environments, (IVEs), are employed in a variety of areas, mainly relating to simulation, entertainment, and education. Sophisticated simulated environments concerning open urban spaces, building interiors, and streets can significantly aid in application areas such as architectural design, civil engineering, traffic and crowd control. IVEs have set new standards in computer-based entertainment, through outstanding examples of computer games involving large, life-like virtual worlds with imaginative scenarios, active user participation in the plot of an interactive drama, virtual story-telling, and many other areas where immersion and believability are key factors.

Similarly to practically every other computer technology, IVEs soon found their way towards the World Wide Web. Although still at an infancy stage, Web-based IVEs seem to be one of the research areas that will keep the academic world engaged for the near future.

In this chapter we first present a short historical overview of the field of Web 3D technology and describe how it came to be integrated with Intelligent Agents, creating the notion of Web based IVA's. Some basic principles of IVA's are presented, followed by a showcase of past and present Web 3D applications.

The combined field of Web-based IVA's is then presented, followed by the presentation of a generic architecture. We finally make some concluding remarks on the present and future of Web IVA technology.

22.2 The Emergence of Web 3D

After its introduction in the early nineties, the World Wide Web quickly found its way towards an enormous global audience, evolving into a new, radical and multi-modal means of communication. Commercialization of the groundbreaking young medium did not take long, and the Web soon turned into a new, fiercely competitive market where each player tried to attract potential customers by putting up a good show.

Every new technology that could make an impression and catch the eye of the public had to be ported into the Web, so that it could be incorporated into commercial sites. Animation, sound and video soon became important elements for most websites and the necessary technology to seamlessly integrate them with the textual content of web pages was developed.

In the same spirit, the rapid evolution of desktop 3D technology over the past decade and its bright prospects for the development of visually compelling applications could not have escaped the attention of the Web community. With Virtual Reality having become one of the new trendy catchphrases in the computer world, everybody wanted to have "something Virtual" or "something 3D" on their websites. A first answer to the increasing demand of the web community for 3D graphics came in 1997, with the standardization of VRML 2.0 [ISO/IEC (1997)], initially presented as a draft in 1996 and a result of earlier attempts to establish a standard for web 3D graphics originating in 1994.

VRML was widely accepted by the community, as it had some very attractive characteristics. It was cross-platform, not only available to sophisticated high-end graphic servers but also humble, end-user computers.

As a public, international standard it was open to everybody, requiring no royalties to be paid. It was based on a text format so there were no special tools required to develop, and it was also a fairly easy language to work with.

Designed with the web in mind from the beginning, VRML could be embedded into HTML pages in a way not much different to video or other, more conventional media. VRML browsers were made available to the public, either as standalone applications or plug-ins to popular Web browsers, with CosmoPlayer [Computer Associates, (2000)], then distributed by Silicon Graphics, probably being the most popular one. Other web-based virtual reality technologies, like QuickTime VR, were also available at the time but VRML was by far accepted as the future.

Fig. 22.1 Screenshot from CosmoPlayer featuring Chomp!, a sample VR application developed by SGI.

The hype about Web-based 3D graphics and VRML soon started disappearing. Low average network speed made it almost impossible to download any virtual world with decent graphics and a considerable size.

Even when fast networks were available, the hardware requirements in order to manipulate a complex virtual environment modeled in an interpreted language were too high, excluding the mass public from the use of the new technology. Interaction was at best limited and inadequate to keep the user engaged for anything more than a few minutes.

The parallel progress of standalone 3D graphics and the gaming industry made their web counterparts look poor in comparison. The additional cease of support by Silicon Graphics, one of the key players in VRML technology, and the burst of the Internet bubble in the late nineties diminished the interest for Web 3D graphics, making it a toy for researchers and Web aficionados.

This temporary cease of evolution of VRML as well as its deficiencies when it came to interaction and behavioral control left the field open for new solutions for Web 3D to be presented, often by small and unknown companies. Representative examples are Java3D [Sun Microsystems], Adobe Atmosphere [Adobe Systems] and WildTangent [WildTangent Inc].

VRML is still a very important solution in the field-it is the oldest and more mature technology of all, and remains the only cross-platform international standard. Although the support of leading software companies was limited and the major browser and plug-in, CosmoPlayer, is not being supported anymore, alternative solutions from small companies have been presented, like Blaxxun [Blaxxun Technologies] and Cortona [Parallel Graphics].

Efforts to develop a new version of VRML are still active, as the Web3D Consortium is working on X3D [Web3DC], an integrated framework for graphics and multimedia on the web. However, X3D is still in a draft form and whether it will be accepted as a standard both by the academic and commercial world remains to be seen.

22.3 The Rise of Intelligent Agents

A few years before the advent of the World Wide Web another important new trend was emerging in the -quite stagnant at the time- field of Artificial Intelligence. The notion of intelligent agents appeared and agent-based approaches gained popularity to the expense of traditional AI techniques [Maes (1990), Woolridge & Jennings (1995)].

Combining intelligence with the potential for autonomy, proactivity and mobility, agents represented a new wave of innovation across an increasingly networked information world and were quickly embraced as a mainstream philosophy by the academic and business community.

These new, unconventional features of intelligent agents were quickly noticed by researchers both in the fields of virtual reality and artificial intelligence as particularly suitable for integration into virtual worlds.

Virtual Reality sounded high-tech, revolutionary and something coming out of a science fiction book, yet users would start losing their interest soon after they got over their initial enthusiasm for their first VR experience.

This was partly due to the fact that there was not much happening in virtual worlds. Visuals were impressive for the first time user, the sense of presence in a computer-generated graphical environment was compelling and watching fully three-dimensional humanoid avatars was a totally new experience for users compared to the TV-like, two-dimensional point of view they were used to.

However, there was something missing. Interaction with the environment was limited, and the avatars seemed more like dummies, aimlessly wandering around rather than behaving in a believable, human-like way. VR researchers realized they had to incorporate some sort of "brains" into their virtual humanoids, and agent technology seemed to fit like a glove.

On the other side, artificial intelligence was already a well-established field. With research work having been carried out for more than thirty years, several advanced techniques and algorithms had been presented and implemented.

The problem was that they had rarely been tested in real-like situations, and most implementations either worked in carefully selected domains or were mainly proof-of-concept, toy examples. Virtual worlds, being more realistic and adequately complex simulation environments seemed to provide the AI community with an ideal test bed to experiment on their new, agent-based techniques and algorithms.

The coupling of AI techniques with VR technology led to the emergence of a new breed of agents, which have become known as *Intelligent Virtual Agents* [Aylett and Cavazza, (2000)], inhabiting computer-generated worlds called *Intelligent Virtual Environments* [Aylett and Luck, (2000)].

22.4 The Basics of Intelligent Virtual Agents

So, let's recapitulate by providing a proper definition of Intelligent Virtual Agents (IVA's), borrowed from the call for the biennial IVA conference [IVA, (2003)], at the moment the most important forum for researchers in the field:

Intelligent Virtual Agents are autonomous, graphically embodied agents in an interactive virtual environment, able to interact intelligently with the environment, other agents, and human users.

Virtual worlds inhabited by IVA's should be able to support enhanced interaction capabilities, as well as provide effective graphical representation means, and are known as Intelligent Virtual Environments.

The term is quite generic and theoretically encompasses both 2D and 3D graphical representations. However, the use of the word "virtual" hints at 3D implementations, which will be the main focus of this discussion.

Although different researchers might have different views on what an Intelligent Virtual Agent exactly is, there are some commonly agreed characteristics [Franklin, (1997)].

First of all, an IVA should be embodied, visually represented in a graphical way, which should be consistent with its attributes as a conceptual entity. IVA's need not necessarily be humanoid; they can be mechanical [Prophet, (2001)], animal-like [Terzopoulos, (1994)] or even fictional entities [Aylett, Horrobin et al, (1999)].

The quality of the graphic model might also vary, from very realistic representations, like in [Kalra et at., (1998)] to more rough but easier to manipulate and less resource-consuming designs. In any case, however, they should be able to move in a convincing manner, similar to the way an equivalent real-world creature would move.

An IVA should also be situated, residing in a virtual world to which it is directly connected usually through a set of sensors, so that it can perceive events taking place in the environment and act accordingly.

It should be aware of its surroundings, able to recognize and manipulate objects, along with being capable to sense the presence of other agents and interact with them.

In addition to the above, an IVA should incorporate some sort of behavioral control. Intelligent behavior in virtual environments is a complex issue, comprising several functions such as communicating, sensing, learning, and reasoning on various levels of abstraction, which all have to be put together. Various approaches have been adopted, especially in respect to reasoning, ranging from high-level symbolic techniques [Lozano, Cavazza, Mead and Charles (2002), Avradinis and Aylett (2003)] to lower-level sub-symbolic approaches.

Although it is beyond the scope of the present discussion to go into greater detail, there are several other issues that have to be considered, such as autonomy, sociability, reactivity, action selection and goal generation. What is probably more important is the fact that the primary aim of researchers in the field is believability [Bates, (1994)], which could briefly be described as a measure of the degree to which an IVA and consequently, the virtual environment it is situated in, helps the user maintain an overall sense of presence.

Believability is different from realism—cartoon-like characters for example can be believable while at the same time being anything but realistic. In other words believability has to do with whether an agent moves and behaves in a way consistent to the user's expectations.

In practice, it is questionable whether a single system exists that supports all the features an agent should theoretically have. IVA's are a particularly tough field, as they consist a meeting point for various technologies and research areas, like Graphics, AI and Psychology, just to name a few.

By nature coupled with an execution system, IVA's present significant difficulties that are not always apparent when one examines Virtual Reality and Artificial Intelligence individually. So, although several theoretically robust intelligent agent architectures exist, they are not readily applicable to Virtual Environments and prove inefficient because of the problems that arise when one tries to link them to a complex execution environment like a virtual world.

22.5 Web 3D Applications-Past and Present

Early implementations of Web-based 3D Virtual worlds were mainly static, with none or limited interaction capabilities. The majority of early works were mostly 3D models the user could rotate and inspect from various angles, rather than virtual worlds one could navigate and explore. Gradually, more complex applications started appearing, using more extensive 3D models and including some sort of interaction as well as integration with HTML textual content.

The VRML 97 version, incorporating the External Authoring Interface (EAI) empowered VRML with Java, which allowed the creation of dynamic applications [McAtamney (2000), Avradinis, Vosinakis & Panayiotopoulos (2000)]. The rise of technologies like Computer Supported Collaborative Work (CSCW) and E-learning led to the introduction of various interesting applications like Virtual Classrooms and Virtual Laboratories, while the design and manufacturing industry, already one of the first and most important users of Virtual Reality exploited the capabilities of the Web to support CSCW and CBT (Computer Based Training) to develop Virtual Collaborative Design, Manufacturing as well as Training applications [Beier (2000)].

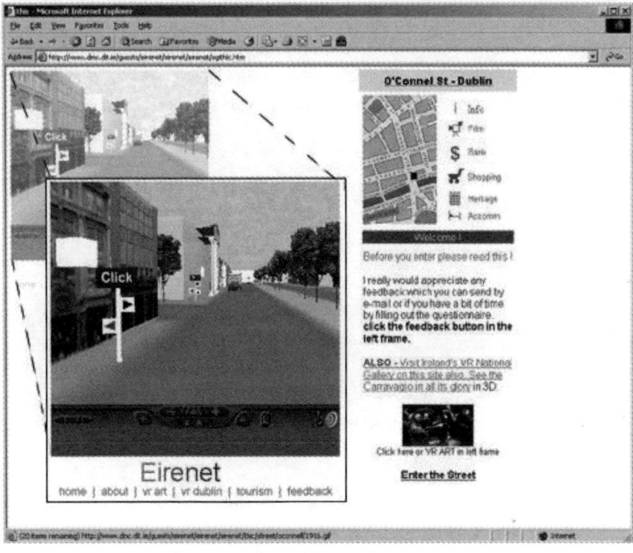

Fig.22.2. Edited screenshot from a virtual guide of O'Connel Street in Dublin developed in VRML by the Dublin Institute of Technology. By clicking on the arrows, the user can navigate to different parts of the street, while his location is also displayed on the map at the top-right corner of the page.

The media industry also came up with some custom solutions for dynamic "virtual agents" on the web, although the results are closer to what one would describe as a "Talking Head" rather than a proper virtual agent. Ananova, the Virtual Newscaster presented by Orange, the UK mobile phone company and its subsidiary, Ananova news agency, is an example of such an application [Ananova (2000)]. A similar one is Vandrea, created by UK's Channel 5 in cooperation with British Telecom's BTExaCT laboratories [BTExaCT (2000)].

However, these applications are still far from what one would call intelligent, as they lack any sort of high-level, automated reasoning capabilities that would allow them to be described as such, not to mention the distance that still exists when one has Intelligent Virtual Agents in mind.

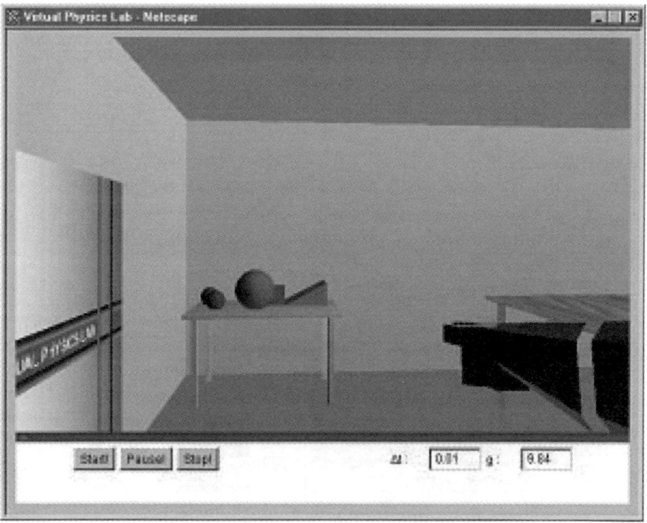

Fig.22.3. Screenshot from the Virtual Physics Laboratory
application (University of Piraeus)

Although Ananova and Vandrea, for example, could be characterized as Virtual Agent implementations, in a broad sense, they lack the key features of situatedness and full-scale embodiment-they are talking heads with no body, located in an empty environment. They may seem alive, but they perform no intelligent task-they convert text to audio and video output, presenting daily news in an appealing way.

Fig 22.4. Ananova and Vandrea, the virtual newscasters

22.6 Intelligent Virtual Agent Applications for the Web

Work towards the integration of intelligent agent techniques started quite soon after the introduction of technologies enabling external control to a virtual environment.

One of the earliest and most frequently cited works is the MAVE (Multiagent Architecture for Virtual Environment) [Coble and Harbison (1998); Coble and Cook (1999)], an agent-oriented architecture developed in VRML, Java and CORBA aiming to support advanced agent functionality in a virtual environment.

A similar research work is the AGILE system [Zhang, Guo and Georganas (2000)] that tried to take things a step further by incorporating emotional agents with modeled personalities.

Works on issues, such as perception and path finding have also been presented, like the "Virtual University Guide" [Panayiotopoulos, Zacharis, and Vosinakis (1999)], a virtual world created according to the ground plans of a real university building, which also included a virtual agent that guides the user within the university.

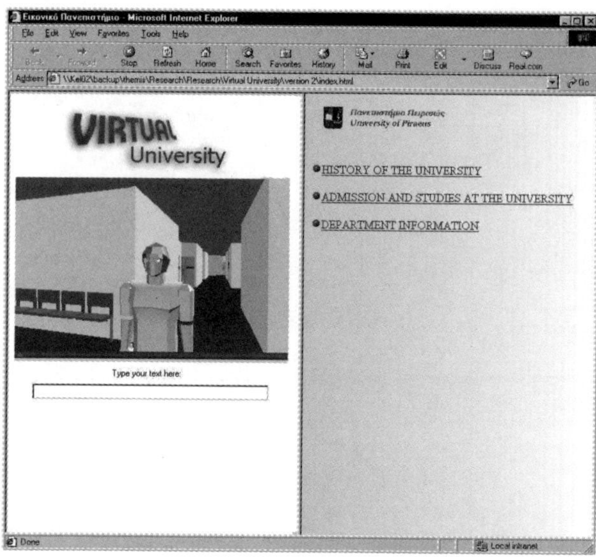

Fig 22.5 Virtual University Application (University of Piraeus).

The need for more descriptive and efficient ways to program intelligent virtual reality applications on the web led to the appearance of techniques integrating a variety of tools and languages.

High-level logic programming languages such as Prolog or DLP were used to provide a reasoning mechanism for web virtual agents, collecting world data from VRML and being able to pass commands to the world through the use of a Java interface [Panayiotopoulos, Katsirelos, Vosinakis and Kousidou (1999); Huang, Eliëns and Visser (2002)].

Techniques like Natural Language Processing were also made available to web-based VR systems, used as a means to communicate with virtual agents, either in virtual chat applications or as interfaces to intelligent assistants in virtual worlds [Jung, Pfeiffer and Zakotnik (2002)].

Lately, more mature approaches towards full-scale intelligent virtual agent environments have been presented [Heylen, Nijholt and Poel, (2001); Jung and Milde (1999)]. As hardware resources become more readily available to users, the creation of more demanding applications becomes feasible, with behavioral control and emotions being more frequently incorporated in Web VR applications.

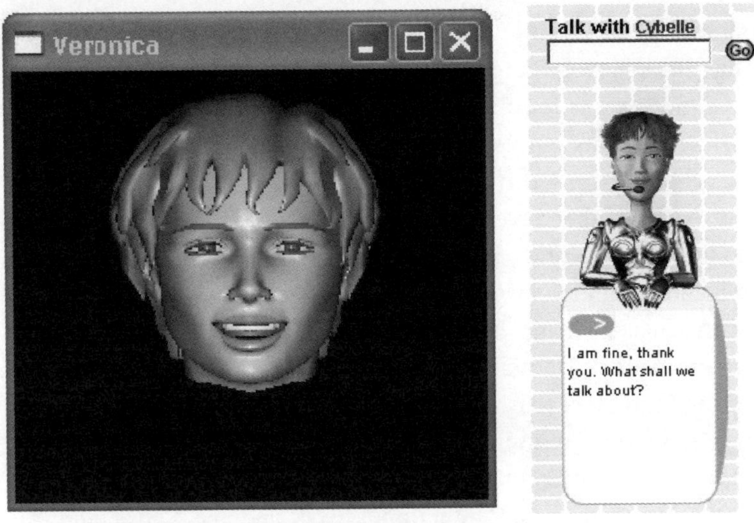

Fig. 22.6. Screenshots from Veronica (University of Piraeus) and Cybelle (http://www.agentland.com), two Eliza-like conversational agents

Fig 22.7 Screenshot from Salford University's VICTEC Project, an application designed to deal with the problem of bullying. The application incorporates emotion support and is developed in WildTangent.

22.7 An IVA Sample Architecture

A basic problem in Intelligent Virtual Environments is the smooth integration of the high-level, intelligent subsystems of an application with the lower-level, graphical representation modules [virtual world itself]. Although it is feasible to direct the graphical subsystem to display and perform actions corresponding to decisions made at a higher level, the reverse process is a difficult task.

How is the higher level going to be informed about changes in the state of the virtual world? How can the success or failure of an action be detected and communicated to the AI subsystem?

For this reason many intelligent virtual agent architectures follow a layered approach, introducing intermediate layers that act as an interface connecting high-level reasoning modules and low-level graphic modules.

A generic description of such a layered architecture follows. It consists of three different layers: the Reasoning and Decision Making Layer, the Perception and Intention Layer, and the Sense and Action Layer.

The Reasoning and Decision Layer, i.e. the cognitive layer, handles all possible decisions and actions in an abstract way, consisting of a reasoning mechanism as well as a knowledge base (KB), where domain and strategic knowledge is stored.

The Perception and Intention Layer, receives an abstract action sequence and transforms it into specific instructions, i.e. it specifies the current intention of the agent. At the same time, receives the sensed geometrical data from the 'physical' layer and transforms them to symbolic abstract relations among objects, stored as ground beliefs in the Belief Database.

The Sense and Action Layer, i.e. the physical layer, contains the appropriate sensors with which it senses the changes of the environment and effectors with which it actually changes the environment.

The described architecture may efficiently direct a virtual agent to perform actions in an intelligent way, in a predefined virtual environment as well as perceive dynamic changes which have not been 'encoded' in its Knowledge Base.

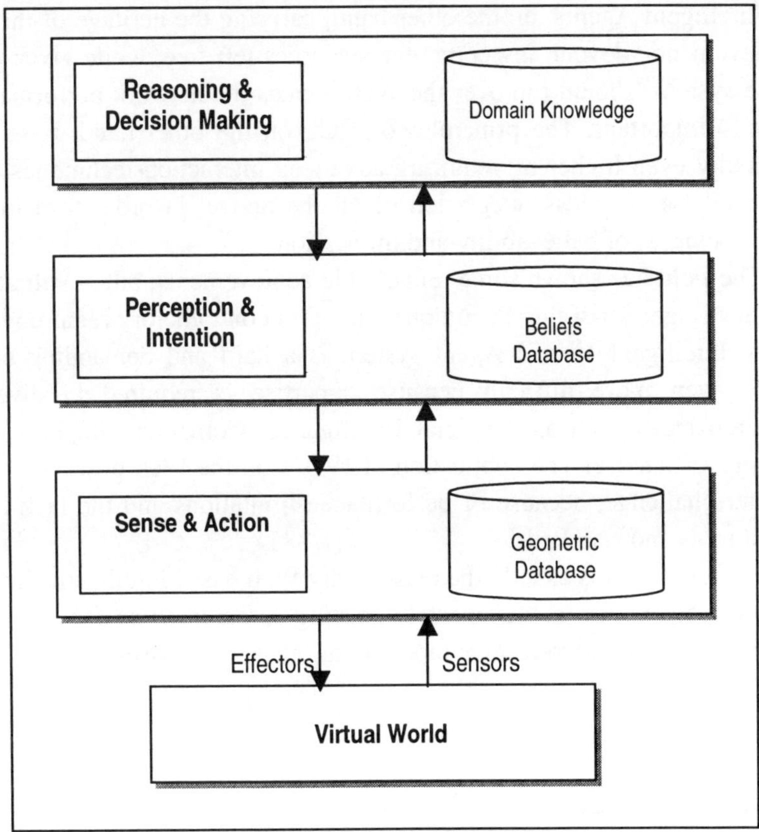

Fig.22.8. A Generic Layered IVA Architecture.

22.8 Conclusions

We have presented a brief overview of the novel field of Intelligent Virtual Agents and their particular application on the Web. The area seems quite challenging, as different demanding technologies must be put together: Virtual Reality demands the best performance in hardware graphic cards and CPU power, in order to permit the user to navigate in real time, in complex, believable and dynamically changing 3D environments.

Intelligent Agents, on the other hand, carrying the heritage of the AI achievements, devour any computer resources left free, while given that these systems should run over the Web, makes the network performance equally important. The principles of HCI, on the other hand, raise the difficulty even higher by requiring advanced interaction techniques and also call for seamless integration of all the above, in order to achieve high standards of believability and immersion.

The field has shown some remarkable achievements, but is still at an infancy stage. Satisfying the unique and often contradictory requirements of an Intelligent Virtual Agent system is a hard and demanding task, made even more difficult because expertise is required in diverse research areas such as Artificial Intelligence, Computer Graphics and Cognitive Science. The application of IVA's on the Web poses an even greater challenge, because of performance limitations and the lack of a set of tools and standards.

However, this is exactly the reason why Web based Intelligent Virtual Agents consist one of the most interesting research areas for the near future, and is bound to receive more attention as time passes.

Acknowledgement

This work has been funded by the University of Piraeus Research Center (KEPP)

Bibliography

4th International Workshop on Intelligent Virtual Agents. (IVA 2003). http://www.sigmedia.org/iva03

Adobe Atmosphere, http://www.adobe.com/products/atmosphere

Avradinis, N., Vosinakis, S., Panayiotopoulos, T. (2000). Using Virtual Reality Techniques to Simulate Physics Experiments. World Conference on Systemics, Cybernetics, Informatics and Information Systems, Orlando, Florida (USA), July 23-26, 2000.

Avradinis, N., Aylett, R. (2003) Agents with no aims: Motivation Based Continuous Planning. Lecture Notes in Artificial Intelligence 2792, Intelligent Virtual Agents. T. Rist et al. (eds), Springer-Verlag, 2003, pp.269-273.

Aylett, R and Cavazza, M. (2000) Intelligent Virtual Environments – A state of the art report. Eurographics 2001 Conference, Manchester, UK, 2001.

Aylett, R., Horrobin, A., O'Hare, J., Osman, A., and Polshaw, M. (1999) Virtual Teletubbies: reapplying robot architecture to virtual agents. Proc. Of the 3rd International Conference on Autonomous Agents, ACM Press, pp 338-339.

Aylett, R. and Luck, M. (2000) Applying artificial intelligence to virtual reality: Intelligent virtual environments. Applied Artificial Intelligence, 14 (1), pp.3-32

Bates, J. (1994). The role of emotions in believable agents. Communications of the ACM 37 (7), pp 122-125.

Beier, K.P. (2000). Web-Based Virtual Reality in Design and Manufacturing Applications. 1st International EuroConference on Computer Applications and Information Technology in the Maritime Industries (COMPIT 2000). Potsdam, Germany, March 29 – April 4, 2000.

Blaxxun Technologies. Blaxxun Contact, Blaxxun 3D. http://www.blaxxun.com

BT ExaCT (2000) http://www.futuretalk.co.uk/avatars/vandrea_main.htm

Cavazza, M., Charles, F., Mead, S.J. and Strachan, A.. (2001). Virtual Actors' Behaviour for 3D Interactive Storytelling. Eurographics 2001 Conference, Manchester, UK, 2001.

Computer Associates, (2000). Cosmo Player 2.1, http://ca.com/cosmo/

Coble, J. and Cook, D. J. (1999). Virtual Environments: An Agent-Based Approach. Proceedings of the AAAI Spring Symposium on Agents with Adjustable Autonomy , 1999.

Coble, J. and Harbison, K. (1998). MAVE: A Multi-agent Architecture for Virtual Environments" Proceedings of 11th International Conference on Industrial and Engineering Applications of Artificial Intelligence and Expert Systems, June 1998.

Charles, F., Lozano, M., Mead, S. J., Bisquerra, A.F., Cavazza, M. (2003). Planning Formalisms and Authoring in Interactive Storytelling. 1st International Conference on Technologies for Interactive Digital Storytelling and Entertainment (TIDSE 03). Darmstadt, Germany. March 24 – 26, 2003

Franklin, S. (1997). Autonomous Agents as Embodied AI. Cybernetics and Systems, 28(6), pp 499-520.

Heylen, D., Nijholt, A., Poel, M. (2001). Embodied agents in virtual environments: The Aveiro project. In: Proceedings European Symposium on Intelligent Technologies, Hybrid Systems and their implementation on Smart Adaptive Systems, Tenerife, Spain, December 2001, ISBN 3-89653-916-7, Verlag Mainz, Wissenschaftsverlag Aachen, pp. 110-111

Huang. Z., Eliëns, A., and Visser, C. (2002). 3D Agent-based Virtual Communities, Proceedings of the 2002 Web3D Conference, ACM Press, 2002.

ISO/IEC (1997). The VRML 97 International Standard (ISO/IEC 14772-1:1997), available at http://www.web3d.org/technicalinfo/specifications/ISO_IEC_14772-All/index.html.

Jung, B. Milde J.-T. (1999). An Open Virtual Environment for Autonomous Agents Using VRML and Java. Proceedings of VRML'99 - Fourth Symposium on the Virtual Reality Modeling Language, ACM, 1999, pp 7-11.

Jung, B., Pfeiffer T. and Zakotnik J. (2002). Natural Language Based Virtual Prototyping on the Web. In C. Geiger et al. (eds.): Proceedings Structured Design of Virtual Environments and 3D-Components. Aachen: Shaker, 2002.

Kalra, P., Magnenat-Thalmann, N., Moccozet, L., Sannier, G., Aubel, A., Thalmann, D. (1998). Real-time Animation of Realistic Virtual Humans. IEEE Computer Graphics and Applications, Vol.18, No.5, pp.42-55, 1998.

Lozano, M., Cavazza, M., Mead, S., Charles. F. (2002). Search Based Planning: A method for character Behaviour. GameOn 2002 - 3rd International Conference on Intelligent Games and Simulation. University of Westminster, London, November 29- 30, 2002

Maes, P. (1990). ed., Designing Autonomous Agents. Cambridge, MA: MIT Press

McAtamney, H. (2000). The National Gallery of Ireland, Virtual Gallery. Proceedings of the VSMM 6th International Conference on Virtual Systems and Multimedia. Ogaki City, Japan. October 2000. Demo available at: http://www.dmc.dit.ie/guests/eirenet/eirenet/pages/vr.htm

Milde J.-T. & Jung B. (2000). Educational Use of VRML and JAVA in Agent-based AI and Computer Graphics. In Future Generation Computer Systems, 17(1), Elsevier, 2000, pp 79-87.

Panayiotopoulos, T., Katsirelos, G., Vosinakis, S., Kousidou, S. (1999). An Intelligent Agent Framework in VRML worlds. In S. Tzafestas (Ed.), Advances in Intelligent Systems – Concepts, Tools and Applications, pp. 219-230, Kluwer Academic Press, 1999.

Panayiotopoulos, T., Zacharis, N., Vosinakis, S. (1999). Intelligent Guidance in a Virtual University, in S. Tzafestas (Ed.), Advances in Intelligent Systems – Concepts, Tools and Applications, pp. 33-42, Kluwer Academic Press.

Panayiotopoulos, T., Anastassakis, G. (2000). Towards a Virtual Reality Intelligent Agent Language. in D. Fotiadis and S.D. Nikolopoulos (Eds), Advances in Informatics, World Scientific, 2000.

Parallel Graphics. Cortona VRML Client.
http://www.parallelgraphics.com/products/cortona/

Prophet, J. (2001). TechnoSphere: "Real" Time "Artificial" Life. Leonardo: The Journal of the International Society for The Arts, Sciences & Technology. Vol 34, Number 4, MIT Press

Ruttkay, Z, Huang, Z., Eliens, A. (2003). Reusable gestures for interactive web agents, Proceedings of the 4th International Working Conference on Intelligent Virtual Agents (IVA'03), Lecture Notes in Artificial Intelligence 2792 (LNAI 2792), R. Aylett, D. Ballin & T. Rist (Eds.), Springer-Verlag, 2003.

Sun Microsustems. (2003). Java 3D API Version 1.3.1
http://java.sun.com/products/java-media/3D/

Terzopoulos, D., Tu, X. and Grzeszczuk, R. (1994). Artificial Fishes : Autonomous locomotion, perception, behavior and learning in a simulated physical world. Artificial Life 1 (4): 327-351, 1994.

Web3D Consortium, http://www.web3d.org/

WildTangent, http://www.wildtangent.com

Wooldridge, M. J. and Jennings, N. R. (1995). Intelligent agents: Theory and practice. Knowledge Engineering Review, 10 (2).

Zhang, Y., Guo, L., and Georganas, N. D. (2000). AGILE: An Architecture for Agent-Based Collaborative and Interactive Virtual Learning Environments. IEEE Globecom'2000 Conference, Nov.-Dec.2000, San Francisco.

CHAPTER 23

DATA MINING FOR NETWORK SECURITY

Guoyin Wang

Institute of Computer Science and Technology,
Chongqing University of Posts and Telecommunications
Chongqing, 400065, P.R.China
E-mail: wanggy@ieee.org

In this chapter, we discuss some key problems in network security and present some possible ways to solve these problems, especially some data mining based methods. The problem of network security and intrusion detection is discussed at first. Then, data mining technique is briefly introduced. The problems, possibilities, and methods of data mining solutions for intrusion detection are further analyzed. Several new techniques such as data reduction, incremental mining, uncertain data mining, and initiative data mining are suggested to solve the problems of intrusion detection systems.

23.1 Introduction of Network Security

With the growing rate of interconnections among computer systems, network based computer systems is playing increasingly vital roles in modern society. They have become the target of intrusions by our enemies and criminals. Network security is becoming a major challenge. In order to meet this challenge, intrusion detection systems (IDS) are being designed to protect the availability, confidentiality and integrity of critical networked information systems.

Though they both relate to network security, an IDS differs from a firewall in that a firewall looks out for intrusions in order to stop them from happening. The firewall limits the access between networks in

501

order to prevent intrusion and does not signal an attack from inside the network. An IDS evaluates a suspected intrusion once it has taken place and signals an alarm. An IDS also watches for attacks that originate from within a system.

Intrusion detection techniques are generally categorized into anomaly detection and misuse detection. Misuse detection systems use patterns of well-known attacks or weak spots of the system to match and identify known intrusion patterns or signatures. Anomaly detection systems attempt to quantify the usual or acceptable behaviors and flag irregular activities that deviate significantly from the established normal usage profiles as anomalies (i.e. potential intrusions).

There are some key differences between anomaly detection and misuse detection techniques. The most significant advantage of misuse detection approaches is that known attacks can be detected fairly reliable and with a low false positive rate. However, the key drawback of misuse detection approaches is that they cannot detect novel attacks against systems that leave different signatures. So, while the false positive rate can be made extremely low, the rate of missed attacks (false negatives) can be extremely high depending on the ingenuity of the attackers. As a result, misuse detection approaches provide little defense against novel attacks, until they can learn to generalize from known signatures of attacks.

Anomaly detection techniques, on the other hand, directly address the problem of detecting novel attacks against systems. Anomaly detection approaches compare current activities against statistical models of past behavior. Any activity sufficiently deviant from the model will be flagged as anomalous (possible attack). It is based on actual user histories and system data to create its internal models rather than pre-defined patterns. Though anomaly detection approaches are powerful in detecting novel attacks, they have their drawbacks as well. It is unable to identify the specific type of attack that is occurring. The most significant disadvantage of anomaly detection approaches is the high rates of false alarm. Moreover, introducing new users into a system may potentially raise one problem. An excessive number of anomaly records will be generated that is caused by the lack of profile information about the new user's behavior as well as by the user's own inexperience with the system.

Another useful classification for intrusion detection systems is according to their data source [Noel *et. al.* (2002)]. To a large extent, the data source determines the types of intrusions that can be detected. The two general categories are host-based detection and network-based detection.

For host-based systems, the data source is collected from an individual host on the network. In particular, these systems employ their host's operating system audit trail as the main source of input. Because host-based systems directly monitor the host data files and operating system processes, they can determine exactly which host resources are the targets of a particular attack.

Intrusion detection systems can be also divided into passive or reactive intrusion detection systems. In a passive system, the IDS detects a potential security breach, logs the information and signals an alert. In a reactive system, the IDS responds to the suspicious activity by logging off a user or by reprogramming the firewall to block network traffic from the suspected malicious source.

Recent research in intrusion detection techniques has shifted to focus from user based intrusion detection to process based intrusion detection. Process based monitoring intrusion detection tools analyze the behavior of executing processes for possible intrusive activity. The premise of process monitoring for intrusion detection is that most computer security violations are made possible by misusing programs. When a program is misused its behavior will differ from its normal usage.

Many events such as GUI events, network packet traffic, or system call traces, et al, could be used for features of an IDS. Two possible approaches to monitoring process behavior are: capturing programs' internal states, or monitoring the operating system to capture external system calls made by a program. The latter option is more attractive in general because it does not require access to source code for instrumentation. It is also possible to audit the computer network, monitor the standard operations on a target systems: logins, command and program execution's, file and device accesses, etc., looking for deviations in usage. Table 23.1 illustrates some features for describing process behaviors.

Table 23.1 Process behavior features.

Telnet Records								
service	flag	hot	Failed_logins	compromised	Root_shell	su	duratior	...
telnet	SF	0	0	0	0	0	10.2	...
telnet	SF	3	0	2	1	0	92.5	...
...	...	...	...	...	...	...	...	...

Shell Command Records				
time	hostname	command	arg1	arg2
am	pascal	mkdir	Dir1	
am	pascal	dvips	dvi	-o
...	...	...	...	...

Network Connection Records								
timestam	duration	service	src_host	dst_host	src_byte	dst_byte	flag	...
lpl	0	http	spoofed_	victim	0	0	S0	...
10.2	2	ftp	A	C	200	300	SF	...
...	...	...	...	...	...		...	...
				...				

Given the rapid development of computer networks, some traditional single-host intrusion detection systems have been modified to monitor a number of hosts on a network. They transfer the monitored information from multiple monitored hosts to a central site for processing. These are termed distributed intrusion detection systems. Example distributed systems are IDES [Denning (1987); Lunt (1993)], NSTAT [Kemmerer (1997)], and AAFID [Spafford and Zamboni (2000)].

Network-based intrusion detection employs network traffic as the main source of input. This involves placing a set of traffic sensors within the network. The sensors typically perform local analysis and detection and report suspicious events to a central location. These sensors are generally easier to harden against attack and to hide from attackers, since they perform only the intrusion detection function.

Recent developments in network oriented intrusion detection have moved the focus from network traffic to the computational infrastructure (the hosts and their operating systems) and the communication infrastructure (the network and its protocols). They use the network as just a source of security-relevant information. Network-based intrusion detection systems have been widened to address large, complex network environments. Examples of this trend include GrIDS (Graph based Intrusion Detection System) [Staniford-Chen *et. al.* (1996)], EMERALD [Neumann and Porras (1999)], NetStat [Vigna and Kemmerer (1998)], and CARDS (Coordinated Attack Response and Detection System) [Yang *et. al.* (2000)].

There are several open questions for intrusion detection techniques [Warrender *et. al.* (1999)]:

- Soundness of approach: Does the approach actually detect intrusions? Is it possible to distinguish anomalies related to intrusions from those related to other factors?

- Completeness of approach: Does the approach detect most, if not all, intrusions, or is a significant proportion of intrusions undetectable by this method?

- Timeliness of approach: Can we detect most intrusions before significant damage is done?

- Choice of metrics, statistical models, and profiles: What metrics, models, and profiles provide the best discriminating power? Which are cost-effective? What are the relationships between certain types of anomalies and different methods of intrusion?

- System design: How should a system based on the model be designed and implemented?

- Feedback: What effect should a detection of an intrusion have on the target system? Should an IDS system automatically direct the system to take certain actions?

- Social implications: How will an intrusion detection system affect the user community it monitors? Will it deter intrusion? Will the users feel their data are better protected? Will it be regarded as a step towards "big brother"? Will its capabilities be misused to that end?

23.2 Introduction of Data Mining

Data mining (also known as Knowledge Discovery in Databases - KDD) has been defined as "The nontrivial extraction of implicit, previously unknown, and potentially useful information from data" [Frawley *et. al.* (1992)]. It uses machine learning, statistical and visualization techniques to discovery and present knowledge in a form that is easily comprehensible to humans.

Data mining tools can scour databases for hidden patterns, finding predictive information that experts may miss because it lies outside their expectations.

Data mining techniques are the result of a long process of research and product development. This evolution began when data was first stored on computers, continued with improvements in data access, and more recently, generated technologies that allow users to navigate through their data in real time. Data mining is ready for application because it is supported by three technologies that are now sufficiently mature: massive data collection, powerful multiprocessor computers, and data mining algorithms.

Data mining algorithms embody techniques that have existed for at least 10 years, but have only recently been implemented as mature, reliable, understandable tools that consistently outperform older statistical methods.

Some commonly used techniques in data mining are:
- Artificial Neural Networks
- Fuzzy Sets
- Rough Sets
- Decision Trees
- Genetic Algorithms
- Nearest Neighbor Method
- Statistics Based Rule Induction
- Linear regression and linear predictive coding
- Etc.

23.3 Problems and Possibilities of Data Mining in Network Security

Most existing systems have security flaws that render them susceptible to intrusions, penetrations, and other forms of abuse. Finding and fixing all these deficiencies is not feasible for technical and economic reasons. Existing systems with known flaws are not easily replaced by systems that are more secure because the systems have attractive features that are missing in the more-secure systems, or else they cannot be replaced for economic reasons. Developing systems that are absolutely secure is extremely difficult, if not generally impossible. Even the most secure systems are vulnerable to abuses by insiders who misuse their privileges. Thus, the development of real-time intrusion detection systems is needed and important. However, real-time detection of previously unseen attacks with high accuracy and a low false alarm rate is still a challenge.

Many recent approaches to intrusion detection have applied data mining techniques. It has been empirically proven to be very effective [Lee *et. al.* (1999); Warrender *et. al.* (1999)].

IBM's emergency response service provides real-time intrusion detection (RTID) services through the Internet for a variety of clients. The emergency response service needs to analyze and respond to thousands of alerts per day. Data mining techniques were used to analyze a database of RTID alerts. They developed profiles of normal alerts and of their clients. Several different types of clients were discovered, each with different alert behaviors and thus different monitoring needs [Manganaris *et. al.* (2000)].

One major drawback of data mining based approaches is that the data required for training is very expensive to produce [Eskin *et. al.* (2000)].

Data mining IDSs collect data from sensors that monitor some aspect of a system. Sensors may monitor network activity, system calls used by user processes, or file system access. They extract predictive features from the raw data stream being monitored to produce formatted data that can be used for detection. Data gathered by sensors is evaluated by a detector using a detection model. This detection model determines whether or not the data is intrusive. Algorithms for building detection models are also usually classified into two categories: misuse detection and anomaly detection.

Misuse detection models are typically obtained by training on a large set of data in which the attacks have been manually labeled. This data is very expensive to produce because each piece of data must be labeled as either normal or some particular attack.

Anomaly detection models compare sensor data to normal patterns learned from a large amount of training data. They require that the data used for training is purely normal and does not contain any attacks. This data can be very expensive because the process of manually cleaning the data is quite time consuming.

Models trained on data gathered from one environment may not perform well in some other environment. This means that in order to obtain the best intrusion detection models, data must be collected from each environment in which the intrusion detection system is to be deployed. The cost of generating data sets can be very expensive and the cost incurred is a significant barrier to IDS deployment.

Because the space of possible malicious behaviors and intruder actions is potentially infinite, it is difficult or impossible to demonstrate complete coverage of the space from a finite training corpus. Furthermore, it is often the previously unseen attack that represents the greatest threat. Finally, for reasons of privacy, it is desirable that a user-based anomaly-detection agent only employ data that originate with the profiled user or are publicly available. Releasing traces of one's own normal behaviors, even to assist the training of someone else's anomaly detector, runs the risk that the data will be abused to subvert the original user's security mechanisms. Thus, we are faced with a learning situation in which only positive instances are available. Learning from only positive examples presents a challenge for classification, since it can easily lead to overgeneralization.

In a dynamic environment such as anomaly detection, the size of the instance dictionary can conceivably grow without bounds, requiring data reduction techniques to reduce the resource consumption of the machine learning system. Possible solutions include removal of instances from the dictionary and representation of instances in another, less space-intensive form.

23.4 Possible Solutions of Data Mining in Network Security

The following criteria should be the goal of intrusion detection systems [Ko (2000)].

- Completeness: All operations in a valid trace should be classified as valid (or normal).
- Consistency: For every invalid trace (or intrusion trace), a valid access specification should classify at least one operation as bad (or invalid).
- Compactness: The specification should be concise so that it can be inspected by a human and be able to use for real-time detection. One simple compactness measure is the number of rules (or clauses) in a specification.
- Predictability: The specification should be able to explain future execution traces, not producing a high false alarm rate.
- Detectability: The specification should fit closely to the actual valid behavior and reject future execution traces which are intrusions.

Intrusion detection techniques based on data mining methods take a data-centric point of view and consider intrusion detection as a data analysis process. Anomaly detection is about finding the normal usage patterns from the audit data, whereas misuse detection is about encoding and matching the intrusion patterns using the audit data. The recent rapid development in data mining has made available a wide variety of algorithms, drawn from the fields of statistics, pattern recognition, machine learning, and database. Several types of algorithms are particularly relevant to this topic [Lee *et. al.* (1999)]:

- Classification: It maps a data item into one of several predefined categories. These algorithms normally output "classifiers", for example, in the form of decision trees or rules. An ideal application in intrusion detection will be to gather sufficient "normal" and "abnormal" audit data for a user or a program, then apply a classification algorithm to learn a classifier that will determine future audit data as belonging to the normal class or the abnormal class.

- Link analysis: It determines relations between fields in the database. Finding out the correlations in audit data will provide insight for selecting the right set of system features for intrusion detection.
- Sequence analysis: It models sequential patterns. These algorithms can help us understand what time-based sequences of audit events are frequently encountered together. These frequent event patterns are important elements of the behavior profile of a user or program.

The accuracy of data mining based detection models depends on sufficient training data and the right feature set.

According to the above analysis of network security and intrusion detection systems, we can find that there are many unsolved problems in intrusion detection systems.

- How to design the model for describing the characteristics of normal behaviors and abnormal behaviors?
- How to design the model for describing the characteristics of specific misuse intrusion behaviors?
- How to reduce the cost of collecting, storing, processing, the huge amounts of source data for mining knowledge of intrusion behaviors?
- How to adjust the intrusion detection systems with the growing of source data at low cost and the changing of users' behaviors?
- How to implement efficient intrusion detections to reduce the damages caused by intrusions?
- How to increase the detection rate while decreasing the false positive rate at the same time.

It should be possible to solve the above problems using some specific data mining techniques. Many data mining techniques have been used to model normal and abnormal behaviors, and many kinds of misuse intrusions. The critical question is how to combine multiple simple detection models into one integrated intrusion detection system.

As we pointed out in the last section, it is very expensive to produce the training data required by data mining based intrusion detection systems. Rough set [Wang (2001)] might be a potential method to solve the problem of reducing the cost of collecting, storing, processing, the huge amounts of source data. Rough set has a unique advantage in data reduction. It can be used to process the data available at present and recommend the importance degrees of different data generated by each sensor for distinguishing each kind of intrusion behaviors from normal behaviors. Thus, we could know what features are important for intrusion detection, and what data is sufficient for each intrusion detection system. We need not to obtain, store, or process unnecessary sensor data.

The data obtained from the IDS monitors increases quickly. The behaviors and methods of intruders often vary also. More and more new technologies are used in intrusion actions. In order to detect these new intrusion behaviors, data mining based intrusion detection systems are required to be updated frequently through mining all collected data, including data mined before and new coming data, again. Generally, data mining processes are time consuming and very expensive. It would be very helpful if incremental data mining method were available. Fortunately, many researchers have developed several data mining algorithms with incremental learning ability, such as rough set and rule tree based incremental knowledge acquisition algorithm [Zheng *et. al.* (2003)], parallel neural networks [Wang and Nie (1999); Wang and Shi (1995)], et al. We need not to mine the data mined before again while mining new coming data. New detection models and knowledge can be extracted from the new coming data and be added into the ones mined from the odd data mined before. Thus, the detection ability of an intrusion detection system can grow itself.

In many cases, we could not obtain the information from all possible sensors. It would be also very expensive to obtain all these data. It would save our time and money if we could mine from partial or incomplete data. In addition, the behaviors of normal computer users and network users differ greatly. Inconsistent data are often generated from detection sensors. Thus, it would be also very important for data mining based intrusion detection systems to deal with uncertain data containing incomplete or inconsistent records. Except for some traditional uncertain data processing techniques like statistical methods, some new techniques for processing uncertain data based on rough set theory were developed in recent years [Wang (2002); Wang and Liu (2000)]. It would be helpful to cope with these problems.

Some intrusion actions might not be noticed even if they have occurred before since the limitation of our knowledge about intrusion behaviors, and new intrusion techniques are developed and used by intruders. Some automatic (self, initiative) data mining algorithms driven by data itself [Wang and He (2003)] would be useful to mine the knowledge of this kind of intrusion actions and improve the detection rate.

23.5 Conclusions

In this chapter, we introduce the current status of intrusion detection systems (IDS) and data mining research, discuss some problems in technologies, methods and models of intrusion detection, and present some possible data mining based ways for solving these problems. Some new techniques like data reduction, incremental mining, uncertain data mining, and initiative data mining are suggested to solve the problems of intrusion detection systems.

Bibliography

Denning, D. E. (1987). An Intrusion-Detection Model, *IEEE Transactions on Software Engineering*, vol. 13, pp. 222-232.

Eskin, E., Miller, M., Zhong, Z. D., Yi, G., Lee, W. A. and Stolfo, S. (2000). Adaptive Model Generation for Intrusion Detection Systems, *Proceedings of the ACMCCS Workshop on Intrusion Detection and Prevention*, Athens, Greece.

Frawley, W., Piatetsky-Shapiro, G. and Matheus, C. (1992). Knowledge Discovery in Databases: An Overview, *AI Magazine*, pp. 213-228.

Kemmerer, R. A. (1997). NSTAT: A Model-based Real-time Network Intrusion Detection System, University of California Santa Barbara Department of Computer Science, Santa Barbara, CA, *Technical Report TR* 1997-18.

Ko, C. (2000). Logic Induction of Valid Behavior Specifications for Intrusion Detection, *2000 IEEE Symposium on Security and Privacy*, Berkeley, California, USA, pp. 142-153.

Lee, W., Stolfo, S. J. and Mok, K. (1999). Data mining in work flow environments: Experiences in intrusion detection, *Proceedings of the 1999 Conference on Knowledge Discovery and data Mining (KDD-99)*.

Lee, W., Stolfo, S. J. and Mok, K. (1999). A Data Mining Framework for Building Intrusion Detection Models, *1999 IEEE Symposium on Security and Privacy*, pp. 120-132.

Lunt, T. F. (1993). A Survey of Intrusion Detection Techniques, *Computers & Security*, vol. 12 (4), pp. 405-418.

Neumann, P. G. and Porras, P. A. (1999). Experience with EMERALD to Date, *Proceedings of First Usenix Workshop on Intrusion Detection and Network Monitoring*, Santa Clara, CA, pp. 73-80.

Manganaris, S., Christensen, M., Zerkle, D. and Hermiz, K. (2000). A Data Mining Analysis of RTID Alarms, *Computer Networks*, vol. 34, pp. 571-577.

Noel, S., Wijesekera, D. and Youman, C. (2002). Modern Intrusion Detection, Data Mining, and Degrees of Attack Guilt, in *Applications of Data Mining in Computer Security*, Daniel Barbarà & Sushil Jajodia (eds.), Kluwer Academic Publishers.

Spafford, E. H. and Zamboni, D. (2000). Intrusion Detection Using Autonomous Agents, *Computer Networks,* vol. 34, pp. 547-570.

Staniford-Chen, S., Cheung, S., Crawford, R., Dilger, M., Frank, J., Hoagland, J., Levitt, K., Wee, C., Yip, R. and Zerkle, D. (1996). GrIDS-A Graph Based Intrusion Detection System for Large Networks, *Proceedings of 19th National Information Systems Security Conference,* Baltimore, MD, pp. 361-370.

Vigna, G. and Kemmerer, R. A. (1998). NetSTAT: A Network-based Intrusion Detection Approach, *Proceedings of 14th Annual Computer Security Applications Conference,* Phoenix, AZ, pp. 25-34.

Warrender, C., Forrest, S. and Pearlmutter, B. (1999). Detecting intrusions using system calls: alternative data models, *1999 IEEE Symposium on Security and privacy,* IEEE Computer Socitey, pp. 133-145.

Wang, G. Y. (2001). Rough Set Theory and Knowledge Acquisition, Xi'an: *Xi'an Jiaotong University Press.*

Wang, G. Y. and Nie, N. (1999). PMSN: A Parallel Multi-Sieving Neural Network Architecture, *Journal of Computer Research and Development,* 36(Suppl.): pp. 21-25.

Wang, G. Y. and Shi, H. B. (1995). Parallel Neural Network Architectures and Their Applications, *Proceedings of International Conference on Neural Networks,* Perth, Australia, pp. III1234-1239.

Wang, G. Y. (2002). Extension of Rough Set under Incomplete Information Systems, *2002 IEEE International Conference on Fuzzy Systems (FUZZ-IEEE),* pp. 1098-1103.

Wang, G. Y. and Liu, F. (2000). The Inconsistency in Rough Set Based Rule Generation, *The Second International Conference on Rough Sets and Current Trends in Computing (RSCTC'2000),* Canada, pp. 370-377.

Wang, G. Y. and He, X. (2003). A Self-learning Model under Uncertain Condition, *Journal of Software,* vol. 14(6), pp. 1096-1102.

Yang, J., Ning, P., Wang, X. S. and Jajodia, S. (2000). CARDS: A Distributed System for Detecting Coordinated Attacks, *Proceedings of IFIP TC11 16th Annual Working Conference on Information Security,* pp. 171-180.

Zheng, Z., Wang, G. Y. and Wu, y. (2003). A Rough Set and Rule Tree Based Incremental knowledge Acquisition Algorithm, LNAI2639, *Springer-Verlag.*

CHAPTER 24

AGENT-SUPPORTED WI INFRASTRUCTURE: CASE STUDIES IN PEER-TO-PEER NETWORKS

Xiaolong Jin[1], Jiming Liu[1], and Yuanshi Wang[2]

[1]*Department of Computer Science,*
Hong Kong Baptist University,
Kowloon Tong, Hong Kong, P.R. China
[2]*Department of Mathematics,*
Zhongshan University,
Guangzhou, P. R. China
E-mail: {jxl, jiming}@comp.hkbu.edu.hk, mcswys@zsu.edu.cn

Since its proposal, Web Intelligence (WI) has quickly grown into an extensively concerned research direction in the computer science community. WI aims at developing and exploring the next generation of the World Wide Web to satisfy the increasing needs of human. In WI research, resource optimization is a fundamental and key problem, which involves two main requirements, a right infrastructure of distributed resources and the corresponding algorithmic support to mobilize resources. Due to the advantages of grids, in particular peer-to-peer grids, such as decentralization and robustness, the next generation of the Web will mainly rely on gridlike resources. This chapter will based on the peer-to-peer infrastructure of gridlike resources explore the corresponding algorithmic support to mobilize resources. Specifically, in this chapter we present a model to characterize the process of task handling among peer-to-peer grid nodes. Our model consists of functional differential equations. Through case studies, (1) we show that our model are effective in characterizing the process of task handling with balanced loads among nodes; (2) we examine the effects of time delay, service time, etc. on the global performance of a peer-to-peer network of grid nodes and show some interesting observations. Based on our model, we further simulate a complete process of task handling on a grid node network.

515

24.1   Introduction

The World Wide Web has become a new medium for resource and information sharing. The Web provides us with world-wide presence and connectivity [Liu (2003a); Liu (2003b)]. It has been making a strong impact on our conventional living, working, and playing ways [Liu (2003a); Liu (2003b); Liu *et al.* (2003)]. But, although the Web is exponentially increasing in its web sites, web pages, and hyperlinks, its development is far behind the increasing speed of human needs. The Web no longer contents the higher and higher needs and expectations of users. *How to make revolutionary innovation in the Web? What will be the next shift of the Web?* In order to answer these questions, based on the current knowledge and expertise in Data-Mining, Autonomous Agents and Multi-Agent Systems, Information Retrieval, and Logic etc. [Liu (2003a)], Zhong, Liu, Yao, and Ohsuga showed great foresight – first proposed the concept of "Web Intelligence" (WI) in 2000 [Liu (2003a); Liu (2003b); Zhong *et al.* (2002); Zhong *et al.* (2000)]. WI aims at exploring and exploiting the essential roles of Artificial Intelligence (AI) and advanced Information Technology (IT) on the next shift of Web-empowered systems and services, in particularl, Web-based life, work, and play. Zhong, Liu, and Yao stated that the next paradigm shift in WI would be towards the notion of *wisdom* [Zhong *et al.* (2003a); Liu (2003a); Liu (2003b)]. Therefore, at present, exploring and developing the *Wisdom Web* is a feasible goal for WI research. The *Wisdom Web* will enable human users to gain *wisdom* of living, working, and playing.

In [Zhong *et al.* (2002); Zhong *et al.* (2003a); Zhong *et al.* (2003b)], Zhong *et al.* stated that WI can be studied on at least four different conceptual levels (See Fig. 24.1), *Internet level, interface level, knowledge level,* and *application level.* The Internet level mainly focuses on addressing the Web technologies and infrastructure, where *resource optimization* is a key problem. It mainly contains two aspects. The first one concerns a right infrastructure of distributed resources. Its goal is to provide not only a new medium for seamless resource and information sharing, but also a type of man-made resources for sustainable knowledge creation and social evolution [Liu (2003b)]. The *Wisdom Web* will mainly rely on *gridlike service agencies* [Liu (2003b)], in particular, peer-to-peer grids because of their advantages, such as decentralization and robustness. The second aspect focuses on algorithmic support to mobilize distributed resources on the Wisdom Web. It has been shown that some nature-inspired rules, such as artificial ant rules [Babaoglu *et al.* (2002); Montresor *et al.* (2002); Resnick (1994)], can be used to mobilize resources on a peer-to-peer network. This chapter will examine the peer-to-peer infrastructure of gridlike resources and explore the corresponding algorithmic support to mobilize resources.

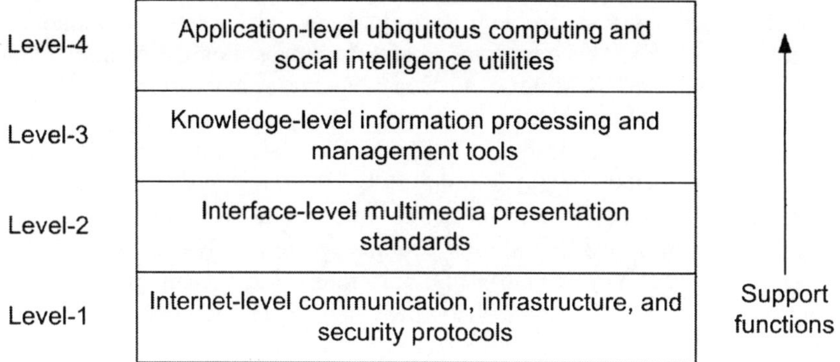

Fig. 24.1 Levels of Web Intelligence.

In the following, we will briefly introduce grid computing and then present the detailed and specific problems we want to addressed.

24.1.1 *Grid Computing*

During the past several decades, the speed of a computer has exponentially increased over one million times [Foster (2000)]. A personal computer today is more powerful than a supercomputer ten years ago [Berman *et al.* (2003a); Foster (2003)]. But, even with such an unimaginable increasing speed, the computer, even the supercomputer today, still cannot satisfy the increasing requirement of large-scale scientific computation in the fields of life sciences, biology, physics, and astronomy [Berman *et al.* (2003a); Foster (2000); Foster and Kesselman (1999b)]. As motivated by this requirement, in early 1980s, 'cluster' technology was proposed, and quickly grew to be a commonly used means to improve the computational power [Foster (2000); Foster and Kesselman (1999b)]. However, some obvious factors limit the development of the 'cluster'. By noticing that computers (including personal computers, workstations, and clusters) in the Internet are often idle, in middle 1990s, the notion of 'the grid' was proposed to share and integrate the idle computing power [Berman *et al.* (2003a); Foster (2000); Foster *et al.* (2003c); Foster and Kesselman (1999b)]. At present, grid computing has become a new IT technology. It not only aims at sharing and integrating geographically distributed computational resources and data resources, but also provides a 'super-supercomputer' which can be seamlessly accessed by the users all over the world, including scientists in the above mentioned scientific fields [Berman *et al.* (2003a); Foster (2000); Foster (2003); Foster and Kesselman (1999b)].

Similar to other new technologies, at the beginning stage of grid comput-ing technology, the first problem is to define widely acceptable standards and protocols. For this problem, Foster and Kesselman [Berman *et al.* (2003a); Foster and Kesselman (1999a); Foster and Kesselman (1999b); Foster *et al.* (2003b); Foster *et al.* (2003a)] and their groups defined two fundamental specifications: *Open Grid Services Architecture* (OGSA), which specifies what a grid should look like, and *Open Grid Services Infrastructure* (OGSI), which specifies how to construct an OGSA grid. They further developed the Globus Toolkit [Foster and Kesselman (1999a); Foster and Kesselman (1999b)]. So far, many large Grid projects have accepted the protocols and services provided by the Globus Toolkit. To illustrate OGSA, OGSI, and Globus Toolkit, in Fig. 24.2 we show a typical grid environment.

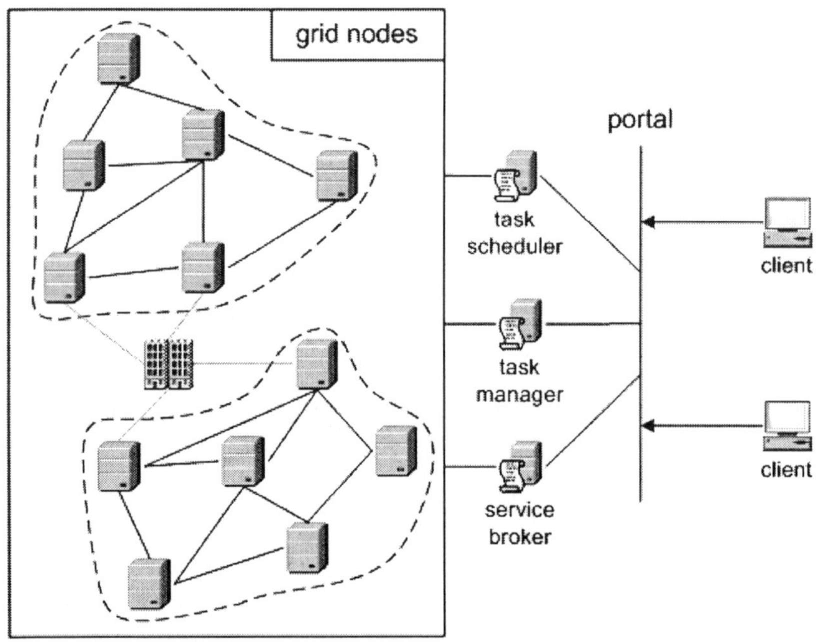

Fig. 24.2   An illustration of a grid environment.

Generally speaking, a grid environment may contain five main compo-nents [Foster and Kesselman (1999a); Foster *et al.* (2003b); Foster *et al.* (2003a); Jacob (2003)]: portal, service broker, task scheduler, task manager, and a network of grid nodes. The portal acts as a user interface, through which a user can log in and use the grid. The portal is also responsible for the security of the whole grid environment. After having logged into the grid, a user can submit a task to the grid. A service broker will check whether or not the grid contains the resources suitable to finish a submitted task. Further, it will check whether or not some resources are available. A task scheduler is responsible for scheduling submitted tasks and arranging them to be served at a proper grid node and at a proper time. A task manager finally launches a submitted task. It is responsible for checking the state of the tasks and collecting the results. In a grid environment, the above four components are optional. However, the nodes, as the core of a grid, are prerequisites. The nodes can be desktops, workstations, and cluters belonging to different LANs, WANs, or the Internet.

Although the task scheduler is a common component of a grid, in some cases, the scheduler is not necessary, such as, in a peer-to-peer grid [Berman *et al.* (2003a); Fox *et al.* (2003)]. In addition, in some applications, it is impossible to schedule a huge number of tasks [Berman *et al.* (2003a); Berman *et al.* (2003b)]. Without a scheduler, tasks are distributed to the network of grid nodes.

24.1.2 *Problem Statements*

According to the above description of a grid environment and especially the peer-to-peer grid node network, here we will concern the following problems:

(1) How can we characterize the global performance of a grid? Can we provide a model to characterize the process of task handling while maintaining balanced loads among grid nodes?
(2) If there are many tasks submitted to a grid, some tasks have to spend some time on finding a suitable node to be served, namely, there is time delay. Each task needs a period of time, called service time, to be served. If we take into account time delay and service time, how do they affect the global performance of a grid?

To address the above problems, in this chapter, we will use differential equation based model, as motivated by the models in [Lerman and Shehory (2000); Wang and Liu (2003); Wang *et al.* (2003)], to describe the process of task handling.

24.1.3 *Organization of the Chapter*

The rest of the chapter is organized as follows: In Section 24.2, we make a brief survey on the related work. Section 24.3 describes an agent-based task handling mechanism and gives basic assumptions in our model. Section 24.4 presents our macroscopic model. Through case studies, Section 24.5 validates the effectiveness of our model and examines the effects of service time, time delay etc. on the global performance of a grid. In Section 24.6, we present a simulation to show how our model can characterize a complete process of task handling on a network of grid nodes. Section 24.7 concludes the chapter and outlines the directions for future work.

24.2   Related Work

In the real world, ants can collect objects (e.g., food) into piles without being controlled by a 'master'. Resnick [Resnick (1994)] successfully simulated this phenomenon by artificial ants and found that with only three simple rules, artificial ants can collect objects into piles:

- The ant wanders around randomly until it encounters an object.
- If the ant is carrying an object, it drops the object and continues to wander randomly.
- If the ant is not carrying an object, it picks the object up and continues to wander.

The goal of Resnick's artificial ants is to collect objects. In order to disperse tasks onto the grid nodes, inspired by Resnick's work, Montresor and Meling [Babaoglu *et al.* (2002); Montresor *et al.* (2002)] developed their artificial ants whose rules are different from those in Resnick's work:

- *SearchMax*: an ant wanders across the network to search overloaded nodes.
- *SearchMin*: an ant wanders across the network to search underloaded nodes.
- *Transfer*: an ant transfers tasks from the most overloaded node to the most underloaded node.

With the above rules, the experiments in [Babaoglu *et al.* (2002); Montresor *et al.* (2002)] showed that the artificial ants can disperse tasks evenly. In one of their experiments, they used 100 idle nodes. Initially, there were 10,000 tasks on a single node. Twenty ants were generated to disperse the tasks. The ants obeyed the above three rules. After 50 iterations, the tasks were evenly dispersed on the idle nodes, that is, there were 100 tasks on each idle node. The experiments in [Babaoglu *et al.* (2002); Montresor *et al.* (2002)] gave empirical simulations of load balancing. However, this kind of microscopic model can only get a final task distribution, but cannot directly describe the global performance of the model. Macroscopic models, on the other hand, can offer such analysis. For more information about macroscopic models, readers are referred to [Hofbauer and Sigmund (1998); Hogg and Huberman (2002); Lerman and Shehory (2000); Nelson and Perelson (2002)].

24.3 Agent-Based Task Handling on a Grid

24.3.1 *The Mechanism*

Agent-based systems have been widely used in peer-to-peer computing [?]. In our models, we will use agents to carry tasks. Then, the movements of agents simulate the transfer of tasks among nodes. The agent-based load balancing and task handling we concern are as follows: Initially, a group of tasks are distributed on a grid. Then, the same number of agents are generated. Each agent carries a task and wanders on the network to search for a suitable team to join and queue. Here, we define the period of time that an agent spends on wandering before joining a team as time delay. An agent will not join a large team because of the possibly long waiting time and its patience. To do so, in our models, we set a maximum size for teams. After having joined a team, an agent can also decide to leave the team and move to other nodes because they prefer to queue at a small team. According to the above description, an agent has three main behaviors: *wandering, queuing,* and *leaving.* In order to have its task finished, an agent must be served by one of the nodes. The service time is assumed to be a constant for each task. An agent only has local information about the sizes of the teams, where it is queuing or which it encounters while wandering. It does not have the global knowledge of the grid environment. After an agent queues at the first place of a team for a unit of service time, its task will be finished and then the agent itself will disappear from the gird environment automatically.

24.3.2 *Assumptions*

Before presenting our models, we make the following basic assumptions as well as their rationalities:

(1) Generally speaking, the nodes on a grid provide the same service(s). Therefore, it is rational to assume that all grid nodes are peer-to-peer.
(2) The tasks are homogeneous. Here, 'homogeneous' means all tasks need the same service and service time. To argue the rationality of this assumption, we consider the situation that, generally speaking, all nodes on a grid can only provide very basic services, for example, addition

operation. If an original task is more complex than an 'addition' task, it has to be decomposed into addition sub-tasks. In this sense, this assumption is rational.

(3) Because tasks are homogeneous, from a global view, the time delay, that a single agent spends on wandering before it finds a suitable node to join, is assumed to be a positive constant; further, we can assume agents follow the same strategies of wandering, queuing, and leaving and occupy the same service time. In other words, all agents are peer-to-peer.

24.4   The Proposed Model

In this section, we construct a macroscopic model to describe the dynamic behavior of task handling while maintaining balanced loads among grid nodes. In doing so, we will consider the factors of time delay, service time etc. Our model will focus on several quantities: the number of wandering agents, the number and size of agent teams. Let y be the number of wandering agents, y_s be the number of agent teams of size s, and m be the maximum team size. Then, obviously, we should have:

$$y \geq 0 \ \text{ and } \ y_s \geq 0 \ (1 \leq s \leq m).$$

Initially, agents are randomly distributed on the grid nodes. They either queue at agent teams or wander on the network.

Based on the previous description and specific assumptions, we have the following general model:

$$\frac{dy_1(t)}{dt} = j_0 y(t - \tau) - j_1 y(t - \tau) y_1(t) + l_2 y_2(t) - l_1 y_1(t)$$
$$+ f_2 y_2(t - \alpha) - f_1 y_1(t - \alpha),$$

$$\frac{dy_s(t)}{dt} = j_{s-1} y(t - \tau) y_{s-1}(t) - j_s y(t - \tau) y_s(t) + l_{s+1} y_{s+1}(t)$$
$$- l_s y_s(t) + f_{s+1} y_{s+1}(t - \alpha) - f_s y_s(t - \alpha), \quad (1 < s < m) \quad (24.1)$$

$$\frac{dy_m(t)}{dt} = j_{m-1} y(t - \tau) y_{m-1}(t) - l_m y_m(t) - f_m y_m(t - \alpha),$$

$$\frac{dy(t)}{dt} = \sum_{s=1}^{m} l_s y_s(t) - \sum_{s=1}^{m-1} j_s y(t - \tau) y_s(t) - j_0 y(t - \tau)$$

$$+ \begin{cases} g(t), & \text{if } t \leq T \\ 0, & \text{if } t > T \end{cases}.$$

In the above equation system, the first three equations characterize the change rate of teams of size 1, s ($1 < s < m$), and m, respectively; The last equation characterizes the change rate of wandering agents. In these equations,

- $\tau > 0$ denotes the period of time between an agent leaves an team and joins another one. Through τ, the model takes into account time delay.
- $\alpha > 0$ denotes the service time of a node to finish a task. Here, we assume all tasks have the same service time to be finished.
- T is a time threshold. When $t < T$, there are new tasks submitted to a grid, and then the same number of new agents are generated.

To understand the equation system, here we will give some more detailed descriptions. First, let us see the second equation, which is a general one. It is suitable to all cases where $1 < s < m$. In the second equation,

(1) $j_{s-1} y(t - \tau) y_{s-1}(t) - j_s y(t - \tau) y_s(t)$ describes the quantitative change of teams of size s caused by wandering agents' joining at certain teams. Specifically,

- $j_{s-1} y(t - \tau) y_{s-1}(t)$ denotes that $j_{s-1} y(t - \tau) y_{s-1}(t)$ wandering agents at time $t - \tau$ meet teams of size $s - 1$ and join them at time t. Then, these teams become teams of size s. Therefore, the number of teams of size s will increase with $j_{s-1} y(t - \tau) y_{s-1}(t)$. Here, $0 < j_{s-1} < 1$ means only a part of teams of size $s - 1$ have a new wandering agent (the same meaning as other j_s).
- $-j_s y(t - \tau) y_s(t)$ denotes that $j_s y(t - \tau) y_s(t)$ wandering agents at time $t - \tau$ meet teams of size s and join them at time t. And, these teams become teams of size $s + 1$. Therefore, the number of teams of size s will decrease with $j_s y(t - \tau) y_s(t)$.

(2) $l_{s+1} y_{s+1}(t) - l_s y_s(t)$ describes the quantitative change of teams of size s caused by queuing agents' leaving. Specifically,

- $l_{s+1} y_{s+1}(t)$ denotes that at time t, the last agents at $l_{s+1} y_{s+1}(t)$ teams of size $s + 1$ leave. Accordingly, these teams become teams of size s. Therefore, the number of teams of size s will decrease with number $l_{s+1} y_{s+1}(t)$. Here, $0 < l_{s+1} < 1$ means only a part of teams of size $s + 1$ have an agent left (the same meaning as other l_s).

- $-l_s y_s(t)$ denotes that at time t, the last agents at $l_s y_s(t)$ teams of size s leave. Then, these teams become teams of size $s - 1$. Therefore, the number of teams of size s will decrease with number $l_s y_s(t)$.

(3) $f_{s+1} y_{s+1}(t - \alpha) - f_s y_s(t - \alpha)$ called "task handling" term, describes the quantitative change of teams of size s, because some queuing agents at the first places have been finished. Specifically,

- $f_{s+1} y_{s+1}(t - \alpha)$ denotes that $f_{s+1} y_{s+1}(t - \alpha)$ teams of size $s + 1$ at time $t - \alpha$ become teams of size s, because the tasks carried by the first agents at these teams are finished. Therefore, the number of teams of size s will increase with number $f_{s+1} y_{s+1}(t - \alpha)$. Here, $0 < f_{s+1} < 1$ means only a part of teams of size $s + 1$ have an agent disappeared (the same meaning as other f_s).
- $-f_s y_s(t - \alpha)$ denotes that $f_s y_s(t - \alpha)$ number of teams of size s at time $t - \alpha$ become teams of size $s - 1$, because the first tasks carried by the first agents at these teams are finished. Hence, the number of teams of size s will decrease with number $f_s y_s(t - \alpha)$.

The first equation is a special case, where $s = 1$. It is similar with the second equation except the first term, $j_0 y(t - \tau)$. $j_0 y(t - \tau)$ denotes that $j_0 y(t - \tau)$ wandering agents at time $t - \tau$ meet idle nodes at time t and form new teams of size one. Then, the number of teams of size one will increase with $j_0 y(t - \tau)$. Note that because we cannot guarantee all wandering agents at time $t - \tau$ will meet an idle node and form a new team, we use j_0 to denote that only a part of wandering agents at $t - \tau$ will form a new team at time t. The third equation is also a special case, where $s = m$. As compared with the second equation, it misses three terms, $-j_m y(t - \tau) y_m t$, $l_{m+1} y_{m+1}(t)$, and $f_{m+1} y_{s+1}(t - \alpha)$, because the maximum size of a team is m. The fourth equation describes the quantitative change of wandering agents, where

- $\sum_{s=1}^{m} l_s y_s(t)$ is the number of agents that leave teams where they are queuing and begin to wander at time t.
- $-\sum_{s=1}^{m-1} j_s y(t - \tau) y_s(t)$ is the number of wandering agents at time $t - \tau$, which meet certain teams and join them to queue at time t.
- $-j_0 y(t - \tau)$ denotes the number of wandering agents that form new teams of size one at time t.
- $g(t)$ denote the number of new incoming wandering agents at time t $(t < T)$.

According to Equation System 24.1, we have the following equation for the total number of agents at time $t + 1$:

$$S(t + 1) = S(t) - \sum_{s=1}^{m} f_s y_s(t - \alpha) + \begin{cases} g(t), & \text{if } t \leq T \\ 0, & \text{if } t > T \end{cases}, \qquad (24.2)$$

where $-\sum_{s=1}^{m} f_s y_s(t - \alpha)$ is the total number of agents, at various teams, whose tasks have been finished at time t, hence they disappear automatically, and $g(t)$ denotes new agents generated for new tasks when $t < T$.

24.5 Case Studies

In this section, we will conduct several case studies to validate our proposed model and, in particular, to examine the effects of time delay τ, service time α, and time threshold T on the performance of a grid. For the sake of convenience, we will set $m = 2$. Hence, Equation System 24.1 and Equation 24.2 can be rewritten as:

$$\frac{dy_1(t)}{dt} = j_0 y(t - \tau) + l_2 y_2(t) - l_1 y_1(t) - j_1 y(t - \tau) y_1(t)$$
$$+ f_2 y_2(t - \alpha) - f_1 y_1(t - \alpha),$$

$$\frac{dy_2(t)}{dt} = j_1 y(t - \tau) y_1(t) - l_2 y_2(t) - f_2 y_2(t - \alpha), \qquad (24.3)$$

$$\frac{dy(t)}{dt} = \sum_{s=1}^{2} l_s y_s(t) - j_1 y(t - \tau) y_1(t) - j_0 y(t - \tau)$$
$$+ \begin{cases} g(t), & \text{if } t \leq T \\ 0, & \text{if } t > T \end{cases},$$

and

$$S(t + 1) = S(t) - \sum_{s=1}^{2} f_s y_s(t - \alpha) + \begin{cases} g(t), & \text{if } t \leq T \\ 0, & \text{if } t > T \end{cases}. \qquad (24.4)$$

Generally speaking, the number of new tasks submitted to a grid at each step is random. In order to simulate the randomness, in this case study, we employ a random function,

$$g(t) = random([0, 50]), \qquad (24.5)$$

to generate a random number and add this number of agents to a grid node network at step $t < T$.

Case study 1. $S(0) = 1000, j_0 = l_1 = l_2 = 0.01, j_1 = 0.0001, \tau = 0, T = 200, \alpha = 5, 10, 20, 40, y(0) = 1000, y_1(0) = 0, y_2(0) = 0.$

The resulting curves corresponding to the first 6000 steps are shown in Fig. 24.3, where in each plot, we inserted a small plot. A small plot depicts the first 1000 steps of the corresponding plot. From Fig. 24.3, we have the following observations:

(1) **All curves can be separated into two phases: increasing phase and decreasing phase.** This phenomenon is caused by the non-zero value of T. When $t \leq T$, a random number of agents are generated to carry the new incoming agents, therefore the curves increase. After t exceeds T, no new task is submitted and no new agent is generated, all tasks are finished gradually and accordingly all agents automatically disappear, therefore the curves gradually decrease to zero.

(2) **The turning points between the increasing phases and the decreasing phases on $y(t)$ curves occur exactly at $t = T$, while those on $y_1(t)$ and $y_2(t)$ curves occur some steps after $t = T$.** This is because all newly generated agents are wandering agents. Only after some wandering steps, these agents will find suitable nodes and join them, and become queuing agents.

(3) At the increasing phase, because at each step, the number of new wandering agents is random, the curves of $y(t)$, $y_1(t)$, and $y_2(t)$ show perturbations. After the turning points, all $y(t)$ curves almost smoothly decrease, but $y_1(t)$ and $y_2(t)$ curves still show perturbations.

(4) For all $y(t)$, $y_1(t)$, and $y_2(t)$ curves, **the larger α, the higher the peaks, but the slower the speed converges to zero.** For example, in the inserted small plot in Fig. 24.3 (c), the peaks corresponding to $\alpha = 5$ and $\alpha = 40$ are around 500 and 1500, respectively. At time $t = 1000$, $y_2(t)$ with $\alpha = 5$ has become zero. But, $y_2(t)$ with $\alpha = 40$ is around 600. We can note the same phenomena occurring at $y(t)$ and $y_1(t)$ curves. These phenomena are caused by the different values of α: For the same number of tasks, the longer the service time of a single task, the longer the service time of all tasks.

Case study 2. $S(0) = 1000, j_0 = l_1 = l_2 = 0.01, j_1 = 0.0001, \tau = 20, T = 200, \alpha = 5, 10, 20, 40, y(0) = 1000, y_1(0) = 0, y_2(0) = 0.$

The resulting curves of Case Study 2 are similar with those of Case Study 1. Therefore, for the sake of space, we do not present those curves here.

Case study 3. $S(0) = 1000, j_0 = l_1 = l_2 = 0.01, j_1 = 0.0001, \tau = 20, T = 200, \alpha = 5, 10, 20, 40, y(0) = 1000, y_1(0) = 0, y_2(0) = 0.$

The result is shown in Fig. 24.4. As compared with Case Studies 1 and

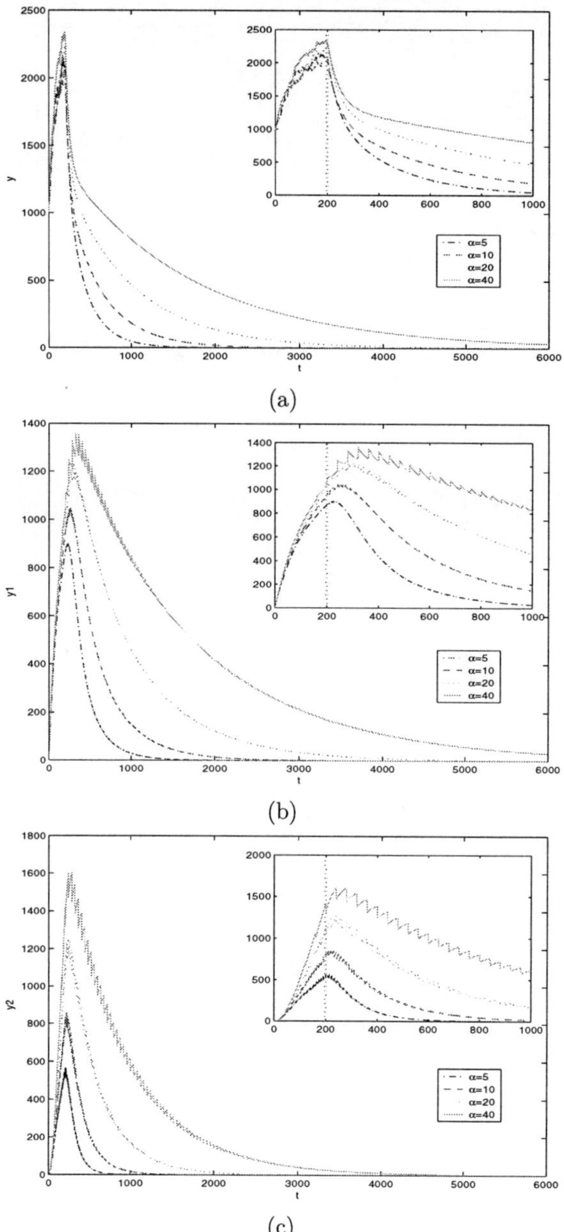

Fig. 24.3 Case study 1 where $S(0) = 1000, j_0 = l_1 = l_2 = 0.01, j_1 = 0.0001, \tau = 0, T = 200, \alpha = 5, 10, 20, 40, y(0) = 1000, y_1(0) = 0, y_2(0) = 0$.

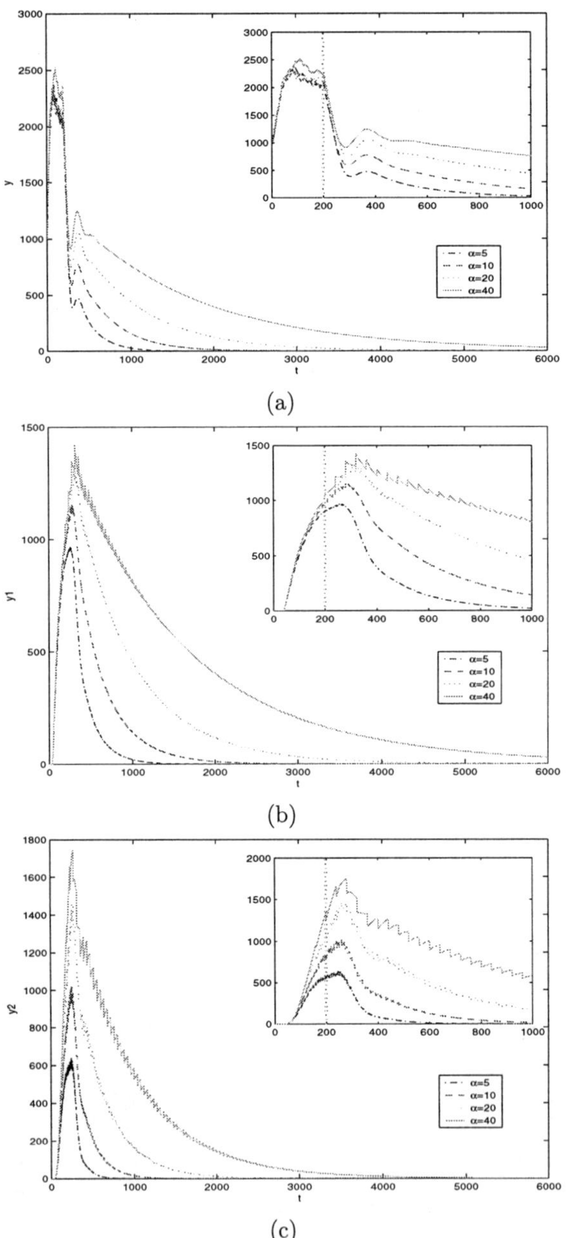

Fig. 24.4   Case study 3 where $S(0) = 1000, j_0 = l_1 = l_2 = 0.01, j_1 = 0.0001, \tau = 40, T = 200, \alpha = 5, 10, 20, 40, y(0) = 1000, y_1(0) = 0, y_2(0) = 0$.

2, Case Study 3 is different from them only on the value of τ. Case Studies 1 and 2 respectively set $\tau = 0$ and 20, while Case Study 3 set $\tau = 40$. Due to this difference, Fig. 24.4 shows the following new phenomena:

(1) $y(t)$ **curves exhibit oscillations at the decreasing phase.** $y_1(t)$ and $y_2(t)$ also seem to exhibit oscillations. But, they are not as clear as those on $y(t)$ curves.
(2) The peaks of $y(t)$ curves no longer occur exactly at $t = T$.

Case study 4. $S(0) = 1000$, $j_0 = l_1 = l_2 = 0.01$, $j_1 = 0.0001$, $\tau = 40, T = 200$, $\alpha = 5, 10, 20, 40$, $y(0) = 1000$, $y_1(0) = 0$, $y_2(0) = 0$.

The resulting curves are shown in Fig. 24.5. As compared with those in Figs. 24.3 and 24.4, $y(t)$ curves show more oscillations than those in Fig. 24.4. Moreover, $y_1(t)$ **and** $y_2(t)$ **curves also show clear oscillations.**

In the above four case studies, we set all agents as wandering agents at the beginning. And, there is no queuing agent. The following case study is slightly different from them, where we set some agents as wandering agents and the others as queuing agents. In addition, in this case study, we will examine the effect of T with different values.

Case study 5. Let $S(0) = 1000, j_0 = l_1 = l_2 = 0.01$, $j_1 = 0.0001$, $\tau = 20, T = 10, 50, 100, 200$, $\alpha = 40, y(0) = 100$, $y_1(0) = 100, y_2(0) = 400$.

Fig. 24.6 shows the result of Case study 5. From Fig. 24.6, we can note that,

(1) $y(t)$ and $y_1(t)$ curves still have two phases, an increasing phase and a decreasing phase. But, $y_2(t)$ curves have one more decreasing phase at the beginning 50 steps (See Fig. 24.6(c)). This is because, at the beginning some steps, compared with the number of wandering agents and queuing agents at teams of size one, there are too many queuing agents at teams of size two. Therefore, some of those agents will leave their original teams and become wandering agents or queuing agents at teams of size one. This is also one of the reasons that cause the sharp increases of $y(t)$ and $y_1(t)$ curves.
(2) In the inserted small plot in Fig. 24.6(a), as T increases from 10 to 200, the peaks of $y(t)$ curves becomes higher and higher. When $T = 200$, the curve shows a plateau phase when t is approximately greater than 100 and less than 200. This is because, as t exceeds 100, there are many wandering agents and queuing agents at teams of size one, consequently more and more wandering agents will find and join teams of size two (See the inserted small plot in Fig. 24.6(c)). The plateau phase means at a step, if there are n new agents, there will be almost the same number of wandering agents that become queuing agents.

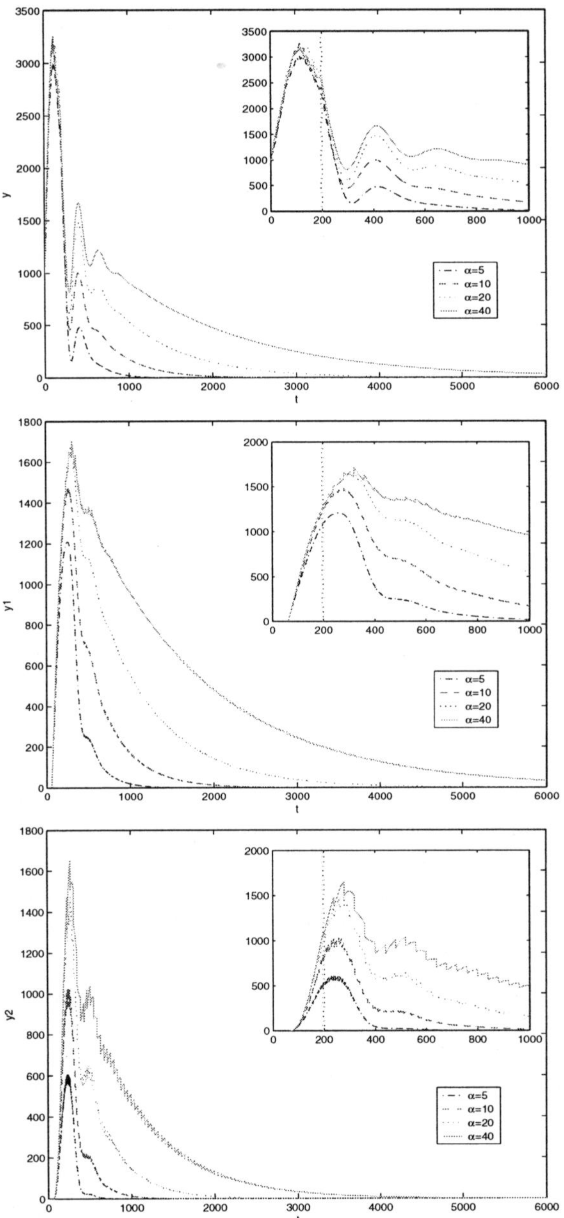

Fig. 24.5   Case study 4 where $S(0) = 1000, j_0 = l_1 = l_2 = 0.01, j_1 = 0.0001, \tau = 60, T = 200, \alpha = 5, 10, 20, 40, y(0) = 1000, y_1(0) = 0, y_2(0) = 0.$

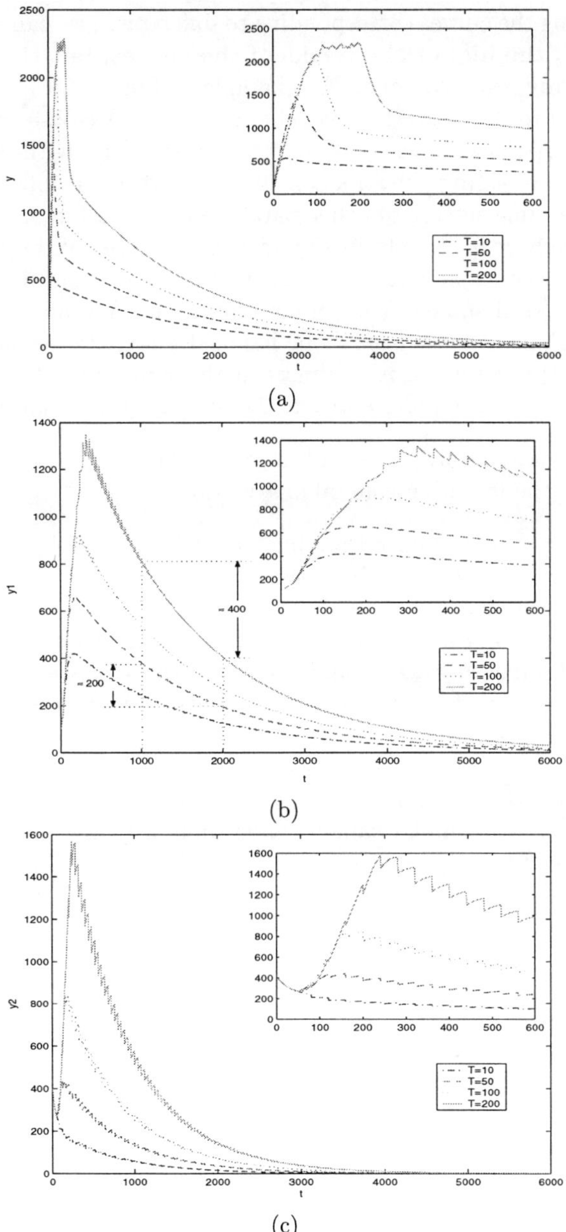

Fig. 24.6   Case study 5 where $S(0) = 1000, j_0 = l_1 = l_2 = 0.01, j_1 = 0.0001, \tau = 20, T = 10, 50, 100, 200, \alpha = 40, y(0) = 100, y_1(0) = 100, y_2(0) = 400$.

(3) Comparing the curves corresponding to different T, we can see that **the larger T, the higher the peaks of the curves, but the faster the speed converges to zero.** For example, in Fig. 24.6(b), as t increases from 1000 to 2000, $y_1(t)$ curve where $T = 200$ decreases with around 400, but $y_1(t)$ curve where $T = 50$ decreases only with 200. This is really an interesting phenomenon. It is caused by the following reason: given the same setting of other parameter, with a larger T, there will be relatively more agents in the grid, then there will be more agents queuing rather than wandering. Therefore, at a certain time, there will be more tasks handled. We can note from Fig. 24.6 that although with a larger T, more tasks need to be handled than with a smaller T, $y(t)$, $y_1(t)$, $y_2(t)$ decrease to zero almost at the same time. In other words, *the more tasks, the more efficient the process of task handling.*

Based on the above five case studies and their results shown in Figs. 24.3-24.6, we have the following general observations:

(1) No matter what the initial parameter settings are, all $y(t)$, $y_1(t)$, and $y_2(t)$ curves, respectively corresponding to the number of wandering agents, the number of teams of size one, and the number of teams of size two, keep non-negative. And, all those curves finally tend to zero. That means all wandering agents and queuing agents disappear because their tasks are finished finally. These are definitely two necessary conditions to show the effectiveness of our model.

(2) As τ increases, the process of task handling exhibits some oscillations. Specifically, the larger τ, the longer the duration of oscillations. Wang *et al.* observed a similar same phenomenon in [Wang *et al.* (2003)].

(3) With different α, the curves show the similar shapes. But, the larger α, the higher the peaks of the curves, and the slower the speed converges to zero. In other words, the larger α, the longer the process of task handling.

(4) With different T, the curves also show the similar shapes. The larger T, the higher the peaks of the curves, and the faster the speed converges to zero.

24.6   A Complete Task Handling Process

In this section, we will use our model to simulate a complete process of task handling on a grid. In the simulation, the parameter setting is as follows: $m = 2$, $S(0) = 0$, $j_0 = l_1 = l_2 = 0.01$, $j_1 = 0.0001$, $f_1 = 0.05$, $f_2 = 0.1$, $\tau = 5$, $\alpha = 20$, $g(t) = rand([0, 100])$. In particular, we set $y(0) = 0$, $y_1(0) = 0$, and $y_2(0) = 0$, that indicates initially, there is no task and no agent. We set $t \in [0, 40000]$ and $T = 38000$, that means the process is relatively long and lots of steps later there is no new task submitted and no new agent generated. Therefore, all tasks are finished finally.

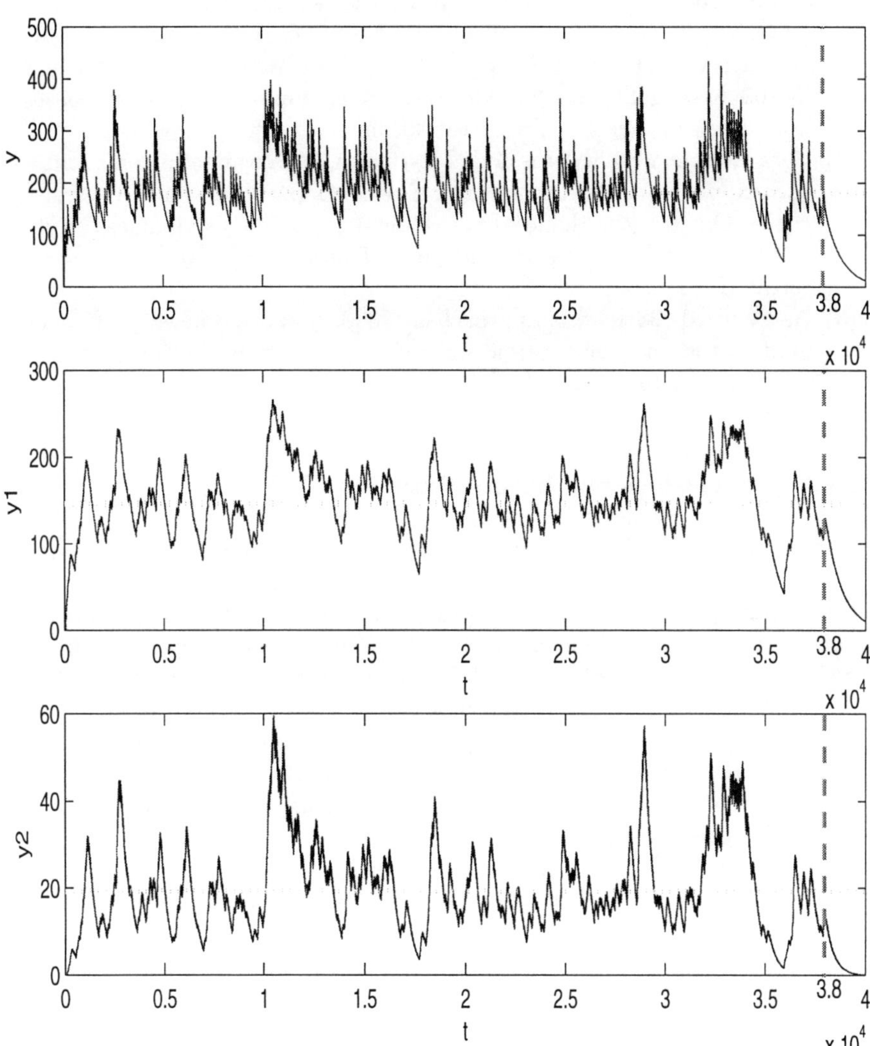

Fig. 24.7 A complete task handling process simulation where $S(0) = 0, j_0 = l_1 = l_2 = 0.01, j_1 = 0.0001, f_1 = 0.05, f_2 = 0.1, \tau = 5, \alpha = 20, y(0) = 0, y_1(0) = 0, y_2(0) = 0, g(t) = rand([0, 100])$.

Fig. 24.7 shows the simulation result, where we have the following observations:

(1) Initially, there is no agent in the grid. Therefore, at the beginning some steps, all $y(t)$, $y_1(t)$, and $y_2(t)$ curves have an increasing phase. After about 1500 steps, all curves approach to an approximately balanced state, where they do not show long time increase or decrease. But, because at each step $t < 38000$, there are a random number of $n \in [0, 100]$ new agents generated for the new incoming tasks, as t increases, $y(t)$, $y_1(t)$, and $y_2(t)$ show perturbations with different swings.
(2) Because each new agent is added to the grid as a wandering one, and at each step the number of new agents are random, $y(t)$ shows a serrated curve. On the other hand, due to time delay τ, the randomness of $y(t)$ will not directly affect $y_1(t)$ and $y_2(t)$. Therefore, they do not show the serrated perturbations.
(3) As t exceeds 38000 and approaches 40000, that is no new agent generated to the gird, $y(t)$, $y_1(t)$, and $y_2(t)$ almost smoothly tend to zero. All tasks are finished and all agents disappear finally.

24.7   Conclusions and Future Work

The World Wide Web has become a new medium for resource and information sharing and leaded us into a new information age. Since it appears, the Web keeps exponentially increasing in its web sites, web pages, and hyperlinks. But, its development is far behind the increasing speed of human needs. In order to explore and develop the next generation of the Web, Zhong, Liu, Yao, and Ohsuga proposed the concept of "Web Intelligence" (WI). They argued WI aims at exploring and exploiting the essential roles of Artificial Intelligence (AI) and advanced Information Technology (IT) on the next shift of Web-based systems, particularly, Web-based life, work, and play. They argued that the next paradigm shift in WI would be the *Wisdom Web*, which will enable uses to gain wisdom of living, working, and playing. In WI as well as the Wisdom Web, resource optimization is a key problem. It mainly consists of two aspects, a right infrastructure of resources and the corresponding algorithmic support to mobilize distributed resources. In order to address these, specifically, in this chapter, we have presented a macroscopic model to describe the global performance of agent-based task handling in a peer-to-peer grid. Our model simulated a general scenario, where new tasks are submitted to a peer-to-peer network of grid nodes and old tasks are finished gradually. Furthermore, we examined the effects of time delay and service time as well as time threshold for new incoming agents on the performance of agent-based task handling. We further simulated a complete process of task handling. Through several case studies, we showed the following observations:

- Our model can successfully simulate the process of task handling in a peer-to-peer grid. Case studies showed that the process of task handling has different phases. Usually, there are two phases: an increasing phase and a decreasing phase. With different parameter settings, the turning points between increasing phasea and decreasing phases will occur in different time and have different values. After the turning points, the process smoothly tends to zero only with some small perturbations. That means all tasks are finished and consequently all agents disappear automatically. In addition, during the process of task handling, the numbers of wandering agents and teams of various sizes keep nonnegative. The above are two necessary conditions of our model.
- Time threshold T seems to be a very interesting factor affecting the performance of task handling on a grid. We have found that the larger time threshold T, the faster the speed of task handling. In Case study 5, we have explained the reason that given the same settings of other parameter, with a larger T, there will be relatively more tasks to be handled than with a smaller T. In this situation, more agents will be queuing agents rather than wandering agents. Therefore, at a certain time, more agents will be handled in the larger T case.
- Service time α of a task determines the speed of task handling: the larger service time, the slower the speed of task handling. For example, in Fig. 24.3, when $\alpha = 5$, our model took around 2000 steps to handle all tasks. On the other hand, when $\alpha = 40$, 6000 steps were not enough for our model to handle those tasks. In fact, it needs 8000 steps. In other words, if service time α decreases from 40 to 5, the process of task handling will increase with a factor of around 4 times.
- Time delay τ is also an interesting factor. We found that as τ increases, the process of task handling will show more and more oscillations. The larger time delay, the longer the duration of oscillations. But, an interesting phenomenon is the speed of task handling is not affected by the oscillations. For example, in Case Studies 1-4 (See Figs. 24.3-24.5) where τ increase from 0 to 60, our model always took 2000 steps to handle all tasks given $\alpha = 5$.

Although our model perhaps does not completely reflect the real process on a grid, we believe it has shown main characteristics of the global performance of a grid.

As for the future work, the following aspects remain open:

- We have experimentally found that the performance of our model greatly depends on service time α, time delay τ, time threshold T, as well as leaving, wandering, and queuing strategies of agents, namely, the parameters l_s and j_s. Therefore, how to determine these parameters such that the tasks are handling in the most efficient way? Can a certain machine learning method, such as, Genetic Algorithm (GA), be used to solve this problem?
- In our model, we have considered service time α, time delay τ, time threshold T, etc. factors, which greatly affect the global performance of a grid. What are the relationships among them keeps unsolved. In addition, some other factors, such as transport cost an agent carries a task from one node to another, should also be considered.
- In our model, we assume all grid nodes are homogeneous. In order to make our model more general, we should focus on the heterogeneous node case at the next step.

Acknowledgement

The authors wish to sincerely thank Mr. Hin Hang Tsang for his helpful discussions with us.

Bibliography

Babaoglu, O., Meling, H., and Montresor, A. (2002). Anthill: A framework for the development of agent-based peer-to-peer systems. In *Proceedings of the 22th International Conference on Distributed Computing Systemsl (ICDCS 2002)*, Vienna, Austria.

Berman, F., Fox, G., and Hey, T., editors (2003a). *Grid computing: making the global infrastructure a reality*. John Wiley and Sons.

Berman, F., Fox, G., and Hey, T. (2003b). The Grid: past, present, future. In F. Berman, G. Fox, and T. Hey, editors, *Grid Computing: Making the Global Infrastructure a Reality*, chapter 1, pages 9–50. JohnWiley and Sons.

Foster, I. (2000). Internet computing and the emerging grid. *Nature Web Matters*. http://www.nature.com/nature/webmatters/Grid/grid.html.

Foster, I. (2003). The Grid: A new infrastructure for 21st century science. In F. Berman, G. Fox, and T. Hey, editors, *Grid Computing: Making the Global Infrastructure a Reality*, chapter 2, pages 51–64. John Wiley and Sons.

Foster, I. and Kesselman, C. (1999a). Globus: A toolkit-based grid architecture. In I. Foster and C. Kesselman, editors, *The Grid: A Blueprint for a New Computing Infrastructure*, chapter 2, pages 259–278. Morgan Kaufman.

Foster, I. and Kesselman, C., editors (1999b). *The Grid: Blueprint for a new computing infrastructure*. Morgan Kaufman.

Foster, I., Kesselman, C., and Tuecke, S. (2003a). The anatomy of the Grid. In F. Berman, G. Fox, and T. Hey, editors, *Grid Computing: Making the Global Infrastructure a Reality*, chapter 6, pages 171–198. John Wiley and Sons.

Foster, I., Kesselman, C., Nick, J. M., and Tuecke, S. (2003b). The physiology of the Grid. In F. Berman, G. Fox, and T. Hey, editors, *Grid Computing: Making the Global Infrastructure a Reality*, chapter 8, pages 217–250. John Wiley and Sons.

Foster, I., Geisler, J., Nickless, B., Smith, W., and Tuecke, S. (2003c). Software infrastructure for the I-WAY high-performance distributed computing experiment. In F. Berman, G. Fox, and T. Hey, editors, *Grid Computing: Making the Global Infrastructure a Reality*, chapter 4, pages 101–116. John Wiley and Sons.

Fox, G., Gannon, D., Ko, S.-H., Sangmi-Lee, Pallickara, S., Pierce, M., Qiu, X., Rao, X., Uyar, A., Wang, M., and Wu, W. (2003). Peer-to-peer grids. In F. Berman, G. Fox, and T. Hey, editors, *Grid Computing: Making the Global Infrastructure a Reality*, chapter 18, pages 471–490. John Wiley and Sons.

Hofbauer, J. and Sigmund, K. (1998). *Evolutionary Games and Replicator Dynamics*. Cambridge University Press.

Hogg, T. and Huberman, B. A. (2002). Dynamics of large autonomous computational systems. Technical Report HPL-2002-77, HP Labs, Palo Alto, USA.

Jacob, B. (2003). Grid computing: What are the key components? *http://www-106.ibm.com/developerworks/grid/*.

Lerman, K. and Shehory, O. (2000). Coalition formation for large-scale electronic markets. In *Proceedings of the 4th International Conference on Multi-Agent Systems (ICMAS 2000)*, pages 167–174.

Liu, J. (2003a). New challenges in the World Wide Wisdom Web (W4) research. In *Proceedings of the 14th International Symposium on Methodologies for Intelligence Systems (ISMIS 2003)*, LNAI 2871, pages 1–6. Springer.

Liu, J. (2003b). Web Intelligence (WI): What makes Wisdom Web? In *Proceedings of the 18th International Joint Conference on Arti.cial Intelligence (IJCAI-03)*, pages 1596–1601, Acapulco, Mexico.

Liu, J., Zhong, N., Yao, Y., and Ras, A. W. (2003). The Wisdom Web: New challenges for Web Intelligence (WI). *Journal of Intelligent Informaion Systems*, **20**(1), 5–9.

Montresor, A., Meling, H., and Babaoglu, O. (2002). Messor: Load-balancing through a swarm of autonomous agents. Technical Report UBLCS-02-08, Department of Computer Science, University of Bologna, Bologna, Italy.

Nelson, P. W. and Perelson, A. S. (2002). Mathematical analysis of delay di.erential equation model of HIV-1 infection. *Mathematical Biosciences*, **179**(1), 73–94.

Resnick, M. (1994). *Turtles, Termites, and Tra.c Jams: Explorations in Massively Parallel Microworlds*. MIT Press.

Wang, Y. and Liu, J. (2003). Macroscopic model for load balancing on grids. In *Proceedings of the 2nd International Joint Conference on Autonomous Agents and Multi-Agent Systems (AAMAS'03)*, pages 804–811, Melbourne, Australia.

Wang, Y., Liu, J., and Jin, X. (2003). Modeling agent-based load balancing with time delays. In *Proceedings of the 2003 IEEE/WIC International Conference on Intelligent Agent Technology (IAT-2003)*, pages 189–195, Halifax, Canada.

Zhong, N., Liu, J., Yao, Y., and Ohsuga, S. (2000). Web Intelligence (WI). In *Proceedings of the 24th IEEE Computer Societh International Computer Software and Application Conference (COMPSAC 2000)*, pages 469–470, Taipei, Taiwan. IEEE Computer Society Press.

Zhong, N., Liu, J., and Yao, Y. (2002). In search of the Wisdom Web. *IEEE Computer*, **35**(11), 27–31.

Zhong, N., Liu, J., and Yao, Y. (2003a). *Web Intelligence*. Springer.

Zhong, N., Liu, J., and Yao, Y. (2003b). Web Intelligence (WI): A new paradigm for developing the Wisdom Web and social network intelligence. In N. Zhong, J. Liu, and Y. Yao, editors, *Web Intelligence*, chapter 1, pages 1–16. Springer.

## CHAPTER 25

INTELLIGENT TECHNOLOGY FOR CONTENT MONITORING ON THE WEB

Mark Last[1], Bracha Shapira[1], Yuval Elovici[1], Omer Zaafrany[1], and Abraham Kandel[2][3]

[1]*Department of Information Systems Engineering*
Ben-Gurion University of the Negev, Beer-Sheva 84105, Israel
[2]*Department of Computer Science and Engineering*
University of South Florida, Tampa, FL, 33620, USA
[3]*Currently at the Faculty of Engineering, Tel-Aviv University, Israel*
E-mail: {mlast, bshapira, zaafrany}@bgumail.bgu.ac.il, elovici@inter.net.il
kandel@csee.usf.edu

International terrorists are increasingly using the Internet for covert communications, collecting information on their topics of interest, and spreading the word about their activities around the world. One way to detect terrorist activities on the Internet is by monitoring the content accessed by web users. This study presents an innovative, DM-based methodology for web content monitoring. The normal behavior of a group of similar users is learned by applying unsupervised clustering algorithms to the textual content of publicly available web pages they usually view. The induced model of normal behavior is used in real-time to reveal anomalous content accessed at a specific computer. To speed-up the detection process, dimensionality reduction is applied to the content data. We evaluate the proposed methodology by ROC analysis.

25.1 Introduction

As shown by the tragic events of September 11, 2001, one of the Internet's threats is the ability of terrorist organizations and other criminal groups to hide their activities among the seemingly infinite volume of traffic it carries [Lemos (2002)]. The use of the Internet as a communication medium for international terrorists is mentioned in [Birnhack and Elkin-Koren (2002)]. Apparently, the Internet is being used by international terrorists for collecting information on their topics of interest and spreading the word about their activities around the world.

Existing *Intrusion Detection Systems* (IDS) would detect terrorists or other criminals using the Internet only in case of abnormal activity at the command level such as password cracking. However, in case of normal but non-legitimate behavior these systems will fail to issue an alarm. For example, they will not detect an employee who is using the web in his regular working hours to read instructions on bomb-making or to view pornography sites. The main goal of our research, initially introduced by us in [Last *et. al.* (2003)] and further enhanced in [Elovici *et. al.* (to appear)] and [Shapira *et. al.* (2003)], is to develop a new method for identification of authorized users with abnormal access patterns to publicly available information on the web.

Certainly, the adoption of strong cryptography by most web sites, including those run or visited by terrorists, will make monitoring of Internet content much harder. As long as this does not happen, using the net as an open-source intelligence tool is "a valuable target of opportunity" [Wilson (2002)]. This research integrates issues from the research fields of computer security, information retrieval, and cluster analysis. An overview of related topics from these research fields is provided by us in [Last *et. al.* (2003)].

This chapter is organized as follows. In Section 2, we present our methodology for Internet content monitoring. Section 3 describes an initial case study that tested the feasibility of the proposed approach. Finally, in Section 4 we outline directions for the next stages of our research.

25.2 Internet Content Monitoring

25.2.1 Methodology Overview

Our new methodology uses the content of web pages browsed by a specific group of users as an input for monitoring user activity. The current version of a system based on our methodology can handle only the *textual* content of web pages excluding images, music, video clips, and other complex data types. Our basic assumption is that textual content normally downloaded by the group members represent their current information needs and can be used as input data for learning the group's normal behavior and for detecting abnormal users. We define user *abnormal behavior* as an access to information that is not expected to be viewed by a member of the user group [Last *et. al.* (2003)]. Since our methodology is based on automated analysis of *web content,* it belongs to the *content mining* area of *web intelligence* [Zhong (2003)].

The suggested methodology supports two modes of operation:

Training Mode

- Identify a group of similar users (e.g., CS students, division employees, etc.).
- Record their web access activities (textual content of downloaded web pages). No recording of individual users' names or IP addresses of their computers is required at this stage.
- Filter out non-textual information (pictures, sounds, etc.).
- Convert each textual web page into a suitable representation (e.g., vector-space model [Last *et. al.* (2003)]).
- Reduce the representation space using a dimensionality reduction technique [Sebastiani (2002)].
- Extract the model of normal behavior by applying techniques of *unsupervised clustering* to the page representations. The resulting clusters represent the group's interests, where each cluster is expected to contain pages related to one topic of the group members' areas of interest.

Monitoring Mode

- Collect the content of pages downloaded by members of the monitored user group. Each user is identified by a "user's computer" having a unique IP address.
- Convert each downloaded web page into a suitable representation (see the training mode above).
- For each downloaded page, find the most similar cluster in the set of clusters that represent the normal behavior.
- Issue an alarm if the similarity between the downloaded page and the most similar cluster is below a pre-defined threshold (lowest similarity is 0 and highest similarity is 1, thus the threshold is in the interval (0,1)).
- Take an action (Respond / Do not respond). The IP address of a monitored computer can be used to locate the suspicious user if he/she is still logged on to the same machine.

In the following sub-sections, we describe in details the normal user behavior training and the suggested network monitoring technique.

25.2.2 The Training Mode

The training part of the methodology, which is operated in batch, defines and represents the normal behavior of a group of users based on the stored content of their web activity. We assume that it is possible to access all public traffic of a group of users by monitoring the Web proxy that is being used by the entire group or by direct packet monitoring on communication lines (see [Feldmann (2000)]). Textual page content is collected by the Sniffer module and sent to the Filter module. The Filter excludes transactions (page views) that do not include enough meaningful textual information. For the included transactions, all the tags related to the content format are removed (for example, the tags of an HTML document are filtered out). The filtered pages are sent to the Vector-Generator module. This module converts the content of each page into a suitable representation, which can be used by clustering algorithms.

The current version of the system based on our methodology represents web pages by the vector-space model that is commonly used in Information Retrieval applications [Salton (1989)]. In the vector space model, a document d is represented by an n-dimensional vector $d=$ $(w_1, w_2, ..., w_n)$, where w_i represents the frequency-based weight of term i in document d. For the sake of simplicity, the vector-space model assumes the index terms in the d vector to be mutually independent. To normalize the elements of each term-frequency vector, we use here the following scheme for calculating the term weights in each document:

$$w_i = \frac{freq_i}{\max_l freq_l} \qquad (25.1)$$

where $freq_i$ is the raw frequency of an index term i in a document d (called *tf* factor)

To indicate if two documents represented as vectors are related, a similarity between them may be computed by using one of the known vector distance measuring methods, such as Euclidian distance or Cosine [Boger *et. al.* (2001); Pierrea *et. al.* (2000)]. This can apply to predicting whether a new document can be related to an existing cluster provided that the document and the cluster centroid have the same representation. Before initiating the cluster analysis, the vectors in the database are normalized so that each vector contains the same number of terms (if a term exists in one vector and not in the other, its weight in the other vector is set to zero).

As shown in [Sequeira and Zaki (2002)], clustering is also an efficient tool for anomaly detection: normality of a new object can be evaluated by its distance from the most similar cluster under the assumption that all clusters have been constructed from purely "normal" data. The Clustering Module accesses the reduced vectors that were collected during the training period and generates n clusters representing the normal topics viewed by the group members. For each cluster, the Group-Representation module computes a centroid vector (denoted by Cv_k) which represents the key terms associated with the corresponding topic. The weight tCv_{ik} of a term i in the centroid vector Cv_k is calculated as follows:

$$tCv_{ik} = \frac{1}{N_k} \sum_{j=1}^{N_k} w_{ij}$$

$$(25.2)$$

where N_k is the total number of vectors in cluster k and w_{ij} is the normalized frequency of term i in vector j.

25.2.3 The Monitoring Mode

The monitoring part is operated in real-time as users surf the Web. The first three modules of the monitoring mode (Sniffer, Filter, and Vector - Generator) have the same pre-processing functionality as in the training mode. The Vector-Generator module converts the user transactions content into a suitable representation (e.g., *access vector av* when using the vector-space model). In order to speed up the real-time detection process we apply a dimensionality reduction algorithm (Figure 25.1). This algorithm, based on [Sebastiani (2002)], reduces the computation time needed to evaluate the similarity between vector pairs by reducing the number of terms in each vector based on the intra-document term frequency.

The Detector uses the clusters representing the "normal user behavior" (that were defined during the training mode) to determine whether the downloaded document is similar to one of the "normal" clusters. This resembles the approach used in some collaborative filtering systems [Hanani *et. al.* (2001)] where relevancy of a document to a user is predicted by comparing the vector representing his or her interests to vectors of users most similar to him or her. In the current version of a system based on our methodology, we use the vector-space model and the cosine similarity measure.

As indicated above, each cluster is represented by a centroid vector. The Detector issues an alarm when the similarity between the access vector and the nearest centroid is below the threshold *tr*:

$$Max\left(\frac{\sum_{i=1}^{m}(tCv_{i1} \cdot tAv_i)}{\sqrt{\sum_{i=1}^{m}tCv_{i1}^2 \cdot \sum_{i=1}^{m}tAv_i^2}}, ..., \frac{\sum_{i=1}^{m}(tCv_{in} \cdot tAv_i)}{\sqrt{\sum_{i=1}^{m}tCv_{in}^2 \cdot \sum_{i=1}^{m}tAv_i^2}} \right) < tr \tag{25.3}$$

Where Cv_k is the k-th centroid vector ($k = 1, ..., n$), Av - the access vector, tCv_{ik} - the i-th   term in the vector Cv_k, tAv_i- the i-th term in the vector Av, and m - the number of unique terms in each vector.

Input:
1. Set of n normalized vectors with m terms each.
2. Dimensionality reduction rate denoted by p (between 0 to 1).
3. The minimum number of non-zero terms in a vector denoted by *MinTerm* (default value = 5 terms). Vector that will have after the reduction less than *MinTerm* terms will be removed from the training set.

Output: Set of n' normalized vectors with m' terms each.

Step1 – Compute the number of occurrences of each of the m terms across the n vectors and store the results in vector v.

Step2– Search in v for the term that has the maximum frequency and store the result in *MaxApp*.

Step3– Compute the lower frequency limit denoted by *tmin=p*MaxApp*.

Step4– Compute the upper frequency limit denoted by *tmax=(1-p)*MaxApp*.

Step5– For $i:=1$ to m do
    If ($v[i]$ > *tmax*) or ($v[i]$ < *tmin*) then remove term
        $v[i]$ from all the n vectors.

Step6 - For $j:=1$ to n do
    If (# of non-zero terms in vector j < *MinTerm*)

Fig 25.1 Dimensionality Reduction Algorithm.

25.3 Empirical Evaluation

25.3.1 *Experimental Settings*

The experimental environment for the initial evaluation of the proposed system included a small network of 11 computers, each having a constant IP address, and a proxy server which was used by all computers to access the web. Ten students representing a homogenous group of "normal" users were instructed to access web sites related to general computer programming subjects. During the experiment the ten users have downloaded about 1000 web pages. In order to simulate a case of "abnormal" behavior, another student was instructed to view 100 pages on a different domain (tourism). The Sniffer, Filter, Vector Generator, Clustering and Detector modules described above were implemented and installed inside the proxy server. We have used the *vcluster* program from the Cluto Clustering Tool [Karypis (2002)] to implement the Clustering module with the "k-way" clustering algorithm and the cosine similarity measure.

25.3.2 *Evaluation Measures*

In order to evaluate the system based on our methodology we adopted performance measures used for intrusion detection system (IDS) evaluation. Performance measures of intrusion detection system (IDS) include accuracy, completeness, performance, efficiency, fault tolerance, timeliness, usability, and adaptivity [Balasubramaniyan *et. al.* (1998); Debar *et. al.* (1999); Lee *et. al.* (2001); Richards (1999); Spafford and Zamboni (2000)] . The most widely used measures are percentage of intrusive actions that are detected by the system (True Positives), percentage of normal actions that the system incorrectly identifies as intrusive (False Positives), and percentage of alarms that are found to represent abnormal behavior out of the total number of alarms (Accuracy). The trade-off between true positives and false positives is usually analyzed by Receiver Operating Characteristic (ROC) curves [Fawcett and Provost (1999)]. Accuracy is also an important parameter, since it measures the *credibility* of an intrusion detection system [Lee

(2002)]. In our initial experiments, we used the following performance measures (based on [Sequeira and Zaki (2002)]):

True Positive Rate (Detection Rate or Completeness): percentage of OTHER (abnormal) downloaded pages that received a similarity rating below the *tr* threshold. In our experiments, "abnormal" pages were obtained from the 11th user that was not a member of the homogenous group.

False Positive Rate: percentage of SELF (normal) downloaded pages that the system incorrectly determines to be abnormal, i.e., the percentage of SELF pages that receive a rating below the *tr* threshold .

Accuracy – percentage of pages that represent OTHER (abnormal) behavior out of the total number of pages that received a similarity rating below the *tr* threshold.

Since no benchmark data on content-based anomaly detection is currently available, our results are compared to the state-of-the-art results achieved with user command-level data [Sequeira and Zaki (2002)].

25.3.3 *Summary of Results*

The original term vectors representing 1000 pages accessed by normal users included 13,949 distinct terms. We have applied to this term set the dimensionality reduction procedure of Fig. 25.1 with reduction rates $p=0.03$ and $p=0.05$. These reduction rates have resulted in a reduced set of 2,012 and 1,139 terms respectively. The number of clusters in the k-way clustering algorithm was set to 20, since in our previous experiments (see [Last *et. al.* (2003)]) this number produced only slightly better results than a much smaller number of clusters (11).

Fig. 25.2 shows the three ROC (Receiver-Operator Characteristic) graphs with dimensionality reduction rates of $p=0$, $p=0.03$ and $p=0.05$ respectively. Every point in the ROC graphs represents an average result of ten cross-validation runs with a given threshold where in each run different 100 vectors were selected at random from the 1000 vectors accessed by normal users. There was no significant change in the performance caused by the dimensionality reduction process with $p=0.03$ though the complexity of the process decreased dramatically (from nearly 14,000 to 2,000 terms). However, with additional dimensionality reduction of $p=0.05$, a minor decrease in the performance was observed.

The graph in Fig. 25.3 describes accuracy as a function of the threshold parameter for different reduction rates. The accuracy chart is consistent with the ROC graph, since it does not indicate a significant difference between $p=0$ and $p=0.03$. In the case of $p=0.05$, we can see that it is possible to reach practically the same level of maximum accuracy though not in the same range of threshold values. The operator of the system may choose an optimal threshold value based on the results demonstrated in Figs. 25.2, and 25.3 and his/her own utility function. The results clearly demonstrate that in this experiment the system reliably detected an abnormal user based on the content of monitored web traffic. For 20 clusters and the dimensionality reduction rate of $p = 0.05$, our prototype system achieved TP=0.987 and FP=0.031 compared to TP=0.7 and FP=0.15 of ADMIT system [Sequeira and Zaki (2002)], which utilized user command-level data.

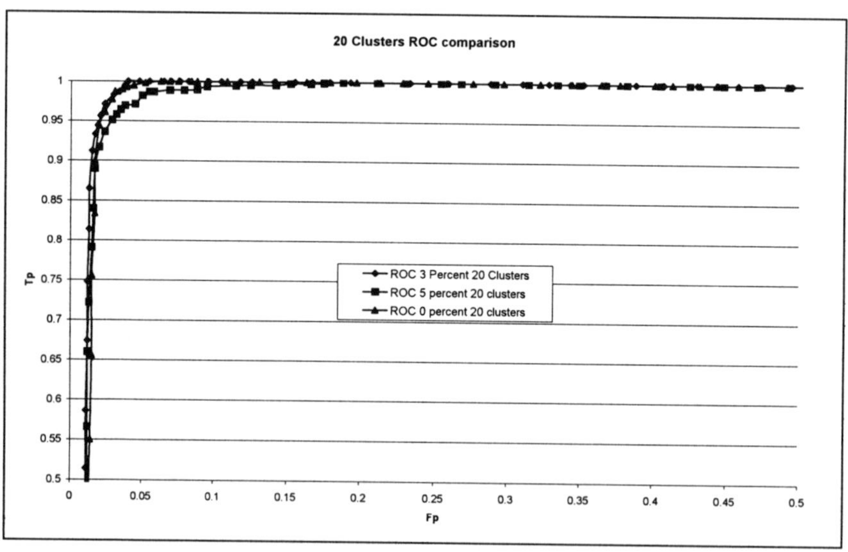

Fig. 25.2 Dimensionality Reduction Effect on ROC Curve.

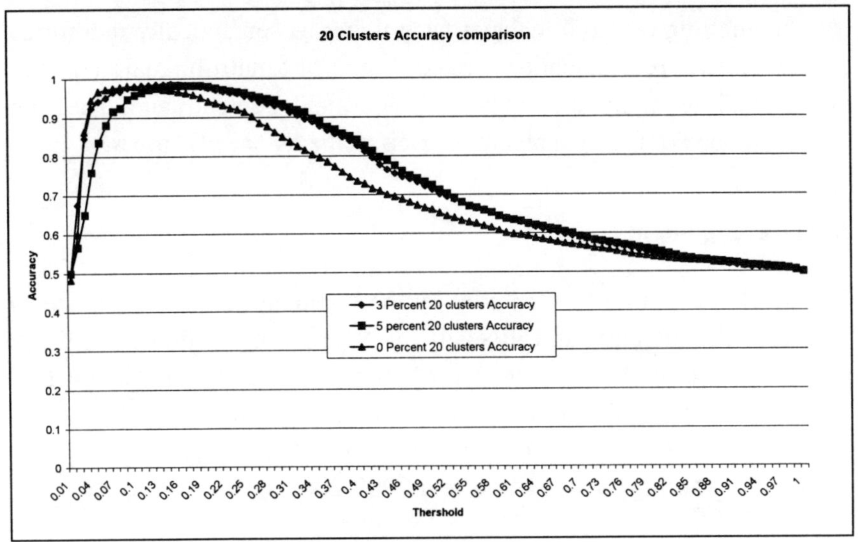

Fig. 25.3 Dimensionality Reduction Effect on Accuracy.

25.5 Conclusions

In this paper, we have presented an innovative, DM-based methodology for content monitoring on the web. The results of an initial case study indicate that the method can be useful for detecting authorized users that perform non-legitimate access to publicly available information. We are fully aware of ethical, privacy and legal issues involved in the usage of the proposed methodology as a tool for monitoring a large number of users who were never engaged in any illegal activity. Though in some countries an organization has a full right to monitor its own computers and some Internet Service Providers even store user-related content automatically [Birnhack and Elkin-Koren (2002)], some other cases may be more problematic from the legal standpoint and we do not intend to solve them in this technical paper. Obviously, we cannot keep ourselves responsible for any future use of this content monitoring methodology like DARPA, the original sponsor of the Internet technology, cannot be kept responsible for the content of all WWW pages including those published by Al-Qaida.

The ongoing research includes such issues as semantically rich forms of document representation, monitoring of multi-lingual content, incremental learning and update of "normal" content, and detecting abnormal behavior from a history of web usage by specific users.

Acknowledgement

This work was partially supported by the National Institute for Systems Teşt and Productivity at University of South Florida under the USA Space and Naval Warfare Systems Command Grant No. N00039-01-1-2248 and by the Fulbright Foundation that has granted Prof. Kandel the Fulbright Research Award at Tel-Aviv University, Faculty of Engineering during the academic year 2003-2004.

Bibliography

Balasubramaniyan, J.S., Garcia-Fernandez, J.O., Isacoff, D., Spafford, E. and Zamboni, D. (1998). An architecture for intrusion detection using autonomous agents, *Proceedings 14th Annual Computer Security Applications Conference*, IEEE Comput. Soc, Los Alamitos, CA, USA, pp. 13-24.

Birnhack M. D. and Elkin-Koren, N. (2002). *Fighting Terror On-Line: The Legal Ramifications of September 11*, Internal Report, The Law and Technology Center, Haifa University.

Boger, Z., Kuflik, T., Shoval, P. and B. Shapira (2001). Automatic keyword identification by artificial neural networks compared to manual identification by users of filtering systems, *Information Processing and Management* 37, pp. 187-198.

Debar, H., Dacier, M. and Wespi, A. (1999). Towards a taxonomy of intrusion-detection systems, *Computer Networks* 31, pp. 805–822.

Elovici, Y., Kandel, A., Last, M., Shapira, B., and Zaafrany, O. (to appear). Using Data Mining Techniques for Detecting Terror-Related Activities on the Web, *Journal of Information Warfare*.

Fawcett, T. and Provost, F. (1999). Activity Monitoring: Noticing interesting changes in behavior, *Proceedings on the Fifth ACM SIGKDD International Conference on Knowledge Discovery and Data Mining*, pp. 53-62.

Feldmann, A. (2000). BLT: Bi-Layer Tracing of HTTP and TCP/IP, *Proceedings of WWW-9*.

Hanani, U., Shapira B. and Shoval P. (2001). Information Filtering: Overview of Issues, Research and Systems, *User Modeling and User-Adapted Interaction (UMUAI)* 11 (3), pp. 203-259.

Karypis, G. (2002). *CLUTO - A Clustering Toolkit, Release 2.0*, University of Minnesota, [http://www-users.cs.umn.edu/~karypis/cluto/download.html].

Last, M., Shapira, B., Elovici, Y., Zaafrany, O. and Kandel, A. (2003). Content-Based Methodology for Anomaly Detection on the Web, in *Advances in Web Intelligence, Proc. AWIC 2003*, Menasalvas Ruiz, E., Segovia, J., and Szczepaniak, P. S. (eds.), LNAI 2663, Springer-Verlag, pp. 113 – 123.

Lee, W., Stolfo, S.J., Chan, P. K., Eskin, E., Fan, W., Miller, M., Hershkop, S. and Zhang, J. (2001). Real Time Data Mining-based Intrusion Detection, *Proceedings of DISCEX II*.

Lee, W. (2002). Applying Data Mining to Intrusion Detection: the Quest for Automation, Efficiency, and Credibility, *SIGKDD Explorations* 4 (2), pp. 35-42.

Lemos, R. (2002). What are the real risks of cyberterrorism, *ZDNet*, August 26, URL: http://zdnet.com.com/2100-1105-955293.html.

Pierrea, S., Kacanb, C. and Probstc, W. (2000). An agent-based approach for integrating user profile into a knowledge management process, *Knowledge-Based Systems* 13, pp. 307-314.

Richards, K. (1999). Network Based Intrusion Detection: A Review of Technologies, *Computers & Security* 18, pp. 671-682.

Salton, G. (1989). Automatic Text Processing: the Transformation, Analysis, and Retrieval of Information by Computer, Addison-Wesley, Reading.

Sebastiani, F. (2002). Machine Learning in Automated Text Categorization, *ACM Computing Surveys* 34 (1), pp. 1–47.

Sequeira K. and Zaki, M. (2002). ADMIT: Anomaly-based Data Mining for Intrusions, *Proceedings of SIGKDD 02*, pp. 386-395.

Shapira, B., Last, M., Elovici, Y., Zaafrany, O., Kandel, A. (2003). Using Data Mining for Detecting Terror-Related Activities on the Web, *Proc. of the 2nd European Conference on Information Warfare and Security (ECIW 2003)*, University of Reading, pp. 271-280.

Spafford, E.H. and Zamboni, D. (2000). Intrusion detection using autonomous agents, *Computer Networks* 34, pp. 547-570.

Wilson, M. (2002). Considering the Net as an Intelligence Tool: Open-Source Intelligence, *Decision Support Systems, Inc.*, [http://www.metatempo.com].

Zhong, N. (2003). Toward Web Intelligence, in *Advances in Web Intelligence, Proc. AWIC 2003*, Menasalvas Ruiz, E., Segovia, J., and Szczepaniak, P. S. (eds.), LNAI 2663, Springer-Verlag, pp. 1-14.

Index

Editors' Biographies

Yan-Qing Zhang received the B.S. and M.S. degrees in computer science and engineering from Tianjin University, China, in 1983 and 1986, respectively, and the Ph.D. degree in computer science and engineering at the University of South Florida, Tampa, in 1997. He is currently an Associate Professor of the Computer Science Department at Georgia State University, Atlanta. From 1997 to 1998, he was with the School of Computer and Information Science at Georgia Southwestern State University, Americus. From 1986 to 1993, he was a Lecturer in the Department of Computer Science and Engineering at Tianjin University. His research interests include hybrid intelligent systems, neural networks, fuzzy logic, evolutionary computation, kernel machines, granular computing, computational Web intelligence, intelligent wired and wireless agents, knowledge discovery and data mining, bioinformatics, medical informatics and fuzzy game theory. He has published six book chapters and over 90 research papers in journals and conferences. He is also the co-author of the book "Compensatory Genetic Fuzzy Neural Networks and Their Applications" published by World Scientific in 1998. He has served as a reviewer for 23 international journals. He has served as a committee member in over 30 international conferences. He is a member of IEEE and ACM.

Abraham Kandel received a B.Sc. from the Technion – Israel Institute of Technology and a M.S. from the University of California, both in Electrical Engineering, and a Ph.D. in Electrical Engineering and Computer Science from the University of New Mexico. Dr. Kandel, a Distinguished University Research Professor and the Endowed Eminent Scholar in Computer Science and Engineering at the University of South Florida, is the Executive Director of the newly established National Institute for Systems Test and Productivity. He was the Chairman of the Computer Science and Engineering Department at the University of South Florida (1991-2003) and the Founding Chairman of the Computer Science Department at Florida State University (1978-1991). He also was the Director of the Institute of Expert Systems and Robotics at FSU and the Director of the State University System Center for Artificial Intelligence at FSU. He is Editor of the *Fuzzy Track–IEEE MICRO*; Area Editor on Fuzzy Hardware for the International Journal "Fuzzy Sets and Systems", an Associate editor of the journals *"IEEE Transactions on Systems, Man, and Cybernetics"*, *"Control Engineering Practice"*, *"International Journal of Pattern Recognition and Artificial Intelligence"* (IJPRAI), and a member of the editorial boards of the international journals *International Journal of Expert Systems: Research and Applications, The Journal of Fuzzy Mathematics; IEEE Transactions on Fuzzy Systems, Fuzzy Systems – Reports and Letters, Engineering Applications for Artificial Intelligence, The Journal of Grey Systems, Applied Computing Review Journal (ACR) – ACM, Journal of Neural Network World, Artificial Intelligence Tools, Fuzzy Economic Review, International Journal of Chaotic Systems and Applications, International Journal of Image and Graphics, Pattern Recognition, Book Series on "Studies in Fuzzy Decision and Control,"* and *BUSEFAL – Bulletin for Studies and Exchange of Fuzziness and its Applications.*

Dr. Kandel has published over 500 research papers for numerous professional publications in Computer Science and Engineering. He is also the author, co-author, editor or co-editor of 38 text books and research monographs in the field. Dr. Kandel is a Fellow of the ACM, Fellow of the IEEE, Fellow of the New York Academy of Sciences, Fellow of AAAS, Fellow of IFSA, as well as a member of NAFIPS, IAPR, ASEE, and Sigma-Xi.

Dr. Kandel has been awarded the College of Engineering Outstanding Research Award, USF, 1993-94; Sigma-Xi Outstanding Faculty Researcher Award, 1995; The Theodore and Venette-Askounes Ashford Distinguished Scholar Award, USF, 1995; MOISIL International Foundation Gold Medal for Lifetime Achievements, 1996; Distinguished Researcher Award, USF, 1997; Professional Excellence Program Award, USF, 1997; Medalist of the Year, Florida Academy of Sciences, 1999; Honorary Scientific Advisor, Romanian Academy of Sciences, 2000.

Tsau Young Lin received his Ph. D from Yale University, and now is a full Professor at Department of Computer Science, San Jose State University - the Metropolitan University of Silicon Valley. He has served as editors, associate editors, members of advisory or editorial board of several international journals, and chairs, co-chairs and members of program committees of conferences. He has edited five books, and published a lot of journal papers and conference papers. His interests include approximation retrievals, data mining, data warehouse, data security, and new computing methodology (fuzzy, granular, Petri net, rough, and soft computing).

Yiyu Yao is a full professor of computer science in the Department of Computer Science, University of Regina, Regina, Saskatchewan, Canada. His research interests are information retrieval, Web intelligence, data mining, fuzzy sets, rough sets, and granular computing. He received a Ph.D. degree from University of Regina, Canada. He has published over 100 journal and conference papers. He is a member of the editorial boards of the Web Intelligence and Agent Systems journal (IOS Press). He has served and is serving as a program co-chair of three international conferences, and as a program committee member in over 20 international conferences. He is a member of IEEE and ACM.